1995

A History of Africa

A History of Africa

J. D. Fage

London
UNWIN HYMAN
Boston   Sydney   Wellington

Published by the Academic Division of
Unwin Hyman Ltd
15/17 Broadwick Street, London W1V 1FP, UK

Unwin Hyman Inc.,
8 Winchester Place, Winchester, Mass. 01890, USA

Allen & Unwin (Australia) Ltd,
8 Napier Street, North Sydney, NSW 2060, Australia

Allen & Unwin (New Zealand) Ltd in association with the
Port Nicholson Press Ltd,
Compusales Building, 75 Ghuznee Street, Wellington 1, New Zealand

First published in 1978
Second edition 1988
Second impression 1990

British Library Cataloguing in Publication Data

Fage, J. D. (John Donnelly), 1921–
    A history of Africa.—2nd edn
1. Africa, to 1986
I. Title
960

ISBN 0 04 445 782 0

Library of Congress Cataloging-in-Publication Data

Applied for

Typeset in 10 on 12 point Garamond and printed in Great Britain by
Butler & Tanner, Frome, Somerset

Contents

Illustrations and maps

A view of Kano, as seen by Henry Barth in 1851. From his *Travels and Discoveries in North and Central Africa*

A lancer of the Sultan of Baghirmi (a territory just to the south-east of Bornu) as seen by the explorer Hugh Clapperton in the 1820s. *Library of the School of African and Oriental Studies*

An eighteenth-century engraving of Khoi-khoi (Hottentots) dismantling their portable encampment and loading it on to their bullocks. *Mansell Collection*

A nineteenth-century drawing of a Trek-Boer waggon and its long span of oxen. *Mansell Collection*

An early train on the Uganda Railway. *Radio Times Hulton Picture Library*

Maps

Author's note

Anybody who embarks single-handedly on an attempt to outline the whole story of human society throughout the whole of one of the major continents of the world faces considerable problems. This is especially so, perhaps, when the continent is Africa, a vast area containing a great number and variety of distinct peoples, each with its own culture and language and each with its own history. Sometimes, too, these histories are as long as any recorded history anywhere; but often they have hardly been recorded at all, and their study has only just begun. This latter situation all too often means that considerable effort must go to establishing the basic chronological narratives of kings and wars and migrations and suchlike before one can begin to discuss, or even to discern, the really human issues in the story of African society. There is also the further complication that this story is not solely an indigenous entity, that human society in Africa has at times been subjected to major forces of change stemming from the neighbouring continents of Asia and Europe.

Perhaps the attempt can be explained, if not entirely justified, with the claim that a single author may be better able to assemble a consistent pattern than any team of specialists each concentrating on the history of a particular African people or region. However, such a pattern must necessarily be conditioned by that author's own specific interests, and also by the extent and variety of his knowledge and experience. Anyone who sets out by his own efforts to be equally knowledgeable on all periods of the history of all parts of the continent would run the risk of becoming so clogged with unassimilable data that he would find it difficult to make his individual contribution to the understanding of the whole. Composing this particular attempt at a history of Africa has certainly served to impress this author with a

sense both of his own limitations and also of the magnitude of his
debt to innumerable other explorers of the African past. Some of these
are, or have been, colleagues and students whom the author would
claim as friends. If, sometimes despite rather than because of their
treatment in this book, these and others recognize ideas which were
once theirs, the author can only hope that they will forgive both him
and the uses to which he may have put them. However, in view of
the variety of the sources which the author has drawn upon, has failed
to notice, or has distorted in their passage through his single mind, it
seems sensible to qualify the assertion that this is a history of human
society in Africa by adding that it can only be a *discursive* account of
such a vast theme.

J.D.F.

Note to the 1979 reprint

I have taken the opportunity of this new printing to make a number
of corrections to the text, many of which are the result of comments
made by readers. I would also like to thank my wife, Jean, for the
hard work she put in on the index.

J.D.F.

Note to the second edition

The first edition of *A History of Africa* was published in 1978, and
for the most part the writing of it had been completed three years
before. In 1975, what had been the Portuguese colonies in Africa had
only just become independent, and the future of what was then called
Rhodesia was far from certain; it therefore seemed best not to attempt
to write any post-colonial history, and to end the book with the
regaining of independence by the colonial territories. But more than
thirty years have now passed since the movement towards independence began to take effect throughout the continent, so for the second
edition an additional chapter has been written which essays to take
the history of Africa up to the end of 1987. Furthermore, during the
last ten or twelve years some significant new research into the history
of Africa has been published – especially, I think, for the long precolonial period. To take some account of this, chapters 1, 5 and 10 have
been extensively rewritten, substantial changes have been made in
chapters 2 and 3, small changes have been made to all the other
chapters, and the Select Bibliography has been revised.

J.D.F.
1 January 1988

Part 1

The internal development of African Society

Chapter 1

The origins of African society

The earliest known evidence anywhere in the world for the existence of man and the emergence of human society comes from East and North-East Africa, from a series of discoveries that stem from Dr Louis Leakey's pioneer excavations at Olduvai Gorge in northern Tanzania. Later finds, by Lake Turkana in Kenya and the river Omo in Ethiopia, for example, have taken the story of human evolution in Africa even further into the past. But the historian need go no further back than the situation disclosed at Olduvai about 1½ to 2 million years ago. Hominids, about 4 feet 6 inches tall, were then living in small groups on lake shores in savannah country, and chipping a rough edge on stones to make crude tools with which they could kill and dismember animal prey. Such tools have been called 'pebble tools', but since stones other than pebbles were also used, most archaeologists now prefer to call them 'choppers'.

The East and North-East African discoveries of Leakey and his successors have taken the story of human evolution right back to the time when man first became distinguishable from other primates. It is usually held that a useful distinction between man and all other animals is man's capacity to make tools, though recently this has become somewhat blurred by the discovery that some apes make what are in effect simple tools. But though the Olduvai hominids had small brains behind their massive faces, they must have possessed a greater ability to learn and to communicate than is normally associated with apes. The use of simple choppers spread throughout the African savannahs and elsewhere in the Old World. However, these implements have not been found in the forest lands of tropical Africa. Earliest man was a creature of the open country. He could not find the game he preyed on in the dense tropical forests, where indeed any kind of movement or of social life would have been very difficult without the use of better tools than he was able to make.

About a million years ago, man began to refine his simple stone choppers, with their single jagged cutting edge, and so evolved better and more specialized stone implements. The most characteristic of these is what was called a 'hand-axe', with two cutting edges meeting in a point; others were scrapers, specialized choppers, and hammerstones. As it happens, hand-axes and the culture represented by them were first recognized in western Europe, and the names which archaeologists gave to them, such as Acheulian, derived from European type-sites. But the earliest hand-axes known today once again come from the Olduvai deposits investigated by Leakey. Thus the first steps towards the evolution of more specialized Stone Age technologies seem also to have been taken by African man. Since this evolution enabled man to become a more efficient hunter, improving his food supply by killing more and larger animals, it became possible for him to live in larger societies.

The African savannahs, with adequate supplies of game animals and with year-round warmth from the sun, seemed to have provided a very suitable environment for early man, at least where there were permanent supplies of water, as on the banks of lakes and rivers. But it could have been the chills of winter which led to the next major technological advance, control of the use of fire, which may have first been discovered in Eurasia. However, by 50 000 to 60 000 years ago, African man was also using fire, a tool with which he could cook and make tender the tougher parts of his prey, and so make a more efficient use of his food supply and allow a further enlargement of the size of his communities.

But over the vast span of hundreds of thousands of years during which man was evolving from his earliest beginnings, there were considerable climatic changes in Africa. The continent did not experience the great Ice Ages which occurred in Europe, but the presence of large ice-caps both to north and south had an appreciable effect on conditions in Africa. During the last European Ice Age, the Würm glaciation between about 70 000 and 10 000 B.C., for example, the eastern part of sub-Saharan Africa was cooler and wetter than it now is, while the western part was cooler and drier. The balance between forest and grassland was appreciably altered. In the east, evergreen montane forests covered a much larger area than they now do, while in West Africa and the Congo basin the effect was to weaken the hold of the moist, dense tropical forests, and to make them more open and habitable. In this situation man was no longer limited to the open savannahs. Equipped with fire, he began to live in the forests also, finding shelter in caves, and making increasing use of a most versatile new raw material, wood, with which he began to make tools which he used alongside his earlier stone and bone implements. With more permanent homes and an improved technology, there was a further increase in the size and complexity of man's social groups. The result was the cultural tradition which the archaeologists called Sangoan (the type-site being at Sango Bay on Lake Victoria in Uganda), recognizable by distinctive stone tools used on trees and timber as well as on animals and their carcasses.

The Sangoan tradition, with various variants and developments, is widely distributed over most of what we now recognize as Negro Africa. It has not been found, however, north of the Sahara nor in those parts of southern Africa which are today grassland or steppe. In the latter, the old hand-axe tradition survived, presumably because it was still suited to the conditions, and here it developed into what archaeologists called the Fauresmith industry. In North Africa, on the other hand, the hand-axe tradition gave way to a new culture, the Mousterian, which was shared with other parts of the Mediterranean basin and the Near East. Since the Mousterian appears in Africa in a fully developed form, it was presumably intrusive.

Between about 35 000 and 8000 B.C. there occurred the highly significant development by which modern man replaced by natural selection all other types of human. In general terms, the practitioners of the Mousterian and Sangoan Stone Age cultures were distinguishable from modern man by their heavy brow and jaw structures. In North Africa these men are called Neanderthal, in line with their fellows in Europe and Asia, while in Africa south of the Equator they were called 'Rhodesioid'. Although modern man is a single, interbreeding species, variations in his environment coupled with limits to his mobility meant that he evolved into a number of variants. These have provided the foundation for the modern concepts of 'race'. Race is a contentious, indeed emotive, theme, and it is as well to try and clarify some aspects of it as they affect Africa before proceeding further.

In the modern world, human race tends to be primarily defined in terms of skin colour, a sharp distinction usually being made between

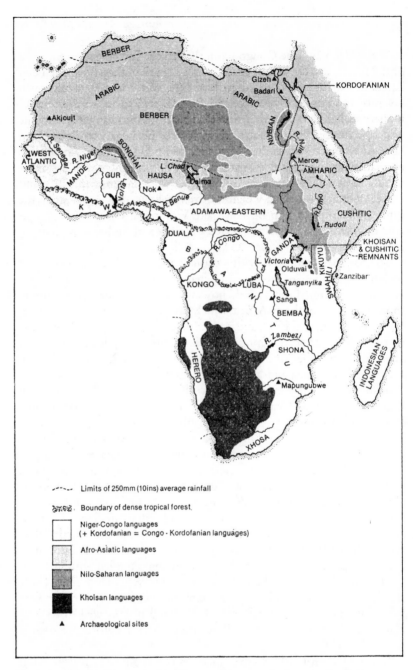

Map 1   Africa: Major geographical factors and present-day language distribution

Limits of 250mm (10ins) average rainfall

Boundary of dense tropical forest.

Niger-Congo languages
(+ Kordofanian = Congo - Kordofanian languages)

Afro-Asiatic languages

Nilo-Saharan languages

Khoisan languages

▲   Archaeological sites

the 'white' and the 'coloured' races, who in Africa are for the most part dark-skinned, and so are called 'Blacks' (which is to be preferred to the older team 'Negroes'). But this criterion of race creates problems for the historian of Africa. In the first place, the distinction has a sharpness which is not in accordance with reality, and it is one which leads on to assumptions about the relative superiority and inferiority of 'white' and 'black' which can be positively dangerous and cloud historical judgement.

Skin pigmentation is essentially due to the combined influences of climate and breeding. Dark skins afford better protection in conditions of bright sunlight and heat; fairer skins, and other genetically associated traits like lighter coloured eyes, are more suited to more diffused lights and colder climates. Thus by and large men who live in the tropics tend to be dark-skinned. But peoples have been moving, meeting and mixing for many thousands of years, and 'white' and 'black' are extremes which hardly exist. Northern and western Europeans, who tend particularly towards fairness, would be better described as 'pinks', while their more southerly and easterly representatives are often quite dark-skinned. Similarly few African Blacks are wholly 'black', and some in fact have skin tones which are little different from those of the darker Europeans.

These problems of colour and nomenclature become particularly difficult in connection with those inhabitants of Africa, mainly in Mediterranean and north-eastern Africa, who are not called Blacks. Europeans, believing – correctly – that these people belong to the same basic stock, usually called Caucasoid, as themselves, tend to think of them as 'whites', and with this there unfortunately often goes the assumption that they are inherently superior to the 'black' people of Africa. This assumption is, for example, the guiding principle of the interpretation of African history offered in such a standard anthropological introduction as C. G. Seligman's *Races of Africa*. In its more recent editions, this actually goes so far as to call the northern Africans 'Europeans'! Earlier they were always referred to as 'Hamites', and the book is full of examples in which these Hamites are supposed to have exerted their superiority over Blacks, most of which can now be seen not to fit the actual historical circumstances. But one problem here is simply that there is no satisfactory general name in modern use for the men of Caucasoid stock who do not live in Asia or Europe, as most Caucasoids do, but who are native to

Africa in that they have been resident there for many thousands of years.

These Africans who are not Blacks, but who are also not always very fair-skinned, are sometimes called Libyan-Berbers, Libyans being the name given to them by the Greek geographers of the first millennium B.C., and Berbers that provided by the Muslim Arabs who entered North Africa from Syria and Arabia from the seventh century A.D. onwards. Both Greek and Arab geographers made a distinction between the Libyans or Berbers and the more southerly Africans, who were called Ethiopians or *al-Sudan*, the name in each case meaning simply 'dark-skinned men'. The fairly general usage 'Hamites' – from the Biblical Ham – as in Seligman, for example, introduces yet another difficulty, that of confusing race with language and culture. Properly the terms 'Hamite' and 'Hamitic' should be used not of an ethnic stock, but for a group of related languages, including Ancient Egyptian and the Berber languages of the rest of North Africa and of much of the Sahara (the first of which has now wholly, and the remainder of which have now mainly, been superseded by Arabic), the so-called Cushitic family of languages in northeastern Africa (including Beja, Somali and Oromo), and some of the languages spoken south of the Sahara between the Niger and Lake Chad, most notably Hausa. But the speakers of Hausa are now universally accepted as Blacks, so it is at once apparent – as indeed should be obvious – that there need be no direct correlation between ethnic and linguistic stocks.

Even as terms of purely linguistic classification, 'Hamite' and 'Hamitic' present difficulties, and are not now much in favour. The view of modern linguists is that there is little if anything to distinguish the Hamitic languages of Africa as a group from the Semitic languages of Arabia and the Near East. Some of the latter, most notably Arabic, but also Amharic, the dominant language of the Ethiopian highlands, are now, as a result of many centuries of culture contact with and settlement by Semitic-speaking peoples, African languages also. It is therefore increasingly accepted that the so-called Hamitic languages of Africa and the so-called Semitic languages, found both in nearer Asia and in Africa, should be classified together in one major language family, for which the best name is 'Afroasiatic'.

An altogether different kind of problem facing the historian of Africa if skin colour is used as the main denominator of race, is that it is something which does not long survive death and burial. Indeed even a man's bones do not usually survive in the earth as well as some of the things he has made, especially perhaps if these are of stone or pottery. This is particularly true of tropical Africa, where a combination of high humidities and acid soils generally means that organic material is unlikely to survive in the earth for any length of time. This is why, so far in this introductory chapter, the history of man in Africa has been sketched mainly in terms of developments in his culture as revealed by those of his tools that have been found by archaeologists. A human culture cannot be confidently assigned to the activity of a specific type of man unless there is a good amount of adequately preserved skeletal material found in proper archaeological context with the cultural evidence, and this is rare in Africa, especially tropical Africa, until comparatively modern times. There is also the problem that any successful new type of tool of general application – and, indeed, any new generally viable cultural idea – must often have tended to spread more widely and quickly than the particular human type, or the particular group of men, which first developed it. For these reasons, it is not at present possible to give any considered account of the processes by which the Neanderthalers and 'Rhodesioids' gave way in Africa to modern men, whether Black or Caucasoid.

However, the cultural evidence after about 35 000 B.C. suggests that man was now evolving particular technologies which were specifically related to particular climatic and geographical situations. One such was the Aterian (named from a type-site at Bir al-Ater in eastern Algeria), which succeeded the Mousterian in north-west Africa and the Sahara, and other specialized local cultures developed in the African tropics. The skeletal evidence suggests that a type of modern man distinct from the Caucasoids of Asia, Europe and northern Africa, and especially adapted to the conditions of the African tropics, may have appeared in East Africa by about 50 000 B.C., and that over about 10 000 or 20 000 years this type evolved by natural selection in two different directions to meet the needs of two different environments. One result was the Black, adapted to the wet conditions of equatorial and West Africa, and the other was a variant more suited to the drier grasslands and savannahs of eastern and southern Africa. The modern representatives of this variant tend to be rather shorter than the Blacks,* and to have yellow or yellowish-brown rather than

---

* This may not be very significant, as there is a good deal of evidence of the influence of diet on stature.

dark skins; as will be seen, they are best called Khoi or Khoisan. North and north-eastern Africa, on the other hand, with a climate and geography similar to those in adjacent parts of Asia and Europe, were open to settlement by the same stock as these lands.

All these stocks were, of course, inter-breeding, so that many degrees of hybridization were – and are – possible. Initially, too, it would seem that the geographical boundaries between them were not as precise as they appear to be today. The situation in modern times is that North and North-East Africa are practically entirely inhabited by Caucasoids, the Khoisan are practically confined to the arid area in the extreme south-west of the continent, in and around the Kalahari desert, while in all the rest of the continent Blacks are dominant. Even as recently as about five thousand years ago, the situation may have been very different.

Caucasoids were certainly the dominant stock, if not the only one, living in North and North-East Africa, but there is also evidence that some Caucasoids were living further south, in at least the northern half of the open highland country which runs southwards from Ethiopia to South Africa. Two of the clues which lead to this conclusion are that the men who practised a local culture called the Kenya Capsian in the dry zone of central Kenya and northern Tanzania around 7000 B.C. seem to have been of Caucasoid type, while in the same area today, there are islands of remnant people, such as the Iraqw, who speak languages which are classified as Cushitic, and therefore belong to the Afroasiatic family. But most of the population of the open country south and east of the equatorial forest seem to have belonged to the Khoisan branch of African man, genetically linked to the Blacks, but distinguishable from them not only by skin colour and some other physical features, but presumably also by language. Certainly the Khoisan languages today are quite distinct from the family of languages spoken by the Blacks; among other things, their phonology makes an unusual use of click sounds. The Khoisan are often called Bushmen and Hottentots, but these terms refer rather to their cultures than to their ethnic stock. Hottentots are those Khoisan who, when Europeans first met with the stock in South Africa some centuries ago, had cattle but no agriculture, while the Bushmen had neither, being entirely Stone Age hunter-gatherers. Khoisan, made up from the Hottentot and Bushman names for themselves, 'Khoikhoi' and 'San' respectively, is certainly to be preferred. There is a fair amount of skeletal evidence for the earlier wide distribution of the Khoisan peoples, and there is also a Khoisan language, Sandawe, surviving today in central Tanzania alongside the Southern Cushitic remnants.

It is more difficult to be confident about the extent of Black habitation 5000 or so years ago. In the first place, as has already been mentioned, the Black seems to be an adaptation to the hot and wet conditions of equatorial and western Africa, that is to just those conditions least suitable for the preservation in the soil of skeletal evidence. It has already been suggested that the tropical forests which cover much of western and equatorial Africa were not a good environment for early human habitation, and the numbers of Blacks initially living actually within those forests were probably not large. Only one skeleton of Black type of any antiquity (about 9000 B.C.) has so far been found in these conditions – in southern Nigeria. Most of the early skeletal evidence for early Blacks is in fact not very early; it relates to the period roughly 5400–2000 B.C., and it comes from the southern Sahara between about 15° and 25°N. This is no doubt simply because the dry soils of this area afford much better conditions for the preservation of bones than exist further south.

But Blacks were not the only inhabitants of the Sahara at this time; there were also Caucasoid peoples there. This introduces a second difficulty in defining the area of Black occupation around 3000 B.C.: on the northern fringes of this area, they were certainly mingled with non-Blacks, and it seems that this was the case on other fringes also. The most dramatic evidence comes in fact from the far north, from the Neolithic cemetery at Badari in Upper Egypt, which must date from about the fourth millennium B.C. Skeletons excavated here have been classified as belonging in about equal proportions to Caucasoid, Black and hybrid types. A similar mingling between Blacks and Caucasoids seems almost certainly to have been the case on the eastern fringe of Black occupation, in Uganda and Ethiopia, and it could well have been the case that there was a considerable overlap also southwards and south-eastwards into the Khoisan area. But here it would hardly be detectable because of the subsequent vast expansion into this area of Blacks from West Africa, which led to speakers of the particular group of languages called Bantu becoming the dominant stock of all the southern half of Africa save only the extreme southwest.

This radical alteration in the population map of Africa – and also a somewhat less dramatic shift in the distribution of population in the Sahara – was the consequence of two great changes in the northern half of the continent between about 8000 and 2000 B.C., one climatic and the other cultural. It was not until about the latter date that the Sahara emerged as the great desert it is today. Earlier it had had an appreciably wetter climate, with the result that it was typically open grassland, supporting considerable game and, in its highlands, a Mediterranean flora. It had also supported an appreciable human population composed, as has been suggested, apparently about equally of Caucasoids and Blacks. But from about 10 000 B.C. onwards, the Saharan climate began to get appreciably drier, until ultimately the desert took over. The other great change was the spread in northern Africa of a series of exceptionally beneficial cultural innovations which had begun to be evident in a particular environment from about 8000 B.C. onwards. These innovations were to bring to an end the long Stone Age period of man's development, and launched him onto a series of cumulatively ever more rapid technological advances which eventually led to the present world civilization.

The beginnings of this process have commonly been called the Neolithic Revolution. The label is not very apt, since the appearance of a series of much more sophisticated and specialized new stone (i.e. 'neolithic') tools, ground and polished rather than simply chipped or flaked, was only one – and not necessarily the most significant – of a number of vital new technological advances, so that the revolution was plural and not solely Neolithic. Other important innovations were the invention of baskets and pottery, in which foods and liquids and other goods could be stored and transported, and the development of more or less permanent huts for man to live in. The real breakthrough, and the foundation for all subsequent human development, came with the discoveries that animals could be tamed and kept and bred and improved, and not simply hunted, and that seeds and roots could be improved and cultivated, and not merely collected or grubbed up from the wild.

The consequence was that man was no longer limited to small bands roaming the wilderness in search of his needs for food and water. He could live in increasingly larger and more permanent settlements, situated close by the best supplies of water for himself, his animals and his crops. He could be more or less certain that he could produce, store and preserve sufficient supplies of food to last him for a season, more or less independently of droughts and floods. Furthermore, some men could devote at least some of their time to specialized pursuits like the making of pottery and baskets and weapons and tools, or even, ultimately, war or government or scholarship. For the Neolithic Revolution was soon followed by the invention of writing – an admirable device for the accumulation and dissemination of knowledge – and the evolution of metallurgy – how to make implements of metal, first of copper and bronze, and then of iron.

It has usually been supposed that the lead in developing these enormously important new techniques was taken by the Near East, where both agriculture and towns had appeared by about 8000 B.C. or even earlier. But recent archaeology has suggested that adjacent parts of Europe and of Africa were not so far behind the Near East as once was thought, and that they need not have owed all their advancement to diffusions from the Near East. But in any case, as far as Africa is concerned, the north-eastern part of the continent is practically part of what Europeans call the Near East. Archaeological activity in Africa was first concentrated mainly on Egypt and the lower Nile valley, and it has long been appreciated that here both animal husbandry and agriculture were established by at least 4000 B.C. More recently it has become apparent that at least some aspects of the Neolithic Revolution extended more or less contemporaneously into other parts of northern Africa. What happened in what is now the Sahara desert and in the region between the Sahara and the northern limits of the tropical forest, the region which is now called the Sudan,* had crucial effects on the distribution of races of man almost throughout the continent.

It is now known that the peoples of the Sahara before it became a desert had pottery as early as peoples of the Near East – certainly by about 6000 B.C., and cattle at least as early as the Egyptians – i.e. by about 4000 B.C. But two or three thousand years later the climate of the Sahara had become much what it is today, and conditions for human habitation had become barely tolerable. Human hunting and

---

* The name comes from the Arabic *Bilad al-Sudan*, i.e. 'the land of the black men', which is equivalent, as has been seen, to the original Greek sense of Ethiopia. There was also an equivalent North African Berber name, *Akal n-Iguinawen*, from which derives the modern term Guinea. But whereas in modern geographic and ethnographic usage, 'Sudan' and 'Sudanic' are applied to the whole belt of territory immediately south of the Sahara which the early Arab geographers saw to be inhabited by Blacks, 'Guinea', because the name came into European languages via the Portuguese, who approached Black Africa from the west by sea, is now used geographically and ethno-graphically only for the southern, forested zone of the Sudan. Today, of course, both Sudan and Guinea also have much more restricted extents in political usage, since four African republics now bear these names, while Ethiopia is really only used for the state of that name.

desiccation had between them destroyed almost all the game, and agriculture was impossible except in a few small areas, the oases, in which there were supplies of underground water. Over most of the Sahara, virtually the only means of human sustenance left was cattle-herding. The cattle competed with agriculture in the oases, greatly to its and their detriment, and eventually cattle-herding came to depend mainly on transhumance, a specialized form of nomadic pastoralism by which cattle were taken deep into the desert only during the short seasons when it afforded some grazing, and spent the rest of the year in better pastures either to the north or the south.

The populations which could be supported in this way were obviously small. They were essentially Libyan-Berbers in the western half of the desert and also to the east of the Nile, the westerners – the ancestors of the modern Tuareg – distinguishing themselves by adopting a custom by which their menfolk were never seen in public without a veil covering the face below the eyes. In between, the desert pastoralists were much more Negroid, and presumably spoke languages which – as will be seen later in this chapter – have now been termed 'Nilo-Saharan'. Most of the earlier population of the Sahara, presumably at least partly cultivators, must have emigrated from the desert towards lands of higher rainfall or where there were at least better supplies of permanent water. It was natural that by and large the Caucasoids would choose to move north and north-east towards their fellows established in the Mediterranean coastlands and in the valley and delta of the lower Nile, while the Blacks from the Sahara tended to move southwards into the Sudan. In both cases the result would be to increase population densities, and so to encourage the development of agriculture as the most effective way to use the available land to support the increased population. There is evidence that population had been increasing in this way for some time in the lower valley and delta of the Nile, thus helping to produce the revolutionary situation which led by about 3000 B.C. to the emergence of Pharaonic Egypt, which is discussed in the following chapter.

What need to be considered here are the subsequent developments in the Sudan. Over and above the increase of population resulting from immigration from the Sahara, the development of agriculture seems to have brought about a substantial increase of population in at least one area, which led to Blacks beginning to settle in the southern half of Africa, where eventually they displaced or absorbed all other populations save only those in the extreme south-west. The sequence of events which led to this result has begun to be discerned only during about the last twenty years, and is therefore nothing like as well known or understood as the broadly parallel sequence concentrated into a single river valley which gave rise to Pharaonic Egypt. Some parallelisms are obvious enough; for example that the Niger valley and the Lake Chad basin afforded somewhat similar conditions for the growth of population to those in the Nile valley, and that the key process was the development of agriculture. Nevertheless, in the present state of knowledge, some argument by analogy and some speculation are inevitable.

However, one major and often accepted speculation is not necessary. This is that the Blacks of the Sudan experienced a Neolithic Revolution that was separate from the Neolithic Revolution of the Near East and Egypt. This has been argued, for example, most cogently in recent years by the anthropologist G. P. Murdock, who has in particular supposed an independent invention of agriculture by the Mande-speaking group of Blacks of the upper Niger valley. If at the relevant period, which would be broadly within the limits 5000 and 2000 B.C., the Sahara had been the desert that it now is, such an argument might be necessary. But – as has been seen – at least at the beginning of this period, the Sahara provided a not unattractive, even in part cultivable, habitat for man, and it was a zone in which Black and Caucasoid peoples met and mingled. The evidence for Saharan agriculture is full of gaps, both chronological and spatial. Nevertheless, as has been pointed out, for example, by the archaeologist Desmond Clark, it is clear enough from the nature of the implements used that the Sahara participated in one single process of agricultural development in common with Egypt and the Near East. There is no reason to suppose that Saharan Blacks did not share in this development equally with Saharan Caucasoids; conceivably perhaps they shared more than equally. The first Saharan potters seem to have been Blacks; furthermore, modern Caucasoids in the Sahara are essentially pastoralists, while such cultivation as there still is, in the oases, is essentially by Blacks.

But the transformation of the Sahara into desert, which was completed by about 2000 B.C., did however mean that thereafter in the Sudan the development of agriculture, and of the Neolithic Revolution generally, did tend to stop being part of the one general Old World process, and became somewhat idiosyncratic. Historians of the west have tended to see this change in terms of sub-Saharan

Africa being cut off from a mainstream of development in the Near East and the eastern Mediterranean which ultimately led to their own civilization. But this is neither really true nor really to the point. Contact across the Sahara desert was never impossible. Even if all else failed, which was not the case, transhumance alone would have ensured the continuance of some contact between North Africa and the Black Sudan. But the Blacks did need to adapt to new conditions the legacy they already possessed before the Sahara became a desert. Furthermore, the subsequent filtration – rather than cessation – of contacts with the north occasioned by the establishment of the desert, afforded them the opportunity to select what subsequent innovations pioneered in the Near East and the eastern Mediterranean seemed to be worth accepting and developing in the new situation in which they found themselves.

The essence of the difference between the situation of the Blacks and other Old World peoples who were experiencing the Neolithic Revolution was that the Blacks were the only people to be confined to a large land mass which (except for its remote southern tip) lay wholly within the tropics. This immediately posed problems for the agriculture they possessed before the growth of the desert confined them to the Sudan and to lands to the south of it. The staple crops, wheat and barley, of the farmers of temperate lands would not flourish in the short growing season of the Sudan, and would not grow at all in the wetter conditions further south. The Black farmers therefore had to turn to develop new seed crops from wild grasses indigenous to the Sudan, thus evolving the various grain crops called millets*, and also domesticating an African rice. The Mande of the upper Niger may have been significant in the development of this African agriculture, but not as original inventors; rather because they inhabited a favourable riverain situation which, like the Nile valley, was unusually close to the Sahara from which some of their ancestors may have come. The evidence does indeed suggest that they were those who first cultivated the African variety of rice, but the major indigenous sub-Saharan grain crops, the millets, seem to have been developed in a number of strains throughout the Sudan. Further south, especially perhaps between modern Ghana and modern Nigeria, where today there is a gap in the tropical forest but where conditions did not favour the development of grain crops, the evolution was probably

* E.g. the *Sorghum* species ('Great Millet'), the *Digitaria* species ('Small Millet'), and the *Pennisetum* species ('Bulrush' or 'Pearl Millet').

initially one of vegeculture rather than of agriculture proper. The African species of yams may have been first cultivated in this forest gap.

There is as yet rather little hard evidence for the dating of the progress of agriculture among the Blacks of the Sudan. But such evidence as there is (see, for example, chapter 3, p. 66) tends to the conclusion that the new cereal crops may have been developed in the savannahs between about 4000 and about 1000 B.C.

The next major development arising out of the Neolithic Revolution was the invention of metal tools and weapons to replace or supplement those made of the earlier raw materials, stone, wood and bone. This was certainly pioneered in the Near East, and the filtering effect of the Sahara desert may help to explain why it was that the smelting of iron ore and the forging of iron or steel implements appears in Black Africa at about the same time as the smelting of copper ores and the manufacture of objects of copper. It is known that copper was mined and worked at two localities in the southernmost western and central Sahara during the first half of the first millennium B.C.; iron was being smelted in the nearby Sudan, by people of the culture first recognized around Nok in what is now northern Nigeria, by at least 500 B.C. Thereafter knowledge of the working of the two metals seems to have spread more or less together, and remarkably rapidly, throughout almost all of sub-Saharan Africa, reaching what is now the Republic of South Africa by about A.D. 400. Elsewhere in the world, it was usual in the history of metallurgy for some millennia of copper working to precede the beginning of iron working. This was presumably because, although iron is a much harder and so more useful metal than copper and its alloys, its ores are much less obviously something out of which objects might be made than are some of the sources of copper, and, after it has been smelted, forging or other further treatment is needed before the metal is usable. As the two metals spread through sub-Saharan Africa, tools and weapons seem always to have been made from iron; the softer metal and its alloys being kept for the manufacture of decorative or symbolic objects. It should also be noted that, while deposits of iron ore may be found virtually throughout Black Africa, workable copper ores are relatively scarce, so that they and their products became highly valued. In the Sudan, copper ores hardly exist at all; it looks therefore as though the people of the Sudan may have taken up iron-working without previously having worked copper. It is difficult to imagine an invention of iron-working by people who had not previously worked the softer metal, so it seems likely that knowledge of iron-working must have been introduced into the Sudan from elsewhere. But exactly how this happened is unknown.

The most general hypothesis is that, after the establishment of the regular use of the metal in the Near East by about 1200 B.C., iron implements were introduced to the North African littoral on which the Phoenicians shortly began to colonize. But it is not thought that the manufacture of iron was developed in Africa on any scale until after the conquest of Egypt by iron-using Assyrians in the seventh century B.C. Following this, Nubia, the land above Egypt in the Nile valley, possessing greater resources of iron ore and especially of the timber needed to smelt it than did Egypt, became a major centre of iron-working from which it is thought that the technology was further diffused into sub-Saharan Africa.

But no evidence has yet been found for the diffusion of iron-working from Nubia westwards through the Sudan. Indeed a habitation site at Daima, just to the south of Lake Chad, which was occupied continuously from about the sixth century B.C. to about the twelfth century A.D., does not seem to have known iron until about the fifth or sixth century A.D. This is about ten centuries later than the known date for iron-working in the Nok culture, which lies further to the west, i.e. further from Nubia. It would not do to hang too much on the negative evidence from the one site at Daima, but it does suggest that it is rather more likely that knowledge of iron-working may have come to the western and central Sudan from the north, across the Sahara from the region of Phoenician settlement, than from the Nile valley in the east. Two additional pieces of evidence would seem to support this view. Knowledge of iron-working is probably unlikely to have been transmitted across the desert simply by its transhumant pastoralists who, among other things, had virtually no supplies of fuel for smelting. But it is known that there was a regular use of wheeled vehicles southwards across the western Sahara, conducted by peoples who lived close to its northern edge, by at least the fifth century B.C., while no equivalent traffic is known to have passed westwards from the Nile valley through the lands of the pastoralists of the eastern Sahara.* Secondly, there is the early evidence for

* Phoenician settlement in North Africa, the development of civilization in Nubia, and the wheeled vehicles in the Sahara are all subjects which are developed further in chapter 2.

copper mining and working in the southernmost western and central Sahara that has already been remarked.

With both wheeled vehicles and copper in the western and central Sahara at the relevant time, it seems plausible to suppose that knowledge of iron-working could have passed from North Africa to the western and central Sudan as quickly as did knowledge of the art of writing and the religion of Islam that brought it in its train. North Africans were hardly converted to Islam before the eighth century, and some West African Blacks were apparently converted by the tenth century at least. Indeed innovations from North Africa seem to have been quickly taken up by the Blacks in the Sudan provided only that they seemed likely to be useful to them in their circumstances. It was doubtless this criterion of utility in the Sudan which explains why the Blacks did *not* adopt the wheel, which other peoples invariably found a most useful invention, and which it seems must certainly have been known to the northernmost Blacks by the fifth century B.C.

As has been seen, the wheel approached West Africa as a means of transport, but though usable on light animal-drawn vehicles in areas of hard-going in the dry Sahara, it must have been much less useful in the Sudan, where wheeled vehicles would have been impracticable in the rainy season without made roads, and where anyway the Senegal and Niger rivers, and Lake Chad and its affluents, were natural waterways affording means for the much more efficient transport of men and goods by canoe. Also, the invention of the equipment to enable animals to be ridden, though appreciably later to the north of the desert than the discovery of how to use animals to draw vehicles, seems to have reached the Sudan hard on its heels. The use of horses and donkeys and, later, of camels for riding and as beasts of burden was much more practicable in the Sudan than their use as draft animals, and so caught on very quickly. It also quickly replaced the use of wheeled vehicles in the Sahara.

The growth of agriculture in the Sudan, reinforced by subsequent technological advances such as iron-working, must have permitted a considerable increase in its population. It is difficult to suppose that, even with the extensive use of land by shifting cultivation, population ever began to outrun the capacity of the land available for farming. But, if aridity was still increasing, or in periods of drought or other natural calamity, it may have become difficult to support people at the new levels of life to which they had become accustomed. On the other hand, the development of food production through agriculture had given time to spare for other pursuits, especially during the dry season between the harvest and the sowing. Bands of restless young men might well use this new leisure to go on excursions into the unknown lands surrounding their villages and farms. While supporting themselves by hunting and fishing, they would naturally keep their eyes open for empty lands and new resources which might offer further opportunities for themselves and their kinsfolk. There was little scope for exploration, and none for expansion, northwards, where the Sahara desert was becoming ever more firmly established. So, if new lands were to be found for settlement and cultivation, they had to be sought to the south. But, with the one exception of the gap between modern Ghana and Nigeria, the land to the south was covered with thick tropical forest, difficult to penetrate even when iron tools had become available, and where the staple crops of the savannah could hardly be grown. On the wide front, therefore, all that was feasible was for small bands to infiltrate the forest or to explore the possibility of outflanking it to the east. Because increasing desiccation had always inclined the early farmers to concentrate their settlements on the banks of rivers and lakes, where as much of the year might be spent in fishing and canoeing as in actual farming, the key to the success of both enterprises seems likely to have been in the disposition of these major water features. Outflanking the forest to the east would have been facilitated by using affluents of Lake Chad like the river Chari, but in the end it would have run into the waterlogged country of the Upper Nile known as the Sudd, an unpromising region for agricultural settlement. Today the western limits of the Sudd coincide with a major cultural and linguistic boundary, with agricultural peoples speaking Niger-Congo languages to the west and pastoral peoples speaking Nilo-Saharan languages to the east (see below, pp. 22–3). However small bands could infiltrate the forest and make some progress by clearing small plots on the banks of streams, gradually developing crops more suitable to the conditions, and placing the emphasis more on vegetables like yams than on grain crops. In one direction really considerable advances were ultimately possible. Successive generations of pioneers advancing through the forest to the south of the Benue tributary of the Niger would in time come to rivers like the Sanga and the Ubangi, and thus gain access to the major central African drainage system of the Congo basin, so that further exploration would ultimately bring them to the wide savannahs to the south and east of the forest. The evidence suggests that such a movement must have occurred, beginning possibly around 2000 B.C. and reaching the savannahs not later than about 300 B.C., with the ultimate result that the people who today are called the Bantu had become the dominant human stock throughout the southern half of Africa save for the extreme south-west, in and around the Kalahari desert, where rainfall was (and is) inadequate to permit of cultivation.

'Bantu' is strictly speaking a term of linguistic classification. It derives from the facts that in the languages spoken by the Black peoples who today provide almost all the inhabitants of the southern half of Africa, some form of the root *ntu* is in general use to mean 'human being', and that these languages have a system of noun classes in which some form of the prefix *ba-* signifies the plural form of the class denoting persons. The 400 or so Bantu languages spoken in the enormous expanse of territory south of a line which runs roughly from Mt Cameroun on the Atlantic coast to Mount Elgon in Uganda, and thence to the east coast near Lamu (albeit with a big re-entrant to the south into central Tanzania), are indeed much more alike in vocabulary and in grammatical structure than is usually the case – even with much smaller areas – with the languages of the Sudan. Thus when, about the mid-nineteenth century, African languages began to be the subject of scientific study, Bantu was seen to be a much more obvious language family than any which could be worked out for the other languages of the Blacks. Though in due course a number of groupings for what came to be called the Sudanic languages were proposed and discussed, the plain fact was that any two adjacent Sudanic peoples, even if culturally very similar, could speak languages so markedly different from one another that their date of separation from any presumed common parent language must have taken place many thousands of years in the past. Any one Bantu language, on the other hand, was likely to be partially intelligible to the speakers of nearby languages, and perhaps not wholly unintelligible to speakers of any other Bantu language, even one spoken some distance away.

It was this unusually close interrelationship of the Bantu languages that provided the first indication that the ancestors of their modern speakers must have occupied the whole southern half of Africa relatively recently and relatively quickly. But other early surmises as to what else this close interrelationship might signify were less apt. It was common to think of the Bantu tongues as a family of languages separate from all other language families of the Blacks. Often the Bantu languages were thought to be so distinct from the other African languages that their speakers could not be 'true Blacks'; it was not unusual, indeed, to think of them as 'Hamiticized Blacks', i.e. to suppose that both their similarities among themselves – cultural as well as linguistic – and their separateness from other black Africans were due to processes of conquest by, and mixing with, 'Hamites'.

The second of these conclusions was very much a value judgement, favoured by those, such as Seligman, who believed in the myth of Hamitic superiority. But neither could be overthrown until enough work had been done in reasonable depth on a substantial number of the multitude of languages that are spoken in Africa, so that the nature and extent of interrelationships between them might be assessed on scientific principles. By the late 1940s, the American linguist, Joseph H. Greenberg, considered that enough was known for him to begin the heroic task of trying to work out an overall, genetic scheme of classification for all the languages of Africa. His method was the classic one first used by the pioneers who had recognized the Indo-European language family. From each of the 800 or so languages spoken in Africa for which he could secure dictionaries or word-lists, Greenberg extracted as many as he could find of a sample of some 400 words with quite basic meanings (e.g. the words for the first ten numerals and for parts of the body, or the words for 'sun' and 'bird', or for 'to eat' or 'to die'). He then compared these words, together with available grammatical evidence, with a view to establishing genetical relationships between the languages.

It was immediately apparent to Greenberg that there was no evidence that the Bantu languages were genetically related to 'Hamitic'. Their grammatical behaviour was different, and so too was their basic vocabulary. The most that could be said was that some word-borrowing had occurred in areas where speakers of two entirely separate language traditions had come into cultural contact.

But by the time that Greenberg was writing, this conclusion was less revolutionary than his eventual decision (1963) that there were only four separate and distinct families of languages in the whole continent. Two of these have already been mentioned, Afroasiatic and Khoisan. The others, which were the language families of the Black peoples, he proposed to call 'Nilo-Saharan' and 'Congo-Kordofanian'.

The 'Nilo-Saharan' languages were spoken by dark-skinned peoples living in the eastern Sahara (for example, the Kanuri, the Teda and the Zaghawa), in the valley of the Niger where it bends north into the desert (Songhai), between the river Chari and the Upper Nile (including Nubian and the 'Nilotic' languages such as Shilluk, Acholi and Nuer), and south-eastwards of this to make an indentation into Bantu country in the dry lands of Kenya and Tanzania east of Lake Victoria, the home of what had previously been called 'Nilo-Hamitic' languages (such as Masai and Nandi).

'Congo-Kordofanian' included a few languages spoken by small groups in Kordofan, in the Sudan Republic, but its main grouping was what Greenberg called 'Niger-Congo'. This comprised the languages spoken by all the agricultural peoples in West Africa from Senegal to eastern Nigeria, and all the Bantu languages of central, eastern and southern Africa. Building on earlier work by Diedrich Westermann, Greenberg confidently asserted that within this major family the status of the Bantu languages, despite their number and their vast spread, was merely a branch of the particular sub-family of the languages spoken by the Blacks living between the river Benue and the Cameroons.*

The overall genetic scheme proposed by Greenberg was so far-sweeping and radical that immediate and universal acceptance of it by other linguists was hardly to be expected. Some of them, indeed, were critical of his methods, pointing to the small sample of words used to establish genetic relationships between the languages and to his use of words from vocabularies which all too often had not been rigorously established. But the negative conclusion that the Bantu languages are not in any real sense 'Hamitic' presents no difficulty, nor does the idea that the Bantu languages are related in some way to the Sudanic languages of West Africa. Furthermore, both 'Nilo-Saharan' and 'Niger-Congo' are illuminating concepts for the historian. An outstanding characteristic of the speakers of Nilo-Saharan languages is that they are predominantly pastoralists. It is therefore possible to surmise that they are the descendants of Blacks of the eastern Sahara and Sudan whose experience of the Neolithic Revolution included the development of animal husbandry and of iron-working, but commonly stopped short of much in the way of agriculture. An obvious explanation for this would be that they inhabited territories with annual rainfalls inadequate to allow of cultivation as a major mode of subsistence. With appreciably greater confidence, it can be

---

* In this book, the old-fashioned English term 'the Cameroons' refers to the coastal region by the Cameroons river and Mt Cameroun, while 'Cameroun' is used for the much larger area of the modern republic and the former colony, which was first German (Kamerun) and then French.

suggested that the ancestors of the speakers of the Niger-Congo languages were the inhabitants of the western Sudan who experienced the full flood of the agricultural revolution, and who consequently expanded over all available lands to the south and south-east.

Greenberg was led to suppose, indeed, that the peopling by Blacks of the southern half of Africa must have taken the form of an overflowing to the south and east by the nearest West African farmers, those of the Benue–Cameroun border area. As a result, the Bantu languages, despite their subordinate genetic status, had become by far the most widespread group of the whole Niger–Congo family. But hardly had this conclusion been published, than it was apparently challenged by the results of another substantial piece of research, that undertaken by Malcolm Guthrie, an older and more cautious British linguist, and one of those who had been most critical of Greenberg's work.

Whereas Greenberg's purpose had been to classify all the languages of Africa (so that he had no choice but to work from the top down using a select list of 'basic' words), Guthrie was interested in the classification only of the Bantu languages. He was therefore able to work from the bottom upwards, examining material from virtually all the Bantu languages, and in the case of 28 of them, selected in part because their data had been well established but also because geographically they were well distributed over the whole Bantu-speaking area, he took into account their whole known vocabularies. Guthrie ended up by assembling some 22 000 sets of cognates, that is to say sets of words, each word coming from a different language, which, when due allowance had been made for shifts of sound and sense according to recognized rules, were sufficiently alike in both respects for it to be confidently asserted that they must descend from a single root in some ancestral language. About 500 of these cognates had a relatively uniform meaning throughout a very wide range of Bantu languages, so that Guthrie concluded that they must be descendants from roots in a language which was the ancestor of all Bantu languages, a 'Proto-Bantu'. A further 1500 were found to exist entirely or predominantly in either westerly or easterly Bantu languages, the inference being that the first split of Proto-Bantu was into western and eastern dialects.

Somewhat to his surprise, Guthrie found that those of his 28 test languages containing the highest proportions, 50 and 54 per cent respectively, of reflexes from the 500 roots common to his Proto-Bantu as a whole, were the languages of the Luba and Bemba, peoples living right in the centre of the present Bantu-speaking area, in south-eastern Zaire and adjacent Zambia. He was led to the conclusion that it was in this region, in and around the Shaba province of modern Zaire, that the speakers of Proto-Bantu must have lived, and that it was from there that their descendants must have subsequently spread out, after their tongues had diverged into western and eastern variants, to occupy the rest of what may now be called Bantu Africa. In the process, their languages diverged even further. Whereas east and west of the 'Bantu nucleus' the divergencies were relatively slight, so that both Kongo on the west coast and Swahili on the east coast had retained 44 per cent of the proto-Bantu roots, they increased as one looked further afield, and particularly in the extreme south-east, where Xhosa had only 26 per cent, and in the far north-west, where the Douala language in Cameroun retained as little as 14 per cent of the roots of Proto-Bantu.

Concerned as he was only with the Bantu languages, Guthrie did not attempt to relate his Proto-Bantu to the Sudanic languages of West Africa. Nevertheless he was in a very general way prepared to accept that there was some connection, and that Proto-Bantu could have had a West African ancestor which might be called 'Pre-Bantu'. But his historical interpretation of the Bantu linguistic pattern which he had discerned, with expansion in all directions – including north-west *towards* West Africa – from a central Shaban nucleus, did not permit him to accept Greenberg's notion of a straightforward over-flowing from the Benue–Cameroun border region into what was to become Bantu Africa. He was left with the idea that a few 'Pre-Bantu' must have moved very quickly along the Congo waterways through the forest until they reached the southern savannahs, where their agriculture could flourish again and they became the Proto-Bantu. Then, as their numbers grew, especially following the introduction of metal technology and of south-east Asian food-crops well suited to the wetter parts of their environment, they spread out in all directions into what is now known as Bantu Africa.

Some support for such a hypothesis comes from the presence of canoeing and fishing terms among the 500 or so roots reconstructable for Proto-Bantu, and also from some scraps of very exiguous literary evidence. When the Indian Ocean coast of Africa was first described in writing, in the Greek sailors' guide of about A.D. 100 known as the *Periplus of the Erythraean Sea*, this coast was called Azania, and no 'Ethiopians', dark-skinned people, were mentioned among its inhabitants. They first appear in the largely fourth-century *Geography* ascribed to Claudius Ptolemy of Alexandria, and then only towards the south, probably on the coast of what today is northern Mozambique, i.e. about the latitude of Guthrie's 'Bantu nucleus'. Cosmas Indicopleustes in the sixth century was to call this southern coast Zingium. After Cosmas, the surviving descriptions of the East African coast are not written in Greek, but in Arabic; Greek-speaking merchants had given way to sea-traders who spoke Arabic, and for them Zingium had become Zanj. Whether Zanj is to be understood as an ethnic or a geographical designation seems to vary with the context in which the name is used; nevertheless, for Mas'udi, a Baghdad geographer of the tenth century, Zanj encompassed the whole known East African coast south of what is now Somalia, i.e. from the present northern limit on the coast of Bantu-speaking Blacks. The inference from these references seems to be, first, that for the early Greek observers, the original 'Azanian' inhabitants of the Indian Coast were not to be distinguished from the peoples they knew on the African shore of the Red Sea, and that therefore they were speakers of Afroasiatic, and most probably Cushitic, languages; and, second, that southwards from Somalia, by the tenth century these Azanians had been replaced by Blacks coming from the south who were presumably ancestors of the modern Bantu-speaking peoples of East Africa.

The suggestion that the spread of the Bantu from a central, Shaban, nucleus was facilitated by the arrival of south-east Asian food-crops is a reasonable one. There is no question but that some of today's most significant sub-Saharan food-crops – including bananas and plantains, the coconut and the sugar-cane, and important varieties of yams and rice – were first brought into cultivation in South-East Asia, and that it was as cultigens that they were introduced into Africa, presumably across its eastern coastline. Some of them had no African equivalents and – more generally – because they had been developed in areas of greater rainfall than most of the sub-Saharan food-crops, they must have made it easier for humans to settle, and to multiply their populations, in the wetter tropical African areas such as the forests and the monsoonal eastern coastlands. Exactly how and when the south-east Asian food-crops came into tropical Africa is not known. However it is plausible to suppose that one route of introduction would have been connected with the colonization of the great

island of Madagascar by Indonesians. Little is known about this colonization beyond the basic fact that the Malagasy language unquestionably belongs to the family of languages spoken in Indonesia. Moreover, since its words for iron and iron-working have cognates in
modern Indonesian languages, while on the other hand it shows no
evidence of Sanskrit or Hindu influences, there are good grounds for
supposing that the colonization of Madagascar must have taken place
after the beginning of the Iron Age in Indonesia and before its languages were subjected to influences from India, that is between the limits
of about A.D. 300 and A.D. 800. The northern end of Madagascar is
in the same latitude as Shaba and Guthrie's presumed Bantu nucleus,
and, since the island was settled by Bantu-speaking Blacks as well as
by emigrants from Indonesia, it does seem that Madagascar would
have provided a suitable route for the transmission of the south-east
Asian foodcrops to the Bantu.

But, attractive though it is, there is really no hard evidence to
substantiate the idea (used in the first edition of this book) that a
central nucleus of Bantu settlement was encouraged to flourish and
expand by the arrival of south-east Asian food-crops. Such a notion
starts, indeed, with a misconception, that the nucleus discerned by
Guthrie has *historical* significance. Its real significance is rather stat-
istical and geographical, for it is reasonable to expect that the largest
common word stock of a widely spread and developing family of
languages is more likely to be central rather than peripheral.
(Conversely, the languages of the family in which the greatest number
of cognates have survived from the original ancestral language are
perhaps more likely to be found on the periphery.) Luckily Guthrie
published all the data on which his conclusions had been based, and
it was therefore possible for other investigators – perhaps most notably
Bernd Heine and Alick Henrici – to rework it. It has been shown
that his conclusions were least convincing for the north-western Bantu
languages, not only in relation to the connection between 'Pre-Bantu'
and the Sudanic languages of West Africa, but also, and importantly,
in the analysis of the Bantu languages of this quadrant. It is now
apparent that the connection with the West African Sudanic languages
is much more like that suggested by Greenberg, and that the pattern
of relationships among the north-western Bantu languages was much
more determined by a southwards drift of peoples from West Africa
than by any movement or influences going in the reverse direction.
This fits in with the opinion of many anthropologists that there is a

considerable degree of cultural continuity from West Africa round the Bight of Biafra to northern Angola.

While there has been general acceptance for Guthrie's concept that the Bantu languages on the eastern side of the continent are sufficiently closely related to mark them off as a group distinct from the others, the later investigators have had difficulty in recognizing any single equivalent grouping for the languages of the western Bantu peoples of the Congo basin and of the savannah lands immediately to its south. It looks as though the expansion in the west must have been by and large slower than expansion in the eastern half of Bantu Africa. Certainly today it is apparent that the eastern languages cover more ground and encompass appreciably more speakers than do the western Bantu languages. Geography does much to explain this. Movement through the Congo basin forest must necessarily have been slower and more piecemeal than movement over the savannah lands character-istic of eastern and south-eastern Africa, and when the westerners came out of the forests, by and large they were faced with drier lands than the easterners, so that ultimately their expansion was totally halted by the Namib and Kalahari deserts. Conversely, the population growth and the expansion of the eastern Bantu is likely to have been helped by the coming of the south-east Asian food-crops to a greater extent than was possible for the western Bantu. But it now seems plain that, if these food-crops did not arrive among the Bantu before somewhere between about A.D. 300 and A.D. 800, it would have been too late to help with their first expansion beyond the Congo basin.

Since the time when Greenberg and Guthrie were working on the linguistic data, a great amount of relevant archaeological evidence has accumulated. Work at a very large number of sites, firmly dated by the radiocarbon technique, has now demonstrated that by about the end of the fourth century A.D. virtually the whole of the present area of Bantu speech from Uganda in the north to as far as the Transvaal in the south was already occupied by iron-working peoples. There is, of course, no means of knowing for certain what languages were spoken by pre-literate ironworkers, but archaeologists have inferred from the pottery and other evidence of their material culture that has survived that in all probability these iron-workers were the ancestors of modern peoples who speak Bantu languages. Guthrie had suggested from his analysis of the linguistic evidence that the Bantu expansion had begun as one of pre-Iron Age fishermen and cultivators, with knowledge of iron working coming in later. The archaeological evidence would seem to support this. Though there are some earlier dates at the end of the B.C. era around Lake Victoria, over almost all the rest of what is now Bantu Africa the dates for the establishment of iron-working lie between about A.D. 100 and about A.D. 400, and the gradient of the dates between north and south is really so slight that it would seem possible that for the most part the people were already *in situ* when knowledge of iron-working reached them. Indeed the coming of iron need not have involved any great migration of people; it could have taken the form of the swift adoption of a valuable new technology by well-established and progressive farming peoples. No more than the south-east Asian crops can knowledge of iron-working be looked to as a primary factor in the Bantu expansion.

It must be appreciated that Bantu-speaking migrants moving out of the Congo basin forests were not moving into uninhabited lands. As has already been remarked (p. 11), the Sandawe survive as an island of Khoisan speech as far north as central Tanzania, and the language of their near neighbours the Hadza may also be classified as Khoisan. In addition it is well known that the south-easternmost Bantu languages such as Zulu and Xhosa incorporate the click consonants characteristic of Khoisan – the most likely explanation for this being intermarriage between incoming Bantu-speakers and local Khoisan. Indeed, the further south they went, the more it is likely that the advance of the Bantu involved the absorption of earlier, rather thinly spread Khoisan populations. In the north-east, the Bantu entered 'Azanian' lands inhabited by peoples speaking southern Cushitic languages. Indeed this was of some importance because there is firm archaeological evidence that modern Kenya and northern Tanzania were the home of a succession of societies, once known as the 'Stone Bowl' cultures, which from about the middle of the third millennium B.C. onwards had cattle and were developing food-producing techniques well suited to the environment. It is unlikely that the Bantu would have brought large cattle with them through the forest, and their cattle terminology suggests that they acquired cattle from eastern African speakers of Cushitic languages, possibly through the mediation of Khoisan-speaking peoples. There is also linguistic evidence to suggest that at a later stage the Bantu may have borrowed the practice of milking directly from Cushitic-speaking peoples in East Africa.

In conclusion, it can be said that the Bantu expansion seems to have begun as a gradual seepage of small groups through the forests of the

Congo basin. The relatively slow and piecemeal nature of this movement in a difficult environment helps to explain the complexity of the
pattern and the interrelationship of the languages in the north-western
quadrant of present-day Bantu Africa. When the advancing Bantu had
penetrated right through the forest, the situation changed. The north-
eastern Bantu in the forest do not seem to have expanded beyond it,
perhaps because to do so would bring them up against Nilo-Saharan
societies that were well adapted to an environment that was at best
marginal for agriculture. But when the Bantu came to the open savannahs beyond the southerly boundaries of the forest, their expansion
seems to have substantially accelerated. Their cereal agriculture could
provide the basis for larger populations than already existed there, but
at the same time they were also able to absorb useful aspects of the
material cultures of, and sometimes also people from, these populations. The earlier societies survived intact only in drier lands which
were at best marginal for agriculture. In the north-east, while Nilo-
Saharan pastoralists were able to hold on to the salient of arid plains
which extend from the south of the modern Sudan Republic into
central Tanzania, Cushitic-speaking peoples – except for the small
groups like the Iraqw which have survived at the southern end of this
salient near the Sandawe and Hatsa – were restricted to an essentially
pastoral existence in the hot lowlands of the Horn. In central and
southern Africa, although there may have been some Caucasoids, the
bulk of the pre-Bantu population seems to have been composed of
the culturally weaker Khoisan. Some of these, in contact with early
Bantu arrivals, may have adopted their use of agriculture and metals,
but in the long run most of them were swamped by, and absorbed
into expanding Bantu-speaking populations. Some of the Khoisan,
being entirely Stone Age hunter-gatherers, were not really absorbable
and in so far as they were not hunted to extinction, survived only by
retreat into the arid refuge of the Kalahari.

The Bantu expansion seems to have been most fruitful on the eastern
side of the continent. On the western side, the Bantu could do little
more than develop their Sudanic inheritance on a new frontier, a
frontier which became increasingly less attractive the further south
they went towards the desert lands of the Namib and the Kalahari.
In the east, on the other hand, the Bantu met with a number of new
stimuli. The first of these was contact with the Cushitic pastoralists
and food-producers, while later on they would be the first to receive
the rewarding new south-east Asian food-crops. In between times, of

course, it would seem that it was in the far north-east that what we now know as Bantu first began to make tools and weapons of iron, and it was from there that knowledge of iron-working was spread through most of the rest of Bantu-speaking Africa.

Chapter 2

Africa and the ancient civilizations of the Near East and the Mediterranean

The post-Neolithic development of human society in Africa, especially in what is now predominantly Black Africa south of the Sahara, has so far been considered, and properly so, essentially as an internal phenomenon free from external influences except, to some extent, along its east coast fronting the Indian Ocean. North of the Sahara, however, Africa was part of the Mediterranean world, and also in close contact with major developments in nearer Asia. One of the earliest great civilizations, that of Pharaonic Egypt, was itself based in Africa. Subsequent Mediterranean civilizations, those of the Phoenicians and Carthage, and of Greece and Rome, also extended to North Africa, while north-eastern Africa was subject to influence and to settlement from the early civilization of southern Arabia. It is therefore necessary to turn back and to consider the influence which these civilizations on the fringes of Africa may have had on the development of human society in the continent as a whole.

The civilization of the Pharaohs, the first of the great civilizations to be established in Africa, was of course founded on African soil. But Egypt was quite unlike any other part of Africa. It was a desert oasis on the grand scale, with alluvial soils of unrivalled fertility, annually renewed by the Nile flood. It was also situated at the great crossroads where Africa met with Asia, and the world of the Mediterranean met with those of the Red Sea and the Indian Ocean, a strategic point of prime importance, attracting people and ideas from all directions. Well before 3000 B.C., the fertility of its soil was permitting its peasant cultivators to produce beyond their immediate needs. There was support for specialized craftsmen and traders, and the cemeteries of the Gerzean culture of about the fourth millennium reveal considerable evidence both of wealth and of a growing inequality in the distribution of this wealth. Then quite suddenly absolute monarchy appears on the scene, first apparently in two kingdoms, one in the delta and the other in the lower Nile valley, and then in the united Egypt ruled by the Pharaohs.

The revolution in man's thinking and organization represented by this development has been dramatically preserved for us by the pyramids. The Gerzean cemeteries, despite the growing inequalities of wealth possessed by their inmates, represent the burials of whole communities, rich and poor alike. With the coming of the Pharaohs, the life of the community became subordinate to, and represented by, the life of the monarch, who was buried in ever-increasing splendour. Initially the royal burials were in shaft tombs developed from the Gerzean model, but with far richer furniture, and with the king going to the other world accompanied by some hundreds of servitors. Then the shaft was surmounted by a great palace-like structure called a *mastaba*, and then smaller *mastabas* were placed on top of this until ultimately the pyramid form was arrived at. The peak of the development was reached in the Great Pyramid of Gizeh, built about 2400 B.C. This was 500 feet high, built of 60 million tons of large stone blocks in a region in which good building stone is scarce, and erected by men who had no iron tools and next to no machinery. Pharaoh was first thought to be the incarnation of the god Horus, and later the son of the sun-god Amun-Re. In either case, he was the interpreter of the heavenly will to man, and the sole arbiter of his existence, of the use of his land for agriculture and of the times of the flood and his planting and harvesting, with his commands made known to the multitude through a vast hierarchy of priests and ministers and bureaucrats and scribes.

It is uncertain exactly what had produced this change. Some authorities, for example Flinders Petrie and W. B. Emery, supposed that it was occasioned by the arrival of a ruling dynastic race from nearer Asia. This may not have been the case, since the valley civilizations of the Near East seem to have evolved their equivalent dynasties rather later than Egypt. It is quite possible, indeed, as Gordon Childe supposed, that the idea of one absolute control over the whole wealth of the land was an autonomous evolution from the unusual circumstances of the delta and lower valley of the Nile, with an ever-growing population penned into its oasis on all sides by the desert, and utterly dependent (much more so than other early valley civilizations) for its well-being on the arrival of the annual flood. The peasant of Gerzean times was already able to grow three times as much food as he and his family needed. But competition for these surpluses could produce disunities, quarrels and wars, which would prevent its full utilization. Unified control of the surplus, on the other hand, would enable part of it to be exported in exchange for useful commodities which Egypt could not provide and which her civilization needed, while the organizers and their growing train of assistants would be supported and recompensed by other parts of the surplus and by the new wealth from trade, and could indulge in conspicuous consumption of which their palaces and temples and pyramids are the memorial. If this was the case, then in Egypt absolute rule by a god-king would have been a local African concept.

It must be appreciated that the alluvial delta and valley of the lower Nile, though admirably suited for the development of a high agriculture which could support a dense population, tended also to be naturally deficient in many materials, such as stone, timber and metals, needed for the support of an advanced material culture. As Egypt became richer and produced a specialized ruling class, so it had a growing need of foreign trade. With desert to both east and west, the only efficient early means of moving goods in any quantity was by water. Short of timber to make sea-going ships, ancient Egypt was never a great sea-going power; as will be seen, much of her trade on the Mediterranean and Red Seas was carried in the ships of foreigners. But locally made river boats could travel up the Nile further into Africa, to Nubia, the land where the Hamitic-speaking peoples were in contact with those of the Negro Sudan, and Egyptian trading and military activity here began about 2500 B.C.

Under the twelfth dynasty of Pharaohs (c. 2000–1780 B.C.), Nubia was colonized to as far as Semna, just above the second cataract. A series of fortified trading posts was established on the banks of the Nile, so that regular supplies of gold and timber and some tropical produce could be brought to Egypt. This colonial venture was halted during the upset to organized government in Egypt associated with the Hyksos, nomad invaders from the east. But it was resumed under the New Kingdom (c. 1580–1050 B.C.), when the frontier of colonial settlement and trade was pushed to the fourth cataract or further by a series of military expeditions against a Nubian chief or chiefs. Towns, palaces and temples were built, governed by viceroys sent out from the Pharaoh's court. Under the viceroy was an Egyptian administration responsible for maintaining orderly conditions for trade and the regular remittance of tribute, so that gold, slaves, timber, ebony, gum, ivory and ostrich feathers began to flow north in increasing quantities.

In the eleventh century B.C., Egypt was beset by civil discords (in which, incidentally, Nubian soldiers played their part). Egyptian control of Nubia faltered, and out of the viceroyalty an independent kingdom emerged, the kingdom of Kush, with its capital supposedly at Napata, just downstream of the fourth cataract. For a space, the power of organized government in Kush was greater than it was in Egypt. Under Kings Kashta and Piankhy (*c.* 770–716 B.C), Kush's armies conquered Egypt, establishing there the twenty-fifth dynasty, which ruled until the Assyrian conquest in 671–666 B.C. The origin of these Kush kings is unknown. They could have been descended from Egyptian settlers or officials, or they may have descended from the chiefly line or lines conquered under the New Kingdom. But if so, they became increasingly Egyptianized, especially perhaps through the influence of the priests of the temple of Amun-Re that was established at Jebel Barkal. After their conquest of Egypt, they certainly thought of themselves as Egyptians, and they began to be buried in pyramids. But their subjects included Blacks as well as Hamitic-speaking peoples, and after their enforced withdrawal from Egypt in the seventh century, Egyptian influence in Kush began to decline. Kush's southern provinces became more important than the northern sector in which Egyptian influence had first become established, and eventually the seat of government was permanently removed to a more southerly capital, Meroe, between the sixth cataract and the Atbara confluence.

There may have been a number of reasons for this shift of Kush towards the south. The most obvious is that, early in the sixth century, Egyptian troops reappeared in Kush. They did not reconquer the kingdom, but they did cause damage to its northern province. They may thus have assisted processes of desiccation begun by the growth of Kush's population and herds. Another factor was that, following the Assyrian conquest of Egypt, iron-working had become an important activity. Northern Kush had inadequate timber to fire the smelters and forges, while southern Kush was both better wooded and provided with greater supplies of iron ore. Then trade along the Nile declined in the wake of the Egyptian sixth-century military activities while, from the third century, trade in the Red Sea began to expand under the direction of Greek merchants from Alexandria, and

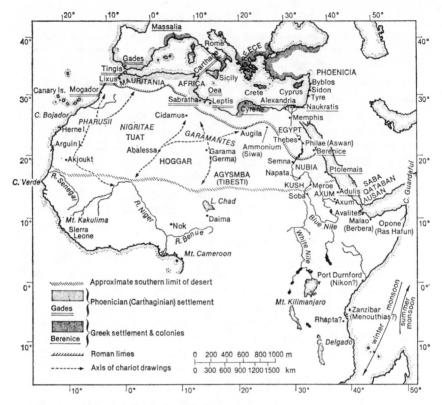

Map 2   Africa and the Ancient World

an increasing proportion of Kush's foreign trade probably began to flow east from Meroe to the Eritrean coast. But here, by the beginning of the Christian era, a new power, the Greek-influenced Semitic kingdom of Axum, was emerging to dominate the trade into the interior. In or before A.D. 350, an army of King Ezana of Axum was sent against Kush. This is usually taken to be the end of the kingdom, but in the inscription in which Ezana recorded his victory, it is noteworthy that there is no mention of Meroe, and the enemy is described as 'the Noba', one of whose towns is called Alwa. Who exactly these Noba were is not altogether certain. But the Romans knew a people in northern Nubia from the third century A.D. onwards whom they called Nobatae, and by the sixth century the former territory of Kush had been organized into three successor kingdoms, of which the northernmost was called in Latin Nobatia and the southernmost Alodia, but in Arabic these names become Nuba and Alwa. It is a fair inference that ancient Meroe had been overwhelmed by the Noba before Ezana's expedition, and that these people later erected three kingdoms in its place.

A common view of the Nubian kingdom ruled from Meroe is that it represents an ancient Egyptian tradition of organized government 'running gradually downhill to a miserable and inglorious end' (as A. J. Arkell put it). It is true that the Egyptian aspect of Meroitic culture declined. There is some indication, for example, that by the beginning of the fourth century B.C., Ancient Egyptian had become a classical language, in use for inscriptions but not in everyday life. By the second century, Egyptian hieroglyphs were being used for inscriptions in Meroitic (a language which has not been wholly deciphered, but which was probably not ancestral to modern Nubian, which may have been introduced by the Noba). Finally, cursive writing was employed. The last kings of Meroe were buried in comparative poverty in ever less pretentious pyramids. But by this time there were no more Egyptian Pharaohs, and Egypt had been subject to the rule of foreigners, Greeks and Romans, for some six centuries. From the African point of view, it is better to see the kingdom of Meroe as a country in which Egyptian and Black traditions could meet and mingle, and where the Sudanic interior could also make some contact with the worlds of Hellenistic Greece, of Rome, and of Red Sea and Indian Ocean trade and culture.

Two aspects of Meroitic Kush have been thought to be of especial significance to the history of sub-Saharan Africa. As has been seen, it is thought that Nubia may have been one of the main channels through which knowledge of iron-working reached the Black peoples. Certainly the vast slag heaps still visible at ancient Meroe suggest that it was a considerable centre for iron industry, likely to influence at least neighbouring peoples in the eastern Sudan. Secondly, and more controversially, it has been supposed that it was also the channel by which aspects of ancient Egyptian culture, the concepts of divine kingship and hierarchical administration in particular, may have reached the Blacks and have influenced their development.

It is commonly argued that the forms of organized monarchical government developed among sub-Saharan Blacks, and probably first evident at some time in the first millennium A.D., display a common pattern. The king, if not necessarily a god himself, was thought to descend from the gods, and was therefore separated from ordinary men by a wealth of ritual. He was rarely seen in public, commonly gave audience from behind some sort of screen, communicated essentially through spokesmen, and was not to be seen performing such mundane functions as eating and drinking. He was the agent of the gods in controlling the use of the land on which his people depended, and determined the times of planting and harvesting and occupied the central role in the great ceremonies appropriate to these times. The fertility of the soil, the regular coming of the rains, and so the whole well-being of the community were thought to be dependent on him and his continued prosperity; his ill-health was a disaster which either had to be concealed or, in some cases, was terminated by his ritual killing. At his death, he was buried in great state together with wives and attendants. At his court there was commonly an important place for a great queen or queen-mother, who was the chief female of the royal family rather than a wife. Under the king there was a hierarchy of great officials to run the court, and to impose order and tribute on the clan and village communities of his subjects. Major items of long-distance trade, such as gold, ivory, copper and salt, were commonly royal monopolies, and the royal court was the prime centre for the major craftsmen of the land, such as workers in gold and the rarer metals, weavers and musicians.

This kind of pattern has been discerned by ethnographers and historians throughout Black Africa: for example, in the lacustrine kingdoms of East Africa, in the Zimbabwe-Monomotapa states in southern Africa, and in West Africa in monarchies like those of Kanem and Benin. There is obviously some affinity with the divine monarchy of Ancient Egypt, though exactly how much is obscure, since flesh and blood has sometimes been given to the earliest Egyptian situation – otherwise known only from archaeological evidence – by analogies drawn from other parts of Africa following modern ethnographic work. However, since the earliest divine monarchy known in Africa is that of Ancient Egypt, it has been strongly argued that the Egyptian model was diffused through the rest of the continent through its southern outpost in Kush. Of course this begs the question of whether the springs of monarchy in Kush were Egyptian-inspired from the beginning, or whether they were an indigenous development which later came under Egyptian influence. But if major concepts of kingship and government were diffused from the Nile valley, it is reasonable to suppose that it was more likely to have been from Kush than from Egypt for, with the single major exception of the spread of the Amun-Re cult westwards along the caravan trails running through oases like Siwa to North-West Africa, there is little evidence for ancient Egyptian influence spreading through the deserts to west and east of the Nile. However it is not easy to see how divine kingship could have been diffused beyond Meroe.

There is little evidence for the spread of Meroitic influence up the White Nile, where the people were 'Nilo-Saharans' who knew nothing of urban civilization and little of long-distance trade. Other explanations seem necessary for the two major manifestations of organized monarchy under sacred kings that have been noted among these Nilotic peoples. One of these is the kingdom of the Shilluk, the power of which reached about as far north as what may be presumed to have been the southern limits of rule from Meroe. But the Shilluk kingdom was developed only about the sixteenth century, that is to say about twelve centuries after the demise of ancient Meroe, and was occasioned, it would seem, by an invasion and conquest by a branch of the Luo, a Nilotic group coming from the *south*. But most Luo – like the Nilotic peoples generally – remained essentially stateless, and the other prime example of divine kingship in a Nilotic context resulted from another Luo conquest, about the same time, of Bantu-speaking agriculturalists far to the south, in what is now Uganda. Here, in the kingdom of Bunyoro, it is sufficiently clear that a southern branch of the Luo, rather than introducing divine kingship to the Bantu, took over a system of monarchy that was already practised in the country.*

If one does want to think in terms of diffusion from Meroe, it is perhaps more plausible to suppose that its style of monarchy found its way up the Blue Nile to influence the Sidama, Cushitic-speaking peoples in the south-western Ethiopian highlands, whose kingdoms such as Kaffa and Enaryea or their precursors may in their turn have influenced Bantu Africa. This could have been through the medium of a Cushitic substratum overrun by the Bantu settlers. Only an explanation such as this might explain how a set of beliefs and practices originating in the Nile valley could have arrived in time to influence the Zimbabwe–Monomotapa Bantu kingdoms so far to the south by about the twelfth century if not earlier.

* See chapter 5.

But this is mere surmise. Hard evidence for Meroitic contacts with the outside world other than Egypt really exists only to the east where, as has been seen, Meroitic influence came to be eclipsed by the rival power of Axum. There is some very tenuous evidence for Nubian influence seeping westward through the Sudan to about as far as Lake Chad (and therefore to Kanem). But in so far as this can be dated, it would seem to relate not to ancient Meroe, but to the Christian kingdoms which arose in its place from about the sixth century A.D. onwards. There is thus nothing here to suggest a strong formative influence from Meroe on the kingdoms of the western Sudan, the earliest known of which, ancient Ghana, was in the far west and was certainly extant by the eighth century, and all of which had their main external links not to the east, but northwards across the Sahara via the Berber nomads of the desert.

Indeed, it is perhaps more reasonable to think that throughout Africa, and particularly perhaps in riverain valleys, divine kingship may have been a more or less natural evolution from the development of agriculture. As a people increased and became increasingly dependent on the crops which their land could grow, and on the water which fed them, so there could have been more need for unified control of their life. Since there was a universal belief in the need to propitiate the spirits of the land and the water, so the mediation of their ancestors in the spirit world became more important. The leader of each society, the lineal descendant of the founding ancestor of the group, the man who had first led them to clear the land and bargain for its use with its spirits, became the prime mediator with the other world, and so more and more invested with supernatural qualities. If this is what did happen, over and over again, then the Pharaonic kingship should be seen not as an ancient Egyptian development which could be diffused from Egypt to the rest of Africa, but rather as a most sophisticated example of a general African development, one formed in the peculiar conditions of the lower Nile valley and delta. As such, it might well, perhaps mainly via Meroe, have been an unusually influential model, so that other divine monarchies, perhaps by any number of indirect or even trivial ways, might be led to adopt and adapt some of its traits.

It has already been remarked that Ancient Egypt was not a great sea-power, and that this was essentially because it lacked timber to build sea-going ships. By 3000 B.C., indeed, it was already importing timber from the port of Byblos in the Lebanon in exchange for manufactured exports such as papyrus (thus, in the long run, providing English with the words 'Bible' and 'paper'). There was also trade with Cyprus for copper (another homonym), and Minoan Crete was becoming an important maritime entrepôt for the eastern Mediterranean. Throughout the area, indeed, the wealth of Egypt was becoming an important stimulus to trade and for the growth of towns and urban civilization, and it was this development which brought to Africa the two major mercantile and maritime peoples of the eastern Mediterranean, the Greeks and the Phoenicians.

Beginning with the trade between Minoan Crete and Egypt, sea-going Greek communities began to prosper and multiply, and so to colonize many lands around the eastern Mediterranean coasts. From the later seventh century B.C., a number of colonies of Greek emigrants were established in the fertile valleys of Cyrenaica (so named from the colony of Cyrene). But these were essentially agricultural settlements, which looked to the Mediterranean for such external contacts as they had, and which exerted little influence on the rest of Africa, from which they were indeed cut off by desert on all sides.

Of much greater importance was the colony of traders which was established about the same time at Naukratis, near the Rosetta mouth of the Nile. With the decline of indigenous Egyptian organization following the Assyrian and Persian invasions, Greek traders came to dominate Egypt's foreign trade and much of its commercial life. In 332 B.C. Greek influence in Egypt was taken a step further with Alexander of Macedon's conquest of the land from the Persians. A new ruling dynasty was established by one of his generals, Ptolemy, and the capital was moved from the Nile to a new city, Alexandria, on the Mediterranean seaboard. Fed by the agricultural wealth of Egypt as well as by the commanding role it assumed as the linchpin in trade between the Mediterranean and the Red Sea and the western Indian Ocean, Alexandria soon became the greatest of all Greek cities, possessing, it is said, a population of 300 000 citizens and as many slaves. Some of its wealth was used to support a lively and truly international intellectual life, in which Greek philosophy and science were fused with the heritage of the ancient valley civilizations of Egypt and Asia, thus providing a platform of knowledge and thought from which major further advances could be made. Judaism was early established here, and in due course Alexandria became the major centre for the development of the religion and philosophy of Christianity.

The great rivals of the Greeks for Mediterranean trade were the Phoenicians. Phoenicia was the Greek name for the coastlands of Syria and Lebanon, inhabited by a Semitic-speaking people who in another context are known to us as the Canaanites. Byblos was one of its earliest ports; later, Tyre and Sidon became its principal cities. With an immediate hinterland that was arid and inhospitable, the Phoenicians naturally looked to the sea for their living, and they were admirably placed to serve as an entrepôt in the trade between the valley civilizations of Mesopotamia and Egypt. In the process they developed no mean civilization of their own, among other things being the inventors of the alphabet, the most flexible of writing systems, and now the basis of all writing throughout the world except in China and Japan.

By and large the Phoenicians were worsted by the Greeks in competition for the maritime trade of Egypt, but further west they more than held their own. Here the main prize was access to the silver and lead and other metals of the Iberian peninsula and other even more remote western European lands. While the Greeks expanded westwards along the northern shores of the Mediterranean, the Phoenician route to the west ran along the African coastline. Rowing against the prevailing westerly winds (they could sail only when the wind came from astern), and preferring to travel by day, beaching their galleys ashore for the night, the Phoenicians required a considerable number of staging posts on this coastline. By about the eighth century B.C., some of these posts west of Cyrenaica were developing into considerable urban colonies.

Even the smaller settlements, seawards-looking and with little interest in the continent at their backs, were probably helping in the processes by which the Berber tribes of the coastal plains and valleys were becoming sedentary agricultural members of a Mediterranean civilization, while their kinsmen on the mountains and steppes of the interior continued as independent, mobile pastoralists. The Phoenician settlements needed foodstuffs to provision themselves and their galleys and sometimes also for export, and the agricultural Berbers received in exchange the manufactured goods of the Mediterranean world. Indeed they received more than this; sharing a common Afroasiatic linguistic and cultural background with the Phoenicians, the Berbers proved particularly receptive to Semitic cultural influences, and Phoenician

influence paved the way for their later acceptance of the great monotheistic religions, first Judaism, and then Christianity and Islam. Even
the pastoralists of the hinterland could not wholly escape the processes
of change. The Phoenician settlements and the areas of developing
agriculture around them provided worthwhile opportunities first for
raiding and plundering, and then increasingly for the exchange of their
cattle and hides and dairy produce for manufactures, and for grain
for the winter feeding of themselves and their herds.

There were three particular areas in which Phoenician staging posts
provided the foundation for the growth of considerable cities. One
of these was what we now know as northern Tunisia, the most sizeable
single area of fertile agricultural land in all north-western Africa. But
the region was also significant for the Phoenicians because of its
strategic situation, commanding the Sicilian narrows, the gateway to
the western Mediterranean. In Sicily itself, the Phoenicians found
themselves in direct and bitter competition with Greek settlers; it thus
became important to them to secure undivided control of the nearby
Tunisian coast and its harbours. Here therefore they concentrated
considerable settlements which, with a secure agricultural base on the
plains behind them, could be independent of support from their
distant homeland. In fact, while Phoenician power at home was
suffering increasingly from attack by mainland Asian peoples such as
the Assyrians and the Persians, their Tunisian colonies began to act
more and more independently. Ultimately, by about the sixth century,
the greatest of these, Carthage, emerged as an independent power
with control over all the other settlements in Africa and the western
Mediterranean. Carthage's increasing imperial and commercial
responsibilities meant that it became a really major city, with a population estimated at some 400 000, and requiring considerable military
as well as naval forces. Therefore during the fourth century it extended
its control over the Tunisian plain to ensure a sure supply both of
foodstuffs and of Berber soldiers for its armies.

The other major areas of Phoenician urban development in north-
western Africa were the region we now call Tripolitania, since here
were the three cities of Lepcis, Oea and Sabratha, and the northern
Atlantic coast of Morocco, where the principal city was Lixus (modern
Larache). The reasons why considerable cities were developed in these
two areas are more obscure. Lixus, it is true, was on the shores of
the next most sizeable area of arable plain in North-West Africa
after northern Tunisia, but Tripoli today has virtually no agricultural

hinterland at all. This was not the case in ancient times, for the Carthaginians (and, after them, the Romans) were highly skilled at agriculture in semi-arid conditions, and in Tripolitania, with the aid of irrigation systems maintained by slave labour, were able to grow both grain and olives, for export as well as local consumption. But even in ancient times Tripoli was very close indeed to the desert.

It seems probable that a considerable part of the importance of Tripolitania and some of that of Lixus was that they lay at the head of trade routes leading south across the Sahara towards the Sudan. It has earlier been suggested that the Phoenicians, as they established themselves along the North African coasts, were far more interested in gaining access to the far west than they were in Africa. The continent north of the Sahara provided little in the way of trading commodities that could not be more expeditiously obtained elsewhere in the Mediterranean. But it seems probable that as the Phoenicians became Carthaginians, in closer touch with the North African Berbers, and more dependent on them for foodstuffs or other commodities to supply their own cities, so as a trading people they would have become interested in the possibility of acquiring valuable or exotic commodities from the lands to the south of them, from the Sahara or even beyond it.

Human contacts across the desert would have remained from the days when the Sahara had been grassland with a comparatively stable population, and subsequently it would have been perpetuated with the aid of transhumance. On both the northern and southern limits of the desert, pastoralists and agriculturalists would have had much to gain from some exchange of their products. It would therefore have been possible for small quantities of goods of tropical African origin to have passed from tribe to tribe across the desert to North Africa, while conversely Mediterranean and Saharan products could have reached the Sudan. Some of the Saharan pastoralists doubtless saw that trading or raiding across the desert – or, for that matter, the raiding of trade crossing the desert – afforded opportunities for enriching desert existence. One such group were the Garamantes of the Fezzan in the central Sahara south of Tripoli, described by Herodotus in the fifth century B.C. as using four-horse chariots to raid the 'Ethiopians'. (Some eight centuries later, Ptolemy was to report that the raids of the Garamantes went as far as a land where there were rhinoceroses.) In the first century B.C. the Roman geographer Strabo wrote about the Saharan chariot raids of more westerly peoples, the

Nigritae, who were probably based on the oasis of Tuat, and the Pharusii, who lived close to the Atlantic seaboard. Herodotus also refers to a route of oases running from the Fezzan to beyond the Hoggar mountains, and to a party of Nazamones from Cyrenaica, who crossed the Sahara in a southwesterly direction until they came to 'a vast tract of marshy country, and beyond it to a town, all the inhabitants of which were of . . . small stature and all black. A great river with crocodiles in it flowed from west to east.' This river is usually supposed to have been the Niger.

The Saharan activities of charioteers like the Garamantes and Pharusii are said to have been for plunder, not for trade, but the one can easily lead to the other. In modern times some confirmation has been found for the ancient stories of charioteering in the Sahara. A large number of rock engravings have been found of wheeled vehicles, each drawn by four four-legged creatures, and these are disposed across the desert along two lines of hard-going (which today provide motorable tracks). One – which supports the report of Herodotus – runs south-west from the Fezzan and Ghadames across the narrowest width of the Sahara to the Niger bend, and the other – supporting Strabo – goes from southern Morocco towards the upper valleys of the Senegal and Niger rivers. These have been interpreted as evidence of trade routes which would have terminated in Tripoli and Lixus respectively.

However, assuming that the wheeled vehicles are indeed chariots, it must be remarked that ancient chariots were light vehicles unsuitable for carrying anything more than one or two charioteers or for going on more than relatively short raids from their base; the evidence would then not indicate significant trans-Saharan trade, but only that there were two routes along which tribe to tribe contact across the Sahara was easier than usual. But the drawings – or some of them – might represent bullock carts, in which case this could be evidence of regular trade of some kind. If so, the nature of the goods being transported is a mystery. No Mediterranean manufactures of any antiquity have ever turned up in archaeological sites in the Sudan west of the Nile valley. The only southern commodity imported into North Africa to have made any impact in the early literary sources is the carbuncle, a precious stone whose identity has not been established, and which in any case would not need to be carried in carts. In later times, a major commodity imported into the Sudan from the Sahara was salt, but this would not have left evidence for archaeologists, and the principal

North African imports from the Sudan included gold dust, slaves, and things like ivory, skins and ostrich feathers. In classical times, there would have been no need to import these last, for the relevant animals still ran wild in North Africa itself. Neither black slaves nor gold dust would have needed carts to transport them, and neither seem to have been present in North Africa in classical times to the extent that they were after the development of regular camel caravan trade across the Sahara around the middle of the first millennium A.D. Nevertheless it does seem as though enough was known to the Carthaginians about the possible advantages of commercial intercourse with the Sudan for them to think of engaging in it directly themselves. As a seafaring people, they were unlikely to challenge the power of the tribes that controlled the desert; their best course would be to explore the prospects for sea trading ventures down the Saharan coastline.

Whereas there is a fair amount of archaeological evidence on the east coast of Africa for the activities in the classical period of visiting traders coming by sea (see Chapter 5), none has been found on the west coast beyond southern Morocco, where Mogador (Essaouira) is the furthest known Carthaginian settlement. The evidence that the Carthaginians may have gone further is entirely literary and its interpretation largely debatable. Herodotus, writing in the fifth century, says that beyond the Strait of Gibraltar, and presumably beyond their furthest settlement, the Carthaginians traded for gold by dumb barter. This form of trade suggests either that the trade was a transient one with people unaccustomed to dealing with strangers, or – more probably – that the Carthaginians wanted to conceal its details from possible competitors.* The *Periplus* of the fourth century, falsely attributed to Scylax, states that from an island called Kerne the Carthaginians traded with a great city of the Ethiopians, albeit not

---

* 'Dumb barter', or 'the silent trade' is a practice quite widely reported when traders from afar first began to deal with people not accustomed to trading with strangers (later occurrences in West Africa are mentioned in chapters 3 and 4). It is said to have operated as follows. The visitors deposit the goods they have to exchange, and then retire out of sight. The local people then approach, and place beside the trade goods the amount of their produce they consider to be a fair exchange, and then retire in their turn. The traders then reappear and, if not satisfied with the exchange, will again withdraw, hoping that more local produce will be forthcoming. But when they are satisfied, they take away the local produce and leave their own goods behind. Whether dumb barter actually occurred in this classical form is another matter. There is reason to believe that, in West Africa at any rate, stories of dumb barter conceal systems of local brokerage (and may have been propagated to protect the interests of the brokers).

for gold, but for skins, ivory and wine (though there is another fourth century source which associates Kerne with gold). Finally, there is the so-called *Periplus* of Hanno, one of the very few Carthaginian writings to have survived, albeit only in a Greek version. Both the authenticity and the interpretation of this are open to debate, but ostensibly it is an account of one or more fifth-century voyages to establish settlements down the Atlantic coast, the most southerly of which was on the island of Kerne, and then to prospect for the possibilities of trade even further afield.

Kerne is presumably one of the islands off the western coast of the Sahara, such as Arguin (which the Portuguese were to use as a trading base in the fifteenth century) or, possibly, an island in or near the mouth of the Senegal, for immediately after Kerne it is said that Hanno sailed up a big river. The main problem with the Hanno *Periplus* lies in assessing how far beyond this the Carthaginian explorers may have ventured. Some would interpret its text as indicating that Hanno got as far as Sierra Leone or even the Cameroons, while others would dismiss the whole second half of the *Periplus* as nothing more than a conflation of ancient myths. From the point of view of the history of Africa, however, the controversy is somewhat sterile. It seems plain that the Carthaginians did explore the possibility of maritime trade with the Sudan, and that they might have quite probably reached its north-western limits about the Senegal. But how far they may have prospected further is immaterial, because it is practically certain that to maintain a regular sea-trade with West Africa lay beyond their effective capabilities. The waterless, inhospitable coast of the Sahara made it virtually impossible to maintain the regular staging posts which were so vital to Carthaginian maritime operations, and trade with its few nomadic inhabitants cannot have been very rewarding. There were also considerable technical navigational problems facing the Carthaginians. They were no longer sailing in the landlocked Mediterranean, but in the wide ocean with its heavy swells beating onto open beaches. Furthermore, both the prevailing wind and the current along the Atlantic coast to as far as Cape Verde came from the north. These would have facilitated a first reconnaissance to the south, but would have made it extremely difficult for their galleys to return home northwards. The Carthaginians may well have concluded that Mediterranean galleys were not suited to the establishment of a regular navigation to and fro along the Atlantic coast south of Morocco.

Thus, however successful and far-reaching Hanno's voyage of discovery may have been, it does not seem to have been followed up by regular maritime traffic with West Africa. Such trade as the Carthaginians had with Black Africa remained indirect, through the mediation of the nomad Berber tribes who dominated the western Sahara. Carthaginian influence in Africa was thus effectively limited to the settled, agricultural areas of North Africa close by their own cities. This influence was naturally strongest in the immediate hinterland of Carthage itself, and secondly in Numidia, the complex of valleys and mountains in western Tunisia and eastern Algeria, where, by the time of Carthage's fatal struggle for survival against Roman imperialism, some Berber chieftains had erected considerable kingdoms to exploit the growing agricultural prosperity of their peoples.

The new power of Rome was not initially much interested in empire in north-western Africa. A much more important focus for Roman interests in Africa lay in Egypt, with its greater agricultural wealth and its access to the rich trade of Asia and the Indian Ocean. Indeed, as Roman imperial power grew, so Egypt slipped almost insensibly into its hands, being finally organized as a formal Roman province in 30 B.C. But long before this, Rome had become involved with Carthage in a conflict for the control of Sicily, which was of vital strategic importance to both empires. Rome continued to fear – or to be jealous of – Carthage even after she had won the day in Sicily (201 B.C.), and eventually in 149 embarked on a war to destroy Carthaginian power in its homeland. This result was achieved in 146 B.C. when, as every schoolboy used to know, the old city of Carthage was utterly destroyed and the land on which it had stood put to the plough.

But this was not the end of the matter. To prevent a resurrection of Carthaginian power, the Romans went on to occupy the Tunisian plains, which they formed into a province which they called Africa. But this brought them into conflict with the adjacent Berber kingdoms, so that Numidia had to be added to the empire to ensure the security of Africa. The Romans then faced a problem which was to plague all imperialists in the African continent, not least the French after their occupation of Algiers in 1830. The borders of their imperial provinces were subject to continual raids from the tribal peoples further afield. Ultimately the Romans were led to occupy almost all the agricultural land from Egypt to Morocco (then called Mauretania), and to establish along the edge of the Saharan steppes a continuous military frontier, the *limes*, which they sought to garrison with regular soldiers.

These men, together with other emigrants seeking new opportunities in the colonies, settled down in the country, and so gave rise to a new stabilized Romano-Berber population. Basing themselves on the exploitation of agriculture to feed imperial Rome and its armies, the Romano-Berbers made North Africa an integral part of the Roman empire, as today the ruins of their numerous cities and forums and theatres and baths and villas bear eloquent witness.

The Roman empire thus consolidated an earlier trend of North African history due to Egyptian, Greek and Phoenician influences. Its agricultural lands and their inhabitants were in effect detached from the African continent and brought firmly within the sphere of Mediterranean civilization, a civilization which now had secured intellectual roots in the marriage of Greek philosophy and Judaism and, by the time of the Emperor Constantine's conversion in A.D. 334, in their common offspring, Christianity. Alexandria remained one of the greatest centres of this civilization, and it was here as much as anywhere else that an aberrant Judaic sect was moulded into the Christian church. The founding father of modern Christian doctrine, Athanasius (*c.* 296–373), was an Alexandrian; so too was his great opponent Arius (*c.* 256–336), the propagator of the heresy which bears his name, who was born in Libya. The new Carthage which the Romans had built was also an important early centre for both Judaism and Christianity, producing in St Augustine (born in Numidia in 354, died as Bishop of Hippo in 430) the greatest of all the early Christian fathers.

The role of early Judaism in North Africa, overlaid as it has been first by Christianity and then by Islam, is not easy to discern, but seems to have been of considerable importance. In addition to preparing the way for the two later Semitic monotheisms, some aspects of Judaism seem to have been early integrated into Berber culture, that of the pastoralists as well as of the settled agriculturalists. It must be remembered that during the ninth century B.C., an important period for Phoenician colonization, there were close relations between Canaan and the kingdoms of Israel and Judah. It seems likely that the settlers in Africa whom we call Phoenicians may well have included people who, had they remained in Palestine, would have become what we now call Jews. Then in 65 B.C. the kingdom of Judaea was brought within the compass of the Roman empire, thus facilitating further contact between its people and the African provinces. When in A.D. 70 this kingdom was destroyed by the Romans, there followed both the great *Diaspora* and a need for the final definition of the emigrants' distinctive faith. It is therefore not surprising that by Roman times there is evidence of considerable Jewish communities living in Egypt and elsewhere in North Africa, not only in the major cities, but also far inland, in the northern Saharan oases, where among other things they seem to have been bankers, financiers and metal-workers associated with the trade across the desert. Their influence on the local Berber tribesmen was thus likely to have been considerable.

The history of Christianity in northern Africa is more clearly documented. The religion had obviously gained considerable support appreciably before the conversion of Constantine. The acceptance of Christianity as the official religion of the Roman empire would presumably have had the effect of spreading it even more widely. But it also created a situation in which ordinary Egyptians and Berbers seem to have felt a need to use their Christianity as an expression of their local particularisms.

Those who held positions of authority or influence in the Roman power structure naturally accepted the official imperial church (the Melkite church, as it came to be called in Egypt). But many of the ordinary people opted for sectarian churches, thus showing that although they were involved in the universal Roman Christian world, they were distinctively Egyptian or Berber members of it. This was most obvious in Egypt, where there evolved what was in effect a native Egyptian church, the church of the Copts, devoted to the Monophysite view of the nature of Christ which, following the Council of Chalcedon in A.D. 451, the rest of Christianity had agreed to be heretical. In north-western Africa there were no doctrinal grounds for conflict with the established church; but something approaching a national church for the country-folk, especially in Numidia, emerged from the conflict over the election of bishops which produced the Donatist schism.

The direct impact of the Roman empire on Africa beyond the *limes* was negligible. Because of the security and prosperity ensured by the empire for the lands at the northern end of the desert tracks, trade may well have increased with people in the Sahara and even possibly with those beyond it. But, as always, it was in the hands of the desert tribes, who were not members of the Roman world, and were wont to raid it as well as trade with it. In an attempt to check raiding and to facilitate trading, the Romans undertook military operations in the Fezzan during the first century A.D., but this was the southernmost limit of their power and their strength there was maintained for only a few decades.

Indeed in their attempts to grapple with the problem of maintaining the *limes* against marauding tribesmen, the Romans may have taken a step which ultimately made impossible the continuance of their African empire. During Ptolemaic times, the camel, an Asian animal, became established in Egypt. The Romans soon saw its value as a beast of burden which could help solve the logistic problems involved in supplying their frontier posts facing the desert, and of quickly reinforcing them should the need arise. But the camel proved to be a two-edged weapon. It was even more useful to the desert tribes as a riding animal, vastly increasing their mobility, enabling them to concentrate swiftly for an attack on the frontier and the lands behind it, and then as quickly to dissolve into the desert and leave no target at which the Roman soldiers could strike back.

By the fifth century, the Roman empire was everywhere crumbling, and North Africa was actually invaded and the province of Africa for a space controlled by the Vandals, a Teutonic tribe who had swarmed through Europe to the Iberian peninsula and across the Strait of Gibraltar from an original homeland between the Oder and Vistula rivers. But in due course the Vandals were merged in the Romano-Berber population and their descendants became subjects of the new Roman empire of Byzantium. The real danger to the empire in Africa was now the Berber camel cavaliers, who were everywhere overrunning and pushing back the *limes*, and developing a new political power of their own which the later Arab historians were to know as the Zenata, a loose confederation of the tribes of the northern Sahara and the adjacent steppe lands. The Byzantine empire in Africa was restricted to Egypt and Cyrenaica, Tripolitania, and the provinces of Africa and Numidia. Everywhere else the old Mediterranean agricultural civilization was being eroded by the advance of the Sahara pastoralists.

But if the political power of the Mediterranean world in Africa was everywhere ebbing, one of the seeds that it had planted had taken firm root on African soil and had even spread deep into the continent. This was the religion and culture of Christianity. The native African churches of Egypt and north-western Africa were eventually to be swamped by the growth of Islam following the Arab conquest of Africa north of the Sahara in the seventh century, but by this time Christianity had already spread further afield. The competing Melkite and Monophysite churches in Egypt sought to enlarge their strength by converting the three kingdoms which had emerged along the upper Nile in Nubia as successors to ancient Meroe. Between the first and third cataracts was Nobatia, or Nuba, with its capital at the modern Faras; beyond the third cataract to as far as ancient Meroe was Makuria (Makurra), with its capital at Old Dongola; and beyond this again was Alodia (Alwa), with its capital at Soba on the lower course of the Blue Nile. During the sixth century, the kings and courts of Nobatia and Alodia were converted by Monophysite missionaries, while the Melkites seem to have secured a comparable success in Makuria. The Nubian ruling classes seem thus to have gained an intellectual and cultural reinforcement for their Meroitic inheritance which helped them maintain the independence of their kingdoms until the fourteenth century, when they finally succumbed to centuries of Muslim infiltration, by traders from Egypt and by bedouin Arab nomad tribes from the desert.

A more remarkable and lasting success was gained by Christianity even further to the south, and once again this was based on earlier heritages from the ancient civilizations. The Semitic inhabitants of south-western Arabia (in and around the modern Yemen) had by early in the first millennium B.C. evolved a distinctive civilization of their own. This had two bases. In the first place, south-western Arabia commanded the junction between the Red Sea and the Western Indian Ocean. Its people were therefore well situated to engage in and to benefit from the trade of the region, the more so since in their own land and in adjacent north-eastern Africa they had access to major sources of two of its most important commercial commodities, incense and spices. Secondly, theirs was the only part of the Arabian peninsula receiving regular rainfall, even if it was only for a few summer months when the south-eastern monsoon touched the Yemeni mountains. Nevertheless, by building dams and by organizing governments to control the irrigation of the valleys, it was possible to develop an agricultural civilization, and a number of major kingdoms arose, of which Saba (Sheba) is the best known and was for some time the most powerful.

At least as early as the seventh century B.C., the south-west Arabians began to expand to nearby Africa. In part they went as traders, seeking supplies of incense, spices and ivory. But, as their own population tended to increase beyond the somewhat restricted agricultural capacity of their homeland, they also became colonists. In the highlands of Eritrea and Ethiopia behind the arid western coastland of the Red Sea, they found conditions for agriculture that were better than those at home, and from these they could penetrate even further into Africa to exploit trade routes for commodities such as ivory, gold and gum. The movement included not only Sabaeans, but also some Arabian Jewish elements.

By the first century A.D., the Semitic colonists, fusing with local Cushitic peoples, who like themselves were also food producers and speakers of Afroasiatic languages, had established their own independent polity, the kingdom of Axum. This evolved a language and writing of its own, Ge'ez (from which modern Amharic is descended), which, though Semitic, was distinct from the Semitic tongues of Arabia. By the third century, through its port of Adulis, Axum was powerful enough for a time to extend its rule across the Red Sea into the Yemen. Foreign traders had been active at Adulis since about the third century B.C., and it was now a major post for the Red Sea and Indian Ocean trade of the Alexandrian Greeks, whose presence shortly brought about the introduction of Christianity into the kingdom. The fourth century saw Axum at the height of its power under King Ezana (c. A.D. 320–50), who is famous not only for his expedition to Kush, but also for the great buildings and obelisks he caused to be erected at Axum, and especially because he was the first king to accept Christianity.

The conversion of Ezana marks a high point for Greek influence at Axum (there are Greek inscriptions from his time as well as those in Ge'ez), and doubtless was to a considerable extent a political move intended to cement the commercial links with Egypt and the Byzantine world that were so important to Axum's prosperity. It also involved Axum in further adventures in the Yemen, where Christianity was in direct competition with Judaism. Early in the sixth century, Dhu Nuwas, the last of the Himyarite kings who had dominated the Yemen after the period of Axumite rule in the third century, was converted to Judaism and embarked on a persecution of Christians. This led to an Axumite invasion of the Yemen under King Ella Asbeha in A.D. 525, and to a further period of Axumite rule there which lasted until the arrival of the Sassanid Persians at the end of the sixth century.

But if originally Christianity in Axum was a religion of the king and the ruling class adopted mainly for politico-economic reasons, it soon became much more than this. Tradition records that, after the Council of Chalcedon, towards the end of the fifth century, Monophysite monks reached Axum. They seem to have been remarkably successful in preaching to a population of mixed Semitic, Cushitic, Judaic and early Christian antecedents, and their work led to the emergence of a distinct national church, with the scriptures translated into Ge'ez. When Cosmas Indicopleustes wrote, in the first half of the sixth century, he regarded Axum as a thoroughly Christianized country. The Ethiopian church, with a strong monastic tradition, capable of maintaining at least a minimum of learning and yet also involving an appreciable proportion of the population, and with a willingness to adopt a syncretic attitude towards traditional Judaic or even pagan beliefs, became a vital element in national life. It created a wide base on which the Axumite tradition of central monarchy could survive the decline of the Hellenistic era in the Red Sea and the shock of the rise of Islamic power to control its trade and its coastlands. The kingdom withdrew into the interior highlands, absorbed more and more essentially African peoples, and so, while remaining steadfastly if idiosyncratically Christian, transformed itself from the Graeco-Semitic kingdom of Axum into the African kingdom of Ethiopia which lasted into the twentieth century.

Chapter 3

The development of states and trade in the Sudan

The accession of Muslim Arabs to power in Africa north of the Sahara and to dominate the trade of the Red Sea and the western Indian Ocean, from the seventh century onwards, led to a considerable increase in the sources of information concerning the development of Black Africa. The Islamic world, the heir to both the Hellenistic and Persian civilizations, to which it added a distinctive contribution of its own, maintained a high level of intellectual inquiry and of scholarship until at least the fourteenth century. The Arabs were best informed about that part of the *Bilad al-Sudan*, 'the land of the Blacks', which was approached by trade routes across the Sahara whose northern termini were in their hands. Arab geographers', historians' and travellers' accounts of the western and central Sudan begin to be of value in the eighth century, and the amount and quality of their information then generally increases up to the work of Ibn Khaldun, the greatest of Arabic historians, who wrote around the turn of the fourteenth century. By this time, when the intellectual life of the main centres of the Muslim world entered into a period of decline, historical scholarship had been established in the Sudan itself, and chronicles written there by African authors are known to have survived from at least the sixteenth century. These written sources of information may be supplemented by some modern archaeology and also by the study of the oral traditions of those kingdoms which survived into modern times.

One of the impressions of the western and central Sudan given by the earliest Arabic authorities, and one that is certainly confirmed by later writers, is that this land was not inhabited simply by tribal societies. It contained organized kingdoms which, though they owed nothing to Islam and were indeed often very strange to Muslim eyes, the Arabs were prepared and able to deal with as they dealt with other non-Muslim states elsewhere. The earliest notable manifestations of these Sudanic kingdoms known to the Arabs seem to have been in two specific areas on the southern fringes of the Sahara. One was just to the north of the upper Niger and Senegal valleys, where the principal state has come to be called Ghana,* and the other was just to the north and north-east of Lake Chad, where the Kanem monarchy of the Saifawa was established. The evidence suggests that the emergence of monarchical government in ancient Ghana was probably somewhat earlier than in Kanem.

The first known reference to the kingdom of Ghana is that of the ninth-century writer al-Fazari. By the end of the ninth and the beginning of the tenth centuries, the writings of Ya'qubi and al-Mas'udi give the idea of a powerful Sudanic kingdom whose monarch exercised some suzerainty over lesser kingdoms. A principal economic activity of the kingdom was the collection of gold from peoples further to the south, and its exchange for Saharan salt and North African manufactures brought south by the Tuareg tribes of the western desert, specifically the Sanhaja, who controlled the caravan routes from Awdaghust, a Sanhaja trading city just north of Ghana, to Sijilmasa, in the oasis of Tafilalt in southern Morocco.

In A.D. 1067–8, the Cordoban geographer al-Bakri was able to put together a fairly comprehensive account of the monarchy, the capital city and the trade of the kingdom of Ghana. The king, who was not the son of his predecessor, but a son of his predecessor's sister, was

---

* This original Ghana should not be confused with its modern namesake, which lies appreciably further to the south and east. It may be noted that the surviving traditions of the Soninke, the native people of ancient Ghana, seem to refer to it as the Kingdom of Wagadu (and Wagadu is the Soninke name for the region in which ancient Ghana was situated). But the Arabic authors – and so history generally – use the name Ghana, for the capital city as well as the kingdom. However, the best informed early authority, al-Bakri, does remark that properly Ghana is the title of the king. The name may thus derive from the Malinke word *gana* or *kana* meaning 'chief', although the name al-Bakri gives for the king reigning in his day is Tunka Manin, and *tunka* certainly means 'chief' in Soninke. It may also be noted that the Timbuctu *tarikhs* (see below) give the name Kaya-Magha for the founding dynasty of Ghana, and *magha* also means chief or ruler. It seems by no means unusual for both states in Black Africa and their capitals to have been known by a name indicating the presence of royalty. Thus Mali in Malinke (and Mande in Soninke) means 'the place where "the master" [*ma*] resides' – and by extension the Malinke or Mande people are 'the people of the king'. Similarly, Yendi, the capital of the kingdom of the Dagomba means 'where the king is'. Or, for a central African example, cf. Kazembe in chapter 5.

an autocrat who communicated with his subjects only indirectly, and was accorded almost divine honours. As well as being the focus of a hierarchy of ministers of state, the king was the centre of an indigenous cult which was carried on by priests in secluded groves near the capital. When he died, he was buried, together with some of his retainers, under a great dome made of timber and earth. He had at his command a considerable army. Al-Bakri says there were 200 000 men, of whom 40 000 were archers. Since his next remark refers to the small size of Ghana's horses, it seems possible that there was also cavalry in the army.* It was doubtless this military power which enabled the king to secure the attendance at his court of a number of lesser 'kings' – perhaps viceroys, perhaps hostages from tributary monarchies. The capital city, also commonly called by the name of Ghana, was composed of two distinct parts. One was an entirely African town built of round mud huts, and it was here that the king had his palace, surrounded by a wall. The other, a few miles away, was a town of stone-built houses inhabited by Muslims and containing a number of mosques. The majority of the Muslims may be presumed to have been trading emigrants from North Africa, but some of them were serving the royal and pagan court as ministers and administrators. The two towns combined to form a sizeable urban complex; the whole of the area between them was to a considerable degree built up. This urbanized region was provisioned by the products of intensive cultivation conducted in its vicinity with water provided by wells. Finally, al-Bakri gives some details of what was obviously a well-organized export–import trade conducted on pack animals, in which the principal commodities were gold, salt, copper and manufactures, and which was subject to organized royal control and taxation.

One interesting point about al-Bakri's extended account of ancient Ghana – and indeed about the Arabic references generally – is that relatively little is said about the actual processes of mining and securing gold, which seems strange since the prosperity of the kingdom and of the trans-Saharan trade were obviously dependent on it. It is obvious, in fact, that they knew little about it. Al-Bakri's actual words are: 'The best gold found in this land comes from the town of Ghiyaro, which is eighteen days' travelling from the city of the king, over a country inhabited by tribes of the Blacks, their dwelling places being contiguous . . . Ghiyaro is twelve miles from [the Niger] and contains

---

* The first explicit mention of cavalry in the western Sudan appears to be al-'Umari's statement (*c.* 1338) that the king of Mali had 10 000 cavalry.

many Muslims.' Al-Mas'udi a century earlier said that the merchants of Ghana secured their gold by dumb barter, and al-Idrisi a century later said that the gold came from 'the land of Wangara', which 'adjoined' the kingdom of Ghana.

It was long supposed that 'Ghiyaro' and 'Wangara' were places where the gold was actually produced, and today the nearest gold-fields which could be regarded as 'contiguous' to or as 'adjoining' ancient Ghana would be the alluvial deposits of Bambuk, along the middle Senegal and its Faleme tributary, and of Boure, around the upper Niger and its tributaries. But the references could equally be to places where there flourished a *trade* in gold. Idrisi's description of a 'land of Wangara' as a large territory subject to annual flooding from surrounding rivers is in fact less apposite to Bambuk and Boure than it is to the inland delta of the Niger between Jenne and Timbuktu. This is not a gold-producing area, but it is productive agricultural and pastoral land, and it is now apparent from archaeological evidence that Jenne, on the southern tributary of the Niger, the river Bani, was already a substantial and flourishing trading city by about the middle of the first millennium. Idrisi's account presents difficulties which can be reduced if one supposes that in reality 'Wangara' was less an area of land than a distinctive group of people inhabiting it, and more specifically a trading group. By the fourteenth century, it is apparent from the evidence of Ibn Battuta (who, unlike Idrisi, actually visited the western Sudan), together with that of Hausa tradition, that terms like 'Wanjara', 'Wanjarata' and 'Wangarawa' did refer to a specialized group of long-distance traders, in origin Soninke – like the people of Ghana – who were Muslims. Al-Bakri's reference to the Muslims in Ghiyaro suggests these Wangara may well have been islamized as early as the eleventh century. Furthermore, since it is known that later on much of the commercial strength of Jenne lay in the role of its merchants in linking trade with the southerly lands of Guinea with the trade across the Sahara to and from Timbuktu (see pp. 89–92), it seems possible that at least some of the gold for which ancient Ghana was famed may have been brought from lands to the south of Jenne, from Lobi country if probably not yet from as far afield as Ashanti. Although the Islam of the merchants engaged in this trade must have reached them via trans-Saharan trade (see pp. 71–2), they would have a strong commercial motive for keeping the Saharan traders – and the Arab world generally – away from direct contact with the gold miners; hence, perhaps, the story of dumb barter with primitive Blacks beyond the realm.

The emergence of a monarchy comparable to Ghana further to the east, in Kanem, seems to have come to the notice of the Arabs somewhat later and their knowledge of it is less precise. At the end of the ninth century Ya'qubi wrote of 'a kingdom of the Zaghawa called Kanem', but added 'their dwellings are huts made of reeds and they have no towns'. The Zaghawa were 'Nilo-Saharan' pastoralists of the eastern Sahara, so that the implication seems to be that the Kanem kings were nomads who had no settled kingdom. This is indeed supported by the earliest traditions of Kanem. A century later, however, al-Muhallabi referred to two towns in Kanem, but what struck him most, because it offended his Muslim principles, was the nature of the monarchy. The people 'exalt and worship the king instead of Allah. They imagine that he does not eat any food. . . . Their religion is the worship of their kings, for they believe that they bring life and death, sickness and health.'

The Arabs' perception of the early history of the kingdom of Kanem is obviously somewhat obscure, while the origins of ancient Ghana, with its early development of organized political and economic life, clearly lay beyond their historical horizon. The first historians to consider the questions of how and when these organized monarchies arose in the Sudan, for example Flora Shaw (Lady Lugard), Maurice Delafosse, Sir Herbert Palmer, or Yves Urvoy, took the general line that such kingdoms resulted from the infiltration and conquest of agricultural Blacks by desert pastoralists who were Hamites (or even Semites; Delafosse, for example, suggested that the kingdom of Ghana was established by 'Judaeo-Syrians').

It is easy to see why such historians took such a view. In the first place, they themselves were representatives of an alien race which had just imposed its domination on the Blacks throughout Africa, and had done so with great ease. They felt that their white race was culturally immeasurably superior to the Blacks, whom they regarded as being at a much more primitive stage of development. They saw themselves as the successors to Muslim invaders and conquerors of Africa from North Africa and the Near East, who also were not Blacks, but Caucasoids akin to themselves. They and their fellow Europeans therefore constructed a view of African history in which the role of the Blacks was essentially passive, in which everything dynamic and constructive was due to alien invaders like themselves. 'Apart from relatively late Semitic influence – whether Phoenician (Carthaginian) and strictly limited, or Arab (Muhammadan) and widely diffused – ', the anthropologist C. G. Seligman wrote as late as 1930, 'the civilizations of Africa are the civilizations of the Hamites, its history the record of these peoples and of their interaction with the two other African stocks, the Negro and the Bushmen, whether this influence was exerted by highly civilized Egyptians or by wider pastoralists . . .'

Some of the flaws in this 'Hamitic hypothesis' have already been indicated. For example, there is nothing Hamitic in the languages of the Bantu whom Seligman supposed to be 'Hamiticized Negroes', and it seems probable indeed that Bantu agriculturalists may have actually displaced and absorbed some Hamitic-speaking peoples. Or again, the language of the black agricultural Hausa is 'Hamitic' – to which one may add that in the early nineteenth century, these Hausa were conquered by the Fulani, admittedly pastoralists, but speakers of a Sudanic language. There is also the general point that the protagonists of the Hamitic hypothesis were often dangerously confusing race, culture and language.

Nevertheless, in addition to the fact that these writers were part of a society which assumed that fair-skinned peoples possessed an inherent superiority over darker-skinned races, 'lesser breeds without the law', there was apparently evidence to support their view of African history. They could actually see nomad tribes from the desert moving into or towards the agricultural lands of West Africa. Tuareg had gained control of the Niger bend cities of Gao and Timbuctu by the end of the eighteenth century, and some were living south of the bend. Arab tribes had been advancing south and west from Nubia towards Kanem and Bornu from about the fourteenth century onwards. Secondly, the earliest traditions of some of the leading states in the history of the western and central Sudan actually said that their monarchies had been founded by immigrants from the north who were not Blacks.

Two important *Tarikhs* (chronicles) composed by Sudanese authors in Timbuctu in the sixteenth and seventeenth centuries stated that the kingdom of Ghana had been founded, appreciably before the Muslim *Hegira* (A.D. 622), by a dynasty called the Kaya-Magha, and that the Kaya-Magha were not Blacks. It was not known for certain what their origins were, but one author thought they were probably of Sanhaja origin. This might seem to be confirmed by one item of the information provided by al-Bakri. He suggests that the system of succession to the Ghana throne was matrilineal, and matrilinealism is characteristic of the veiled Tuareg Berbers, to whom the Sanhaja belonged before they became Arabized. On the other hand, the life styles of the king's court and of his pagan subjects look to be thoroughly Sudanic, and the *Tarikhs* say that the people of the kingdom were Soninke (i.e. northern Mande, as opposed to southern Mande, or Malinke) and also that the original Kaya-Magha dynasty was eventually replaced by Black kings.

The Saifawa dynasty, who ruled Kanem and its successor kingdom in Bornu continuously from the tenth to the nineteenth centuries, claimed to descend from an eponymous ancestor, Saif ibn Dhu Yazan, who lived in the Yemen in the sixth century, in the time of Dhu Nuwas and of Ella Asbeha's Axumite conquest. When and how such a dynasty might have arrived as far away as Kanem is obviously an open question. But it is interesting that the traditions of the early kings state that they took their wives only from the nobility of the Tebu (or Teda), east-central Saharan pastoralists akin to the Zaghawa. This affords some confirmation for the view of the origins of the kingdom taken by Ya'qubi and al-Muhallabi in the ninth and tenth centuries, and suggests that, with nomadic peoples like the Zaghawa and Tebu as intermediaries, the foundation of the monarchy could have been in some way linked with events around the Red Sea in which the Yemen, Axum and Nubia were all involved. The first Saifawa king regarded as being wholly of local extraction does not seem to have reigned until about the beginning of the thirteenth century.

These local opinions as to the origins of the Ghana and Kanem kings can be matched elsewhere. For instance, the Songhai kingdom below the Niger bend also claimed a Yemeni origin for its first dynasty. Between Kanem and Songhai, the legends of the relatively small Hausa kingdoms begin with concepts of a Canaanite who tried unsuccessfully to become 'king of Tripoli', and with one Bayajidda, 'son of the king of Baghdad'. The latter might be identified with the historical Abu Yazid, a Kharijite leader who was killed leading an unsuccessful revolt against Fatimid rule in Tunisia in A.D. 947,[*] and whose followers subsequently dispersed into the Sahara.

Even more remarkable, perhaps, is the Kisra legend which survived

[*] See chapter 7.

into modern times as a sub-stratum of historical memory among peoples along the valley of the Benue and up the Niger to the borders of Songhai territory. The story line of this legend, which has a number of variants, goes as follows. Kisra was king of the Parsi or Baghdadshi (i.e. Persians) who, before Muhammad's conquest of Mecca (A.D. 630), waged war against the Rumi (i.e. Byzantines) in Egypt. He occupied Egypt for a space, but then was forced to flee up the Nile to 'Nupata', where he asked to be allowed to settle. The King of Nupata (sometimes called Mesi, i.e. Messiah) consulted his familiar spirit, Issa (Jesus), who advised instead that Kisra should be asked to conquer to the west, and that the king of Nupata should follow him. Kisra went off and eventually reached the Benue and Niger valleys, while the king of Nupata arrived in Gobir (northern Hausaland) where he founded a kingdom from which all the Hausa states derived. Kisra died at Bussa (north-west Nigeria), but he or his followers were responsible for the foundation of the kingdoms of Borgu (in north-west Nigeria and adjacent Dahomey), Nupe (north of the Niger-Benue confluence), of Kwararafa or Jukun (on the Benue), and, further south, of Igala and Yorubaland.

The beginning of this story is recognizable history. Kisra is Chosroes (Khosru) II, the Sassanid ruler of Persia from 590 to 628. The Sassanids were then everywhere advancing in the west against Christendom and in 616, shortly after their expulsion of the Axumites from the Yemen, their army occupied Egypt, holding it until expelled by Heraclius ten years later. Chosroes is not known to have gone to Egypt in person, and was murdered in his own palace at Ctesiphon in 628. But it is not impossible that, after their expulsion from Egypt, some Persians sought refuge up the Nile and ultimately became absorbed in the Christian kingdoms of Nubia (in whose art some Persian influence seems to be visible). More broadly, the end of the sixth century and the beginning of the seventh was a period of great upheaval in the lands around the Red Sea. There was first the period of Persian ascendancy and the withdrawal of Axum from Arabia, and then, after 622–30, the advent of Islam and the establishment of its ascendancy in Egypt and on the African coasts of the Red Sea. The Christians of Arabia and of the Nubian and Axum kingdoms could not but have been affected by these momentous developments. Although it is highly unlikely that any significant number of actual Nubians or Yemenis or Persians ever found their way to Kanem or beyond, it is by no means absurd to suppose that a series of reactions was set up by which echoes of the great events in North-East Africa and the Red Sea, passing through the mobile Saharan peoples like the Zaghawa and Tebu, reached right across Africa to as far even as the valleys of the Niger and the Benue.

The most plausible explanation of the legends of great heroes like Kisra or members of Saif's line or Bayajidda coming to the Sudan from the east and north is that they were probably a device adopted by Sudanic kingdoms to put their origins into relation – chronological, geographic and thematic – with what they might have seen as a mainstream of historical development in the Near East and North-East Africa. There would certainly be a need for such a device following the arrival of Islam in the Sudan and its acceptance by many of its ruling dynasties (however much these may have needed at the same time to keep up the traditional customs and obligations of their ancestors). One objection to such an explanation is that some of the legends, not least that of Kisra, have been maintained essentially by pagan societies. In modern Borgu, for example, although the Kisra story is widely known, it exists in a folk culture which does not meet with the approval of Muslim society. But recent work has suggested that this objection may be more apparent than real.* Knowledge of Arab history and legend need not have been introduced and spread solely by a new class of literate Muslim scholars and historians. Even today, for example, the Koran is known as much by rote and recitation as it is by reading (and initially this would have been more so), and traditional Arab and Berber society certainly prized the arts of the bard and the story-teller. Acquaintance with the prestigeful world from which Islam had sprung, and a desire to establish connections with it, would thus spread faster and further – for example along the trade routes developed by islamized Sudanic merchants – than would effective conversion to the new religion. So the *griots* (bards) and the keepers of traditions in even pagan kingdoms could easily incorporate Near Eastern folklore with their traditional recitations, and adapt it to the purposes of their patrons and rulers. It should be noted, too, that figures like Saif and Kisra and Bayajidda are not exactly Muslim heroes; rather the first two are anti-heroes of Islamic lore and legend, while Abu Yazid was a defeated rebel against one of the first major dynasties in African Islam.

Nevertheless there still remains the important point that there can

---

* The argument that follows is owed by the author to his colleague Paulo Farias.

be little doubt that the lands of the agricultural peoples of the Sudan immediately south of the Sahara have in fact been subject for centuries to raids, infiltration, conquest and settlement by nomadic pastoralists coming from the desert. Such desert peoples must equally have always had some sort of contact with the peoples of North and North-East Africa.

It is not difficult to construct a model of the process of interaction between pastoral and agricultural peoples in the border zone between Sahara and Sudan. Groups of mobile horsemen would be thrust out southwards from the desert by the incessant quarrels of its tribes, by a growth of human or cattle populations, by an unusually dry season, or by simple desire for trade or adventure. They would pasture their animals in the expanses of bush between the agricultural villages, and exchange some of their meat, hides and dairy produce for the products of the fields and of the village craftsmen. At first they would have no fixed base, and have no fixed, formal political relationship with the village chiefs. But they would come to cast covetous eyes on the comparative wealth and stability of agricultural society, and the mobility born of their possession of horses and camels would enable them to plunder this with ever-growing confidence. Their own feuds and alliances would thus become entangled with the politics of the village peoples. Their leaders would become allied through marriage with some of the leading village families, and so gain some claim to overlordship of the villages and their fields. Ultimately the incomers, with their cavalry and the strong sense of group discipline needed for survival in the desert, would gain territorial control and settle down as a ruling nobility levying tribute on the farmers and remitting some of it to the fixed capital of their king. But in course of time, king and nobles alike could become through intermarriage racially and linguistically little to be distinguished from the common people.

This is not a fanciful picture. It is, for example, comparable to the pattern which Ibn Khaldun discerned to have happened time and time again to the north of the Sahara, and which was to play a central part in his philosophy of history. Equally, and perhaps more to the point, it can readily be pieced together from surviving Sudanic traditions, most notably perhaps those of Kanem, but also, for example, in the smaller kingdoms of the Mossi and Dagomba further to the west and south. A similar model was also worked out for the region of Air, once inhabited largely by Hausa but now predominantly a Tuareg domain, by one of the early European historians of West Africa, Yves Urvoy.

But it would seem that Urvoy and his contemporaries with a similar background fell into serious error in their interpretation of the nature and significance of this interaction between 'Hamites' and Blacks on the southern fringes of the Sahara. Since the more active participants in it were the northerners, they concluded that it was their culture and their traditions of government which triumphed, so that the resultant kingdoms were not Sudanic, but 'Hamitic'. But in almost all the arts of life, it was the Blacks who were the more advanced. While the incomers were pastoralists with no permanent habitations, the Blacks were sedentary agriculturalists with villages and even towns.

It is now clear that there were already substantial towns in the western Sudan by the second half of the first millennium. The ruins at Koumbi Saleh in southern Mauritania, which correspond with the position of ancient Ghana and with al-Bakri's description of it, date from at least the late ninth century and at its peak, from about the twelfth to fifteenth centuries, the city occupied about 200 acres. The mound which represents the first site of Jenne has demonstrated the existence of a town of some 80 acres flourishing from about the mid eighth century to about 1100. Other settlement mounds are known from further down the Niger and into the central Sudan; few have been excavated, but that at Daima, already mentioned, 30 feet high at its centre and extending in all over something like 30 acres, represents the residue of continuous human occupation, perhaps only of a sizeable village, over something like eighteen centuries from about the sixth century B.C. North and east of Lake Chad, sizeable brick-built ruins are known. Evidence of early urbanization also extends southwards into Guinea. For example, at Ife, traditionally the first centre of Yoruba settlement, the excavation of extensive potsherd pavements has shown that this ostensibly urban feature dates from at least the eleventh century A.D. This evidence so far to the south, for a culture which claims to have come from the north, suggests once again that the Blacks of the western and central Sudan would probably have had towns by the times indicated in tradition for the arrival of such legendary heroes as Bayajidda or the Saifawa. Such towns were presumably the market, ritual and political centres for progressive agricultural societies, and their growth and their geographical spread must have been encouraged by the emergence, around the middle of the first millennium, of regular camel caravan trade across the Sahara.

At this point it is worth considering another model – complementary rather than alternative to the one already sketched – of the interaction between pastoral and farming peoples in the Sahel, the borderland between the Sahara and the Sudan. Raiding by desert pastoralists would encourage the farmers of the Sudan to group together in larger and more defensible communities. Villages would be preferred to dispersed family homesteads, and ultimately some villages could develop into fortifiable towns. These changes in the spatial distribution of population would doubtless engender socio-political changes also. It might be expected that the more senior or the more forceful family heads would acquire some authority, certainly for specific military purposes and thus eventually in defined political spheres also, over the heads of other family units. This model is even less theoretical than the earlier one. In its spatial aspects, at least, it is supported by important archaeological evidence from the Tichit-Walata escarpment. Here the work of Patrick Munson has afforded what would seem to be the earliest clear evidence, about 1000 B.C., of the cultivation of local Sudanic cereals. The farmers responsible began by living on the shores of the lakes which once existed in this region, but by about 1000 B.C. they were concentrating their dwellings in fortified cliff top villages of considerable size. Since these were obviously not the best places for cereal cultivation, the obvious inference is that the farmers were seeking shelter from raiding pastoralists. By about 400 B.C., the villages had been abandoned, presumably because the region had become unfit for cultivation due to the combined effects of pastoralism and desiccation. It is also significant that this Tichit-Walata escarpment lies just to the north of the presumed site of the capital of ancient Ghana, the first known truly effective political and military mobilization by the Blacks of West Africa.

Obviously the wealth, facilities and pleasures which towns like Koumbi Saleh could offer would have become powerful magnets attracting pastoral peoples to leave the desert to settle in the Sudan, and the more settled they became the more they must have been absorbed in and acculturated to the Sudan's agricultural and urban society. But this still leaves open the question whether organized monarchical government was an innovation of the newcomers, or whether it was found by them when they arrived for them to take over. The general argument of this book is that organized government under divine or sacred kings is most likely, as in Egypt, to have evolved among agricultural peoples. In the Sudan, therefore, it seems preferable to regard it as being an indigenous development, and not an introduction of pastoralists coming in from the Sahara.

Nevertheless the incoming pastoralists had an important political role, and just as the history of modern England has been commonly thought of as beginning with the Norman conquest in 1066, so the Sudanic traditions may be right in their indication that the history of pre-colonial West Africa takes a new departure from infiltrations and conquests of roughly the same period. For one thing, as has already been suggested, the newcomers could have brought with them some characteristic traits of monarchical ritual which they had picked up, however indirectly, from their contacts with North-East and northern Africa. Perhaps more cogently, their advent must have meant a considerable enlargement of the scale of political organization, and perhaps too a more precise institutionalization of its modes of operation. These things would result from a number of factors. Their possession of horses and their access to regular supplies of such animals in a land in which they could be bred only with considerable difficulty, must have enabled them to exert power over appreciably greater distances than earlier rulers could. Then too, the fact that they were newcomers with no established ties with the cultivated land and the religious cults associated with it, afforded them a larger field for political manoeuvre than their predecessors. They needed to legitimize their rule by marriage with the Sudanic ruling families, but they could choose which families and on what terms, so that some of the resulting offspring would become overlords with increased power and others merely tributary vassals.

The political processes represented in the founding traditions of the states of the western and central Sudan which have survived to be incorporated into modern historiography would therefore represent the conversion of small political units, city states or even village states, into larger kingdoms requiring more – and more precisely defined – organized administration. The development of the organized monarchies discernible by about the tenth century would thus be a two-stage process, with the seeds of kingship lying deep in the Neolithic Revolution of the Sudanic Blacks, and its ultimate flowering being the result of centuries of interaction between these Blacks and their pastoral neighbours in the Sahara which stimulated these seeds to develop and grow. The strongest historical traditions are naturally those stemming from the latest and most successful lines of kings. But in the earliest legends of Kanem, Songhai, and the kingdoms of the Hausa and the Mossi and Dagomba, for example, it seems possible to discern, however dimly, earlier stages of development to be associated with earlier invaders, or even with the original structures of late Neolithic society.

In this context it is probably significant that the earliest major kingdoms known to the Arabs in North Africa lay just to the north of areas that must have been particularly favourable to early agricultural and Iron Age development. Ghana lay just north of the upper Niger and Senegal valleys, and Kanem just north of the Lake Chad basin. That these kingdoms were not actually in these favoured areas, but on the frontiers of the desert north of them, suggests that Saharan contacts and trade may have played an important role in stimulating the rise of the earliest of the greater monarchies. Alternatively, of course, it could be an optical illusion. It was just in these areas accessible over the trade routes from North Africa that the outside world could first know of the existence of major West African kingdoms. Equally, the economic self-interest of these kingdoms would deny foreigners coming from the north access to knowledge of comparable kingdoms further south. Al-Bakri, for example, does mention the existence of two kingdoms to the south of ancient Ghana, but we know practically nothing of these beyond the names he gives for them, Malal and Daw.

But indigenous traditions are practically unanimous in giving a picture of major political growth in West Africa spreading from north to south, from the fringes of the desert deeper into the Sudan, and from the Sudan into Guinea. Political grounds for believing that this is historically a correct picture have already been given, and the economic evidence leads to the same conclusion.

Ever since the emergence of the desert, or even before, the border between the Sahara and the Sudan had been a significant one. This was not only because it was here that the Blacks were in contact with other peoples and cultures, but also because it was a major ecological divide between cultivable land and land suited only for pastoralism, and also, with the nomad Saharan peoples as the link, between the African tropics and the temperate lands bordering the Mediterranean. It must always therefore have been an important trading frontier, and it was no accident that the ancient chariot routes led directly across the desert towards the most promising lands for agricultural development and, in the case of Ghana, gold-bearing lands also. Very obviously in the case of Ghana, somewhat less clearly perhaps in the case of Kanem, it would seem that an important motive for the development of considerable kingdoms here was the economic one of engrossing the Sudanic exports which Saharan and North African peoples desired to have, and of controlling the distribution in the Sudan of the goods received in exchange.

An important part of the early Arabic information concerning ancient Ghana is economic in character – as may be seen from al-Bakri's account. To al-Fazari, the earliest Arabic source, Ghana was essentially 'the land of gold', while anecdotes stressing its wealth abound in later accounts. One of the best known is the story told by Ibn Hawqal, himself a merchant, who wrote in the tenth century. He says that when he was in the southern Moroccan caravan centre of Sijilmasa, he saw a 'cheque' (i.e. a note of account) from a merchant in Awdaghust to the value of 40 000 dinars (equivalent to £20 000 in gold sovereigns, or 100 000 silver dollars, and many times this in modern currencies). If trans-Saharan trade was indeed being carried on on this sort of scale and with this degree of sophistication as early as the tenth century, and not only in gold, but also in salt (sometimes said to have been exchanged for gold weight for weight), copper, and general merchandise, then it can readily be seen that the economic motives for the extension of empire south of the Sahara must have been considerable, at least in ancient Ghana. The economic evidence concerning Kanem in the early Arabic authorities is slight, but this is doubtless simply because Kanem did not have access to sources of gold comparable with Ghana's, and so did not attract so much attention. Nevertheless it did lie due south of the Fezzan, the land of the ancient Garamantes. When its monarchy was strongest, it always sought to expand to the Fezzan, and its power was certainly sometimes effective as far as Bilma, an important source of salt for the Sudan. In later times, the road from Tripoli and Tunisia via the Fezzan and Bilma to Lake Chad and Hausaland was one of the most important caravan routes. It would therefore seem quite probable that commercial motives played at least some part in the emergence of organized government in Kanem. It has been suggested, indeed, that these would relate to the development of a trade to North Africa in black slaves.

In ancient Ghana, and in its successor states, ancient Mali and the Songhai empire of Gao, the economic motives for empire seem quite explicit. The ruling groups sought to extend their power across the essentially north–south lines of trade, so that all the valuable exports of the western Sudan would come into their hands. Their capitals and other trading towns thus gained control of the goods sought by traders from the Sahara and North Africa, and equally their agents secured control of the distribution of Saharan and North African goods in the Sudan. The means by which Sudanic produce was secured varied. As has been seen, the early Arabic accounts suggest that gold was obtained on the southern frontiers of Ghana by trading with the less sophisticated peoples who actually won the gold in alluvial diggings. Ultimately, as is clear in Mali and Songhai, a specialized class of Sudanese merchants evolved in close alliance with the rulers, whose trade (and also that of the northern merchants) was subject to regular royal tolls and taxes. In the case of gold, certainly, the trade was so subject to royal control that it seems to have been virtually a state monopoly, with the actual traders in effect either servants or licensees of the king. It also seems that a large part of the Sudanese produce collected in the capital and other urban centres arrived in the form of tribute from vassal peoples. Certainly the effect of the trading system was to concentrate wealth in the hands of the king and the ruling class. Part of this wealth could be used to buy horses and arms, and so to create an army which was much more powerful than any other possible concentrations of force. With this army, it was possible to extend both the royal control of tribute and trade even further afield, and thus further to increase the wealth of the monarchy and its adherents. The more wealthy and powerful the monarchy, the more clients it could attract to its service, and the fewer there were available to support rival rulers. Equally it became possible to recruit ever more slaves for service in the palace and in the government and army, and to create new units of production in the fields and in craft industry, which could supplement, if not replace, the production of the traditional family units.

But the conduct of caravans across the Sahara, which had helped stimulate larger economic and political units to emerge in the Sudan, was always the affair of the Saharan tribes descended from the ancient Garamantes and Pharusii, and specifically of the Sanhaja and Tuareg. The advent of the camel made possible a substantial increase in the volume and regularity of trans-Saharan trading. This was fully developed by the merchants, by now Arabs as well as Jews, who financed the caravans sent out from northern oases like Tafilalt and Wargla. But the fortunes of these merchants and of the desert camel-eers were necessarily affected by changes in the political balance in North Africa following upon its conquest by the Arabs (Chapter 6). Thus by the eleventh century, Sanhaja power in Tafilalt, where their northern caravan base, Sijilmasa, was situated, was threatened by the advance of the Zenata from the east.

The rise of organized kingdoms in the Sudan could equally pose problems for the Saharan tribes. As the power of the Ghana kings increased, so they cast envious eyes on the trade brought to them by the veiled Sanhaja, and sought to extend their control northwards at their expense. Since the Sanhaja were divided into a number of competing tribal factions, the Lamtuna, Godala and Masufa, they gradually lost ground. By about the end of the tenth century their principal southern trading centre, Awdaghust, had become tributary to Ghana. However, the Sanhaja had already experienced some degree of Islamic influence, and early in the following century one of their tribal chiefs may well have glimpsed that Islam might provide a unifying principle which would help them to redress the balance. A Muslim divine from southern Morocco, 'Abd Allah ibn Yasin, was persuaded to come and preach to the Sanhaja. After early struggles and vicissitudes, his rigid puritan form of Islam gained control of the Sanhaja tribes and formed them into the militant federation known to history as the Almoravids.*

By the middle of the eleventh century, the Almoravids had regained control for the Sanhaja of the western trans-Saharan caravan route and of its termini in Sijilmasa and Awdaghust. Ghana itself came under their influence and at least its ruling and merchant classes became Muslims. With their economic base secure, the army of the Almoravids then left the desert to engage in the conquest of the settled and wealthy Islamic lands of North-West Africa and the Iberian peninsula that is discussed in Chapter 7. Here our concern is with the Sudanic states, and the plain fact is that, despite the Islamization in Ghana that followed the rise of the Almoravids, the main lines of

---

* The name Almoravids derives from the Arabic *al-Murabitun*, 'people of the *ribat*'. The normal meaning of *ribat* is a fortified monastery in which military as well as religious instruction was given. It was therefore assumed, reasonably enough given the character of their movement, that the Almoravids had such a base, and scholars spent some time arguing where its remains might be. However, recent research has demon-strated that in this case *ribat* need not have this material significance, and that *al-Murabitun* meant something more like 'people of the persuasion'.

political development in the western Sudan remained pagan and Sudanic until at least the seventeenth century.

The Arabic sources indicate that Ghana was not the first Sudanic state to accept Islam. This honour is usually given to Takrur, a smaller kingdom in the Senegal valley to the south-west of Ghana, whose king and court are said to have been converted some decades earlier. In fact, trans-Saharan trade provided means by which Islam could approach all the Sudanic peoples immediately to the south of the desert. Al-Muhallabi (end of the tenth century) refers to the conversion of the king of 'Kawkaw', which may be the same as the 'Kuku' which had a Muslim king in al-Bakri's time, and perhaps these are names for the early Songhai capital at Kukiya. Al-Bakri also reports the conversion of a king of Malal, while the arrival of Islam at the court of Kanem is ascribed to the time of a king who was probably on the throne towards the end of the eleventh century. But this early acceptance of Islam in the western and central Sudan seems generally to have been essentially restricted to ruling and – in the western Sudan especially – merchant classes.

There were obvious reasons why Sudanic rulers and traders should have been receptive to Islam; for example that it facilitated their increasingly important relations with traders and rulers in the Sahara and North Africa, or that it provided them with a literacy which was valuable for the maintenance of diplomatic, administrative and commercial correspondence and records. But the acceptance of Islam by kings in the Sudan was usually something of a façade. If it were more than this, then it would destroy an essential basis of their power as successors to the founding ancestors of their societies, the original pagan kings who had first made the compacts with the world of the spirits and the gods on which the prosperity of their peoples and their agriculture were popularly thought to depend.

In Ghana and adjacent lesser kingdoms like Takrur which were subject to the influence of the Sanhaja and the Almoravids, but probably only here, eleventh-century Islam went further, and could affect the whole basis of society. In the long run this was to have important effects throughout the western Sudan through the spread of a thoroughly islamized merchant class. But more immediately the Almoravid outburst may have served to accelerate processes of change that were undermining the agricultural base for Sudanic power in this region so close to the desert. The economic and political success of Ghana would have brought increases in the populations of people and cattle which were bound to tax the available natural resources of water, soil and timber. It was possible to some extent to withstand this so long as new wealth continued to be brought in from long-distance trade. But the initial militancy of the Almoravids no doubt discouraged some merchants from sending their goods through the western Sahara, and after the Sanhaja had secured complete control both of the western route and its termini, conditions did not improve. Once the Almoravids had moved on, the desert Sanhaja dissolved again into their factions, each looking for the maximum short-term advantage, and all seeking to acquire and pasture more cattle at the expense of settled farmers. Thus agriculture as well as trade was threatened. Gradually the northern and central lands of the kingdom were converted into desert so that ultimately their cities had to be abandoned. Increasingly trans-Saharan traders chose to use the more central routes leading to the Niger bend rather than to go through the disturbed western Sahara to arrive in an impoverished western Sudan. The decline of both agriculture and trade meant less revenue for the maintainance of the fabric of the Ghana kingdom. More southerly Mande peoples, whose agriculture had not been disrupted and who lived closer to the Niger, which afforded both better conditions for agriculture and a fine natural trade route north-eastwards to the Niger bend, began to break away from Ghana's control, and so still further to diminish the resources available to its government. It is possible indeed that, in an attempt to remedy this situation, the Ghana capital was moved further south. Al-Idrisi (c. 1150) refers to it as being situated on the Niger, but perhaps, with the decay of communication over the western trans-Saharan routes, this city was not the capital of Ghana itself, but of one of the former vassal states which were now independent.

Indeed a struggle was now developing between more southerly Mande groups to take over the inheritance of ancient Ghana. Initially supremacy seems to have passed to a people called the Susu, whose king, Sumanguru, is said to have conquered and made tributary what was left of Ghana at the beginning of the thirteenth century. But Sumanguru's power was challenged by another Mande group, the Keita, originally it would seem traders from lower down the Niger, who were endeavouring to develop political control over a number of earlier kingdoms in the upper Niger valley which were doubtless represented by al-Bakri's Malal and Daw. Tradition has it that eventually, after prolonged warfare, the Keita produced a king, Sundiata, who overthrew Sumanguru and went on to capture the Ghana capital, thus laying the foundations for the new Mande empire of Mali.

Sundiata, who is thought to have reigned between about 1230 and about 1255, is an archetype of the Sudanic kings of the period. On the one hand, he is the great hero figure of Mande legend, many of whose successes are ascribed to his command of magic. On the other hand, Sundiata is also presented as coming from a Muslim background. It is indeed reasonable to suppose that the Keita, as traders, had been islamized, and his immediate successor, his son Uli (c. 1255–70), was the first of many subsequent *Mansa* of Mali to make the pilgrimage to Mecca.

The Timbuctu *Tarikhs* regard the empire founded by Sundiata as a natural continuation of ancient Ghana. This would seem to be a correct view of history. Ancient Ghana, at least in its later stages, was controlled by Soninke ruling and trading classes who aimed to monopolize the local trade of the western Sudan and its connections with the trans-Saharan trade. Mali was the creation of a more southerly Mande group, possessing better agricultural resources and a more direct control over alluvial gold-fields, who aimed to control the whole Sudan to at least as far as the Niger bend, where the new southern termini for the trans-Saharan trade, Timbuctu and Gao, were situated. In this Sundiata and his successors were remarkably successful, and by the fourteenth century, from their capital at Niani, on or near the upper Niger, they were controlling an empire appreciably greater than ancient Ghana's. It reached some 1250 miles from the Atlantic in the west to the borders of modern northern Nigeria in the east, and from such southern Saharan caravan centres as Awdaghust, Walata (to which the Muslim merchants from Ghana had fled after the occupation of its capital by Sumanguru) and Tadmakka (Es-Souk) in the north, to the borders of the Guinea forests in the south-west, a maximum extent of about 600 miles.

The central axis of this empire, and its main line of communication, was the river Niger. But navigation of the Niger downstream of about modern Segu was in the hands of a non-Mande people, the Songhai. The beginnings of Songhai history go back to the first millennium, when they were essentially farmers and fisherfolk inhabiting the banks of the Niger in Dendi, between the Niger bend and Borgu. But their fishermen were continually extending their operations upstream, and this brought the Songhai into closer contact with the trade using the short route across the Sahara to the Niger bend. Two consequences of this were to consolidate the growth of central monarchy among the Songhai, and also to shift its centre northwards, the capital being moved about 1100 A.D. from Kukiya, in Dendi, to Gao. By the time of the rise of the Keita to power in Mali, Songhai canoemen were operating to as far west as the major Mande trading centre of Jenne. Control over the Songhai domains and operations thus became of major importance to the Keita. This seems to have been achieved about the third quarter of the thirteenth century, and to have been maintained, though possibly with some interruptions, to about the beginning of the fifteenth century.

Control of Songhai enabled Mande merchants to extend so far to the east as to bring international trade and Islam to the small Hausa kingdoms, where they were known as Wangarawa (i.e. 'people from Wangara' or, more probably, simply 'Mande merchants'). Local tradition suggests that the first Wangarawa may have arrived in Hausa-land in the fourteenth century, and that they were certainly well established by the following century. More generally, control of Songhai enabled Mali to achieve a peak of prosperity and power. The empire was firmly placed on the map (literally, was well as figuratively, for it appears on the *mappa-mundi* drawn in 1339 by Angelo Dulcert, a member of the great school of cartographers then active in Majorca), by the magnificent pilgrimage to Mecca via Egypt which was conducted by *Mansa* Musa (1312–37) in 1324–5. Musa is variously reported to have crossed the Sahara with 8000 to 15 000 retainers, and to have taken so much gold with him – and to have spent it so lavishly – that the value of the metal in Egypt was depreciated by 12 per cent. Clearly such a pilgrimage had more than religious motives; it must also have been intended to cement political, economic and cultural ties with the Islamic world. There are some indications that this was achieved. For example, from about this time it is known that there was some kind of a hostel in Cairo for students from the Sudan, while Musa is said to have taken home with him an Andalusian poet and architect, as-Sahili, who built mosques in Gao and Timbuctu and also a palace in the latter town. It is probably from about this period, indeed, that the foundations were laid for the traditions of Islamic scholarship in Sudanic towns like Timbuctu and Walata which was to produce, as well as works of religion and philosophy, the *Tarikhs* which are such a valuable source for modern historians.

But the best sources for thirteenth- and fourteenth-century Mali history are in fact North African writers: al-'Umari (1301–49) and

Makrisi (1360–1442), who relied to a considerable extent on evidence connected with Musa's visit to Cairo; Ibn Khaldun (1332–1406), whose service at the courts of Tunis and Fez and as a *mufti* in Cairo provided him with sufficient information to devote a chapter of his great history to 'the kings of the Sudan' (essentially of Mali); and Ibn Battuta (1304–68), a Moroccan who rounded off a lifetime of travel through most of the known world, and to as far afield as China, by a tour through the dominions of Mali during 1352–3. The picture given of fourteenth-century Mali by these sophisticated inhabitants of a Muslim world which was then at its own apogee of civilization and scholarship is a remarkably favourable one.

Ibn Battuta, for example, travelling through the length and breadth of the large empire, is always commenting on the ease of travel. The security and prosperity were such that there was no need to travel in large parties with armed guards, or to carry provisions or to make advance arrangements, for provisions could be bought and safe lodging found in every village. 'The Negroes possess some admirable qualities. They are seldom unjust, and have a greater abhorrence of injustice than any other people. Their sultan shows no mercy to anyone who is guilty of the least act of it. There is complete security in their country. Neither traveller nor inhabitant in it has anything to fear from robbers or men of violence.'

The reader is in fact left with an impression of an orderly system of law and government, and of a prospering economic life and urban civilization as good as anything that might then be found in western Europe, and which were maintained over a remarkably large area. He may also be left with the impression that this was an Islamic civilization, maintained by Muslim religion, law, administration and scholarship. But this is an illusion stemming from the fact that the Arabic authorities depended for their information in the last resort essentially on visiting Sudanese Muslims of the ruling and mercantile classes or, in the case of Ibn Battuta, on the fact that he could really only communicate with people in the larger towns, which had a considerable immigrant North African population which we know was to some extent administered as a separate *regnum in regno*. The truth of the matter may be better gauged by two pieces of information given by al-'Umari. In the one, it is said that *Mansa* Musa did not know until his pilgrimage that under Muslim law he should not have more than four wives. The other, more significantly perhaps, indicates that pagan and magical practices were common among Musa's subjects, and that he feared to push the cause of islamization too far because he knew that to do so would diminish the production of gold (and doubtless also of other products of the soil) which was so essential to the imperial economy.

In short, the empire was maintained by the exercise of dominion, for their own profit, of a quasi-Islamic ruling class and a more genuinely Islamic merchant class, by force (al-'Umari writes of an army of 100 000, with 10 000 cavalry), over a congeries of traditional social groups who believed in a world of spirits and pagan gods, and who thought that their prosperity depended on the maintenance of traditional relations with this other world. As far as his Mande subjects were concerned, a large part of the *Mansa*'s position derived from his claimed descent from Sundiata, the magician hero who had initiated the new and larger Mande community.

But Mali at its peak included many peoples who were not Mande and did not share Mande traditions and beliefs, and it could only maintain its control over these vassals so long as its central power remained united, and remained stronger than any regionally based power which could be brought against it. There had already been at least one period, at the end of the thirteenth century, when these things were in doubt. Eventually the central government had then only been maintained by the usurpation of authority by one Sakura, not himself a Keita, but one of their freed-slave retainers, who managed to secure control of the army. Suleiman, the *Mansa* in Ibn Battuta's time, may also not have been in the direct line of succession, and after his death in 1360, various factions of the royal family began to compete with each other for power. In such a situation, the power lying in some of the principal vassal territories could become of critical importance. These might be controlled through viceroys who were members of the *Mansarin*, who would thus have a claim to the central authority in Mali itself, but who also might secure local bases of power by marriage into the local chiefly lines. Alternatively, members of local ruling families might have been brought as hostages to the *Mansa*'s court. There they would have acquired knowledge of how the central power was manipulated and maintained, and even perhaps have made alliances with the competing factions within the imperial family.

Mali's relations with Songhai were of especial importance if it wanted to maintain its empire intact. One of the Timbuctu *Tarikhs* says that, at some time, two brothers of the Songhai royal family had escaped from the *Mansa*'s court, where they had been employed as officers in the Mali army, and returned home to Gao. The result was a revival of the Songhai monarchy, no doubt with lessons learnt from Malian experience.* The Songhai kings adopted a new title, *Sonni*, and by about 1400 were acting independently, since one of them is then reported to have sacked the Mali capital, Niani.

Eventually the Sonni dynasty produced a king *Sonni* Ali (1464–92), who stands in Songhai tradition as the great innovator; a hero-magician – but also in some degree a Muslim – comparable with Sundiata in Mande lore. A lifetime of campaigning destroyed the military power of Mali and restricted its empire to the valleys of the Gambia and the upper Niger and the immediately adjacent lands. North of this there emerged independent kingdoms of the Tukolor and of Diara. From Jenne eastwards, *Sonni* Ali and his successor Muhammad (1493–1528) built up a new empire ruled from the Songhai capital of Gao. Its extent to the south was limited by new independent kingdoms created within the Niger bend by Mossi cavaliers who had come from the east (see chapter 4). However, the Songhai empire, attempting to assert its suzerainty over the Hausa kingdoms to the borders of Bornu, achieved an east–west extent that was comparable with that of Mali at its peak, while to the north its power reached appreciably further, encompassing Air in the north-east, and in the north-west reaching five hundred miles or so across the Sahara to the important salt deposits of Taghaza and Taudeni.

Sonni Ali received a mixed reception from the authors of the *Tarikhs*. He was 'a man of great force and restless energy', ceaselessly campaigning and always victorious, but he was also 'the tyrant, the debauchee, the damned, the oppressor'. This dualism is a reflection of strains in the make-up of the empire he founded which were to mean that it was to be neither as stable nor as long-lasting as Mali. *Sonni* Ali represented a Songhai reaction against Malian imperialism; his strength as a Songhai king rested on his role as the champion of their traditional, local paganism. He seems therefore to have shown deliberate hostility to the Muslim divines and scholars of the major towns, Timbuctu especially, representatives of a universalist doctrine which had served Mali's imperial purposes. At the same time, however, *Sonni* Ali was an imperialist himself, and needed aspects of Mande Muslim experience if he were to be able to establish a political

* There is extant a fragment of a seventeenth-century chronicle which avers that the new dynasty was of Mande origin.

system which could successfully embrace a number of non-Songhai peoples.

Just how important this dichotomy was, was shown immediately after his death, when his heir was put aside and power was taken by one of his generals, Muhammad Ture, himself a Mande, who established a new dynasty, that of the Askiyas. It was also shown, later on, by Muhammad's own failure to establish an orderly succession. The history of the Songhai empire of Gao between *Askiya* Muhammad's deposition by his sons in 1528 and its destruction by conquerors from Morocco in 1591 may almost be said to have been a continual struggle between two political groups, one with colours that were Songhai, pagan and nationalist, and the other proclaiming a Mali-type Muslim universalism. The deepness of the division between the two factions goes far to explain the easy victory achieved by the small Moroccan expeditionary force which crossed the desert to Gao and Timbuctu in 1590–91.

Thereafter the Songhai kings, like their predecessors of Mali, ruled only a small remnant kingdom, in their case in Dendi. There were no longer any politically effective upholders of the idea which had had its birth in ancient Ghana, that of one major empire engrossing tribute and trade from the whole western Sudan for the benefit of essentially Mande ruling and mercantile classes. Thereafter, too, for reasons of North African as well as Sudanic history, the principal trans-Saharan trade roads ran even further east than they had when Mali and Songhai were the principal Sudanic states, from Tunisia and Tripoli to Kanem and Hausaland.

The history of Kanem, as has been seen earlier, can be interpreted in some measure as an attempt to build up the same sort of empire as Ghana had further west. Doubtless the conversion of its kings, the *Mais*, to Islam about the end of the eleventh century is some measure of the growing influence of trans-Saharan traders. By the beginning of the thirteenth century, the capital established at Njimi controlled the territory to the south of Kanem around Lake Chad, while to the north, Saifawa power extended to the salt deposits at Bilma and the oasis of Djado. Its influence was felt more widely afield, in the north to the Fezzan and to the south-west over at least the nearer Hausa kingdoms. But there then followed some three centuries of internecine strife among factions of the Saifawa ruling group. There was also growing trouble with the Bulala, a pastoral group comparable to the original Zaghawa who had originally put the kingdom together, but whose influence was destructive, not constructive, as they were competing for power with the Saifawa rulers. Eventually the *Mais* were forced to withdraw from Kanem, and to seek to re-establish their kingdom from a new southern base at Ngazargamu, in the erstwhile province of Bornu to the south-west of Lake Chad.

During the sixteenth century, this new Saifawa kingdom in Bornu became increasingly powerful. The Bulala, though remaining as rulers of Kanem, were made tributary, and Saifawa influence was once again felt in Hausaland. By the end of the century, effective relations had been established with the Ottoman Turks who were now in control of Egypt and Tripoli, with the result that *Mai* Idris Alawma (*c.* 1560–*c.* 1590) secured supplies of firearms, and instruction for his soldiers in their use and the appropriate tactics, and was also able to recruit an Arab camelry. As a result he became possessed of a force appreciably greater than any which could be brought against him, and he began to convert his kingdom into a unitary state governed according to Islamic principles. But once again the Saifawa line failed to maintain its imperial strength. There were continual frontier wars with the Hausa to the west and the Jukun to the south, while Tuareg tribes began to encroach from the desert in the north. The Saifawa princes sought to escape from these troubles by competing with each other for the ritual and pleasures of the palace, and their empire gradually dissolved.

The ups and downs of organized monarchy and imperial power in Kanem and Bornu were probably no greater than those in the more westerly area which the kings of Ghana, Mali and Songhai sought in turn to control over the same length of time. Politically, indeed, there was doubtless rather more continuity in Kanem-Bornu. But the Saifawa system seems never to have exerted a consistent wider influence comparable with the ever-growing influence of the Mande. It is of considerable interest, for example, that Islam is said to have come to the Hausa kingdoms, on the very borders of Bornu, from Mali, which was many hundreds of miles away. Once again the explanation seems to be connected with the point that the economic motives for empire seem to have been weaker, or at least less successful, in Kanem and Bornu. Certainly no Kanuri merchant class emerged which could compare with that of the Mande. The resources available for commercial exploitation may have been less – certainly there can have been no very direct access to sources of gold – or the country lay too open to infiltration from desert pastoralists from the north and north-east,

the Bulala, the Tuareg tribes, or the Shuwa Arabs. After the coming of
the Mande traders, the much smaller Hausa kingdoms, albeit subject at
times to military pressures from both Kanem-Bornu and Songhai,
succeeded in making a much more effective use of their resources. By
the sixteenth century, they were producing agricultural surpluses and
developing manufactures of metal-ware, cloth and leather.* These
were to make them the prime Sudanic market for trans-Saharan
traders, and moreover enabled them, despite their lack of political
unity, to build up a system of trade and trade-routes to more southerly
regions which was to rival that of the Mande merchants further to the
west. The influence of the politico-economic systems of the Mande
and of the Hausa and Kanem-Bornu on the peoples of the Guinea
lands to the south of the western and central Sudan must now be
examined.

* What Europeans know as 'Morocco leather', because initially they imported it
from Morocco, had probably often been imported by Morocco from the Sudan.

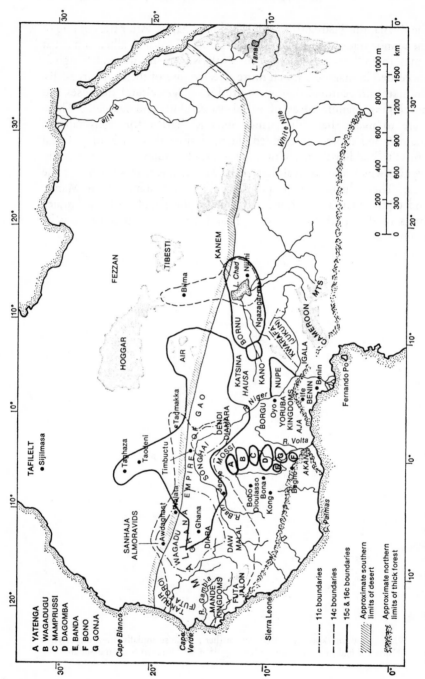

Map 3 *States and empires in the western and central Sudan, c. eleventh to c. sixteenth centuries*

A YATENGA
B WAGADUGU
C MAMPRUSSI
D DAGOMBA
E BANDA
F BONO
G GONJA

TAFILELT
• Sijilmasa

FEZZAN

TIBESTI

HOGGAR

AIR

KANEM

BORNU
L. Chad
• Bilma
• Njimi
Ngazagamu

TAGHAZA •
Taodeni •

SANHAJA
ALMORAVIDS
• Awdaghast
WAGADU
• Ghana
DIARA
• Walata
Timbuctu •
Tadmakka •

MALI EMPIRE

SONGHAI EMPIRE
OF GAO

DENDI
DIAMARA

KATSINA
HAUSA
KANO

• Jenne

R. Bani

DAW
MALAL

TAKRUR (TEKROI)
R. Gambia
FUTA
JALON
MANDE
KINGDOMS

BOBO
Diouassso •
Kong •

MOSSI
A
B
C
D
E
F
G
Bighu •
Bona •

AKAN

BORGU
Oyo •
YORUBA
KINGDOMS
• Ife
AJA
BENIN
• Benin
NUPE
IGALA
KWARAFA
(JUKUN)
CAMEROON MTS

R. Volta
C. Palmas

Sierra Leone

Cape Blanco

Cape Verde

R. Niger

White Nile

R. Nile

L. Tana

Fernando Po

------ 11c boundaries
– – – 14c boundaries
——— 15c & 16c boundaries
////// Approximate southern limits of desert
Approximate northern limits of thick forest

0   200   400   600   800   1000 m
0   300   600   900   1200   1500 km

30°   20°   10°   0°
30°   20°   10°   0°   10°

Chapter 4

The development of states and trade in Guinea

The widespread Mande political and commercial system whose origins and development have been sketched in the previous chapter could hardly have existed without affecting more southerly West African Blacks in the region of Guinea. Equally, the Kisra story suggests that movements which occasioned the emergence of considerable organized monarchies in the central Sudan did not stop there, but also had repercussions further to the south. In general, it seems sufficiently clear that the economic and political revolutions evident in the western and central Sudan from about the middle of the first millennium naturally tended to overflow to influence developments elsewhere in West Africa.

However this overflowing seems relatively rarely to have involved direct political intervention by states of the Sudan in the affairs of the Guinea peoples. At least in some measure, the explanation for this seems to be a technical military one. The power of the rulers in the Sudan beyond the metropolitan territories that were inhabited by their own ethnic groups depended on their possession of superior military force. The key arm in their armies became cavalry, an ideal weapon for the swift and economic exercise of force over long distances in the open grassland savannahs. Moreover, through their control of the southern termini of the trans-Saharan trade routes, and so of the importation of horses suitable for military use, they had a monopoly of this weapon. But the further south cavalry were used, the less effective they became. It was difficult to deploy them effectively in the woodland savannahs; in the forest it was impossible, horses could move only in single file along the narrow, winding paths made by foot-travellers. The further south cavalry penetrated, the more easily they could be out-fought by much less costly local levies of bowmen and swordsmen. This was admirably demonstrated after the Moroccan conquest of Songhai. The invaders were able to hold the major towns of the Niger bend without much difficulty, but whenever they tried to come to grips with the Songhai kings who had taken refuge in the scrubland of Dendi, their forces were ambushed and made to retreat.

In this context it is therefore important to remember that there is one area of Guinea, between the lower Volta and the south-western border of modern Nigeria, where, because the rainfall is unusually low for the latitude, there is no thick forest even in the coastlands, and where even the woodland belts are thinner and less dense. As it happens, this area lies almost directly south of the borderland, east of the Niger bend, between what might be termed the Mande and the Chadic zones of the Sudan. The forest lands immediately on either side of it, in what today are southern Ghana and western Nigeria, were thus unusually open to influences from the north.

The widest deployment of political and economic power in the Sudan before the seventeenth century was undoubtedly that stemming from Mande initiative in the successive empires of Ghana and of Mali (and to some extent of Songhai also). This certainly did have direct political consequences in the lands immediately to the west and south of the Mande heartland around the upper reaches of the Niger and Senegal rivers. Here, extending from the lower Senegal to western Liberia, were a congeries of peoples such as the Tukolor, Wolof, Serer, Diola, Tenda, Pepel, Bullom (or Sherbro), Temne, Kissi and Gola. Linguists are agreed that the languages of these peoples form a 'West Atlantic' sub-family of the Niger-Congo language family which is quite distinct from the sub-family comprising the various Mande languages and dialects. In general it would seem that these 'West Atlantic' peoples were Blacks who possessed cattle and considerable agricultural skills (including sometimes crop rotation), and who had a high level of village life and industry (including metal working), but who had not developed much in the way of long-distance trade or of sizeable and positive political structures to compare with the Mande, perhaps in part because the latter intervened between them and the direct stimulus of trans-Saharan contacts.

However, one ethnic group speaking a West Atlantic language was totally different from all the others, and its history from about the eleventh century turned out to have such momentous consequences for so large a part of West Africa, that its relationship with the growth of Mande trade and empire should first be considered. This is the people known in English as the Fulani. This is because the British first came into contact with them in northern Nigeria, where they adopted the Hausa name for them. In fact their own name for themselves is Fulbe, and in the singular, Pulo, from which derives their name in the considerable French literature, which is Peul (occasionally Poular).

Although, as will be seen, some Fulani today are sedentary and urban, historically they are to be distinguished from all other West African peoples because their basic way of life was mobile pastoralism. The Fulani have also been distinguished from other West Africans anthropometrically, it being said that they are more slender, and with straighter noses and hair and thinner lips than are normal among West African Blacks. Also, though Fulani can be as dark-skinned as any, others have notably fairer or redder skins. This combination of distinctive cultural and physical features has given rise to the idea that the original Fulani were a Saharan pastoral people, possibly even Nilo-Saharans, who had migrated westwards along the southern limits of the desert.

If this were so, it must have been a migration of prehistory, because the earliest possible glimpse of the Fulani in historic times suggests that they were one of the groups of cattle-herders in the region in which the Soninke (i.e. northern Mande) kingdom of Ghana developed. One result of the growth of this settled agricultural society was to disperse pastoralists outwards. The ancestors of the modern Fulani seem to have chosen to settle to the south-west, in the steppe-lands astride the middle Senegal valley. It was presumably here that, if perhaps they were not originally of West African origin, they acquired their present language through mixing with local peoples, for its closest relations are the languages of the Serer and Wolof peoples of the lower Senegal and Gambia valleys. But with the emergence of the organized kingdom of Takrur, their pastoral way of life must have again been threatened. Some of them chose to participate in settled (and Muslim) society, and became the people now called Tukolor (or Toucouleur). This is the French version of a name meaning 'people of Takrur', and in their colony of the Senegal, the French used the names Tukolor and Fulani more or less interchangeably; their languages, indeed, are essentially the same.

But other Fulani did not accept the settled and Islamic way of life, and about the eleventh century sought to preserve their traditional pagan pastoralism by filtering eastwards through the grasslands of the Sudan between about 10° and 15° N. By the fifteenth century, they had settled in considerable numbers in the Futa Jalon highlands and in and around Masina, the inland delta of the Niger upstream of Timbuctu. They were also beginning to appear in Hausaland, where today there are perhaps some four million people of Fulani descent. By the sixteenth century, the leading elements of the Fulani migration were in Bornu, and by the eighteenth large numbers of them were settling on the grassy uplands of Cameroun.

This remarkable emigration was characterized by the fact that, except in the far west (Futa Toro – the ancient Takrur – and Futa Jalon), the Fulani generally neither displaced nor mixed with the earlier inhabitants of the lands in which they settled. They remained distinct communities, each under its own leader or guide, the *ardo*, continually moving themselves and their herds through the bush pastures around the fields of the agricultural villages. Their relationship with the governments and economies of the sedentary communities – rather like that of gypsies in Europe – was essentially a symbiotic one. They were willing to exchange their dairy produce, skins and, occasionally, cattle for some of the products of settled society, but not to participate in it. Many Fulani, indeed, maintained this way of life intact into the twentieth century. However, in course of time some Fulani did break away from this distinctive pagan pastoralism to settle, not in the villages of the agriculturalists, but in the growing urban centres, and there they were converted to Islam. It is not known how this happened, but it may well have been because the towns, with their developed networks of trade, afforded by far the best markets for the Fulani to dispose of their produce and to acquire what little in the way of goods and facilities they required from the rest of the world, so that some Fulani settled in them initially as factors for their rural brethren.* Since the growth of towns and trade in the Sudan to as far east as Hausaland was often connected with Mande initiatives, it might be said almost that the growth of Mande power and trade tended to pull as well as to push the Fulani eastwards.

The urban Fulani of the dispersion maintained their ethnic links not only with the wandering herdsmen in the rural districts, but also with the islamized Fulani and Tukolor populations concentrated in

---

* It has been remarked by E. F. Gautier, of the northern Saharan steppes, that nomads have a much greater use for towns than they have for agricultural settlements.

Futa Toro and Futa Jalon in the far west. Thus when in the eighteenth century these latter began to reorganize traditional West African society into something akin to Muslim theocracies, the network of Muslim Fulani communities in the towns throughout the rest of the western and central Sudan, together with the ties that these urban communities had with the very much larger numbers of mobile pagan Fulani in the surrounding countryside, enabled the ideas of Muslim reformation and revolution to spread very rapidly and forcefully over very great distances.

Other results of the growth of organized Mande power and trade in the western Sudan were less dramatic and far-reaching than the Fulani dispersion, but nevertheless brought significant change to the West Atlantic peoples bordering the Mande homeland to the west and south. Groups of refugees from the state-forming revolutions (sometimes also, perhaps, from the early stages of the Fulani dispersion) came to settle in the West Atlantic lands. The most notable of these were the Susu, who, as has been seen earlier, were unsuccessful contenders for the legacy of ancient Ghana, their king Sumanguru being defeated by the Keita leader, Sundiata, the founder of the great Mali empire. The Susu today live close by the sea between the Temne and the Serer, thus forming a Mande-speaking wedge into the territory of the West Atlantic languages.

Other groups of Mande-speakers moved west or south towards the coast as traders or conquerors. In the case of traders, an important incentive was probably access to the supplies of salt obtainable from the coast. The close connection at this time between trade and state-formation, specifically perhaps because tribute provided an easy means of acquiring surpluses for trade, has already been remarked. Certainly the growth of Mande trade towards the coastlands led to a number of Mande pioneers carving out kingdoms for themselves in emulation of the major model of Mali. There seem to have been two major axes for the Mande expansion. One was along the line of the river Gambia, a most useful artery for trade, which rises within a few miles of the sources of the Faleme, one of the major tributaries of the Senegal, whose head-waters were firmly in Mande occupation. The other, separated from the Gambia by the Futa Jalon massif which the Fulani were occupying, ran south into modern Sierra Leone close by the Susu settlement. In both areas, political organizations were established under rulers called *farimas*. Initially these seem often to have paid tribute to Mali, and even after the decline of the great Mali power in the later fifteenth century, they maintained some idea of its ultimate supremacy.

A final Mande contribution to the ethnic and political geography of the West Atlantic lands came when these were invaded from the east during the first half of the sixteenth century by marauding bands of conquerors called the Mane. There is really no room for doubt, from the evidence of their dress and weapons (which were observed at the time by Europeans), as well as from the evidence of their language, that the Mane were in origin Mande soldiers. But how they came to be advancing parallel to the coast from the *east*, is another matter. External sources cannot take them back further than about the middle of the Liberian coastline. But there is a Mane tradition, recorded in writing about 1625, to the effect that they first reached the coast close by a Portuguese fortress. This, it seems, can only have been on the Gold Coast (i.e. the coast of modern Ghana) some 600 miles further east. There is no corroboration for this either in Portuguese records (but these are notoriously defective for the period), or in the surviving traditions of modern Ghanaian peoples. But in view of what will be said shortly about Mande connections with the Gold Coast, it would be by no means impossible for a Mande military contingent to have got there over the trade roads leading south-east from Jenne. Its decision to return home westwards along the coast could conceivably have been in some way connected with the rise of Songhai military power along the middle Niger. Since there is certainly some evidence that Mande as far west as the Gambia knew about other Mande trading activities in the Gold Coast hinterland, such a decision need not have been such a step into the unknown as might have been supposed.

Be this as it may, by about the 1540s the Mane were advancing westwards parallel to the coastline of modern Liberia, fighting in turn with each tribal group that they came across. They were almost invariably successful. Following each victory, some of them settled down as overlords of a new petty state, while others were enabled to sweep up in their train some of the local people as auxiliaries (called Sumbas) and, thus reinforced, to continue to further victories further west still. The Mane advance was really only halted when, in the north-west of what is now Sierra Leone, they came up against the Susu, like themselves a Mande people, and possessing similar weapons, military organization and tactics.

The end result of the Mane conquests was considerably to compli-
cate the ethnic situation in the southern and south-eastern borderland
of West Atlantic territory. It seems to have been these conquests
which established the Mande-speaking Mende as the dominant stock
of southern Sierra Leone. Further north, the Loko are also Mande-
speaking, but there is reason to believe that their ethnic base was
originally of 'West Atlantic' origin. Their neighbours, the Temne,
though speaking a West Atlantic language, seem to have an aristocracy
of Mane origin, and it seems that some chieftaincies among the Kru,
the dominant stock of much of modern Liberia, may have arisen in
the same way.

Mande influence in lands to the east of Liberia, in the modern
republics of the Ivory Coast and Ghana, seems to have been primarily
commercial in intent, though, as the speculation about the early
history of the Mane may have already suggested, this could and did
occasion considerable consequences in the political sphere. It was
connected with the expansion of the specialized class of Muslim Mande
traders called the Dyula, who seem in origin to have been connected
with, if not identical with, the Soninke Wangara gold traders
mentioned in chapter 3. (It has been pointed out that there are contexts
in which the terms 'Dyula' and 'Wangara' are used interchangeably.*)
As far as Dyula (or Wangara) expansion to the south and south-east
is concerned, a key factor was the development of the city of Jenne,
an important early centre for long-distance trading activity. Dyula
basing themselves on Jenne can really only have done so with a view
to opening up trade towards the south. The city is not situated on
the Niger, the main line of communication through the Mali empire
from west to east, but on its southern tributary, the river Bani, which
here pursues a somewhat tortuous course through marshy country
roughly parallel to the Niger, which it joins just south of Timbuctu.
Jenne therefore does not have good natural communications with
the Mande heartland in the west but, protected by the surrounding
marshland, it is a good base for merchants desiring to connect trade
to and from the south and south-east with the trans-Saharan routes
terminating at Timbuctu and other towns of the Niger bend.

There were two major commodities originating to the south and
south-east which were bound to excite the interests of traders in the
Mande world. The first of these was gold. There were appreciable

---

* For the Soninke, *dyula* is simply a word meaning 'trader', but outside areas of
Mande speech, it has come to have an ethnic connotation.

deposits in the country of the Lobi in the valley of the Black Volta only about 300 miles S.S.E. of Jenne. Beyond this, gold could be won in alluvial washings or by digging relatively shallow mines in many places in the forests of the southern Ivory Coast and of modern Ghana. In the latter, indeed, in and close to the valleys of the rivers Ofin and Ankobra, lay what have turned out to be the richest gold deposits in all West Africa. All these would have been of interest since it is unlikely that the alluvial deposits of Bambuk and Boure could meet growing demands for the metal, in increasingly sophisticated West African societies as well as for trans-Saharan trade. (Certainly their output in modern times has been insignificant compared with that from modern Ghana; their exploitation is essentially only a dry season occupation for farmers.)

The second southern commodity of major interest to northern merchants was the kola nut, the product of trees which grew wild in the tropical forest. The nut when chewed has a pleasantly refreshing flavour, and it plays a role in the etiquette of hospitality and social intercourse not unlike that of coffee in Arab lands. Since it is also mildly stimulating, it was of some interest to Muslim communities that were by law denied the pleasures of alcohol. There are a number of varieties of kola tree, but the one which gives the nuts most favoured by trade and social usage, the *Cola nitida*, was native to the forests from Sierra Leone to modern Ghana.

There were probably already some islands of settlement of Mande-speaking peoples to the south of Jenne (and also to the east, towards Hausaland), notably the peoples known as Samo and Busa, and these may have helped provide stepping-stones by which Dyula merchants could advance. Their practice was to establish settlements close by the villages of the more important pagan rulers, thus apparently repeating the pattern evident in ancient Ghana, with its Muslim merchant quarter alongside the pagan capital. The first major settlement south of Jenne was Bobo-Dioulasso, the very name indicating the situation, since this can only mean 'the Dyula settlement in the country of the Bobo'. South of Bobo-Dioulasso, another principal Dyula centre was Kong, about 350 miles from Jenne, from which a number of trade routes radiated out towards the forestlands of the Ivory Coast and eastern Liberia. But even today these lands are relatively little developed by human occupation, and five hundred or so years ago they may have been very thinly peopled. The most lucrative trade routes seem to have gone further east, either directly from Jenne, for

example towards the gold-bearing Lobi lands, or from Bobo-Dioulasso and Kong towards the lands inhabited by the Akan-speaking
peoples who today are the dominant stock of the southern half of
the Republic of Ghana. By about 1300, there were important Dyula
settlements at Begho, south-east of Kong in a gap in the Banda Hills,
and seventy miles beyond this at Bono-Mansu, near modern Tekyiman
in the Brong country of northern Ashanti.*

When in the fifteenth century the Portuguese were involved in
trying to gain access to the gold trade of West Africa by sea, their
agents managed to secure a fair amount of information about the trade
from Jenne to the lands of the Akan, and this is reflected in the
writings of Cadamosto (c. 1455), Pacheco Pereira (c. 1505), Valentim
Fernandes (1507) and João de Barros (1552). The first three of these
all secured their information from the region of the Gambia, where,
of course, the Portuguese could make contact with the fringes of the
empire of Mali. The most lucrative aspect of the trade seems to have
been the time-honoured exchange of Saharan salt for West African
gold. The salt was carried by camel from the Sahara to Timbuctu in
large blocks of up to 200 pounds each (a camel would carry two such),
and then shipped in, presumably Songhai, canoes (each of which might
carry some 20 tons or so) to Jenne, where it was worth something like
8 ounces of gold (£32 or $160, when these currencies were on a gold
standard) per hundred pounds. This was roughly twice its value at
Timbuctu, so the trade was pretty lucrative. If Fernandes is to be
believed, a Wangara merchant in business at Jenne might have a
turnover of something like £30 000 gold ($150 000) a year. Other
goods imported to Jenne by the same means, and presumably also re-
exported to the south, included brass and copper, blue and red cloths,
silk and spices. At Jenne, the salt (and doubtless other commodities
as well) was broken down into headloads, and taken south by caravans
of one or two hundred porters. The Portuguese sources indicate that
at the end of the dry season the merchants would return north with
slaves and gold dust. Part of these commodities would be retained in
the Sudan; part would be remitted further north to buy salt and North
African merchandise. The Portuguese were mainly interested in this
trade in so far as it concerned gold, but doubtless on the northwards

---

* Conceivably the name Bono-Mansu may have a significance similar to Bobo-
Dioulasso, namely 'the Man[de] settlement in Bono (Brong) country' (though *man* is
also the root of the Akan word for kingdom, *oman*, and *aman* in the plural).

journey many of the porters would be carrying loads of kola nuts (a commodity of less interest to the Portuguese).

Pacheco Pereira, and also one of the Timbuctu *Tarikhs*, mention some of the places to which the Dyula caravans from Jenne went. The important market was clearly 'the land of Toom', and specifically perhaps its town of Bitu. Both names are perfectly recognizable, Ton and Tonawa ('people of Ton') being Mande and Hausa names respectively for the Akan, while Bitu is still the Hausa name for Begho. According to Pacheco's informants, the people of 'Toom' were strange dog-headed monsters with whom dumb barter was the rule, but Fernandes, stressing that the trade with them was the absolute monopoly of the Wangara (i.e. Dyula), in effect provides the explanation for such a story.

In about the fourteenth century, the Akan seem to have been predominantly inhabitants, not of the forestlands in which lay the richest gold resources, but of the savannah immediately north of it. One result of the arrival in their country of Dyula traders seems to have been to encourage the emergence of positive kingdoms controlling the outlets of the forest paths along which the gold was brought. (Once again there seems to be an instructive parallel with ancient Ghana.) Certainly the first known Akan kingdoms lay north of the forest or in its fringes, rather than in the forest proper. Close by the Lobi gold mines was Bona, originally, it seems, an Akan state, though it was conquered from Dagomba towards the end of the sixteenth century. The two most important early kingdoms were probably Banda, ruled from the strategic site of Begho controlling the gap in the hills through which the main trade route ran towards Kong, and Bono, with its capital at Bono-Mansu. Both these towns had, of course, important Dyula settlements. It has been claimed that the Bono monarchy, in the form in which it existed up to its conquest by Ashanti in 1722–3, was founded in 1295. A stricter interpretation of the traditional evidence, however, suggests that a date nearer 1420 would be more reasonable. This date (and, at a pinch, the earlier one also) fits well with the conception that the political growth of the Bono kingdom is to be associated with the development of the trade route from Jenne, and the rise of Banda was presumably roughly contemporary.

Bono's main direction of expansion seems to have been south-east, parallel to the northern edge of the forest, which here slopes away to the south towards the coast and the gap in the Akwapim-Togo hills through which the Volta flows towards the sea and the gradually widening strip of grassland which runs from about Sekondi eastwards to Nigeria. Attention has already been drawn to the importance of this coastal region, and to the fact that early agriculturalists were not well equipped to live in the dense equatorial forests. It may well have been round the forest through the Volta gap that the ancestors of the southern Akan group, generally known as Fante, first reached the coastlands south of the forest and west of Accra, where they mingled with earlier inhabitants and, by the time of the arrival of the Portuguese by sea in the 1470s, had established a number of small kingdoms. Some of these kingdoms seem to have maintained traditions linking them with Bono.

Obviously the forest cannot have been uninhabited at this time, else the gold would not have been got out to towns like Bono-Mansu and Begho. But it was probably thinly peopled (as today are the non-auriferous regions of the forest to the west in the Ivory Coast and Liberia), or perhaps working for gold was essentially a seasonal occupation for bands of men from the savannah. But equally obviously, with increasing appreciation of the wealth to be gained from the gold-trade, there was every incentive for the Akan to settle permanently in the forest in strength. This would be facilitated as they acquired south-east Asian foodcrops.

By the time of the arrival of the Portuguese on the coast, there was already a significant nucleus of Akan settlement and economic and political activity in the forest with its southern boundary roughly on the rivers Ofin and Pra, corresponding to the modern Ashanti state of Adansi. Although its own name was Akyerekyere, it was known to Europeans on the coast as Akany and Twifo (or Twifu). These are significant names. Akany (or 'Accany') is obvious enough, and to the European merchants throughout the sixteenth and seventeenth centuries the 'Accanees' were renowned as the best traders in gold. Twifo, translatable as 'the Twi people', is equally meaningful, since Twi is the name of one of the two major Akan languages in Ghana (the other being Fante).

Not very much is now known of Akany and/or Twifo. We cannot be sure, for example, whether it was one or two kingdoms, or indeed if it was anything more than some first nucleus of Akan trade and settlement in the forest. The reason is simply that it did not survive the great economic and political explosions occasioned among the forest Akan through the emergence, as a result of European maritime initiatives, of important new and highly competitive southern markets for their gold that were alternative to the older northern markets of the Dyula system. But it is invariably thought of as highly significant for later Akan development. For the nineteenth-century Ghanaian historian, C. C. Reindorf, Akany was 'the first seat of the Akan nation . . . from whom the others acquired knowledge and wisdom'. The ruling dynasties of many of the later important Akan kingdoms traced their descent to Akany or Twifo, and the development of these is viewed as being connected with the establishment of the Dyula trade route from the north. Thus the rulers of Akwamu, one of the three major kingdoms which competed for the trade with the Europeans in the seventeenth century, preserve the tradition that their ancestors came from Twifo, before that from Dormaa (just south of Begho), and before that from Kong. Down to the twentieth century, links were still preserved with Dormaa.

It has even been suggested that the royal families of Akwamu and other Akan states were in fact of Dyula origin. This is probably to push the evidence unnecessarily far. Perhaps the most that can be said is that the new economic opportunities presented by the Dyula would serve to stimulate some traditional leaders of Akan kinship groups to develop more positive and extensive political power; that Muslim Dyula leaders may often have been useful advisers to them in these processes; and that sometimes the leading families on the two sides may have become allied, and so to some extent merged, in marriage. But the institutions and customs of the Akan states seem to have been developed from indigenous bases, for example the great yam festivals or matrilineal inheritance to office, and even as late as 1798 a major Akan king, Osei Kwame of Ashanti, could be deposed for being too partial to Muslims.

It is however known from seventeenth- and eighteenth-century history that the Mande Dyula certainly could seize the political initiative in areas in which they had settled when it was in their interest to do so. But sometimes in Akan areas this may have been, at least in part, a reaction to the growing strength of Akan polities. This seems to have been one of the factors at work in the Mande creation in the early seventeenth century of the new state of Gonja.

Gonja is a barren district immediately north of Bono, sparsely inhabited except around its fringes, but important to the Dyula traders because through or close by it ran some of the major trade routes to the Akan gold and kola producing areas. By the early seventeenth century, conditions for these traders were notably less good than they had been initially. In the first place, the Bono monarchy was now so strong and extensive that it must have been able to a considerable extent to dictate its own terms for allowing the Dyula to purchase the gold and kola coming out of the forest lying beyond its southern border. Secondly, since about the end of the fifteenth century, a new military kingdom, Dagomba, had been developing and expanding immediately to the north-east of Gonja. Dagomba's conquest of Bona was doubtless upsetting for the Dyula, but even more important may have been the fact that at Daboya, on the White Volta, Dagomba had come into possession of the only important source of salt in the region. No doubt its kings were keen to exploit this to their own advantage, and to the disadvantage of the trading position of the Dyula. A third factor in the situation was that the Dyula were no longer the sole group of international traders operating in the area. The *Kano Chronicle** records the opening up of trade between Hausaland and Gonja, specifically for kola nuts, during the time of kings who must have been reigning during the middle or the second half of the fifteenth century. There is in fact a reference to merchants from Gonja trading to Hausaland; if this were the case, they may have been Dyula/Wangara. But Leo Africanus, referring to conditions in the early 1500s, wrote of merchants in Hausaland becoming 'very rich because they go with their goods into distant countries and because they are, towards the south, in close touch with a country where large quantities of gold are found', and this surely refers to Hausa merchants trading to Akan countries. Thus it would seem that, by the sixteenth century at least, the Dyula traders in Gonja must have been meeting with competition from traders from Hausaland.

The reaction of the Dyula in the Bono-Banda-Gonja region to this general worsening of their position seems to have been to call on the services of Mande soldier-adventurers. Where these came from is not exactly clear from the available sources. They may have come from the north, where the rise of Songhai military power from about 1464 onwards may have meant a lessening of opportunities for at least some Mande soldiers, or they may have already been resident in the region,

---

* The *Kano Chronicle* has survived in an Arabic manuscript which is thought to date only from the end of the nineteenth century, and the chronological evidence it gives for kings of Kano is not universally accepted. But it is presumably based on earlier chronicles or on oral tradition current at the time it was written, and by any computation the references to Gonja must relate to the period suggested above.

for example as guards for the Dyula traders. The evidence suggests that these warriors first occupied Begho and then advanced into Gonja, where they set up a state which began to expand at the expense of both Bono and Dagomba. The latter was forced to move its capital, Yendi, from close by Daboya to its present site further east. The various Akan and Gur-speaking peoples inhabiting the new state were parcelled out among the leaders of the Mande bands, one of whom was recognized as king. The constitution of the kingdom suggests parallels at once with Dagomba and with Akan political organization. But Gonja was not a fruitful land in which to try to maintain a centralized government, neither Dagomba power to the north nor Akan power to the south had been finally destroyed, and the new kingdom rapidly declined in strength as each band of conquerors became more and more integrated with its local community.

The Dyula presence and changes in the balance of power occasioned political upheavals in other places besides Gonja. In the seventeenth century, tensions between the Muslims and the local pagans in Begho erupted into a destructive war which eventually led to the total abandonment of the Banda capital. The local people eventually settled in a number of towns further east, while the Dyula withdrew to the west, to the further side of the Banda hills, where they established the new trading centre of Bonduku. About 1730, there was similar trouble at Kong, where the Dyula succeeded in taking over political power for themselves. This change could well have been associated, as the final eclipse of Gonja certainly was, with the rise of Ashanti as a power controlling virtually all the Akan of the forest and their important produce.

The references to Hausa merchants and to the rise of Dagomba power (which was linked with Hausa trade) serve as a reminder that in modern Ghana the Dyula were operating in a region of Guinea that was open also to political and economic influences stemming from the central Sudan. The lack of forest in the coastlands east of the Volta meant that the territory of modern Ghana was particularly open to eastern influences. Indeed, two groups of its peoples, the Dagomba and the Mamprussi and their kindred in the north, and the Gã, Adangme and Ewe in the south-east, maintain traditions of origin to the effect that their ancestors came from the east.

In the case of Dagomba and Mamprussi, and of the related Mossi people to the north of them in the Republic of Burkina Faso, these traditions have been pretty thoroughly analysed, and their early

history can now be outlined with considerable confidence. The kingdoms of Dagomba and Mamprussi, the two major Mossi kingdoms
of Wagadugu and Yatenga (or Wahiguya), and also a number of lesser
monarchies, were all established by mounted invaders who overran
the Volta basin from the east during the fifteenth century, having
perhaps appeared on its eastern borders towards the end of the
previous century. Before this, perhaps between about the eleventh
and fourteenth centuries, similar cavaliers had apparently organized a
number of kingdoms further to the east in Diamare, a territory just
to the south of the Dendi homeland of the Songhai, on either side of
the Niger where the towns of Niamey and Say now are. Certainly
the Timbuctu *Tarikhs* report raids of what they call Mossi against
the major towns of the Niger bend, which seem to have occurred
intermittently between about 1260 and 1480, and these raiders seem
to have come originally from Diamare. Undoubtedly what brought
these raids to an end, and what may well have led to the extinction
of the Diamare kingdoms, was the growth of Songhai military power
in the Niger bend from the time of *Sonni* Ali onwards. By the time
of *Askiya* Muhammad (1493–1529) and *Askiya* Daoud (1549–1582),
the Songhai armies were taking the war into the enemy's country and
destroying his towns.

It is possible that the establishment of the kingdoms which survived
into modern times in the Volta basin may in some way have been
connected with this change in the balance of power further north and
east. In any case, from a base which was close by the north-eastern
corner of modern Ghana, the ancestors of the rulers of Mamprussi,
Dagomba, Wagadugu, Yatenga and other kingdoms began to spread
out in a westerly direction about the middle of the fifteenth century,
using their cavalry to conquer and levy tribute on many of the homesteads of the local Voltaic or Gur-speaking agricultural peoples. Sometimes the priest-kings of the local animist cults were killed and
displaced. More normally, perhaps, the invaders took wives from
their families, and thus established claims to the overlordship of the
land by right as well as by conquest. In any case the result was to
establish an authoritarian, hierarchical nobility over the autochthonous kinship groups, and to weld these into unitary kingdoms. In
due course, the stock of the conquerors merged with the local stocks,
but holders of titles of nobility and power retained the ability to
trace descent from the original conquerors, and their badge was the

possession of horses, albeit in time of war the cavalry were reinforced by levies of local archers.

The means by which the Mossi–Dagomba group of kingdoms were created are very reminiscent of the means by which, some seven centuries or so before, the Zaghawa had established the kingdom of Kanem to the north of Lake Chad. Indeed, bearing in mind that apparently there were earlier Mossi kingdoms in Diamare, there seems no doubt that the creators of the Volta basin states were, together perhaps with the early Songhai kings, westerly offshoots from state-forming processes which were earlier active around Lake Chad. It is not too difficult to imagine young men from the cavalier nobilities of peoples like the Zaghawa or Bulala striking out westwards to create new estates for themselves. Perhaps the pagan pre-Wangara Hausa polities were born in this way, then the kingdoms in Diamare and Dendi, following which the cycle would have been repeated further west still.

If this could happen to the west of Kanem, it could equally happen in the zone of open country to the south-west which reaches right down to the coast. This does in fact appear to be the case, and here the Kisra legend would seem to provide a useful (though not a unique) model. It suggests that the cycle of expansion and conquest, followed by the organization of kingdoms, and then expansion and conquest and state organization even further afield, may have proceeded across West Africa from the region of Lake Chad and Hausaland in two main streams. One of these is the line already considered, which probably also involved the kingdoms in Borgu (in which land Kisra himself is said to have died), immediately south of Diamare. The other would run in a more southerly direction from Hausaland and Borgu, embracing the Jukun state on the Benue which the Hausa called Kwararafa, the Nupe kingdom just north of the Benue-Niger confluence, the Igala kingdom south of Nupe, the Yoruba kingdoms to the south-west of Nupe and the south of Borgu, the Benin kingdom to the east of the Yoruba, and the kingdoms of the Aja to their west. Beyond the Aja, who are a branch of the Ewe, lay the small states of the Adangme and Gã in south-eastern Ghana.

The rulers of these kingdoms, and of a number of other kingdoms besides, looked back to the east or north-east (in the case of Benin, to Yorubaland) as the direction from which their ancestors had come. In some cases, little more can be said than this. The Jukun today survive as little more than a remnant group with little interest in the past of the empire they once controlled northwards to the borders of Hausa and Bornu. Such of its history as survives is known mainly from the histories of the Hausa states, especially Kano, and of Bornu, to both of which kingdoms the Jukun seem to have paid tribute in about the fifteenth and sixteenth centuries. In the seventeenth century, however, they were a formidable military power which could ravage the territory of both Hausa and Bornu. The subsequent decline and disintegration of their state may be connected with the arrival of the Fulani in the region in the eighteenth century. Nupe was certainly subjected to Fulani conquest, in the nineteenth century, following on a period of civil warfare, and as a result little of its earlier history is remembered either. There is a further complication in that what appears to have been the arrival of a new dynasty from Igala about 1500 has virtually completely extinguished any traditions of Nupe history before that time. The past of the Igala themselves is viewed today mainly in terms of successive political influences stemming from the Yoruba, Benin, and the Jukun, and it is difficult, if not impossible, to establish a satisfactory chronological framework for this history.

There is in fact much to be said for the view that the Jukun, Nupe, Yoruba and Benin kingdoms, and probably also the Borgu kingdoms, were brought about by a common political process, or series of processes, but it is only perhaps in Yorubaland and Benin that it is possible to get much idea of what may have been involved. In the case of Benin, the first explanation of this is that it kept its polity intact until the very end of the nineteenth century, and a very valuable recension of its tradition was written by one of its own chiefs, J. U. Egharevba. From the 1480s onwards, the kingdom was also in contact with Europeans, and their records can usefully be used as a check on the traditional history since that time. As for the Yoruba, while they were engaged in a destructive series of internecine wars almost throughout the nineteenth century, they have developed a remarkably strong sense of the identity of their culture. They have been aided in this, somewhat paradoxically, by the fact that they were open to Christian missions, and hence to western education, as early as the 1840s. The foundation for any investigation into the Yoruba past is in fact a *History* completed by a Yoruba pastor, known to history as the Reverend Samuel Johnson, in 1897. Finally, for both Yorubaland and Benin, a fair amount of archaeological evidence is now available.

Modern interest in Benin and its history in fact really began with the very large numbers of pieces of its court art, mainly castings in brass, but also including some notable work in ivory, which were looted from Benin City following the British expedition against it in 1897. Shortly after this, in 1910, the German ethnographer, Leo Frobenius, first revealed to the outside world the existence of an even finer tradition of sculpture in brass and terracotta from Ife, traditionally the city from which the Yoruba had dispersed to found their kingdoms. Knowledge of this art has subsequently been greatly increased by archaeological investigations. A large part of the Ife finds are life-size representations of the heads of ancient kings and queens in a style of striking beauty and of a naturalism hitherto unsuspected of African artists. Some of the Benin brasswork also takes the form of the representation of royal heads, initially also naturalistic, but then increasingly stylized, but one of its major achievements is the large series of cast brass plaques (of which about a thousand in all are known), representing scenes from Benin history and legend, that once adorned the royal palace in Benin City.

The naturalistic strain in the art of Ife and Benin, together with the high degree of technical skill needed to make such fine brass castings by the lost wax process, at once led Europeans to suppose that some non-African influence must have been involved. But if this were so, it must have been a very ancient one, since some at least of the Benin plaques had been seen as early as the mid-seventeenth century, when a Dutch writer referred to the king's palace as having 'wooden pillars encased with copper, where their victories are depicted', while Benin tradition asserted that the art of brass casting had been brought to Benin from Ife in the time of a king who probably ruled something like a century before the arrival of the Portuguese.

Recent archaeological research has confirmed the antiquity of the cultures which produced the art of Ife and Benin, and has also demonstrated that no external influence need have been at work. The modern view is that the sculpture of Ife and Benin could have evolved quite naturally out of the sculpture of the Nok culture, which produced fine terracotta figurines, and has been dated to the period 900 B.C.–A.D. 200. The area in which Nok culture artifacts have been found extends from western Hausaland across the Benue into Jukun territory, while fine brasswork in the Ife-Benin tradition is also known from Nupe and Igala.

The only innovation from outside need have been the art of lost wax casting in copper alloys. But there are a number of reasons why this may not have been as significant as has been supposed. In the first place, the metal sculpture is only, as it were, the gilt on the gingerbread. The area has produced equally fine work in terracotta, stone and ivory, and much fine work is still done in wood and calabash, materials which are not very likely to survive in the archaeological record. Secondly, the Nok culture affords evidence that metallurgical skills in iron, and also tin, were early established in the area. The main problem may have been that of securing adequate supplies of metal. The nearest known historical copper workings are in Air and in the lower Congo, both about 800 miles away, but the production in the first seems to have been too slight, and in any case the copper used for casting the sculptures was almost invariably in the form of brass or bronze, in which copper is alloyed with other metals such as zinc, tin and lead. It is practically certain that brass at least was not made in sub-Saharan Africa, so there is a strong possibility that much of the metal may have come from outside, through trans-Saharan trade and eventually, after about 1480, via the European sea-borne trade, both of which are known to have transported large quantities of the copper alloys. As for the lost wax process of casting, it could have been used for tin at Nok, and anyway it was widely used for brass or bronze in eastern Guinea, from the lands of the Akan in the west (their most famous work being the fine small sculptured weights with which they weighed their gold-dust) to Cameroun in the east. The oldest metal sculptures so far identified in this region are the magnificent bronzes excavated at Igbo-Ukwu in eastern Nigeria, which have been dated to the ninth century A.D., and are, incidentally, in a style which appears to be quite different from that of the Ife-Benin tradition.

The sophistication of the art of Ife and Benin suggests that it must have been associated with kingly or priestly functions in a wealthy and a highly organized society. It has already been said that the Benin plaques once decorated the royal palace; it is also known that the brass heads were used on ancestral altars also in the palace, while the most likely use for the naturalistic Ife heads was on effigies used in state funerals. Dutch visitors of the seventeenth century thought it fair to compare the Benin capital with such major towns of the contemporary Netherlands as Amsterdam and Haarlem. Modern archaeology has shown that it was a walled city of about a mile square, with a further complex of walled enclosures extending into the surrounding countryside sometimes for many miles. It has also demonstrated that the site was certainly being occupied, and by a culture corresponding to the culture observed by the seventeenth-century visitors, by about the thirteenth century.

This affords striking confirmation of the inference from the list of kings preserved in Benin tradition that the origins of the dynasty conquered by the British at the end of the nineteenth century might go back to about A.D. 1300 or 1200. But Benin tradition asserts, not only that brass-casting was introduced from Ife to Benin after this dynasty had been established (on the foundations, it would seem, of an even older monarchy or monarchies), but also that the dynasty itself was due to the initiative of an Ife prince, Oranmiyan. It is certain that in more recent times Benin kings sent to Ife for confirmation of their accession and received messengers from Ife, while tradition suggests that originally the heads of Benin kings were sent to Ife for burial.

The best established Yoruba traditions today came not from Ife, but from Oyo, which was the dominant Yoruba state of the seventeenth and eighteenth centuries, and whose traditions are enshrined in Johnson's great *History of the Yorubas*. However, Oyo tradition certainly confirms Benin's view of its relationship to Ife. Oranmiyan appears in it as Oranyan, a grandson of the founder of Ife, Oduduwa, and reputedly also the first king of Oyo. Furthermore it is claimed that all the other Yoruba kingdoms were founded by descendants of Oduduwa who went out from Ife.

These first Yoruba kings are clearly legendary, more gods than men, and the first remembered king of Oyo who looks like a historical figure is probably Aganju, traditionally a grandson of Oranyan, but whose reign is unlikely to have been before about the end of the fifteenth century. However, there seems no reason to question the concept that many other dynasties of the area, including that of Benin, were the creation of emigrants from Ife, and there is now no doubt whatsoever that the actual town of Ife is older than anything that has been found at Benin and, indeed, that it is of very considerable antiquity. Both terracotta and brass sculptures have now been found there in a context datable to the eleventh or twelfth centuries, while the excavation of pits in what is reputedly the burial ground for the heads of Benin kings has produced dates as early as the ninth and tenth centuries A.D. For that matter, it is now known that there was a considerable settlement at the first site of Oyo by about 1100.

When it is added that one version of the Oduduwa legends tells a story of an emigration from Arabia via Bornu and northern Hausaland that is reminiscent of the Kisra story, it is difficult to escape the conclusion that Benin and the Yoruba kingdoms were the creation of bands of immigrants who entered the lands of agricultural, metal-using communities, such as those of the ancient Nok culture, from the north and north-east. Some support for this view may come from the fact that there is a separate tradition about Oduduwa, which is a myth of his coming from heaven to create the world at Ife. This would seem to be a reflection of the belief that a Yoruba society and culture existed before the formation of the kingdoms that lasted into the nineteenth century. The formation of new territorial kingdoms by invaders is, of course, the process that has been suggested to have occurred rather earlier in Kanem/Bornu and in Hausaland, and possibly rather later in the Volta basin, and which it seems fair to assume also operated in Borgu and Nupe and among the Jukun and Igala.

In the south, as in the north, the success of the newcomers may possibly have been connected with their possession of cavalry. Shango, the Yoruba god of war, but also represented as a son of Oranyan, is typically a horseman. The armies of Oyo, which in the seventeenth century extended its power south-westwards through the open country on the edge of the forestlands to the Aja states close by the coast in Dahomey, were apparently essentially composed of cavalry. It is true that today the Yoruba are often thought of as forest dwellers. But many of them still live in the savannahs to the north; the early history of Oyo suggests a continual jostling for power with the other savannah kingdoms of Borgu and Nupe; and the present concentration of population in the forest may well be in part a consequence of Fulani pressure in the nineteenth century. Ife, it is true, is just in the forest, but only just, and the newcomers may well have been attracted to it as an important cult centre of the peoples they were bent on dominating. Benin, on the other hand, is well into the forest, but even here, where horses can hardly survive, let alone be effective in warfare, kings and nobles always sought to appear in public on horse-back (as both its brass plaques and seventeenth- and eighteenth-century visitors bear witness).

Another characteristic of the newcomers may have been that they were town-builders. The size and complexity of Benin City has already been noted, while the modern Yoruba typically live only in towns, from which farmers may sally out very long distances to reach their farms. These towns were walled and of considerable size. The circuit of the outer walls at Ife, for example, was about nine miles, while the Oyo capital before the nineteenth century may have had outer walls about sixteen miles in length. This recalls the situation in Hausaland, where the walls of Kano and Katsina, for example, were both about fourteen miles around. However, there is evidence that not all the area within the walls was built up. This was certainly so in Hausaland in the nineteenth century when, for example, the traveller Henry Barth thought that in Kano some 30 000 people occupied only about one-third of the enclosed space, and in Katsina about 8000 occupied only about one-sixth of the area within the walls. Although, as archaeologists have shown both at Ife and Benin, the question of city walls in this region is a very complex one, it does look as though the idea of walling could have been to provide a shelter large enough to support all the subjects of the king and their animals for some length of time if need be. If this were so, then perhaps the origin of the walled cities is to be seen in the first sanctuaries established by the incomers in a potentially hostile country, or, alternatively, in the refuges established by the invaded peoples.

Considerable remains of earthworks are known to exist at Tado and Nuatsi, which lie on a line running westwards from Ketu, the westernmost Yoruba state, roughly parallel to the sea and about sixty miles from it. Ewe and some Gã traditions recall this line as one along which their ancestors emigrated, while Tado is recalled as the point from which the Aja peoples dispersed over their present country, and Nuatsi as the dispersal point for the Ewe. It looks therefore as though the state-building impulse continued westwards from Yorubaland along this axis. Perhaps this was a line of refuge taken by rulers who had been displaced by the Yoruba state-builders, for at the far west of the line the early Gã rulers seem to have been priest-kings of very small communities, while in the east the Aja kings seem to have been subject to a fair degree of Yoruba influence (though this may simply be a consequence of Oyo expansion in the seventeenth and eighteenth centuries). The earthworks have not been excavated by archaeologists, but the dispersal of the Aja from Tado is traditionally supposed to have been about the middle of the sixteenth century, and the arrival of the Gã on the Accra plains to have been about the same time or a little earlier.

The processes of state formation in the eastern half of Guinea have so far been looked at essentially in terms of military occupation and of political motivation. The evidence available does not really permit of any overall economic interpretation of the kind that was attempted for western Guinea. This is perhaps not surprising. As has been said, the origination of states in the central Sudan seems to have been much less obviously inspired by commercial motives than was the case further west, while long-distance trading in the central Sudan, and from it to eastern Guinea, seems to a considerable degree to have been stimulated by the influence of Mande traders who reached the Hausa kingdoms from the west in the fourteenth century. But if the hypothesis is accepted that the eastern Guinea kingdoms known to history were created by the constant branching-out from earlier established monarchies of splinter groups bent on conquest, then clearly one of the motives for these groups would be economic gain, the desire to possess and to exploit new estates of their own. If the argument on p. 63 above is taken to its logical conclusion, then the stories of the migrations of Kisra and of other conquerors could be as much evidence of the growth of trade routes along which traders spread the stories than they would be of actual conquests. In any case, bearing in mind both the nature of the interaction further to the north, between the Sahara and the Sudan, and the antiquity of the Nok culture, much of the conquerors' energies could well have been devoted to the taking over, and the exploitation and development, of earlier kingdoms, and such kingdoms could well have had their own trade networks. Since the memory of these kingdoms would be largely erased by the conquests, it may be difficult to discover historical evidence to substantiate such a view. But it does seem to be supported, for example, when one considers that the ancestors of the Mossi-Dagomba kings moved, in the reverse direction, along the same axis as that used by the Mande Wangara traders to reach Hausaland. If the chronological correlation here is obscure, it can still be said that an important early Mossi activity was raiding the wealth of the Niger bend cities.

The art evidence alone suggests that some of the new kingdoms brought their rulers very considerable wealth. Much of this was doubtless from tribute, but some of it must also have been through trade. The brass and bronze used in Ife and Benin, and in the Akan states too, must have been brought from somewhere, and presumably in exchange for some local produce. Our knowledge of early trade and its patterns in eastern Guinea is scanty, but there is increasing evidence that it may have been considerable.

An important clue here seems to be the site excavated by Thurstan Shaw at Igbo-Ukwu and dated, as has been mentioned, to as early as the ninth century. The finds here included the burial of a man who could only have been a wealthy monarch or priest-king, and considerable evidence of trade. Yet Igbo-Ukwu is in the country of the eastern Ibo, where no tradition of monarchy was thought to have existed, and which was thought too to have lain outside any system of long-distance trade until the advent of European traders to the coast. In such a situation, it was not easy to see how such wealth could have been accumulated. But recent work has suggested that, before the European arrival, the communities of the Niger delta and the creeks eastwards to the Cameroons were sending salt and dried fish northwards to exchange for agricultural produce, and that there was also an east–west trade to as far west as southern Yorubaland in some specialized manufactures.

This is substantiated by the records of the early Portuguese traders on the coast in the sixteenth century. The early Portuguese were not great innovators of trade in Africa. For one thing, they had little of their own to export which would interest African buyers. Their practice was generally to seize on local trade and to exploit it for their own purposes. Their main concern, as has been said, was with obtaining gold from the Gold Coast (i.e. the coast of modern Ghana). In one sense, this was not difficult since there was already an active trading community among the Akan close by the coast (Dyula, Akany and other merchants from the hinterland were seen on the coast as early as *c.* 1500). But this community had to be supplied with goods it wanted to buy. Initially the Portuguese imported, among other things, considerable quantities of Moroccan cloth, which conceivably had already been reaching the Akan in smaller amounts overland. But they soon also discovered that they could secure commodities in demand on the Gold Coast from nearer at hand. At first the Portuguese went mainly to Benin for these, not because Benin itself was a great producer, but because in the Benin kingdom there was a well-organized trading system easily accessible from the sea. (Later the extent to which this system was subject to royal control in the king's interest was too much for them, and they traded instead with Itsekiri and Ijaw outside Benin control.) One of the principal Portuguese imports into Benin and adjacent territory was brassware, and among the major exports to the Gold Coast were Yoruba cloth, beads (some possibly from Ife, which manufactured glass at this time, others, stone beads, probably from the upper Benue), and slaves.

There can then be little doubt that trade was a factor in the accumulation of wealth and in the development of monarchical power in eastern Guinea, even if it may have been a less formative influence here than in western Guinea. It is even possible that the trading network from Benin and the Niger delta country could have reached as far south as the mouth of the Congo, which would have been a good source of copper, and to which Fante canoes are said to have been sailing as late as the seventeenth century.

Chapter 5

States and trade in North-East and Bantu Africa

What is known or may be conjectured about the prehistory of the Bantu-speaking peoples who today occupy almost all of Africa south of a line from the Cameroons to the Kenya–Somalia border on the Indian Ocean coast has been sketched in chapter 1. There seem to have been only two factors restricting Bantu settlement in this enormous area. One was obviously the numerical and cultural strength of the peoples that were already inhabiting the territories into which the Bantu were moving. Secondly there was a geographical factor: by and large the Bantu were not interested in settling lands where agriculture could not be relied upon to provide subsistence, which was usually because the annual rainfall was inadequate or insufficiently reliable.

In most of the vast area into which the Bantu advanced, the earlier inhabitants were probably speakers of Khoisan languages, whose surviving remnants are the small-statured, yellowish-skinned Khoikhoi (or 'Hottentots') and the San Bushmen. The distinction between the two is primarily cultural. The Khoikhoi are pastoralists and possess the skills of pottery, basketry, weaving and metal-working. What remain of the San are still nomadic, Stone Age hunter-gatherers, and it is possible that this was the general cultural state of the Khoisan when the Bantu appeared on the scene. If so, their population density would have been very much lower than that attainable by the agricultural Bantu, with the result that they were unable to resist the advance of the latter. They were either exterminated, impressed and ultimately assimilated into the society and culture of the Bantu groups, or left to withdraw into areas the Bantu did not find attractive for settlement. The largest of these was the increasingly arid region in the extreme south-west of the continent which culminates in the Namib desert and the near desert of the Kalahari. Today almost all the surviving Khoikhoi are distributed round the fringes of this dry country, and it is in the Kalahari itself that the few surviving San practise their hunting and gathering. Other, and larger remnant communities of small-statured hunter-gatherers survive in another difficult geographical environment, the Congo basin forest, and especially the high, very wet and relatively cold Ituri forest of north-eastern Zaire. These are generally referred to as Pygmies and Pygmoids. However it is not known whether their ancestors were originally Khoisan-speakers, since today all these small-statured forest groups speak the languages of Bantu communities with which they live in relations of symbiosis or subordination.

The aridity of the extreme south-west of the continent is an extreme consequence of the fact that most of the rainfall in southern Africa comes in the summer from the Indian Ocean. South of about 20°S latitude, more than half of the upland interior receives on average less than 400 mm (16 in.) of rainfall a year, and thus is unfavourable for agriculture. So, although there is good archaeological evidence to show that Iron Age farmers were across the Limpopo and beginning to settle the Transvaal, Swaziland and Natal from about the fourth century onwards, their subsequent progress in southern Africa was relatively slow. Cattle became increasingly important in their economy and society, and settlement was concentrated in the better-watered coastal lowlands before it advanced into the dryer interior. Significant settlement of the high veld grasslands seems to have begun only about 1300, and on the coast the Bantu may not have reached the Kei river much before the sixteenth century (when there is firm evidence for their presence from the narratives of shipwrecked Portuguese sailors). The reason why the languages of the south-easternmost Bantu have been so noticeably influenced by Khoisan speech is doubtless because their final expansion was a slow and tentative advance by no very great numbers of people, and much of it must have been effected by absorbing many of the existing Khoisan-speaking inhabitants into their own social structures.

In the north-east there was also dry land, a great tongue stretching south from the near desert that runs from around Lake Turkana (Rudolf) towards southern Somalia, and separating the westerly lacustrine and highland regions which the Bantu had occupied from the coastlands they had colonized in the east. But aridity was not the only problem faced by the Bantu in this quarter. If they wanted to advance further they had to compete for possession of the land with militant tribes of mobile pastoralists speaking 'Nilo-Saharan' or even 'Hamitic' languages.

Today the ethnic pattern along the north-eastern Bantu frontier is one of some complexity. The great tongue of dry land stretching south from the Lake Turkana area through central Kenya into north central Tanzania is mainly occupied by the most southerly Nilo-Saharans, speakers of the so-called 'Nilo-Hamitic' languages, such as the pastoral Masai and, to their north, the Kipsigi, Nandi and Samburu. But east of the southern Masai there are remnant groups speaking either Hamitic or Khoisan languages, e.g. the Iraqw and Sandawe. To the north-east of the Masai, there is a considerable bulge of Bantu territory occupied by tribes, such as the Kamba and Kikuyu, who may have advanced from the region of the coast in southern Somalia. To the north and north-west of the Nilo-Hamites are other Nilo-Saharans, the so-called 'Nilotes', such as the Luo, Acholi, Dinka and Nuer, whose territory stretches northwards down the White Nile towards ancient Meroe. To the north-east is the Horn of Africa inhabited by speakers of Afroasiatic languages, whether mobile pastoralists like the Cushitic-speaking Somali and Oromo (Galla) of the arid lowlands, or agriculturalists like the Semitic-speaking peoples who colonized the Ethiopian highlands from the north-east from the ancient kingdom of Axum, or the Cushitic-speaking Sidama of the more southerly highlands.

This is a simplified picture even for the present-day distribution. It would be extremely rash to attempt any sketch of what the position may have been when the first Bantu arrived on the scene two thousand or so years ago. All the evidence available suggests that throughout the last two millennia there has been a tidal ebb and flow of population in this north-eastern Bantu borderland and beyond it; indeed, that this region of Africa has seen, even within the last five hundred years, population movements of a scale and type which are probably unusual in African history of this period. A term such as 'Nilo-Hamites' itself illustrates the point. Linguistically, as we have seen, it means little. Culturally, however, it may mean those 'Nilotes', i.e. people of the upper White Nile, who had moved into territory previously occupied by 'Hamitic'-speaking pastoralists, some of whose culture they have absorbed. Cross-acculturation is in fact typical of the area. Thus systems of age-grades are found indiscriminately among some of the most north-easterly Bantu, such as the Kikuyu, some of the Nilo-

Hamitic and Nilotic peoples, and among the southern Cushites (with whom the cyclical age-grade system is supposed to have originated).* Again, it is probably in this area that the Bantu acquired first cattle, and later the art of milking cattle, probably from Cushitic-speaking peoples.

About the most that can be said, perhaps, is that in most of the first millennium the Bantu were advancing northwards (though avoiding the tongue of dry land from Lake Turkana to central Tanzania), absorbing Stone-Age hunter-gatherers, and also absorbing, or displacing northwards, Cushitic-speaking peoples who had cattle and some agriculture. But by the end of the first millennium, the tide seems by and large to have begun to flow in the other direction. Cushitic peoples in the Horn of Africa were taking to extensive pastoralism on a large scale. The expansion of pastoral Somali to the west and south-west seems to have set off a vast movement of Oromo, the main line of which was clockwise round the southern edge of the Ethiopian highlands, and which was to culminate in the sixteenth century in the invasion of these highlands from both south and west. Oromo also displaced the northernmost Bantu on the coast, and caused them to move west towards the forested foothills of Mount Kenya. But the change that most affected the Bantu was that about A.D. 700 pastoral Nilotes and their herds began to move south to the west of Lake Turkana. Some of these Nilotes were to end up by conquering and ruling Bantu monarchies to the north of Lake Victoria; others, in greater numbers, were to settle and mix with less politically organized Bantu-speaking peoples to the east of the lake, the result being peoples like the modern Luo. More generally Nilotic influence seems to have induced changes in the society and economy of Bantu-speaking peoples that better fitted them for the occupation of dryer lands than those which they had first preferred for settlement. Two of the more obvious of these changes were an increased emphasis on the keeping and milking of cattle, and the dispersal of human settlement rather than concentrating it in sizeable villages near rivers and lakes. Such changes were being experienced as far south as the Zambezi and the Limpopo as early as the tenth and eleventh centuries, and in

* An age-grade system divides the male population into grades of boys, warriors and elders. All boys born within a given period of years belong to a particular, named grade; at the appropriate time, all are formally initiated into the status of warriors. After a set interval of years, this grade will be ceremonially installed as elders (or perhaps as junior elders), eligible for marriage and responsible for government, and the grade junior to it will be installed as the warriors of the nation.

due course they were obviously to facilitate the Bantu settlement of dryer lands even further to the south.

But it would be a mistake to seek to understand what was happening in the far north-east from around A.D. 700 onwards simply in terms of predominantly pastoral Cushitic and Nilo-Saharan peoples reacting to pressures previously exerted on the region by expanding Bantu-speaking farmers. It must not be forgotten that throughout these times the Red Sea and Indian coasts were open to foreign trade and settlement, and that the organized monarchy shaped by early southern Arabian colonization and by Christianity was in being in the northern Ethiopian highlands. By about the fourteenth century, if not earlier, organized kingdoms also existed among the Sidama of the south-western highlands and among the Bantu to the north and west of Lake Victoria.

After the seventh century, external relations with North-East Africa were a monopoly of Muslim Arabs, for the most part from the Red Sea and Persian Gulf coasts of Arabia itself, but with connections with the rest of the Muslim world from Egypt to India and even beyond. The relations that developed between the Muslim Arabs who settled on the African coasts of the Red Sea and the Gulf of Aden and the Christian kingdom of Ethiopia that had evolved from ancient Axum were not initially unfriendly. Christians were 'people of the book', the Christian king of Axum had traditionally been more friendly to Muhammad than most other potentates, and the Axumites were recognized as being themselves south Arabians in origin. No attempt seems to have been made to extirpate the Christian kingdom, which indeed was still allowed to send to Egypt for Monophysite bishops to head its church (and continued to do this, indeed, until the twentieth century). But the rise of Islam and its power in the Red Sea inevitably cut off the Ethiopian kingdom from the commercial and cultural links with the Greek and Mediterranean worlds which had been so vital to its earlier development. If it were to survive, it had to come to terms with Africa; to resist, to advance inland against, and to conquer and to acculturate, pagan African peoples, for the most part Cushites. This was the main preoccupation of Ethiopian kings, soldiers and churchmen from the eleventh to the thirteenth centuries, the 'dark ages' of Ethiopian history.

Initially Christian Ethiopia all but went under, but from the end of the thirteenth century it began to blossom forth under what is called the restored Solomonic dynasty,* which consolidated the concept of an African Christian kingdom with its own tradition and literature in Ge'ez. But Ge'ez was now a classical, clerical language; the everyday language of the kingdom was Amharic, a Semitic language descended from Ge'ez but with Cushitic accretions. The centre of the kingdom was now in the province of Amhara, close by Lake Tana, some 200 miles to the south of Axum, in Tigre, which was now a frontier province, while the southern boundary of the kingdom extended to the loop of the river Abay (Blue Nile) running south from Lake Tana.

In the Eritrean coastlands, colonies of Arab merchants and settlers were converting to Islam the local Cushitic tribesmen – Saho, Afar and Somali – and erecting Muslim kingdoms bent on expansion. Christian Ethiopia, though dependent on the Muslims for such trade as it had, was able to resist them politically. The main route for the advance of trade and Islam into the interior thus came to run further south, through the southern highlands. The advance was directed from Zeila, a Red Sea port which was the capital of Ifat, the most successful of the Muslim sultanates. The city state of Harar became a permanent inland base for Muslim traders, and beyond this the search for supplies of gold, ivory and slaves took them into Shoa and to Sidama territory, where new Muslim polities such as Hadya and Bali were organized.

Ifat was in effect recreating the old trade route which had once linked Meroe to the sea, and on which Axum had risen to prosperity. Not unnaturally the newly consolidated Ethiopian monarchy reacted against this growth of Muslim power. Beginning with the reign of Amda Syon (1314–44), the great hero of the restored dynasty, a series of wars was directed against Ifat and the inland Muslim governments. The political hold of the Muslims in the interior beyond Harar was weakened, and Ifat itself was forced for a time to pay tribute. But the Muslims shifted their base to Adal, a little further to the east, and continued to trade with the interior, though along a route further to the south through lowland country into which the Ethiopian soldiers disliked to venture. In the sixteenth century, when the advent of Ottoman Turkish sea-power to the Red Sea provided the Muslims with a steady supply of firearms, the balance of power shifted once again. Ahmad ibn Ibrahim Gran (1507–42) of Adal re-established the inland Muslim empire and threatened to overrun Ethiopia itself.

The Christian kingdom was probably only saved from extinction

---

* The dynasty cultivated the legend that the first king of Ethiopia was the offspring of an alliance between Solomon and the Queen of Sheba.

by the dramatic appearance in 1541, after some years of embassies passing to and from Portugal, of a small but well-armed and disciplined expeditionary force of Portuguese musketeers. In 1542, after a series of bitter engagements involving heavy casualties, the surviving Portuguese joined with the Ethiopians in a great battle in which the Adal army was routed and Gran himself killed. Any further threat from Adal was soon prevented when hordes of pagan Oromo began to advance across its line of communication with the interior. But the Oromo provided a menace to Christian Ethiopia which was far more insidious and difficult to deal with than the armies from Adal. Their pastoralists were soon advancing *en masse* into the highlands along a front running from the south-east round to the west. The very tradition of centralized Christian monarchy, and indeed of the organized agricultural way of life that gave it support, began to crumble, and three centuries were to pass before the Oromo menace was contained.

The external dangers and the internal problems faced by the Christian state and church in Ethiopia from the seventh century onwards were such that there can have been little opportunity for the kingdom to have exerted much positive influence on the Black peoples to its west and south. If significant influences did touch Blacks in the Nile valley and the Great Lakes region from the Ethiopian highlands, it is perhaps more likely that they came from or through the kingdoms which developed among the Sidama. The Sidama were essentially the Cushitic-speaking agricultural peoples of the southern highlands who had so far escaped the Semitic influence and colonization which had led to the emergence first of Axum, and then of the Christian Ethiopian monarchy in the northern highlands. Little is known of their history before the coming to them of Muslim traders from Zeila, which led to the more eastern and northern Sidama being incorporated into Muslim states like Bali and Hadya. But the wars of Amda Syon and his successors prevented their permanent islamization, and indeed led to some nominal conversion to Christianity.

In the far south-west, beyond the river Omo, Sidama peoples erected a number of small kingdoms which, though in touch with the traders from Zeila, seem to have largely escaped both early Muslim and early Christian influences, and to have remained essentially pagan. The origin of these monarchies is obscure. Surviving traditions of the best-known kingdom, Kaffa (others were Jimma, Janjero and Enaryea), cannot take its monarchy back beyond about 1400 at the earliest. They suggest that it was the creation of waves of immigrant nobility coming from the north who conquered and organized autochthonous peoples who might have been Nilotes. But this concept of the origin of the Sidama kingdoms seems likely to be a reflection of the later dominance of Amharic Ethiopia. It is possible that the western Sidama tradition of monarchy could be appreciably older than the fifteenth century. Early Arabic and Ethiopic texts say that in the tenth century Christian Ethiopia was being threatened by attacks from a people ruled by a queen. One interpretation of the name given for this people, Hamuya (which is otherwise unknown), would place them in, or close by Sidama country south of the river Abay. The reference to a queen-regent is reminiscent of the tradition, reflected in the Acts of the Apostles, that latter-day Meroe was ruled by queens called Candace. But the origin of this tradition is doubtless that between 160 B.C. and A.D. 15, five out of about eleven rulers of Kush seem to have been women, while Candace is a Meroitic word meaning 'queen' or 'queen-mother' (and thus was a title, not a name).

In 1613–14, as it happens, a Portuguese Jesuit named Antonio Fernandes visited Enaryea and Janjero, while a fair amount is known of Kaffa from twentieth-century researches. As a result it is possible to build up some picture of these Sidama monarchies before they were overlain by conquests from Oromo who later became islamized, or by the late nineteenth-century advance of the Christian Ethiopian kingdom. In addition to cattle-herding, there was a rich agriculture, involving ploughs like those of ancient Egypt and the production of cotton and coffee as well as foodcrops. Cloth, cattle and salt were traded to adjacent Blacks in exchange for gold (which the Sidama produced themselves to a limited extent). Small iron bars were used as currency. On this not inconsiderable economic base, there had been erected monarchies in which the status of the kings was at least semi-divine and in which queen-mothers played an important role. When the king died, his body was wrapped in an ox-hide and, after the election of one of his sons to the throne by the council, was buried with elaborate ritual, including the sacrifice of many cows, in a shaft grave.

Some of the customs and ceremonial attaching to monarchy in the Sidama kingdoms are reminiscent of those in some of the lacustrine Bantu kingdoms, and the possibility that Sidama monarchy might have some relation to Meroitic monarchy has already been hinted at. However, both connections are entirely speculative, and they cannot provide a firm foundation for any further speculation that the basic idea of divine kingship reached Bantu kingdoms by diffusion from the historical Nile valley kingdoms of Egypt and Nubia. If a concept of diffusion is thought to be needed, it seems far more likely – as argued in chapter 2 – that it ran through a pre-historic Cushitic stratum overrun by the Bantu expansion.

Nevertheless the pagan Sidama kingdoms as they existed from about the beginning of the fifteenth century, or possibly even earlier, certainly occupied a highly significant geographical position. Communication with Nubia was possible along the line of the Blue Nile, with the Nilotes along the valley of the river Sobat, with the Lake Turkana basin down the river Omo, and along the line of the Webi Shibeli with the Indian Ocean coastlands of Somalia, where traders from Arabia were established from at least the seventh century. Since the Sidama undoubtedly provided a link through which trade and influences from the Red Sea world could reach the Nilotes, they could equally have passed on to these peoples ideas which had their proximate genesis in either Meroe or Axum. All this is important because it is certain that some Nilotic groups emigrated to found kingdoms both to the north and south of their homeland.

But there is no reason why movements of Nilotes and other Nilo-Saharan peoples need have been solely or even mainly due to influences reaching them through the Sidama kingdoms. It has already been suggested that the southern migration of 'Nilo-Hamites' might have been set in motion by Oromo pressure on the lands of the Lake Turkana basin. In so far as the Oromo migrations were themselves caused by the expansion of Somali pastoralism in the Horn, it is conceivable that the cause of these enormous population movements may have been in some way connected with the growth of Arab trade and settlement on the Somali coasts from about the seventh century onwards. But if so, then once again we are led back to the idea of developments in the Red Sea basin as the ultimate cause of Nilotic population movements. Alternatively, of course, these movements may have been due to purely local factors, growth of population or – as with any pastoral people – the growth of herds leading to the overgrazing of the local pastures.

The first major Nilotic population movement about which something is known is that of the Luo, who began to move out from an original homeland between the northern end of Lake Turkana and the headwaters of the Sobat somewhat before the sixteenth century. The story of the Luo migrations is a complex one which cannot be fully told here. The important point to grasp is that there were two quite distinct types of Luo settlement. One took the form of mass movements of herdsmen who mixed with the earlier inhabitants of the lands they entered and created new ethnic groupings speaking Nilotic languages. This was the origin, for instance, of the modern Acholi and Alur peoples in north-eastern Uganda. Further south still, on the eastern shores of Lake Victoria, there is a large group of people who call themselves Luo and who speak a Nilotic language, but who are the result of mixing between immigrant Luo pastoral settlers and local Bantu agriculturalists. All these societies are essentially stateless. But elsewhere, both in Shillukland to the north of the confluence of the Sobat with the White Nile, and in Bantu territory in the north-west of modern Uganda, smaller groups of Luo immigrants appeared on the scene about 1500 as the founders of kingly dynasties.

Even more interesting, perhaps, neither to north nor south were these small Luo groups the only dynasty-founding invaders to have arrived on the scene from the direction of the upper Nile valleys and south-western Ethiopia. Also about 1500, what was left of the ancient kingdom of Alwa (Alodia) was conquered by black immigrants called the Funj who founded a dynasty which ruled from Sennar until it was conquered in 1821 by an army sent from Egypt by Muhammad 'Ali. The origins of the Funj are a matter of some argument, but possibly the most likely explanation is that they may have been herdsmen coming from further up the Blue Nile. Secondly, the Luo group known as the Bito who founded the dynasties which ruled the Bantu kingdoms of Bunyoro, Toro and Buganda, which survived into the twentieth century, achieved this result by conquering and taking over the institutions of an earlier kingdom which may likewise have been created by immigrants from the north. Not a great deal is now remembered of this kingdom except in Bunyoro, which it is clear inherited most of the central territory of the earlier polity. Here the predecessor kingdom is called Kitara, and in it the agricultural Bantu were ruled by pastoral kings and nobles called the Chwezi, who are said to have departed to the south when the Bito arrived. In Buganda, further to the west and more on the fringes of the old Kitara, the Chwezi period seems to be subsumed in a legend of a great hero called Kintu, who is said to have come from the north-east and to have first brought the various Bantu clans together under one central authority.

It is apparent from the form of these legends that the original Bito were comparative barbarians who were conscious that they were taking over a political and economic system considerably more advanced than any they had known before. Indeed, as Luo, they must have come from a society governed through age-sets rather than by kings or chiefs. The Bito sought to legitimize their accession to power in Bunyoro by claiming that the Chwezi had invited them to come; that they had peacefully taken over the palaces, regalia, herds and wives of their predecessors, who had cheerfully gone off to the south; and that the Chwezi wives had instructed them in the duties of kingship. In Buganda the new dynasty claimed to be the result of an alliance between a descendant of Kintu and a daughter of the first Bito king of Bunyoro. But, as Professor Oliver has pointed out, the real nature of the Luo invasion of Kitara is apparent from the tradition of the more southerly kingdom of Rwanda which the Luo did not succeed in conquering. Here reference is made to a terrifying invasion of Banyoro (i.e. people of Bunyoro) who, at a time which must have been equivalent to the early sixteenth century, appeared on the scene to ravage the land, to kill the cattle, and to enslave the women and children.

There is some archaeological confirmation of the conquest in that tradition asserts that the last Chwezi stronghold was in the vast earthworks at Bigo, on the southern limits of the land occupied by the invading Bito and on the northern border of Ankole. Excavation of these earthworks has shown that they were occupied around 1350–1500, and that the basic structure (though not the vast size of the complex as a whole) is essentially similar to royal enclosures that were in use in Ankole and Rwanda until the nineteenth century. There is in fact no doubt that the Chwezi kings were part of the pastoral group, variously known as Hima or Tutsi, who remained into the colonial period as the ruling nobility in the kingdoms of Ankole, Rwanda and Burundi to the south of Toro, the most southerly Bito conquest. The name Chwezi (together with those of Gabu and Ranzi, said to have been in some way associated with the Chwezi in the government of Kitara) is still in fact a Hima clan name.

The social structure of the kingdoms that developed from the Bito conquest was much more homogeneous than that of the Hima states or, presumably, of Kitara. In Rwanda, for example, the ruling Tutsi were an endogamous caste constituting some 10 per cent of the population, and were clearly distinguishable from the rest of the population both physically and functionally. They were taller (average stature

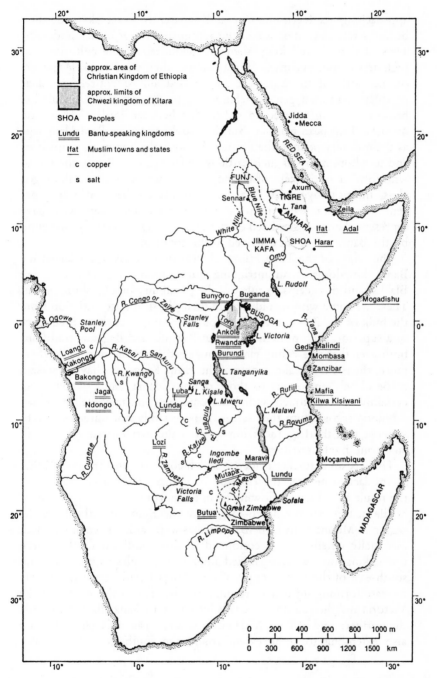

Map 4   *North-east and Bantu Africa,* c. *thirteenth to* c. *seventeenth centuries*

approaching six feet), slimmer and apparently fairer skinned; their business was government and the administration of justice under the aegis of their sacred king; their life permitted of the cultivation of high arts of poetry, music and basketry; they were the sole owners of the cattle of the kingdom and existed almost entirely on their products; and their general relationship to the rest of the population has been not unfairly compared to that between lords and serfs on medieval European manors. But they spoke the same Bantu language as the ordinary people, the Hutu, who were the hoe-using cultivators and to whom many of their cattle were farmed out. Below the Hutu, who formed 85 per cent of the population, was a further, submerged class, the near pygmoid Twa, who constituted the remaining 5 per cent. The Twa were hunters and potters, and may well have represented an unassimilated element of the original population found by the Bantu when they arrived in the country.

The origin of the Tutsi/Hima/Chwezi ruling class in the lacustrine Bantu kingdoms is an intriguing question. Serologically they are Blacks, and this seems to rule out the possibility of a Cushitic origin. There are some who would explain their physical differentiation from the bulk of the Bantu-speaking population simply as the consequence of a superior, high protein, diet. But Rwanda and Baganda traditions both aver that this ruling class immigrated from the north. Further-more, the royal burial customs of the Hima Kingdoms have been said to be closely analogous to those of the Sidama states, which were certainly in close touch with Nilotic peoples and may well have had a Nilotic sub-stratum themselves. It is certainly not unreasonable to suppose that the Luo incursion was not the first Nilotic invasion of lacustrine Bantu territory.

There is some further evidence which could support the notion that in the lacustrine area the erection of monarchical governments was the result of influences flowing from the north in a number of waves. While in the extreme north-east, from the Kenya coastlands to the region of Mount Kenya, the Bantu tribes were, as has been mentioned, essentially chiefless, and continued in this condition until modern times, kingdoms were organized among the peoples to the south and south-east of the Hima states. The traditional evidence in fact points to state-forming influences running southwards to the west of Lake Victoria and then south-eastwards into western Tanzania and towards the northern end of Lake Malawi. In western Tanzania generally, and also extending to some extent round the southern end of 'Nilo-

Hamitic' territory into north-eastern Tanzania, there is a common tradition of chieftaincy which resembles the lacustrine model, and which is ascribed to the coming of cattle-owning strangers from the north or north-west. But it is significant to note that the cattle brought by the strangers were not the big long-horned cattle of the Hima and Tutsi, but a smaller short-horned breed which is not now found in the lacustrine kingdoms. It looks therefore as though the state-builders of western Tanzania must have left the Uganda region before the coming of the Hima.

Among the Bantu of Tanzania, the scale of monarchical organization tended to be on a very much smaller scale than it was further north. The principles were the same, but sometimes the king might have only a few thousand subjects. This may well reflect the fact that the land was much less suitable for agriculture than the well-watered volcanic and alluvial soils of the lacustrine region, so that the communities were naturally poorer and the opportunities for royal aggrandizement therefore less. But it also suggests that the building up of substantial kingdoms by immigrants in the lacustrine region proceeded by stages, and that only the first stage might have reached as far south as Tanzania. The question then arises as to what any such immigrants had to build on; whether they had to begin with a stateless kind of society, like that found among the Kenya Bantu, or whether they found communities who already had within themselves the seeds from which the notion of divine kingship could grow and prosper.

It is tolerably clear that the chieflessness of the Kenyan Bantu cannot be used as evidence that this was the 'natural' state of Bantu society. There is a great deal of evidence, besides that of the age-grade systems, to show that their social as well as their political structures have been greatly influenced by mixing and exchange with their Cushitic and 'Nilo-Hamitic' neighbours. It is necessary then to proceed further south, to consider what is known of early Bantu history beyond modern Tanzania, in territory which might be thought to be too remote to have been penetrated by Nilotic influences. However, these more southerly Bantu did not develop in total isolation. They were certainly subject to influence from Indian Ocean trade and settlement on the east African coastline, and the course of this trade and settlement should first be chronicled.

Navigation of the Indian Ocean seems to have presented early seafarers with far less problems than navigation of the Atlantic. As has already been mentioned, an important factor here was the northern Indian Ocean's system of monsoon winds, blowing steadily towards the African coast during the winter months, and away from it towards India and the Arabian peninsula during the summer. It was therefore possible for regular trans-oceanic commerce to be developed to and from eastern Africa appreciably earlier and with simpler vessels than was the case with the Atlantic coasts. As has been mentioned in chapter 2, sailors from the Red Sea trading system commanded by Hellenistic Egypt were certainly acquainted with the northern half of the Indian Ocean coast of Africa by about A.D. 100. The *Periplus of the Erythrean Sea* mentions a town called Rhapta as the most southerly trading place in 'Azania', and this is most usually supposed to have been somewhere in the Rufiji delta. In the form in which it is now known to us, Ptolemy's *Geography* is thought to reflect the geographical knowledge which had accumulated in Alexandria by about the fourth century. From this it is apparent that Greek sailors were acquainted with the coast to as far as Cape Delgado at least. They also knew of an island called 'Menouthias', which could have been Madagascar or one of the Comoro Islands. (They seem too to have had some concept of the inland geography of East Africa with its great lakes and snow-capped mountains.)

It would in fact be reasonable to suppose that Hellenistic navigation would normally cease about the northern end of the Mozambique channel between Africa and Madagascar, because this represents the southerly limit of reliable monsoon winds. The picture given by the *Periplus* and by Ptolemy is in fact confirmed by finds on the coast of Hellenistic, Roman, Byzantine and Persian coins, from the period between the third century B.C. and the fourth century A.D. The main concentration of these finds is on the southern Somalia coast, thus suggesting a concentration on trade with the southern Ethiopian highlands occupied by the Sidama. But these coins have also been found as far south as the islands of Zanzibar and Mafia. Similar coin finds have been made in western India, so that there is little doubt that during the last few centuries B.C. and the first few centuries A.D., there was an established system of maritime trade linking the countries bordering the western Indian Ocean, and that it was largely operated by Greek or Graeco-Roman merchants based in Egypt. Their interest in North-East Africa would be as a source of spices, incense, gum, ivory, gold and slaves. This system seems also to have linked up with trade in the eastern Indian Ocean and beyond, since there is some evidence that Chinese merchants of this period had some knowledge of East Africa.

In about the fourth century, the Greek hold on western Indian Ocean trade decayed because of the rise of the naval power of Sassanid Persia, and perhaps also in part because of the development of over-land routes of trade in north-eastern Africa from Axum. In the seventh century, however, Muslim Arabs destroyed Sassanid power, and also secured control of Egypt and the Red Sea coastlands, while from the eleventh century onwards, Muslims also began to penetrate north-western India. It was therefore possible for the western Indian Ocean trading system to be re-created by Arab merchants.

The first Arab settlements on the East African coast seem to have been temporary encampments of folk who may have been as much or more fishermen as traders, and who were also probably pre-Islamic. By the ninth and tenth centuries, however, there is evidence for quite substantial Muslim towns on the coast, especially perhaps on the Somali coast, but also on the islands of Zanzibar and Pemba. Building was at first in mud, but by at least the beginning of the twelfth century, substantial buildings, mosques and possibly also forts and palaces, were being built in coral stone. At about the end of the twelfth century, there settled at Kilwa Kisiwani,* an island off the southern Tanzanian coast about 160 miles north of Cape Delgado, what the *Kilwa Chronicle* (the earliest known of a number of local histories written in Arabic, and apparently composed about 1520) calls 'the Shirazi'. It is probably wrong to think that the Shirazi came from Shiraz in Persia. It is more likely that they went to Kilwa from the southern Somali coast (though doubtless as traders there they would have had connections with the Persian Gulf region). The Shirazi decision to re-settle lower down the coast marks a shift of emphasis in the Muslim trade with eastern Africa; trade with the southern coast was becoming more lucrative than trade with the northern coast. There is some evidence that about the end of the thirteenth century yet another group of traders followed the Shirazi south, and replaced them as rulers of Kilwa.

There is no question that from about 1200 Kilwa began to be the most prosperous of the east-coast trading cities, and that there was a further marked increase in prosperity after about 1300. Ibn Battuta, who visited Kilwa in 1331, thought it 'one of the finest and most

---

* That is, 'Kilwa on the island'. There are now two further towns in the vicinity which also bear the name Kilwa.

substantially built towns' he had seen. The ruins of its Great Mosque are still plain for all to see, and recent excavation of what must have been the royal palace indicates that it was a magnificent structure erected probably in the early fourteenth century in a style reminiscent of Umayyad and Abbassid architecture of some 500 years earlier. Among the thirty-seven other coastal towns which were flourishing by this time were (from south to north) Kismani on Mafia Island, Kizimkazi on the island of Zanzibar, Mombasa, Gedi (now totally ruined and abandoned), Malindi, and Mogadishu, many of which are known from contemporary Arab or sixteenth-century Portuguese accounts, and in many of which substantial archaeological work has been done. Even the smaller towns could cover forty to fifty acres, all had substantial stone buildings, and all have revealed substantial evidence of their commercial prosperity, especially in the fourteenth and fifteenth centuries. The most striking evidence for this is perhaps the substantial quantities of Chinese porcelain that have been found. This is important archaeologically because it can be accurately dated: most of it is of the time of the Ming dynasty (1368–1620). Porcelain was presumably only a luxury good; the import staples seem to have been trade beads, very large numbers of which have been found, and cloth, which leaves little or no archaeological record. Another index of commercial prosperity and sophistication is that coins, usually of copper, were minted at three at least of the coastal towns, at Kilwa from the time of a king who reigned from 1277 to 1294, at Mogadishu certainly from about c. 1322, and at Zanzibar probably from some time in the fifteenth century.

The trading settlements provided a powerful acculturating influence on the coastal Bantu. Ibn Battuta said of Kilwa that 'the greater part of its inhabitants are Zanj of very black complexion'. The general result of Arab settlement, indeed, was to create along the length of the coast the homogeneous, urban-centred Islamic culture of the Swahili (from the Arabic Sahel, 'coast'; hence Swahili, 'people of the coast'). The Swahili language is undoubtedly Bantu, though with a considerable vocabulary of borrowings from Arabic, and from about the thirteenth century onwards it began to supersede Arabic as the everyday speech of the coastal towns. Folk literature probably began to be written in Swahili by about the sixteenth century; during the nineteenth century it began to replace Arabic as the language for historical writing, and by the twentieth century it had replaced it for all purposes. In the nineteenth century, with the growth of inland trade routes, the use of Swahili began to spread into the interior. Today it is the national language of Tanzania, and is widely understood over the whole eastern half of central Africa from northern Kenya to Mozambique, and to as far west as the upper Congo.

Nevertheless, before the nineteenth century, the coastal trading towns seem to have exerted virtually no influence on the peoples of the interior lying behind the coastal districts of Kenya and Tanzania. The archaeological research that has been undertaken in this region has made to all intents and purposes no finds of coastal or Indian Ocean provenance datable to earlier than the later eighteenth century. In one sense this is easily enough explicable. Within fifty to eighty miles inland from this coast, the environment begins to change from the mixed forest and savannah lands watered by the monsoon rains to a country of inhospitable thorn scrub. For much of its length this ecological boundary is also matched by the ethnic frontier between the coastal Bantu agricultural peoples and semi-nomadic pastoralists. Thus both environmental and ethnic and cultural factors militated against the development of trade routes inland from the coast. The problem then is rather to account for the presence on this coast of so many Muslim trading towns and for the development of their rich and sophisticated Arab-Swahili society.

What seems to have happened is that the early Arab traders on the Somali coast, trading with the interior for spices, incense, ivory, slaves and gold, must have begun to prospect with the monsoon winds to see whether they could find further supplies of these desirable commodities further south. Ivory and slaves were certainly to be obtained from the southern coastlands, and the demand for both was growing in the sophisticated lands from Egypt to India with their wider Mediterranean and further Asian trading links. It is known, for example, that Zanj slaves were employed in salt-mining near Basra as early as the ninth century, while African ivory was more easily carved than Asian, and so was in demand as far afield as both western Europe and China. Al-Idrisi, in his description of the coast (written in 1154, but presumably relying on somewhat earlier information), also says that in the neighbourhood of Malindi a deposit of high-grade iron ore was discovered, and it proved profitable to work this for export to India. But some time between the date of Idrisi's information and that of Abu al-Fida, who wrote in the early fourteenth century, a much more momentous discovery was made, namely that on the coasts close to the southern limits of monsoon navigation it was possible to trade for gold. It must have been this discovery that led to the 'Shirazi' migration, and to Kilwa supplanting Mogadishu, in southern Somalia, as the major trading centre, though at the time of Ibn Battuta's visit in 1331, the latter was still apparently the larger and culturally more developed town.

The gold that was obtainable on the southernmost monsoon coast came from the territory now called Zimbabwe, and Arab or Swahili merchants were soon exploiting trade routes to it. The first of these presumably ran south-westwards overland from Kilwa and the coast immediately south of it, following the line of river valleys like that of the Rovuma, which run from the highlands around the southern end of Lake Malawi. These would have brought the traders to the Zambezi valley and so to a number of routes of access to the Zimbabwean high veld where the gold was mined. But discovery of the Zambezi would have suggested that, despite the uncertainty of the monsoon winds in the Mozambique channel, it would be easier to reach Zimbabwe from outports of Kilwa on the coast further south. The chief of these became Sofala, on an island close by the coast about midway between the Zambezi delta and the mouth of the river Sabi. If the *Kilwa Chronicle* is to be believed, the town of Sofala must have been founded (perhaps only taken over) from Kilwa very shortly after the Shirazi migration, i.e. about the end of the twelfth century.

It is a clear implication from this southern extension of the Arab East African trading system that gold was already being mined in Zimbabwe. This was undoubtedly the case. Twentieth-century Zimbabwe, of course, has been a not inconsiderable producer of gold, and it has been said that 'there is scarcely a modern mine . . . which is not on the site of an "ancient working"' (Summers). Originally, it seems, gold was very widely found in the Zimbabwean highlands close to the surface, and there are innumerable remains of early workings down to a depth of as much as 100 feet. It is not easy to date the workings themselves, the more so since so many of them have been interfered with by modern prospectors or miners, but the balance of the cultural evidence that may be associated with them suggests that gold was certainly being extracted from the Zimbabwean highlands by the eleventh century.

It was at one time suggested that the techniques used in the early gold-mines in Zimbabwe were so similar to those once used in southern India that the mines must have been opened up in response to an outside initiative. Indian Ocean traders would certainly have been interested in new sources of gold, the more so as the gold resources of southern India were becoming exhausted by the fourth century. It is not perhaps totally impossible to imagine some precursors of the Arab–Swahili traders on the east coast prospecting inland, south of the barriers of the thorn scrub and its pastoral tribes, perhaps primarily in search of wider sources of ivory, coming across gold outcrops and, realizing their significance, sending for pioneer miners from southern India to begin their exploitation. But, quite apart from the facts that the techniques used in any particular mining situation are bound to some extent to be determined by the circumstances in which the ore is found, and that early technology did not present a vast variety of possible techniques, when early Zimbabwean gold-mining is considered in the perspective of contemporary archaeological evidence available in central and southern Africa as a whole, there is really no need to think that any outside influence was needed to get it started.

It has already been seen how quickly all the Bantu had taken to iron-working and, although iron ores are much more widely and commonly found in their lands than other metallic ores, there is adequate evidence to show that they were keen to work these, and skilful at it, wherever these ores were recognized. There is evidence for the working and smelting of copper ores in the Shaba province of modern Zaire, about 500 miles north of the Zimbabwean gold workings, from as early as the fourth or fifth century. Copper shares with gold the characteristics of being an attractively bright metal that is soft and easy to work into attractive shapes; compared with the more common metal iron, it is also relatively imperishable. Copper is therefore a good material for the manufacture of adornments and objects of prestige, the more so if gold is not readily available. This is very well demonstrated in the vast cemeteries which have been partially excavated at Sanga and Katoto in the upper Lualaba valley in Zaire. These were in use between about the seventh and seventeenth centuries, and by about the eleventh and twelfth centuries – even though Sanga is about 150 miles away from the nearest known source of copper, and Katoto even further – men, women and children were being buried together with considerable quantities of elaborate copper bracelets, necklaces and other jewellery. As time went on, the graves also contained increasingly large numbers of small X-shaped copper ignots; these can only have been regarded as emblems of wealth, perhaps even as currency. Further south, in Zambia, in Zimbabwe itself, and to the south of Zimbabwe in the northern Transvaal, there is quite extensive evidence for the mining and working of copper from about the eighth century onwards. It is also known that, in both Zimbabwe and the northern Transvaal, tin was mined and also alloyed with copper to produce bronze. With such experience in the extraction and working of metals, there seems no reason to suppose that in Zimbabwe the indigenous Bantu would not themselves have embarked on the mining and working of gold as soon as they had recognized the ore and its possibilities.

However it is important to note that from about the eighth century onwards quite a few of the prehistoric sites which have been excavated in central Africa, up to as much as 1000 miles from the east coast, have produced small numbers of objects, such as glass and shell beads and cowrie shells, which can only have been brought into the interior from the Indian Ocean. It would stretch credulity too far to suggest that foreign traders had penetrated halfway across the continent by the eighth century. One is therefore led to conclude that by this time the Bantu communities of central and southern Africa were already sufficiently advanced as to organize trade for themselves over considerable distances. It may be presumed that all these communities were usually self-sufficient in the necessities of life, such as foodstuffs, housing and pottery, the materials of which in any case tended to be bulky and so difficult to transport. But at least three raw materials needed or desired by advancing Iron Age societies were unevenly distributed. Good salt could only be obtained from the coasts, or from occasional salt-pans in the interior which would acquire considerable economic significance. Accessible outcrops of copper from which to make objects of adornment and prestige were readily available only in limited areas. Iron ore was much more generally distributed, but high-grade ores are comparatively rare, and it may therefore be supposed that the peoples adjacent to these would gain an appreciable lead in the manufacture of good quality tools (especially hoes) and weapons.* Thus exchange would develop, and it would not be unreasonable to suppose that by about the eighth century the interior network of trade would have come into contact with the external

* It has been pointed out that the better qualities of clay suitable for pot-making are also unevenly distributed, so that the same argument would apply to pottery. But pots are fragile and bulky in proportion to their value, so that it is difficult to imagine trade in them over any substantial distances.

demand for African staples from the Indian Ocean traders (especially since the coast would often be the nearest good source of salt). If the mining of gold started on the Zimbabwe plateau in about the eleventh century, it would be reasonable to expect that by the end of the twelfth century sufficient of the metal had arrived on the coast to serve as a magnet strong enough to draw these traders, the 'Shirazi' in particular, southwards to Kilwa and Sofala, from which they were ultimately to seek to penetrate the interior themselves.

By about the fourteenth century, the link-up between Indian Ocean trade and the internal network of exchange is certainly attested by the excavations which have been conducted at Ingombe Ilede, close by the point where the river Kafue, flowing south from Shaba through Zambia, joins the Zambezi in about the middle of its course. These revealed fourteenth and fifteenth century graves containing rich ornaments in gold and copper, X-shaped copper ingots and wire, cotton cloth, ivory, and Indian Ocean glass and shell beads. There are several points of interest here. In the first place, there are no nearby sources of either gold or copper; all the goods made of these metals must have been carried at least 100 miles from north or south. Since also there was no trace of permanent and contemporary dwellings, it is a pretty fair inference that these goods had been brought deliberately for exchange with the Indian Ocean beads, and probably too for exchange with cloth (though some of this may have been of local manufacture) and, doubtless, salt, and that fourteenth-century Ingombe Ilede was a trading encampment rather than a place of permanent habitation. Finally, the wealth displayed in the graves suggests that they represent the burials of a developed chiefly or merchant class (if in fact the two would not be the same).

When, about a century later, the Portuguese arrived in South-East Africa attracted by its gold-trade (they captured both Sofala and Kilwa in 1505), the picture becomes relatively plain. There were organized kingdoms in the interior with which it was well worth trading, and the Portuguese endeavoured to do this by establishing trading settlements or fairs up the Zambezi (certainly to as far as within 100 miles of Ingombe Ilede), and also up the valley of its southern tributary, the Mazoe, onto the north-western Zimbabwean plateau. Moreover it is apparent that these trading settlements were established in the wake of earlier penetration by Arab-Swahili merchants.

Modern Zimbabwe was the seat of some of the best known of the early kingdoms of the southern Bantu. More work has probably been done here than elsewhere on the surviving oral traditions, which seem to reach back to about 1400. But just as important if not more so are the facts that, because of its gold, this was the area of central Africa most explored by the Portuguese in the sixteenth century; and that it was here and southwards into the Transvaal, that the early Bantu kingdoms built in stone, thus giving rise to durable and often very impressive ruins that have fascinated explorers and archaeologists for more than a century.

In all, something like 200 stone-built ruins are known to exist in Zimbabwe and in adjacent areas of Mozambique and the Transvaal. The first European reaction to them was that sub-Saharan Africans did not build in stone (and, indeed, were incapable of building in stone), and that therefore the ruins must have been built by foreigners – Arab, Sabaean or even Phoenician builders were suggested at various times. In fact the reason why stone-building was rare in sub-Saharan Africa was essentially that good building stone is rare. Mud is much more readily available and, whether burnt or sun-dried, can with less difficulty and labour be used to give as good or better results. This is especially so if care is taken to maintain it properly from the effects of rain, though, once this is neglected, mud buildings will collapse into shapeless heaps which are vastly more difficult for archaeologists to find and interpret than are stone ruins.

In the Zimbabwe region, however, it so happens that the country is covered with stone outcrops, many of which weather naturally into layers from about three to seven inches thick, which can easily be split to produce building blocks with at least two parallel faces. So not unnaturally the Bantu who settled there used stone for building, not for all purposes (their actual living spaces normally continued to be round huts of mud with pole and thatch roofs), but when they wanted to build really big structures, or to construct platforms on which they could build huts on hillsides, or to join such dwellings into fortified ensembles. It is clear from the techniques they used, dry stone walling without mortar and without bonded joints, that the Zimbabwean builders were originating for themselves, and were in no way influenced by other architectures, as, for example, the Islamic buildings of coral stone on the coast. There are in fact many other instances of stone-building in the interior of sub-Saharan Africa where the conditions were suitable for it, for example at Engaruka in northern Tanzania. But in Zimbabwe the stone ruins are remarkable for their splendour and sheer size; indeed, the name of the country is derived from an indigenous term for them, probably *dzimba dzem-babwe*, 'houses of stone'. The most famous, 'Great Zimbabwe', extends over something like sixty acres, and includes some walls that are 30 feet high and up to 15 feet thick at the base, and many of which have elaborate patterning, for example in a chevron form. It is apparent that sites such as this can only represent the royal capitals of cult centres of considerable states with developed political and economic systems, and capable of mobilizing and directing consider-able resources of trained and disciplined labour.

The investigations of archaeologists at Great Zimbabwe and many other sites over some eighty years indicate that these ruins are to be associated with a culture which developed out of the agricultural and iron-using society of the Leopard's Kopje people of the first millennium. This culture began to build in stone quite widely some-where about the twelfth century, and by this time Great Zimbabwe itself was already a site of considerable prestige. The most splendid achievements at Great Zimbabwe can be dated to the fourteenth and fifteenth centuries, and are associated with growing prosperity, indi-cated by the presence for the first time in any large quantity of imported porcelains and beads. This development at the centre is reflected by a growing amount of stone building of comparable sophis-tication, albeit on smaller scales, elsewhere in Zimbabwe, particularly to the south and west, thus suggesting some growth of population, certainly of population under the control or influence of the centre. But after about the middle of the fifteenth century, stone-building seems virtually to have ceased until the seventeenth or eighteenth centuries, when a more limited area to the south-west of Great Zimbabwe experienced a revival of stone-building and of prosperity and power apparently equal to anything that had gone before.

The archaeological picture begins to acquire flesh if there is added to it what is known from the coast and from local tradition. Through the exploitation of the available agricultural and mineral resources, and with the stimulus provided by growing trade with the coast, some traditional leaders who combined chiefly and priestly functions began to acquire the status of divine rulers, developing military strength by securing increasing numbers of clients and followers at the expense of neighbours and rivals, and investing their wealth in large herds of cattle which were pastured in the adjacent lowlands during the plateau's dry season and whose meat could be used to reward their retainers. Their cult-centres where access could be had to the high God through the spirits of their ancestors, often situated in the hill fortresses or caves close by which many of the best ruins are found, would thus become more potent than others, thus enabling them to attract even more clients and wealth and trade and power. The culmination of this process came from about the twelfth century onwards, so that in the fourteenth century virtually all the gold-bearing highlands may have been under the rule of one great king-priest at Great Zimbabwe, or of kinglets who gave allegiance to him. It is no doubt significant that it is to the thirteenth century that is dated the beginning of the commercial pre-eminence of Kilwa on the east coast, and the growth of its and Sofala's gold-trade with the interior.

About the later fourteenth century, the build-up at and from Great Zimbabwe comes to an end. It remained into modern times as a major cult-centre for the Shona peoples of modern Zimbabwe, who are the descendants of the people of its imperial greatness, but it was never again a centre of political importance. What seems to have happened is that the Great Zimbabwe structure had been emulated by a number of competing dynasties. Three of these dynasties seem to have achieved major success, each for a time achieving a hegemony over an area of the same sort of size as that dominated by the rulers of Great Zimbabwe.

The first of these dynasties is that best known by the name given to its ruler by the sixteenth-century Portuguese, 'Monomotapa', derived from *Mwene Mutapa*, 'lord (or master) pillager', his praise name. This was the creation of a ruling group which, with its followers, moved northwards off the plateau in the early fifteenth century to conquer and dominate the peoples of the southern side of the middle Zambezi valley between Tete and Zumbo from *zimbabwes* which, for want of good building stone, were made with timber and mud. The background to this move, and indeed to the emergence of the other rival dynasties such as those of Changamire and of Torwa, may well have been some considerable economic and political disruption on the plateau. It has been suggested that this may have been connected in some way with the Sotho groups who at this time were moving southwards between the highlands and the Kalahari. But it is perhaps more likely that it was the result of one or more natural disasters, such as droughts, crop failures or cattle epidemics, in a situation where the growth of human or cattle populations may have been putting critical pressures on the resources of the land. However a more specific explanation for the particular move of the Monomotapa dynasty towards the Zambezi lies with the tradition that they migrated to secure better supplies of salt. This may be interpreted more broadly to mean that the Monomotapa group wanted to make better contact with the important Arab–Swahili controlled main artery of trade along the Zambezi. (It might be remarked that the site of Great Zimbabwe was somewhat eccentric both in relation to the major trade routes and to the major sources of gold.) The importance of long-distance trade to the Zimbabwe successor states would seem to be illustrated by the history of the Changamire dynasty. This is first heard of when it attempted, in the 1490s, to challenge the power of the Monomotapa in the southern Zambezi lowlands, but was defeated. Later on, however, in the late seventeenth century, the Changamire reappear as the successful challengers for the power and wealth of the Torwa, the dynasty which, from the late fifteenth century onwards had developed a hegemony over the substantial area of the plateau known as Butwa to the south-west of the old centre at Great Zimbabwe, an area which was being fertilized by trade routes running to and from the coastal emporium which the Arabs had developed at Sofala, and which the Portuguese had occupied in 1505. While Monomotapa decayed following active Portuguese penetration between about 1575 and 1666, Butwa, possibly in alliance with Muslim traders operating up the Sabi valley, prospered and gained ground, and eventually, at the end of the seventeenth century, expelled the Portuguese from their interior trading fairs in the highlands. Butwa's success can of course be equated with the seventeenth- and eighteenth-century recrudescence of stone-building in the south-west.

The combination of archaeological, traditional, Arabic and Portuguese sources allows the history of the Bantu kingdoms of the Zimbabwe plateau to be reconstructed in greater depth than is possible elsewhere in central and southern Bantu territory. But it is perfectly plain that by the end of the fifteenth century, at least, these were by no means the only substantial Bantu kingdoms of central Africa. By the seventeenth century there was, for example, a Maravi* polity challenging Monomotapa from north of the Zambezi and reaching to the southern end of Lake Malawi. But not very much is known of its history. The best known other early Bantu kingdoms are those on the west coast on either side of the lower Congo. This is because the Portuguese arrived in the Kongo kingdom of the Bakongo, immedi-

* This is the same word as the modern Malawi.

ately south of the Congo estuary, in 1482, with the result that for the next two or more centuries this kingdom and its neighbours were under the close observation of the Portuguese and of Catholic missionaries. In addition to the Kongo kingdom, which had a coastline of some 150 miles and reached inland for about 250 miles to the valley of the river Kwango, there were a number of smaller and possibly once tributary kingdoms, such as Loango and Kakongo to the north of the Congo mouth, and in the south, Ndongo.

From traditional information which began to be collected shortly after the Portuguese arrived, it can be said that the Kongo kingdom was formed through the conquest of a number of earlier, smaller Bantu kingdoms. Traces of this were evident in the Portuguese period, when the king, called the *Mani-Kongo* (*mani* being equivalent to *mwene*), was the head of a hierarchy of provincial and sub-provincial chiefs (also called *mani*, i.e. 'lord') who were appointed by him and under whom were the traditional villages with their traditional heads. The king, who had little more than a bodyguard of soldiers at his direct disposal, depended on his lords for levies in time of war, and it was a council of these lords who elected him from among eligible members of the royal family. It looks then as though the kingdom was erected by a conquering nobility moving into the land, and the traditional evidence would suggest that this was from the country above Malebo (Stanley) Pool and probably around 1400.

Why this nobility should have acted in this way, is not wholly clear. Obviously there was profit in organizing a large kingdom, and the Bakongo state had a regular system of taxes and a central treasury. But why should the conquerors come from the north-east into this particular territory? Part of the answer may perhaps be seen from the rapid organization by the Portuguese after their arrival of trading caravans into the interior under leaders called *pombeiros*,* who, though initially Portuguese, were very soon half-castes or even African slaves. In return for Portuguese imports, coastal salt, and shells from Luanda called *nzimbu*, which were currency in Kongo, these *pombeiros* brought ivory, copper, slaves and raphia cloth down to the coast from beyond Malebo Pool. The Portuguese can hardly have acted in this way, and so quickly, if there had not already been evidence on the coast that these commodities could be got from the interior. (It has already been remarked that the Portuguese were rarely

---

* A *pombeiro* is one who travels to trade in a *pombo*, a market or fair. There is no doubt that such markets existed before the coming of the Portuguese.

initiators of new trade.) Also the fact that the Bakongo had an established currency, as did other coastal states (Loango, for example, used raphia cloth), suggests that these states already had a considerable degree of commercial sophistication. There may thus have been commercial reasons why people from the interior should want to get control of the coastlands, to secure their supplies of salt, for example (and even conceivably to export their copper, as was hinted at the end of chapter 4).

The Kongo kingdom and its neighbours lay at the north-western extremity of the savannahs into which the Bantu debouched when they emerged from the Congo basin forests. Its ruling nobility seems to have organized the smaller kingdoms of the land at much the same time as the Bantu polity ruled from Great Zimbabwe, which was also probably built up from smaller units, was at its peak, and this was towards the other extreme of the savannahs far away to the south-east. It might therefore be asked whether both these sets of political initiatives may not have drawn inspiration from more central Bantu achievements about which less is known, because they have left less solid archaeological memorials and were more remote from observation by literate observers.

In a somewhat negative way, there is no great problem here. Professor Oliver has used the term *mwene* (which in Kongo became *mani*) as a label for the kind of political organization characteristic of those Bantu peoples towards the south of Tanzania and beyond who were not organized by force into more positive kingdoms by Nilotes or Nilotic offshoots coming from the north. This kind of political organization, operating perhaps more through religious and magical persuasions and through kinship ties than by overtly political means, was based on the presumed capacity of the chief descendant of the ancestral founder of a community to communicate with the other world, and, via his ancestral spirits and other spirits of the land and water, to placate the forces of nature, so vital to the prosperity of agricultural communities, better than any other mortal. It was clearly basic to the Bantu world generally, as it was in that of the West African farmers from which the Bantu had sprung. In Zimbabwe, Monomotapa and Butwa, this kind of organization seems to have proved its capacity to grow and transform itself until it was operating on a national scale. Both here and in the region of the lower Congo, the idea of gaining wealth through trading and taxing the surplus produce of the soil seems to have provided the necessary incentive.

The more difficult question to answer is whether the same incentive was producing equally impressive results in more central parts of the vast Bantu area. One difficulty here is that rather little archaeological work has been done in Zaire and Angola compared with what has been achieved in the region from Zambia southwards. The rich material found with the burials at Sanga and Kotoko indicates that surpluses, sophisticated manufactures supported by them, and long-distance trade were all apparent right in the heart of Bantu Africa by at least the eleventh century. But the general opinion is that the burials do not provide any evidence for social stratification, and therefore that one cannot be sure that the considerable material resources available were exploited to support any major political superstructure. There is very little information as yet available on this point other than the oral traditions of the central African Bantu kingdoms that happened to survive into the colonial period. Though such traditions can be guides for an understanding of the past which in all probability reach back for four or five centuries, they are notoriously deficient in reliable chronology, and they provide little or no evidence relating to anything other than narrowly *political* history as the victorious survivors want it to be remembered. But the political history they do relate suggests a process of the continual flowering, decay and dispersion of the concepts of political statehood.

Two peoples seem to have had central parts in this process, the Luba, who live astride the upper Lomami valley, and the Lunda who live just to the west of them. Both peoples possessed extensive kingdoms by the end of the seventeenth century. The major Luba state (there appear to have been two smaller ones just west of it) occupied an area of about 20 000 square miles. Its traditions aver that it was founded by immigrants from the north-east, who built up the kingdom from smaller political units at a time which may have been somewhere between the limits 1400 and 1500. The Lunda kingdom, or empire, for it was about three times as big as the major Luba kingdom, occupied the territory between the Bushmaie and Kwilu rivers, and from the upper reaches of the river Kasai in the south to its westward-flowing stretch in the north. The traditional evidence is that it was built up by emigrants coming from Lubaland at a time which must have been somewhere in the sixteenth century. The evidence also suggests that these Luba emigrants had learnt from experience in their own homeland, in that they were somewhat more successful than they had been there in integrating the ancestral heads of the local agricultural communities into their own political hierarchy without creating strains and tensions.

In the seventeenth and eighteenth centuries, many other kingdoms of the Lunda type were created, mainly to the south of Lunda itself. One of these was the Lozi kingdom in and around the flood plains of the upper Zambezi, which was probably founded in the seventeenth century. Others were specifically offshoots of the Lunda empire, ruled by kings entitled Kazembe, who seem to have begun by being the leaders of raiding or trading parties sent out by the Lunda rulers. The most famous of these were the Kazembe who created a kingdom around the Luapula valley between Lake Mweru and Shaba (see chapter 12).

The Jaga and Imbangala groups who appeared in the eastern borders of the Bakongo kingdom in the latter part of the sixteenth century, and whose military activities did much to hasten the decline of a polity already weakened by Portuguese interference in its affairs, may also be considered in this context. 'Jaga' is the English form (which would be better rendered 'Yaka') of a term the Portuguese used generically to cover marauding bands of warrior-adventurers who began to enter their sphere of interest in Kongo and Angola from the east in the second half of the sixteenth century; the Imbangala were a particular band which may have been larger and more coherent than was usual. These bands behaved very much like the Mane, their contemporaries in the Sierra Leone region further north, being permanently mobilized for war and highly mobile, and accustomed to overwhelm settled communities by surprise attack and then to incorporate their captives in their own society. An end result of their activities was the appearance of a series of small military kingdoms along the eastern border of the Kongo kingdom, the largest and most stable of which was the Imbangala kingdom of Kasanje on the upper Kwango. It used to be thought that the Jaga had arrived on the scene from Lubaland, and that the Imbangala had advanced from Lundaland. It is now known that the immediate starting points for their attacks lay in the immediate hinterland of the Kongo kingdom, which they envied for its trade and wealth, the more so when their own lands were subject to periodic droughts.

There were other bands, more dimly perceivable than the Jaga and Imbangala, which seem to have played a comparable role on the other side of Bantu Africa. These were the groups known to the Portuguese as 'Zimba', who appeared from the interior as raiders of the eastern coastlands between Kilwa and Mombasa in the second half of the sixteenth century and the first three-quarters of the seventeenth. The Maravi empire seems to have been the end result of a series of invasive raids into the lands immediately north of the lower Zambezi, and Maravi tradition claims a Luba origin for their first kings. It is probably fair to say that, although the actual raiders of the Kongo kingdom from the east, and of the Zambezi valley and Monomotapa from the north, may not have originated from Luba or Lunda at first, or even at second or third remove, they were symptomatic of a continuing instability which prevented the Bantu peoples living in the centre of the continent from making the most of their political heritage in any lasting ways. There seems to have been no lack of people with the necessary knowledge and desire to organize farming villages into political kingdoms; indeed there may have been too many of them. A kingdom would rarely remain stable and undivided for long before groups of its nobility would begin to compete for the throne and its power. As a result of the struggle, the kingdom might split into two or more fragments, or its outlying provinces would become independent, or the defeated contestants would move away and seek to build anew outside what they had not been able to take for themselves within.

It is not easy to be certain what the underlying problems may have been here. It is obvious enough that the Bantu kingdoms tended to suffer by not having a clear right to succession to their thrones, and from the difficulty of securing the continuing loyalty of subject peoples with different traditions from their own at any distance from the centre of power. But these problems applied equally to West African kingdoms, whose stability by and large appears to have been greater than that of Bantu kingdoms. But some Bantu kingdoms seem to have been much more successful than others. These include the northern lacustrine group and, of the kingdoms in central Africa, the Congo and Zimbabwe groups (at least until these were infiltrated by the Portuguese), and also the Lozi kingdom and the Kazembe kingdom of the Luapula, both of which lasted well into the nineteenth century. The stability of the lacustrine kingdoms might have something to do with the fact that their ruling classes were not in origin Bantu. But it is also doubtless to be associated with the fact that their lands were unusually well-watered and fertile and so productive, and this was probably a paramount factor for the Lozi. The Lozi kingdom excepted, the central African kingdoms had a much more marginal environment. They were in highland areas with poorer soils and without great lakes,* and largely dependent on rivers for their water. A series of poor rainy seasons might therefore create a critical situation for the crops and herds of populations growing in size with the growth of organized governments. The most successful kingdoms in this sort of environment were, together with Kazembe of the Luapula, those on the edges of the system, the Congo and Zimbabwe groups. These last had the advantage that they were in or close by the coastlands which provided a contrast of environment, and so enabled stable trade systems to develop and to supplement the production of wealth from agriculture. The Zimbabwe group also had the great advantages of mineral wealth and of access to the Indian Ocean trade system. Kazembe, far from the sea, also had appreciable mineral wealth and, throughout the eighteenth and nineteenth centuries, was in firm contact with both east and west coasts through established caravan routes.

The conclusion for central Africa seems then to be that in those regions where there were no major sources of mineral wealth, where everyone was producing the same agricultural crops in the same environment, and in an environment which might prove critical for agricultural production as population increased and if the dry seasons were protracted, there was little possibility of augmenting through long-distance trade such surpluses as agriculture might produce. Kingdoms could not develop beyond a certain point therefore, and they were unlikely to survive major crises of agricultural scarcity. This would be the context in which groups like the Jaga and Imbangala, the Zimba and the founding Kazembes of the Luapula would strike out from the interior towards the coastlands and their trade, or – in the case of the Kazembes – towards a major source of mineral wealth which was linked to the coast by major trade routes.

Nevertheless, even if conditions were often unfavourable for its stability and growth, the evidence does suggest that the Bantu of central Africa did have a basic concept of monarchical organization, of *mwene*-ship. It seems sensible to presume, therefore, that the same concept was also possessed, at least in embryo, by those Bantu-speaking peoples who settled lands west and north of Lake Victoria. *Mwene*-ship would have been encouraged to develop in this more favourable environment. The Nilotic peoples who conquered the

---

* It is worth noting, perhaps, that there seems to have been an unusually stable, though very small, Luba polity called Kikonja on the northern shore of Lake Kisale.

northern lacustrine Bantu would therefore seem more likely to have been feeding on and expanding a local concept of monarchy rather than introducing a new one of their own.

Part 2

The impact of Islam

Chapter 6

The rise of Islam and the Arab empire in North Africa

Islam, a civilization as well as a religion, was the first major external influence upon the course of African history. Within about four centuries of the Arab conquest of North Africa that began with the invasion of Egypt in A.D. 639, the population of the continent north of the Sahara had become predominantly Muslim in religion and Arabic in speech. Islam then spread across the Sahara, becoming the dominant faith in all Africa north of about 8°N latitude, and making appreciable inroads further south, to as far as the coast in modern Nigeria, into Uganda and north-eastern Zaire, and down the eastern coastlands to as far as Mozambique.

The influence of Islam thus preceded that of western Europe in Africa by many centuries, and it was in no way extinguished by the subsequent European domination of the continent. In some respects, indeed, the colonial period tended to entrench and even to extend the sway of Islam and its culture. Today Islam is far and away the most important of the world religions in Africa. Christianity was greatly advanced by European penetration in the nineteenth and twentieth centuries, but it has always remained the religion of a minority. Indeed in only five countries can it claim the adherence of more than a third of the population – the Republic of South Africa, Zambia, Malawi, Zaire and Uganda. But 90 per cent or more of all Africans north of the Sahara are Muslims, and so too are the majorities of the populations of present-day Senegal, Gambia, Guinea, Mali, Niger, Nigeria, Chad, the Republic of the Sudan, Somalia and even Ethiopia.

But in the modern world generally, the concepts of the civilization developed in western Europe tend to have an appreciably wider currency than those of Islam and its civilization. If Islam's impact on

Africa and its history is to be properly appreciated, it seems sensible to begin with a short excursus on its origins and on the history of its principal propagators, the Arabs.

The root *'arab* means either desert or the nomadic pastoralists, the bedouin, who inhabit desert, and desert is essentially what Arabia is. Except for its south-western corner, the Yemen, no part of the Arabian peninsula receives more than about ten inches of rain a year, and it has no perennial rivers. Man is engaged in a continual struggle for survival, and a man by himself is in great danger. The Arabs consequently developed a very strong spirit of community based on the concept of kinship. They grouped themselves in tribes, each regarding itself as the children (*banu*) of the ancestral founder of the tribe, and each governed by an elected leader (*sayyid* or *shaykh*) who was responsible to a council of family and clan heads. Although there was some concept of a supreme deity, Allah, for practical purposes each tribe had its own god whose presence was symbolized by a rock or some other natural object. Each tribe competed fiercely with every other for possession of the best pastures and for access to the best supplies of water.

Three factors combined to give these warring tribes the important place that Arabs have acquired in world history. The first was the position of their peninsula joining the worlds of Asia and the Indian Ocean with those of Europe, Africa and the Mediterranean. From the most ancient times, major land and sea routes of world trade either crossed Arabia or ran close by its Red Sea and Persian Gulf coasts. Thus, with obvious limits to the wealth which they could win from their land or their herds, Arabians were constantly attracted to make a living as traders, conducting caravans across their territory or sailing to and fro along and beyond its coasts, or by raiding or levying tribute on the traders. Secondly, the northern half of Arabia abutted onto the Fertile Crescent, rich agricultural lands in which developed some of the leading early civilizations. Arabs were constantly raiding these lands, and with every increase in their own population they tended to overflow into them as conquerors and settlers. Thus the peoples of the Fertile Crescent tended to become arabized, while some at least of the Arabs acquired the arts and tastes of settled life.

Finally there is a more imponderable factor, which may perhaps be most simply expressed by observing that the Arabs are a 'Semitic' people. Although they themselves were initially on the fringes of Semitic civilization in Mesopotamia and Syria, this meant that they were associated with two of the major developments of early intellectual history. The first of these was linguistic. The Semitic languages in general, and perhaps Arabic in particular, developed into remarkably flexible, expressive and poetic systems for communicating ideas, and Semitic peoples invented and were the first to develop the alphabet, the most flexible system of writing and so the most stimulating way of preserving ideas for later development. Thus when the Muslim Arabs expanded out of Arabia into Syria, Mesopotamia, Persia, Egypt and the Byzantine world, they were unusually well equipped to synthesize and take further the intellectual heritage of the civilizations of these lands. But to make this synthesis purposeful and productive, the Arabs needed to contribute a guiding principle of their own, and this they did through their version – itself a synthesis – of the second great Semitic contribution to intellectual development, monotheism, the idea that all humanity was subordinate to the will of one God.

The concept of the universal submission (*Islam*) of all men to the will of the one God, a vital principle for the competitive Arab tribes to accept if they were to unite and to make their mark on history, was the core of the teaching of the Prophet Muhammad who was born at Mecca about A.D. 570. Mecca was a significant centre for such a prophet. It was a great caravan centre containing a shrine, the Ka'ba, of more than purely local significance, and to it and through it passed many Arabs, and also many of the Jews and Christians who had already proclaimed the principle of the one God. Muhammad was to draw considerably on the tradition and experience of these two earlier monotheistic religions. It was indeed from the Archangel Gabriel that, about 610, he heard the momentous message that he was to be the unique instrument through whom the true will of God was to be revealed to all mankind.

Lā ilāhā illā Allāhu: Muhammadun rasūlu Allahi: even to the non-Arabist and the non-Muslim, the Arabic has a direct poetry lacking in the English translation – 'There is no God but God: Muhammad is the messenger of God.' This is the kernel of Muhammad's teaching, the essential creed of Islam that is preserved in the Koran, the series of revelations Muhammad claimed to have received directly from God, and which were written down by his disciples partly during his lifetime, but for the most part after his death, when a permanent record of his teaching was needed. Compared with the Jewish and Christian scriptures, the Koran is a short and simple text (though not a systematically arranged one), and its teaching is expressed in the

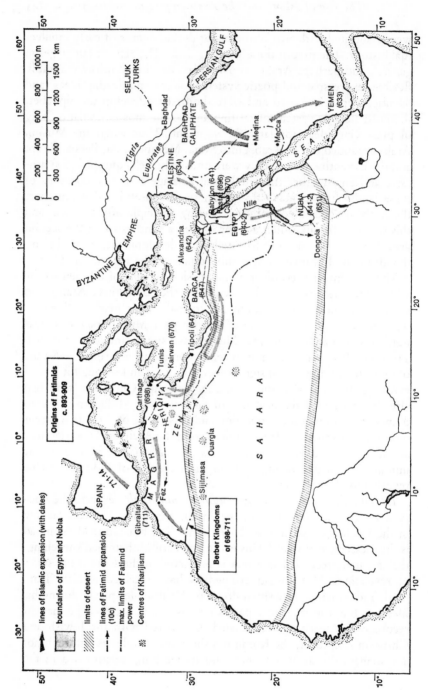

Map 5   The expansion of Islam in North Africa

lines of Islamic expansion (with dates)

boundaries of Egypt and Nubia

limits of desert

lines of Fatimid expansion (10c)

max. limits of Fatimid power

Centres of Kharijism

Origins of Fatimids
c. 893-909

Berber Kingdoms
of 698-711

SELJUK
TURKS

Baghdad

Tigris

Euphrates

BAGHDAD
CALIPHATE

PERSIAN GULF

•Medina

•Mecca

YEMEN
(633)

PALESTINE
(634)

R E D   S E A

Babylon (641)
Fustat (696)
Cairo 970

Nile

Alexandria
(642)

EGYPT
(640-2)

NUBA
(651)

Dongola

NUBA (641-2)

BYZANTINE   EMPIRE

BARCA
(647)

Tripoli (647)

Kairwan (670)

Tunis

Carthage
(698)

M A G H R I B

I F R I Q I Y A

Z E N A T A

Ouargla

Sijilmasa

S   A   H   A   R   A

Fez

SPAIN

Gibraltar
(711)

711-14

1000 m

km

0   200   400   600   800   900 1200 1500
0   300   600   900

very beautiful and direct style which became the standard of classical Arabic.

The essence of Muhammad's teaching is that a man is a true believer, a *Muslim* – one who has submitted himself to, is at peace with, the will of God – if he makes the great profession of faith that there is only the one God and that it is through Muhammad that his will is revealed, and if he also carries out four major ritual obligations. First, irrespective of where he is and what he may be doing, he should pray to God at five set times each day. It is to be noted that this is private prayer; there are also congregational prayers on Fridays at midday, but these are led by a prayer leader (*imam*) rather than a priest. There is little concept of an organized priesthood intervening between God and the individual. The second obligation is that of giving alms. But this was quite soon replaced in Muslim communities by the levying of a regular contribution, *zakat*, theoretically one tenth of each man's income, to provide a fund not only for the poor and needy but also for the advancement of Islam and its government. Thirdly, Muslims, like Jews and Christians, are enjoined to fast, and it is obligatory to fast between sunrise and sunset during the month of Ramadan. Finally, every Muslim is enjoined if possible to make the pilgrimage (*hajj*) to Mecca at least once in his lifetime.

Once men have submitted to the will of the one God, they are all equal in his sight, and in Islam all men are in a very real sense brothers, partaking equally in the duties of prayer, almsgiving, fasting and the pilgrimage without any discrimination of status, wealth, kinship or race. This was a momentous message to preach to the competing Arab tribes. If it were accepted, the tribal brotherhoods would surrender to a universal brotherhood, their united energies would be turned outward, and, with the hardness, discipline and militancy developed in the conditions of their desert life, they would be a formidable people.

But as might be expected, the doctrine that there was an equality which transcended tribal status and tribal divisions did not commend itself to the wealthy traders of the Quraysh who governed Mecca. In A.D. 622 Muhammad and such followers as he had gained therefore accepted an invitation to establish themselves in the rival town of Medina, about 300 miles from Mecca, which then had no established government. It was from this move, the *Hegira* (departure), that the Muslims came to date their era; rightly so, because it was from this time that the movement begun by Muhammad commenced to gain in strength and emerged as an organized community, based on faith, not kinship, which could challenge the tribal principle and indeed develop into a world government.

Mecca was conquered in 630, and by the time of Muhammad's death two years later, Islam had triumphed throughout Arabia. Competing Arab tribesmen then poured out in an overwhelming burst of energy which overran the adjacent lands of the Byzantine and Sassanid Persian empires, and by the beginning of the eighth century had conquered as far east as the Indus and as far west as the Iberian peninsula. These vast conquests do not seem to have been planned. They were in essence a consequence of the fact that, dissuaded from fighting each other, the Arab tribes had quickly found it extremely profitable to conquer and exploit the fertile, civilized lands beyond their Arabian desert. Thus 'Amr ibn al-'As, the conqueror of Egypt in 639–41, is said to have been motivated largely by jealousy of others' achievements in Syria and Iraq.

The governance of this vast empire raised large issues, some of which the Muslims never satisfactorily solved and some of which are especially relevant to the history of Islam in Africa, and it is as well that these issues should be briefly set out before this history is considered.

In theory the Arabs were now a single community, the community of God's people, of the only true believers, and equal membership of this community was open to the people they had conquered when they too became believers, Muslims, as sooner or later they almost invariably did. But in practice there were still rivalries and jealousies among the Arabs and between their tribes, and the Arabs as a whole expected to receive reward for their exertions at the expense of the people they had conquered. While Muhammad was alive, there was no problem. The only real ruler of, and law-giver for God's community was God himself, and it was axiomatic that Muhammad was the sole interpreter of God's will. But Muhammad died on the eve of Islam's imperial success; he had not designated his successor nor indicated how a successor to him might be chosen; and he was survived by only one of his children, a daughter, Fatimah.

In the strictest sense, no successor to Muhammad was possible: no one else was likely to receive the same direct revelation of the will of God, or if there were such a man, he would be selected by God and not by other men. But for practical purposes, there had to be some leadership, some means of interpreting, not the will of God, but the

Koran and the traditions (*hadith*) about Muhammad, so as to produce decisions and laws to deal with the manifest problems of an earthly government whose scale and responsibilities were continually growing. Hence it was accepted that there should be a Caliph (*khalifa*), a 'lieutenant', not the lieutenant of God on earth (because this could only be Muhammad himself), but the lieutenant successor to Muhammad. But even in 632, there was no unanimity as to how this successor should be determined. The main division was between those who had emigrated with Muhammad from Mecca, or who had rallied to his support at Medina, who claimed that as the original Companions of the Prophet they should choose his successor, and the Legitimists, who argued that Muhammad could not have meant to leave the succession to chance, and that therefore the succession must be inherent in Fatimah and her children.

At first the Companions carried the day, and the first four Caliphs (632–61), who ruled from Medina, were chosen from their own number, though all those chosen were also relatives of Muhammad, and the last, 'Ali, was Fatimah's husband. The election of these first four Caliphs (the so-called 'orthodox Caliphs', accepted as such by all Muslims) was not seriously disputed until 'Ali came to power in the wake of the assassination of his predecessor, 'Uthman, by mutineers from the Egyptian army. This murder of a Caliph by fellow Muslims did serious damage to the religious and moral power of the office. 'Ali's authority was quite widely challenged, and not least by one of the provincial governors, Mu'awiya. Mu'awiya was govenor of Syria, which was now the real military and political heart of the empire, the central link between the rich conquered provinces of Iraq in the east and Egypt in the west, while Medina and Mecca in the Hejaz, for all their religious significance, were becoming something of a political backwater. The dispute between Mu'awiya and 'Ali was submitted to arbitration in 659, with the result that 'Ali was declared to have abdicated. When, two years later, 'Ali was murdered, Mu'awiya was generally accepted as Caliph throughout the empire. This was the beginning of the Umayyad dynasty which ruled Islam from Damascus, the Syrian capital, until 750.

But the processes by which 'Ali had been replaced by Mu'awiya had created fundamental divisions in Islam. The most basic of these is the division between Sunni and Shi'ite Islam. The Sunnis are the believers in the *Sunna*, that is to say the orthodox tradition of Islam. They were the majority who went along with the political reality, and accepted Mu'awiya and his successors as Caliphs. The Shi'ites, on the other hand, were those who believed that Mu'awiya was a usurper, and that the Caliphate continued to reside of right in the descendants of 'Ali and Fatimah. Two consequences of Shi'ism may be noted, both of which were to affect Africa. One was the mystical concept that, although 'Ali's descendants did not have temporal power, they remained as hidden *imams* possessing spiritual ascendancy. This concept became involved with another, that of the *Mahdi* who would prepare for a second coming of Muhammad; eventually the hidden *imam* would declare himself the Mahdi. A more immediately practical consequence was that any movement of political dissent had only to find a real or putative descendant of 'Ali and Fatimah, and declare him to be the Caliph, to legitimize its claim to power.

One other minority movement should be noted. This was Kharijism, which though by no means as important as Shi'ism (which still has its modern adherents), was of quite considerable consequence in the early history of Islam in Africa. The Kharijites, 'the seceders', were in origin supporters of 'Ali who objected that the judicial process of arbitration by which 'Ali had been deposed was human interference with the will of God. They came to believe that the only true way of interpreting God's will on earth was by ascertaining the general will. This in effect was a return to the old Arab tribal doctrine of government based on consent. Kharijism therefore proved particularly attractive to particularist tribal groups within Islam, whereas the appeal of Shi'ism was rather to suppressed majorities.

Islam came to Africa with the incursion into the lands north of the Sahara of competitive bands of Arabs from Syria and Arabia. These bands were often quite small. 'Amr ibn al-'As, for example, was able to conquer Egypt, a land of perhaps fifteen million people, with forces which probably never exceeded about 12 000 men. This first conquest was possible in fact only because the Arabs were fighting not the Egyptians, but the forces of the Byzantine empire, and the Byzantine rulers of Egypt were not loved by the native Egyptians. They were foreigners, seeking to exploit the land and people of Egypt for their own purposes and profit. Even their Christianity was foreign, for they regarded the Monophysite native Coptic church as heretical, and sought to replace it with their own imperial, Melkite church.

'Amr faced serious opposition only from the fortress of Babylon, at the head of the Nile delta, and from the Byzantine naval base at their capital at Alexandria. Babylon surrendered in 641, and in the following year 'Amr was able to conclude a treaty with the Coptic Patriarch at Alexandria. Following this, the Byzantine forces evacuated the city, and, on the understanding that the Egyptians would pay an annual poll tax (*gizya*) of 2 dinars* per adult male and another tax (*kharaj*) levied on the productivity of the land, 'Amr agreed that there would be no interference with the religion, church, property or land of the native Egyptians. The Arabs in effect simply replaced the Byzantine nobles and officials as landholders and administrators. Their administration was soon drawing a revenue from Egypt of some twelve million dinars a year, any surplus of which was meant to be remitted to the caliphal government at Damascus. On the whole this was an efficient administration, which, for example, restored and extended irrigation works which had been neglected during the Byzantine period, and which realized that any attempt to increase the revenue further was likely to be non-productive in that it would create unrest and revolt among its Egyptian subjects. The most significant change was to move the capital of Egypt. Alexandria was no longer a suitable seat of government, since the Byzantine navy still commanded the sea (and, indeed, permitted a brief reoccupation of the city in 645–6), while the Arab lines of communication from Syria and the Hejaz ran overland to the head of the delta. So a new site was chosen at Fustat, close by Babylon, and just south of the modern Cairo.

Egypt was such a profitable fief of the Arab empire that there was great competition for its governorship. During the first 128 years of Arab rule, there were no less than 108 governors, each of whom arrived with a train of five or ten thousand Arab soldiers and retainers, all of whom expected to receive jobs or lands. By and large the growth in the productivity and trade of Egypt under the Arab empire, and the increase in the area of irrigated land, made it possible to accommodate this growing Arab population without undue strain. The Arabs lived mainly in the towns, and did not seek to dispossess the Copts on the land, and the latter's rights under the treaty of 642 were not seriously interfered with. There was certainly no great desire to convert Christians to Islam, because this would reduce the conquerors' revenue from taxation. But within a century, there were something like a million Arabs in Egypt. An ever-increasing number of Egyptians became associated with the Arabs as wives, servants and retainers of various kinds, and these tended to adopt their masters' religion. Other

* The dinar was a gold coin equivalent to a gold half-sovereign or $2.50.

Egyptians would convert to Islam so as to avoid paying the taxes levied on non-Muslims. By about A.D. 750, it is thought that there were probably no more than about five million Coptic Christians remaining. The vast bulk of the population were what the Arabs called *Mawali*; assimilated Muslims.

There was no reason why the Arab invasion of Africa should stop in Egypt. Nubia was invaded in 641–2 and again ten years later, but its conquest was not proceeded with. The reasons why this was so are not explicitly stated in the exiguous early sources. But one factor seems to have been simply that an attempt to conquer Nubia was a very different and appreciably more difficult business than the conquest of Egypt. In Egypt, the Arabs had only to defeat the Byzantine army of occupation for the land to fall into their hands and for the Egyptians almost to welcome them as their deliverers from Byzantine oppression. In Nubia, however, the Arabs had to face an organized native Christian government which descended from earlier monarchies which had long been accustomed to fighting against interference in their affairs from Egyptian rulers. There is evidence that the Arabs found the archers of the Nubian army redoubtable opponents. The first few Arabs on the scene must therefore have concluded that it would be much more profitable for them to settle down in Egypt as exploiters of its riches than to continue campaigning, at increasing distances from their base, against the growing resistance of much larger Nubian forces. It therefore seemed sensible to seek an accommodation with the Nubians which might suit the interests of both parties.

This in effect was secured by a treaty concluded with the Christian king at Dongola, who by this time was apparently ruling the territory of both the earlier kingdoms of Nuba and Makurra. By this treaty, the Nubians were granted freedom from attack from Egypt in return for their promise to pay an annual tribute of slaves and their granting of freedom of trade and religion to visiting Muslims. The Nubians also apparently received a substantial amount of corn, horses and other supplies from Egypt, and there is reason to believe that this gift was repeated in later years. The Arabs therefore gained freedom to trade in Nubia for the slaves and gold and other commodities which Egypt had long looked to the Sudan to provide, while the Nubians seem to have been assured in their turn of supplies of the commodities they looked for from Egypt.

This treaty is said to have remained in force for 600 years. Since it

allowed the Arabs freedom of movement in the Nile valley to as far
as Alwa, the infiltration not only of their merchants but also of
bedouin from Arabia eventually secured for them the possession of
the land they had been reluctant to take by force. The hold of Christianity and the fabric of organized government were both gradually
eroded until between 1250 and 1340 the Christian monarchy based at
Dongola finally went under, to be replaced by a congeries of petty
tribal principalities. Following this there seems to have been a great
rush of competing Arab tribes into the southern kingdom of Alwa,
but here some semblance of centralized government was preserved
by the Funj, though partly perhaps through their success in allying
themselves with some Arab tribes against the others.

The Arabs quickly extended their hold over Cyrenaica and Tripoli,
which had been part of the Byzantine territory under Alexandria, but
their advance further into the Maghrib (i.e. 'the west') was by no
means as easy. Between Cyrenaica and the agricultural wealth of the
Tunisian plain in the Byzantine province of Africa (*Ifriqiya* in Arabic),
the Sahara desert reached to the coast. The Arabs were well used to
moving striking forces rapidly across desert or near desert. But they
had a long coastal flank open to attack from the Byzantine fleets
which commanded the sea, while the Byzantine forces in Ifriqiya
could easily be reinforced through their naval base at Carthage. It was
therefore extremely difficult for the Arabs to secure permanent control
of the Maghrib until they had developed a naval power of their own,
and they did not finally succeed in overcoming the Byzantine navy
until the very end of the seventh century. But Byzantine sea-power
was not the only danger to their advance into the Maghrib; there were
other foes as well. Beyond the Aures mountains which commanded
the southern Ifriqiyan plain lay the Numidian kingdoms which had
for centuries been accustomed to resisting foreign conquest, while the
northern fringes of the Sahara from Tripoli westwards were the home
of another even more independently minded group of Berbers, the
Zenata tribes, as adept in the use of camels in mobile warfare as were
the Arab bedouin themselves.

Early Arab ventures into the Maghrib therefore were as much in
the nature of reconnaissances as they were of attempts at conquest.
The Arabs were not in a position to venture very far until after 670,
when they succeeded in establishing a base for themselves in southern
Ifriqiya at Kairwan. But their first major expedition beyond Kairwan,
'Uqba ibn Nafi's sally to as far as Morocco, ended in disaster in 683

when, returning towards Kairwan, his army was trapped and wiped out by the forces of a Numidian coalition under King Kussaila. For a time Kairwan itself was lost to the Arabs. But there was no cooperation between the Arabs' enemies. Both Numidians and Zenata sought to wrest the Ifriqiyan plain from Byzantine control. The Arabs were therefore enabled to recover, and to take their foes one at a time. First the Numidians were defeated. Then in 695–8, with the advent of Arab sea-power, it proved possible to conquer and dismantle the Byzantine stronghold of Carthage (and shortly to build nearby the new Arab city of Tunis). Finally in 702 the Arabs decisively defeated a great coalition of Zenata tribes which had been built up under a queen remembered as Kahina.* Secure in their possession of the resources of the richest part of the Maghrib, the Arabs were then able to press on swiftly further west with forces swelled by Berber recruits. By 711, the whole of North-West Africa was nominally under their control, and a mixed Arab-Berber army was embarking on further conquests across the Strait of Gibraltar.

The whole of the western conquests, in Spain – which was equally part of the Maghrib – as well as in Africa, was officially placed under Arab governors residing at Kairwan. But this government was really only effective over the agricultural lands of Ifriqiya, which were easily open to settlement by Arabs coming from the east, and which had had a settled Byzantine administration which could be restored to exploit the land in the Arab interest. Here therefore there developed a mixed Arab-Berber Muslim society not so very different from the society of Muslim Egypt. In due course the Arab mobilization of Ifriqiyan resources, together with their assimilation of the local Romano-Greek civilization, led to a flowering in Ifriqiya of much the same Islamic civilization as was developing in Egypt, albeit somewhat later in the day and with somewhat less rapport with the other great centres of early Muslim culture in Syria and Iraq. There was a flourishing urban and intellectual life, with notable mosques and palaces being built, and lively schools of theology, law and science developing. In due course the urban and agricultural Berbers became assimilated into this civilization, more completely in fact than was the case in Egypt, where the Christian church had stronger roots as a vehicle for local feeling and was never completely extinguished,

* Literally, 'the priestess'.

whereas in Ifriqiya Christianity had virtually disappeared by the eighth century.

Elsewhere in the Maghrib, however, traditional Berber society continued with but little change, except that there seems to have been a very rapid acceptance of the basic tenets of Islam. The idea of monotheism was no novelty to the Berbers; they were prepared for it through centuries of contact with Judaism and Christianity. The pastoral Berber tribes, indeed, seem to have accepted Islam in much the same kind of spirit as the Arab bedouin, with whom they had obvious similarities. Not bothering themselves with its finer religious and ethical points, and in fact retaining many aspects of their traditional beliefs in spirits, and local shrines and holy men, they could see in Islam new outlets for imperial ambitions. The Muslim armies that swept into the Iberian peninsula and southern France from 711 onwards were as much Berber as they were Arab.

By this time, indeed, the concept of one polity under an Arab caliph, in which Muslim Arabs ruled peoples of many races and creeds from the Atlantic to the Indus, was beginning to fade. One problem, that of the reduction of revenue due to the growth of the Mawali, was solved under the later Umayyads by the ingenious decision that it was not the occupier of a piece of land who paid the *kharaj*, but the land itself. Thus if *kharaj* had been due before the occupier became a Muslim, it continued to be due thereafter. But if this legal device solved the one problem, it merely intensified a larger one. This was that the Arabs could not give the Mawali the equality of status that was their due as Muslims without reducing their own power and status as a ruling aristocracy of immigrant conquerors. There were also new emigrants continually coming out of Arabia who felt that the first conquerors were denying them the share of the spoils of empire that was their right as Arabs, and these were only too ready to appeal to traditional Arab tribal loyalties to whip up support against those who were monopolizing power and wealth. In the provinces, the right of the Umayyads to govern the whole empire came to be increasingly disregarded, and in the 740s it was challenged even in Syria itself.

In an Islamic context, both Arab and Mawali dissidents naturally had recourse to Shi'ite and Kharijite views, and it was a Shi'ite movement based in the eastern empire which finally in 750 overthrew the Umayyads and established the new caliphal dynasty of the Abbasids. The Abbasids ruled not from Damascus, but from a new capital,

Baghdad, in Iraq, the richest province of the eastern empire in which lay their main strength. As a consequence, the whole character of the empire came to change. Iraq, the ancient Mesopotamia, had been the seat of an ancient civilization centred round the dynastic exploitation of riverain agriculture, and it had lucrative trading links with other seats of ancient eastern civilizations in Persia, the Indus valley and beyond. It was also the province which had the richest and most successful Mawali class. Baghdad therefore was in a very different environment from Damascus, on the border of the Syrian desert, and significant essentially because it was a suitable point from which conquering desert Arabs could seek to maintain their military supremacy both to east and west.

In Baghdad, the Caliphs ceased to be primarily soldiers or even primarily Arabs. The Umayyads had been tribal shaykhs who, although they borrowed much from the Byzantine system of centralized administration they had found in Syria, Egypt and elsewhere, still aimed to govern with the assent and assistance of other Arab tribal leaders. The Abbasids, on the other hand, drew more on the model of Sassanid Persia, and developed into oriental despots claiming divine authority for their rule: they called themselves the Caliphs of God, not the Caliphs of the Prophet. They became increasingly remote from the people, surrounding themselves with layer upon layer of bureaucrats and slaves selected for their ability and willingness to serve the caliphal interest. All power and prestige now derived from the Caliph, and not in the last resort from the support of Arab tribesmen. Beyond the immediate circle of the court, the keys to advancement and wealth were no longer military valour, but success in business or banking, law or scholarship. Baghdad became the commercial capital of Asia, and the shining centre of Islamic culture and learning at their glorious peak, but there was no longer an Arab empire.

If there were to be an empire at all, it could be maintained only through the development of a professional army. This the Abbasids recruited from Turkish slaves, Mamluks, selected from the slave markets of central Asia for their strength and courage. However, the Mamluks became Muslims, and some of them were so able that as generals and ministers they became in due course the effective rulers of the empire. But Baghdad was not an ideal centre from which to seek to control the lands beyond Syria, and the new Caliphate was never wholly accepted in the west. Once firmly in power, the Abbasids abandoned their Shi'ism and became firmly orthodox, thus hoping to secure wide support for their regime. But one result was simply to increase the appeal of Shi'ism, and of Kharijism also, to western Muslims who had no desire to send tribute to a remote eastern ruler. The old western empire was in fact already dissolving into a congeries of independent Muslim states.

Chapter 7

The Muslim states and empires of North Africa

Abbasid authority was never acknowledged in the remotest west; the Muslims in Spain, for example, chose to give shelter to a refugee branch of the Umayyads. Within fifty years, the government of Ifriqiya had become the hereditary possession of one of its local Arab families, the Aghlabids. In Egypt, however, the title to government became the gift of the leading Turkish favourites at the caliphal court at Baghdad, and these sent their own favourite slaves to rule from al-Askar, a new palace-city built just to the north of Fustat. But in 872, one of these, Ibn Tulun, more ambitious than his predecessors, ceased to send tribute to his master in Baghdad, built up his own army of black slaves, and developed Egypt into a kingdom strong enough to wrest Syria from the Caliphate. Ibn Tulun's private empire did not long survive his death in 884; nevertheless he had established a pattern which was to persist into the nineteenth century. Conquering Arabs and native Copts had now merged in Egypt into one homogeneous and essentially Muslim population. If efficiently managed, this population produced enough wealth for any governor coming from the nominal source of authority in the Islamic world to raise an army of his own, and to enable him to turn Egypt *de facto* into an independent kingdom with its own imperial ambitions. These ambitions usually looked east, to the strategically important lands and prestigeful centres of Syria and the Hejaz, which strong rulers of Egypt almost invariably sought to control. They were never much concerned to extend their power to the west. A strong Egyptian government often claimed suzerainty in Cyrenaica, but real power there was increasingly in the hands of bedouin tribes. Beyond Cyrenaica, the desert reached to the sea, and beyond this again Ifriqiya could support an organized government of its own.

The Aghlabids indeed developed a centralized, autocratic adminis-tration in Ifriqiya which was not unlike that of Baghdad or al-Askar. But they had appreciably less scope for extending its sway. In the south their agricultural lands shaded insensibly into the desert domi-nated by the pastoral Zenata Berbers. From the west they were menaced by the equally independently minded Berbers of the Aures and Kabyle mountains. These Berbers on their frontiers had accepted Islam, but this did not involve any desire to accept the authority of an imperial government. They chose rather to look in Islam for concepts which might be used to strengthen and justify their local particularisms. Both Shi'ism and Kharijism were early at hand to be used in this way.

Missionaries of a moderate Kharijite persuasion, the Ibadites, arrived in the Maghrib early in the eighth century. They soon found fertile ground for their preaching among the Berber camel nomads in the steppes and northern Saharan fringes from the south of Tripoli to southern Morocco. Around oases such as those of Wargla and Tafilalt, little Ibadite principalities emerged, and from the more westerly of these, raids were made against Aghlabid territories whose Berber inhabitants were often willing to rise against an Arab government. Tripoli and even Kairwan itself were briefly in Ibadite hands in the middle of the eighth century. The largest and most stable Ibadite state was Tahert in the highlands of central Algeria, where between about A.D. 760 and 900 there flourished an ingenious compromise between organized Muslim government and traditional Berber tribalism. The kingdom was led by *imams*, who, though they were elected by and were responsible to a council of tribal elders, possessed something of an administrative hierarchy under their personal command.

Outside Tahert, little is known of these Ibadite regimes, but they were undoubtedly significant in the history of the diffusion of Islam in Africa because, of course, it was from northern oases such as Wargla and Tafilalt that there ran the trade routes to the western and central Sudan. Trans-Saharan trade seems to have been increasing at this time with the growth of Sudanic monarchies such as Ghana and Kanem. The great caravan base of Sijilmasa in the oasis of Tafilalt, the departure point for caravans to Walata and Ghana, was founded about 800. There seems no question that the merchants who intro-duced Islam to West Africa were of the Ibadite persuasion. Though

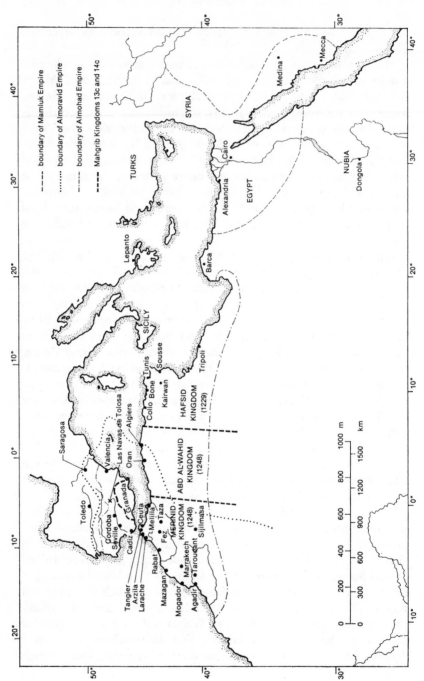

Map 6 Muslim states and empires in North Africa

boundary of Mamluk Empire
boundary of Almoravid Empire
boundary of Almohad Empire
Mahgrib Kingdoms 13c and 14c

TURKS

SYRIA

Medina •

Mecca •

Alexandria

Cairo

EGYPT

NUBIA

Dongola •

Barca

Tripoli

Sousse

Tunis
Collo Bone
Kairwan

HAFSID
KINGDOM
(1229)

Lepanto

SICILY

Saragosa

Valencia •
Las Navas de Tolosa
Oran
Algiers

ABD AL-WAHID
KINGDOM
(1248)

Toledo

Cordoba
Seville
Cadiz
Granada
Ceuta
Melilla

Fez • Taza
MERNID
KINGDOM
(1248)

Marrakech
Taroudant
Sijilmasa

Tangier
Arzila
Larache
Rabat
Mazagan
Mogador
Agadir

km

0   200   400   600   800   1000 m
0   300   600   900   1200   1500

the political passivity of almost all the early Muslims in West Africa was doubtless basically due to the fact that they were traders with no interest in changing organized Sudanic governments, and lacking any military strength with which to attempt any such change, it may not be without significance also that Kharijism was a form of Islam which expected its adherents to respect local sovereignty and custom.

The eighth century also saw the first tentative appearance of Shi'ism in the Maghrib. This was in the far west, in Morocco, which, after Tunisia, contains the only sizeable block of arable plain readily providing adequate resources for the long-term support of a stable monarchy. Here in the 780s, shortly after the fall of the Umayyads, an Arab called Idris ibn 'Abd Allah emerged who claimed descent from Fatimah and 'Ali, and began to build up a kingdom which he ruled from the new town of Fez. He was succeeded by a son, by a Berber wife, also called Idris, and thereby planted a seed from which the concept of an organized Berber monarchy in Morocco might grow. Initially, however, it could not survive the particularist drives of the Berber tribesmen of the Atlas mountains and the adjacent Saharan steppes, and the Idrisid monarchy was not continued after 828.

A more dramatic success attended the propaganda of Shi'ite emissaries who arrived in the eastern Maghrib from the Yemen towards the end of the ninth century. Their teaching that the existing Muslim regimes were not legitimate found a ready response among the Kutama Berbers of the Kabyle mountains. These were long accustomed to resist the pretension of Ifriqiyan governments to control them, and were glad of any excuse to raid their agricultural lands. It soon appeared that the Ifriqiyan peasantry was as ready to rise against Aghlabid taxation, and by 915 a Shi'ite Mahdi had been set up as a Fatimid Caliph at Kairwan.

A Fatimid Mahdi needs must aspire to the Caliphate of all Islam. But before any successful advance could be made against the Muslim strongholds in Egypt and beyond, it was necessary for the Fatimids to secure their position in, and to mobilize the resources of, the Maghrib. This was the main preoccupation of their caliphs during the first half century of their rule. Ceaseless campaigns were fought in the west until the Berber tribes had acknowledged their supremacy and the Kharijite kingdoms had been extinguished. Finally, in 969, the Caliph al-Mu'izz was strong enough to mount a successful conquest of Egypt. Four years later, he removed to Egypt himself, together with his court and treasury, and the coffins of his ancestors. Here he established yet another palace-city as the seat of his administration; this was *al-Kahira*, from which derives our name Cairo.

With the Fatimid conquest of Egypt, the original Arab conquest of North Africa had in effect been reversed. Berbers from the Maghrib had established an empire which reached all the way from Morocco to Egypt, and which indeed was soon engaged in the conquest of the Arab lands of Syria and the Hejaz. However, they did not succeed in expanding any further to the east. They were not welcomed in their new eastern territories, where they were viewed not only as foreign conquerors but also, because of their Shi'ism, as heretics. As will be seen, they very soon lost the support of the Maghribi tribesmen who had provided the initial impulse for their eastern conquests, while the Berber soldiers who had come to Egypt with them wanted to settle down and enjoy the fruits of conquest in its cities, and could no longer be trusted to be loyal and effective soldiers. As with the Abbasids or with Ibn Tulun, the maintenance of their power, and of their income from Egyptian agriculture, came to depend on their employment of a slave army, in their case both of Turks and Sudanese. But these soldiers developed interests of their own which the Fatimids lacked the authority to control. By 1065–73, which was a period of bad harvests, sections of the army were raiding the peasantry and destroying the economic basis of Fatimid power. Order was restored only by recalling to Egypt the garrison of their Syrian province. Its commander, Badr al-Jamali, became chief minister, and soon the Fatimids were rulers only in name.

The recall of the Syrian army meant the end of the Fatimid empire. There was no defence against the Saljuk Turks who were then overrunning the Baghdad Caliphate from the east. By 1076 both Syria and the Hejaz were in their hands. Then, at the end of the century, another foreign enemy appeared in the form of the European Crusaders, who by 1124 were strongly established in Syria and Palestine. The ideal of a universal Islamic polity had become an empty dream. Indeed Islam was fighting for survival, first against a new militant, western Christendom, and then, when this had been rebuffed by the middle of the thirteenth century, against Mongol hordes advancing from the east.

The two rival Caliphs, the Abbasid Caliph at Baghdad and the Fatimid at Cairo, were both now prisoners in a gigantic power struggle which was to occupy the Near East for the next three centuries. In this struggle, Egypt, the gateway to Africa and western Islam, and important for the resources which its agricultural and commercial wealth afforded, came to play a pivotal role. But except in that its resources were used to keep both pagan Mongols and Christian Europeans out of Africa, it was a role that was more part of Near Eastern than of African history, and it must be very briefly dealt with here.

In essence what happened was that Syria was saved from the Crusaders by the rise to power there of a great Turkish soldier, Nur al-Din. Nur al-Din, aware of the importance of securing his flank, sent his equally able Kurdish lieutenant, Salah al-Din ibn Ayyub (Saladin), to govern Egypt. By the 1170s, Saladin had taken the name as well as the reality of power in Egypt, establishing a hereditary Ayyubid sultanate which reigned until 1250. By this time the objectives of Nur al-Din and Saladin had been largely achieved. The wealth of Egypt was effectively mobilized to keep the Crusaders out of Egypt and to thrust them back in Syria (though they did not abandon their last fortress there until 1291). Ironically part of this achievement was due to the establishment of Egypt as a new major entrepôt for trade between Europe and Asia. The sailors and merchants of the Italian city-states, whose rise to dominate the trade of the eastern Mediterranean had in part been based on the contracts they had secured to transport Crusaders to the Levant, were encouraged to come to Egypt and there to buy the increasing quantities of oriental luxury goods that the growing wealth of southern Europe could demand.

The basis of Ayyubid power became their army of some 12 000 Mamluks,* who were systematically recruited as youths from Asia. Initially they were for the most part Turks; later on, in the fourteenth and fifteenth centuries, the Egyptian Mamluks were mainly of Circassian or of Mongol origin. The new recruits received a rigorous military training in the citadel at Cairo, and then were posted to regiments whose *amirs*, or commanders, had risen by merit through the ranks. In the thirteenth and fourteenth centuries, this was probably the finest professional army anywhere in the world. The *amirs* were able, forceful and ambitious men, and shortly after the death of Saladin,

---

* The meaning of *mamluk* is 'owned', 'belonging to', hence a slave, but more specifically a man of Caucasoid stock captured in war or purchased in a slave market; another word for slave is *'abd* (plural *'abid*), but the sense is rather different (cf. the common Muslim name 'Abdallah, i.e. 'slave to God'), and *'abid* are usually black, as were the *'abid* of Mulay Ismail of Morocco (see below p. 182).

their council became the effective government of Egypt. In 1250 they rid themselves of the Ayyubids, henceforward electing one of their own council as sultan. This self-perpetuating military oligarchy remained in undisputed control of Egypt until its conquest by the Ottoman Turks in 1516–17, and its power was not finally destroyed until the advent of Muhammad 'Ali at the beginning of the nineteenth century.

It is customary to divide the pre-Ottoman Mamluks into the Bahri Mamluks, who ruled until 1382, and the Burgi Mamluks, who were in control during 1382–1517.* The Bahri Mamluks were remarkably successful administrators and generals, and admirably completed the work begun by Saladin. Under Baybars (1260–77) and Kala'un (1277–91), the last Crusaders were cleared from Syria. More importantly, the whole western world was saved from the menace of invasion by the Mongols who had carried all before them in the east: a series of defeats in northern Syria finally checked their advance. (Out of the wreckage of the eastern Caliphate, Baybars plucked one of the Abbasids, and installed him as Caliph at Cairo to give a lustre of legitimacy to Mamluk power.) These considerable military feats were achieved without doing any damage to Egypt's agriculture and trade, both of which prospered under the management of the early Mamluks. They were active in maintaining irrigation and in developing trade relations with Europe and Asia, and so secured adequate revenue both for the support of their administration and army, and for themselves as landowners.

After Kala'un's death, the sultanate was monopolized by members of his family until Circassian *amirs* staged a palace revolution and brought his dynasty to an end. The Burgi Mamluk period proved nothing like as glorious. The *amirs* were continually competing for power among themselves (the average tenure of office of one of their sultans was only about five years). Naked force and bribery became the accepted weapons of political life, each man seeking to exploit the revenues from his land and his office to the maximum personal advantage to himself. The efficiency of the army declined, with the result that there was a decline in the revenues from the provinces which the Bahri Mamluks had acquired in Syria, the Hejaz and Nubia. There

---

* 'Bahri Mamluks' means 'the river Mamluks', so called because their dominant element were the cavalry quartered in barracks on Roda island in the Nile opposite Fustat; in the later period, the dominant Mamluk force was that quartered in the Cairo citadel or *Burg* (i.e. tower).

was thus even more incentive to increase the demands on farmers and traders. There were peasant revolts which were brutally suppressed, and it is thought that both Egypt's agricultural productivity and the size of her population declined. Duties on the important transit trade passing through Egypt were increased, and the Mamluks themselves tried to monopolize commerce in such major items as spices and sugar entering from Asia and metals and timber from Europe, with the consequence that the principal European merchants, the Venetians, began to threaten to withdraw altogether from Egyptian trade.

Towards the end of the fifteenth century, both Egypt's commanding position in east–west trade and its political independence began to be threatened by new external factors. The Ottoman Turks had emerged as a major military power in Asia Minor. Mamluk military technology was still medieval, based on the use of bowmen and armoured cavaliers. The Turks, on the other hand, were becoming masters of the new arts of cannon warfare and of the deployment of regiments of musketeers. Maintenance of the defence of the Mamluk frontier with the Ottomans in Syria was already placing an intolerable burden on the Egyptian economy, when suddenly one of its main resources virtually disappeared. In 1498 the Portuguese admiral Vasco da Gama arrived in India by sailing directly from Europe round Africa. The Mediterranean–Red Sea route via Egypt was no longer the only means by which Europeans could satisfy their growing demand for Asian produce. Within a few years the Portuguese were flooding western European markets with goods imported in bulk at prices with which the Venetians and other Italian merchants could not compete. The Mamluk navy proved as powerless to destroy Portuguese power in the Indian Ocean as their army was to keep out the Turks. In a rapid campaign in 1516–17, the Ottoman soldiers of Selim I marched across Syria and entered Cairo. Egypt had become a province in an Ottoman Empire whose ruler was soon to inherit the title of Caliph from the last of the Abbasids.

While Egypt was involved in the great struggles which have just been chronicled, the Maghrib was left very much to itself. When the Fatimids had left Ifriqiya in 973, they had entrusted the viceroyalty of their western empire to the Zirids. These were a Sanhaja Berber chiefly family from the Kabyle mountains who had fought for the Fatimids against Zenata and Ibadite attacks on Ifriqiya, and who had provided soldiers for the Fatimid campaigns in the western Maghrib.

When it was clear that the Fatimids would never return to Ifriqiya, the Zirids set about converting their viceroyalty into an independent kingdom, though it was not until 1048 that they took the final, decisive step of dropping the name of the Fatimid Caliph from the Friday congregational prayers and substituting that of the Caliph of Baghdad.

On a more limited scale, the Zirids were in fact acting rather as the Fatimids had done, and the results in the Maghrib were not dissimilar. Just as the Fatimids had preferred Egypt to the Maghrib, so the Zirids preferred the wealth and culture of the Ifriqiyan plains to the business of keeping watch on the western Maghrib from their homeland in the Kabyle mountains. They lost control of the Kabyles to a rival branch of their family, the Hammadids, and over the rest of the Maghrib to the west, the Zenata became the dominant power.

After the Zirids had formally repudiated their allegiance in 1048, the Fatimids seem to have decided to destroy what they could not control, and dispatched against the Maghrib a number of bedouin Arab tribes, recently arrived from Arabia, who had been causing trouble for them in Syria and Egypt. The chief of these were the Banu Hilal and the Banu Sulaym. From 1051 onwards, these tribes began to invade the Maghrib from the west, the Hilal close by the sea and the Sulaym further south, in the steppe lands. It is thought that within the space of a few years, something like 200 000 bedouin herdsmen had descended on the Maghrib seeking profit and plunder at the expense of settled society.

The Arabic authorities viewed the advent of the bedouin as a major disaster for the Maghrib. In a famous passage, Ibn Khaldun, the noblest of the Arab historians, who was born in Tunis in 1332 and died at Cairo in 1406, likened the bedouin in the Maghrib to a swarm of locusts, destroying all in their path. Throughout his account of them they are referred to as brigands or bandits who oppressed the people, who interrupted trade and waylaid peaceful travellers. They were always sacking towns and villages, cutting down trees and filling in the wells, and turning prosperous farmland into an empty wilderness. The conclusion is that an ordered, settled society, based on the cultivation of crops and orchards with carefully organized water supplies, a society which the first Arabs had inherited and developed from Roman and Carthaginian foundations, was in the space of a few years totally ruined by this incursion of nomadic pastoralists.

However, despite his sophisticated scholarship, Ibn Khaldun's view of the bedouin invasions cannot be wholly dispassionate. Indeed it is coloured simply because he was a great scholar writing at the very end of a noble tradition, when the world of classical Islamic culture and scholarship was beginning to crumble, in part as the result of a series of barbarian invasions – of Turks, Mongols and Tartars. He was bound to see the bedouin invasion of the Maghrib in this light. In reality, the heritage of civilization in the Maghrib must already have been considerably eroded by the rise of the Zenata, and there is plenty in the history of dynasties like the Aghlabids, Idrisids, Fatimids and Zirids to indicate that the claims of settled society and of organized government to prevail in the Maghrib over dissident tribalism were by no means undisputed before the coming of the bedouin.

Nevertheless the conquest and settlement of the Maghrib by the bedouin tribes does mark a watershed in its history. Hitherto the Arabs in North-West Africa had been rather like their Roman and Phoenician predecessors. They were a numerically small upper class, who had settled for the most part in the towns. Here they had absorbed the traditions of urban civilization and settled administration, and had assisted in the acculturation of like-minded Berber aristocracies, such as the Idrisids or Zirids. It was only this urban, ruling class that spoke Arabic as its first language, and it was the Arabic of the Koran – of philosophy, science and classical education, of bureaucratic administration and of international commerce. The bulk of the population, though islamized, remained Berbers, speaking Berber dialects (thus, for example, Berber was the language of the Kharijite regime in Tahert) and – except in Ifriqiya – maintaining their traditional Berber tribal allegiances.

A great change was wrought by the advent of some hundreds of thousands of tribal Arab bedouin. They may have been like destructive locusts, but they were perhaps more like a high tide sweeping over a shoreline. Only a few places escaped the flood. Elsewhere the tide swept clean. Old Berber tribal associations were dissolved. The Zenata, for example, eventually disappeared completely from history; camel nomads themselves, they simply became absorbed in the society and tribalisms of the bedouin. More generally, Arabic and something of its culture were increasingly adopted by the Berbers, but at a much lower level than the old classical language and culture of the towns. The Arabic, for example, was non-literate, an Arabic of many local colloquialisms and variants, hardly intelligible to Arabs and strangers from other parts of the Muslim world. Berber tribes survived in mountain fastnesses, and to some extent in the Sahara. But other bedouin pressed westwards in the wake of the Hilal and Sulaym, and in course of time the traditional Berber languages and tribal society remained only in pockets of the Kabyle and High Atlas mountains and among the Tuareg of the central Sahara.

The old high Islamic culture of the towns was not destroyed, but it became penned in and isolated, and lost the possibility of advancing further either in space or time. In the eastern Maghrib, the organized kingdoms of the Zirids and Hammadids were reduced to small coastal principalities around Mahdiya and Bougie respectively. But the bedouin did not begin to arrive in western Maghrib in any numbers before about the middle of the twelfth century. Here, in Morocco, the old ideals of a universal Islamic empire remained alive for a space, and indeed were brought to new peaks of glory, but by two movements of tribal Berbers.

The first of these was the Almoravids, the confederation of western desert Sanhaja under a militant, puritanical Muslim leadership, whose activities in relation to the Sudanic kingdom of Ghana in the eleventh century have already been discussed. But the main thrust of Almoravid arms was northwards. Sijilmasa and the oases of Tafilalt, the main departure point for the Sanhaja caravan trade to Awdaghust and Ghana, were being overrun by the advance of Zenata camel nomads through the North African steppes from the east in the aftermath of the withdrawal of Fatimid power. Beyond Tafilalt lay the agricultural plains of Morocco, with its urban civilization in Fez and in coastal towns whose history went back to Carthaginian times. Beyond Morocco was Muslim Spain, which had also formed part of the empires of Carthage and Rome, and had prospered greatly under Umayyad rule, but which in the eleventh century was divided among more than a dozen petty Muslim *amirs* who were proving incapable of joining together to stem the Christian reconquest from the north.

Once the Almoravids had regained control of Tafilalt for the Sanhaja (1055–6), there was a considerable pull on them to extend their conquests further. Their appetite for conquest had been whetted, and many of the Moroccan tribes, albeit agriculturalists, were also Sanhaja brethren ready to welcome help against the Zenata. By 1082 the whole of Morocco and much of western Algeria had been brought under the command of Ibn Tashfin, who made his capital at the town of Marrakesh, which the Almoravids had founded in 1070 to command the Moroccan plains from the south. It is from this time, rather than from that of the Idrisids two centuries earlier, that one can date the effective establishment of the concept of one Islamic kingdom ruling all the people of Morocco; it is from Marrakesh, incidentally, that the European name Morocco derives.* In 1086, Ibn Tashfin felt strong enough to respond to one of a series of appeals for aid against the Christians from the Muslims of Spain. But the Almoravids found the Spanish *amirs* indifferent allies, weak and divided among themselves, and yet looking down on them as ignorant barbarians from the desert. So they ended up not only by stemming the Christian reconquest, but also by bringing all Muslim Spain under their direct rule. When in 1106 Ibn Tashfin died, he was the ruler of an Islamic empire as extensive as and more powerful than that possessed by the Fatimids at the other end of the Mediterranean.

However, Ibn Tashfin's successors proved unable to maintain this empire. The Almoravids quickly concentrated on exploiting the fruits of their conquest, and soon began to lose the characteristics that had ensured their initial success, the hardy discipline and military vigour nurtured by life in the desert, and the puritanical Islam which had united their tribal energies. They quickly provided a perfect illustration of Ibn Khaldun's dictum that history was a cyclical process in which pastoral nomads invaded, conquered and organized agricultural civilization, but after about three generations lost their identity and sense of purpose. Becoming an exploitative, ruling and taxing class themselves, the Almoravids could no longer appeal to the Moroccans, even to the Moroccan Sanhaja, as their liberators from Zenata oppression and exactions. The Moroccans came to share the view of the Spanish Muslims that the Almoravids were nothing more than alien, barbarian upstarts from the desert. Soon they were only able to maintain their power over their fellow Muslims by recruiting an army of Christian mercenaries and renegades from Spain.

During the 1120s, a movement of reaction against Almoravid rule began to emerge among the Masmuda tribes in the High Atlas. The Masmuda were traditional foes of the Sanhaja tribes, from whose Saharan members the Almoravids had been recruited, but shape and purpose were given to their own movement by their acceptance of the religious teaching of a local divine called Ibn Tumart. This teaching evolved out of the mystical developments in Islam which are called Sufism.

* For Arabic speakers, Morocco is *Al-Maghrib al-Aqsa*, i.e. 'the furthest west'.

In essence Sufism was a reaction to the formalization and seculariz-
ation that developed in Islam as its leaders became more and more
preoccupied with the legal procedures and administrative modes
needed to deal with the practical problems of governing God's
community as it actually existed on earth. Spiritually inclined men
began to consider that the formal leaders of Islam were interposing
an excessive amount of human apparatus between the individual
believer and the revelation of God's will through Muhammad. They
also noted that in the process they were acquiring increasing and
ungodly amounts of personal power and wealth. The Sufis, therefore,
were those who preached asceticism (the literal meaning of the word
sufi is one who wears a shirt of undyed wool), and the importance
for each individual Muslim of seeking God for himself in his own
best way. As Sufism began to gain ground, from the eleventh century
onwards, it began to acquire its own sort of organization, though
without compromising its basic principles. Certain individuals had
achieved such sanctity and holiness through their ways of seeking
God that they attracted to themselves disciples who wished also to
learn these ways. Some of these disciples might then go off and in
due course themselves attract pupils. Thus there developed *tariqas*,
expanding brotherhoods or chains of teachers devoted to the teaching
of a particular way ('way' is the literal translation of *tariqa*; plural
turuq) as the best means of achieving the true Islam.

Though the major developments in the evolution of these mystical
currents of thinking took place in eastern Islam, Sufism found a ready
response among Berber tribesmen in the Maghrib. These had been
ready enough to accept the major tenets of Islam, but they saw no
reason why this should mean the imposition on them of codes of
administrative control, of law and taxation, that were alien to their
traditional tribal ways of life. Hence their acceptance of Shi'ism and
Kharijism as weapons against early Arab imperialism. In Morocco in
the twelfth century, the oppressors, the traducers of Islam, were
themselves Berbers – the Almoravids, who had first promised freedom
from perversions of the will of God, but who had then institutionalized this will as much as any Arab government had done. A simple
tribal reaction was not enough. It needed to be demonstrated that
Almoravid rule was ungodly, and new principles for the interpretation
of God's will needed to be found which fitted more closely with
traditional customs and beliefs. Since Berber tribal society had always
given particular sanctity to the cults of local shrines and local saints,

here was a fertile soil for Sufism to take root and to provide a religious justification for warfare against the Almoravids.

Ibn Tumart, the man of the hour, was a Masmuda divine from the southern Atlas who had studied in the religious schools of Iraq and Egypt just at the time when Sufism was reaching its finest peak in the teaching of the Baghdad philosopher al-Ghazali (1058–1111). Returning to the Maghrib, he had acquired a few disciples, but his teaching was regarded with disfavour by the established governments, and it was not until he arrived among his own Masmuda tribesmen in the Atlas, probably about 1122, that he began to acquire any considerable following. The core of his message was an emphasis on the central feature of Muslim belief, the essential oneness of God. Hence his followers became known as *al-Muwah-hidun*, 'the people of unity (*tawhid*)', which Europeans have corrupted into Almohads. From this starting point, Ibn Tumart went on to claim that God was so much one, so unique, that any attempt by men to interpret his will in terms of laws and legal decisions of universal application, must be perversions of the essential truth. Thus the Almoravids, in their preoccupation with the mundane business of administering and raising taxes for the benefit of their administration and themselves, had become unlawful rulers unjustly interposing themselves between God and man. Each individual must seek direct contact with God to assess his will for himself, and the way to do this was through his own purity of heart: only the pure in heart shall see God.

The teaching of Ibn Tumart quickly received support not only from the Masmuda, but also from Zenata who had equally been conquered by the Almoravids, and who indeed provided some of Ibn Tumart's most notable converts. A council of ten was created to help Ibn Tumart govern the growing community, and a final religious seal was put on its rebellion by his declaration that he was the Mahdi, sent to restore rightful Islam. Ibn Tumart died in 1130, but he had nominated a *Khalifa* to succeed him. This was 'Abd al-Mu'min, a Zenata who, as well as being one of Ibn Tumart's first disciples, soon proved himself to be a more than able political and military leader. The Almoravids did not appreciate the danger of the challenge to their authority until it was too late, and by 1141 the whole of the Atlas had acknowledged 'Abd al-Mu'min. The Masmuda and their Zenata allies then swept down to conquer the Moroccan plains, and by 1147 the Almohad Caliph was ruling at Marrakesh.

The Almohads were immediately invited into Muslim Spain, where the Almoravid administration had broken down, and where the disunited *amirs* were losing ground to new Christian attacks. The dispatch of an Almohad army stabilized the situation for the time being. But 'Abd al-Mu'min was more concerned with the increasing chaos that was being caused in the eastern Maghrib by the bedouin Arabs, and by the advantage that was being taken of it by the Normans, who had established themselves in Sicily and were beginning to make inroads into Ifriqiya. So, after their conquest of Morocco, the main strength of Almohad arms was directed to the east, with the result that by about 1160 the whole of the Maghrib as far as Tripoli had been brought under their control.

The empire of the Almohads, combining in one dominion the whole of the Maghrib and Muslim Spain, unquestionably marks the apogee of Berber power and civilization under the inspiration of Islam. Once in power, 'Abd al-Mu'min and his associates could not continue with the Sufi idealism which had initially proved so attractive to their tribal supporters. They developed a *makhzin*, a professional administration, which they recruited for the most part from Muslim Spain, which had a longer and higher tradition of culture and scholarship than almost any part of their African domains except possibly Ifriqiya. A prime purpose of this *makhzin* was the efficient levying of *kharaj* on the agricultural lands, and a substantial proportion of this revenue was needed for the maintenance of an army which, together with a fleet, could protect the frontiers from attack and, within them, check the disruption of organized society by the pastoral tribes.

Following on the earlier expansion of organized government in the western Maghrib under the Almoravids, the results were impressive. Commerce flourished throughout the Maghrib, and merchants were attracted to it from Pisa, Genoa and Marseilles as well as from Muslim Spain. Urban life prospered and, with the help of Spanish Muslims, there were notable achievements in architecture and other such civilized arts as music, philosophy and medicine. Some of these were not without influence on the civilization which southern Europeans were beginning to erect at the close of their dark age. The writings of Ibn Rushd, known in Europe as Averroës (1126–98), who held an appointment at the Almohad court, were one of the principal means of introducing Europeans to the philosophy of Aristotle, and he also had an important influence on Aquinas and the development of Christian theology.

But however successful or glorious the achievement of the Almohads, the century of dominion by a Berber dynasty over all the Maghrib and its Berber peoples did not create a lasting sense of national identity of the type that was then beginning to emerge for some western European peoples, for example for the Portuguese or English or French. The very concept was difficult, if not impossible, for the Berbers of this time to grasp. Their basic loyalties were to their own tribes, and they could not readily contemplate larger or other units than such groupings of these tribes as the Sanhaja or the Masmuda. From this standpoint, indeed, the activities of the Almo-hads were divisive and not constructive. They were a banding together of some Masmuda and some Zenata to dominate other tribes. It is significant that as soon as the movement began to achieve the chance of major success, i.e. from about 1145, no new tribes were admitted to the original confederacy.

There was also, of course, a basic tribal division in the confederacy itself, that between Masmuda and Zenata. This was not unduly significant so long as the Almohads continued to be successful and so long as there was an orderly succession to power at the centre. 'Abd al-Mu'min was such an outstanding and successful Caliph that he had no problem in securing the succession for his descendants, and the first two of these, his son, Abu Ya'qub (1163–84), and his grandson Ya'qub al-Mansur (1184–99), proved to have much the same qualities as the founder of the dynasty. The fourth Caliph, Muhammad al-Nasir, however, came to the throne as a timid youth of eighteen, and in 1213 abdicated in favour of his son, Yusuf al-Mustansir, a boy of sixteen. In these circumstances, it was all too easy, as it was in any Muslim kingdom following the initial example of competition between the Companions and the descendants of Muhammad, to question the right of one family to rule. Competition for the Caliphate between candidates supported by the various tribal leaders was more or less inevitable.

It must also be appreciated that the Almohad Caliphate, even at the height of its power, was always subject to considerable and almost intolerable military strains. Their Iberian frontier had to be continually defended against aggressive Spanish and Portuguese kings determined to drive the Muslims from the peninsula. There was a long and exhausting war against the Banu Ghaniya, an offshoot from the Almoravids, who had succeeded in retaining control of the Balearic Islands. In 1187 they descended on the eastern Maghrib with a force of Zenata and bedouin warriors. The Almohad government, based at Marrakesh in the extreme west of the Maghrib, was forced to appreciate the impracticality, especially in view of the mountainous nature and poor communications of most of their empire, of simultaneously conducting campaigns 600 miles to the north on their Spanish frontier, and 800 or more miles away in the eastern Maghrib against the Banu Ghaniya. Eventually they entrusted the control of their affairs in the east to a notable general of the Hafsid family, one of the first Masmuda chiefly lines to rally to their cause (thus unwittingly taking a step which was to lead to the effective splitting of their empire into two). Even so, it was not until 1212 that the Banu Ghaniya were finally defeated.

A third military problem facing the Almohads was that of dealing with the Arab bedouin who were steadily eroding the resources and power of their government in the plateau and steppe lands west of Ifriqiya. This middle part of the Maghrib, with little agricultural wealth and few natural lines of communication behind its narrow coastal plain, and with no obvious political or military centre (and, indeed, with no real name of its own until after 1830 when the French conquered it through Algiers), was difficult enough to control even at the best of times. The Almohads hit upon the stratagem of inviting the bedouin into Morocco, supposing that they would be easier to control if they were more under the eye of their government, and that they might employ their destructive energies to good account by recruiting their menfolk for the considerable armies they needed to maintain in Spain and Ifriqiya. They were successful in this last, for in the later Almohad period bedouin soldiers predominated in their fighting troops. But once Almohad power began to crack at the centre, it became obvious that bedouin warriors were just as willing to serve factional leaders as they were to serve the Caliph of the day. All the Almohads had succeeded in doing was to extend the range of bedouin activity, and to bring a virulent disruptive force into their own home-land at a time when they were already losing the control of affairs in the eastern Maghrib, and in the north were being increasingly hard pressed by the Christian reconquest.

In 1212 the united forces of the Christian kings of Spain inflicted a major defeat on al-Nasir's army at Las Navas de Tolosa. A further disaster in the following year led directly to al-Nasir's abdication and death, and meant the beginning of the end both for Islam in the Iberian peninsula and for the Almohad dynasty and its empire. Within fifty years, Moorish rule in Spain was confined to the one emirate of

Granada in the extreme south-east of the peninsula. By 1230, Ifriqiya, Tripolitania and eastern Algeria had become an independent state ruled by Hafsid kings at Tunis. Almohad Caliphs continued to reign, at least in name, at Marrakesh until 1269. But the reality of the situation in Morocco after the early death of al-Mustansir in 1224 was a series of internecine conflicts between tribal factions each seeking to instal its own candidate as Caliph. In these conflicts, the extent of territory controlled by the *makhzin* steadily diminished, and the only gainers were the bedouin and Zenata whom all sides indiscriminately employed as warriors. In the end, two of the competing factions emerged with some claim to authority over a reasonable extent of territory. These were the Marinids, chiefs of a Zenata tribe, who from 1269 controlled from Fez what was left of the Moroccan domain of the Almohads and Almoravids, and the 'Abd al-Wadids (or Ziyanids), another Zenata group, who built up a kingdom from a seat of government at Tlemcen, a town commanding the major land route from Morocco to the east.

The tripartite division of the Maghrib between the Hafsids, the 'Abd al-Wadids and the Marinids produced a political pattern for the Maghrib which was to endure into modern times. Traditions of monarchical government had been firmly established both in the east, in Ifriqiya or – as it is now appropriate to call it – Tunisia, and in the west, in Morocco. Both these territories had considerable areas of agricultural land which could be organized to provide revenues, an administration and an army which could hold pastoral tribes at bay. In both, the tradition of monarchy became sufficiently strong to maintain independence against, or, in the case of Tunisia, to survive the advance of, major Mediterranean powers – the Ottoman Turks, Spain and Portugal – until the nineteenth and twentieth centuries. In between Tunisia and Morocco lay lands corresponding to the modern Algeria, which had no major area of agricultural territory and no obvious metropolitan centre, and where it was much more difficult to mobilize resources for the maintenance of organized government.

The 'Abd al-Wadids were therefore the least successful of the heirs of the Almohads. Emerging out of the contest for power in Morocco, they sought to control the central Maghrib from the west. Tlemcen, indeed, is very close to what became the eastern frontier of the Moroccan kingdom, and the writ of the 'Abd al-Wadids rarely extended over the whole of what we now know as Algeria. The kings at Tunis were usually strong enough to maintain their power

westwards to about as far as Bougie. 'Abd al-Wadid kings continued
to reign at Tlemcen until 1554, though from the end of the fourteenth
century they usually acknowledged the suzerainty of either Fez or
Tunis. But the reality of power in the central Maghrib passed to the
pastoral tribes, originally Zenata but eventually absorbed into the
bedouin Arab tribal system. The 'Abd al-Wadid kingdom was in no
position to survive attack from major Mediterranean sea-powers and,
after a period of Spanish supremacy, eventually went under to the
Ottoman Turkish corsairs who in the middle of the sixteenth century
established themselves in the major towns on its coast.

The most stable and prosperous of the Maghribi kingdoms was that
of Tunis, which possessed the largest area of agricultural land, and
the longest tradition of organized government, stretching back in
Muslim times to the Aghlabids and beyond this to the days of Rome
and Carthage. The Hafsids never developed military power to the
same extent as the Moroccan dynasties. Tunisia was invaded by
Marinid armies in the middle of the fourteenth century, and was never
wholly free from European attacks (there were, for example, French
crusades against its coastal cities in 1270 and 1390). Eventually after
1534 the Hafsid dynasty went under to attacks first from Spain and
then from the Turks. But compared with other parts of the Maghrib,
the rulers at Tunis did succeed to a remarkable extent in maintaining
a lively economy and a high degree of urban civilization. Wool,
leather, grain, dates and olive oil were exported to the Levant and
southern Europe, and from 1231 onwards a series of treaties were
concluded with Venice, Pisa, Genoa, Florence and Aragon under
which European merchants were attracted to settle in Tunis, which
became a commercial centre of some importance. This independent
economy survived the formal establishment of Ottoman suzerainty in
the 1570s, and was able to compete with a similar quasi-independent
regime in Tripoli for the lion's share of the trade across the Sahara
with the central Sudan.

In Morocco, the balance between organized monarchy exploiting
agricultural and commercial wealth through a *makhzin* and a tribal
society dominated by the pastoral peoples of the Atlas and Saharan
steppes was initially a very narrow one. There was the further problem
that after 1415, with the reconquest of the Iberian peninsula virtually
complete (totally so after 1492, when the combined monarchy of
Aragon and Castile finally extinguished the emirate of Granada), first
Portuguese and then Spanish kings were determined to take the

crusade against Islam across into Moroccan territory. From 1415 onwards, when the Portuguese captured the fortress town of Ceuta opposite Gibraltar, few of the major towns of the Moroccan coastline did not spend some time in Iberian occupation. South of Mazagan, the Moroccans were able to keep out the invaders after the 1540s, but from Mazagan northwards, important towns like Larache (the ancient Lixus), Arzila, Tangier, Ceuta and Melilla remained in foreign hands until the end of the seventeenth century or even later.

In the long run, however, the two dangers of Christian conquest and Berber tribalism tended to cancel themselves out, and even in effect to strengthen the cause of national monarchy in Morocco. Thus when in the middle of the fifteenth century, the Marinid sultans were proving powerless in the face of European aggression, a rival branch of this southern Zenata tribal group, the Wattasids, appeared on the scene to take over the monarchy and to expedite the war against the infidel. A century later, when the Wattasids had lost their original impetus and the Christians were again gaining ground, they too were pushed aside by another chiefly line from southern Morocco, the Sa'dids, who were of Arab origin and indeed claimed to be *sharifs*, that is descendants of Muhammad. The Sa'dids took possession of Marrakesh in 1525 and of Fez in 1554, but preferred the southern capital, from which they ruled with the title of Caliph. By this time a further threat to Moroccan independence was arriving on the scene in the form of the Ottoman Turkish corsairs.

Morocco had now become a focal point in an international struggle for control of the western Mediterranean which was not unlike the earlier struggle for power in the Near East which had embroiled Egypt, except that here the major contestants, the Ottoman Turks and western Europeans under Spanish leadership, fought at sea rather than on land. The major issue was settled by the disastrous defeat inflicted on the Turkish fleet near Lepanto in 1571, after which the Turks posed no major naval threat to the western Mediterranean. Up to 1576, Moroccan independence was preserved by a tortuous combination of diplomacy and force in which some members of the Sa'did family were to be found allying themselves with Spain to check the Turks, and others allying themselves with the Turks against Spain. But then the air cleared. The Caliph 'Abd al-Malik, who had long served the Ottomans and had come to power with their support, but who was also very much a man of the western Mediterranean, and a speaker of both Spanish and Italian, entered into negotiations with

Spain. His predecessor, who had taken refuge there, was expelled, but shortly invaded Morocco in company with the young king Sebastian of Portugal and a large army. In 1578 this army was annihilated by 'Abd al-Malik's Moroccan troops at the great 'Battle of the Three Kings' at al-Ksar al-Kabir (Alcazarquivir) in which both the Portuguese king and the Moroccan pretender were killed.

'Abd al-Malik himself died immediately after the battle, but his victory had secured for his brother, the equally sophisticated Ahmad al-Mansur (1578–1603), a position of power for the Moroccan monarchy both at home and abroad that had hardly been approached since the time of the first Almohads. Al-Mansur continued the work of the first Sa'did Caliph, his father, Muhammad al-Shaykh, in consolidating the *makhzin*, developing local industry through royal monopolies, and, to counterbalance the Iberian and Italian interests, attracting English merchants who bought sugar, gum and saltpetre, and supplied cloth and munitions (and, apparently, Irish marble for the palace at Marrakesh!). He even sought to convert the English interest into a political and military alliance with Queen Elizabeth against Philip II of Spain. Seldom in its history has Morocco been more outward looking than it was under the Sa'dids.

Al-Mansur's most dramatic action was in 1590–1, when he sent an army across the Sahara to conquer the Songhai empire of Gao. Trade with the Sudan was undoubtedly of some importance to Morocco; among other things it was a source of gold for the diplomatic and military exertions of its rulers. However, al-Mansur's advisers were by no means agreed with him that it was in their country's interest to attempt to control the whole trade across the desert together with the sources of supply in the Sudan. But since al-Shayk's time, the Sa'dids had been concerned that Songhai power had been extended so far to the north, and so close to their own territory, as to secure control over Taghaza, where there was major exploitation of the deposits of the salt which was so valuable in the trade with the Sudan. There had already been skirmishes between desert allies of the two kingdoms in the 1540s and 1550s, and it is possible that an earlier, unsuccessful, Moroccan expedition had been sent out against the Songhai in the 1580s. In 1582, it seems certain that the Sa'dids secured control over Taghaza. But the slaves who mined the salt had fled, and were then employed instead on other deposits at Taudeni, 200 miles nearer Gao. What seems to have tipped the scale in deciding al-Mansur to order the conquest of Songhai in 1590 was news of the weakness of its monarchy in the face of its internal divisions (see chapter 3).

It was not an easy task to exert effective military force across more than a thousand miles of desert trails; only a small force could be sent. It had therefore to be composed of hardy and experienced soldiers who, despite the rigours of the march, would be able to maintain their discipline and fitness sufficiently to win a decisive victory immediately after their arrival against superior numbers, who would be fighting on and in defence of their home territory. The 4000 soldiers sent were all hardened warriors from the campaigns in the western Mediterranean lands, Moorish emigrants from Spain, Christian renegades or captives, Turks and Moroccan cavaliers. Rather more than half the force were musketeers, and some cannon were also taken. The commander, Judar Pasha, and some of his principal officers were Christian renegades. 8000 camels and 1000 horses were provided to transport the large amounts of ammunition, equipment, food and water which were necessary if the army were to arrive and fight successfully on the other side of the desert.

After a twenty-week march, something like half this force arrived in fighting order on the Niger about halfway between Gao and Timbuctu, and early in 1591 they met with the army of *Askiya* Ishak at Tondibi just outside Gao. The Moroccans were outnumbered by probably something like twenty to one. But their discipline was good, while there were dissensions within the Songhai ranks, and, whether the Moroccan musketeers and gunners were efficient or not, especially after their long desert march, neither the Songhai soldiers nor their horses had faced firearms and their noise before. Ishak's army was routed, the survivors and the king himself fleeing across the Niger which, for lack of boats, the Moroccans could not cross. Following this signal victory, Judar and his men had little difficulty in occupying the major cities of the Songhai empire, Gao, Timbuctu and Jenne, where in the first few years they were able to secure large quantities of gold in the form of booty and tribute which could be remitted to Morocco.

However, the long-term results of the Moroccan expedition against Songhai were nothing like as impressive as the initial victory. The Moorish and European soldiers suffered seriously from disease in their new environment, and needed continual reinforcement from across the Sahara to maintain their fighting strength. Even so they proved quite incapable of conquering the remnant kingdom of the *Askiyas*

which remained in the Songhai homeland of Dendi lower down the
Niger. What was just as serious, if not more so, they were unable to
conquer or control any great amount of the territory of the old
Songhai empire outside the three cities of Timbuctu (which became
their headquarters), Gao and Jenne. This had consequences which
were to negate al-Mansur's dream of a remunerative empire in the
Sudan. There was a disruption of the old system of trade and imperial
order established by the Mande and maintained by them and the
Songhai kings for five centuries or more. There was a decline in the
flow of trade, including the highly important gold trade, into the
Niger bend cities along the routes leading to and from the Mande
lands in the west and the Akan and other peoples and states to the
south. The Songhai down the Niger to the east and the Mande
upstream in the west pursued completely independent policies, and
the Tuareg also began to disrupt the caravan routes across the Sahara
along which trade and tribute had to pass to reach Morocco, and
Moroccan reinforcements to reach the Sudan.

In all, something like 20 000 further soldiers may have been sent
out from Morocco in attempts to complete the work of conquest in
the Sudan. But the Sa'dids could ill afford to spare troops of the
required quality, and after al-Mansur's death in 1603, his successors
began to wonder whether the returns from the conquest were
commensurate with the effort needed to maintain it. Eventually the
situation in the Sudan was reviewed, and in 1618 the decision was
taken to abandon it. Left to their own devices, the surviving soldiers
in the Sudan took to electing their own leaders, a *kaid* in each of the
three cities, and a *pasha* in overall command, at least in name, for
continual competition for office did not make for orderly government.
In 1660 nominal allegiance to Morocco was repudiated, the Friday
prayers being thenceforward said in the name of the *pasha* of the day.
By this time, of course, the Moroccans had all taken Sudanese wives,
and the rulers of Timbuctu, Gao and Jenne had become the self-
perpetuating aristocracy known as the *Arma*. But soon they were not
even masters of their own cities. From the end of the seventeenth
century, Gao was tributary to the Tuareg (and was ultimately occupied
by them in 1770), while Jenne sometimes paid tribute to the Fulani and
sometimes to the Mande kings at Segu. Timbuctu became tributary to
Segu in 1727, but then passed under Tuareg control, finally being
occupied by them in 1787.

Such evidence as there is suggests that initially the Sudanese venture was very remunerative to the Sa'dids, but that ultimately it became a drain on their resources. There are contemporary sources which suggest that the combined annual tribute due from Timbuctu and Gao may have been in excess of 300 000 gold pounds ($1 500 000), and that due from Jenne about a tenth of this. It is also said that when finally, after various political ups and downs, Judar returned to Morocco in 1599, he brought with him gold-dust worth some 600 000 gold pounds ($3 000 000) and large numbers of slaves. Other commodities reaching Morocco from the Sudan included ivory, ebony, pepper and civet. How much of this wealth actually reached the caliphal treasury at Marrakesh is another matter. But al-Mansur seems to have been sufficiently enriched to build considerable fortifications at Fez and Larache, to import skilled craftsmen from Europe and England, and to develop the sugar industry which was the mainstay of the English trade with southern Morocco. His successor, his son Mulay Zaydan (1603–28), thought it worthwhile to style himself king of the Sudanese cities as well as Caliph.

There is some indication that substantial tribute may still have been arriving in Morocco from the Sudan in 1607. But it cannot have been very long after this that Mulay Zaydan sent out the commissioner whose report led to the abandonment of the Sudan in 1618. After this, of course, tribute can no longer have been expected. Presumably the wealth initially transmitted from the Sudan must have been that actually available at the time from the cities of Timbuctu, Gao and Jenne. But these cities were wealthy only as trading emporia. When, as a result of the Moroccan conquest, their trading links with their Sudanic hinterland were disrupted, they must have become considerably impoverished. Furthermore, the Moroccan venture had also been to the disadvantage of the Tuareg tribes who operated the caravan routes, via Taudeni and Taghaza and their saltmines, to Morocco. These retaliated by attacking both the Moroccans' cities in the Sudan and their even more vulnerable line of communication across the desert. There is thus reason to believe that little wealth may have been coming back from the Sudan after about twenty years of the Moroccan conquest, and, furthermore, that the important trade route from southern Morocco to the Niger bend may have become disorganized as a result of this action. Certainly, by the eighteenth century the dominant trans-Saharan routes seem to have been those between Tunisia and Tripoli and the region of Hausaland and Lake Chad.

But an important factor in this shift of trade routes must have been the relative political and economic stabilities of the respective termini. It has already been remarked how the Hausa kingdoms and their trade began to develop following the destruction of the Songhai empire and the consequent weakening of the Mande (Wangara-Dyula) trading system in the western Sudan, and how Tunisia and Tripoli prospered from the time of the Hafsids onwards. On the other hand, not only had the stability and prosperity of the western Sudan been disrupted by the Moroccan conquest; after al-Mansur's death, the cause of organized monarchy in Morocco itself suffered serious upsets.

Al-Mansur's succession was disputed among his three sons, and Mulay Zaydan never really controlled Fez and northern Morocco. One consequence was the advance of Spain to take most of the northern ports. Another was the eventual rise to power of yet another dynasty from southern Morocco, the Filali, Arab *sharifs* from Tafilalt. During the 1660s, Mulay al-Rachid of the Filali line secured possession of all Morocco, but anarchy broke out again after his death in 1672, and it was not until 1677 that his son, Mulay Ismail, had the whole country under his control.

The dangers facing organized monarchy in Morocco, from competitive and dissident tribes, and from Spanish pressures in the north and Turkish pressures in the east, were clearly formidable. However, Mulay Ismail was an ambitious, indeed ruthless, king and, coming to the throne as a young man of twenty-six, was able to reign for fifty-five years. If gold was no longer readily obtainable from the Sudan, it was still possible to secure black slaves from the Saharan oases and from Segu and Timbuctu. By this means Ismail built up a large slave army, the *'Abid*,* up to 150 000 strong, which would have no undesirable political affiliations and whose interests would be the same as those of the dynasty. (Later on the *'Abid* were mainly recruited and trained from the slaves' own children.)

This thoroughly professional army enabled Ismail to win back for Morocco all the European holdings except for two fortress peninsulas (Ceuta and Melilla) and two islands (Alcuhemas and Velez) on or off the Mediterranean coast, which Spain was able to hold on to, and, on the Atlantic coast, Mazagan, which Portugal held until 1769. He then endeavoured to push back the Turkish corsairs from eastern Algeria. In some respects, Ismail's policy for Morocco was not

* See note on p. 163.

unreminiscent of that of his French contemporary, Louis XIV (with whom he exchanged a number of embassies). All aspects of his people's life were subordinated to the glory of the monarchy, and European slaves were employed to build a magnificent new palace-capital at Meknes. So long as he himself was alive, his system worked: no one could dispute his political and military power, buttressed as it was with rigid royal control of the trade with European merchants on the coast and of trans-Saharan exchange through Tafilalt. But after his death, his descendants and the tribal chiefs became involved in continuing struggles for power. For the most part sultans were made and unmade by the commanders of the '*Abid*, and the area of Morocco subject to any sort of consistent central authority became virtually confined to the two separate areas of plain commanded by Fez and Marrakesh. Thus preoccupied with its own internal dissensions, Morocco had little constructive role to play in its external relations. The main activity of its ports, indeed, became piracy against the growing numbers of European ships passing by its coasts. In this respect, they were not unlike the ports of the rest of the Maghrib under the Ottomans.

The advancement of Turkish interests in Africa beyond Egypt was due to their development of sea-power, largely through their recruitment of Greek sailors from the islands and coastlands of the Aegean. The Turks quickly obtained mastery of the Red Sea, but they were unable to develop this to much purpose because they failed to defeat Portuguese naval power in the western Indian Ocean. Control of the Indian Ocean and its trade passed firmly into the hands of European sea-powers using the route round the Cape of Good Hope, and for three centuries the Red Sea ceased to be of any significance in world trade. When the Red Sea again became important, following the opening of the Suez Canal in 1869, the change was due to western European initiative, and took place at a time when the Ottoman Turks were no longer a power of any significance.

In Mediterranean Africa, largely as a result of the leadership of the two Barbarossa brothers, Khair al-Din and 'Aruj, the Turks were initially successful enough. By the third quarter of the sixteenth century, the Ottoman Porte was claiming an empire to as far west as the Moroccan border. This empire has been little studied by modern historians, but it seems safe to say that the actual control exercised by the Porte over its African provinces was minimal. Turkish sea-power was never the disciplined force their armies were. Their Greek seamen were always perhaps as much or more motivated by the desire for personal plunder and profit as they were by that of extending Ottoman rule, and after the decline of centrally organized fleets following Lepanto, the Porte tended to lose any power to control the course of events in Africa.

By the beginning of the eighteenth century, Egypt was the only one of four African pashaliks to which governors were still regularly sent out from Istanbul. But even so, power was less in Turkish hands than in those of the Mamluk aristocracy. This had passed into the least impressive and most self-centred phase of its long history. With the decline of Egypt's transit trade, an increasingly heavy burden of taxation was placed on the peasantry. But nothing was done to maintain the efficiency of the agricultural system; irrigation decayed, and once-fertile lands became more and more subject to encroachment from the desert and the bedouin tribes.

In Cyrenaica, which was nominally part of the Egyptian pashalik, the bedouin took over completely. Turkish pashas continued to be sent to Tripoli until 1714, but the office then became hereditary in the Karamanli family until 1835–6, when Turkish troops were sent to regain control following a disputed succession. But by this time the government at Tripoli had no more power in the hinterland than suited the convenience of its desert tribes.

The course of events in Tunisia was somewhere between that in Tripoli and that in Egypt. Tunis continued to receive pashas from Istanbul until the beginning of the eighteenth century, but real power resided with the officers of the original Turkish army of occupation and their descendants by local wives. From 1590 onwards, these were electing one of their number as a supreme commander, the Dey, who was effectively the autocrat who ruled the country. However, the Deys came to leave more and more of the day-to-day work of running the army and raising the taxes to a subordinate officer, the Bey, with the result that his power tended to grow at the expense of their own. Between 1702 and 1710, a Bey called Husain took the name as well as the reality of power: the office of Dey was abolished, and the title of pasha became hereditary in his family. By this time there was little to distinguish the descendants of the original Turkish army from the ordinary people of Tunisia. The Husainids indeed had restored the situation which had existed under the Hafsids: by the standards of the place and time, Tunisia had a prosperous and stable monarchy accepted both by its own subjects and by the major Mediterranean powers.

The only real innovation due to the Turks in North Africa was in the borderland between Tunisia and Morocco, for it was here, at Algiers, that the Barbarossas and their successors, who had won Tripoli and Tunisia for the Turks, had chosen to make their head-quarters. Hitherto a place of no significance, Algiers was important to these corsairs as an advanced base from which they could direct operations against Morocco and the western Christians. It was undoubtedly due to their efforts that the Moroccans were held back just to the west of Tlemcen. But with the decline of formal Turkish naval power after Lepanto, the corsair Beys at Algiers lost their mari-time empire east of Bone and became a purely local power. Since the Algerian hinterland was neither very productive nor easy to control, the corsairs controlling its ports converted the Turkish war against western Europe into a means of earning profits for themselves and revenue for their state. Merchant ships and their cargoes were captured, and their crews and passengers either enslaved or held to ransom.

By the middle of the seventeenth century, this kind of corsairing was a profitable business, employing some seventy vessels, some of which were large enough to be used in ventures outside the Mediter-ranean. Algiers itself had a population of some 100 000, about a third of whom were slaves, skilled men being employed at their trades, the others as labourers or as oarsmen in the galleys. The ransoming of the more important or wealthy captives was itself an important busi-ness, in which quite a few Europeans were engaged as resident agents. However, corsairing became less remunerative with the rise of organ-ized European navies from the later seventeenth century onwards. By 1788 there were said to be at Algiers only ten ships employed in corsairing, and only some 800 European slaves. This decline in the state's major industry led to a shift of power in Algiers itself. The Beys, the leaders of the seafaring corsairs, were superseded by the Deys, the commanders of the soldiers the corsairs had brought with them to garrison their conquests. These had originally been mainly Anatolians but, like their fellows in Tunisia, they had settled down and married local women and formed themselves into a hereditary urban ruling class. In 1711 the military commander, the Dey, took the office of pasha from the Bey of the time, and henceforward ruled as an autocrat. But his state was now increasingly stagnant and anarchic. Corsairing was no longer so profitable, yet its continued existence made it difficult to develop much in the way of peaceful trade; the main recourse of the Deys was to use their soldiers to seek to wring tribute from the tribes of the interior. In this way it is thought that perhaps a sixth of modern Algeria was brought under the intermittent authority of provincial officers who were expected to render account at Algiers every three years.

During 1793–1815, the preoccupation of the European navies with their own wars permitted some revival of corsairing. But the main effect of this was to draw the attention of Europeans to the lack of order that existed so close to their own lands on the other side of the Mediterranean, and to suggest to them that it would benefit their own civilization and commerce if they were themselves to control affairs in North Africa.

Chapter 8

The advance of Islam in West Africa

It is sometimes said that the Moroccan invasion was a disaster for the western Sudan which led to centuries of stagnation for two of the most important formative influences in its history, the development of organized commerce and the advance of Islam. What the Moroccan conquest certainly did do was to make impossible the further continuance of the concept of a single Sudanic imperium seeking to organize and to profit from the trade and tribute of all the savannahlands from the Atlantic to Hausaland. This concept had dominated the history of the western Sudan for six or more centuries. It had originated in ancient Ghana, and was subsequently developed by the Mande in association with the Songhai – initially junior, and then equal, partners – in the great empires of Mali and Gao. The main artery of this imperium had been the river Niger, and the commercial cities of the Niger bend had become its heart. When these cities remained in the possession of Moroccan conquerors who lacked the power to advance further, this main artery was severed and the heart cut from the body.

But it would be wrong to suppose that either trade or Islam could flourish in West Africa only under the protection of major empires. In the east, Hausa merchants were building up a trading network to compare with that of the Mande Dyula in the west, and which could successfully compete with it where the two commercial systems touched on each other in the lands north of the Gold Coast. Yet the political units of the Hausa remained small and divided among themselves. It is also apparent from the history of the Songhai empire of Gao (and, for that matter, from Hausa history too) that the appearance of Islam occasioned strains in Sudanic political systems which might well outweigh such benefits as it might bring to their rulers.

Kings and their machineries of government might appear to be isla-mized, but the principles of Sudanic royal power remained pagan. In the last resort, the authority of a king, and the legitimacy of the force he could use to maintain his authority, derived from his acceptance by his subjects as the descendant of the founding ancestor of the people. Thus the king, with the help of the priests associated with him, became the unique means of establishing, via the ancestral spirits, a right relationship between the people and the supernatural forces on which the people's life was dependent. However useful and prestigeful the presence of Islam might be in normal times, in any major crisis – such as when *Sonni* Ali was fighting to re-establish Songhai indepen-dence, or when Kanejegi of Kano (*c.* 1400) was losing in war against the rival Hausa kingdom of Zaria – Islam was likely to be viewed as an alien aberration which the state must repress. To profess that there was but the one God for both kinsmen and strangers was treasonable; the ancestral religion of the people must be reaffirmed.

By occupying the Niger bend, the Moroccans pushed the old Sudanic traditions of pagan imperium away into the wings, and opened up the stage of empire in the western Sudan to new actors and a new drama. They did not do this consciously. They tried in fact to make their will known to their subjects through *Askiyas* and other Songhai or Mande officers bearing traditional titles who were their puppets. Until about 1650, indeed, the Arma still saw point in engaging in campaigns against the independent Songhai *Askiya* who had retreated upstream into Dendi. It is a moot point as to whether these campaigns were ended because of the decline of the Arma's own power, or because they finally realized that the traditional *Askiya* was no longer a foe worth bothering with. In fact from the 1630s onwards the Songhai state in Dendi was dissolving into a series of petty chieftaincies.

This collapse of the imperial concept among the Songhai was prob-ably the inevitable consequence of losing control over the middle Niger and the junction of its trade with the trans-Saharan trade in the islamized cities of the Niger bend; there was no longer the revenue or the expertise available to maintain administration on a major scale. Much the same thing seems to have happened to the old Mali *Mansas* who, despite their defeats by *Sonni* Ali and the *Askiyas*, sought to maintain an independent kingdom in the upper Niger valley beyond Jenne. (Jenne itself, protected by its surrounding marshland, main-tained a fair degree of autonomy under both the Songhai and the

Arma.) But ultimately the Keita *Mansas* declined into the position of petty chiefs reigning at the original birthplace of their dynasty, Kangaba.

However, the Mande territory around the upper Niger was not as devoid of new political initiatives as was the Songhai land of Dendi. The reason is probably that, although there was no longer any control by the Mande over the river down to the trading cities of the Niger bend, their homeland still possessed both appreciable wealth and a developed trading system. The gold of Bambuk and Boure may now have been of relatively minor importance compared with that of the Akan lands further east, but there was still a demand for it and for other commodities, slaves especially, both across the Sahara and now also at the coasts where Europeans were trading. From the economic point of view, the dominant influence became that of a group of Soninke traders called the Boirey (Boare), who controlled a network of commercial colonies from a base at Segu. But this agricultural Mande territory was subject to infiltration by other peoples as well as Soninke traders. Bozo fishermen of Songhai origin could be absorbed into the Boirey system as canoemen, but Fulani pastoralists were a potential menace to it.

The Boirey sought to control the Fulani by enlisting them as military allies. The result was that by the early seventeenth century, interrelated groups of mixed Soninke and Fulani descent, the Massassi, were beginning to claim military and political suzerainty over the local Mande cultivators, who from about this time onwards began to be known as Bambara. This name is first recorded in the Timbuctu *Tarikhs*, where it has the connotation 'pagan Mande'. However, this is an expression of the viewpoint of the *'ulama*, the sophisticated divines and scholars of the Muslim communities of the Niger bend cities. The Massassi were not necessarily more unacquainted with Islam than other Sudanic rulers of the time. They had Muslim clerics in their entourages and, when it suited their interests, acted in Islamic ways (and the Soninke traders were essentially Muslim). But Massassi political actions were in no way Islamic; they were concerned with converting the clan and age-grade structures of traditional Bambara society into associations of serfs and clients subordinate to their will as war-leaders.

Massassi political structures tended to be very dependent on the personalities of their leaders, but from about 1650 onwards, one particular family, the Kulubali, produced a number of outstanding

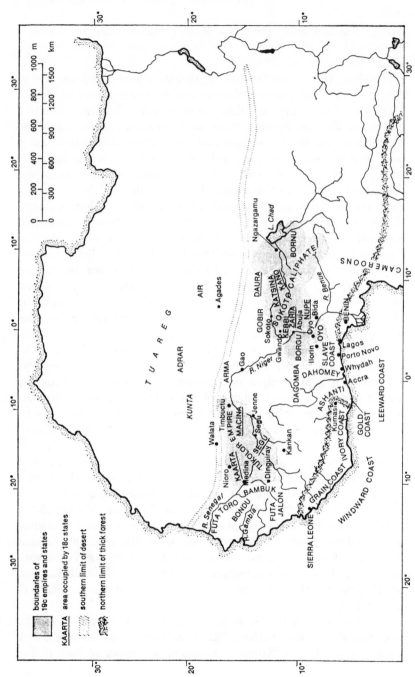

Map 7 West Africa in the eighteenth and nineteenth centuries

boundaries of
19c empires and states

KAARTA   area occupied by 18c states

southern limit of desert

northern limit of thick forest

1000 m

0 200 400 600 800 1000 m
0 300 600 900 1200 1500 km

TUAREG

ADRAR

KUNTA

AIR

• Agades

• Walata

• Timbuctu

Gao

R. Niger

ARMA

Nioro •

Medina •

KAARTA EMPIRE

• Dinguiray

MACINA

Segu

SEGU

TUKOLOR

Jenne •

• Kankan

R. Senegal

FUTA TORO

BONDU

BAMBUK

FUTA
JALON

R. Gambia

SIERRA LEONE

GRAIN COAST

IVORY COAST

WINDWARD COAST

ASHANTI

Kumasi •

GOLD
COAST

LEEWARD COAST

Accra

Whydah

DAHOMEY

SLAVE
COAST

Porto Novo

Lagos

DAGOMBA

BORGU

Ilorin •

OYO

Oyo •

NUPE

• Bida

BENIN

Abuja •

GOBIR

Sokoto •

Gwandu •

KEBBI

SOKOTO
ZARIA
CALIPHATE

DAURA

RATSINA

KANO

BORNU

Ngazargamu

• L. Chad

R. Benue

CAMEROONS

men. By the time of Mamari Kulubali (1712–55), it is possible to recognize a kingdom ruled from Segu which was acknowledged by all the surrounding Bambara, Bozo, Soninke and Fulani. A Massassi group which did not acknowledge his authority was forced away to the north-west, establishing there the rival Bambara kingdom of Kaarta in a predominantly Soninke territory. After Mamari's death, there was a Bambara reaction against absolute personal rule, and in the ensuing struggles for the succession, the Kulubali were destroyed. But another family continued the pattern and was able to extend its sway. Ngola Diara (1766–90) secured the subjection of the Fulani of Masina and levied tribute on Jenne and Timbuctu, and Mansong Diara (1790–1808) would probably have gained possession of Kaarta had its Soninke inhabitants not secured the protection of a neighbouring Berber tribe whose clients they became.

It was in fact Berbers from the Sahara who were the principal immediate gainers from the collapse of the Mande-Songhai imperium following the Moroccan conquest of the Niger bend. Increasing desiccation and political upsets in the north – the arrival of the Arab bedouin in particular – were bringing a number of tribes south towards the farms, trade and cities of the Sudan. Whereas the Songhai had exerted a Sudanic suzerainty to as far north as Taghaza, these tribes were now independent agents, free to profit from trans-Saharan trade and Sudanic agriculture as they chose. Thus the eastern branch of the Kunta tribe came virtually to monopolize the salt trade north of Timbuctu, while to the east of them and north of Gao the Barabich preferred rather to raid caravans or to levy protection money on them.

To some extent the political sway of Songhai was replaced by the establishment of tribal confederations, such as those of the Tadmakka and the Aulliminden in and around Adrar, or the Kel Air confederation around Agades. But confederations of desert pastoralists competing with each other for grazing land and control over the caravan routes could themselves produce instabilities and pressures to drive tribes to the south. Thus in the middle of the seventeenth century, the Tadmakka left Adrar after dispute with the Aulliminden and settled south of the Niger bend. Subsequently the Aulliminden expanded to the south-west to reach the Niger south of Gao. The relationships between these two groups and the Arma were at first equivocal. They were happy to raid the Niger bend cities and farms when opportunity offered, but equally they were prepared to acknowledge the overall suzerainty of the Arma and engage in military expeditions on their behalf. But the Arma's employment of desert warriors as mercenaries, in their own internal disputes as well as on expeditions to assert their authority, led to a steady erosion of their own power. By the 1730s, the Tadmakka were the dominant power in and around Timbuctu, and the Aulliminden to the east of that city. During the 1750s, however, the Tadmakka were weakened by internal quarrels, and the development of an alliance between the Aulliminden and the Kunta was beginning to mean that the Tadmakka were no more an effective power than the Arma they had themselves superseded.

The pastoral tribes of the western and central Sahara have thus far been regarded as Berbers. They were indeed a branch of the Libyan-Berber race, and the Berber stock is still the essential basis of their population. But from the fifteenth century onwards, the Saharan Berbers became subject to much the same pressures from Muslim bedouin Arabs as were transforming the Berbers of the Maghrib.

These pressures were strongest in the western Sahara, into which the bedouin spread in considerable numbers, and where the desert Sanhaja tribes had given allegiance to Islam since the time of the Almoravids. The consequence was that the western desert Berbers became completely arabized in language and culture; thus, for example, the matrilinealism and the veiling of the lower part of the face by the men, which had so aroused the interest of the first Arab commentators, completely disappeared. So did the Berber tribal structure, which was replaced by a structure tracing the origin of the tribes to Arab ancestors. Terms like Sanhaja (*zanaja, znaga*, etc.) survive today only with the connotation of people who are serfs to or tributaries of an Arab aristocracy. The bedouin groups who entered the central Sahara, however, were smaller and more fragmented. The result was that, although the central Saharan Berbers became islamized, their language and many of their customs (for example, the wearing of the veil by men, whereas – unusually for Muslims – the women go unveiled) prevailed, and the Arab groups were absorbed as tributaries into the Berber tribal system.

It is thus common, and often convenient, to call the modern western Saharan tribes 'Arabs' and the central Saharan tribes 'Tuareg', though in both cases the reality is more complicated. (Among other things, both groups have an appreciable lowest caste of Black origin, descended from the original cultivators of the oases or from slaves who had been bought or captured.) A point of considerable importance in both areas is that a military aristocracy of one ethnic origin (Arab in the west, Berber or Tuareg in the central Sahara) was commonly controlling client or tributary groups of the other. Denied access to military power, some of these other groups (of Berber origin in the west, of Arab origin in the centre) sought compensation in the development of a parallel power based on religious sanctity and learning, becoming the so-called 'clerical' or '*zawaya*' tribes.* Such, for example, were the Kel al-Suq among the Tadmakka.

In the eighteenth century, the Kunta became an unusually influential clerical tribe. The Kunta were in origin western Saharan Berbers who had become mediators between the Berber tribes and the Banu Hassan Arabs. A substantial part of the Kunta had moved eastwards to the north of Timbuctu where, as has been said, they engaged in the salt trade. Here they also came under the influence of Muhammad al-Maghili. Al-Maghili was a notable divine from Tlemcen, whose preaching had occasioned a notorious persecution of Jews in Tuat and Tafilalt in 1492, and who had subsequently sought patrons on the other side of the Sahara, writing a treatise on the duties of Islamic rulers for King Rimfa of Kano and also serving *Askiya* Muhammad of Gao. Tradition asserts that it was al-Maghili who introduced the Qadiriyya to the western Sudan. This was the first of the Sufi orders to be influential in West Africa, and certainly the Kunta clerisy became involved in this order.

The Kunta produced a number of notable divines of their own and, during the second half of the eighteenth century, they had a religious leader whose importance far transcended their own tribal limits. This was Sidi Mukhtar (1729–1811) who, in addition to possessing outstanding personal qualities of learning, sanctity and leadership, represented an impressive spiritual tradition, leading back through Sidi ʻUmar al-Shaykh, commonly regarded as a contemporary and colleague of al-Maghili, to an early fifteenth-century divine in the earliest stages of modern Kunta history in Tuat. From 1757 onwards, Sidi Mukhtar al-Kunti,† unchallenged as the dominating figure among the Kunta, began to assert his spiritual ascendancy by acting as a mediator in the many disputes among all the neighbouring Tuareg. His position was consolidated by the fact that all the other Qadiri

---

* Elsewhere, *zawiya* (plural *zawaya*) has much the same physical meaning as *ribat*, i.e. a centre of religious instruction.

† The name means 'Saint (Holy Man) Mukhtar of the Kunta'.

shaykhs came to recognize his supremacy. Ultimately Mukhtar came to have unchallenged spiritual authority among all the desert tribes from Walata in the west to Adrar in the east, and Tuareg power in the Niger bend was concentrated into a single alliance dominated by the Kunta and Aulliminden. With the decline of the Tadmakka, the Aulliminden were the most powerful military group, while, since the Barabich and other tribes had been dissuaded by Mukhtar from pillaging Kunta commerce, the Kunta, as well as providing spiritual leadership, had also become some of the most important traders of the region.

The importance of Mukhtar al-Kunti was not confined to this consolidation of Tuareg power over the Niger bend. He has been credited with the authorship of as many as three hundred treatises on Islam and its role in the world. His teaching and his pupils provided powerful force and reinforcement for the advancement of Islam throughout the Negro peoples of the western and central Sudan. The spread of the Qadiriyya order received a great impetus. The arrival of the Sufi *tariqas*, the Qadiriyya first and foremost, meant that Islam was no longer simply a private religion for a specialized merchant class organizing the long-distance trade of pagan communities, and for a few scholars in the major trading cities, a religion which basically pagan kings might also sometimes choose to profess because it gave them the use of a superior, prestigeful kind of literate magic. Islam continued to spread peacefully along the trade routes, but increasing numbers of its carriers were now members of the *tariqa* orders. As such they had a positive obligation to eschew syncretism, and to preach and to establish the truth of the one God and of the universal brotherhood of man subordinate to his will alone. They also had the training to do this effectively, to establish schools where all could begin to learn the Koran and from which some might go on to study it and the religion embodied in it in some depth, to convert the heathen, and to train and send out disciples who would spread their work ever more widely. Thus a town like Kankan, deep in the heart of pagan Mande country beyond Segu, where Soninke and Kunta traders settled in some numbers during the seventeenth century, became an important centre for the propagation of Islam even further to the south and west. The later trading settlement of Salaga, in the Gonja hinterland of the Akan, served much the same function further to the east.

Strongly organized Black polities, such as the kingdoms of the

Mossi, Dagomba and Akan, in which the power of the king was firmly based on the kinship organization of the people, could and did resist this new, more sophisticated infiltration of Islam, and continued to maintain the old Sudanic traditions of government which might use but which were never wholly committed to the new religion. In an ethnically and socially non-coherent area like Gonja, on the other hand, Islam could be a useful ally to the work of would-be state builders, used to justify with a supreme law what they were trying to achieve by force.

But the really significant new development lay in the new appeal of strict Islam to groups of people who were either excluded from the traditional socio-political structures or who, to the extent that they were subject to them, felt that such rights as these structures gave them were outweighed by the burden of the obligations – of tribute, taxation and military service, for example – placed upon them. For such groups, acceptance of Islam provided a means by which the legality of the traditional system might be challenged. The system could be shown to be a denial of the essential brotherhood and equality of man, irrespective of his ethnic and social origins, while Islam provided a set of principles by which a new, rightful society might be run. And not only run, but established as well, for the achievement of Islam – surrender to the will of the true God – need not only be by peaceful means. As H. F. C. Smith once wrote: 'It was easy for anyone learned in the *shari'a* [the canon law of Islam] to show that a position of political and social subordination for proper Muslims in pagan or nominally islamized areas could not be tolerated. There was a clear canonical obligation, not only of flight (*hijra*)* from the country of the pagans (*dar al-harb*), but also of *jihad* against pagans who were oppressors.' Thus, if a Muslim society (*dar al-Islam*, 'the abode of Islam') could not be brought about by persuasion, it should be achieved by force; rebellion or war (*jihad*, 'religious war') was at once lawful and obligatory.

Although the Qadiriyya, the first of the *tariqas* to reach and to spread in West Africa, was more quietist than the Tijaniyya, the much younger order which followed in its path in the nineteenth century,†

---

* Or *hegira*.

† The Qadiriyya developed out of the teaching of 'Abd al-Qadir al-Jilani, who taught at Baghdad about fifty years after al-Ghazali, the first great Sufi philosopher, and died in 1166. The Tijaniyya is a much more specifically African Sufi brotherhood, which resulted from the teaching of the Moroccan divine, Ahmad al-Tijani (1737–1815).

its divines were well instructed in the *shari'a*, and so capable of preaching *jihad* should the circumstances seem to demand it and suggest that there was a reasonable chance of it succeeding. In the eighteenth and nineteenth centuries, there was one important ethnic group which possessed a highly developed class of Muslim clerics which became particularly adept in grasping that the circumstances for *jihad* did apply to them. This was the Fulani.

As has been seen, Fulani herdsmen were spread throughout the western and central Sudan, pasturing their cattle on the uncultivated grasslands around and between the agricultural holdings of other Blacks. They were joined in self-regulating communities under their own leaders, the *ardo*, which were separate and distinct from the socio-political structures of the agricultural communities. Initially the Fulani dispersion and expansion may have caused very little problem. Although the agricultural communities may between them have had claims to the possession of all the land, their populations were not great and – even allowing for shifting cultivation and bush fallowing – the amounts they actually needed to cultivate were only a very small proportion of the total. Thus there would have been plenty of land available for the Fulani herds. But with the growth of settled government, so the agricultural communities became larger, richer and more powerful and ambitious. At the same time, the numbers of the Fulani and their cattle also increased. Thus the rulers of the settled communities sought to control and contain the Fulani for the protection and benefit of themselves and their subjects. They sought from them increased tribute, and rent for the use of the grazing lands; they employed them to look after their own cattle and to fight for them in their wars. But since the Fulani were strangers outside the social organizations of the settled communities, they secured no rights or privileges in compensation for these exactions and services. They had, for example, no voice in the processes by which the rulers were chosen; the rulers were in no sense their representatives, with a traditional obligation to act in their interests (and certainly an obligation not to act against their traditional interests).

The pastoral Fulani (*boroje*) were pagans, but some of their kin had settled in the towns. Here they were as much or more unprivileged strangers as the *boroje* were outside. They maintained links with the *boroje*, but in the towns it was virtually impossible for them to participate in or reproduce for themselves the traditional Fulani cults.

On the other hand, since they were strangers, they could not join the ancestral cults of the peoples among whom they were living. But the towns also tended to contain communities of Wangara, Soninke or Dyula traders who were Muslims, and the Fulani were drawn to these for any number of reasons. These too were often stranger communities which, like their own, were not part of the local pagan societies. The Muslims were traders, and trading interests may well have brought some Fulani to settle in the towns. Unlike the traditional pagan cults with their ancestor worship, Islam was not ethnocentric; it was an article of its faith that all Muslims were brothers. Finally, the Fulani themselves had originated from Futa Toro which, in the time of the ancient kingdom of Takrur, had been one of the first parts of West Africa to be islamized. Reluctance to accept Islamic control may have been one of the original motives for Fulani emigration from Takrur, but they still had kinship links with its Tukolor people. Moreover by the seventeenth century the Tukolor and the western Fulani had nurtured a new Muslim clerical class, the *torodbe*. Some of these followed up and lived in more or less permanent camps among the Fulani who had spread eastwards through the savannah. They could communicate with these pastoralists in their own language, yet some among the *torodbe* became among the most notable Arabic scholars of the western and central Sudan. As such they could also readily communicate with the Tuareg divines. These were also scholars living in a pastoral society, so that it was easy for an affinity to develop between the two clerical groups, one result of which was the spread of the Qadiriyya among the *torodbe*.

Thus Islam gained a footing among the Fulani and, with the general decline of Mande influence following the Moroccan invasion, Fulani clerics joined with those of the Tuareg in the leadership of Muslim scholarship in the Sudan. They were thus well acquainted with the doctrines which argued that pagan societies which denied them full rights had no legal justification, and which could indeed be used to create a new form of society in which Islam would have its rightful place and the Fulani would have as many rights as anyone else. Furthermore, in the *boroje* lay widely spread reservoirs of manpower, already accustomed to the use of force, whether in self-defence or in the service of others. They were also free from contamination by the societies the Fulani clerics wished to reform or destroy, and they were all linked together by the same nexus of kinship, and by a common language that the clerics themselves could use for their effective mobilization.

The *jihad* was not new in West African history. From the Islamic point of view, the Almoravid activities in ancient Ghana could be thought of as a *jihad* which had resulted in the conversion of the heathen. But the Almoravids were strangers invading West Africa from the desert, so that their activities are to be distinguished from the later *jihads* deliberately launched by Fulani or Tukolor clerics, for these were themselves West Africans objecting to the treatment accorded to West African Muslims and minorities by other West Africans. Nevertheless it is not without interest that the later *jihads* occurred first in the far western Sudan, in the lands immediately south of the Almoravid sphere of operations, where Islam had made considerable headway even before the coming of the *tariqas* and of the stimulation to Muslim revivalism provided by the Kunta, and where it would seem that some tradition of *jihad* remained from the early days of the first introduction of Islam.

The *jihads* of the seventeenth and eighteenth centuries in the western Sudan have not received as much attention from historians as have the more widespread *jihads* which followed in the nineteenth century. On the basis of present knowledge, it would appear that the first movement that might justify the name *jihad* was that by which a Fulani dynasty secured control of Bondu in the middle of the seventeenth century. Bondu is a region just south of the middle Senegal, which was originally inhabited, somewhat sparsely perhaps, by Mande-speaking farmers. It would seem that what happened here was that the immigration of Fulani from nearby Futa Toro, lower down the Senegal, together probably with a growth of population among the Mande, produced tensions which led ultimately to a cleric from Futa Toro called Malik Si (d. 1699?) organizing the Fulani to create a new political unit over which he ruled with the title *eliman* (i.e. *al-imam*).

It is quite possible that this was by no means the only tentative of this kind at this time where Fulani herdsmen were pressing in some numbers into agricultural lands south of the Senegal valley not far from the reservoirs of Tukolor-Fulani population and of Muslim clerisy in Futa Toro. But if so, other such ventures must have been less successful and have left less historical memorial. What is certain is that from about 1725 onwards numbers of Fulani began to act in this way, in concert to some extent with Muslim Soninke traders, further south still, in Futa Jalon, and that their actions not only had lasting consequences in Futa Jalon itself, but also a wide influence on other Fulani or Tukolor clerics throughout West Africa.

The arrival of Fulani herdsmen from Takrur on the Futa Jalon highlands dates from the later part of the fifteenth century. The local people (Jalonke) were Mandingo and Susu farmers with not much political organization beyond the village level, and the Fulani pursued their usual practice of settling as strangers on the unused lands of the Jalonke village units. By the beginning of the eighteenth century, Fulani immigration and population growth was such that some of their settlements were in effect towns. Their herds were encroaching on the agricultural lands of the Jalonke, and they were increasingly resentful of Jalonke taxation of their wealth and trade in cattle and hides. Soninke traders shared similar resentments, the more so as, with the presence of Europeans on the coast who were demanding increasing quantities of hides and slaves, trade and the acquisition of wealth through trade were becoming increasingly important throughout the region.

The Soninke were Muslims, and from early in the seventeenth century onwards, *torodbe* had also been appearing to preach the merits of Islam to the Fulani. The developments in Bondu in the later part of the century doubtless gave added point to their message, and by the early 1700s Muslim Fulani leaders were challenging the right of the Jalonke chiefs to tax the Fulani and to control the allocation of land to them. It is difficult from the available evidence to see much sign of central planning in the resultant *jihad*. A number of Muslim leaders seem to have risen more or less spontaneously against Jalonke authority, first in northern Futa Jalon, where *torodbe* influence had first arrived and where it was initially strongest, and then – from about 1726 onwards – in the south. By about 1750, the socio-political balance had been reversed, and Jalonke chiefs had become tributary to Fulani overlords throughout the territory. Some sort of central authority for the new Fulani polities was thought to be desirable, and initially a leading local cleric, Alfa Ibrahim, who had studied under an *imam* of Kankan, was recognized as *amir al-mu'minin*, 'Commander of the Faithful'. In practice there was considerable competition for power between the leading families of each of the Fulani groups in Futa Jalon, and also rivalry between the clerics and the more successful military leaders. It was one of the latter, Ibrahim

Sori, a cousin of Alfa's, who succeeded him and who consolidated the military supremacy of the Fulani under his authority as *almami*.

Ibrahim Sori's motives have been interpreted as being as much economic as religious. Certainly he seems to have tried to consolidate the economic strength of the new regime by bringing all the trade with the coast under state control. European cloth, iron and weapons were replacing the indigenous products and, in the circumstances of the time, could best be secured in exchange for slaves, and success in war was a prime means of securing slaves, not only for export, but also for purposes of local production and power. But however successful in this respect, Ibrahim Sori did not succeed in creating a unitary state. Ultimately the Jalonke became Muslim and accepted members of Fulani society. But the office of *almami* remained elective in the hands of the heirs of the Fulani leaders who had participated in the original *jihad*, and tended in practice to alternate between members of two factions, a clerical party represented by the descendants of Alfa, and a more militant and secular tradition represented by the descendants of Ibrahim Sori.

The success of the Fulani *jihad* in Futa Jalon undoubtedly influenced the *jihad* which began in Futa Toro about 1769. This, of course, was the homeland of the *torodbe*, but the ruling clans, though Tukolor, were pagans, not Muslims. Moreover they were by no means united, and their continuing competitions for power led to incessant exactions and pillaging at the expense of their more peaceful brethren. It was not difficult for a *torodbe* shaykh, Sulayman Bal, to denounce this regime as unlawful and to build up a Muslim reaction to it. By 1776 a new state had been established in which the divine law of Islam was administered by an *almami* elected from among the families of the principal clerics who had rallied to him.

Shortly after this there developed the most famous of the *jihads*, that launched in 1804 by the Fulani Shehu (i.e. shaykh) Usuman dan Fodio (1754–1817), in what is now northern Nigeria, which resulted in the creation of a Muslim empire over some 180 000 square miles and perhaps ten million people. The size and strength of this empire have always attracted notice. More recently, increasing attention has been paid to its history through studies of its considerable literary output, mainly in Arabic but also to some extent in the languages of the Fulani and Hausa. Usuman dan Fodio and his two principal lieutenants, his brother Abdullahi and his son Muhammad Bello, are alone known to be the authors of over 260 works – books and treatises

on religion, law, politics and history, and also poetry. There seems
little doubt that this was by far the most literate and intellectual of
the West African *jihads*, with the result that both the thinking behind
it and the actual course of events can be studied in some detail.

Usuman was born and spent almost all his life in the Hausa state
of Gobir. This was not a prosperous and relatively stable trading state
like Kano or Katsina. It was on the northern frontier of Hausaland,
and had been subject to continual invasion and erosion from the
Tuareg tribes who had established themselves in and around Aïr
(which may have been the original home of the Gobirawa). In the
eighteenth century the Gobirawa were seeking to re-establish their
state at the expense of the two states of Zamfara and Kebbi to the
west of Katsina. This was something of a frontier zone, with arid
uplands between the river valleys, which were unattractive to agricultural settlement, an area in which the interests of the Hausa-Bornu
political systems met and competed with those of the Niger valley.
Zamfara had probably never been politically strong, while the Kebbi
kingdom had been founded by a Songhai general who had
subsequently declared his independence of the *Askiya*. With the decay
of Songhai power following the Moroccan invasion, and the weakening of the eastern states with the rise of Kwararafa, this area was
open to conquest from the Gobirawa. They imposed their rule over
the agricultural peasantry, pushed the Zamfara kings southwards and
made those of Kebbi tributary, and established their capital at Alkalawa on the river Rima.

Since the territory of the new Gobir had been a frontier zone thinly
populated by Hausa farmers, it had a considerable Fulani population
grouped around a number of defensive settlements. Neither the local
Hausa nor the Fulani looked with favour on the establishment of a
Gobir aristocracy and government in their land. But only the Fulani
had the political and military organization to stand out against it, and
tension began to build up between the two. Most of the Fulani were
pagan *boroje*, but there were Muslim Fulani in the towns, and among
the pastoralists there were clans of more recent arrivals from the west
who were also Muslims, *torodbe* in effect.

Usuman dan Fodio belonged to one of these *torodbe* families which
had established itself at Degel, a settlement some fifty miles west of
Alkalawa. With his background, he must certainly have known about
the successful *jihads* in Futa Toro and Futa Jalon, but his own career
was conditioned more by his own education and his own experiences

in Gobir. He was a Qadiri, and thus acquainted with the teaching by which al-Maghili had attempted to reform Songhai and Hausa governments three centuries earlier, and also with the work of Mukhtar al-Kunti in the Niger bend in his own time. His own teachers, however, were local shaykhs and Jibril ibn 'Umar, a Tuareg divine in Aïr, who held extreme views of the value of *jihad* for achieving a just government. Usuman's younger brother Abdullahi was also a pupil of Jibril's, and it is clear from their writings that they secured an unusually good grounding in classical Arabic, in the *shari'a*, and in all the traditional Islamic sciences.

Usuman was thus well equipped to know what an ideal Islamic society and government should be, and to know that the Hausa kingdoms, despite the professed Islam of their kings and the presence of *mallams* (the Hausa form of the Arabic *mu'allim*, 'teacher') at their courts, did not measure up to this ideal. However, this did not lead him immediately to the conclusion that *jihad* was the only solution. (In this respect, his younger brother was a more apt pupil of Jibril's; he may indeed have spent a longer time with this master.) The active preaching and study tours which the Shehu embarked on in Gobir and Zamfara from 1774 onwards seem to have developed the purpose of building up the Fulani into a truly Islamic community which could command the respect of the Gobir authorities, and so influence them towards reform by both moral and political strength. In this respect Usuman's tactics seem to have been different from those of the *torodbe* in the two Futas. These seem to have supposed that local conditions were so disordered and the traditional rulers so unequivocally pagan that if Islam were to be achieved it could only be through *jihad*. In Hausaland, on the other hand, even in Gobir, there was a sufficient tradition of organized government – which, if not consistently and truly Islamic, at least accorded some respect for Islam and allowed its adherents a definite, if subordinate, role in society – to make it seem worthwhile to attempt to achieve the true Islam by reforming and taking over the established system.

Initially this policy seemed to have some chance of succeeding. Just before his death (1789?), the king of Gobir for the last twenty years, Bawa, agreed that there could be an Islamic community, based at Degel, of the kind that Usuman wanted, and that he would not interfere with it or its growth. It is also said that Bawa's two brothers, Yakubu and Nafata (c. 1789–c. 1801), and his nephew, Yunfa, who succeeded him, each secured Usuman's blessing at their accession, and that Yunfa was sent to Usuman to be educated and that he secured the throne with his support. But the policy of peaceful infiltration miscarried. Weakened by its long series of wars in the past and also subject to attack from Katsina, the Gobir monarchy was bound to become resentful of the over-mighty subject and his people at Degel. Nafata revoked the privileges accorded to the community by Bawa, and Degel was organized for self-defence. In 1802 Yunfa summoned Usuman to Alkalawa, and apparently attempted to secure his assassination. Accommodation between the two regimes was now impossible: the failure of the assassination attempt had only confirmed Usuman's superior sanctity, not merely among his own followers, but also among superstitious Hausa. Yunfa then attacked, not Degel itself, but some of Usuman's outlying supporters. Usuman retaliated by freeing some of the captured Muslims, and was then faced with a demand to abandon Degel or see it destroyed.

Usuman knew what the answer should be; already in 1802 he had set out the obligations of withdrawal (*hegira*) and *jihad* against the pagan. In 1804, therefore, the whole Degel community withdrew to the west, outlying supporters were called in, and relations with Gobir were finally broken when Usuman was persuaded to assume the office of *Sarkin Musulmi* (i.e. *amir al-mu'minin*). Early attacks from Yunfa's army forced further withdrawals on the community but did not succeed in destroying it. The Muslims established themselves in Kebbi in 1805, capturing its capital, and setting up a permanent base at what was to become their town of Gwandu a few miles to the west. Both sides were now appealing for wider aid. But the kings of the other Hausa states neglected Yunfa's message that the fire that he had failed to put out in Gobir had got out of control. They were too busy trying to deal with similar fires themselves. From all over Hausaland and beyond, Fulani emissaries had come in to secure Usuman's blessing and to return with his flag to raise the *jihad*. In fact the *jihad* was more quickly successful elsewhere than it was in Gobir and Kebbi. Zaria fell to the *jihad* in 1804, its king and principal men fleeing to establish a new kingdom further south at Abuja, and most other major Hausa centres had fallen by the time that Katsina and Kano were occupied in 1807. The decisive battle in Gobir, in which Yunfa was killed, was not fought until 1808, while Kebbi, with a new capital at Argungu, hardly more than twenty miles from Gwandu, was never really overcome.

The reasons for this are connected with the composition of the competing forces. Fulani, Hausa and Tuareg could be found fighting on both sides. Initially however, although the *mallam* core of Usuman's community was mainly Fulani with some Tuareg, and only about 20 per cent Hausa, the *jihad* received a good measure of at least tacit support from the Hausa peasantry, who had no love for their new Gobirawa masters, while Yunfa's main allies were Tuareg, who had no wish to see Gobir's land controlled by a competing pastoral group, namely the Fulani, with peasant allies. But as the campaigns continued around and between Gwandu and Alkalawa, the Fulani community and soldiers could only be supplied at the expense of the Hausa farmers, who consequently became estranged from the movement. Full control over the local peasantry in Gobir and Zamfara was not finally secured until the later 1830s, by which time, though Kebbi remained a source of trouble, danger from the Tuareg had largely disappeared because of the success among them of a *jihad* parallel to that among the Fulani. Elsewhere in Hausaland, however, the joining together in a united aggression of the mobile forces which the Fulani possessed for the defence of their widely dispersed settlements proved more than a match for the formal armies of the Hausa kings and nobles. There was no prolonged campaigning, and the Hausa commoners had no cause for complaint against a movement which promised them – as well as the Muslims and the Fulani – relief from arbitrary government and taxation. Furthermore the *jihad* did not stop in Hausaland, but was quickly pressed forward into other, usually more pagan, lands where all its members, Hausa as well as Fulani, could win both spiritual credit and material rewards.

Eventually men bearing the Shehu's flag, or their successors, established something like fifteen major Muslim emirates and perhaps as many lesser governments. Only four of these – Katsina, Kano, Zaria and Daura – were Hausa kingdoms taken over by the Fulani. Beyond them, the outstanding successes of the flag-bearers were to the south and south-east. A number of new emirates were created in areas which hitherto had been essentially both pagan and stateless, including such major units as the emirate of Bauchi in the hill and plateau country south of Kano, and the vast emirate of Adamawa in the grasslands of northern Cameroun. Beyond Zaria, though Abuja remained an independent Hausa kingdom of the old type, Fulani settled in Nupe were able to make increasing capital out of a succession dispute in this old pagan kingdom. By 1856, they had finally succeeded here in establishing a new Fulani state ruled from a new capital, Bida. Beyond

Nupe across the Niger was the Yoruba power of Oyo, whose government was in some disarray by the beginning of the nineteenth century
(see chapter 11). There was already some Fulani settlement in northern
Yorubaland, and Islam was already gaining ground there. When Oyo's
northern governor sought aid from Fulani and Hausa mercenaries in
a rebellion against his king in 1817, the *jihad* took root, and northern
Yorubaland became the Fulani emirate of Ilorin.

Apart from the problem of Kebbi in the north-west, the only
major resistance met by the Fulani *jihad* was in the east. The ancient
monarchy of Bornu was incapable of mobilizing effective resistance
to its local Fulani when these joined in the *jihad*, and its *Mai* lost his
capital, Ngazargamu, to them as early as 1808. But Islam had been
more thoroughly established in Kanem-Bornu than anywhere in
Hausaland, and it had its own clerics who were not prepared to accept
that the Fulani *mallams* had any monopoly of Islamic rectitude. It
also had its own mobile pastoralists, the Kanembu. A Kanembu cleric,
Muhammad al-Kanami, arose to organize a spirited resistance to the
Fulani, and to engage in an epistolary duel with Muhammad Bello on
the legality of the *jihad* against the Bornu kingdom. By 1811 the
Fulani had been repulsed by forces very similar to their own, and
their power in Bornu was eventually restricted to four small emirates
in what had been its western marches with Hausaland. In Bornu itself,
the authority of the *Mais* of the Saifawa line was superseded by a new
power wielded by al-Kanami, who ruled with the title of Shehu. By
1826 he had firmly established an Islamic state throughout Bornu and
Kanem. In 1846 the *Mai* of the day refused to continue as the puppet
of al-Kanami's son, Shehu 'Umar, but was defeated and executed.
This was the end of the ancient Saifawa dynasty.

In view of the piecemeal manner in which the empire initiated by
Usuman dan Fodio had been constructed, and also of its vast size –
it was a two months' journey to cross it from north to south and
three or four months from west to east – its control and administration
were not a simple matter. One thing was not in dispute, namely that,
under God, supreme authority rested with Usuman and his heirs,
who bore the titles of Shehu or Shaykh, Sarkin Musulmi and Caliph.
But Usuman was by inclination a scholar and divine; in addition,
when the *jihad* began, he was already fifty. The practical direction of
affairs was from the beginning entrusted to a number of lieutenants,
of whom the two most prominent became his more militant brother,
Abdullahi, and his son, Muhammad Bello. Abdullahi, twelve years

his junior, and Bello, who was twenty-three at the beginning of the *jihad*, proved able to combine scholarship with effective administration and leadership. By 1812 these two had become viziers responsible for western and eastern departments of state respectively. The seat of Abdullahi's administration eventually became Gwandu, while Bello established himself sixty miles away to the north-east, where he had had his war camp at the strategic confluence of the Sokoto and Rima rivers, and where he came to build the new walled town of Sokoto.

Initially it may have been supposed that the western department under Abdullahi was the more important. The war against Kebbi on the north-western frontier was the most immediately pressing problem, and beyond Kebbi lay important potential allies for the advancement of true Islam, the Kunta on the Niger bend and, beyond them, another Fulani state in Masina, which had been conquered under the leadership of Seku Ahmadu, a divine who had consulted with Usuman dan Fodio before launching a *jihad* of his own (see below). In the event, the failure to subdue Kebbi made it impossible to achieve any grand western alliance. Eventually the eastern Fulani agreed that Ahmadu was an independent *amir al-mu'minin* who was not tributary to their own Caliph. In addition, the Fulani *jihad* in the south-east proceeded much more swiftly and decisively than that in Nupe and Yorubaland to the south-west, so that Bello quickly came to oversee a much larger (and less troublesome) amount of territory than his uncle. Just before his death in 1817, Usuman came to live in Sokoto, and it was Bello (d. 1837) and his heirs there who succeeded as Shehu and Caliph. However, the principle was maintained that the western part of the empire should be supervised through Abdullahi (d. 1828) and his heirs, who became emirs of Gwandu.

In Sokoto and Gwandu, traditional Muslim governments were instituted on a model which originated in the Abbasid Caliphate. These ruled directly over the two emirates which had been constructed from Usuman's original *jihad* at the expense of Gobir and Zamfara, both of which ceased to exist, and to some extent of Kebbi also. Beyond these territories, the two emirs were accepted as being responsible for ensuring that administration, justice and taxation were efficiently and fairly carried out in the other emirates according to the principles of the *shari'a*. But the actual structure of government in Kano, Katsina, Zaria and Daura was that which the Hausa kings had built up over the centuries – though a Fulani aristocracy had now replaced the old

Hausa aristocracy – and by and large it was this structure which was extended into the new emirates. This structure had to be reformed in the interests of Muslim law, fair taxation, and efficient and honest administration. There was no great problem at first, because the flag-bearers who became the first emirs were primarily clerics and scholars: when there was competition for the office, Usuman had usually chosen the most devout and learned candidate. In addition, he, Abdullahi and Bello were all prolific writers of treatises on the principles of sound Muslim government, some of which were addressed to particular emirs rather than to the world at large.

What was more difficult was to maintain the honesty and efficiency of the system once it had been set up. Scholars could not have won or maintained the *jihad* by themselves; they needed soldiers, and they got these primarily through the support of the traditional Fulani clan-leaders, and these needed to be rewarded with land and offices. These political alliances tended to be consolidated through marriage, and, initially perhaps at lower levels in the new states, there were also obvious advantages for the new Fulani ruling class in contracting marriage alliances with some of the old Hausa families. Thus the rulers became less clerical and scholarly, and less able to appreciate principles which were best expressed through Arabic. The scholarly class continued, but it was less integrated with the administration, whose everyday language eventually became Hausa (which was written in Arabic script).

Against this, the Caliphate maintained the principle that an emir's powers derived from it alone, and this was accepted because in the last resort the Caliph was the sole interpreter of the absolute law of Islam. Emirs were expected to remit tribute via officials of the Caliphate or of Gwandu, and their accession to power required confirmation from Sokoto or Gwandu. The Caliph and the Emir of Gwandu sought to maintain control through chancelleries for the regular conduct of correspondence, through sending their officers on tours of inspection or mediation, and by contracting their own marriage alliances with the families of the provincial emirs. Detailed studies of the administrations of Zaria and Nupe have shown that these controls were by no means ineffective. The Hausa peasantry were still subject to landlords, and the new landlord class was, initially at least, an alien one less subject to the dictates of custom. But on the other hand, both landlords and peasants were now islamized and operating within a framework of general law and principle, which militated against arbitrary oppression, and made for greater security and efficiency. Within the empire, if not on its fringes, there was also far less danger to agriculture and trade from raids and warfare. Certainly the trade and industries of the Hausa cities and of new centres such as Bida were manifestly prospering after the *jihad*. This is quite clear, for example, for Hausaland proper, from the comprehensive account given by the explorer Henry Barth, who spent some years there in the 1850s.

The system of Fulani government in Nigeria undoubtedly developed both particularisms and abuses. But equally undoubtedly it was still a going concern when, in the early years of the twentieth century, it was conquered by the British. Its relative lack of resistance to the conquest, certainly of concerted imperial resistance, was perhaps less the result of any decadence than of self-confidence. The emirs were quite sure that the principles of a true Islamic society could not be overthrown by a handful of Christian adventurers. When it became clear that in fact the British were prepared to accept and respect these principles, and to work through them and their administrative expression in the emirs' governments, to implement their own rule, resistance became less relevant. In the event, the Muslim Fulani empire in northern Nigeria outlived the British empire.

Some mention has already been made of Seku (Shaykh) Ahmadu's parallel Muslim Fulani empire in Masina which resulted from a *jihad* practically contemporary with that of Usuman dan Fodio. It has also been noticed that this riverain area astride the Niger and Bani upstream of Timbuctu had been subject to a considerable degree of settlement by Fulani herdsmen from the fifteenth century onwards. These lived under their own *ardo* alongside Mande and Songhai farmers and fishermen. In the seventeenth century, Masina was nominally under the Arma of Timbuctu and Jenne, but in fact the *ardo* began to act increasingly independently of external restraints. They and their people were thus resentful of the rather more effective authority over Masina which was established by the Bambara of Segu in the eighteenth century. Since this authority was essentially that of pagan strangers, the *torodbe* among them doubtless began to gain in influence.

Ahmadu ibn Hammadi (c. 1775–1844) was a leading member of this clerical class, a Qadiri whose intellectual development had been influenced by his proximity to the influence of Mukhtar al-Kunti and the *'ulama* (divines) of the ancient Islamic centre of Jenne. His actual *jihad*, however, was very much influenced by the example of Usuman dan Fodio in Hausaland. It began about 1818 when he came into open conflict with the local *ardo*, and the latter was unwise enough to appeal to his suzerain at Segu for military assistance. Pagan Fulani, as well as Muslims, quickly rallied to Ahmadu's banner, and very soon he was master of a kingdom of some 50 000 square miles, which included within its borders both Jenne and Timbuctu. This kingdom was administered in five provinces, each under an emir. But there was never any doubt that these were under the absolute theocratic control of Ahmadu, who reigned as *amir al-mu'minin* at a new town he had built for himself fifty miles north-east of Jenne and which he called Hamdallahi ('Praise be to God'). This absolutism, combined with what appears to be both a lack of doctrinal depth and an increasing intolerance in Ahmadu's government, which estranged the clerics of Jenne, Timbuctu and the Kunta, provoked considerable dissensions within the state after his death. This facilitated its conquest in 1862 by the third of the great West African jihadists of the nineteenth century, al-Hajj 'Umar ibn Tal.

Ah-Hajj 'Umar (*c.* 1795–1864) was a Tukolor *torodbe* from Futa Toro. The honorific *al-Hajj* indicates that he had made the pilgrimage to Mecca (something not accomplished by either Usuman or Ahmadu). He was in fact away from his homeland for about twenty years. Twelve of them seem to have been spent at Sokoto, where he was associated with Muhammad Bello's court, took one of his daughters to wife, and wrote at least one important book. A goodly number of his writings have survived, and he would appear to have been both a more learned man generally, and better acquainted with the principles of Muslim Fulani *jihad* in West Africa, than Ahmadu ibn Hammadi. But the influences upon him were much wider than those of the Sokoto jihadists – and also much more modern (for the inspiration of the Sokoto *jihad* was essentially one of returning to the straightforward purity which was somewhat idealistically supposed to have existed in the earlier days of Islam). He had also spent some time with al-Kanami in Bornu. More importantly, he had been to Egypt, and to Mecca itself, and had presumably had contact with its shaykhs and with those of the great centre of learning at the al-Azhar mosque at Cairo. He must therefore have been conscious at once of the Islamic revivalism of the Wahhabi movement in Arabia against the dead hand of Ottoman rule, and of the manner in which Muhammad 'Ali was trying to drag Egypt into the nineteenth century after its successive occupations by French and British soldiers (and French scientists). Furthermore he had joined the new Tijaniyya order founded by a Moroccan shaykh who had died only in 1815, and had become accepted as its leader in the western Sudan. This was a much more disciplined, determined and active body than the older Qadiriyya; its members had a definite moral obligation to achieve rightful Islam quickly, by force if need be.

All these influences must have been active in 'Umar when eventually he arrived home in the Futa region with some followers from Hausaland in about 1840. Within a few years he was estranged from the local *torodbe* among whom he had been brought up. In 1849, with such disciples and supporters as he had, he conducted a *hegira* to Dinguiray on the borders of Futa Jalon and Bambuk, where he established a *ribat*. This was far more than a religious sanctuary for the training of recruits to the Tijaniyya – for the most part from among the younger and more ambitious Fulani and Tukolor *torodbe* of the region. It was also a power base which was deliberately conceived of as providing the nucleus for an army and a state. As such it attracted able and ambitious clients from many walks of life and from a variety of ethnic groups. The community was strengthened through trade and the acquisition of slaves and other worldly goods, some of which could be traded with European merchants on the coast for firearms and other equipment.

The result was that when in 1852 the men of Dinguiray came into open conflict with the local Bambara authorities, they were better equipped – in a modern, material sense, as much as spiritually – for the resultant *jihad* than any of their predecessors in West Africa. The initial direction of the *jihad* was northwards, through the gold-bearing lands of Bambuk and Boure towards the upper Senegal, and its first major success, in 1854, was the defeat of the Bambara kingdom of Kaarta and the occupation of its capital, Nyoro. But this may have been a diversion, or perhaps the securing of a flank. Subsequent events suggest that 'Umar's main objective may have been the lower Senegal, in which lay his own homeland of Futa Toro, whose valley was a major artery of trade with the outside world, and up which French troops were conquering Muslims in their desire to gain access to what they were convinced was a rich hinterland. However, two years of campaigning (1857–9) against the French in Galam proved to 'Umar that he was not strong enough to dislodge them from their fortified frontier post at Medina. But if he had to leave the Senegal itself to Christian imperialists, he could at least secure and control the hinterland at which they were aiming, and by 1861 'Umar had defeated and occupied the Bambara kingdom of Segu on the upper Niger.

This victory became a turning point in 'Umar's career. The Fulani of Masina had refused to cooperate with him against Segu, which they regarded as being within their Qadiri sphere. Some Fulani soldiers indeed fought with the Bambara against 'Umar's army, and their Caliph wrote letters of protest to 'Umar in much the same vein as al-Kanami had written to Usuman dan Fodio. But 'Umar could not accept that Muslim leadership lay elsewhere than with himself and the Tijaniyya, and his next step was to bring the Fulani of Masina under his authority. Hamdallahi was taken and destroyed, and by 1863 'Umar's army was in Timbuctu. But these actions provoked a bitter reaction in which Fulani and Bambara, Qadiri and Kunta shaykhs, and urban *'ulama* all joined. In the following year, 'Umar was killed trying to suppress the Masina resistance to his regime, and he passed on a very disturbed inheritance, in Segu as well as Masina, to the son who succeeded him, Ahmadu Seku.

Although 'Umar's activities led to the extensive, if not always very deep, conversion of the pagans of the lands in which his armies operated, and also to the establishment of the Tijaniyya as the dominant religious brotherhood in the western half of West Africa (from which it subsequently spread eastwards at the expense of the Qadiriyya), he does not seem to have been as successful as Usuman dan Fodio in establishing an orderly government. Captains and bands of his disciples, equipped with guns and horses, were detached from the army to control each conquered territory. These men were exempt from taxation, and when 'Umar's supreme authority was removed by his death, they tended to become exploitative and competitive groups which were very difficult for such central government as there was to control. Faced with revolt from the Fulani and Bambara, Ahmadu Seku had little opportunity to secure the effective cooperation even of those provincial leaders who were relatives or close associates of his father. When he had his own opportunities to appoint to office, he tended to select men who were loyal slaves or came from subject peoples. It is possible that by the later 1870s Ahmadu was beginning to get the situation under control; certainly an able cousin had brought Masina to order. But if so, it was too late. On the southern borders of his territories, a remarkable soldier-trader, Samori, was busy assembling a new Mande empire, while in 1879 the French began an advance to and along the Niger from the west that was to destroy the military and political power of the Tijani Tukolor state.

Part 3

Africa in the age of European expansion

Chapter 9

The beginnings of European enterprise in Africa

In 1415, the Portuguese took the fortress-town of Ceuta from the Moroccans, and shortly afterwards they embarked on some sixty years of exploration of the Atlantic and Indian Ocean coasts of Africa. This led to the establishment of the first of a series of European footholds on these coasts which were to bring sub-Saharan Africa into closer relations with the rest of the world than ever before in its history. From these, by the end of the nineteenth century, Europeans were to advance to conquer and control virtually the whole continent. The motives which occasioned this European expansion which was so radically to change the history of Africa belong properly to European history. What is important in African history is what the Europeans did when they entered the continent, and the effect of their presence and their actions on African societies which hitherto had followed an essentially autonomous development.

Nevertheless, the actions of Europeans in Africa cannot be wholly understood without some consideration of the reasons which brought them to the continent. Initially these derived from the situation in the Mediterranean which had arisen after the rise of Islam. The establishment of Islamic civilization and power throughout the Near East and northern Africa, and also in the southern peripheries of Europe, provided southern Europeans at once with a major challenge and with new ideas and opportunities. Their first major reaction to the challenge, the Crusades, ultimately demonstrated that Europe was not yet sufficiently strong or united to advance with a counter-attack on the heart of the Islamic world. (And it is to be noted that Africa played its part in the military and political defeat of the Europeans through the mobilization of Egypt's resources by the Ayyubids and

Mamluks.) However, the Crusades did open up new opportunities, which Italian city-states were particularly quick to exploit, for southern Europeans to enter into commercial relations and intellectual dialogue with the major world civilization of the middle ages.

The Islamic civilization had made more of the intellectual heritage of the ancient civilizations than Europeans had been able to do. The Muslim occupation of lands like Sicily and the Iberian peninsula provided opportunities for Europeans to rediscover ancient Greek philosophy and to partake of the subsequent advances in science and mathematics made in the Islamic world. Of particular importance in relation to the subsequent European expansion was the widening of geographical horizons brought by contacts with Islamic peoples, and the acquisition of technologies which were to enable Europeans to venture into this wider world with confidence and purpose. Islam reached as far afield as China in the east and the Sudan in the south. With the compass, the astrolabe, and the astronomic knowledge and expertise of the Muslims, it became possible to construct representations of this wider world which were more accurate, positive and comprehensive than the schematic *mappae mundi* of the high middle ages. Here in fact it was southern Europeans, albeit men in close touch with the Islamic world, who made the major syntheses from which further advance was possible. By the fourteenth century, cartographers, largely of Jewish extraction, who were first based in Italian cities like Genoa, Venice and Pisa, but who later were centred principally in the Balearic island of Majorca, were drawing the charts, called *portolani*, of the Mediterranean and Black Sea coasts, which are the ancestors of all modern maritime charts. It will be recalled that it was one of these map-makers, Angelino Dulcert of Majorca, who first placed ancient Mali on a map (1339). A later Majorcan atlas, attributed to Abraham Cresques, drawn for Charles V of France *c.* 1375, depicts the western Sudan quite recognizably, with the major cities of Niani, Timbuctu and Gao in the right relative positions. (See plate, p. 313.)

That it was southern Europeans, rather than members of the Muslim world, who so usefully capitalized on the skills and knowledge that were available by the fourteenth century, may be explained by the fact that by this time the initiative in trade and navigation in the Mediterranean had passed to the Italian entrepreneurs and seamen whose first major maritime ventures had been to transport the Crusaders to the Levant. Christian fleets regained control of the Mediterranean, and the Italian city-states were soon establishing resident commercial agents in the major ports of the Near East, Egypt and North Africa. A flourishing trade developed in which European exports of timber, metalware and slaves were exchanged for the luxury produce which Muslim merchants could provide and which Europeans could increasingly afford – spices, perfumes, drugs, silks and other fine cloths, precious stones, sugar, ivory and gold.

Few of these commodities originated in the Near East or North Africa. Most were brought there by merchants of the Muslim world from market to market along trade routes which stretched back across the Sahara, or down the Red Sea and Persian Gulf to India, south-eastern Asia or the east coast of Africa. The amount of these goods available for re-export to Europe was of necessity therefore relatively small, and their prices tended to be high. In face of a growing European demand, this situation tended to be exacerbated by the fact that one particular group of Italians, the Venetians, partly because of their traditional ties with Byzantium and because of the close relations they succeeded in establishing with the Egyptian Mamluks, ended by engrossing the lion's share of the most lucrative trade, that with the ports of the eastern Mediterranean. Their competitors became increasingly confined to the less lucrative trade of the Maghrib west of Tripoli or to intermittent ventures into the Black Sea. In these circumstances it was not surprising that some of their competitors, most notably perhaps the Genoese, began to wonder whether they might not secure better supplies of the goods in demand in Europe more cheaply by by-passing the Mediterranean ports and by venturing to sources of supply beyond the political control of their Muslim rulers.

This idea became more practicable as more became known of the world beyond the Mediterranean. The journeys of members of the Venetain Marco Polo family (and of some other travellers) in Asia are the best known of the European explorations of the time, in part because of their great range, but also because Europeans were more interested in Asia than they were in Africa. Apart from gold, Africa was not known to produce many of the commodities which Europeans desired, nor was it known to have much in the way of organized civilizations with which it would be worth establishing commercial relations. However, some not inconsiderable exploring journeys were also undertaken in Africa.

The idea that there was a Christian king and government in Ethiopia with which it might be advantageous to establish relations had never

wholly faded in western Europe, though initially there was some
doubt as to where exactly Ethiopia might be. Indeed, the general
conception – no doubt derived from the fact that it was most accessible
from the east – was that Ethiopia belonged to Asia rather than to
Africa: its king was therefore 'Prester John of the Indies'. However,
the need of the Ethiopians to send to the Coptic Patriarch at Alexandria each time they wanted a new head of their church, and the fact
that this church also had a monastery in Jerusalem, meant that contact
of some kind with Ethiopia never wholly lapsed. After the restoration
of the fortunes of central monarchy under the Shoan dynasty in the
later thirteenth century, it was possible for both sides to begin to
think of establishing more effective relations. A Dominican mission
was sent to Ethiopia in the fourteenth century via Nubia, but thereafter this route was blocked by the growth of Muslim control over
the upper Nile valley. Nevertheless there remained an intermittent
trickle, via the Near East and the Red Sea, of European clerics and
other travellers going to Ethiopia and of Ethiopian envoys to Rome
and to other major centres of south-western Europe.

Whatever the resultant gain to European geographical knowledge
of north-eastern Africa, it must have been clear that, so long as the
Mamluks and the Venetians remained powerful and closely allied,
there was no opening for rival European merchants to the trade of
either Asia or Africa through the Levant and the Red Sea. But whereas
Venice naturally looked eastwards down the Adriatic towards Byzantium and Egypt, her major competitors – Genoa, Pisa and Florence
– were on the western side of the Italian peninsula, and their natural
relations were more with the lands of the western Mediterranean,
southern France, the Balearic islands, Catalonia and Aragon, and the
western Maghrib. There were in fact a number of European journeys
into or across the Sahara, some of which seem to have been in the
nature of deliberate commercial explorations. Towards the end of the
thirteenth century, a Catalan cardinal, Raymond Lull, a pioneer in
the European study of Arabic, sent a mission to North Africa, one
member of which seems to have succeeded in accompanying a caravan
across the Sahara. Antonio Malfante, a Genoese merchant agent,
certainly gathered information about trans-Saharan trade in Tuat in
1447, and in 1469–70 a Florentine, Benedetto Dei, seems to have
succeeded in reaching Timbuctu.

But while it was not impossible for Europeans to reconnoitre the
Saharan trade or even that of the Sudan, it must have quickly become

obvious that neither the governments of North Africa nor the established Muslim traders of the Maghrib and the Sahara would willingly allow Europeans to compete in the trade with the Sudan overland. The Italian city-states possessed no military strength sufficient to allow them to force a way into the trans-Saharan trade against North African resistance; such power and skills as they possessed were essentially maritime. So, quite early on, some Italians conceived the idea of trading with Africa and Asia by sea. In 1291, shortly after the rediscovery of the Canary Islands, a Genoese merchant family called Vivaldi sent out an expedition through the Strait of Gibraltar, apparently with the express purpose of circumnavigating Africa. It may in fact have succeeded in this aim, for there is a hint that the end of the expedition came with shipwreck close by the entrance of the Red Sea. But, whatever the fate of the Vivaldi venture, the Italians must soon have appreciated – as had the Carthaginians nearly two thousand years earlier – that Mediterranean galleys were not suitable vehicles with which to develop and maintain trade in the great oceans.

In the fourteenth and fifteenth centuries, therefore, enterprising Italians who were unable to compete with the Venetians in the eastern Mediterranean, were equally finding their ambitions blocked in the west also. They lacked power to force their way into North Africa; neither did they possess ships and experience suitable for the conquest of the problems of oceanic navigation and commerce. However, both these things were developing in the Iberian peninsula. By the middle of the thirteenth century, Christian Iberians had had more than four centuries of experience of aggressive warfare against Muslim powers. Their crusade for the reconquest of their peninsula had had results very different from the splendid but ultimately futile crusades in the Levant. In the first place, it had been successful. By 1257, the Moors had been expelled from all but the small emirate of Granada in the extreme south-east. Secondly, in the reconquest, the Iberians had developed not only considerable military strength, but also strong institutions of monarchical government capable of focussing national energies to the one end of the defeat and expulsion of the Moors. Furthermore, on the maritime side, the Iberians living on the Atlantic coasts had evolved types of ship capable of development for long oceanic voyages. Unlike the Mediterranean galleys, which were designed primarily to be rowed by large numbers of oarsmen, and which were consequently long, slender and low in the water, and therefore fragile, difficult to manoeuvre and easily foundered, the

Iberian vessels were designed to be sailed, and were broad, high and strong, and – once the lateen sail had been borrowed from the Muslims and added to the traditional square rig – suited to manoeuvring even in high seas or coastal shallows. By the beginning of the thirteenth century, the Iberians had gained sufficient experience and skill in the use of such vessels to exploit the rich fishing of the Atlantic shelf to as far south as southern Morocco.

In this situation, ambitious Italians, particularly perhaps Genoese, began to seek employment for their capital and for their mercantile, navigational and cartographical expertise in the west. Genoese admirals went to organize navies for Portugal, Castile and France; the map-makers moved to Majorca; and Italian captains and super-cargoes sailed on Portuguese, Castilian and Catalonian ships to explore new commercial opportunities, especially perhaps in the Canaries and further to the south and west. Although it was men from Castile and France who first embarked on the conquest and colonization of the Canary Islands, it was Portugal which first fully grasped the possibilities of combining Italian capital and commercial and technical skills with Iberian Atlantic experience in one strong national enterprise under royal direction.

The Portuguese ports, looking south and west over the broad ocean, were obvious bases from which to embark on the exploration of the possibilities of maritime trade with Africa. It is true that Portugal did not have the resources of Castile, which also had an Atlantic coastline – albeit a shorter one – which was even closer to Africa. But until 1492, when they finally conquered Granada and also merged their dynasty with that of the other major Iberian power, Aragon, the rulers of Castile were hardly in a position to give high priority to western adventures. Portugal, on the other hand, had rid itself of Moorish neighbours by completing the conquest of the Algarve during the early thirteenth century. It was then faced with the problem of how to develop this devastated and depopulated southern province, and in the Aviz dynasty it had a new line of kings determined to maintain its power and independence against its more powerful neighbour. It was therefore both possible and politically advantageous for Portugal to continue the crusade against the Moors into Africa, and there were obvious incentives for her to look there for fresh resources.

With the conquest of Ceuta in 1415, Portugal became launched on a series of campaigns to conquer territory in Morocco. In the sixteenth century the newly united Spanish kingdom joined in, albeit on the

Mediterranean coastline rather than on the Atlantic front which attracted the Portuguese. The resultant wars have been looked at already, from the North African point of view, in chapter 7. Little need be said of them here except that by the end of the sixteenth century it had become apparent that, fighting on their own soil, the Moors were able to hold their own. Neither Portugal nor Spain were able to extend their power beyond a handful of coastal footholds. However, the possession of some Moroccan territory from 1415 onwards obviously gave the Portuguese better opportunities to learn about the trans-Saharan trade and the lands across the Sahara than before, and, possibly too, better opportunities than other Europeans.

Among those who participated in this knowledge was a younger son of the first Aviz king, John I, Prince Henry (1394–1460), who had taken part in the capture of Ceuta and had become its first Portuguese governor. The idea developed in his mind, and in that of his brother Pedro, that Portuguese resources might be more profitably engaged in a maritime outflanking of Moroccan power than in a direct assault on it. About 1419 Henry became associated with the exploring voyages southwards and westwards into the Atlantic which were to give him the name of Henry the Navigator. Apart from the discovery and subsequent colonization of Madeira (*c.* 1419) and the Azores (*c.* 1439), the initial results were not very impressive. Hitherto the accepted limit for both Christian and Muslim navigation on the Atlantic coast of Africa had been Cape Bojador, in the same latitude as the Canary Islands, and about 300 miles south of the southern limits of habitable Moroccan territory along the Wadi Dra which runs to the sea from the region of Tafilalt. Bojador is a considerable cape, extending out into the ocean for some miles, and apt to be invested with fog or with heavy surf. Muslim sailors are said to have conceived the notion that it was impossible to return from beyond it. Certainly the prevailing wind and current, both running from the north, made this difficult. Moreover, for some 800 miles beyond the cape, there was nothing but the waterless, surf-bound and very thinly habited coastline of the Sahara.

It was not until 1434 that this formidable technical and psycho-logical obstacle was overcome, but thereafter Henry's enterprise began to gather momentum. In 1443 Henry established himself permanently at Sagres, on Cape Vincent, the most south-westerly point of Europe, and devoted his major energies to the direction of a carefully coordi-nated national exploring venture. Each year his captains probed further along the African coast, accurately noting its hydrography, its peoples and their customs and their economic life. The information so gathered was meticulously recorded and examined by some of the best geographers, cartographers and astronomers of the day, and collated with the information obtainable from other travellers and from the accepted geographers of both the Christian and Muslim worlds. Thus each new captain who set out from Portugal could have better knowledge, maps and equipment, and so greater confidence and more chance of success than his predecessors.

Henry's public motives have been recorded for us by a contemporary court chronicler, Gomes Eannes de Zurara (or Azurara). 'He desired to know what lands there were beyond the Canary Islands and . . . Cape Bojador, for up to that time no one knew . . .' He wanted to do this for two reasons. First, if in the newly discovered lands 'there should be any population of Christians, or any harbours where men could enter without peril', the Portuguese, as the first sea-traders from Europe, might be able to trade in bulk with low costs and great profit to themselves and the natives. Secondly, 'because every wise man is moved . . . to know the strength of his enemy', Henry wanted to find out 'the full extent of the Infidels' power', and to see whether beyond these limits there might be any Christian princes to aid him against the Muslims.

Zurara's references to the search for Christians and Christian princes with which Portugal might ally herself in her crusade against Islam, and so outflank Muslim power in the Mediterranean, seem to show clearly enough that Henry was hoping that his sailors might reach Ethiopia or even India, in which also Christian communities were thought to be. Circumnavigation of Africa and entry into the Indian Ocean and its trading system thus seem to have been aims of Henry's enterprise from the outset. But what no one could tell at the beginning was how long these aims might take to achieve, or how practicable it might be to establish regular communication with the Indian Ocean with the ships, equipment and navigational techniques available. It was therefore of some importance – although Zurara does not say so directly (perhaps because it was so obvious) – that the Portuguese knew from their knowledge of Arab geography and from their contacts with Morocco, that if they could pass beyond the western edge of the Sahara desert they should quite quickly arrive close by the West African territories with which North Africa traded for gold. If the Portuguese could divert this gold trade, or some of it, then their Moroccan foes might be weakened. They would also acquire supplies of bullion which would provide invaluable capital for the more ambitious enterprise, and which were also very necessary to enable them to purchase the spices and other goods which Europeans wanted from Asia (where, at this time, there was practically no market for European goods).

It is noteworthy how the process of Portuguese exploration accelerated by stages. The first stage, simply gathering enough momentum to pass beyond Cape Bojador, took something like fifteen years. After this, only ten years were required to explore about 1000 miles of Saharan coastline and to arrive (in 1444) at Cape Verde, significantly 'the green cape', a land where once again there was permanent vegetation, and where lived the Black peoples whom the Portuguese called *Guineus* (from the Moroccan Berber word for blacks), with whom the North Africans traded for gold but who were independent of their political control. Some time was needed to assimilate this discovery and its commercial possibilities. But by the time of Henry's death sixteen years later, in 1460, his captains had reached as far as Sierra Leone, 600 miles further to the south-east, and the Cape Verde Islands had been discovered and were being colonized to serve as a permanent base for trade with the adjacent Guinean coasts.

The fact that Prince Henry was no longer there to spur things on led to a slackening of momentum after 1460, and for a time the emphasis of Portuguese royal policy shifted back to Morocco. But private entrepreneurs were now willing to continue the work of exploration. From the 1440s onwards, the voyages of Henry's captains had begun to reveal increasingly attractive commercial possibilities, first of exploiting the rich fishing banks south of Cape Bojador, and then, from the Senegal mouth and Cape Verde onwards, of obtaining from the Blacks of Guinea not only gold, but also slaves, who could be used to exploit the empty lands of the Algarve or the Atlantic islands. The possibilities of this early African trade may be judged by the statement that a Portuguese company operating from the Algarve port of Lagos is said to have made profits during 1450–58 of 600 per cent. The Portuguese were soon grappling with the problem of rival European traders, especially from the Andalusian ports of Castile. Diplomacy secured them Papal Bulls giving them exclusive rights based on the claim of prior discovery. More practically, fortified bases were built on the island of Arguin (off the Saharan coast south of

Cape Blanco) and at Santiago in the Cape Verde Islands, from which Portuguese interests might be protected.

By 1469 the prospects of African trade and discovery were such as to inspire a prominent Lisbon merchant, Fernão Gomes, to secure a five-year lease of the trade beyond Sierra Leone on condition that his ships discovered a hundred leagues (about 400 miles) of new coastline a year. This contract was subsequently extended to 1475, by which time Gomes had kept his bargain. His captains had discovered the islands of Fernando Po and São Thomé, nearly 2000 miles east of Sierra Leone, and had proceeded some distance further south to cross the equator. In so doing, they had made a find of major importance. In 1471 they had discovered the land which the Portuguese called *Mina*, literally 'the mine', and which later Europeans were to know as the Gold Coast, the coast of modern Ghana, whose peoples from about the mouth of the river Tano to Accra displayed abundant evidence of their hinterland's wealth in gold. The short-term economic aim of Henry's enterprise, to tap the gold wealth of West Africa beyond the control of Islam, had been realized. Within a few years the Portuguese were securing from trade on the Gold Coast an average of something like 13 000 oz of gold a year, at that time a sizeable proportion of the total world supply.

There were three immediate and important consequences of the discovery of the Gold Coast. First, the Portuguese crown decided not to extend Gomes's contract any further. The trade of the Gold Coast was of such value that it should be brought under direct royal control. Secondly, to ensure this, and also to try and exclude the other European traders, Castilians especially, who were also rushing to try and exploit the new discovery, King John II decided that a third major fortified base was necessary. In 1482 an expedition was sent out to select the most suitable site for this on the Gold Coast. Its commander, Diogo d'Azambuja, chose a rocky promontory about midway on the coast and, after some initial difficulty with the local ruler and his people, secured permission to begin the construction of the impressive castle called São Jorge da Mina (now known as Elmina). Finally, with the confidence gained from the successes of Gomes's captains, and with the wealth obtainable from trade on the Gold Coast behind them, sailors in the direct employ of the Crown stepped up the rate of exploration even further. The mouth of the Congo, 500 miles south of the Equator, was reached by Diogo Cão in the same year that Elmina was begun. Less than six years later, in 1488, Bartolomeu Dias was over 2000 miles further south, rounding the tip of Africa and making a first tentative European foray into the southern Indian Ocean.

At this point there was another pause in the maritime expansion of the Portuguese. They were aware that in the Indian Ocean there was both a set pattern of navigation based on the monsoon winds, and also a long-established and complex maritime trading system linking the Near East and the East African coast with India, and India with the East Indies and the Far East. The Portuguese must have realized that they could not simply thrust forward into the Indian Ocean as they had into the Atlantic, where there were no established patterns of navigation and trade, but that they should first survey the Indian Ocean systems and decide how these might be best exploited to their advantage. Thus at the same time as Bartolomeu Dias was sent out to find the southern entry into the Indian Ocean, John II was also sending out exploring agents into the Indian Ocean lands by the established routes of communication through the Near East. It was obviously thought necessary to await their reports before proceeding further.

The most successful of these travellers was Pero de Covilhã, who left Portugal in 1487, the same year as Dias, in company with Affonso da Paiva. Paiva's mission was to go to Ethiopia, but he died before he got there. In 1488, however, Covilhã investigated the spice markets of the western coast of India, and then took ship in an Arab dhow for the Persian Gulf and East Africa. It seems likely that he travelled along the East African coast to as far as Sofala, the port for the gold trade of central Africa, and the southern limit of Arab commerce. If so, he came within about 1200 miles of the furthest point reached by Dias. In 1490 Covilhã was at Cairo on his way home when he was met by a messenger from John II who instructed him to complete Paiva's mission by going to Ethiopia. This Covilhã did, and he was well received at the Ethiopian court. But he was not allowed to return, and he continued to live there until his death some thirty years later.

It seems likely that some report of Covilhã's findings up to 1490 was sent back to Lisbon from Cairo. A number of factors may explain why it was that it was not until 1497 that Vasco da Gama was sent out on his voyage to India and back via the Cape of Good Hope and the East African coast. Some of these were purely Portuguese, for example the illness and death (1495) of John II. Time was probably spent on discovering a better sailing route through the South Atlantic than that used by Dias. To find the southern limit of Africa, Dias had necessarily kept close by the coast. This meant that south of the equator he was proceeding against the prevailing wind and current. Vasco da Gama, on the other hand, like all subsequent Europeans sailing to the Indian Ocean, followed a more favourable course by going much further westwards into the Atlantic. Then, of course, wholly exceptional care was needed to fit out a fleet for a voyage which was more than twice as long as any that Europeans had yet accomplished and one, moreover, which was deliberately trespassing into an established Muslim naval preserve. Finally, there was also probably a natural desire to await the fuller report on Indian Ocean conditions that Covilhã would have given had he been able to return to Lisbon.

In the event, when Vasco da Gama set out in 1497, he seems to have been well informed about the general strategy of his journey, but somewhat less understanding about some of the particular problems he was to face. This seems to have bred a sense of insecurity which led da Gama and his immediate successors to use force where it may not always have been necessary, and thus perhaps needlessly to antagonize local peoples, particularly perhaps on the East African coast.

Da Gama sailed directly to South Africa, making a landfall just north of the Cape, and then proceeded along the coast to Mozambique, where a pilot was secured for the East African coast. He then called at both Kilwa and Mombasa which, with Mozambique, were allied in the gold trade with Sofala, and where he was received with suspicion, and then at Malindi, which was hostile to Mombasa, and where another pilot was secured to take the Portuguese across the Indian Ocean to the spice port of Calicut, where they arrived in May 1498. When, a little over a year later, da Gama had returned to Lisbon, he had done and seen enough to convince the Portuguese authorities that the major aim of the enterprise begun three-quarters of a century earlier by Henry the Navigator was within their grasp. It would be entirely practicable to deploy Portuguese naval power in the Indian Ocean in such a way that the bulk of the Asian goods in demand in Europe would be taken there in Portuguese ships sailing directly to and fro around Africa. Da Gama's voyage was immediately followed up by the dispatch of annual fleets, the first of which, under Pero Cabral (1499–1501), discovered Brazil on the way. In 1502, da Gama, on a second voyage, began to impose Portuguese suzerainty on the major East African ports, and then between 1505 and 1515 the first two Portuguese viceroys for the Indies, Francisco de Almeida and Afonso de Albuquerque, laid the foundations for Portuguese control of the Indian Ocean.

A permanent headquarters was established at Goa on the western coast of India; and control of the main shipping routes was secured by capturing Malacca, commanding the entrance to the China Sea, and Ormuz and Socotra at the mouths of the Persian Gulf and Red Sea respectively, and by controlling or neutralizing all the main East African ports. Malindi's hostility to Mombasa and Kilwa had already secured its allegiance for the Portuguese, and that of Zanzibar, not yet a major place of trade, was also secured without much difficulty. But Mombasa was sacked in 1505 (and again in 1528), and force or the threat of force was used to establish Portuguese forts at Kilwa, Sofala and Mozambique, which were needed to secure control over the East African gold trade. Kilwa was subsequently abandoned, while Mozambique, which had a better harbour for the Portuguese Indiamen (which were larger than most of the Arab vessels), and was in a more suitable position for ships sailing to India from the south up the channel between Africa and Madagascar, was developed into the local Portuguese headquarters under the Viceroy at Goa. When first Egyptian and then Ottoman fleets tried to dispute Portuguese control of the western Indian Ocean, they were decisively defeated.

Although men of many nationalities, including Italians, Spaniards, Flemings and Frenchmen, had initially shared in or competed with the early Portuguese voyages to explore the coasts of Africa and to develop trade with them, by the 1490s the Portuguese had the field virtually to themselves. They were thus effectually the sole pioneers of European trade south of the Equator on the west coast and along the whole east coast to the mouth of the Red Sea. The discovery of the Gold Coast and the subsequent acceleration of Portuguese exploration had demonstrated to the Portuguese crown what rich prizes lay within its grasp, and determined it to take steps to exclude other Europeans from access to them. Portugal's most dangerous competitors were the sailors and merchants of Castile, especially if they were backed by the full power of their government. But from 1492 onwards, the exploitation of the New World discovered by Columbus for the newly united kingdom of Castile and Aragon provided a more than adequate outlet for Spanish maritime energy and imperial ambitions. Spain's claims to the Americas were confirmed by Papal Bulls comparable to those earlier secured by Portugal for her African discoveries, and in 1494 areas of dispute between the two monarchies were settled by the treaty of Tordesillas, which in effect divided the world into distinct Spanish and Portuguese spheres of interest. This treaty did not, of course, bar seafarers of other nations, and during the first half of the sixteenth century there were a number of French and English trading ventures to Africa. But none of these voyages penetrated further afield than the Gulf of Guinea, so that the Portuguese monopoly of trade beyond this remained intact, and neither the French nor the English governments provided sufficient backing for their individual merchants concerned with the trade to Guinea to enable them to make any serious impression on the power deployed there by the Portuguese state. After about 1560, with the French and the English increasingly absorbed in domestic affairs or in raids on Spanish America, Portugal had virtually no competition at all in the African trade until, at the very end of the century, following upon the Dutch rebellion against their Spanish sovereign, who since 1580 had become king of Portugal as well, Dutch traders began to appear on the scene.

For rather more than a century, then, Portugal held an almost unbroken monopoly of European relations with tropical Africa. But her government sought to exploit it only in selected areas and for selected purposes. Compared with Spain or France, sixteenth-century Portugal was not a rich or powerful country, nor did she possess the advantages which were subsequently to make the United Netherlands and England into major commercial and maritime powers. Her population was small, no more than 1½ millions, inadequate to develop all her cultivable land, and she had very little in the way of minerals or industry. Indeed, as has been suggested, this very poverty and lack of population may originally have served as incentives to overseas expansion. But this expansion had been so spectacularly successful that by the early years of the sixteenth century Portugal had imperial interests stretching halfway round the globe, from Brazil to the Moluccas. She was hard put to it to find men to control, maintain and exploit her vast empire, certainly to find enough competent and trustworthy men. She also found it increasingly difficult to build and maintain sufficient ships to maintain her empire's long lines of communication and to carry its trade. Disease and shipwreck exacerbated the situation. A Portuguese sailor, soldier or official setting out for India had rather less than one chance in two of getting there alive.

It has been calculated that, of 912 ships sent to the Indies during 1500–1635, only 768 arrived, while only 470 ever returned to Portugal, and whereas in the first decade of the sixteenth century an average of some fourteen ships a year were sent out to India, by the 1630s the annual average was down to three.

The trade of Asia, which had for centuries been exporting commodities, spices especially, for which there was a lively demand in Europe, was by and large more highly valued than trade with Africa. It was also easier and more economical for the Portuguese to turn this trade to their advantage by seizing the strategic points commanding the established navigational system of the Indian Ocean than it was to employ their limited resources in inducing African societies, which outside the western Sudan and the east coast had had little or no contact with inter-continental trade, to develop exports of value to Europe. The principle of Portuguese policy in Africa was therefore to keep territorial and administrative responsibilities to the minimum necessary to control already extant commercial activities which could benefit Portuguese trade in Europe or elsewhere in her empire.

The same principle applied equally to Asia (or, for that matter, to Brazil), but the opportunities for applying it to Africa were appreciably fewer, because in the last resort the only things which Africa seemed to offer that were really of value to the Portuguese scheme were gold and slaves. Long stretches of the African coasts were almost totally ignored by the Portuguese because their inhabitants apparently did not possess the first, and had no established trading systems offering the second for sale. The most extensive of these was the 3000 miles of coastline from southern Angola right round to Sofala. This was simply an obstacle which had to be sailed round to reach India. On the east coast, Portuguese aims were effectively only two, to explore the possibilities of developing a working alliance with the Christian monarchy of Ethiopia, and to secure control of the export of gold from the mines of the Monomotapa country. So long as the sailors and traders of the Muslim towns on the 2500 miles of coast between Mozambique and Adal did not interfere with these aims, they were left very much to themselves.

Albuquerque had sent envoys to the Ethiopian court about 1510, but, like Covilhã, they were not permitted to leave the country. Another mission, sent out in 1520, was more successful in that after six years' residence it was allowed to return home, and it occasioned the first modern descriptions of the country and people, their church and government. But the Ethiopian authorities were not at all oncoming in response to Portuguese advances until they woke up to the dangers involved in Ottoman control of the Red Sea (Massawa, the main port of entry to Ethiopia, was captured by the Turks in 1536), the consequent acquisition of firearms by the Muslims of the area, and the opening of Ahmad Gran's offensive against them from Adal. In 1541, Portugal responded to King Lebna Dengel's appeal for aid by sending the small expeditionary force (commanded by a son of Vasco da Gama) which proved invaluable in helping to stave off a Muslim conquest of the Christian kingdom. The survivors of the Portuguese expedition stayed on in Ethiopia and were joined by Jesuit missionaries. The consequences included the training of Ethiopian soldiers in the use of firearms; the emergence of a permanent capital for the king (who hitherto had been in constant progress round his provinces) at Gondar, close by Lake Tana, where the Portuguese built royal castles; and, eventually in 1622, the conversion of King Susenyos to western Catholicism. But later missionaries were tactless in their exploitation of this advantage, and provoked a national reaction against interference with the traditional church. By 1648 the Jesuits had been expelled, other western missionaries were denied admission to the kingdom, and for the next two centuries Ethiopia deliberately cut itself off from contacts with the outside world. Its Christian church and kingdom became atrophied, and, in the face of renewed advances from the Oromo and from Islam, their authority over the Ethiopian highlands steadily shrank.

Thus the Portuguese intervention in Ethiopian affairs that had begun in 1541 achieved little. They were never strong enough to defeat Ottoman naval power in the Red Sea. Contact with Ethiopia could therefore only be intermittent, its landlocked kingdom became value-less to Portugal as an ally, and eventually it lacked not only the strength but also the will to help her.

In the long run, the Portuguese intervention in the gold trade from Monomotapa was also counter-productive. The initial idea was that if the Portuguese controlled Sofala, the principal outlet for this trade, where they built a fort in 1505, then the gold would come into their hands readily enough. But the gold was brought down from the interior by Muslim merchants who were more experienced and skilled than the Portuguese in inland travel, in trade with the Bantu, and in supplying suitable Asian commodities for which the latter were prepared to exchange their gold or ivory. Moreover, the Portuguese attacks on the principal coastal bases of the Muslim traders indicated the hostility of their intentions, and the Muslims had no wish to trade with the Portuguese if they could avoid it. Some gold did reach the Portuguese, but less than they had expected, and only fitfully. By about 1530 it was apparent that the supply was inadequate even to pay for the cost of the fort and establishment at Sofala, and that the bulk of the trade with the interior had been diverted to a selection of creeks and small ports north of Sofala whence it was shipped off in small vessels that could slip through the Portuguese attempts at control.

The Portuguese therefore needed to reconnoitre the mining areas and the routes to them for themselves, and then, if possible, to emulate the Muslim merchants and to establish inland trading places. The first of these things was successfully undertaken in two journeys made in 1514 by Antonio Fernandes. Efforts were then made to communicate with the Monomatapa kingdom by advancing up the navigable lower Zambezi, posts being established at Sena and Tete in the 1530s. From these, small groups of Portuguese advanced into the gold-producing highlands and, both expelling the Muslim traders and following their example, began to build small fortified trading settlements called 'fairs'. But the Portuguese wanted to go beyond this, and control the Mwene Mutapa and his kingdom. The first serious attempt at this took the form of a Jesuit mission in 1560–61 under Gonçalo da Silveira, the aim being to convert the king and his court and so link them to the Portuguese interest. After apparent initial success, however, the missionaries and their converts were killed, apparently at the instigation of hostile Muslims. There followed an ambitious military attempt at conquest in 1572 under Francisco de Barreto, but this ended in disaster, due as much to the fevers of the Zambezi valley as to Shona resistance.

Three years later, however, the Portuguese were able to conclude a treaty with the Mwene Mutapa under which the Muslims were to be expelled and the Portuguese were permitted to trade, to mine and to conduct missionary work. The explanation of this treaty on the African side seems to have been that the Mwene Mutapa's authority was declining, and that the Portuguese were seen as useful allies to help maintain it. In the 1640s, indeed, they seem to have been strong enough to penetrate into the southern kingdom of Butwa, and to restore to his throne a king who had been expelled by the Muslim traders. But this represents the high point of Portuguese power and influence. They were never strong in the south, while in the north their intervention in affairs on the side of the Mwene Mutapa by and large weakened, rather than strengthened, his regime. As the power of the Portuguese increased, so his income from their traders in the form of gifts and taxes decreased, and more of his land and people came under their direct control. On the other hand, the Portuguese authorities were neither in firm enough control of the situation in the interior, nor deriving enough revenue from it, to replace the Mwene Mutapa's law and government with their own. Individual Portuguese adventurers secured *prazos*, grants of land, initially from the African authorities and later from the government at Mozambique and, often consolidating their authority by marrying into local chiefly families, forced local people to become their retainers or slaves and began to build up petty kingdoms of their own. By this time little gold was forthcoming; such wealth as there was to be exploited was mainly in the form of slaves and ivory. The major power of the region became the new Zimbabwe-type kingdom of the Changamire away to the south-west in what is now called Matabeleland. Towards the end of the seventeenth century, the Mwene Mutapa called on the Changamire for aid against the Portuguese. These were driven off the plateau, but equally the result was the virtual extinction of the northern kingdom.

On the western side of Africa, the main focus of Portuguese attention was not unnaturally Mina, or the Gold Coast. This was not easy for them to control. There were a number of paths along which trade flowed between the coast and the interior, and the coastlands themselves were divided between ten or a dozen small kingdoms – Akan-speaking in the west and centre, Gã or Adangme in the east – which competed with each other for the trade. On the other hand, the very fact of this political division gave the Portuguese some advantage. It is noteworthy that their first fort, Elmina, was built on the boundary between the two states of Komenda and Afutu. Furthermore, once the Africans had realized that the Portuguese were no longer going to allow casual trade with any visiting ship, there was something of an incentive for an African king to agree to negotiate with the Portuguese for the building of a fort on his territory. Eventually the Portuguese built three other major forts besides Elmina, at Axim in the far west, at Shama at the mouth of the river Pra (which was the first point at which they had traded), and, east of Elmina, at the place on the coast of the Gã kingdom which became known as Accra, and which was the most easterly point at which appreciable supplies of gold were available.

In each case, some sort of agreement seems to have been reached between the Portuguese and the local ruler. There is no contemporary documentary record of the terms of these agreements, but it is more than probable that they were the prototypes of the later agreements concluded by the Dutch and English with African kings when they in their turn came to build or to occupy forts on the Gold Coast, and which were embodied in written documents called 'Notes'. Essentially what was involved was that the African king accepted a European fort on his people's coast, and the Europeans agreed to make regular payments of trade goods to the king. On the African side, these payments seem to have been regarded as rent or tribute by which the Europeans, like any other strangers, acknowledged the supremacy of the local ruler. It is doubtful, however, whether the Portuguese looked at them in this way. In their eyes, their forts were overseas possessions of the Portuguese crown, and the payments made to the African rulers were most probably regarded as presents to secure their goodwill and to facilitate trade with them and their people.

The forts, strongly built structures of stone or brick on the very edge of the sea, were manned by Portuguese soldiers and officials, and served as depots where gold could be regularly collected and where stores of trade goods were maintained. They were not primarily intended for defence against local Africans or as means for their political domination. Few people other than fishermen and saltmakers lived on the coast at this time, and the major towns and political centres were in the interior. The extension of Portuguese political or military power into the interior was neither necessary nor really advisable, as the Portuguese were occupying points on the boundary of a well-developed trading system in which merchants from the interior were already coming to the coastal states for purposes of commercial exchange. The main role of the forts and the ships based on them was to keep other Europeans away from trading with the Africans, and to make the Portuguese the sole European purchasers of gold and suppliers of the imports that the Africans took in exchange. But this did not mean that the Portuguese exerted no political and military power on the coast. Communities of merchants and brokers, and of the slaves and artisans needed to serve the forts, developed around their walls, and these often came to accept their governors as the local authorities *de facto*. Equally, the Portuguese would undertake punitive expeditions against coastal peoples or king-doms which, seeking to escape the monopoly which the Portuguese claimed, traded with visiting ships from other European countries. However, in the last resort, the Portuguese – and the other Europeans who followed them to the Gold Coast – could not maintain a fort in face of concerted local hostility. The Africans could deny the Euro-peans access to water or provisions, or indeed boycott a fort altogether if they wished. As early as 1576, the Gã king must have decided that the disadvantages of having such over-mighty subjects on his territory outweighed the commercial gains. The Portuguese fort at Accra was destroyed, and for the next half century there was very little commer-cial intercourse between the Gã and any Europeans.

In a good year in the sixteenth century, the Portuguese might obtain about £60 000 ($300 000) of gold from their Mina forts. Obviously in return they had to supply the Gold Coast traders with goods which the latter accepted as being of equivalent value. This the Portuguese did not find very easy. Clearly there was no established African demand for European goods. Furthermore, Portugal was not well endowed with minerals or with industry to produce goods for export. She was therefore an entrepôt trader, buying goods from abroad and re-selling them abroad. The commodities most in demand on the Gold Coast which she did attempt to supply seem to have been metalware and raw metals, cloth and clothing, beads and slaves. Europe supplied metals, brass in particular, which were cheaper than the metals which Africans produced. It also supplied some of the cloth and beads, though initially European varieties of these were not well adjusted to African tastes, and it was often better to secure supplies from Asia. But some cloth and beads and all the slaves sold on the Gold Coast were purchased through trade elsewhere in Africa. Initially much of the cloth was of North African manufacture, while both cloth and beads were brought from lands to the east of the Gold Coast. In both cases there is an implication that goods from these regions may have been reaching the Gold Coast, albeit doubtless in smaller quantities, prior to the Portuguese arrival, and that all the Portuguese did was to fasten their hold on already established African trades. (This was certainly the pattern of their activity in the Indian Ocean.) Slaves were also brought from coasts to the east, but this was doubtless a new departure occasioned by the African merchants' need of porters to carry back into the interior goods which were much more bulky than the gold for which they had exchanged them, and also by the need for labour to increase gold production in forest lands which were presumably then thinly peopled.

Initially it was to Benin that the Portuguese looked as their main West African source of cloth, beads and slaves for their Gold Coast trade. Benin was not in fact a major producer of cloth or beads, but its organized state was in touch with people who were, the Yoruba and Ibo, for example, and through them with other producers even further afield. Also, until their Indian trade was established, the Portuguese were further interested in Benin as a source of peppers. In addition they were intrigued by the fact that its king, though clearly very powerful, sent to another potentate in the interior for confirmation of his accession, and that among the insignia which the Benin messengers brought back with them were metal crosses. Initially the Portuguese leapt to the conclusion that this inland potentate must be Prester John. In fact the name given to him, Ogane, suggests that he was the *Oni* (king) of Ife, still called Oghene in Benin, and by the early sixteenth century, the progress of their discoveries must have given the Portuguese a much better idea of the true distance from Benin to Ethiopia.

From about 1487 the Portuguese occupied a trading post at the Benin river port of Ughoton, though probably not continuously, but this seems to have been abandoned in 1507. The prime reason for this must have been that it was not producing the expected results, and the explanation of this seems to have been that the centralized kingdom of Benin would only allow trade with the Portuguese on its own terms. Although it possessed many slaves, and at the time was capturing numerous prisoners of war, its king seems to have been reluctant to supply either the quantity or quality of slaves that the Portuguese wanted. By 1516, indeed, the latter were virtually excluded from buying male slaves. Other factors in the Portuguese withdrawal were that they were no longer interested in African peppers (which were not the type preferred in Europe), and the high death rate from disease in the Niger delta – though this did not prevent them from operating elsewhere in the delta beyond Benin control. However, the main bases for delta trade were henceforward to be in the islands of the Gulf of Guinea, São Thomé in particular.

In 1514 the king of Benin sent an embassy to Portugal, in part to complain about the activities of traders from São Thomé and Principe, but also to invite Christian missionaries. This obviously suggested to the Portuguese a means of establishing their influence over the king and his administration and policy, and missionaries were duly sent. It seems, in fact, that what the king really wanted, at a time when he was in some political and military difficulty, was firearms. However, the indigenous social and political system was too strong to be penetrated by the resources the Portuguese could deploy, and the Portuguese were not willing to sell arms to people who were not their Christian allies. For the best part of two centuries, therefore, Benin virtually cut itself off from contacts with Europe: European trade was something it chose to do without.

Portuguese settlement of the islands of the Gulf of Guinea started about 1485. They were relatively healthy, and their situation in relation to the trade winds made them ideal places for ships going from Guinea back towards Europe or across to Brazil to call for water and provisions or for repairs. Except for Fernando Po, the largest and nearest to the coast, and of which the Portuguese took little notice, they were also uninhabited. They were therefore obvious places for Portuguese settlement. However, despite grants of land and of free trade with the mainland, few Portuguese wanted to settle so far afield in the tropics, and much of such Portuguese colonization as there was was effected by deporting undesirables and Jews. However these few settlers quickly appreciated that the islands' combination of volcanic soils and high rainfall made them highly suitable for the cultivation of tropical crops for the European market. Of these the most important was sugar, originally an Asian product fetching very high prices in Europe as a luxury good. Attempts to grow the sugar cane in southern Europe had not been very rewarding, but it was being grown very profitably in Madeira and the other Atlantic islands after their discovery, and from there it was introduced to São Thomé and the other Gulf of Guinea islands with outstanding success.

However, sugar cultivation requires a great deal of labour. Soon the colonists of São Thomé and Principe were looking for slaves not simply to send to the markets of the Gold Coast or of the Atlantic islands and Portugal, but for their own plantations. The numbers of slaves successfully supplied to all the earlier markets seem to have been small, possibly no more than an average of 600 to 700 a year. But a substantial labour force was needed to clear and maintain sugar plantations on the Gulf of Guinea islands, and it is thought that these alone absorbed an average of about 1000 slaves a year during the first quarter of the sixteenth century, and not much less than this during the next fifty years. By this time, i.e. the 1570s, the number of slaves in the islands was so large as to make it difficult to control them, and thereafter both the import of slaves for the islands' plantations and the islands' plantation economy itself sharply declined. The focus for the production of tropical produce on plantations under Portuguese management had now in fact shifted across the Atlantic, to Brazil, to which many of the São Thomé planters emigrated, and to the Spanish colonies in the Caribbean islands and tropical America. Consequently São Thomé's economic role reverted from plantation production to one of being once again an entrepôt base in a maritime slave trade. But this trade was now on an appreciably larger scale, for the demand for slaves in the Americas was infinitely greater than the demand had been in the local African trade or in the Atlantic off-shore islands or in Europe.

But even before this, the São Thomé settlers had begun to look further afield than the Niger delta for the slaves they needed. Increasingly their attention was drawn to the Kongo kingdom, just south of the lower Congo, and to its satellite states both north of the river and further south. The Portuguese were obviously impressed by the size, organization and trading system of the Kongo kingdom which they had first touched in 1482, and it was here that they undertook their most ambitious attempt to secure control of an area of African territory by christianization and peaceful penetration. Embassies were soon passing between the courts of Portugal and Kongo, and in 1491 the first of a series of contingents of priests and skilled artisans was sent out to begin the conversion of the kingdom into a Christian state under Portuguese protection. In return for its modernizing aid, the Portuguese crown expected to receive a monopoly of Kongo's trade and other relations with the outside world, and a base from which it might be possible, via the Congo river, to establish direct overland communication with Ethiopia and the Mwene Mutapa.

Doubtless, as a political ally, the kingdom of the Bakongo was less valued than Ethiopia, and as an economic goal less attractive than the Mwene Mutapa's kingdom, but it did offer some advantages. It was more accessible than either. It was linked to its neighbours and to the interior by a network of trade routes, along which flowed commodities like salt, copper, shells and cloth (both of the latter being valued as currency), and which the Portuguese might hope to dominate and develop. Politically it was possibly better organized than its Bantu contemporary on the other side of central Africa, and yet its monarchy and its national ethos were not so strong as to be likely to resist

Portuguese influences, as they were resisted in both Ethiopia and Benin. Indeed the initial success of the Portuguese plans for the Bakongo seems to have been largely due to the welcome given to the Portuguese by a son of the king who was ruling at the time of their arrival.

Though this king, Nzinga Kuwu, accepted baptism in 1491, by the time of his death in 1506 he had for many years returned to the pagan practices of his ancestors. The election of a successor was the responsibility of the principal officers and provincial rulers of the kingdom, and in 1506, as doubtless often before, this led to a struggle for power between a number of contenders and their supporting factions. The victor was Nzinga Kuwu's son Mvemba Nzinga, who had been baptized Afonso, and who seems to have been a convinced Christian and a firm supporter of the Portuguese modernization programme. It seems likely that his motive was to use Christian thinking and Portuguese technical support to strengthen the position of the monarchy *vis-à-vis* that of the nobility. Certainly Afonso succeeded in getting the succession limited to his own direct descendants.

But by the middle 1520s, the schemes of both the Portuguese crown and of the Bakongo king were going wrong. The root of the trouble was that Lisbon's plan for a royal monopoly of Kongo trade conflicted with the grant already made of trading rights on the mainland to the settlers of São Thomé. The latter, as has been seen, simply wanted as many slaves as they could get. By as early as 1506 they were organizing slave caravans into the interior of the Kongo kingdom, and they cared nothing for the policies of Lisbon and Afonso. Lisbon was too far away to control the situation, and the priests and officials it could maintain in the Kongo too few. In 1526, for example, there were only four priests in the Kongo although fifty were needed. São Thomé was much closer, and its traders much more numerous. By the second quarter of the sixteenth century, about a third of all slaves being taken out of Africa by the Portuguese were coming from the Congo region.

In 1526 Afonso tried to ban all trade and to expel all Europeans except priests and teachers. But this was impossible. By now many Bakongo chiefs were actively engaging in slave trading and raiding, and the slave trade was a major economic activity of the kingdom. So Afonso was forced to turn to an attempt to bring the trade under royal control. One result of this was to cause many of the São Thomé traders to shift their attentions to areas not under his direct authority, and notably to the nominally tributary kingdom of Ndongo further south (whose ruler was the *Ngola* – hence 'Angola'). In 1556 the official Portuguese faction persuaded Afonso's successor, Diogo (*c.* 1545–61) to go to war with Ndongo, but he was disastrously defeated. A few years later, further trouble struck the Bakongo kingdom in the form of the Jaga invasions. These were repelled by King Alvare I in 1572, but from this time on the official Portuguese cause in Kongo was lost.

When Alvare had restored internal order, he looked for external aid not to Portugal, but directly to the Vatican. By the beginning of the seventeenth century, although the Portuguese crown maintained that Kongo was still under its suzerainty, because of the independent spirit maintained by its rulers its attempt to control the kingdom had effectually been abandoned. Official Portuguese interest shifted south to Ndongo, and to a policy of direct colonization. In 1571 a young Portuguese nobleman, Paulo Dias, was given a charter or commission (*donatario*) to colonize Angola at his own expense. In 1575–6 a base was established at Luanda, and Dias and his followers embarked on a career of conquest. More than a century of warfare followed, involving many African peoples, including the Imbangala and Bakongo as well as the Mbundu of Ndongo, and also – during 1641–8 the Dutch. But the end result was the destruction of African political authority, and its replacement by a colonial system. By the end of the seventeenth century, three Portuguese towns, Luanda and Benguela on the coast and Massangano in the interior, constituted an arrowhead penetrating west central Africa, on which was based a system of military captaincies seeking the maximum exploitation of the surrounding territory. Initial dreams of rich silver mines in the interior had faded, agricultural colonization had failed, and the *raison d'être* of the whole enterprise had become to mount trading caravans and raids to secure as many slaves as possible for the mines and plantations of Portugal's transatlantic colony in Brazil.

It now remains to consider Portuguese activity in West Africa west and north of the Gold Coast. This was neither very successful nor very considerable. An early attempt to intercept the trans-Saharan trade from Arguin was soon abandoned. Thereafter the main activity was the trade which the settlers of the Cape Verde Islands conducted with the adjacent coastlands of Upper Guinea. This became concentrated on the coast from the mouth of the Gambia to about the modern border between Sierra Leone and Liberia. This coast possessed numerous rivers, creeks and offshore islands to encourage commercial penetration, and also represented the south-western fringes of the Mande trading system. By contrast, much of the coast further east, especially the modern Ivory Coast and the coast from Accra to Lagos, was surf-bound open beach which was dangerous to shipping. In the Ivory Coast and modern Liberia, the coast also fronted dense and thinly populated forests which backed onto mountainous lands, with the result that these areas had been little penetrated by the trading system originating in the Sudan.

As well as obtaining slaves to help in the development of the empty lands of southern Portugal and the Atlantic islands, the Portuguese hoped that they might be able to penetrate through the Upper Guinea coastlands to open up direct commercial and other relations with Mali and its resources of gold. But the empire of Mali was in decline by the fifteenth century, while the Portuguese were nothing like strong enough to advance effectively into the interior, and to weld the various Mande principalities and the congeries of heterogeneous peoples of the region into a new trading system directed to their interests. The one large Upper Guinea polity that was close to the coast, and so accessible to the Portuguese, was the so-called Djolof (i.e. Wolof) empire between the lower Senegal and the Gambia, i.e. in the western-most Sudan. This had probably come into being less than a century before their own arrival on the scene. It seems to have been in some measure a response to the decay in this area first of the influence of Takrur and then of that of Mali. A group of Wolof leaders, influenced by the political, commercial and islamizing examples of these states, sought to fill the vacuum caused by their decline by instituting a hierarchical control of their own over the other Wolof and Serer chiefdoms. In the 1480s, the Portuguese took advantage of a dispute among this Wolof ruling class to convert one of its members, whom they called 'Prince Bemoym', into a Christian vassal of their own king. But Bemoym was soon killed in mysterious circumstances, and it does not seem that the Portuguese scheme to control the Wolof polity as they later sought to control Kongo ever really got off the ground. Nevertheless, the introduction of European trade seems to have been a factor which weakened Wolof control over their empire. On the coast, it eventually dissolved into its component parts, the small kingdoms of Walo, Cayor, Baol, Sine and Saloum.

Portuguese influence in the Upper Guinea coastlands was quickly reduced to a number of petty coastal trading settlements in which men from the Cape Verde Islands had informally established themselves to do what business they could with the Mande traders and the local peoples. In course of time these trader-settlers, the *lançados*, allied themselves with and married into the African trading and ruling families, and, like the later holders of *prazos* in the Zambezi valley, became members of African society rather than representatives of a Portuguese imperial system. All attempts to control them, for example by revoking the trading privileges of the Cape Verde islanders, failed, and by the second half of the sixteenth century they were already demonstrating – for example in their dealings with the English slave trader, John Hawkins – that they were motivated by local and not by Portuguese interests.

It may be doubted whether the period of Portuguese monopoly in the development of European trade and other relations with the coast-lands of tropical Africa from the Senegal to Somalia had much significant effect on the course of African history. As has been indicated, large stretches of the coast were altogether ignored by the Portuguese. Where they were active, as in Upper Guinea, the Gold Coast, the Gulf of Guinea, Angola or on the east coast from Sofala to Mozambique, their main strength lay in offshore islands, like the Cape Verde Islands or São Thomé, or in forts or settlements built on the very edge of the sea, like the Gold Coast forts, Luanda, Sofala and Mozambique (and their first settlements in the last three were all in fact originally on small islands). The essential pattern of their activity was not to develop new trade or to establish territorial colonies, but to turn existing African trade or political systems to their advantage. On the Gold Coast, they were largely successful in a commercial sense. But even here, trade more than about 100 miles from the coast kept to its traditional inwards-orientation. The most that happened was that new sources of gold production nearer to the coast than most of those originally exploited by African chiefs and merchants began to be developed more intensively, but developed by Africans and not by the Portuguese, and for their own profit as well as that of the Portuguese.

Elsewhere the Portuguese largely failed in their original purposes – in Upper Guinea, in Benin, in the Kongo kingdom, in Ethiopia, on the East African coast. This did lead them in some cases to undertake positive steps to advance inland by force, for example Barreto's expedition in the Zambezi valley and Dias's conquest in Angola, both originating in the 1570s. But of these, only Dias's initiative really achieved a profitable outcome for the imperial economy, and only after a century of effort and only really owing to the energies of individual *conquistadores*. These *conquistadores* were often a law to themselves, and elsewhere the successful Portuguese in Africa – like the *lançados* of the Upper Guinea coastlands or the *prazo* holders in the Zambezi valley – were those who had largely emancipated themselves from the control of church and state, and had become more or less acculturated to African society.

Except in a few relatively small areas – the coastal states of the Gold Coast, Kongo, Angola, the Zambezi valley, the trading cities of the east coast – the political and economic life of tropical African peoples continued much as it had done before the century of Henry the Navigator and Vasco da Gama. The Portuguese were in fact harbingers of change rather than actual agents of change: African societies were far stronger than the Portuguese could ever be in Africa. Yet things were changing. In the coastlands from the Senegal to Angola, the Portuguese language or Africanized versions of it became a lingua franca for foreign trade and for the acquisition of new ideas. Some elements of the original christianization of the Bakongo kingdom lingered on into modern colonial times, and some knowledge of a wider world and of new kinds of social mobility filtered much more widely into Africa. Although the technological distance between western European society and African society was very much less than it was to become in the eighteenth and nineteenth centuries, some Africans acquired new knowledge and new skills. Above all perhaps, African farmers were introduced to new crops, usually of tropical American provenance, such as maize and cassava, which in given circumstances could be more productive than their older cultigens, and which therefore were sometimes quickly taken up and adopted wherever they could usefully be grown. Thus within about fifty years of Columbus's voyage, two varieties of maize had reached Nigeria by two different routes, one along the west coast, and the other through the Mediterranean and across the Sahara. By the end of the seventeenth century, it was known virtually throughout tropical Africa.

Finally, the significance of the Portuguese expansion to embrace the coasts of tropical Africa in the fifteenth and sixteenth centuries was that they showed other Europeans, with greater maritime and commercial strength than they themselves had, that there was profit to be made out of contact with Africa. By the end of the sixteenth century, the Portuguese example had also shown western Europeans that the prime value of Africa for them was not as a source of gold or spices, or as an expanding frontier for Christendom, but as a continent where slaves could be secured for the exploitation of the Americas.

Chapter 10

The first stage of the impact of world trade on tropical Africa: the export slave trade

In the first decade of the seventeenth century, the Dutch East India Company destroyed Portuguese power in the Indian Ocean, and between 1637 and 1642, the Dutch West India Company seized all the major Portuguese establishments on the western coast of Africa. It was these initiatives, rather than the early Portuguese ventures – in the perspective of African history, these must be viewed as no more than a tentative reconnaissance – which led to the incorporation of tropical Africa into a dynamic world trading system dominated by western Europeans. Ultimately this system was to generate sufficient power and momentum to lead to European political control of the whole of the continent.

But this outcome could hardly have been envisaged at the time. In the first place, the reasons which led the Dutch to form two major trading companies, each with a charter giving it a monopoly of the United Netherlands' trade within its half of the world, arose from a purely domestic European situation. The people of the northern Netherlands were in revolt against their Spanish sovereign, Philip II, who, following upon the disaster to the Aviz dynasty occasioned by its defeat at al-Ksar al-Kabir in 1579, had also become king of Portugal. Netherlands merchants had become principal distributors in northern Europe of the Asian, African and American produce flowing from the Spanish and Portuguese empires. In an attempt to punish the rebels and to diminish their powers of resistance, Philip closed the Iberian ports to their ships. The merchants and government of the United Netherlands were therefore led to create national overseas companies strong enough to engage directly in commercial ventures on the Atlantic and Indian Oceans and to attack and destroy Spanish and Portuguese naval power on them.

The East Indies seemed a riper field for exploitation than the West. The spice trade was still seen as the major prize, and Portuguese power in the east was viewed – correctly – as more fragile than Spanish power in the Americas, which was territorial as well as maritime. A twelve year truce (1609–21) in the war with Spain further delayed the setting up of a Dutch West India Company to match the East India Company established in 1602.

As is sufficiently indicated by their names, neither company was principally concerned with Africa. It is true that in the middle of the seventeenth century the East India Company established the base close by the Cape of Good Hope which was to lead to the spread of European settlement throughout the temperate lands of southern Africa. But the effective consolidation of this settlement had to wait until after the industrialization of western Europe, and the very different conditions produced by this, in nineteenth-century Africa as well as in Europe – and by this time, the Company had long disappeared from the scene. Furthermore, the dispersion of European settlers in southern Africa occurred despite, rather than because of Company policy, which was rigidly concerned with securing control of the East Indies spice trade.

As has been seen, the Portuguese scheme to exploit this hinged on the possession of a base in India from which it was sought to dominate the whole monsoon-based Indian Ocean trading system. But with better ships and techniques of sailing and navigation than the Portuguese had possessed, the Dutch were able to ignore the monsoon winds altogether. Their ships sailed with the trade winds from the Cape of Good Hope until they had made enough easting to turn north, and to arrive directly in the East Indies through the Sunda Strait between the islands of Sumatra and Java. Only two bases were needed to ensure control of this route: one close by the Sunda Strait, Batavia (the modern Jakarta), which became the overseas headquarters of the Company; and one about halfway between Europe and the East Indies which would also guard the entrance to the Indian Ocean. Initially St Helena was tried for this purpose, but in 1652, in the face of growing French and English competition, the decision was taken to establish the settlement from which Cape Town was to develop. Thus the network of bases which the Portuguese had established round the shores of the Indian Ocean all the way from Mozambique to Malacca came to have no useful purpose so far as the major aim of European enterprise in that ocean was concerned.

East Africa therefore became of little account in the European scheme of things in the Indian Ocean. This remained the case even when, baulked by the Dutch in the East Indies, French and English East India Companies concentrated their activities on the Indian sub-continent. Their ships therefore sailed closer to the East African coast, sometimes indeed using the Mozambique channel. But their only interest in the western Indian Ocean was to have ports of call equi-valent to Cape Town, and for this purpose Mauritius, Madagascar and the Comoro Islands were more suitable than the mainland. The growth of sugar planting in the Mascarene islands of Mauritius and Réunion after these islands had become French colonies in the early eighteenth century occasioned a concern with sources of slave labour, but even so, French interests did not take root on the East African coast. They were constantly frustrated by English sea-power, while Madagascar was a nearer source of supply. Early in the nineteenth century, of course, Europeans ceased dealing in slaves, and Mauritius became a British colony.

The Portuguese were left with a string of East African bases which they could neither properly develop nor defend, and the way was clear for a revival of Muslim trade and sea-power in the western Indian Ocean. The community that led the way was the Omani Arabs of the barren coastlands of Arabia close by the mouth of the Persian Gulf. People here had always looked to the sea for a living, whether as merchants or as pirates. The Portuguese had sought to control their activities and those of the Persian Gulf sailors generally by occupying Hormuz and the principal Omani settlement, Muscat, on either side of the entrance to the Gulf. In 1650, the Omani threw them out of Muscat, and two years later they went on to capture Zanzibar, which had considerable potential as an entrepôt for the trade of the East African coast. In 1698, the Omani took Fort Jesus at Mombasa, the principal bastion of Portuguese power on the northern half of the coast. There was a brief Portuguese reoccupation of this fort in 1728–9, when the Omani governors of Mombasa and Zanzibar were at loggerheads, but from 1698 onwards, Portuguese power in East Africa was effectively limited to the coastlands south of Cape Delgado and to the lower Zambezi valley. North of this, the Omani had secured the restoration of a purely Muslim trading system linking the

East African coastal towns with the lands of the Red Sea, the Persian Gulf and north-western India.

Thus from about the middle of the seventeenth century to at least the middle of the nineteenth, when Europeans referred to the 'African Trade', to all intents and purposes they meant their trade with western Africa, and for the most part, indeed, their trade with the coast from the Senegal to about the Congo. The value of this trade increased continuously throughout the period. By the last quarter of the eighteenth century, Europe's exports to this coast were probably worth something of the order of £2 000 000 ($10 000 000) or more a year. This was a not insignificant proportion of Europe's overseas trade, and probably represents something like a tenfold increase on its value in the early seventeenth century. But until circumstances began to change during the first half of the nineteenth century, by far the largest part of this European trade with West Africa was subsidiary to Europe's interests in the Americas. It was based on the exportation of one commodity, African slaves, for service on American plantations growing tropical produce for sale in western Europe.

Moreover, the growth of Europe's trade with West Africa did not obviously lead to any great growth of European power there. Rather the reverse was the case, for, in Guinea in particular, African kings and their peoples responded to the increase of foreign trade very much as some kings and peoples of the Sudan had earlier responded to the growth of trade across the Sahara. Larger, more powerful, and more commercially oriented African political structures were developed. There was thus neither need nor opportunity for seventeenth- and eighteenth-century Europeans to seek to establish political power in western Africa; indeed, their inroads into the continent were appreciably less than those undertaken by the Portuguese in the previous century. Nevertheless, a web of interaction between Africans and Europeans was being woven and, in the nineteenth century, when Europeans ceased to be interested in slaves for the Americas, and when their new industrial societies were evolving new patterns of overseas trade and empire, this was to lead more or less inevitably to the establishment of European rule over virtually all tropical Africa.

The new African trade was pioneered by the Dutch West India Company following its success, in the later 1630s, in conquering appreciable areas of northern Brazil from the Portuguese. The dominant economic activity there was the plantation production of sugar and other tropical produce for the European market. The plantations were entirely dependent for their labour on a supply of slaves from Africa, and it was to ensure their continuing prosperity that from 1637 onwards the Company's governor in Brazil, Maurice of Nassau, initiated a programme to conquer the Portuguese bases in western Africa. By 1642 this had been almost uniformly successful, and for the space of a few years the Dutch Company seemed to have in its grasp the whole supply of African slaves to the Americas.

In fact this success was illusory. Modern research suggests that even at the height of its success in the early 1640s, the Dutch West India Company did not succeed in transporting to America more than about 3000 slaves a year – which may not have been more than a half, or even a third, of the total. In the first place, following Portugal's independence from Spanish rule in 1640, there was a considerable recrudescence of Portuguese colonial energy. By 1645, the Dutch had been expelled from Brazil, and by 1648 the Portuguese, whose resistance in the interior of Angola had never been totally overcome, had succeeded in recovering both that colony and also their islands in the Gulf of Guinea. Thus the Portuguese largely regained control of the Atlantic slave trade south of the equator. North of the equator, however, the Dutch remained in a strong position. They retained the important forts on the Gold Coast, at Elmina, Axim and Shama, which they had captured from the Portuguese, and added to these more forts of their own construction. For the rest of the century, indeed, the Dutch remained the strongest European trading power on the Gold Coast, which itself remained the main focus of European activity in Guinea. They also began to develop trade on the coast east of the Volta, which soon became known as the Slave Coast, and until 1677 they possessed the important island fortress of Goree, from which it was possible to control much of the sea trade of Upper Guinea. From all these places they could ship slaves, via Curaçao and other islands which they still held in the West Indies, to meet the needs of the Spanish mainland colonists and of the English and French planters who were now settling the lesser Antilles.

But the very success of the Dutch West India Company proved its undoing. Mercantilist governments in England and France were not prepared to allow their American colonists to become tied to Dutch merchants for their supplies of slaves and other forms of capital, with the resultant possibility that much of the marketing of their produce in Europe would also be in Dutch hands. Moreover, just as the Dutch disruption of Spanish naval power in the Caribbean had cleared the way for English and French settlement there, so too their demolition of the Portuguese monopoly of Europe's trade with West Africa facilitated the emergence of national English and French African or West Indian companies to compete with the Dutch in the business of buying African slaves for sale to planters in the New World. Competition for the American trade, which necessarily involved competition for trade in West Africa as well, was an important motive for the wars between the Netherlands, England and France which were a principal theme in European history from 1652 to 1713. These were to end with the virtual elimination of the Dutch as a major trading power, and the initiation of a century of struggle for overseas trade and empire between Britain and France. But long before this stage had been reached, the English and French companies were by no means the only competitors of the Dutch West India Company in West Africa. Portuguese or Brazilian merchants reappeared in the trade north of the equator, while other European governments, notably those of Sweden, Denmark and Brandenburg, joined with those of Britain and France in emulating the Dutch model of creating national slave trading companies. Since there were also substantial numbers of Dutch merchants opposed to the monopoly granted to the Dutch West India Company, there was no shortage of skills or of capital to enable these rival companies to become established.

The second half of the seventeenth century was therefore one in which a number of major European trading companies were competing for the trade of the West African coastlands. The competition was the more bitter because, during the many wars of the time (or even outside them), the companies, as the representatives of their nations' interests in Africa, might expect to call upon the armed support of the new national navies. Because of this, much of the competition in West Africa centred around the possession of coastal forts. Many of the details of this competition belong more to European than to African history, and here little more need be done than to assess the results that were discernible by the beginning of the eighteenth century – by and large a period of stability in Europe's relations with West Africa.

The French, who in 1639 had established themselves on an island at the mouth of the Senegal, where twenty years later they began to build the fort and town of St Louis, and who in 1677 had captured Goree from the Dutch, achieved a position of dominance in the European trade on the coast from the Senegal to the Gambia which in the event was little affected by the British habit of occupying Goree and St Louis during the sea wars of the eighteenth century. The Gambia itself, however, became the scene of continuing competition between the British, who had first occupied James Island in its estuary in 1618 and had built a fort there in 1664, and the French, who maintained an establishment nearby at Albreda from the 1670s onwards. The rivers and islands south of the Gambia were essentially a preserve of Portuguese traders, and the Portuguese had long maintained a fort and settlement at Cacheu, while the coast from the Sierra Leone river to Sherbro Island was predominantly a scene for British activities. South and east of this, the Grain or Pepper Coast (corresponding to the coast of modern Liberia) and the Ivory Coast attracted little permanent European settlement.

On the other hand, the Gold Coast, immediately east of the Ivory Coast, was the scene of the most intense European competition, English, Swedes, Danes and Brandenburgers all joining with the Dutch in the struggle for the possession of forts on its shores. By the early eighteenth century, however, a pattern had emerged which was to last for a century and a half. The Swedes and the Brandenburgers had both been eliminated, and Danish activity had been restricted to Accra and the coast to the east of it. Along the rest of the coast, from Accra to west of Axim, eleven Dutch forts were being challenged by eight British. The British forts tended to be less well built, armed and garrisoned, but, as the eighteenth century developed, they were securing the lion's share of the trade. This was partly because Britain had overtaken the Netherlands as the major world trading power, and because her new industries were producing goods for export in a volume and at prices with which no one else could compete. But it was also because the British were opening their African trade to a host of individual merchants, whereas the Dutch held to the policy that it should remain the monopoly of their West India Company.

The period of violent, armed competition was now over, and the restriction of trade to monopoly companies, which alone could hope to meet the expense of maintaining strong forts and garrisons on the coast, was now an anachronism and, indeed, prejudicial to trading profits. Over long stretches of the coast, African communities were now thoroughly accustomed to, and well organized for the business of dealing with Europeans; there was trade enough for all. The new situation began to be reflected on the Slave Coast, east of Accra to about Lagos, to which European traders had begun to turn their attention with the growth of the demand for slaves in the Americas in the second half of the seventeenth century. The sandy *terre de barre* here was not suited for the erection of coastal forts of stone or brick as on the Gold Coast, and the Aja kings, doubtless hoping to avoid the development of European *imperia in imperiis* of the kind that had developed on that coast, required the Europeans to build their trading depots close by their palaces in their capitals a little way inland. Consequently, while the Dutch, English and French companies, as well as Portuguese traders, all became established on the Slave Coast, their local heads developed the powers and responsibilities of consuls or ambassadors rather than becoming embryo colonial governors, as was the case on the Gold Coast. Thus the way was clear for the growth of individual European trading activities, controlled less by the European monopoly companies than by the economic regimes maintained by the African kings.

As the American demand for slaves further increased, and as European activities extended even further afield, to the Niger delta, to the Cameroons, and south to the Congo mouth and the northern limits of the Angolan territory under Portuguese control, so the new pattern of trade became even more manifest. There were no shore bases under the exclusive control of one or other of the European monopoly companies. The right to trade was the prerogative of the African rulers, and was commonly granted to any European who was prepared to acknowledge African sovereignty and to pay the required dues and taxes.

Though Europeans were prepared to exchange their goods – principally cloth (often originally of Asian origin, but by the end of the eighteenth century increasingly of European manufacture); raw metals and manufactured hardware; muskets, shot and powder; brandy, rum and gin; and beads and other trinkets – for any African product which could bring them a profit, it was the ever-increasing American demand for slaves which principally explains the wide expansion and great growth of European trading activity from the middle of the seventeenth century onwards. There was, of course, a continuing demand for gold, but this was available in appreciable quantities only on the Gold Coast. Initially ivory was also an important commodity, and one that was available almost anywhere on the coast. But, by the end of the eighteenth century, the increasing availability of guns for hunting was depleting the supply of elephants within ready reach of the coastlands except where (as, for example, on the Ivory Coast) these remained thinly populated by humans. There was also a demand for gum arabic from Senegambia, and for dye-woods and hardwoods from the forests further south. But none of these commodities could compete in value or in general availability with slaves. Indeed the intensity of the late seventeenth-century competition for the possession of forts on the Gold Coast was due as much to the fact that, through the earlier gold trade, the African communities here were very well organized for dealing with the Europeans and for supplying them with their requirements, as it was to the fact that gold could still be bought in appreciable quantities. By the end of the eighteenth century, indeed, this was not always the case. There were some years when, because some of the more accessible deposits were becoming worked out, and more generally because the well-organized Gold Coast kingdoms required to retain more of their production to meet the needs of their own expanding state and commercial systems, Europeans were actually importing gold to buy slaves.*

The demand for slaves derived, of course, from the vast expansion of the labour-intensive plantations which Europeans had developed in the Americas. The New World surpassed Europe and the Atlantic and Gulf of Guinea islands as a market for African slaves in the third quarter of the sixteenth century. But its absorption of African labour remained relatively small until the Iberian monopoly of its exploitation was broken by the actions of the Dutch West India Company in the second quarter of the seventeenth century. From then on, the numbers of African slaves taken to the Americas grew steadily up to about the 1790s, when the French Revolutionary and Napoleonic Wars began to disrupt traffic across the Atlantic. After the restoration of peace in 1815, the Atlantic slave trade began to revive. But Europeans had now begun actively to question the morality of trading in men, and since at the same time their more prospering economies had reached a stage when investment in slaves seemed less remunerative than investment in other means of production, measures began to be taken to outlaw the slave trade. During the 1830s, these began to have some effect north of the equator. One consequence of this was for the volume of trade south of the equator to increase, but by the end of the 1860s the whole Atlantic trade was coming to a close, the ultimately determinant factor being the abolition of slavery in the Americas.

When looking back at the Atlantic slave trade, historians and others

---

* To this it may be added that Portuguese merchants had little to offer in exchange for slaves that was acceptable to the Africans other than gold and tobacco from Brazil.

were for long accustomed to think that the number of African slaves taken to the Americas must have amounted to at least 15 millions, and that it could well have been appreciably greater. Thus in 1936, R. R. Kuczynski, one of the first modern demographers to apply himself to African data, regarded 15 millions as 'rather a conservative figure'. But in the 1960s, Professor Philip D. Curtin realized that this commonly accepted figure of at least 15 millions derived merely from estimates made in 1861 by an American publicist; later writers had taken it up without inquiring into its authenticity. Curtin therefore set himself to survey as much of the literature relating to the import of slaves into the Americas, or their export westwards from Africa, as was necessary to establish reasonably reliable estimates for all the various regions and periods of the trade. Where he could find no consensus for the volume of a particular aspect of the trade, or where there was a gap in a series of published figures, he constructed new estimates which seemed to him best to fit the particular circumstances. In this way he arrived at an estimated grand total for the number of African slaves imported into the Americas of only 9 566 000.

The limitations of the exercise undertaken by Curtin are well set out in the preface to the book in which his work was published. He thought he would have done well if his figures were within plus or minus 20 per cent of the reality; elsewhere he wrote 'it is extremely unlikely that the ultimate total will turn out to be less than 8 000 000 or more than 10 500 000'. However his book served to inspire other historians to search among archives for runs of first-hand figures showing the volume of the Atlantic slave trade in particular places at particular times, and some of these historians, coming upon data which do not match with Curtin's figures, have been extremely critical of them. But this is to mistake his purpose, which was simply to get a better idea of the volume of the Atlantic slave trade, both in total and in its various aspects and phases, than the almost totally unsubstantiated estimates that had previously been uncritically accepted by scholars (including the present writer) who ought to have known better. In this, Curtin certainly succeeded. Over nearly two decades, the work of many 'dig-deepers' has demonstrated that some of his figures may have been too small, but overall his underestimates have been balanced by other figures that seem to have been too high. The result of the work done since the publication of Curtin's book – which in 1982 was conveniently summarized and interpreted by Professor Paul E. Lovejoy – has been to provide revised estimates which in grand total arrive at much the same result as that produced by Curtin. The main trends of the trade as discerned in 1982 are set out in Table 1.

Table 1   *Estimated numbers of African slaves landed overseas by European traders**

	to Old World destinations		to the Americas		totals
	totals	annual average	totals	annual average	
1451–1525	76 000	1 000			
1526–50	31 300	1 200	12 500	500	
1551–75	26 300	1 000	34 700	1 400	
1576–1600	16 300	600	96 000	3 800	293 000
1601–25	12 800	500	249 000	10 000	
1626–50	6 600	300	236 000	9 500	
1651–75	3 000	120	368 000	15 000	
1676–1700	2 700	100	616 000	25 000	1 494 000
1701–20			626 000	31 000	
1721–40			870 000	43 000	
1741–60			1 007 000	50 000	
1761–80			1 148 000	57 000	
1781–1800			1 561 000	78 000	5 212 000
1801–20			980 000	49 000	
1821–67			1 803 000	38 000	2 783 000
totals	175 000		9 607 000		9 782 000

* The sources for this table are Philip D. Curtin, *The Atlantic Slave Trade: A Census* (1969), especially his Tables 33 and 34, and Paul E. Lovejoy, 'The volume of the Atlantic slave trade: a synthesis', *Journal of African History*, vol. 23 (1982) pp. 473–501, especially his Tables 2–6. Lovejoy's book, *Transformations in Slavery: A History of Slavery in Africa* (1983), contains further information including, for example, estimates for the trans-Saharan, Red Sea and Indian Ocean export slave trades.

It must be emphasized that the figures in Table 1 are estimates for the numbers of Africans *landed overseas*, for the most part, of course, in the Americas. Such estimates are obviously relevant to the demographic history of the New World, but what those concerned with the history of African peoples want to know is how many men and women *left Africa*. Curtin worked primarily from figures for slaves landed overseas because he thought that by and large these were more reliable than those available for slaves shipped from Africa. Lovejoy accepted this up to 1700, but thereafter thought it feasible and better to use figures for slaves shipped from Africa. The figures given in Table 1 for the eighteenth and nineteenth centuries have therefore been calculated from Lovejoy's figures by allowing for an average loss of life en route of 15 per cent. The data available for these two centuries enables such an average to be calculated with some confidence. For earlier times, the loss of life at sea is likely to have been higher – though exactly how much higher is uncertain. But if the fairly conservative rate of loss of 20 per cent is assumed for times up to 1700, it is possible to suggest that the loss of people from Africa may have been of the order of the estimates given in Table 2.

Table 2 *Estimated numbers of men and women taken from Africa by the Atlantic trade*

	total exported	annual averages
1451–1601	367 000	
1601–1700	1 867 000	19 000
1701–1800	6 133 000	61 000
1801–1867	3 274 000	33 000
total	11 641 000	

This was undoubtedly one of the greatest population movements in history, and certainly the largest migration by sea before the great European emigration, also primarily to the Americas, which developed as the Atlantic slave trade was beginning to end. But it was not, of course, the only export of slaves from tropical Africa. For centuries Blacks had been taken northwards across the Sahara and down the Nile, and also across the Red Sea and the Indian Ocean. However, information on the numbers involved in these slave trades is nothing like as good as that for the Atlantic trade.

There is very little good quantitative data for the slave trade across the Sahara to North Africa. Such information as there is suggests that, although there is evidence of the presence of Blacks in North Africa in classical times, a systematic trans-Saharan slave trade on any scale probably did not develop until after the introduction of the camel and, more particularly, until after the Arab conquest of North Africa. The marching of men and women across a waterless desert must always have presented great problems, and prior to the ninth century it is thought unlikely that imports into North Africa can have averaged more than about 1000 a year. However from about the ninth century onwards there is evidence for an organized trans-Saharan trade in slaves.* The exiguous data available suggests that it may have averaged something like 6000 or 7000 slaves a year until the 1880s (after which it was rapidly extinguished), though with peaks in the tenth and eleventh centuries at about 8700 slave imports a year and in the first eighty years of the nineteenth century possibly as high as 14 500. Allowing for losses in transit and for slaves retained in Saharan societies, during the greater part of the period when the Atlantic trade was flourishing it is possible to suppose that an average of somewhere between 7000 and 9000 men and women a year could have been lost to Black Africa as a result of the trans-Saharan trade. A significantly greater rate of loss would have been incurred only in the first three-quarters of the nineteenth century (when the Atlantic trade was in decline). The trans-Saharan trade may therefore have in total removed from Black Africa almost as many people – some nine or ten millions – as did the Atlantic trade. If it be asked why such numbers appear to have made a much less obvious impact on the ethnic composition of the populations of North African and adjacent Near Eastern lands than was made on that of many American countries, it might be argued that a long-continuing infiltration of only a few thousand Blacks a year is unlikely to have led to such obvious results as the compression of the bulk of the Atlantic slave trade into little more than two recent centuries. Conversely it might be suggested that it would have been a good deal less damaging to the exporting populations in Black Africa. But more than numbers alone needs to be considered. While the slaves imported into the Americas were predominantly male, and efforts were commonly made to maintain a reservoir of black labour separate from white society, a large proportion of the slaves taken across the Sahara were female and were absorbed into the recipient populations as wives or concubines (and many of the younger males seem to have been converted into eunuchs). Therefore the Blacks taken across the Sahara would have been more easily assimilable than those taken to the Americas. In addition, the loss of potential wives and mothers would have made

* The data that follow, for the Red Sea and Indian Ocean slave trades as well for that across the Sahara, are based on Ralph A. Austen, 'The trans-Saharan slave trade: a tentative census', in Henry A. Gemery & Jan S. Hogendorn (eds), *The uncommon market* (1979), pp. 23–76, as modified by tables 7.1 and 7.7 in Lovejoy's book.

the demographic damage to Black African populations relatively greater than the numbers alone might suggest.

The export of slaves by sea from the Red Sea and Indian Ocean coasts seems to have been like the Atlantic trade in that the major volume of the exports was apparently concentrated in a relatively short and recent period. The quantitative data available are no better than those available for the trans-Saharan trade. The best estimates available suggest that from about A.D. 800 to 1700, exports to the Near and Middle East and to western India might have averaged about 3000 a year, with 2000 going from the Red Sea coast and the remainder from the Indian Ocean coast. In the 1700s it seems likely that the two coasts may have shared equally in a slave trade averaging about 4000 a year. It is generally agreed that the volume of the trade began to increase substantially from about the beginning of the nineteenth century, but there is argument as to the numbers that were actually exported. This is in large measure because a considerable but uncertain number of slaves brought down from the interior to the Indian Ocean coast were retained for employment on plantations in the coastlands and on the off-shore islands. The most reasonable estimate perhaps is that altogether something like 900 000 slaves may have been exported to Asian destinations in the nineteenth century, about half from the Red Sea coast and half from the Indian Ocean coast. By about the middle of the century, the growth was attracting the attention of the European interests that were then opposed to slave trading, with the result that increasingly effective measures were taken against it. The export of slaves from the Indian Ocean coast had virtually ceased by the 1870s, and by the 1890s the Red Sea trade had been reduced to a trickle.

The development of the Indian Ocean trade in the earlier nineteenth century coincides with a marked build-up of Omani power on the east coast which began towards the close of the previous century, and which culminated in 1840 in the removal of their major seat of government from Muscat to Zanzibar. With this, and backed with finance from Indian merchants resident at Zanzibar, there was associated a totally new development in which Arab-Swahili caravans went inland from the coast to the great lakes of East Africa and ultimately as far as the upper Congo. A principal cause of this seems to have been a growing European and Asian demand for ivory from East Africa, itself due in some measure to the demands of the rising European middle class for goods such as billiard balls and pianos, but also no doubt associated with the decline in exports of ivory from West Africa (which, via the European companies, had also traded with Asia, where African ivory was valued since it was better suited to carving than Asian ivory). But it is also clear that it was this new exploitation of trade routes from the east coast into the interior that made possible the great growth of the Indian Ocean slave trade from about 1800 onwards. Conversely, however, bearing in mind the previous absence of any such system of trade routes into the interior under the control of coastal merchants in the whole region between Somalia and the Zambezi, it is reasonable to conclude that the export of slaves from East Africa prior to 1800 was not on any very great scale. But for the first seventy or so years of the nineteenth century, exports of slaves from the Swahili coast seem likely to have averaged at least 6000 slaves a year, and for the first ninety years exports across the Red Sea seem likely to have averaged at least 5000 a year. In other words, for the greater part of the century slaves may have been exported to Asian destinations at the rate of at least 11 000 a year; some authorities would double this figure.

From the continental perspective, then, there would seem little question but that the significant period of the export slave trade in Africa runs from about the middle of the seventeenth century, when the Atlantic trade began to assume major dimensions, to about the middle of the nineteenth, after which the sea-borne slave trades were all rapidly extinguished. During this period of some 200 years, the evidence suggests that something like 14 000 000 men and women may have been taken out of Black Africa. The distribution through time would seem to have followed something like the following pattern:

Table 3 *Estimated totals of slaves exported from Black Africa, c. 1650–c. 1870*

	Atlantic trade	Saharan trade	Indian Ocean and Red Sea trades	totals	annual average
1651–1700	1 230 000	350 000	150 000	1 730 000	35 000
1701–1750	2 350 000	350 000	200 000	2 900 000	58 000
1751–1800	3 780 000	350 000	200 000	4 330 000	87 000
1801–c. 1870	3 270 000	1 015 000	770 000	5 055 000	72 000
totals	10 630 000	2 065 000	1 320 000	14 015 000	

The impact of these export trades obviously varied from one region of Black Africa to another. So far as the Atlantic trade was concerned, almost all the slaves were taken from the west coast, which was closest to the source of the demand in the Americas and was where Europeans had first established satisfactory trading relationships. It was only as the demand reached its peak towards the end of the eighteenth century, and when, in the nineteenth century, the measures taken against the Atlantic slave trade were initially concentrated north of the equator, that any significant numbers of slaves were taken by Europeans from eastern Africa – to the French plantations on the Mascarene islands as well as to America – and for these destinations together the total probably did not exceed 500 000. During the period of some 200 years when the export slave trades were at their height, West Africa north of the equator contributed something like 5 700 000 slaves to the Atlantic trade and must also have provided some proportion – possibly a half – of the 2 065 000 or so slaves exported across the Sahara. The other half would have been drawn from the eastern Sudan which, together with the Horn of Africa, would also have contributed something like 750 000 slaves to the Red Sea trade. South of the equator, Bantu Africa was divided between two slave-trading networks, feeding the Atlantic and the Indian Ocean systems respectively, the former taking about 4 550 000 slaves during these 200 years and the latter something like 750 000 (including slaves for the Mascarenes as well as for Asian lands, but excluding the substantial numbers retained for plantations on the east coast and its offshore islands).

While it is possible to construct broad estimates of the numbers of slaves exported between *c*. 1650 and *c*. 1870 from major regions such as the Sudan, West Africa or Bantu Africa, it is much more difficult to judge how each of such regions may have been affected by such a substantial depletion of its human resources. For one thing, we really have no idea how many other lives may have been lost in the business of securing slaves for export and in bringing them down to the coast. Such contemporary estimates as there are – for example the oft-quoted mid-nineteenth-century statement of David Livingstone that for every slave exported from east central Africa ten other human beings lost their lives – are hardly more than guesses. In Livingstone's case, it is reasonable to assume that his judgement was coloured both by the appalling scenes he had witnessed and by a compulsion to use his evidence to secure the maximum support for the European anti-slave trade campaign. It also needs to be appreciated that such estimates relate only to particular parts of Africa at particular points of time: in Livingstone's case it must be remembered that his travels were largely limited to the bands of territory within which the Arab–Swahili traders themselves moved. Neither the activities of these traders nor the overall environment in which they operated were necessarily typical of other regions or of other times. There can be no question but that weak or sick slaves could be killed or left to die along the trails that led to the coast, and that raids and wars were among the means used to secure slaves, thus occasioning further loss of life, whether directly, or indirectly through the destruction of crops, cattle and shelter or the spread of disease. But it is equally true that such destruction could result from natural disasters, such as drought or flood and pestilence, and that these natural disasters could also lead to slaves being provided for the trade – and to population fleeing to strengthen the resources of societies in more favourable environments (something which made it easier for them to acquire and trade in slaves).

It is frankly impossible to make any firm assessment of the total effect on Black Africa of the monstrous rape of its life, manpower and productivity by the export slave trades. Even the most elementary issue, namely the extent to which the export of slaves affected the size and growth of populations, cannot really be tackled, since usually nothing but the crudest estimates exist for the size of African populations, their rates of natural increase, or their geographical distribution, for any period before the present century.

For what it is worth, demographers, basing themselves on current data, have supposed that in 1650, when the Atlantic slave trade really began to take off, the population of the whole continent may have been about 100 000 000, and that up to that time it may have been growing at the low rate of 0.12 or 0.11 per cent per annum. South of the Sahara, Black Africa is unlikely to have had more than four-fifths of the total population, so when the export slave trades began to reach their peak, the affected population would have been at most 80 000 000. An annual natural increase, i.e. an excess of birth over deaths, of 0.11 per cent, i.e. of about 88 000, would have been well above the 35 000 which has been suggested as the estimated mean annual loss due directly to the export slave trades in the second half of the seventeenth century. On the other hand, the estimated mean annual direct losses suggested for the second half of the eighteenth century and the first half of the nineteenth – 87 000 and 72 000 respectively – seem to have been of the same order of magnitude as the estimated annual natural increase. Indeed, the demographers assume that during 1650–1800 the population of the continent as a whole remained static at around 100 000 000. By implication, therefore, they must also suppose that the indirect loss of life due to slave trading was fairly minimal.*

Of course the incidence of the export slave trades was not felt uniformly through sub-Saharan Africa. There was, for instance, the important difference – already indicated – between the trade conducted by Christian Europeans to the Americas and the Muslim-conducted trades to North African and Asian lands, namely that the former preferred to acquire men rather than women, and also adults rather than children, while with the latter the preferences tended to be reversed. It is known that the ratio of men to women exported by the Atlantic trade averaged about 2 to 1, and something like the reverse of this ratio may be relevant to the Muslim trades. The consequence, bearing in mind that African societies were polygynous, was that the capacity for making good losses inflicted by an export slave trade would be higher where the trade was to the Americas than where it was to North Africa or Asia. Furthermore, of course, not all regions were equally touched by export slave trades, while some societies were more able than others to resist damage from a slave trade – or, indeed, to profit from it. In West Africa, for instance, there had been an essential continuity of population and population growth, and of social, economic and cultural evolution, ever since its inhabitants had embarked on agriculture and metallurgy some two or more millennia before the period of greatest slave-trading. Its societies, in Guinea as well as in the western Sudan, had commonly been accustomed to coping with – and trying to profit from – the demands of foreign traders before such traders came to demand slaves in any numbers. It may therefore be presumed that they were able to organize their affairs so as to minimize damage from slave trading. But to the east and south of the Cameroons, a new departure had been made with the coming of the Bantu-speakers who, for the most part, were the intro-

---

* See, for example, Colin Clark, *Population Growth and Land Use* (1967). After 1800, the demographers postulate an increasingly rapid growth of population, with a mean rate of annual increase of 0.19 per cent for the nineteenth century as a whole, until in the twentieth century one comes to the growth rates of around 3 per cent per annum that are now established for many African countries.

ducers of agriculture and metal-working. Except in so far as the north-western Bantu had been able to maintain some cultural and economic continuity with nearby West Africa, and had also shared with it in the earliest expansion of European trade, and the people of a narrow band along the east coast and around the Zambezi valley had been touched by Indian Ocean trade, Bantu Africa had also been largely remote from outside trade or influence until it began to experience the dramatic increases in the Atlantic and Indian Ocean demands for slaves. It may be supposed, therefore, that it should have been more seriously affected by them. Yet there is some evidence, from Congo and Angola for example, to show that some affected populations did not decline in numbers, or that the combined effects of drought, famine and disease were as or more important than the export slave trade in restraining population growth.

For sub-Saharan Africa as a whole, perhaps only three generaliz-ations are possible. First, that the export of people to other parts of the world, together with the concomitant indirect losses of life involved in slaving, was obviously a major constraint on population growth (though the further generalization that these things actually led to widespread depopulation needs closer examination). Secondly, that it was essentially through the slave trade that sub-Saharan African societies were first brought into contact with the rapid changes that were occurring in the modern world as a consequence of the rise of western European economic power. Thirdly, that the combined effects of this enforced emigration of people and of this new contact with the outside world were a major force for change in Black Africa, and by the end of the eighteenth century and the beginning of the nine-teenth, when export slaving reached its peak, probably *the* major force for change.

Chapter 11

West Africa during the slave trade era

In West Africa it seems unlikely that the export slave trade would have had any dramatically adverse effect on the size of the population as a whole. The crucial period would have been the eighteenth century, for which it has been estimated that on average something like 38 000 people a year were being taken from the coasts between the Senegal and the Cameroons plus perhaps up to another 4000 across the Sahara. Though such an estimate can only be very rough, it does not seem that a loss of population of this order need have been excessively damaging. The present-day population and growth rates suggest that in 1700 the population of West Africa cannot have been much less than about 25 000 000. Excesses of births over deaths may have been about 0.15 per cent per annum at the beginning of the century, and nearer 0.19 per cent at the end. Since 42 000 is 0.17 per cent of 25 000 000, the direct loss of population due to the slave trade during the eighteenth century seems unlikely to have done much more than halt population growth. For other periods the demographic effect would have been relatively slighter.

This is a very crude calculation indeed, but in the absence of much in the way of direct information about West African populations during the slave trade era, not much can be done to refine it. However, some points can be made. For example, it is known that women constituted only about a third of the slaves taken to the Americas. It is also the case that African men who could afford it were polygynous. Therefore the number of births may not have been as much reduced as would have been the case had the European settlers in the Americas taken as many women slaves as they took men. On the other hand, of course, they looked for fit slaves in the prime of life, which was thought to lie between the ages of about twelve and thirty-five for men and about twelve and twenty-five for women. It may therefore be argued that the Atlantic slave trade attacked the stratum of the population that was biologically (and also economically) the most active and productive. However, as will be seen, it looks as though many West African authorities were quite well aware of this danger. For example, the narratives of the European slave traders are full of warnings against buying slaves who had been doctored and prepared so as to conceal deficiencies due to age or ill-health. It might also be argued that the demand for slaves for export led to an increase in warfare and raiding, and hence to an increased destruction of life, and of the property, production and general security needed to sustain life and growth. But again, as will be seen, this is at least open to question.

It is obvious that the average annual rate of loss for the eighteenth century could conceal substantial departures from the average, so that there might have been periods when the pressure of slave exports on the population was appreciably greater than the average would suggest. To some extent, this was so. The acceleration in slave exports which had begun in the previous century continued until about 1740, and some decline is evident after the 1780s. But taking the century as a whole, the maximum variation from the average is only about 25 per cent, and by and large it is the consistency in the annual figures, especially from the 1740s onwards, rather than any variations in them, which strikes the attention. Together with the conclusion on the following point, this seems to be a factor of some significance.

It is also obvious that the export of slaves need not have been evenly distributed over the whole length of the coastline, so that some parts of West Africa could have been more seriously affected than the overall figures might suggest. However there is evidence that the numbers of slaves exported from each part of the coast tended to be related to the size of the population from which they came. Thus as the demand increased, it was met by taking more slaves from the coasts to the east of the Gold Coast. Except in special circumstances like those created by the *jihad* in Futa Jalon, the contribution to the trade from Upper Guinea tended to decline. There seems little doubt why this was so. In modern times, that part of West Africa east of a line corresponding more or less to the western boundary of modern Ghana (i.e. the old Gold Coast) extended northwards to meet the Niger and the Sahara at Timbuctu, though very much the same size as the area to the west of this line, contains something like two and a half times as many people. (In the 1950s, for example, the overall population density of the six political units in the eastern half was about thirty persons to the square mile, as compared with about twelve for the eight countries in the western half.) Indeed, the coastlands and immediate hinterlands of the eastern half, i.e. of Lower Guinea, contain some of the most densely populated areas in all tropical Africa. Densities as high as 700 or more persons to the square mile can be found among the Ibo and Tiv in the hinterland of the Niger delta, and not far short of these in Yoruba and Aja country. The available evidence suggests that this contrast between Upper and Lower Guinea is not a new development, but that it was also characteristic of the slave trade era. It is also significant that the coastlands of Lower Guinea, the homelands of the Akan, Aja, Yoruba and Benin peoples, had much higher levels of economic and political development than were generally to be met with in the Upper Guinea coastlands (where, by and large, major economic and political initiatives were the preserve of immigrant traders and settlers from the Sudan). They also had good commercial connections with similar areas of high population and economic and political development in the interior.

In general, it seems permissible to infer that West African communities sold slaves for export with some regard to their capacity to do so without causing serious damage to their populations and economies and their chances of growth. It would seem that, as the slave trade developed on each particular segment of the coast, so commonly a level of exports was quite soon reached which thereafter was rarely exceeded, and usually only when the political or military situation was an unusual one. This may be substantiated from the estimates given in Table 4 for slaves exported from various West African regions in the eighteenth century.*

It should be appreciated that, whereas in the earliest days of the export slave trade from West Africa, Europeans had occasionally captured some of the slaves themselves, by the eighteenth century it

---

* These data are adapted from Table 3.4 in Paul E. Lovejoy, *Transformations in Slavery: A History of Slavery in Africa* (1983). The principal differences between it and the equivalent table in the first edition (which was based on Table 66 in Curtin's *The Atlantic Slave Trade*) are that it covers shipments in Portuguese and Dutch ships as well as in English and French vessels, and that, following the criticisms by Adam Jones and Marion Johnson (*Journal of African History*, vol. 21, pp. 17–34) of Curtin's allocation of exports to a 'Windward Coast' between Sierra Leone and the Gold Coast, these exports have been reallocated between the Sierra Leone region, the Gold Coast and the Slave Coast (see Lovejoy's note to his table).

Table 4   *A regional distribution of eighteenth-century slave exports from West Africa (estimates only)*

Coastal region	Early peak		Subsequent decades with average numbers of slaves exported in them		Decades with exports in excess of early peak
	Decade	Slaves exported			
Senegambia	1711–20	30 900	8	19 000	0
Sierra Leone	1761–70	108 100*	3	62 500	0
Gold Coast	1741–50	91 400	5	71 200	1
Slave Coast	1711–20	169 300	8	118 500	0
Bight of Biafra	1791–1800	185 400	0	—	—

* The 1760s exports from the Sierra Leone region seem to have been unusually large, no doubt as a consequence of the Futa Jalon *jihad*. The previous peak, in the 1740s was 45 200; the figure for the 1770s is 82 000, and for the 1780s 47 200.

was extremely unusual for slaves to be procured other than by purchase from the established African rulers or from merchants who were themselves often operating under some kind of royal licence or control. In effect these Africans seem to have been consciously or unconsciously weighing up whether their interest would be better served by concentrating exclusively on building up the local labour force, or by exchanging some of it for the commodities which were offered for sale by the Europeans. These were essentially manufactures, such as cloth, metals and hardware, which European industrial technologies could produce more cheaply and efficiently with less labour than could West Africa, or such as muskets, which West Africa did not produce at all, but which were valued as emblems of power, or as means by which more labour could be procured (for domestic use as well as for export) and agricultural productivity increased (by keeping down wild animals and birds). There are in fact at least two instances in which one can almost see a ruling group making its choice. As has been seen, the kings of Benin decided as early as 1516 that it was not in their interests to allow an uncontrolled export of slaves. Towards the end of the seventeenth century, however, the controls were relaxed. Presumably this was because by this time the politico-economic structure of the kingdom was thought to be suffering compared with those of its neighbours by its relative lack of trade with the Europeans, or simply because the rising demand for slaves in the Americas had increased the relative value of the goods offered in exchange for them. Secondly, in 1727–8, King Agaja of Dahomey, apparently trying to increase his and his kingdom's returns from the slave trade, took steps which had the inadvertent result of temporarily diminishing the number of slaves purchased by the European traders. But by the time of his successor Tegbesu, who came to power in 1740, the trade had increased again: slaves were the only significant resource Dahoman kings could command to secure the goods, such as muskets and gunpowder, which they wanted from the Europeans.

Rather less than half of the slaves supplied from West Africa to European traders seem to have come from the societies that sold them. They might broadly be termed the 'unfortunates' in those societies, men and women who had become outcasts from the close-knit system of interdependence provided by the extended family, who had offended against persons of position and power, or who simply had no kin or friends of influence to prevent their being kidnapped and sold, and they included those who had been convicted of crimes or of adultery or witchcraft, debtors and those who had already been sold or pledged to a creditor in respect of a debt, and men and women who had some mental or physical deficiency. The remainder had been taken from other societies by force, sometimes in raids specifically organized for the purpose, but more commonly because they had been captured in war. All such people could be retained as slaves by those who had captured, bought or condemned them. Alternatively they might be executed (if they were criminals or prisoners of war) or used as human sacrifices in an ancestral or land cult, or they could be offered for sale to other Africans or to Europeans who wanted to purchase slaves.

Quite a lively debate developed among Europeans as to whether these processes of enslavement, and especially warfare, were deliberately exploited to procure slaves and, more specifically, slaves for the Atlantic slave trade. In the nineteenth century, in particular, the anti-slave-trade interest claimed that they were. From this it was originally argued that the abolition of the Atlantic trade would bring considerable benefit to African societies, enabling them to concentrate on more peaceful and productive pursuits. Then, when the cessation of the export slave trade apparently brought no diminution of African slavery, slave raids and wars, their continuance was used as an argument justifying European conquest and colonial rule. Earlier, however, in the eighteenth century, there were some European slave traders who held that enslavement and warfare were natural features of West African society (and, indeed, went on to claim that Europeans were actually doing a service to the cause of humanity by rescuing the victims!).

In fact both parties were slanting the evidence to suit their own interest. The basic factor underlying all African attitudes, not only to slavery and slave trading, but to any form of economic activity, was that people were a very scarce resource in relation to cultivable land and other resources, such as mineral deposits. In comparison with most other parts of sub-Saharan Africa, West Africa was in fact comparatively well endowed with people, but even so, an estimated population in 1700 of 25 000 000 would represent an overall population density of only about twelve persons to the square mile. This is about the same density of population as there was in western Europe in the high middle ages about the eleventh century. In the particular circumstances of western Europe, the key to economic and political survival and to subsequent development lay through what is called feudalism. Africa, in somewhat different historical circumstances, evolved systems of dependence which were not all that different, but for which the word 'slavery' is most commonly used.

In a situation in which there was an abundance of land but a scarcity of people, traditional village societies based on ties of kinship and engaged in subsistence agriculture were unable to take advantage of all the opportunities arising when they were touched by growing external demands for scarce and valuable commodities such as gold, salt, copper or ivory. There was a shortage of people available to act as traders and carriers, to work in the mines, to provide the political organization and military security to enable trade to flow freely, or to provide food and other support for those withdrawn from the subsistence sector to engage in these new activities. The solution lay in the emergence of kings powerful enough to impress labour and to secure tribute; and the growth of monarchies, with their courts and the craftsmen, officials, priests and soldiers serving the needs of their courts and governments, meant that the process of converting ordinary men and women into slaves, clients or tributaries was further accelerated.

Europeans have tended to view this process in the light of their own experience as the exploiters of African slaves in the Americas. In West Africa, some slaves were employed simply as agricultural labourers – and sometimes in conditions of considerable hardship – on the estates of kings and other great men. But more generally they were regarded as additions to the social group headed by their master and, although they could never wholly escape the stigma of their slave origin, in course of time they and their descendants – especially if these came by marriage with a free member of the group – became integral members of it, acquiring or inheriting property much like other members. At the lowest levels, then, they became members of the family unit. At the highest levels they could become trusted traders or soldiers or court officials; indeed, they sometimes seem to have been preferred for the important roles, because their slave status or origin meant that their authority was solely a reflection of their master's authority, so that theoretically they could not usurp it for themselves.

The prime importance of slaves then was not as articles of commerce, but as means by which larger and more effective units of population might be created than resulted simply from kinship ties. In West Africa, as has been seen, the evidence suggests that this mobilization of scarce human resources, and the attendant politicization of society, was first evident in the Sudan in association with the growth of trans-Saharan trade, and that it was subsequently extended into Guinea as the practice of long-distance trading was itself extended. In one important respect, the growth of political authority served economic or commercial needs more directly than might be supposed. Where communications were indifferent, money scarce, and an indigenous trading community only beginning to emerge, one of the best means of accumulating a surplus of produce in one place that was sufficient to attract foreign traders, was by levying tribute on the surrounding peoples.

If there were no viable alternative, then tribute could be levied in people, and slaves might then be exchanged for the desirable goods brought by long-distance traders. But in general slaves (and clients and other dependants) were valued less as trade goods themselves, than as a resource which needed to be accumulated to produce goods for export, and to support the economic and political superstructures needed for trade to flourish. The prime motive for warfare and raiding in Africa, then, was not to secure slaves for sale and export, but to secure adequate quantities of this resource and to diminish the amounts available to rivals.

But in this process of change, men and women acquired an economic value which had been inconceivable before, when they were not thought of as individuals, but rather as the component elements of kinship-based social groupings. Now, not only had these social atoms become splittable, but an individual man, a slave, tended to become the yardstick by which other resources – horses, guns, parcels of trade goods, quantities of agricultural produce – were measured. While in Europe from about the fourteenth century onwards the wealth of a kingdom was commonly assessed in terms of the amount of bullion it could command, so in West Africa from much the same time it was assessed in terms of its numbers of people. Because they had a measurable economic value, these people could be disposed of if it was thought the national interest would gain as a result. Thus, just as a mercantilist European state was prepared, for example, to exchange gold or silver for Asian spices with the expectation that it might regain more gold or silver by selling these spices to other Europeans who had no access to the Asian markets (perhaps because the state used its strength to prevent such access), so a successful African kingdom which itself had accumulated relatively large stocks of people was prepared to dispose of some of them to secure the goods which its ruling class valued, especially if these goods enabled it to increase its power at the expense of its rivals, and so to replenish its manpower. Horses, in the Sudan, and muskets, in Guinea, could fulfil this role very directly; cheap cloth, metals and hardware did so indirectly by increasing the recipient kingdom's inland trading potential.

Thus on the Guinea coast, as slaves became far and away the commodity most in demand among the European traders, the West African ruling and merchant classes organized themselves to export slaves to their own maximum advantage, balancing the expenditure of their most valuable resource against the concurrent rewards, including that of being better able to replace their loss of people. The balance was most readily achieved by the complex of kingdoms from the Gold Coast to Benin, where state formation was already well advanced, and where fruitful trading relations had already been established with the interior and with earlier European traders on the coast. In Upper Guinea, the results were more tenuous. The Grain and Ivory Coasts remained thinly populated forest lands in which political and economic organization was slow to develop. Further west and north, population still tended to be thin, and the new trade had to compete with the long-established trading system of the westernmost Sudan. Its main beneficiaries were immigrant Mande and Fulani traders and political adventurers from the Sudan, who did not have much care for the interests of the local societies, and time was needed before viable new political and economic units could emerge under their control.

In many ways the most spectacular developments occurred in and around the Niger delta between Benin and the Cameroons. The coastal mangrove swamps of this region were an impossible environment for agriculture, and on the sandspits besides the many coastal inlets, resourceful members of peoples like the Ijaw and the Efik had come to develop villages which lived by canoe fishing and trading. They could exchange some of their fish for the agricultural and other produce of the interior, and their mastery of the river network of the delta also enabled them to engage profitably in a variety of transit trades, from east to west as well as from north to south. As early as c. 1500, if Pacheco Pereira is to be believed, one at least of these villages, probably the modern Bonny, had developed into a community of some 2000 dwellings. Thus when Europeans came in search of slaves, this was already a mobile, commercially minded and outward looking society. Moreover the river network it commanded gave easy access to the exceptionally densely populated country of the Ibo. The archaeological evidence from Igbo-Ukwu suggests that the Ibo had early achieved considerable economic sophistication. This could well have encouraged population growth and the over-exploitation of a not very good natural environment, one with poor soils and a shortage of water, and so to hold back – or perhaps to undermine – political growth. In the twentieth century, the Ibo sought to solve their problems by a great investment in western education and by emigrating to seek jobs all over Nigeria. In the later eighteenth and early nineteenth centuries, they provided an apparently inexhaustible reservoir of slave labour.

From what is known about the organization of Ibo trade at this time, it would seem that a principal role in it was taken by the Aro. At Arochuku, about sixty miles from the sea and close by the Cross river, the Aro possessed an oracle which commanded universal respect among their fellow Ibo. Reinforcing its authority by the recruitment of mercenary soldiers, they were able to establish a network of trading settlements throughout Iboland. One result was that by the end of the eighteenth century, one European observer thought that three-quarters of the slaves exported from Bonny, one of the principal delta ports, were of Ibo origin.

The general effects in Guinea of the growth of the Atlantic slave trade were of two kinds, those due to its particular character as a trade in people, and those due to the fact that the continuing growth in this demand for people spearheaded a great increase both in the volume of major trading activities, and in the number of people and the extent of territory involved in such activities. The growing American demand for African slaves meant that many more European traders were active on the West African coast than before, and that there was a comparable increase in African trading activity. Each side was eager to make profits wherever there was opportunity to do so. Gold, gum, timber, hides and palm oil either remained or became of interest to European merchants, and these also needed to buy substantial quantities of foodstuffs to provide for their slaves during the Atlantic crossing. On the African side, the production or collection, and the transport of all these things needed to be organized, and so too did the distribution and retailing of the European goods received in exchange. It has sometimes been argued that the increasing imports of European goods like cloth, metals and metalware, and spirits undermined indigenous African economic activities and was socially deleterious. But there is considerable evidence that Africans were often discriminating in their purchases. It is probably more to the point to argue that they bought only those goods which they regarded as better value than their own products, and that the net result was an increase, not a decrease, in African production and economic activity generally.* There was probably also an increase in general living standards, even though new distinctions were being made between rich and poor, haves and have-nots. Thus the increase in imports of Indian, European or American cloth meant that more people could afford to clothe themselves rather than that local manufacture ceased (or, so far as there is evidence, declined).

Using as yardsticks the average numbers of slaves exported from Guinea at the beginning of the eighteenth century (say 30 000) and when the export slave trade was at its height towards the end of the

---

* The major criterion seems to have been comparative labour cost. African iron-smelting, for example, was a laborious and time-consuming process. It sometimes ended up with the destruction of the smelting furnace, so that a new one had to be constructed when more raw iron was needed. A great amount of labour was also involved in forging the raw metal into usable forms. In the manufacture of cloth, a wholly disproportionate amount of labour was involved in spinning enough yarn to keep a single weaver fully occupied. There is evidence that as early as the sixteenth century, West Africans were buying second-hand European cloth to unravel to obtain cheap yarn for their own weavers. Thus by importing part-processed materials from Europe, African metal and cloth workers could concentrate on blacksmithing and weaving respectively, and so produce more goods at less cost in labour.

century (say 50 000), and the average nominal value of the trade goods exchanged for a slave at these times (say £15 ($75) and £25 ($125) respectively), and assuming that no more than a quarter of European trade was in commodities other than slaves, it is reasonable to suppose that the combined value of Guinea's exports and imports by sea, which would have been negligible prior to 1500, might have reached a sum of the order of about £1 200 000 ($6 000 000) a year by the beginning of the eighteenth century, and of about £3 400 000 ($17 000 000) a year during the peak period of the slave trade towards the end of that century.*

A threefold increase in foreign trade on the Guinea coasts during the eighteenth century must have acted as a considerable stimulus to indigenous commercial activity. One index of this was the spread of regular systems of currency. Currencies appear early in the European accounts of Guinea (and, for that matter, in the even earlier Arabic accounts of the West African Sudan), and it seems certain that they were essentially indigenous creations. But the growth of trade ensured that in each major commercial area, a single currency became the accepted money of account – for example, iron bars in Upper Guinea and also in much of the Niger delta, cowrie shells on the Slave Coast and gold-dust on the Gold Coast – and that regular exchange rates became established where these currencies met with each other and with European moneys of account.

Another feature was the emergence of a new class of men to which the term 'merchant princes' is commonly applied. These were men, often of humble, indeed sometimes of slave origin, who had used their commercial acumen to break out from some of the restrictions of traditional communal society, to accumulate personal wealth and clients and slaves bound to them alone, and sometimes, indeed, to use these things to achieve positions of power rivalling those of the traditional kings and courts. This class was naturally most in evidence on or close by the coast, and a good deal is known about such figures as John Kabes of Komenda (*fl. c.* 1683–1720), John Konny of Ahanta (*fl.* 1711–24) and Edward Barter (*fl. c.* 1690–1702) of Cape Coast, to name only Gold Coast examples. Such men could also arise in interior countries. One example whose career has recently been investigated is Jibril Dobla, the leading trader in Dagomba at the end of the

---

* These are not inconsiderable figures by the standards of the eighteenth century. Thus in 1760, on the eve of her major industrialization, Britain, then the major trading nation of western Europe, had foreign trade officially valued at £13 500 000.

eighteenth century, and a considerable figure in political competition in that kingdom. Jibril was a Muslim of Hausa origin, and on the coast, as the names quoted above may suggest, the new men made intelligent use of the opportunities presented by the European presence. They often began their careers in the service of European traders, acquiring some European education in the process: thus Barter had visited England. Some European traders had settled more or less permanently on the coast and, through their marriages with local women, established families which remained important in commercial and political life into the twentieth century. One such was the Brew family on the Gold Coast, another the Olympios who produced the first president of the modern Republic of Togo. On the Slave Coast, indeed, a whole new intermediary class emerged, the so-called Brazilians, some of part Portuguese descent, but many pure-blooded Africans who had returned from slavery in Brazil and established themselves in coastal society and trade. Whatever their origins, the strength of the new class lay in its ability to make the best of two worlds, exploiting family links with African society on the one hand, and on the other ensuring that they could deal with the Europeans on an equal basis, often by sending their sons to be educated in Europe.*

Nowhere was social change due to the growth of trade more in evidence than in the region extending from the Niger delta to the Cross river. Here the original fishing villages by the mouths of the rivers that led into the interior grew in size and wealth until they were nothing less than city-states controlled by oligarchies composed of the leading traders. The key to the growth of these states, as also to individual wealth and power, lay in the acquisition of the considerable quantities of slaves that were needed to man the trading canoes and to fill a growing number of other commercial, political, military and productive roles. Ultimately the kinship structure of society was in many respects replaced by a system of wards, or 'Houses', in which large groups of people of varying origins, both freemen and slaves, were bound together by economic self-interest, and whose leaders would compete with one another for the major offices of the state. This was an environment in which individuals could advance almost irrespective of their original status in society. Thus in the nineteenth century, an Ibo slave, Ja Ja, became head of one of the Houses at

* The first West African known to have graduated from a European university is Anton Wilhelm Amo, a Nzima from the western Gold Coast, who during 1727–40 studied at Halle and Wittenberg, and also lectured at these universities and at Jena.

Bonny, one of the principal states of the delta. Under his leadership, this House became so successful that the other Houses had to fight to preserve their independence. When, finally, they secured the expulsion of Ja Ja and his people, these established nearby the rival trading state of Opobo, which then went on to take away much of Bonny's trade.

But the Niger delta situation was virtually unique in that, at the beginning of the commercial revolution brought about by the Atlantic slave trade, society was already considerably dependent on trade, and was led by men who, as traders themselves, could turn the new conditions to advantage. Elsewhere on the coast the effect of the growth of trade, and of contacts with European society in some of its more aggressive and individualistic aspects, was rather to dissolve the bonds which held African communities together, and to create dangerous new tensions between the new men and the traditional authorities. This process was exacerbated by the competition and rivalry between the various groups of European merchants and their African allies. The coastal states, hitherto on the remotest fringe of the major areas of economic and political change, which were in the Sudan, tended anyway to be small and limited in their resources. Sometimes they split into still smaller units, as when, at the end of. the seventeenth century, John Kabes quarrelled both with the traditional king of Komenda and with the Dutch, the major traders there, and set himself up as an independent power aligned with the English interest. More widely, the traditional authorities began to lose their power to control the situation, and society began to dissolve into an anarchic free for all.

This undoubtedly facilitated an expansion in the local slave trade: more people were kidnapped, or accused of crime or adultery or witchcraft, or arraigned for debt, and so sold into slavery, than was normal. But it also created difficulties for inland peoples who had acquired an interest in trade with the coast. It became difficult for them to send their merchants down to the coast in security; difficult, indeed, for them to establish any stable and mutually beneficial relations with the coastal communities. Their social and political systems, on the other hand, were not subject to the cankers affecting the coastal peoples; rather the increase of trade was presenting their authorities with an increased range of opportunities. The traditional rulers remained in command of the situation and in control of trade. Skilful princes and their commercial henchmen or associates were able to exploit the new opportunities as those of the Sudan had done before them, so that their kinship groups acquired more slaves and clients and wealth than others, with the result that their power could be exercised over wider areas than before, and the numbers of their slaves and clients and tributaries still further enlarged.

This pattern of change has been well studied for the Akan peoples in the forest lands behind the Gold Coast. During the first half of the seventeenth century, the new opportunities arising from the growth of trade at and with the coast would seem to have stimulated intense competition among ambitious princelings of the Akany-Twifu region. By about 1660, those of Denkyira had succeeded in imposing their control over many of the peoples of this important gold-bearing area, and they went on to build an empire northwards along the historic trade routes leading to Banda and Bono. Until the 1670s, Denkyira was content to trade with the Europeans via intermediaries. But her kings then turned to conquer states lying between them and the sea, so that by the end of the century they had acquired a paramountcy over the whole western Gold Coast and its hinterland.

By this time the rival empire of Akwamu had arisen on the eastern Gold Coast, led by another group of men who had at one time been associated with the Akany-Twifu area, but who had by 1629 established themselves in the hinterland of Accra, with their capital about forty miles from the sea. The land here was by no means devoid of gold resources, but they were less concentrated than they were further west, and Akwamu had to compete for them with the states of Akyem, on its eastern border. The ambitions of the Akwamu kings therefore became concentrated more on securing control of as many as possible of the paths leading from the coast into the interior along which trade with the Europeans was conducted. The competition with Akyem limited their success to the west. But during 1677–81 they conquered Accra, hitherto the major kingdom on the eastern Gold Coast, and thus secured direct access to and overlordship of the Dutch, English and Danish forts on its coast, and they then continued until, by 1702, the whole slave-exporting coast eastwards to close by Whydah had been brought under their control or influence.

The competition which developed between Denkyira and Akwamu (and, to a lesser extent, the Akyem kings) for control of Gold Coast empire and trade, led quite quickly to their downfall and to the emergence of the new super-power of Ashanti, which was to dominate practically all the territory of modern Ghana until its conquest by the British at the end of the nineteenth century. The origins of Ashanti again lie with developments in the nuclear Akan forest area of Akany and Twifu. The seventeenth-century growth of population and economic and political competition here would seem to have induced six or seven small kinship groups to emigrate towards the north central area of the Gold Coast forest, where a number of trade paths from the coast tended to converge and join with the major trade routes from the western and central Sudan which were operated by Mande-Dyula and Hausa merchants respectively. Here the emigrants settled down, conquered and absorbed local Akan peoples, and erected a number of petty kingdoms. The need for mutual support against hostile strangers and to resist the exactions of Denkyira, which shortly forced them to become its tributaries, led these small Ashanti states into closer combination. Eventually, towards the end of the seventeenth century, they came together in a permanent union in which all the other kings accepted the supremacy of the king of the state of Kumasi. Rituals and ceremonies were established to ensure that henceforward he and his heirs were to be not only *Kumasihene* (king of Kumasi), but also *Asantehene*. The other kings remained supreme in their own states, but the kings of Kumasi became the accepted guardians of a wider national interest, even if it was difficult to pursue this in practice without the concurrence and support of the other kings, who acted as the supreme political and military council.

The first *Asantehene* was Osei Tutu (*fl. c.* 1680–?1717). It is significant that, as a young man and a potential heir to the Kumasi kingship, he had been sent to serve at the court of Denkyira; that, following an indiscretion there, he then went to spend some time at the court of Akwamu; and that it was from Akwamu, and with Akwamu political and military support, that he had acceded to power in Ashanti. He and his advisers obviously gained a great deal from these early associations. Ashanti military organization and tactics were based on Akwamu experience; while perhaps the prime lesson from Denkyira was of the importance of not being too over-bearing towards conquered peoples. In the war of liberation which Osei Tutu directed against Denkyira in 1698–1701, while Ashanti received arms and other support from Akwamu, Denkyira's tributaries deserted her. She found it difficult to get supplies of muskets and powder from the coast and, once she had been defeated, her empire dissolved overnight, leaving Ashanti unchallenged as the major power in the western forestlands.

Osei Tutu (or possibly, his successor)* was killed in 1717 in a war with Akyem, which alone among the southern Gold Coast states had supported Denkyira during 1698–1701. A factor in this disaster seems to have been treachery on the part of a contingent from Akwamu, which was doubtless concerned at the growth in power of what had originally been a junior ally. As a result, Ashanti did not intervene to help Akwamu when it was attacked from Akyem in 1730. Akwamu suffered a serious defeat, following which its empire immediately broke up into a congeries of petty kingdoms. In the more westerly of these, Akyem influence was of major importance, but any growth of an Akyem empire to replace that of Akwamu was prevented both by disunity among the Akyem leaders and by Ashanti campaigns against them during the 1740s.

However, initially, the main aim of Ashanti's external policy was to secure control over the major trade routes and the resources of people in its hinterland. Bono had been conquered and absorbed in 1724. Then, when further progress towards the north-west was checked by the growth of Dyula political power, Ashanti established a stable relationship with the Hausa trading system in the north-east, overrunning Gonja and subjecting the Dagomba kingdom to a protectorate. But Ashanti also needed a stable relationship with the coastlands and with the European traders there if it were to gain the maximum benefit from this sizeable empire. Occasional punitive campaigns against southern states did not give Ashanti traders the security they required, the more so as these campaigns were leading the Fante states of the central Gold Coast, which had the most closely developed relations with the European traders, to come together – with some European support – in a federation designed to resist Ashanti pressures. In 1765, then, there took place the first major Ashanti invasion of the coastlands. The Fante states survived this, but it achieved the important result of splitting the European interest. While the British by and large preferred to stand by their Fante trading partners, the Dutch, losing ground to the British in the coastal trade, began to believe that their best recourse might be to accept Ashanti as the paramount African power and to concentrate on developing their relations with it. When in 1806–07, Ashanti armies finally overran the Fante states, they came into direct confrontation with the

* Professors Priestley and Wilks have argued that Osei Tutu died in 1712, and that it was his successor who was killed in battle in 1717 – and, as a result, deliberately forgotten by Ashanti tradition.

Above A San Bushmen rock painting showing an encounter between them and the Bantu. The Bushmen are the small men, armed with bows and arrows, on the left, who are apparently trying to make off with cattle they have taken from the Bantu. The latter, the tall black men armed with spears and shields, are chasing after the raiders.

Below A Saharan rock engraving of a horse-drawn chariot driven by a warrior with a lance.

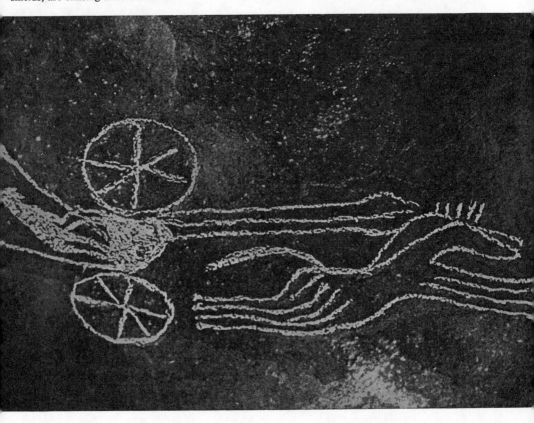

The pyramids of Gizeh, near the modern Cairo.

Some of the pyramids of ancient Meroe.

Above left A terracotta head from the Nok culture.

Above A terracotta head from ancient Ife.

Left One of the brass or bronze plaques that once adorned the royal palace at Benin City. This one represents a Portuguese officer. Note the holes at the top by which the plaque was fixed.

Two views of Great Zimbabwe. *Above* A general view of some of the Valley Ruins, with the great Elliptical Building prominent at top right. *Below* Part of the wall of the Elliptical Building, showing chevron decoration towards the top.

British, and from this was to spring the major theme of nineteenth-century Gold Coast political history.

On and behind the Slave Coast, the course of events in the seventeenth and eighteenth centuries followed much the same pattern as it did on the Gold Coast. Initially there may have been less political disunity here. The power of Benin was felt as far west as Lagos, where, about the middle of the sixteenth century, a Benin dynasty had been established, and among the Aja states, Allada seems to have enjoyed an ultimate paramountcy. But the coastal kingdoms, like those on the Gold Coast, were very small, rarely extending over more than about 400 square miles, and among the Aja there was little positive political authority. The power of a king depended entirely on the degree of support he received from the heads of the major lineages and families in the community. Similarly the authority of the kings of Allada over the other Aja kings was also essentially familial, resting on their acceptance of his seniority and ritual superiority in the royal line from which they all claimed descent.

Thus when, from about 1670 onwards, the kings of Allada began to follow a policy of attracting Europeans to their inland capital with the idea of making it the sole focus among the Aja for the new trade they brought, the results were disastrous. The export slave trade rapidly increased, from annual exports of probably not more than 3000 slaves a year to a peak which has been thought to be as high as 18 000. But politically and socially disruptive forces had been set in motion which the Allada rulers lacked any power to control. The nominally satellite Aja kings began to act independently with ever less care for Allada policy; and within their states, and within Allada itself, private and personal interests quickly came to override those of the community at large. None of the kings had any command of force to restore his authority, and efforts to restore order by enlisting the services of Akwamu or Accra forces (the king of Accra and many of his supporters had fled to Little Popo on the Slave Coast when his kingdom had been conquered by Akwamu) or other mercenaries only added to the confusion. The Europeans were able to exploit this situation by gaining firm footholds in the coastal kingdoms, especially in Whydah, whose kings were made and unmade according to the balance of European power on the coast, and ceased to tender any effective allegiance to Allada.

The increasing disorder on the Slave Coast brought reactions from two inland states. The first of these came from Dahomey, a kingdom created by an offshoot of the Allada royal line which, like the founders of Ashanti (and at about the same time), had struck out to the north to establish its fortunes by conquering and organizing small kinship groups in the interior. In the process, from their capital at Abomey, some seventy miles from the coast, they evolved an authoritarian form of government and society in which each individual owed direct allegiance to the king and was his to dispose of for whatever political economic or military purpose he chose. In 1724, the army of King Agaja of Dahomey (1708?–40) conquered Allada, and then, with somewhat more difficulty, it went on during 1727–32 to impose his will on Whydah and the other coastal kingdoms except the one which became known as Porto Novo, in the far south-east, in which refugees from Allada managed to remain independent. Elsewhere, however, the old Aja kings were swept away, and their ineffective governments replaced by a system of viceroys owing absolute obedience to the Dahoman monarch.

But though the Dahoman conquests succeeded in imposing a single effective system of law and order over the whole Aja country except for Porto Novo, their kings' authority did not go unchallenged. In 1726, the enlarged kingdom was subjected to the first of a series of invasions from the Yoruba kingdom of Oyo, whose capital, Old Oyo, lay more than 200 miles to the north-east of Abomey. Little is known about Oyo before the sixteenth century. It was on the remote northern fringe of Yorubaland, and such importance as it had was presumably derived from its position on the trading and military frontier between Yorubaland and the outside world of the Sudan. What is known of Oyo's sixteenth-century history suggests that at this time it was entirely involved in the power rivalries of the south-central Sudan. It suffered disastrous invasions from Nupe which led its kings to take refuge in Borgu, with whose rulers they were allied by marriage. It is possible, indeed, that the dynasty which regained control of Oyo at the end of the century may have been partly at least of Borgu descent. It obviously could well have been through the Borgu connection that Oyo gained the horses and the technical expertise to raise the cavalry which during the following two centuries were used to establish and control a considerable empire.

In the early seventeenth century, Oyo armies began to conquer towards the south. It seems certain from the surviving traditions that a principal motive for this was to try and secure control of the trade routes which were bringing salt and some European goods from the coast into the interior. Conquest directly to the south, into the forest country occupied by other Yoruba kingdoms, was a matter of some difficulty, doubtless because the forest inhibited the effective deployment of cavalry and also, perhaps, because advances in this direction could bring Oyo into conflict with the established power of Benin, with which, indeed, a frontier was shortly agreed. Thus by the second half of the century, the main thrust of Oyo arms was directed to the south-west, through more open country from which access could be gained to such southern and western Yoruba peoples as the Egba, the Egbado and the Nago, and to the Aja and their ports on the Slave Coast. By the 1690s, Oyo armies were campaigning successfully close to the sea in Aja territory.

Although some of the people exported from the Slave Coast must have been enslaved as a result of the disruption of society in the comparatively densely populated Aja country, or of the wars and raids by which Dahomey built up its power, it is also clear that a principal commercial function of the Aja communities in the seventeenth and eighteenth centuries was to provide the hinterland with salt and European goods, and slaves were one of the principal commodities received at the coast in exchange. As early as the 1660s, Yoruba traders were of sufficient importance on the Slave Coast for one European report to suggest that the Yoruba language, rather than any Aja dialect, was the lingua franca of trade, and by the close of the eighteenth century at least it would seem that Hausa traders were also in evidence there. By the beginning of the eighteenth century, Oyo dominated the greater part of the immediate hinterland of the Aja country. Thus the incorporation of almost all the Aja into a single, centralized polity under the absolute control of the kings of Dahomey posed an immediate challenge to Oyo interests.

This challenge was met, almost as soon as it was mounted, by a series of campaigns in 1726–30 in which the Oyo cavalry carried all before them. Central Dahomey was devastated, and its king and government were for a time forced to reside elsewhere. Dahomey had no alternative but to seek peace on Oyo terms, which involved the regular payment of tribute and the recognition of an eastern boundary beyond which Oyo interests were to be paramount. It was undoubtedly this Oyo intervention which preserved the independence of the old Allada royal line at Porto Novo; and this and other eastern ports like Badagri and Lagos subsequently became the main outlets for Yoruba trade and, indeed, began to eclipse Whydah as centres for the export of slaves. Under Agaja's successors, Dahomey recovered its integrity, and part of the explanation for the rise of the slave trade at Porto Novo and other places on the eastern Slave Coast was that they were free of the authoritarian controls imposed at Whydah and elsewhere under Dahoman jurisdiction. But any attempt made by the Dahoman kings to throw off their dependence on Oyo, or to extend their system of control onto the eastern ports protected by Oyo, was consistently frustrated for nearly a century. It was only when, in the early nineteenth century, the Oyo empire suddenly collapsed, that Dahomey was able to regain its independence and its freedom of action to the east.

The seeds of Oyo's collapse lay in internal political problems which can be traced back to at least the 1750s, and which were of a kind that tended to afflict all major West African states, and not least those which had risen to prominence in Lower Guinea against the background of the increasing trading opportunities of the seventeenth and eighteenth centuries. Essentially there were two problems, though these often overlapped. First there was the problem of how a particular royal line, whose right to rule sprang from its descent from the founding ancestor of a particular kinship group, could preserve this right, and develop its power accordingly, as this group and its initial following of clients and slaves extended its control over other kinship groups which owed it no natural allegiance. Secondly, there was the problem of retaining the monopoly of power in a situation in which the rewards of power were continually increasing and so exciting the ambitions of others: tributary rulers who had a natural claim to authority among their own people, or other members of the imperial ruling group – royals and non-royals alike – who wanted a larger share in the proceeds of empire, or some combination of both of these. This problem tended to be accentuated by the fact that usually no particular member of the royal line had an automatic right to succeed to the throne: the succession was commonly a matter of the metropolitan elders choosing a suitable candidate from among its members. Consequently the death of any king was likely to produce active competition for the succession.

Of the Guinea kingdoms whose seventeenth- and eighteenth-century history has just been outlined, only Dahomey seems to have escaped serious trouble. The explanation probably lies in the circumstances in which this kingdom was originally built up, its kings forcing their authority on the members of defeated alien descent groups which subsequently ceased to have any political significance. No doubt, too, this tradition of absolute royal power was reinforced by the subsequent struggle to maintain the kingdom against the pressures from Oyo. Benin, of course, had risen to power before the commercial revolution caused by the Atlantic slave trade. However, towards the end of the seventeenth century, when the question of a more active involvement in this trade was being debated, and when therefore the allocation of the rewards from this involvement must also have been in question, competition between the *Oba* and the principal chiefs of his court developed into open conflict. The monarchy seems only to have been saved by allying itself with the chiefs of the people of the capital. One consequence of this conflict was that henceforward the power of the palace chiefs was circumscribed by establishing a rule of primogeniture to govern succession to the throne.

Little is known of the internal organization of the Denkyira monarchy and empire. However, the Denkyira kings seem to have evolved no system of imperial administration for the kingdoms they conquered, but allowed their traditional rulers to remain in office so long as they remitted sufficient tribute. It would seem that it was excessive demands for tribute that served to provoke the successful rebellion of the Ashanti and, once Denkyira had been defeated, all the once tributary kings immediately reclaimed their independence. Akwamu, on the other hand, tried to establish a more lasting imperial fabric by sending out members of its royal line to govern the peoples it had conquered. But these sought to facilitate their task by marrying into the traditional local ruling families. Thus the Akwamu system completely defeated its object: the provincial rulers secured sure local allegiances and power bases, while at the same time retaining their right to compete for authority at the centre. The Akyem defeat of Akwamu in 1730 was facilitated by the fact that the governor of Accra, its richest province, as the uncle of the *Akwamuhene* of the time, was challenging his right to rule. As with Denkyira, serious military defeat led to the immediate dissolution of the empire, though with the difference that in this case the former provinces which escaped coming under Akyem influence did not, with independence, regain entirely their old shapes or constitutions, but continued to show the influence of Akwamu models.

As has already been suggested, Ashanti could learn from Akwamu and Denkyira weaknesses as well as from their successes. But it had the additional problem that its initial ruling group was not a unitary one, but a coalition in which at first the *Asantehene* was not much more than *primus inter pares*. Osei Tutu, the first *Asantehene*, and his immediate successors thus faced a problem of building up the central power so that it was unquestionably greater than that of any of the other constituent states of the union. They sought to do this by claiming overlordship of many of the union's initial conquests for their own throne as the representative of the larger national interest. But they entrusted the day-to-day oversight of these conquered provinces to the divisional chiefs of their capital, with the result that by the middle of the eighteenth century, these Kumasi chiefs commanded a major share of the fruits of empire and began to seek to dictate policy. In the later 1740s, *Asantehene* Opoku Ware had to fight to regain control with the help of the other kings of the union, with the result that when, in 1750, he died, an uncertain heritage was left for his successor. Eventually what saved the Ashanti union and ensured its continuance into the nineteenth century, was the recruitment by Osei Kwadwo (1764–77) and his successors of a corps of professional administrators, police, soldiers and entrepreneurs who were totally unconnected with the traditional power structures in Kumasi or the other constituent kingdoms of the union, and owed their positions entirely to the faithfulness and efficiency with which they carried out imperial policy.

The evolution of this career bureaucracy could not prevent major crises developing when the Kumasi chiefs and the rulers of the other states were finding a new *Asantehene*, but it did give the new incumbent a machine of his own by which to restore his authority, especially over tributaries, which commonly used the interregna to reclaim their independence. In the Oyo empire, the *Alafins* also developed their own administrative system to control Oyo's conquests, and they staffed this for the most part with palace slaves whose power derived directly and uniquely from the monarch. But their problem was that they owed their position to election by the traditional chiefs of the lineages of their capital; that these had the right to require their ritual suicide if they did not perform their duties in accordance with tradition; and that the *Alafin*'s administration did not control the army of the capital, which remained responsible to the metropolitan chiefs and their leader, the *Basorun*. The *Basorun* of the period 1754–74, Gaha, and his colleagues, no doubt envious of the extent to which through his slave administration the *Alafin* was engrossing the major fruits of empire, exploited their traditional powers to ensure that no *Alafin* survived for more than a year or two. But Gaha overreached himself. Unlike the *Alafin*, and the other Yoruba rulers now subordinated to Oyo, all of whom claimed descent from the first Yoruba kings at Ife, Gaha had no prescriptive claim to rule. Therefore when he attempted to replace the *Alafins'* imperial administration with one recruited from his own kin and slaves, he incurred widespread hostility. Eventually, the last of the *Alafins* he had made, Abiodun, regained control with the help of the provincial rulers.

When (c. 1789) Abiodun died, the Oyo empire was more extensive than ever before. But the provincial rulers who had helped restore Abiodun to power soon became restive at the extent to which the proceeds of empire were controlled and enjoyed by the *Alafin* and his servants. In the 1790s, following upon defeats suffered by Oyo in wars against Borgu and Nupe, the provincial chiefs, led by Afonja, the viceroy of the north based at Ilorin, joined with the *Basorun* and the Oyo chiefs to remove the *Alafin*. Afonja seems to have hoped for the succession for himself. When this was denied him, he declared his independence of Oyo. He was able to sustain this against all attempts against him by enlisting the aid of Fulani and Hausa mercenaries from the north, and thus maintaining his cavalry power while denying supplies of horses and, indeed, any access to northern trade, to Oyo. In such a situation, the power of the *Alafins* to control the other Yoruba kings rapidly fell away, and when in 1817, following the Fulani *jihad* in Hausaland, the northerners took over power in Ilorin for themselves and shortly began to conquer to the south, the Oyo empire broke down into a congeries of competing principalities.

One further question remains to be discussed, namely the extent to which the increase in the scale of monarchies in Lower Guinea in the seventeenth and eighteenth centuries was due to their use of firearms. It is clear that, when the Portuguese monopoly had been broken, the importation of guns and ammunition became an important and most competitive element in European trading on the coast. By the eighteenth century, it seems likely that every year on average at least 200 000 muskets were being imported into West Africa. It might therefore be supposed that a significant element in the new power politics was the acquisition of these weapons by kingdoms trading to the coast. These could use them to conquer and enslave peoples further in the interior, who were denied access to firearms, while the captured slaves would be important in considerable measure because they could be used to purchase still more guns.

But it is doubtful whether the evidence supports such a simplistic model. It is true that Akwamu's success was associated with its musketeers and its evolution of suitable tactics for their employment, and Denkyira's defeat is ascribed to its southerly tributaries conspiring to deny it supplies of guns and powder while Akwamu ensured that Ashanti both got guns and knew how to use them. But it should be noted that here is a case of a state with direct access to the coast, Akwamu, supplying firearms to one in the interior, Ashanti, which might – and in fact did – become a serious rival. Equally, when, towards the end of the eighteenth century, Ashanti had consolidated its hold on Dagomba in the far north, it provided the kings of the latter with the means to add a corps of musketeers to their army. It needs also to be stressed that Oyo's victories, including those over Dahomey, which certainly had firearms, are ascribed entirely to its use of cavalry; indeed muskets did not come into common use among the Yoruba before their civil wars in the nineteenth century. There is also an eye-witness account of the first major engagement, in 1744, between an Ashanti army, which had muskets, and a Dagomba force which had no guns and in which cavalry were the élite arm, and it is clear that this ended in deadlock, neither side being able to overcome the other.

It would seem that cheap trade muskets, inherently slow-firing, and difficult to operate and maintain in the humid tropics, were not necessarily an effective weapon. Their effectiveness depended on such things as the amount and quality of the training given to the musketeers, how well their weapons were maintained, and whether adequate supplies of good quality gunpowder were available. If it chose its ground well, a well-organized army relying on cavalry, or perhaps even on bowmen, might be at least a match for a sizeable force of not very efficient musketeers. But the key words are 'effective' and 'well-organized', and the societies most likely to get quantities of firearms and to give them a prominent place in their military system were the well-organized and effective monarchies. In African terms, firearms were expensive, not only to buy, but to keep in working order and adequately supplied with powder. They thus fulfilled in Guinea a role comparable to that of horses in the Sudan (and in this respect, Oyo was in origin a Sudanese kingdom). Only great kings could afford to have them in significant numbers, and to supply them to their followers. Guns, like horses, were thus symbols of power, and also elements in the growth of royal power at the expense of that of small kinship groups both within and without the kingdom. Some ambitious traditional leaders were bound to try and turn the new opportunities arising from the growth of trade in Guinea to the economic and political advantage of themselves and their followers, and they would have done this without firearms had none been available – as indeed Oyo did, since for it access to supplies of horses made guns essentially superfluous. But once the new, expensive, prestigious element of firearms entered the situation, so the successful new kings sought to secure them and to exploit them, using them to equip and reward their followers and allies, and trying to deny them to those they sought to dominate. Though always second to the urge to secure and dispose of more people, control over the acquisition and distribution of firearms became an important part of the process by which the power of the new monarchies was extended at the expense of the traditional social groups.

Chapter 12

Bantu Africa, c. 1600 to c. 1870

Before the later part of the eighteenth century, the greater part of
Bantu Africa was little affected, at least in any direct sense, by the
swelling tide of world trade which induced such spectacular changes
in West Africa, especially in lower Guinea. The Portuguese interventions in the Kongo and Monomotapa kingdoms led only to the
destruction of these two major early Bantu politico-economic initiatives. The new pattern of Portuguese interest in western Bantu Africa,
in Angola, was not fully established until the 1680s, and it was not
until about the same time that other European traders interested in
the acquisition of slaves for the Americas began to devote much
attention to the coastlands between Angola and the Cameroons.
Active European interest of any kind on the east coast hardly existed
before the end of the eighteenth century. The Portuguese maintained
a tenuous occupation along the Mozambique coast and in the lower
Zambezi valley, but they had lost the initiative, which to the south
lay with Changamire and to the north with the Omani and the other
Arab or Swahili traders of the coast.

The societies of the Changamire kingdom in Butwa and of the
Portuguese *prazo*-holders in the Zambezi valley seem both to have
been basically inward looking. The Changamire developed a firm
administrative as well as military control over their subjects. This
secured the efficient remission of tribute, in the form of surplus
foodstuffs, cattle and tobacco, and prestige items such as gold, ivory
and cloth, to the principal political centres established by the kings
and their leading feudatories at such places as Dhlo Dhlo and Khami,
where there was much new building in stone, essentially for purposes
of prestige and display. Foreign traders were rigidly excluded, and all

prestigious activities, such as weaving, carving in ivory and stone, and
– above all – the mining and working of gold were subject to royal
control. The kingdom is not known to have exerted any significant
influence on surrounding peoples. Some trade with the outside was
deemed necessary, to secure luxury imports, such as porcelains, for
the court, and – during the eighteenth century – firearms also. Much
of this was also firmly under royal control. For example, official
caravans were sent from time to time during most of the eighteenth
century to the Portuguese post at Zumbo on the Zambezi to secure
cloth, beads, hardware, guns and porcelain.

In return for this, the Portuguese in the Zambezi valley and also
on the eastern frontier of the Changamire kingdom in Manyika might
in a good year receive as much as £100 000 ($500 000) of gold. But
they were almost entirely dependent for this on the whims of the king
of the day; the prime purpose of the major economic activities of the
kingdom was to enrich the kings and their courts. Until the end of
the eighteenth century, and the rise of the export slave trade, the
economy of the Portuguese *prazos* seems to have been essentially
equally self-centred, their slaves being used to secure tribute and
supplies from African communities whose agriculture was little above
the subsistence level. Apart from the occasional consignments of gold
received from Butwa, and a little gold secured locally, there was little
available to export to the outside world except some ivory and a few
surplus slaves.

Butwa and the Portuguese *prazos* along the Zambezi valley seem
indeed to have been remarkably little affected by such links with the
outside world as they had. But it is even more remarkable that, until
the last years of the eighteenth century, they seem to have been
essentially the only parts of eastern Bantu Africa to have had any
direct contacts at all with the coast. At first sight it is difficult to see
what could have attracted the Omani and other Arab traders during
the course of the seventeenth century to take over control from the
Portuguese of the coastal towns north of Cape Delgado. Prior to the
arrival of the Portuguese in the early sixteenth century, the prosperity
of these coastal settlements had been tied up with the trade southwards
to Kilwa and Sofala, and hence with the gold trade with Monomotapa.
But this Arab–Swahili gold trade does not seem to have survived the
Portuguese occupation of the Zambezi valley and the subsequent
decline of Monomotapa. Apart from this, the east-coast towns seem
to have been denied access to the interior by the tribes of militant

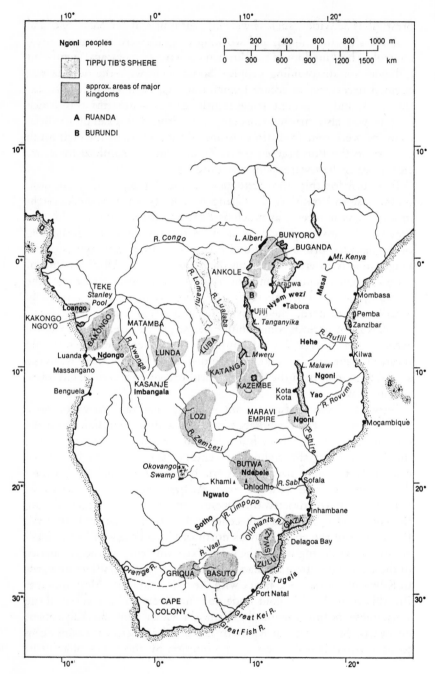

Legend

Ngoni peoples

 TIPPU TIB'S SPHERE

approx. areas of major kingdoms

A RUANDA
B BURUNDI

Map labels

10°   0°   10°   20°

0 200 400 600 800 1000 m
0 300 600 900 1200 1500 km

R. Congo   L. Albert   BUNYORO   BUGANDA   ▲Mt. Kenya

ANKOLE   A B   Karagwa   Masai

TEKE   Stanley Pool   R. Lomami   R. Lualaba   Nyamwezi   Mombasa

Loango   Ujiji   •Tabora

KAKONGO   NGOYO   BAKONGO   MATAMBA   R. Kwango   LUBA   L. Tanganyika   Pemba   Zanzibar

Luanda   **Ndongo**   LUNDA   R. Rufiji

Massangano   KASANJE   **Imbangala**   KATANGA   L. Mweru   Hehe   Kilwa

Benguela   KAZEMBE   Kota Kota   L. Malawi   **Ngoni**   Yao   R. Rovuma

LOZI   MARAVI EMPIRE   **Ngoni**   Moçambique

R. Zambezi   R. Shire

Okovango Swamp   BUTWA   **Ndebele**

Khami▲   Dhlodhlo   R. Sabi   Sofala

Ngwato   Inhambane

Sotho   R. Limpopo   Oliphant's R.   GAZA

R. Vaal   SWAZI   Delagoa Bay

Orange R.   GRIQUA   BASUTO   ZULU   R. Tugela

Port Natal

CAPE COLONY   Great Kei R.   Great Fish R.

Map 8   Bantu Africa c. *1600* – c. *1870*

herdsmen and hunters who subsisted in the belt of arid and inhospitable thorn scrub running parallel to the coast south from the semi-
desert of Somalia to close to the northern end of Lake Malawi.

However, the coastal strip itself was well watered, fertile and
adequately peopled. It could therefore be exploited to produce foodstuffs and some commercial crops, such as coconuts and copra and
oil seeds, as well as cowrie shells, for trade, and purely domestic
production might be boosted by the enslavement of some of the local
population for work on plantations, and also, in some degree, for
export. When, under Seyyid Said (1806–56), the Omani empire on
the East African coast was fully developed, a considerable part of its
wealth was still derived in this way, most notably through Said's
personal development of clove planting on the islands of Zanzibar and
Pemba. Hitherto, cloves had only been produced on the Moluccas
and adjacent islands in the East Indies. These had not been able to
keep pace with the demand, with the result that cloves had continued
to be a rather scarce and expensive spice. By the time of Said's death,
clove production by Arab landholders with slave labourers was the
dominant agricultural activity on Zanzibar and Pemba, and exports
were already worth something like £60 000 ($300 000) a year. Eventu-
ally, by the early twentieth century, Zanzibar and Pemba were
producing something like four-fifths of the world's supply of cloves.

The dry lands immediately behind the coastal strip were also not
entirely devoid of products of economic interest. One of these was
gum copal, exports of which through Zanzibar were worth about
£35 000 ($175 000) a year by the mid-nineteenth century. But their
most precious resource was ivory, which was probably comparatively
abundant at the time of the Omani arrival simply because, where the
human population was thin, the numbers of elephants (and other
game) were considerable. The development of trade into and across
the zone of thorn scrub seems to have been largely connected with
the eighteenth- and nineteenth-century growth of the external demand
for African ivory. Reliable data for the export of ivory from East
Africa are not available before the 1850s, but by this time Zanzibar
was already exporting about 500 000 pounds a year (worth about
£150 000 ($750 000), and exports remained near this level until the
1890s (and by this time, the price of ivory had risen nearly tenfold).

This growth in the demand for ivory meant that mainland peoples
who had access to numbers of elephants and who had developed skills
in hunting them began to see that they had within their grasp a

resource of considerable value. When they began to exhaust their local supplies of ivory (and the pace and scale on which this was done can be readily appreciated from the fact that for every 100 pounds of ivory, at least one elephant had to be killed), they began to organize hunting bands to penetrate further into the interior to find more elephants. Since they would have to trek down to the coast to exchange their tusks for trade goods, so in effect they began to develop trade routes and, indeed, to become traders, for example exchanging some of their goods from the coast with interior peoples to secure grain and other foodstuffs to help support them on their inland expeditions. Finally, as elephants became even scarcer, so the travellers might become primarily traders, exchanging coastal trade goods for stocks of ivory built up over a whole season by the interior chiefs as a result of their own people's hunting activities.

Thus, for example, the Nyika people of the immediate hinterland of Mombasa built up a hunting and trading network, especially to the north-west, until, by the later eighteenth century, they were getting a large part of their ivory from the Kamba, in and around the foothills of Mount Kenya. The Kamba, perhaps more mobile and better hunters than the Nyika, and certainly with access to more elephants, began to play the game for their own account, pushing further into the interior, and also expanding their own hunting and trading and colonizing activities to lands to the west and south of Nyika territory, until by the 1840s the Kamba and Nyika between them were dominating the trade of the whole area from the Laikipia plateau north of Mount Kenya to almost as far south as the hinterland of Kilwa. South of this, the hinterland was better watered and more productive. The early trade of the Yao who lived along the Rovuma to the south-west of Kilwa seems to have been connected with the peregrinations through their country, peddling their wares, of specialized iron-workers. As these touched the coast, so an exchange developed between Yao iron-wares, tobacco and skins, and coastal salt, cloth and beads. But the subsequent expansion of the Yao to Lake Malawi may well have been associated with the search for ivory before, in the late eighteenth and in the nineteenth centuries, it became primarily connected with slaving.

Although there is no evidence for this, it seems reasonable to surmise that it may have been through the activities of people like the Kamba that the attention of the Nyamwezi in the west of modern Tanzania was drawn to the possibilities of trade with the coast. The result was that towards the end of the eighteenth century, a few luxury goods began to find their way from the coast to northern lacustrine kingdoms like Ankole and Buganda. Hitherto these kingdoms had been isolated from the outside world. Fertile soils and adequate supplies of water permitted the growth of populations to densities unusual in Bantu Africa, and the production of agricultural surpluses sufficient to allow tribute-levying kings to maintain elaborate courts and administrations. Each kingdom was economically self-sufficient for most purposes, and if it were lacking in a resource of some significance, it could be secured by exchange with one of its neighbours. Thus the principal supplier of raw and manufactured iron was Bunyoro, which had the best deposits of accessible high-grade iron ore. Bunyoro also possessed one of the two major sources of salt in the northern lacustrine region, while a number of states, including Ankole and Buganda, competed with each other for possession of or access to the second, at Katwe on Lake Edward. Buganda specialized in the manufacture of bark-cloth, which became a luxury good when exported to the other kingdoms, while the best tobacco was grown in Ankole and the best coffee came from Buganda and Bunyoro.

The Nyamwezi, on the highlands of north central Tanzania immediately south of Lake Victoria, can be regarded as south-easterly outliers of the lacustrine kingdoms. However, their political units were very much smaller, and their settlements were much more widely dispersed over a generally poorer environment. Therefore their people had to travel much longer distances to secure access to the important resources, such as salt, iron and fish, which were unevenly distributed over their area. Thus when, probably in the second half of the eighteenth century, the Nyamwezi were touched by the coastal demand for ivory, they seem quickly to have appreciated that they were in a key position to operate a trading system directly linking the hitherto quite separate economies of the coast and of the lacustrine states. This must have proved a profitable enterprise. Soon a major long-distance trade route was developed linking the coast near Zanzibar to Nyamwezi, and thence running north-westwards to Buganda, with branches directly northwards to Lake Victoria and westwards to Lake Tanganyika and, eventually, south towards Lake Malawi.

However, the success of the Nyamwezi in organizing trade along these routes quickly incurred competition from the Omani who were established at Zanzibar. There was constant jostling for power in their homeland in Arabia, and their position as traders exploiting relations

between the Persian Gulf and the western Indian Ocean was threatened by their neighbours, the Jawasmi, and by the rise of the Wahhabi
movement on the Arabian mainland. Following a bitter struggle for
the succession to power among the Omani at Muscat in 1804–6, the
eventual victor, the young Seyyid Said bin Sultan, gradually came to
the conclusion that his interests would be better served if he opted
out of Arabian affairs altogether, and used his naval resources to
develop his power and his people's trade on the coast of East Africa.
Hitherto Omani political authority there hardly existed beyond the
islands of Zanzibar and Pemba; in the mainland towns, Said's predecessors had been content to accept as governors the leaders of the
dominant local Arab families. But from 1822 onwards, Said used his
navy to assert his direct authority on the coastal towns, the last of
these, Mombasa, falling to him in 1837. Finally, in 1840, he himself
moved permanently to Zanzibar, leaving his interests at Muscat to a
regent.

Said made Zanzibar the focal point of a secure and prosperous
coastal trading empire which had the general aim of opening up the
resources of East Africa for the benefit of the Indian Ocean trading
community, and the more specific purpose of controlling their exploitation to the benefit alike of his public revenue and his private income
as the leading trader and landholder at Zanzibar. One of his major
economic initiatives, the development of clove planting on the islands,
which dates from the 1830s, has already been mentioned. The other
was the organization of large, armed Arab-Swahili trading caravans
to penetrate inland along the trade routes pioneered by the Nyamwezi.
Capital to support both these enterprises was readily available from
Indian merchants, who had long been trading to East Africa, and who
now established themselves in considerable numbers at Zanzibar, to
sell the cloth and other Indian merchandise which was required for
the mainland trade, and to purchase East African produce for export
to Asia.

In the eighteenth century, as has been seen, the most sought-after
product of the mainland was undoubtedly ivory. But by the time Said
turned his attention to East Africa, there was already also a growing
export trade in slaves. For centuries, of course, there had been a
market for African slaves in Muslim Asia from Arabia to north-
western India. But until the later eighteenth century, the Arab traders
who sought to meet this demand do not seem to have operated much
further afield than Somalia, and it may well have been that it was

European initiatives at this time that first stimulated the Arab and Swahili merchants further south to develop an export slave trade on any scale. In 1776, for example, an enterprising French trader had negotiated with the Sultan of Kilwa for a regular annual supply of slaves which he could transport to Mauritius. It was also about this time, or a little later, that the insatiable American demand for African labour led the Portuguese to develop an active export slave trade from their Mozambique and Zambezi territories. This last activity must certainly have come to the notice of Arab traders if, indeed, they did not to some extent participate in it themselves.

By the beginning of the nineteenth century, at any rate, the merchant community in what was to become the Omani coastal trading empire directed from Zanzibar was fully alive to the profits which could be gained by exporting slaves from East Africa to other parts of the north-western Indian Ocean. In addition, of course, from the 1830s onwards, labour was also required for the new clove plantations in Zanzibar and Pemba. Thus a primary object of the caravans going into the interior was to secure slaves as well as ivory, with the result that during *c.* 1840–70, on average something like 18 000 slaves a year may have been taken away from the mainland, about two-thirds of whom went to the clove plantations.

By the 1840s, annual caravans from the coast under Said's flag were reaching as far as Ujiji on Lake Tanganyika and Karagwe to the west of Lake Victoria, in both of which some Zanzibari merchants settled as permanent agents for their operations, as they also did at the important junction of trade routes at Tabora in Nyamwezi. By the 1860s, east-coast traders were reaching halfway across the continent into the basin of the upper Congo and Shaba, and they were also well established around the northern shores of Lake Malawi.

The political and social consequences of this irruption of external trade into eastern Bantu Africa were considerable. In what today is mainland Tanzania, traditional life was largely disrupted for all except the non-Bantu pastoral peoples speaking Nilo-Saharan languages, like the Masai, who remained hostile and aloof (and whose major concentrations further north shielded from change the Bantu of the Kenya highlands). Except in the immediate vicinity of major settlements like Tabora and Ujiji, the men from the coast, relatively few in numbers and essentially concerned with trading profits, did not usually seek political authority. But the regular passages of their armed caravans, their occasional direct forays in search of slaves, and the muskets which (together with cloth and other goods brought from the coast) they were willing to exchange with local chiefs for ivory and slaves, were all necessarily extremely disruptive of traditional authority, and there was no lack of unscrupulous local men who sought to profit from the situation by embarking on careers of plunder and conquest. The pattern was essentially one of exchanging some ivory and a few unfortunate men and women for muskets and other prestigious trade goods, such as cotton cloth, and using these to build up followings of adventurers and clients, who were employed to acquire mastery over larger resources of people and ivory, some of the stocks of which could be exchanged for further guns and trade goods. The most successful of these new war-lords or warrior kings was a young Nyamwezi chief, Mirambo, who by the 1870s was strong enough to begin to dictate terms to the coastal traders settled in, or seeking to pass through Nyamwezi.

Further afield, however, the men from the coast tended to come up against traditional African rulers whose political and economic control over their peoples was more strongly entrenched, and different tactics were followed. The northern lacustrine monarchies in particular had a secure hold over large numbers of people and considerable areas of territory. Furthermore, as has been seen, they had their own trading system which, if somewhat limited in scope and development, was within its own terms an international one, while their taste for imports from the coast had already been whetted by the Nyamwezi traders. Their kings were thus prepared to barter some of the stocks of ivory and other commodities held at their courts for such imports as they thought it desirable to have, but they insisted that the coastal traders should operate – as earlier traders had done – under their control. From their point of view indeed, the Zanzibari merchants were merely a new variety of clients. The kings were unwilling to allow these clients to acquire any substantial numbers of slaves, and trade with the coast tended to be concentrated on the exchange of ivory for trade goods, especially perhaps for guns and powder, and for cowrie shells. The terms of exchange were generally very favourable to the Zanzibaris, for hitherto there had been little or no commercial market for the ivory of the lacustrine area, the kings were keen to acquire fire-arms, and cowries were quickly in demand as a local currency (the lack of which seems earlier to have held back the commercial development of lacustrine society). Royal power thus remained intact, and indeed increased, with the kings maintaining firm control both of major trading transactions and of the increasingly specialized and lucrative pursuits of securing fresh supplies of ivory through hunting and local trading.

However, one important consequence of the coming of long-distance trade to the northern lacustrine kingdoms was to accentuate a change in their internal balance of power which had begun in the seventeenth century. At this time the largest and most powerful kingdom was the northernmost one, Bunyoro, which had inherited the prestige and much of the territory of the ancient Kitara. Buganda, between Bunyoro and Lake Victoria, was initially a much smaller kingdom, but – perhaps both because it was smaller, and because it needed to withstand the pressure of Bunyoro – its kings came to develop a much more positive and centralized form of government. In the middle of the seventeenth century they were thus able to seize the chance presented by disastrous defeats suffered by Bunyoro in southern campaigns in Ankole and Karagwe to begin to extend their territory round the shores of the lake to the east and north-east and to the south and south-west. They also developed canoe traffic on the lake itself. Thus when long-distance traders began to appear on the scene in the south-west, in Karagwe, and to some degree also on the southern and south-eastern shores of the lake, Buganda was in an ideal position to benefit from their trade and to control their access to Bunyoro and, moreover, its access to firearms. So, in the nineteenth century, especially under the forceful and long-reigning *Kabakas* Suna (c. 1830–56) and Mutesa (1856–84), both the power of the Buganda monarchy over its subjects and its territorial expansion were greatly accelerated. Ultimately Bunyoro was confined to a small triangle between Buganda, Lake Albert and the Victoria Nile, where from the 1860s onwards it also had to suffer attacks from militant slave-traders approaching down the Albert Nile from the empire established in the Sudan by Muhammad 'Ali's Egypt.*

Another interesting example of a people on the fringes of the Zanzibar trading empire gaining in wealth, power and territory is the Yao of the far south-east. The southern hinterland of Kilwa was appreciably more thickly populated than any other region of the interior so near and so accessible to the coast, while around Lake Malawi, and especially on the Shire highlands south of the lake, population densities matched those of the far less accessible, and

* This is discussed in chapter 14.

politically resistant, lacustrine kingdoms of the far north-west. It seems certain that it was this southern region which provided the largest share of the slaves for the Indian Ocean trade. But the coastal traders themselves were far from securing a monopoly of its exploitation.

As has been seen, the Yao had developed their own indigenous trading system before the rise of the Zanzibar trading empire. The growth in the coastal demand stimulated them to expand up the tributaries of the Rovuma towards the south-eastern shores of Lake Malawi and the Shire highlands in search of more ivory and slaves. Hunters and traders may have been in the van of this advance, but in the process the Yao began to develop militant territorial chieftaincies each competing to maximize its human resources as well as its commercial wealth. Indeed, the increase in foreign trade served to stimulate a transformation of society from a complex of village units into nascent kingdoms centred on sizeable towns.

This was essentially an indigenous process. The most notable direct foreign influence on these Yao chieftaincies was that, by the later nineteenth century, they were becoming increasingly islamized, with the result that their status as equal partners in the changes wrought by the growth of Arab-Swahili trade from the coast tended to be further confirmed. The coastal traders themselves, however, controlled the situation only along more northerly routes to the Malawi basin. Their principal bases were established at the northern end of the lake or, like Kota Kota, on its western shore reached by crossing the lake. Here, in a land where traditional society was disintegrating in the face of raids from the Yao and invasions of Ngoni (see below), the Zanzibaris had little alternative but to attempt to take political control for themselves. However, the most ambitious and successful example of this tactic was on the extreme westernmost boundary of the Zanzibar trading system in the upper Congo basin beyond Lake Tanganyika. Here, in Manyema, a far-seeing entrepreneur of mixed Arab and Bantu descent, usually known as Tippu Tib, seems to have come to the conclusion that indiscriminate raiding of the kind which so horrified Livingstone when he witnessed it in 1871, was not the best way to exploit one of the last major reserves of ivory in central Africa. He began instead during the early 1870s to build up a territorial empire which reached as far west as the river Lomami, and to seek to exploit its wealth by regular systems of taxation and tribute levied by political agents responsible to him.

In Manyema, as also in and around Katanga, where he had operated in the 1860s before settling on the upper Congo, Tippu Tib and east-coast trade were reaching halfway across the continent, and so encroaching into an area which was as accessible from the west coast as it was from the east, and which indeed had not been unaffected by developments on the west coast. But before passing to these, it is necessary to make some assessment of the success of the east-coast commercial empire based on Seyyid Said's regime at Zanzibar.

In economic terms, there is no question but that the Zanzibari empire was enormously successful, and there is also no doubt that the peak of this success was associated with Seyyid Said's personal initiatives as a ruler and as the leading entrepreneur of his empire. It is thought that government revenue at Zanzibar had been of the order of £10 000 ($50 000) a year in the 1820s, when he first became actively concerned in East African affairs, and that it had risen to about £50 000 ($250 000) a year by the 1850s, the decade of his death. Most of this derived from duties on the trade passing through its port, and in the 1850s the combined value of its exports and imports was of the order of £1 500 000 ($7 500 000) a year, making Zanzibar the richest seaport in tropical Africa. By this time, European hostility to the maritime slave trade had been extended to the Indian Ocean, with the result that there was every incentive to conceal the contribution which the trade in slaves was making to this commercial prosperity. However, it seems unlikely to have been less than a quarter (an estimate deriving from that part of the ruler's revenue thought to derive from duties on the slave trade), and at most not more than a half (an estimate deriving from the known values of exports of ivory, cloves, cowries, gum copal and oilseeds which, as has been seen, were still important items of trade).

Much of Zanzibar's foreign trade was with Asia, particularly with India, but it was also a significant market for French, German, British and American traders (the latter providing by far the largest proportion of East Africa's imports of cloth). American, British and French consuls had all been appointed to Zanzibar before Said's death, and a representative of the German Hanseatic League followed soon after. One consequence of this diplomatic recognition, following upon Zanzibar's commercial pre-eminence, was to suggest to the outside world that Zanzibar was also politically the paramount power in East

Africa. In fact outside the islands and the mainland ports on which they could bring to bear their naval strength, Said and his successors had influence rather than power. Traders proceeding into the interior carried his flag, and gained prestige from it. But once away from the coast they were effectively their own masters, and as has been seen, they were for the most part motivated by the desire to achieve trading profits rather than by any ambition to establish a political influence unless – as was the case with Tippu Tib and perhaps at Kota Kota – this seemed the best way to commercial gain. In fact the political structure of the Zanzibar trading empire was extremely fragile. Even Said's hold on the coast depended very much on his acceptance by the major European powers, and in particular on the extent to which his actions served the interest of the British, who possessed ultimate naval paramountcy in the Indian Ocean, and who were also overlords in India, on which Zanzibar was dependent for capital and as a major market for its exports. Once the Europeans, the British in particular, had decided to take active measures against the Indian Ocean slave trade, Zanzibar and its network of trade routes into the interior served mainly to provide a means by which European interests could sweep into and secure control over all East Africa and its peoples.

On the west coast of Bantu Africa north of the Congo estuary, the seventeenth- and eighteenth-century pattern of European trading and of African responses to the growth of trade was very similar to that found in Guinea at the same time. The Cameroon and Gabon coasts were backed by tropical forest as dense as that to be found behind the Grain and Ivory Coasts, and even more extensive, with the result that population was equally thin, and political and economic organiz- ation similarly little developed. But immediately north of the Congo estuary, the forest thinned out and gave access to a hinterland of wooded savannahs, and here there was a complex of small kingdoms very similar to the larger Kongo kingdom south of the estuary. Orig- inally, indeed, these kingdoms – among which Loango became pre- eminent, others being Kakongo and Ngoyo (or Ngoy) – may have been tributary satellites of Kongo, but they would seem to have gained their effective independence even before the decay of the latter kingdom under Portuguese pressures. They had been neglected by the Portuguese, who had enough on their hands in Kongo, and also, it would seem, because they had more centralized systems of govern- ment (perhaps a reflection of the smaller size of the political units) so that their kings could successfully discourage the export slave trade in the interest of building up their own manpower.

In the early· seventeenth century, Loango and its neighbours naturally therefore attracted the attention of European traders, first and foremost the Dutch, who were beginning to compete with the Portuguese. The local kings and their subordinate aristocracy proved ready to exchange copper, which they obtained from trade with interior peoples such as the Teke, dye-woods, locally manufactured palm-cloth (which was used as currency in Angola), and, above all, some of the considerable stocks of ivory which they maintained as prestige goods, in return for European exports. Initially the Dutch were not interested in slaving. When they were, following their Brazilian conquests, they turned to Angola, and it was only after the failure of their attempt to expel the Portuguese from their colony there, that they began to look to the Loango coast for slaves.

By the 1670s, there was an increasing demand on Loango and its neighbours to supply slaves, not only to the Dutch, but also to French, English and Portuguese merchants, and royal attitudes towards their export began to change. The kings remained sufficiently in control of the situation to frustrate attempts by the European merchants to establish permanent forts on the coast or monopolies over its trade. But their traders were sent on organized expeditions into the interior to secure slaves as well as ivory (elephants now being scarce in the coastlands) for export. One consequence was a considerable stimulation of commercial activity in the interior, with the Teke north of Malebo Pool emerging as considerable middlemen. In Loango, however, a new trading class emerged to challenge the monopoly of authority hitherto exercised by the traditional ruler and nobility. By the end of the eighteenth century, the competition for power was leading to the decline of the kingdom, and the Europeans were increasingly turning their attention to the smaller states of Kakongo and Ngoyo.

South of the Congo estuary, the dominant theme in the coastlands from 1575 onwards was Portugal's attempt to establish a territorial colony. This went through three phases. In the first thirty years, the aims of the Portuguese were not unlike those of the Spanish *conquistadores* in America, to secure mineral wealth and estates which they could exploit. They were not very successful, partly because the supposed silver mines in the interior were a myth,* but mainly because the resistance of the Mbundu kingdom of Ndongo, ruled by the *Ngola*, and of the Imbangala warrior groups, who had recently arrived in Angola and Kongo, proved stronger than they had anticipated. The Portuguese were effectively kept off the interior plateau, and were restricted to a narrow strip of unhealthy lowlands running inland from Luanda between the rivers Bengo and Kwanga to their fortified frontier post at Massangano.

After 1605, the emphasis of Portuguese policy shifted to securing slaves for export. Some slaves were acquired by levying tribute on such Mbundu chiefs as had been conquered. Others were bought by sending trading agents to the markets, or *pombos*, in the interior. Initially, these *pombeiros*, as they were called, were Europeans, but they soon became half-castes or even themselves African slaves. Finally, the Portuguese became even more African in their methods by making the acquisition of captives a primary purpose of their military campaigns. As a result, the old kingdom of Ndongo was conquered. But once it had been plundered, the supply of slaves naturally decreased. The Portuguese then played for a time at rebuilding Ndongo as a slaving partner, an idea which was not unattractive to the remarkable queen, Nzinga, who had seized power in 1624, since she needed help to establish her authority over the Mbundu lineages. But the Portuguese wanted more than Nzinga was willing to concede, with the consequence that the Portuguese resumed their campaigning while Nzinga sought military support from bands of Imbangala. But this alliance also broke down, and eventually Nzinga abandoned the old Ndongo territory to a Portuguese puppet, and herself withdrew eastwards to establish a new kingdom in Matamba close by the one which was being established in the Kwango valley by substantial numbers of Imbangala who had come together under a leader who had the title of *Kasanje*. Both these new polities lay effectively beyond the reach of the Portuguese.

Matters had reached this stage when, in 1641, troops of the Dutch West India Company landed at Luanda, and shortly went on to try and expel the Portuguese from the colony of which it was the capital. Both Queen Nzinga and the Kongo king welcomed the newcomers as allies. But the Portuguese countered this by coming to terms with Kasanje, which kingdom was furthest from the danger presented by

* At this time, similar, equally mythical, wealth in silver was also thought to lie in East Africa, north of the Zambezi.

their colonial ambitions, and, revived by the arrival of an energetic new governor, Salvador de Sá, expelled the Dutch (1648). They subsequently went on to inflict a defeat on Kongo (1665) which led to the final extinction of centralized government in this kingdom. It was thus opened up to the slave traders, and since Kasanje was also trading with the Portuguese, only Matamba remained outside the Portuguese orbit. Portuguese interventions and campaigns in Matamba did not succeed in subverting its independence, but in 1683 an agreement was reached by which the Portuguese, and the Portuguese alone among Europeans, were given access to its markets. Matamba could not really afford to stand out against the new order Portugal had established in relations between Angolan rulers and the outside world.

However, although during the 1680s the Portuguese also embarked from Benguela, 250 miles south of Luanda, on the military and commercial penetration of the Ovimbundu kingdoms in the highlands south of Ndongo, it cannot be said that their slave trade in Angola and the Congo was flourishing during the next century. Part of their difficulty lay in a conflict between the officials and soldiers sent out from Portugal, who wanted quick results by military means, and those who had settled permanently in the colony, who preferred to try and cultivate good trading relations with the interior nations. More importantly, as the terms of the 1683 agreement with Matamba indicate, the Portuguese were now facing active competition from other Europeans who could offer more attractive terms of trade than the Portuguese. The Dutch, English and French could generally provide better and cheaper trade goods than the Portuguese, while the Portuguese government made things worse for its traders by refusing, until 1767, to countenance the sale of firearms to Africans, and by monopolizing the purchase of ivory at an artificially low price. Consequently the inland states preferred to route their exports, of slaves as well as ivory, to parts of the coast, for example around the Congo mouth, which were not under Portuguese control. Portuguese efforts to counter this, whether by military expeditions into the interior or by extending their control along the coast, were largely ineffective. Indeed their situation improved only when their rivals ceased to come to buy slaves, first as a consequence of the Revolutionary and Napoleonic wars in Europe, and then because they had banned the slave trade. Portugal did not do this until 1836, and the law was not enforced in Angola before 1845.

The real root of the matter, of course, was that the Portuguese were powerless to influence the commercial policies of the inland states beyond about 200 miles from the coast. The evidence seems to suggest that the arrival of the Portuguese on the west coast may have provided ambitious members of west-central Bantu societies with a useful widening of their economic horizons. But the early policies of the Portuguese towards kingdoms like Kongo and Ndongo did not altogether encourage the development of stable and fruitful trading relations between the coast and the interior. Eventually, as has just been seen, the result was the consolidation of Kasanje and Matamba as new kingdoms which were beyond the military reach of the Portuguese, and so able to determine the terms on which trade was to be allowed to reach the Europeans on the coast. Their bargaining position was, of course, strengthened by the growing competition among the European traders that became evident from the later seventeenth century onwards.

By the beginning of the following century, Kasanje and Matamba had emerged as focal points at which ivory and slaves coming from a wide area of the interior were marshalled for onwards transmission to what their ruling and trading classes saw as the most profitable coastal outlets for dealing with the Europeans. During the course of the eighteenth century, this organized export trade, together with the steady increase in its volume due to the growth of the Atlantic slave trade, helped to reshape political organization in the interior. There is evidence that about 1700, the major Luba kingdom, in the far east, with its centre between the Lualaba (upper Congo) and Lomami rivers, began to expand, but that the expansion was associated with increasingly bitter competition for the throne, so that ultimately central authority collapsed, leaving the vacuum which Tippu Tib was later able to exploit. However, in the east, in the Chambezi valley beyond Lake Mweru, Luba emigrants succeeded during the eighteenth century in establishing new chieftaincies over the Bemba, and in the early nineteenth century the demands on these for ivory and slaves for the Zanzibar trade together with the pressures that were felt from the Ngoni (see below) tended to lead to the consolidation and extension of their power. Later, however, while their raiding activities increased, their political organization seems to have begun to weaken.

It has indeed been earlier suggested that a weakness of Luba kingdoms was their failure to integrate local community heads successfully into their own political hierarchy, and also that this weakness was less evident among their Lunda neighbours, whose politicization they had inspired. The Lunda, of course, lay between Lubaland and Kasanje and Matamba, and there seems no doubt that by the eighteenth century, under the impulse of the trade reaching them through these middlemen kingdoms, there was an increase of Lunda political and economic activity. First, the authority of the monarch, the *Mwato Yamvo*, over the Lunda homeland was increased, and it was also extended to the west towards Kasanje and Matamba, so that his centralized system of tribute and trade was brought into closer and more effective contact with the trading network leading to the Atlantic coast. But Lunda could not provide from its own resources all the slaves and ivory for which there was a market in the west without weakening its own society and its imperial political and economic superstructure. So, secondly, the *Mwata Yamvo* began to send out sizeable raiding parties to conquer and to exploit the surrounding peoples, especially to the south and south-east. These latter-day equivalents of the Jaga and Imbangala were unlike their prototypes in that they were commanded by officers, commonly called *Kazembe*, who were relatives or subordinates of the *Mwato Yamvo*, and who continued, at least in name, to recognize his supremacy even when they had settled down and built up new kingdoms among the peoples they had conquered.

The most famous of these satellite kingdoms was the one which became known simply as Kazembe (more accurately, perhaps, Kazembe's), which was established in the middle of the eighteenth century around the Luapula valley between Lake Mweru and Shaba. This was – and indeed is – an area of considerable importance. It is a highland country, containing a number of lakes and salt-pans, which is the watershed between the Congo and Zambezi basins. It lies just to the south of Lubaland, and immediately west of the gap between Lakes Malawi and Tanganyika leading to the Nyamwezi trading system. In addition to its salt, it has good sources of iron ore and it has the richest deposits of copper in all Africa. As has been seen, it was part of the original area of Bantu settlement and development, and ever since then it seems to have supported some of the richest and most developed societies of Bantu Africa.

It was therefore an ideal place to establish a new kingdom, its mineral wealth supplementing the benefits of its position as a commercial cross-roads linking the Atlantic trade with that of the Nyamwezi and Yao in East Africa and that of the Portuguese along the Zambezi. Indeed it soon became a magnet for Portuguese ambitions. In 1798,

Kazembe's capital near Lake Mweru was reached from the east by an expedition led by Dr Francisco Lacerda, governor on the Zambezi, and in 1806 from the west by two Angolan *pombeiros*. The latter continued to the Portuguese post of Tete on the Zambezi, ultimately returning to Angola in 1816, thus anticipating by half a century Livingstone's famous trans-continental journey. The expeditions of Lacerda and the *pombeiros*, and later exploits by such men as Gamitto, from the Zambezi, and Silva Porto, from Benguela, became the basis for subsequent Portuguese claims to this strategic and mineral-rich centre of the continent lying between their long-established Mozambique and Angola colonies. But the Portuguese lacked the strength to turn these pretensions into reality, and ultimately Kazembe and the neighbouring central African kingdoms fell to the more effective imperialisms of Leopold of the Belgians and Cecil Rhodes.

As for the central Lunda hegemony, it does not seem to have been able to adapt to the new conditions resulting from the ending of the slave trade in Angola after 1845. Its political superstructure had been closely connected with the collection and accumulation of slaves. When this activity ceased to produce useful revenue, it collapsed. The dominant traders now became the Cokwe, a people of Lunda origin, who concentrated on the acquisition of ivory – by now the major staple of long-distance trade – from the little developed lands to the south-west of the old Lunda centres. But their organization revolved around long-ranging hunting expeditions in search of increasingly elusive elephants, and it had not produced much in the way of central government by the onset of the colonial period.

The decay of the central Lunda power of the *Mwato Yamvo* left those of its offshoots which had a broader economic base to continue as independent kingdoms. The Kazembe state is obviously the pre-eminent example, though there may be a parallel in the Lozi (Barotse) kingdom south-west of Shaba in the fertile floodplains of the upper Zambezi. It would seem likely that this kingdom was also created by Lunda emigrants who, probably rather earlier than the Kazembe conquests in Katanga, conquered peoples who may have been influenced by the Monomotapa states.

The efforts of the Portuguese to open direct contact with Kazembe's kingdom seem to have been a factor in the growth of its independence of the *Mwata Yamvo*, encouraging it to look east instead of west for outlets for its trade. But it was not the Portuguese who benefited from Kazembe's about-face, but first the Nyamwezi and then Zanzibari traders. Nyamwezi trade with Kazembe, for ivory and copper, seems to have begun about 1800, and a Nyamwezi group, the Yeke, settled permanently in the kingdom. In the 1860s, their leader, Msiri or Msidi, exploited local political rivalries to establish his own kingdom in Shaba, in the south-west of the Kazembe's territories. The resultant political disunity and the general decline of the Kazembe's authority were then very fruitfully exploited by armed slave-hunting caravans of Zanzibari traders, one of whose leaders was Tippu Tib.

From the 1820s onwards, large areas of central and eastern Africa began to experience invasion and conquest by bands of warriors pushing northwards as a result of revolutionary changes that had been taking place among the south-easternmost Bantu. Little has so far been said about the history of the frontier-lands of the Bantu in the far south of Africa. However, Bantu-speaking peoples had been settling the country south of the Limpopo (which marks the north-eastern boundary of the modern Republic of South Africa) from at least the fourth century, and by about 1600 they had established a basic pattern of settlement which can be seen even today. This pattern was primarily determined by the amount of rainfall available since, unlike the earlier inhabitants, who were Stone Age hunter-gatherers – the San (Bushmen) – or pastoralists – the Khoikhoi (Hottentots) – the southern Bantu, though accumulating cattle as the prime expression of wealth and power in their societies, depended for their basic subsistence on agriculture. But except for a small area near the coast in the south-west, which has winter rains and a Mediterranean climate, and which is where the first Europeans chose to settle, rainfall in South Africa is essentially dependent on monsoon winds from the Indian Ocean. While rainfall between the east coast and the Drakensberg mountains averages 750–1250 mm (30–50 in.) a year, the interior plateau, the high veld, becomes increasingly arid towards the west until, beyond a line running from the coast between the modern towns of East London and Port Elizabeth through the modern Kimberley, the average rainfall becomes less than 400 mm (16 in.) a year, and any serious agriculture is virtually impossible. The Bantu therefore chose to settle only in the eastern half of the modern Republic. While San and Khoikhoi communities survived in the west, in the east they were totally displaced or absorbed.

It is possible to surmise that the Bantu settlement occurred in two stages, and that these are reflected today in the major linguistic and

Above right A section from the *Catalan Atlas*, drawn in Majorca in 1375 for Charles V of France. Along the top can be seen a line of the northern oases from which North African caravans set out for the Sudan. Sijilmasa (Sijilmessa) is prominent towards the left, while further right and somewhat lower is Tuat (Vadia), just below which is marked Taghaza (Tagaza), one of the principal Saharan salt deposits. To the left of Sijilmasa, the legend says, 'Through this place pass the merchants who go to the land of the Negroes of Guinea, which place they call the valley of the Dra.' Guinea (Ginyia) is marked in capitals in the centre, while below and to the left is marked Sudan (Sudam). To the left of this, about where ancient Ghana was, is depicted a cameleer of the veiled desert Berbers, Sanhaja or Tuareg, with the legend, 'All this country is inhabited by people who veil their mouths; only their eyes are visible. They live in tents and have camel caravans . . .' The other figure, to the right, is described as follows: 'This Negro lord is called Musa Mali (Mussa Melly), lord of the Negroes of Guinea. The gold which is found in his country is so abundant that he is the richest and most noble lord in all the land.' To the left of his throne is marked Timbuctu (Tenbuch), and further left and slightly lower is the capital city of Mali (Ciutat de Melly); to the right of his throne is Gao (Geugeu). At the bottom is a representation of the river Niger, apparently indicating the inland delta which lies above Timbuctu.

Below right Seventeenth-century Dutch shipping off the great Gold Coast castle of São Jorge de Mina (Elmina), begun by the Portuguese in 1482. On the hill at the back is the smaller Fort Santiago, built by the Dutch to prevent enemies bombarding São Jorge (as they themselves had done when they captured it in 1637) from the landward side.

Above An air view of the ruins of the Great Mosque at Kilwa, which was probably completed in the fifteenth century.

Below A view of Kano, as seen by the traveller Henry Barth in 1851.

A lancer of the Sultan of Baghirmi (a territory just to the south-east of Bornu) as seen by the explorer Hugh Clapperton in the 1820s.

Below An eighteenth-century engraving of Khoikhoi (Hottentots) dismantling their portable encampment and loading it on to their bullocks.

Above A nineteenth-century drawing of a Trek-Boer waggon and its long span of oxen.

Below An early train on the Uganda Railway; note the Indian railway officials and passengers.

social division of the southern Bantu between the Nguni and the Sotho peoples. In the first stage, ancestors of the modern Nguni settled on the best agricultural land between the east coast and the Drakensberg. This left the wetter eastern high veld available for the Sotho, whose earlier history may have been connected in some way with the developments immediately to the north which produced the Zimbabwe-Monomotapa group of states. While the early Nguni seem to have lived in relatively small kingship groups, the early Sotho may well have had larger political units. They certainly built substantial stone-walled settlements, the largest of which are thought to have had populations of several thousands. But what is known of the early history of both the Nguni and the Sotho suggests that their political systems were very far from stable: segments of the royal lineages were continually breaking away and establishing new politico-social units. These must often have involved the conquest and absorption of neighbouring peoples, but the ideal seems to have been a tightly-knit group separated from its neighbours by uninhabited grazing land.

During the course of the eighteenth century, this continuing process of segmentation, fission and fusion began to reach critical proportions among the northern Nguni. It is not entirely clear what the reasons for this may have been. It seems reasonable to suppose that increasing contacts with the outside world may have played their part. By the mid-eighteenth century, the Portuguese were securing substantial quantities of ivory and slaves from trade at their settlement at Inhambane, on the coast some 300 miles south of Sofala and about 100 miles north of the mouth of the Limpopo, and English, Dutch, French and Portuguese traders were all showing interest in ivory trading at Delagoa Bay, about 200 miles further down the coast. Small quantities of copper were also reaching the coast, and probably all the southern Bantu were being linked by a growing network of internal trade. Thus it seems reasonable to suppose that the economic rewards of political competition were generally increasing. But a more general explanation for growing tension among the northern Nguni may have simply been the growth of population, which was doubtless accelerated as a consequence of the coming of maize to South-East Africa in the eighteenth century.

Maize offered the general advantage of higher yields over the millets which were the staple indigenous African grainstuffs, while more specifically the humid Indian Ocean coastland environment is one in which millets are prone to disease but which suited the cultivation of maize. Thus the introduction of maize cultivation permitted an increased density of settlement and a better chance of accumulating surpluses and avoiding famine. The result would be increased exploitation of the best soils for cultivation and increased demand for grazing for the larger herds in which wealth was invested. It seems possible that by the beginning of the nineteenth century, the processes of soil exhaustion and soil denudation, today so characteristic of the territories of the south-easternmost Bantu, may already have begun to show. At all events, by this time it seems to have become increasingly difficult for any one group of the northern Nguni to secure all the land thought necessary for the support of its society without seeking to attack and push back its neighbours. However, each successful attack could only be a short-term palliative. It not only tended to build up pressure for the neighbouring groups, but it also tended merely to increase the size of the problem for the aggressors, since their victory was only too likely to lead to their acquiring cattle, and possibly people as well, from the vanquished, and so to their requiring even more land.

Thus there began the *Mfecane* or *Difaqane*, the time of crushing and enforced migration, in which the troubles afflicting the northern Nguni were most successfully exploited by two successive warrior kings, Dingiswayo (*fl. c.* 1800–*c.* 1818) and Shaka (*c.* 1818–28). Dingiswayo sought a solution to the problems afflicting his small group, the Mthethwa, by taking its young men by regular age-groups out of ordinary society and maintaining them as regiments of a standing army. By the time of his death, this army had secured Dingiswayo's paramountcy over all other Nguni in an area of about 4000 square miles between the Umfolozi and Tugela rivers. The conquered chieftaincies were allowed to continue so long as they remained loyal, but their power and wealth were limited by the conscription of many of their young men and cattle for Dingiswayo's army and herds. After his death at the hands of a rival empire-builder, Zwide, this system was taken over and further developed by one of his regimental commanders, Shaka, who belonged to the royal line of the Zulu, one of the small groups conquered by Dingiswayo, and the result was the birth of the Zulu kingdom and nation.

Unlike Dingiswayo, Shaka believed in total war. Hitherto the main weapon had been the throwing spear, which might or might not hit the foe. This was replaced by the short, stabbing assegai, which could be used over and over again in the same battle, and discipline and tactics were evolved to allow large Zulu forces to approach the enemy unseen and unheard, and then overwhelm them in a sudden hand-to-hand onslaught. The ruling families of the defeated were totally eliminated, and Shaka had little hesitation in ordering wholesale massacres if he thought it expedient. The survivors were directly incorporated into the Zulu nation and regiments, and their cattle became Shaka's own, which he farmed out to his soldiers, who were allowed the use of their milk. The dominion built by Dingiswayo was extended to the north by the conquest of Zwide's rival kingdom, while all the country beyond the Tugela to as far south as the river Umzimkulu, and from the coast to the Drakensberg, perhaps 15 000 square miles, was virtually denuded of its original population, becoming a vast Zulu campaigning ground and cattle-run.

The consequences of this military explosion in South-East Africa were truly enormous. Refugees fleeing southwards from Shaka's regiments created considerable disturbance and renewed pressure on the available land for the southern Nguni, who were now also feeling the pressure of advancing European settlement on their southern and western frontier (see chapter 14). Other refugees fled west across the Drakensberg into Sotho territory, or to the north. These were accompanied or followed by armed bands led by unsuccessful rivals of Shaka, dissident generals of his army, or desperate leaders who saw no means of survival for themselves and their followers save by emulating his methods. The result was a complete reorganization of the political landscape.

A large area of the high veld was emptied of its inhabitants, much as the land south of Zululand had been. The agents here were firstly the raiding bands of mixed Nguni and Sotho refugees that the contemporary Europeans called 'Mantatees' (MaNthatisi, a woman, was one of their principal leaders), and secondly the warriors led by a dissident Zulu general, Mzilikazi, who in 1822 established himself on the high veld between the Vaal and Limpopo rivers, and there began to build up on the Zulu model the new conquest kingdom of the Ndebele. Those Sotho peoples who survived these onslaughts did so either by withdrawing to the west, to the confines of the Kalahari desert, or by fleeing to base themselves in or around the southern mountain fastness now known as Lesotho. Here from the mid-1820s onwards, Mosheshwe (d. 1870), originally no more than a minor Sotho chief, displayed remarkable military and political skills in uniting the refugees with the local people into a kingdom able to withstand not only the *Difaqane* but also subsequent European pressures. Another kingdom of refuge and survival was built up, albeit more on the Zulu model, to the north of Zululand by two Nguni chiefs, Sobhuza (*fl. c.* 1815–*c.* 1836), and his son, Mswazi (r. *c.* 1840–68), the latter giving his name to the state which, like Lesotho, has survived into the present century.

The people brought together in the Swazi kingdom included some Sotho, but were mainly Nguni, and the early history of the Swazi was involved with the consequences of the earlier rivalry in northern Zululand between Dingiswayo and Zwide. After the latter's defeat by Shaka in 1819, two of his military leaders, Shoshangane (d. 1858) and Zwangendaba (d. *c.* 1845)), took their followers northwards on careers of adventure. The former quickly established his paramountcy over the Tsonga peoples behind the coast between Delagoa Bay and the Zambezi, sacking the Portuguese posts at Inhambane, Sena and Delagoa Bay, and creating the Gaza kingdom. About 1835, he quarrelled with Zwangendaba, who thereupon led his people on an epic march through Butwa and across the Zambezi, then continuing northwards to the west of Lake Malawi to the country of the Fipa by the south-eastern shores of Lake Tanganyika.

This was the origin of the Ngoni* chieftaincies which began to emerge in south-central East Africa from about 1840 onwards. Zwangendaba's men were a Nguni army on the march, attacking and plundering each people they came across, and adding the able-bodied survivors to their own strength. Such a continually enlarging, mobile body, of increasingly heterogeneous ethnic origin yet dominated by a competitive military ethos, was naturally fissiparous. Some groups had already broken away during the northwards march, and after Zwangendaba's death, rival heirs and sub-chiefs led their men in all directions. Some raided north-west towards the Congo and north-east to Ujiji and Nyamwezi. But these seem to have been only small groups, which sometimes had the interesting long-term effect of encouraging peoples who hitherto had little in the way of central monarchical government to unite under leaders capable of organizing armies which could meet and defeat the Ngoni on their own terms. An outstanding example of this process occurred among the Hehe in the Tanganyika highlands to the south-east of Nyamwezi which itself,

* Ngoni, of course, is simply the eastern Bantu variant of the southern Bantu Nguni. Similarly, in East African history, Zwangendaba becomes Zongendaba.

under Mirambo, was strong enough to subdue and absorb the last of the northern marauders.

The activities of these northernmost Ngoni doubtless helped to increase the supply of slaves to Zanzibar, but, following Zwangendaba's death, the bulk of the Ngoni moved south to busy themselves in creating conquest states in the fertile and well-populated regions around Lake Malawi. The coming of the Ngoni, together with the more or less simultaneous expansion of the Yao towards the lake and the Shire highlands to the south of it, totally disrupted the rather loose association of chiefdoms under a titular head that is commonly called the Maravi Empire. In the seventeenth century, its power had reached to the coast, but more recently its centre had been in the Cewa country to the west and south-west of Lake Malawi.* Except in the four major areas where the Ngoni settled and organized Zulu-type kingdoms in which their language came to prevail, the Malawi basin and the Shire highlands became a territory in which orderly agricultural and village life was constantly subject to interruption by itinerant brigands and refugees. It therefore became an ideal hunting ground for Yao and Zanzibari slave traders, and doubtless the total insecurity was one of the factors behind the assumption of political authority by those of the latter who based themselves at Kota Kota.

In 1836–7, Mzilikazi's kingdom on the Transvaal high veld, which had already been harassed by Zulu raids, became involved in hostilities with the Boer trekkers advancing from the Cape Colony (see p. 359). He therefore decided to withdraw his Ndebele, who now included many people of Sotho origins, north across the Limpopo. Here it would seem that the ancient Butwa polity had not survived the earlier shock of Zwangendaba's invasion. The Ndebele quickly made themselves masters of the south-western Shona tribes. These were incorporated in the kingdom which the European colonists who were to follow them half a century later were to call Matabeleland (a corruption of Ndebele and its Bantu plural prefix 'ama-'), while the north-eastern Shona were subjected to raids in search of cattle and human recruits for Mzilikazi's kingdom. The Sotho to the south-west and the Lozi to the north-west across the Zambezi were also subject to Ndebele

* The ethnic and linguistic nomenclature in this region is somewhat confusing. Malawi, the modern name for the lake and the territory called Nyasa and Nyasaland in the colonial period, is simply a variant of Maravi. The people of the old Maravi empire live in the south of modern Malawi and in adjacent areas of Mozambique and Zambia, and all speak dialects of the language now called Nyanja. The Cewa are their largest group.

attacks, but both these peoples were able to hold their own. In the first case, this was due in large measure to the leadership of Khama, the ruler (1865–1923) of the Ngwato, the northernmost Sotho group, who lived at a time when it was possible for him to balance the danger from the Ndebele by exploiting the growing interest in the western Sotho territories (the modern Botswana) of European missionaries and traders and, ultimately, of British officials. In the second case, survival was also associated with a Sotho group, the Kololo, originally refugees from the *Difaqane*, who were led by their chief, Sebetwane (d. 1851), northwards through Botswana and across the Zambezi, where they were able to secure control of the resources of the Lozi kingdom. The Kololo themselves, emigrants from temperate highlands, soon succumbed to the malaria of the Zambezi valley. However, their conquest served to stimulate a revival of Lozi political leadership, which led on to a considerable expansion of the kingdom.

In conclusion, some attempt should be made to assess the general effects of the opening up of Bantu Africa, from the seventeenth century onwards, to forces of change generated by world trade, and especially by the unrestricted overseas demands for African slaves. The general picture given by the travellers from the outside world who, following the inspiration of David Livingstone, began increasingly to penetrate Bantu Africa from the 1850s onwards, is one of the near-universal destruction of peaceful, village agricultural society, and its replacement by chaos and barbarism. The blame for this was laid on wars and raids to secure slaves for robber societies and economies both outside and inside Africa, and the only remedy seen was the introduction – if necessary, the imposition – of European commerce, Christianity and colonization to extirpate such crimes against humanity, and to lead Africans back to the path to civilization.

This picture remains a popular western stereotype even today, and of course it is an article of faith for the Europeans who have taken root in southern Africa. But while it was based on observation at first hand, it was also to a considerable extent shaped by the preconceptions of the observers. Mid- and late-nineteenth-century Europeans were generally convinced that their Christian, scientific and industrial society was intrinsically far superior to anything that Africa had produced, or could produce unaided, and specifically that slavery and slave-raiding were wrong – at once inhumane and economically inefficient. However, the West African history that is now being written seems to suggest that, in African conditions, institutions of servitude could be used to build up societies which could offer enlarged opportunities for the achievement of wealth and security. Perhaps, too, the subsequent development of European society has shown that Victorians tended to exaggerate not only the importance, but also the reality of the personal liberties that they thought were being surrendered to gain these opportunities. There was certainly much death and destruction in the history of Bantu Africa in the seventeenth, eighteenth and nineteenth centuries. However, as has already been suggested, the Europeans, exploring as they did along the Zanzibari trade paths and in the wake of the Nguni and Ngoni conquests, may have seen more than a fair sample. (Nor, incidentally, did their transformation into colonial rulers automatically end such destruction; this was already apparent in Angola, and was soon to be seen, for example, in the Congo, in Rhodesia, and with the campaigns of 1914–18 in East Africa.) But some orderly Bantu states survived or more than survived during this period: both the Lozi kingdom and Buganda were seized upon by the explorers and early missionaries as fertile soils for the implanting of the new seeds for the redemption of African society. Some new orderly states arose out of the chaos, for example the kingdoms of Mosheshwe, Khama and Queen Nzinga, and perhaps of Kasanje and Mirambo and Mwaka of the Hehe. Nor can anyone say for certain that the new Nguni and Ngoni polities would not have developed beyond their origins in military despotisms for, within a generation or two, they were all subjected to equally arbitrary European military conquests.

Nevertheless, it is probably true that, as has already been suggested, conditions for the development of stable large-scale societies were not generally as propitious in Bantu Africa as they were in West Africa. Outside a few favoured lacustrine or coastal regions, the good soils and the adequate supplies of water and people needed to build up stable and prospering states on an agricultural base were generally lacking. Moreover, compared with the West Africans, the Bantu were also late starters in the business of learning how to exploit their resources and to build up and diversify their populations and their economies. The impact of world trade fell upon most of them both late and suddenly. Bantu peoples had usually had very little time to construct their own systems of government and trade before they were assaulted by militant external demands for the most readily extractable of their scarce resources, ivory and people. These demands were often levied by aliens who had penetrated their society and who cared little for its welfare or its future. Slaves became 'black ivory', and the acquisition of them, like the acquisition of ivory, was as much a hunting as it was a trading activity, and no one bothered at the loss of life involved.

It has been seen that, in terms of the total number of slaves taken away, the demand on Bantu Africa was of much the same size as that on West Africa. But the load was concentrated in a shorter period of time and spread over a much wider area. A rough calculation suggests that the area from which most of the Bantu export slaves were taken must have been at least three times greater than that which bore the brunt of the trade in West Africa (which, as has been seen, was the thickly populated region of Lower Guinea). In modern times, Bantu population densities generally are comparable not with those of Lower Guinea, but with Upper Guinea, which, it has been suggested, was too thinly populated to contribute significantly to the Atlantic slave trade. It is indeed tempting to think that in Bantu Africa, the export slave trade, often externally rather than internally organized, may itself have been a principal cause of these relatively low population densities. In fact it is difficult to substantiate this. Two of the principal exceptions to the general picture are the well-watered and now densely populated basins of Lake Malawi and Lake Victoria. The former was extensively exploited for slaves, the latter was relatively little touched, yet there is little significant difference between their modern population densities. A similar point can be made in relation to the more typical areas of relatively thin population. In recent times, mainland Tanzania, which was subjected to intense slaving, has had an average population density greater than that of Zimbabwe, a territory little if at all affected by the export slave trade. This suggests that the underlying explanations for the relatively low population densities that characterize Bantu Africa were the relatively late date of its settlement by farming societies, and recurrent droughts, famines and epidemics, which impeded agricultural exploitation and made the accumulation of surpluses a difficult and risky business.

But this in itself leads to the further conclusion that, except for the islands of better soils and water supplies and of dense population, the general picture in Bantu Africa at the time that it was hit by the external demands for slaves and ivory, was one in which the numbers of people available to ensure a reasonable and orderly exploitation of the soil and of other resources were critically low. If this were so,

then to take so many people away, and to do so by political, military
and economic methods which seem generally cruder than were needed
in West Africa, and in a shorter period of time, must often have been
extremely damaging to Bantu society.

Chapter 13

The expansion of European power during the nineteenth century, 1:

General considerations; West Africa

A variety of explanations has been advanced to account for the explosive European competition for colonies that swept over Africa during the last quarter of the nineteenth century, and which ended with virtually the whole continent being partitioned between a number of European powers. One view, implicit for example in works by such eminent modern historians as A. J. P. Taylor and W. L. Langer, is that, from about the 1860s onwards, the rivalries between the great powers in Europe became so acute that they more or less inevitably spilled over into Africa and other parts of the non-European world. These regions therefore were treated as bargaining counters and *points d'appui* in what was essentially an intra-European conflict. It is certainly possible, for example, to interpret Bismarck's sudden support for the aspirations of the German colonial party in 1884–5 in this sense – and it may also be noted that Britain required German support if France were to be outvoted on the Egyptian Debt Commission established in 1880.* But such an explanation presents some difficulties as an overall interpretation for the colonial scramble in Africa. The most obvious of these is that the scramble did not involve all the major European powers and – if there are good non-

---

* See below chapter 14, page 374. (It has also been suggested, of course, that Bismarck's espousal of the colonial cause was motivated by reasons of internal German politics.)

African reasons for this – that some states of little or no weight in the European struggle, such as Portugal, Belgium and Spain, were in one way or another active participants in it.

However, another argument, which was advanced at the time by European colonial propagandists, is not unrelated to the explanation that the scramble was due to intra-European rivalries. The core of this argument, as expressed for example from the 1870s onwards by the French economist, P. Leroy-Beaulieu, was that Britain was the richest and most developed nation in Europe during the first three-quarters of the nineteenth century, and that since she was then the only one possessing a sizeable overseas empire, the possession of empire was essential if a European nation were to be rich and powerful. This kind of reasoning may well lie behind Italy's bid for empire in North-East Africa and Libya, where to a large extent she was belatedly following what appeared to be the example not only of Britain, but also of France and Germany (and, indeed, of her own great Roman ancestors). But if Britain was the prime exemplar, as she was, then the real relationship between wealth and empire seems to have been the reverse of that postulated by Leroy-Beaulieu and his kind. They were arguing that the acquisition of colonies was necessary if there were to be major growth in European foreign trade and industry. In fact, in the British case, the historical evidence suggests rather that it was Britain's primacy in European overseas trade and in the development of manufacturing industry which had led her, alone among the European powers, to acquire a sizeable overseas empire prior to the 1870s.

However, what people believe can well be more important in determining their actions than the actual facts of the situation. This observation is also relevant to an interpretation of the scramble which was first cogently advanced at its climax in J. A. Hobson's *Imperialism* (1902), and which was subsequently taken up and developed into part of the dogma of socialist thought by Lenin and others. In essence this interpretation boils down to the contention that it was only by finding new markets and new sources of cheap raw materials outside the continent that the momentum of industrial and commercial growth in the rich countries of western Europe could be maintained and, indeed, the capitalist system saved from collapse.

This may well have been so. On the other hand, it is easy to demonstrate that European traders and investors showed very little interest in the greater part of Africa. North Africa, of course, had long been part of a Mediterranean trading system involving the merchants of southern Europe, while South Africa had recently become a focus of interest following the discovery of its mineral wealth. (It is worth pointing out that Hobson wrote his book at a time when many liberally-minded men, such as he was, were aghast at the methods of British imperialism employed in South Africa to control its minerals.) But in 1897 the value of the foreign trade of all Africa south of the Sahara was only £66 000 000 ($330 000 000), of which South Africa alone accounted for two-thirds, while in 1929, after a quarter of a century of European control, it had risen only to £340 000 000 ($1 700 000 000), of which South Africa contributed one half. The foreign trade of just one European country, the United Kingdom, was worth thirteen times as much as in 1900 and six times as much in 1929. Again, by 1913, foreign – mainly European – investment in Africa south of the Sahara was worth about £650 000 000 ($3 250 000 000) and by 1929 it had increased to about £1 200 000 000 ($6 000 000 000). But in each case rather more than half the investment was in South Africa, and *tropical* Africa's share of the world's total foreign investments amounted to only some 4 per cent in 1913 and 7 per cent in 1929.

There can be no doubt that in matters of trade and investment, Europeans found it more profitable, and thought it safer, to deal with more developed parts of the world. In fact, in 1913, about 80 per cent of British and French and 90 per cent of German foreign investment was in other European countries or, if outside Europe, was in territories which had long been settled by Europeans and where considerable development had already taken place – for example in North and South America and Australia. It may also be remarked that, after Britain, France and Germany (in that order), the largest overseas investment came from the United States, which acquired little formal empire overseas and, of course, none in Africa.

Africa, tropical Africa in particular, was then of little real importance to European traders and investors at the time of the scramble – and the situation had not greatly improved even after a quarter of a century or more of European control of the continent. On the other hand, however, until colonial control had been established – and, in many cases, for some time afterwards – there was little or no exact knowledge of the resources available in Africa or of the problems which might be involved in developing them profitably. It was thus possible for those who were interested in colonial adventures, whether for their own personal, or for national, purposes of gain or prestige, to make extravagant claims about Africa's agricultural or mineral wealth or the numbers of its potential customers for European trade. Thus in 1898, a British War Office intelligence report (which might be thought to have been a sober source) said of the Bahr el Ghazal, even today one of the least accessible and most impoverished regions of Africa, that it was 'well watered and fertile' and held out the promise of 'considerable developments, agricultural, pastoral and mineral, in the hands of a civilized power'. Similarly, in the 1880s, when the French were actively engaged in their conquest of the western Sudan, responsible government ministers could talk of finding there a market of 88 000 000 or more people. When the conquest had been completed and stock could be taken, the reality was found to be nearer 10 000 000, and the lack of communications and development meant that they were a very indifferent market for French trade and industry. Again, following the discovery of the gold wealth of the Transvaal, Cecil Rhodes, who had his own political reasons for occupying the territories to the north of it, was able to claim that these were even more richly mineralized. Between 1889 and 1910, he and his successors were able to secure nearly £12 000 000 ($60 000 000) of capital to enable his British South Africa Company to occupy these territories. But, in the event, this so stretched the resources of the company that no dividend was paid to investors in it before 1924.

More recently, it has been cogently argued by some economic historians such as A. G. Hopkins, that, in West Africa at least, Europeans felt driven to advance into and to conquer the interior less by the lure of its potential wealth than by the difficulties that their traders were experiencing in the coastal trade during the period of depression in world trade from 1874 to 1896. During the nineteenth century, Europe's trade with West Africa had become focussed on Guinea's agricultural produce, especially vegetable oils and oilseeds – palm oil and kernels, and groundnuts. But by the late 1880s, for example, the world market price for a ton of palm oil, which had previously been around £50 ($250), had fallen to as low as about £20. At such price levels, there was virtually no profit to be made from the trade in West African oil produce. European traders therefore began to press for direct access to the producing areas in the hinterland. They argued that not only would this cut out the African middleman traders and their need for profits, but also that the estab-

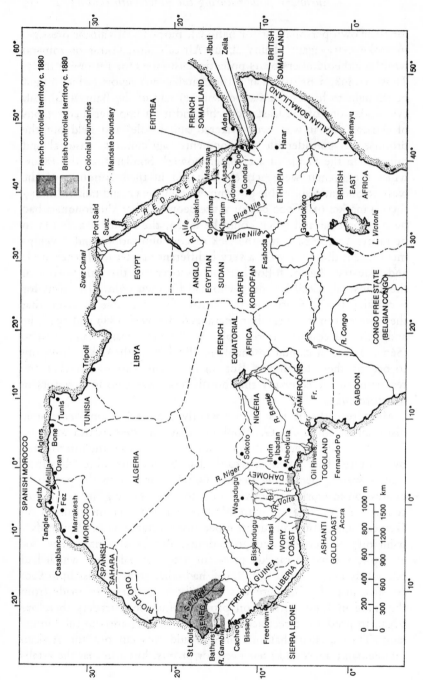

Map 9   Northern Africa during the era of European expansion

lishment in the interior of European systems of transport (e.g. railways) and methods of trading would provide more economical means by which palm oil and other produce might be bulked and brought down to the coast for export. It was further argued that these things could not be quickly and efficiently done unless European political control were also extended into the interior.

This West African example, which is well supported by evidence, suggests that important factors in precipitating the scramble for African colonies were the nature and extent of the European interests that were already involved in the continent, and the extent to which Europeans had persuaded themselves that these were thwarted or frustrated by the indigenous African authorities. This approach to an explanation of the European scramble can be seen in Professor Hargreaves's *Prelude to the Partition of West Africa* (1963) (though this does not go further back than the 1860s). It is also implicit in one of the most important modern works on the partition generally, *Africa and the Victorians* (1961), by Professors Ronald Robinson and John Gallagher. This points to the importance of the strategic and financial or commercial interests which Europeans acquired in two key areas, in Egypt following the opening of the Suez Canal in 1869, and in South Africa following the discovery of its mineral wealth, diamonds in 1867, but more especially gold in 1886. In brief, Robinson and Gallagher argue that what precipitated the scramble for African colonies was the reaction of other European powers, notably France and Germany, to the paramountcy which Britain achieved in Egypt in 1882 and shortly began to achieve in South Africa also.

But *Africa and the Victorians* is Eurocentric, even Anglocentric (its subtitle is 'The Official Mind of Imperialism'). Moreover Egypt and South Africa, however important, were not the only areas of the continent in which Europeans had become seriously entangled, while to concentrate on these entanglements as the precipitating factors for the partition does not do justice to its chronology. It has been shown, for example, that the origins of France's colonial advance in West Africa can be traced back many years before she had any need to recoup her imperial fortunes because of the British pre-emption of Egypt, and the decisive step in this advance was probably taken in 1879, when her troops began to move across from the valley of the upper Senegal to that of the upper Niger. Other critics of Robinson and Gallagher have suggested that the precipitating factor was the focussing on the Congo of the long-held colonial ambitions of

Leopold II of the Belgians. This was evident by 1876, and led quickly not only to the treaty-making competition in the lower Congo between his agent, H. M. Stanley, and the French explorer, Savorgnan de Brazza, but also to reactions from Portugal and Britain, whose interests in the region were of appreciably longer standing. No one would dispute that this Congo imbroglio led directly to the first European partition conference, the Berlin Conference of 1884–5.

But a considerably longer perspective is needed to understand why by the 1870s the French were established on the Senegal or, for that matter, why the British had formed colonies in Sierra Leone, on the Gold Coast, at Lagos and in South Africa; why such colonial interests could engender further imperial advances; or why Leopold was interested in the Congo, and Stanley and De Brazza were making treaties there. The starting-point must be the nature of the European interests that already existed at the beginning of the nineteenth century in both West and South Africa, and how these were modified by the decisions taken between 1792 and 1836 by the European nations trading to Africa to cease dealing in African slaves and, in some cases, to intervene against both the slave trade and slavery in Africa itself. These decisions unlocked powerful forces for change in many African societies. This was not least because they came to be accompanied by a full-scale campaign to establish Christianity throughout sub-Saharan Africa, for the missionaries believed not only that slavery and trading or warfare to secure slaves must be totally eradicated, but also that there was no future at all for African societies unless they agreed to be educated on a European model. In South Africa, the deployment of these new forces, and the local reaction to them – the reaction of Europeans of an older era as much as of the Africans – led incidentally to an increasing interest in the affairs of central and East Africa. This interest took root the more easily because a new European strategic concern with the Red Sea and the western Indian Ocean had been developing since the later eighteenth century. This in its turn was a consequence of another factor of major long-term importance in explaining the European partition, namely that it had become abundantly clear that Ottoman power no longer provided a shield keeping Europe out of North Africa.

The European scramble for African colonies that became so virulent in the 1880s and 1890s must in fact be seen as the culminating stage in a process of interaction between Europeans and Africans which had been growing in momentum and intensity over a much longer period, certainly since the close of the eighteenth and the beginning of the nineteenth century. At this time, vital decisions were taken in Europe – with regard to the abolition of slavery and slave trading, and intervention in the affairs of North and South, West and East Africa – which were to lead to more and more confrontations between Europeans and Africans. These confrontations were of a nature which was increasingly different from those which had taken place before, in the long period since the fifteenth century, when the Iberians had mounted their first campaigns in Morocco and had pioneered European trade and colonization and Christian conversion round the sub-Saharan coastline. The confrontations then had been between societies that were very different, but which were not unequal in material or moral strength, at least in tropical African conditions. During the eighteenth century, European civilization was achieving the full maturity that is exemplified in the scientific, industrial and French revolutions. By the beginning of the nineteenth century, it possessed means to create material wealth and power unparalleled in the history of mankind, and with these it had gained truly enormous moral strength and purpose. In any clash between European and African interests or beliefs, Europe now possessed both the material means – steampower, firepower, medical power – to impose its will upon Africa, and the moral strength – the certainty that European civilization would prevail, and also that it was in the interest of the African peoples that it should do so.

In West Africa, the European interest was a very considerable one by the end of the eighteenth century, the result of some four centuries of cumulative commercial intercourse. This interest was not diminished when, beginning in 1792, the various European nations involved came to outlaw the traffic in slaves which had hitherto been the mainstay of their trade. Two points need to be borne in mind here.

In the first place, even when the Atlantic slave trade had been Europe's dominant interest in West Africa, slaves had never been the only commodity sought there. Leaving out of account the considerable quantities of foodstuffs that were purchased to feed the slaves on the voyage to America, the Europeans were prepared to buy any African product for which they could see a profitable market, and the list includes gold, ivory, timber, gum and vegetable oils. Secondly, the change in the European attitude towards the slave trade and slavery occurred gradually. Some seventy years elapsed between the first prohibition of the slave trade by a European state (Denmark in 1792) and the final cessation of the export of slaves from West Africa. Abolition of the slave trade was promoted principally by those northern nations, Britain chief among them, which were experiencing the industrial revolution and the Protestant evangelical revival, and it was accepted reluctantly and under pressure by more conservative southern European societies, more especially those of Spain and Portugal. Thus so long as there continued to be a market for slaves in the Americas, African slaves continued to be exported, and higher profits compensated for the decline in numbers and for the increasing risks involved in engaging illicitly in the trade.

Nevertheless, however gradual the process, the ending of the export slave trade did produce a major crisis in the long-established relationship between West Africa and Europe. From the later seventeenth century onwards, the buying and selling of slaves had become the dominant and most profitable aspect of this relationship for both sides. It was therefore by no means straightforward to develop alternative export staples to take the place of slaves. Some Europeans eventually decided to abandon, or were forced to restrict, their West African interests. Thus first the Danes (1850) and then the Dutch (1872) withdrew from the Gold Coast forts which they had occupied since the seventeenth century, while such Portuguese activity as remained was reduced to a small area around Cacheu and Bissao and other settlements founded from the Cape Verde Islands. But both Britain and France possessed commercial interests that were so committed, morally as well as financially, to the trade with West Africa, that withdrawal from it was never really in question.

There can be no doubt about the substantial nature of the British trading interest in West Africa. In the quarter century before the abolition of the British slave trade in 1807, British ships had carried some two-thirds of the slaves taken from West Africa to the Americas (and nearly half of all the African slaves taken across the Atlantic). A sizeable proportion of British shipping, trading and manufacturing capital had become dependent on selling goods to Africa, and to West Africa in particular. This was particularly the case with the fast-growing port of Liverpool (which by the 1790s was handling about three-quarters of the British slave trade, involving it in the dispatch of up to a hundred or so ships a year), and with the cotton manufacturing towns of Lancashire and the metal goods industries of south Yorkshire and the Midlands which formed its commercial hinterland.

These interests therefore become involved in the search for, and the development of, alternative African exports to replace the slaves which had been the staple of the earlier commerce.

The French interest cannot be so surely demonstrated in economic terms. France's economy was far less dependent on foreign trade than was Britain's. Furthermore, during 1793–1815 her old West African trading empire had been largely ruined by British sea-power. But this had bred a determination that the British should not have things all their own way in West Africa. The result was that, subject to the exigencies of an ever-changing domestic political scene, those French merchants and others who were interested in rebuilding old, or in developing new, interests in West Africa could expect some official support.

By and large the Europeans, with their highly diversified, industrialized economies, possessing considerable reserves of capital and a rapidly increasing command of technical resources, were able to adapt to the new conditions of the West African trade more effectively and rapidly than the Africans. This was particularly so because, as has been seen, the old staple of foreign trade in West Africa, namely slave trading, had been very intimately bound up with the rise of new monarchical governments and societies. From the commercial point of view, these were in effect cumbersome state monopolies which – rather like the old seventeenth-century European monopoly trading companies – could not readily or quickly change the nature of their activities. Their difficulty was compounded by the fact that the major commercial consideration of the Europeans, the replacement of slaves as an export staple by other commodities, did not really enter at all into the thinking of the men who governed and managed these African societies. Their primary aim was to maintain and to develop their political and economic power over as many people as possible: the export slave trade was for them only a by-product of this. At the same time, however, it was a by-product on which they had become increasingly dependent for the purchase of the means by which their power could be maintained and developed, and which therefore they were extremely unwilling to forgo. The systems they commanded, oriented as much or more to political as to commercial ends, thus had no incentive to produce alternative goods for export, and in fact were ill-adapted to doing so. The new staples of foreign trade that emerged in the nineteenth century, like palm oil and kernels and groundnuts and, ultimately, crops like cocoa and coffee, were not most effectively produced and marketed by major state organizations, but by hosts of enterprising small men, who could respond freely and quickly to the varying stimuli of world market forces. It was these small-scale producers and collectors and traders with whom the nineteenth-century European traders struck up alliances. Efforts made by the traditional authorities to control the new situation began to appear increasingly obstructive and old-fashioned. Economic and political strains began to appear in West African societies which led many Europeans to conclude that their own legitimate interests might be better served if they withdrew from the old, traditional alliances with African rulers, and themselves took over political control.

This shift in European political attitudes was accentuated because the merchants were not now the only Europeans on the scene in West Africa. From the 1790s onwards, European explorers began to penetrate behind the screen of slave-trading states on the coast to see what alternative resources might be developed for foreign trade. In the following decade, Christian missionaries began to establish themselves in the coastlands. Seeking to repair the moral damage caused by slavery and slave trading, they were most successful in implanting themselves in areas in which European trade and its changing demands had had the greatest effect. In such places, indeed, some Africans became divorced from the norms of African society and accepted the missionary claim that the adoption of European modes of thought and action presented the best means of preserving or restoring social stability and of achieving progress. In this way, some Africans themselves became important agents in the processes drawing Europe into closer involvement with Africa.

But some time was to elapse before either these consequences of the missionary implantation or the full implications of the explorers' work were to become evident. More direct and immediate results flowed from the appearance alongside the traders on the West African coasts of European naval, military and political agents, more especially of the French and British governments. Essentially there were two reasons for the arrival of European government officials on the West African scene.

First, if the laws of European states prohibiting their citizens from engaging in the slave trade were to be effective, the places where they needed to be enforced were not in Europe itself, but on the African or American coasts where the slavers actually conducted their trade. For a number of compelling reasons, it was Britain that took the lead in anti-slave-trade enforcement on the coasts of West Africa. As has been seen, Britain's share of the old Atlantic slave trade in the eighteenth century had been much greater than that of any other nation. Her anti-slave-trade campaign had therefore to generate the greatest moral and political force in order to succeed. Equally, from the economic point of view, Britain had the strongest incentive to replace her old slave trade with what was now called 'legitimate trade', and also to block any competition from other Europeans – or from Americans or Africans – who wanted to continue a trade in slaves which might impede the development of British legitimate trade. Finally, although both the governments of France and of the United States did from time to time mount naval anti-slave-trade patrols in African waters, only nineteenth-century Britain possessed a navy big enough to enable this to be done on anything approaching the scale, or with the continuity required, to have a reasonable chance of preventing slaves being exported from Africa.

Secondly, both the French and the British governments felt a growing need to impose their will on African authorities. On the French side, this was essentially because their traders needed some political, and naval or military, backing if they were to make headway against their stronger and more strongly established British competitors. Thus, for example, during 1838–42, a naval officer, Bouët-Willaumez, negotiated treaties with coastal rulers to establish trading posts at a number of points on the West African coast. Many of these were subsequently abandoned, but it can fairly be said that effective French interest in what ultimately became their colonies of Guinea, the Ivory Coast, and Gabon dates from this time. Also, in 1843 the old French fort at Whydah was reoccupied, and during the next twenty years a fair amount of official backing was given to French merchants trading on the old Slave Coast. In this manner the French gained a number of *points d'appui* between the areas of established British and Portuguese interest on the West African coast, and from these formal colonies could be developed in the period of intensive colonial competition from the 1870s onwards.

However, in 1817, following the peace settlement after the Napoleonic wars, the French had also been able to return to the Senegal, the one area in which they had been strongly established in the previous century, and St Louis and Goree and two up-river posts were reoccupied. Since African labour could no longer be exported, an attempt was made to employ it locally, on plantations which would grow the same crops as had been produced in the West Indies. But within five years, this scheme had failed. The Senegalese did not want to labour on European plantations, and the Europeans were inept in their management in conditions of soil and climate that they did not properly understand. Thereafter French attention was somewhat diverted from the Senegal by the coastal trading tentatives already mentioned. In 1854, however, it was decided that the administration of these, from Goree, should be separated from that of the Senegal, at St Louis. A new governor was appointed for the latter, Louis Faidherbe, an army officer who had participated in the conquest of Algeria and who had already established a rapport with the French merchants at St Louis.

Faidherbe was persuaded that it was futile for French fortunes on the Senegal to be dependent on the whims of the interior traders. His subsequent actions provided a blueprint for the establishment of profitable colonies in tropical Africa at minimum cost to European tax-payers. He recruited an army of African soldiers, trained and led by European officers, and used it to impose French control on an area of territory and a number of people sufficient to provide the French merchants operating from St Louis with a viable hinterland. He was lucky in that, in the 1840s, the latter had begun to appreciate that, in the face of an ever-increasing European demand for vegetable oils, groundnut oil could be an acceptable supplement to the Mediterranean staple of olive oil, while Senegalese farmers were learning that their dry sandy soils were well suited to ground-nut production, and that this could give them useful cash returns. The revenue from the groundnut and more traditional trades enabled Faidherbe to provide an efficient administration for the territory conquered by his soldiers. It also provided the beginnings of a modern, state education system, which had the purpose of training Senegalese to be efficient assistants to the French in the management and exploitation of their country.

When Faidherbe finally returned home in 1864, he had advanced French power in the western Sudan to the limits of navigation on the river Senegal, over 300 miles from the sea, and he had decisively halted the advance of al-Hajj 'Umar's empire in the contrary direction. Once France had recovered from the decline and fall of her Second Empire, nothing was more natural than that imperially minded planners in Paris and ambitious military commanders in Senegal should seek to continue his work. If al-Hajj 'Umar's empire could be conquered, then the French would have advanced to the navigable upper Niger, thus gaining access to the whole western Sudan.

Prior to the new conditions brought about by the world trade depression in the 1870s, British officials in West Africa were perhaps rarely as openly aggressive in taking action in the British trading interest as Bouët-Willaumez and Faidherbe had shown that French officials could be. The official attitude was the *laissez-faire* one that what British merchants did was their own business, and that if they were not strong enough to stand on their own feet in Africa or other foreign territories, they had no business to be there. But it was accepted that it was the duty of the British government to act against the slave trade, especially where it was impeding the development of legitimate trade. British anti-slave-trade activities came to include the negotiation of treaties with African as well as with European authorities, and the taking of political and naval initiatives to ensure the observance of these treaties, or even to force them upon reluctant governments. The result in practice was that there was as much or more British interference in West African affairs as there was French interference, even if the British were somewhat slower than the French had been in the Senegal to come to the logical conclusion that their ends might best be achieved by using force to set up territorial colonies. In each case there were two policy objectives; to stop the slave trade, and to establish profitable legitimate trade in its place. If the French officials tended to put rather more emphasis on advancing the interests of French traders, which had as a consequence a reduction in the old slave trade, while the British laid more stress on fighting the slave trade, which had the consequence that British trading interests were advanced, the results from the African point of view were hardly distinguishable.

The first consequence in West Africa of the British campaigns against slavery and the slave trade was the establishment in 1792 (after an earlier false start) at Freetown on the Sierra Leone peninsula of a settlement of freed slaves. Initially this was a private venture of British philanthropists who had launched a company with the purpose of resettling in Africa former slaves from Britain and British North America, and of trying to recoup the costs of the settlement and its administration from the profits of legitimate trade. But such profits proved elusive so long as the slave trade continued in the vicinity, and further difficulties arose when the settlers and the company's officials failed to see eye to eye on such matters as land and rents and local government. In 1808, however, the nascent colony's future was secured when, after an interim period of grants-in-aid, the British government agreed to take over responsibility for it. It needed Freetown's harbour as a base from which British warships could operate in the wars with France and in anti-slave-trade patrolling off the West African coast. During the next sixty years, the population of the colony was swollen by the landing of some 60 000 men and women liberated from captured slave ships.

In 1814, the governorship of Sierra Leone was entrusted to Sir Charles Macarthy, an energetic military officer, who believed that the best way to stop the slave trade was to extend British control over the major places of export within his reach. His local initiatives to this end were not wholly discountenanced by the Colonial Office, which in 1821 extended his jurisdiction to include the British settlements on the Gambia and the Gold Coast. On the Gold Coast, Macarthy quickly concluded that the British and anti-slave-trade interest necessitated military action against Ashanti in concert with the Fante and the Danes. But in 1824 this led to his defeat and death in a battle with the Ashanti. Though, two years later, the military fortunes of the allies were re-established, this setback caused the Colonial Office to count the cost of Macarthy's policy. A fourfold increase in administrative expenditure had not been justified by any worthwhile increase in British trade. It was therefore decided that the Gold Coast forts should be abandoned, and the competence of the Freetown governor restricted to Sierra Leone and the settlement of Bathurst, at Banjul in the Gambia, where British traders had established themselves when they had left Goree in 1816–17.

However, the handful of British merchants trading to the Gold Coast refused to accept this retrogressive measure. They secured authority to set up their own administration for the few forts they still occupied. The man they appointed in 1830 as their local administrator, George Maclean, proved skilful in re-establishing peaceful relations with Ashanti while at the same time winning and preserving the confidence of the coastal Africans. The result was that an informal British jurisdiction was established over the Fante and Gã states, and that within ten years the value of British trade on the Gold Coast had been nearly quadrupled, exports and imports combined reaching some £750 000 ($3 750 000) a year. But the legal basis for Maclean's jurisdiction was obscure; he himself argued that he had no right to take active measures against slave traders who were not British subjects. In 1843, therefore, the Colonial Office decided that it must resume control over his Gold Coast colony. But the Colonial Office officials who succeeded Maclean, though sometimes equally ambitious, were less experienced and adroit in their dealings with both Ashanti and the coastal peoples. Trade swiftly declined to the 1830 level. Though the Danish forts were taken over in 1850, the continued presence of Dutch forts on the coast prevented the raising of an effective revenue from customs duties, and an attempt to levy a poll tax incurred open hostility from the coastal peoples. By the 1860s, Ashanti armies were again threatening the coastlands, and in 1865 a Parliamentary Select Committee recommended that British official commitments in West Africa should once again be restricted to Sierra Leone.

The truth was that, despite the British involvement in the Gold Coast and the relatively heavy cost of this, it was now a minor British interest commercially. The new staple of British trade with West Africa was palm oil, purchases of which were amounting to about £500 000 ($2 500 000) a year by the 1850s, and to about £1 500 000 ($7 500 000) a year by the 1860s. Though oil palms grew throughout a belt lying just behind the coast, and the oil from their fruit was always an important article of local consumption and trade, negligible quantities of palm oil were available for export from the formal British colonies. Initially something like nine-tenths of the British palm oil trade was with the Niger delta.

Transport by canoe on the many waterways of this region provided a better and cheaper way of bringing the oil down to the coast than was possible with headloading or cask rolling, but this cannot be the only explanation of the early primacy of the delta in the oil trade (which, of course, gave it its nineteenth-century name, the Oil Rivers). It would seem that this must lie in an almost unique combination of two factors. The Ibo hinterland of the delta had an unusually dense population in relation to its indifferent agricultural environment. Thus it had both a greater need to make use of the semi-wild oil palms than was usual, and more labour with which to collect the fruit and to manufacture the oil and to bulk it for trade. Secondly, the small, competitive city-states of the delta, controlled as they were by merchant oligarchies that were naturally responsive to economic stimuli, were ideally fitted to exploit this situation when their European trading partners began to ask for oil instead of – or as well as – slaves.

When the European demand for palm oil began to exceed the

delta's capacity for supplying it, the trade also began to take root in neighbouring Yorubaland until, by the 1860s, this was supplying almost as much oil as the delta. It may be noted that this too was an unusually thickly populated region, and that the centralized control which Oyo had once sought to exert over its economic and political life had now totally broken down. Neither the Dahomans, to the west, nor the Fulani, seeking to advance from the north, succeeded in taking full advantage of this situation for their own imperial purposes. The Yoruba reorganized themselves around a number of local nuclei. Some of these, like Ijebu or New Oyo, were the seats of traditional kings, but others, notably the metropolises of Ibadan and Abeokuta (which played the prime roles in repulsing the Fulani and Dahomey respectively), were new foundations attracting men and women from many parts of Yorubaland. In these societies, economic and political opportunism became the rule. The ablest and most ambitious sought to achieve security by building up the largest possible retinue of retainers and clients; lesser men chose to ally themselves with one or other of these new leaders.

From the political point of view, the result was often chaotic, whether within a new city like Ibadan or Abeokuta (or even one of the more traditional towns) or in the country as a whole, where there was almost continuous warfare. But from the economic point of view, there were boundless new opportunities. Each of the new leaders sought to achieve maximum returns for and with his following. Initially one result was a boom in the export slave trade. But this led the British, who were already blockading the Dahomey coast, to take active measures to stop the export of slaves further to the east. In 1851 force was used to expel the king of Lagos and to install a rival who had promised to forbid the slave trade, together with a British consul to keep an eye on him. When this did not work very well, Lagos was annexed as a colony, and the British began to extend their jurisdiction to neighbouring ports, like Palma and Lecki to the east and Badagri to the west. Thus the new men in Yorubaland, like their counterparts in the delta, came to rely more and more on the palm oil trade as the mainstay of external commerce. Competition for control of the trade routes to the European merchants sheltering under British suzerainty at Lagos came to be a major theme of the later Yoruba wars. Not unnaturally, then, both these merchants and the officials responsible for the welfare of the infant British colony began to wonder whether their and its interests might not be better served by extending British control over the hinterland.

The call for action in the interior was not confined to Europeans. The bulk of the population in their major settlements at Lagos and Sierra Leone, on the lower Senegal and the Gold Coast, was not white, but black. By the 1860s many leading local men, most of whom were involved in trade, were also anxious to see what they considered to be the benefits of European civilization taken into the interior. Though they were by no means agreed among themselves as to whether this might best be done by the advancement of European colonial rule, or by some reform of African society, in either case they saw themselves as acting as principal agents of change.

This modernizing element in African coastal society was partly a consequence of the acculturation that had been going on for centuries in and around the European trading forts and settlements in such places as the Gold Coast and the lower Senegal. But it had been given a totally new impetus and sense of direction by the work of the European missionaries who began to flock to Africa from the end of the eighteenth century onwards. Christian missions in Africa were not, of course, a novelty. But the early missions had been very closely associated with the first flush of European expansion from Portugal and Spain, and little of their influence survived outside the remaining Portuguese colonies. When in the second half of the nineteenth century, new Catholic missionary societies were founded, such as the White Fathers (1868) and the Lyons Society for African Missions (1877), one of the reasons for their foundation, and certainly for the attention they gave to tropical Africa, was the growing activity there of new Protestant missionary societies.

The pioneers were the Moravian Brethren, who sent out their first missionaries, to South and to West Africa, as early as 1737. But little success attended these early ventures, and the real spur for Protestant missionary activity came from the religious revival in Britain during the course of the eighteenth century. The evangelicals were concerned to advance their cause wherever they could, and they were drawn to Africa both because Britain, alone among the Protestant countries of Europe, had a substantial interest there, and because they took a leading part in the British anti-slave-trade movement. They thus felt a duty to bring the Christian message to the African protégés recently acquired by Britain in Sierra Leone and the Cape Colony.

With the arrival of missionaries of the Church Missionary Society at Sierra Leone in 1804, followed by the first Wesleyan Methodist missionary in 1811, and of missionaries of the London Missionary Society at the Cape in 1799 (following upon a renewed Moravian initiative seven years before), these two colonies became established as the prime bases from which Protestant (and predominantly British)* mission activity was to spread throughout sub-Saharan Africa. The purpose of this activity was not simply to spread the word of God, even if this were a sufficient end and reward in itself. From the beginning, the advancement of Christianity in Africa was seen as a practical weapon in the moral campaign against the slave trade and slavery, as a means by which African society might be redeemed from a barbarism which was thought to be largely due to these things, and as a recompense for the wrong done to Africa by the encouragement thought to have been given to them by Europeans in their own Atlantic slave trade.

In the event, the missions were singularly unsuccessful in making any significant impact on organized African societies until after these had been subjected to colonial conquest at the end of the nineteenth and beginning of the twentieth centuries. African authorities quickly appreciated that the Christian message was subversive of their political and social order, while the missionaries soon found that their sense of their own moral superiority was not an adequate weapon with which to convert and reshape African societies which were determined to maintain their spiritual independence. The African kingdoms in which the missionaries made some headway before c. 1900 were usually ones whose rulers were subject to considerable outside pressure, and who therefore saw in the missionaries potentially valuable political allies or mediators. In particular, missionaries were thought especially suited for helping to deal with pressures from Europeans seeking African lands for settlement. This was not the case in West Africa, and in this political sphere the major missionary successes were in southern and central Africa, for example in Khama's Botswana, Mosheshwe's Lesotho or Lewanika's Loziland. But even

* It may however be observed that some British missionary societies, in particular the Church Missionary Society, the major missionary arm of the Church of England, at first experienced considerable difficulty in persuading the established clergy to venture overseas. Many of its most notable early missionaries, for example J. F. Schön, S. W. Koelle and J. L. Krapf, were recruited from Germany. The missions of the British nonconformist churches, however, had much less of a problem in finding their missionaries, perhaps because they were happy to recruit from lower social classes.

in such cases it did not necessarily follow that the missionaries gained many actual converts or that there was any very significant change in traditional society before the advent of colonial rule. Buganda is virtually unique as an example of an African kingdom, unrivalled in its own sphere, and reached by missionaries (in 1877) in advance of other European influences, in which their preaching quickly gained considerable numbers of converts. The reasons for this must be looked for, it would seem, in an unusual combination of local circumstances: the success of the *Kabakas* in creating under themselves an open society, and one in which little authority was left to the traditional priesthood; and the arrival, hardly more than a dozen years before, in the train of the Zanzibaris, of the other major world religion in African history, Islam. This then was a situation in which ambitious young men could eagerly dispute the relative merits of Christianity and Islam as avenues for their own advancement.

In West Africa, as for that matter in South Africa, the major early successes of the missionaries were in areas where traditional society no longer had a strong hold on ordinary people. Sierra Leone provided an ideal foothold. In and around Freetown there were growing numbers of individuals who had been cut away from their original societies by enslavement, and who had subsequently been reassembled in an alien, if African, locality by the exercise of European power. They had little in common other than the coincidence of their subjection to these two arbitrary external forces, and it was really only through some exploitation of the second, and apparently more powerful, of these forces that they could hope to achieve any communal identity. The first liberated Africans landed at Freetown from North America and England had themselves brought with them seeds of evangelical Christianity. Even more urgently than the missionary societies in Britain, they sensed that here lay the key to their salvation, to the establishment and growth of a new society. In the event, the key lay rather less with the Christian faith than with Christian education. If the missionaries started schools so that Africans could learn to read the Bible, Africans learnt, and demanded ever more schools, so that they could use some of Europe's knowledge to ensure their own self-preservation and advancement.

Within little more than a generation, a distinct Creole community was forming among the liberated Africans of Sierra Leone, one which was determined to share with its British mentors in the exploitation and transformation of West Africa. In Sierra Leone itself, the Creole presence was an alien one tending to create resistances among the local Africans, so that opportunities for the Creoles were often less good than they were elsewhere, particularly in and around the trading settlements on the coast from the Gold Coast eastwards. By the mid-nineteenth century, traders, artisans, clerks, teachers, priests, doctors, lawyers and administrators from the Sierra Leone Creole community were sharing in or competing with British activities all along the coast. The white missionaries followed in their converts' footsteps, with the result that new avenues of change were presented to other Africans on an ever-widening front. Individuals who were inspired or tempted by the new opportunities did not usually dissociate themselves from their local societies as completely as the Sierra Leone Creoles had been forced to do. Rather they offered to the traditional leaders cooperation or challenges through which they hoped to transform their societies so that they would move with the forces of change and not be broken by them.

In the eastward advance of the liberated Africans and the white missionaries from Sierra Leone, two areas became of particular importance. The first was the Gold Coast, where centuries of less formal culture contact had already gone far to prepare the ground for the emergence of a European-influenced coastal élite which was as capable of taking advantage of the new initiatives in religion and education as were the Sierra Leonians. The other was southern Yoruba-baland, disrupted by the incessant rivalries and warfare attending the demise of the Oyo empire. These had had the consequence that Yoruba formed by far the largest single ethnic group among the men and women taken from slave ships by the British navy and landed in Sierra Leone. Yoruba probably accounted for a third or more of the liberated African population, and they seem too to have been the only group to retain a major sense of ethnic cohesion and purpose. By the 1830s, some of them had developed commercial interests strong enough to allow them to acquire small ships and to begin trading with Yoruba ports like Badagri and Lagos. These men quickly appreciated that the competition for power in the hinterland of these ports was producing an open society which offered considerable opportunities for men of skill and initiative. Appreciable numbers of Sierra Leone Yoruba soon began to return to their homeland, especially to the new city of Abeokuta.

Abeokuta had been established, under a quasi-republican govern-ment, as a place of refuge for southern Yoruba fleeing from the wars generally, and in particular from the militant pretensions of the rival new foundation of Ibadan. This looked to achieve pre-eminence over all other southern Yoruba as its reward for saving them from being overrun by the Fulani and Hausa who had constituted northern Yorubaland into the Muslim emirate of Ilorin. Missionaries quickly followed the Saro (as the Yoruba called the re-emigrants), firmly establishing themselves in Abeokuta during 1846–7. A modernizing element had now entered Yoruba society and politics. It stressed the importance of developing links with the outside world, based on the increasingly important export of palm oil to British merchants in Lagos, and of maintaining these links against attack from the more traditionally oriented politics of Ibadan and Dahomey. It sought, too, to establish a literate and bureaucratic government in Abeokuta.

Sierra Leone's influence on the course of West African history in the nineteenth century proved to be appreciably greater than that of the other settlements for freed slaves that were established in emulation of Freetown – on the Grain Coast, on Fernando Po Island, and by the Gabon estuary. This was essentially because of the large numbers of its settlers and because of their close association with the considerable British interest. The Libreville settlement established by the French on the Gabon in 1839–48 could not produce equivalent results because the number of slaves liberated there by French naval action was very much smaller. The settlements established from 1821 onwards by private United States initiatives on the Grain Coast also languished in part from lack of numbers (about 15 000 American Blacks were landed there, and about 5 000 slaves taken by the US Navy on the high seas). But the main problem here was that the settlers had no recognized government backing them in their struggle for survival against the local African peoples or the activities of hostile European traders. It was the lack of formal US support which eventually led the settlers in 1847 to seek international recognition and status through their declaration of the Republic of Liberia. But for the next hundred years the resources available to the Republic were never commensurate with its ambitions. In the event, its survival was largely a by-product of the mutual jealousies of the colonial powers.

The Fernando Po settlement was a British venture arising from the inconvenience of having Freetown as the only naval base and freed slave settlement on such a long coastline. But the British occupation of the island in 1827 awoke the government of Spain to the fact that in 1778 it had acquired title to it from Portugal, and in 1834 the

British navy abandoned its base there. Nevertheless this brief British occupation, and the continuing presence on Fernando Po of a small liberated African community, attracted the attention of British missionaries and traders. The island served them as a base for the projection of their activities onto the coastal societies from Lagos to the Cameroons. But compared with Sierra Leone, the lead here remained with Europeans. The most notable of these was the English trader, John Beecroft, who, arriving in 1828, stayed on when the navy left, for a time administering the island's affairs under the Spanish flag. Beecroft's activities became concentrated in the Niger delta, whose waterways he explored, and where he achieved such useful success in mediating between European traders and competing African authorities that in 1849 he was appointed the first British consul for the Bights of Benin and Biafra (i.e. for the coast from Dahomey to the Cameroons). In his last years before his death in 1854, one of Beecroft's major concerns became the promotion of legitimate British trade in the fight against the slave trade on the Dahomey and Yoruba coasts, and he was a prime agent in bringing about the British naval action that conquered Lagos in 1851.

Up to the 1870s, the work of spreading a Christian European influence in West Africa was essentially a partnership between Europeans and Africans, and it would not have advanced as rapidly as it did without the latter – Senegalese *tirailleurs* and the so-called 'Hausa' mercenaries in the British service, as well as the sophisticated urban élites of St Louis and Goree, Freetown and Monrovia, the Gold Coast, Lagos and Abeokuta. Yet if sizeable areas of the coastlands were being transformed by this partnership, it had little effect beyond these. Men like the Saro, Samuel Ajai Crowther, who in 1864 became the first Bishop of the CMS Niger Mission; the West-Indian-born Dr E. W. Blyden, whose active career in Liberia, Sierra Leone and Lagos spanned the years 1851–1911, and embraced exploration as well as pioneer work in education and in attempting a rational synthesis of African, Christian and Muslim ways of thoughts and life; or the Fante surveyor, G. E. Ferguson, who led British expeditions to the Gold Coast hinterland in the 1890s – these and men like them were just as much strangers to the interior African societies as any European. Major kingdoms as close to the sea as Ashanti, Dahomey and Benin remained totally antagonistic to the new order of things.

From the mid-1850s onwards, the protagonists of change began to chafe at their confinement to the coastlands; the interior presented them with a challenge which could not be resisted if they wanted to maintain their claim to superiority. Over the previous sixty years, a notable line of explorers, beginning with Mungo Park and culminating in Henry Barth, had revealed to the outside world the interior geography of West Africa. It was known in particular that the river Niger and its Benue tributary between them afforded a major highway traversing the central and western Sudan, and that practicable access to it could be had both through the Oil Rivers and from the upper Senegal and Gambia rivers. The Liverpool shipbuilder McGregor Laird and the surgeon consul W. B. Baikie had demonstrated on the lower Niger that, with steamships and quinine, Europeans could make practical use of this highway, while on the Senegal Faidherbe had shown the results that might be achieved if European strength were used to break or by-pass the traditional African systems which had hitherto linked the interior to the coast.

In 1873, therefore, the British Colonial Office decided that it could no longer allow its Gold Coast possessions to remain subject to the threat of Ashanti invasion. The way was meticulously prepared for a striking force of European soldiers to march to, and to sack the Ashanti capital, Kumasi. It was hoped that this would serve as a salutary lesson which would break the psychological dam which was holding back the forces of progress. But this was to underestimate the strength of African resistance. In 1900, Ashanti had to be systematically conquered and the conquest consolidated by the construction of a railway to Kumasi from the coast. The French were more experienced and realistic. When during 1879–83 their forces advanced to the Niger from the upper Senegal, their purpose was not merely to defeat the Tukolor state but to add it to their empire, and as early as 1882 work was commenced on a railway to link the two rivers.

Officialdom was also initially hesitant in the major sphere of British commercial interest, the delta and lower river of the Niger and the adjacent Lagos hinterland. In the 1860s and 1870s, it was hoped that the open access required for European civilization and for British trade could be gained through the consular influence pioneered by Beecroft and through the advance of the missions. Indeed Baikie and Crowther were able to take these things as far into the interior as Lokoja, at the Benue–Niger confluence. But two factors led to the eventual abandonment of this concept of informal empire. As with Ashanti, the British had underestimated the determination and the strength of the African authorities – the coastal merchant princes, such as Ja Ja of Opobo or Nana Olomu of the Itsekiris (Warri), just as much as the Fulani emirs of Nupe and Ilorin – to resist changes that were inimical to their own interests. In the long run, conquest and occupation became the solutions. The second factor was that, by the 1870s, British primacy in the trade in the delta and lower Niger and at Lagos was being challenged by traders from other European countries, notably from France and Germany. German traders established a considerable footing in trade at Lagos. But since Britain was already in political control there, this was not as serious as the entry during the 1870s of French competitors into the trade that small British companies were conducting in the delta and on the lower Niger. Here the Europeans were competing not only for a market which was becoming marginal as the world price for palm produce fell, but also for the political favours of a multiplicity of rival African authorities. In the event, British paramountcy on the lower Niger was secured not by government action, but by the intervention of a young ex-army officer, George Goldie, who had become involved in one of the firms trading there. By 1884, Goldie had amalgamated the British companies and used their combined strength to buy out the French. He then began to develop his National African Company into a major political and military force aiming to control the lower Niger absolutely, and to forestall the French advance down the river from the Senegal by ensuring that the most prosperous part of the Sudan, the Sokoto Fulani empire, would become a British preserve.

The annexations on the coasts of Dahomey and Togo by France and Germany in 1883 and 1884, which drove a wedge between the British colonies of the Gold Coast and Lagos, and also the German annexation of 1884 in the Cameroons, hitherto a major seat of British merchant and mission activity, finally persuaded the British government of the importance of Goldie's activities. It responded by declaring its own Oil Rivers Protectorate (1885) and by granting a charter (1886) to Goldie's company, henceforward the Royal Niger Company, which made it its formal agent for the advancement of British interests up the river. The arrival of the French in Dahomey and of Goldie's soldiers in Nupe and Ilorin finally persuaded the British authorities to heed the arguments of the Lagos community and to assume direct responsibility for Yorubaland.

By this time, the scramble for West Africa was already in full spate. In outline it was an attempt by the French to secure as much territory as possible by advancing eastwards down the Niger and by linking these conquests in the Sudan to the sea wherever the coast was not already in British, Portuguese, Liberian or (after 1884) German hands, and a slowly mobilized counter-offensive by Britain to procure a satisfactory share of the hinterlands of those coastal regions where her merchant and missionary interests had been most successful. In the far west the British secured some hinterland for Sierra Leone and acquired both banks along the nearly 300 miles of navigation on the river Gambia. But their colony of the Gambia became merely an enclave in French territory, thus confirming the river Senegal as the main access to the western Sudan (though its navigational deficiencies eventually involved the French in a very substantial railway building programme).

The French had not found it difficult to defeat and destroy the military structure ruling the Tukolor empire. But they did experience tough resistance from another new African empire which was being formed south of the Tukolor territories more or less contemporaneously with their own advance. This was the empire created by Samori who, though a Muslim, and making increasing use of Islamic concepts in the administration of his empire, was reverting to earlier principles of West African state organization than those of the jihadists. Samori, who was born about 1830, was a Dyula trader and soldier engaged in building what might be termed a traditional Mande empire. By the mid-1860s, the nucleus of this had been established around Bissandugu, to the south of the upper Niger, and not far from Samori's birthplace. During the first stage of the French advance, from the Senegal to the Niger, when their main goal was the defeat of the Tukolor power, they preferred to deal with Samori by diplomacy rather than force. But when they began to move further along the Niger to the east, they felt the need to protect their exposed flank in the south-west. Troops were therefore sent against Samori, and in 1891 these captured Bissandugu. However, Samori's response was to move the centre of his operations eastwards towards the middle Volta, where he continued hostilities against the French and also came into conflict with the British advancing from the Gold Coast. It was not until 1898 that the French finally defeated and captured Samori.

This complication delayed the French advance, and helped produce a different balance in the partition between France and Britain east of Timbuctu. French forces were not established in Borgu (which they approached from the south, not from the west) until 1894, or in

Mossi territory until 1896. There was thus time for British commercial interests to persuade the Colonial Office to enter into treaty relations with the African rulers in the hinterland of the Gold Coast and Ashanti, and for these interests themselves, in the form of Goldie's agents, to secure treaties in what was to become the Protectorate of Northern Nigeria and even to begin to try and occupy this sizeable territory. It was therefore possible for Britain to negotiate agreements with France by which the latter accepted the primacy of British interests in these areas. With the advent of Joseph Chamberlain to the Colonial Office in 1895, and its formation two years later of a West African Frontier Force of African soldiers under regular British officers, Britain finally agreed to match force with force, and to use this force to convert her share of the partition into effective colonies. The result was that though France gained an enormous West African empire, and one more than three times as large as Britain's, the major plums in terms of trade and population were denied to her. France was allowed to extend her empire to as far east as Lake Chad, and there to link up with her thrusts from North Africa and the Congo, only through the southern marches of the Sahara.

During the processes of rapid colonial expansion and conquest that began in the 1870s, West Africans lost more than the independence of their traditional polities. They lost the ability to compete equally in the commercial exploitation of their territories. Hitherto almost all the trade in the interior had been in African hands. The advent in the 1850s of regular steamship lines had also enabled their major merchants on the coast to engage in the business of trading with Europe on their own account. But the trade depression hit African merchants even more than it did European traders. The more enterprising Europeans not only became determined to break into the interior trade. They were in a much better position than the Africans to join together in larger enterprises which could secure substantial credits from European banks and replace damaging competition by establishing monopolies of trade along the rivers and – above all – the new European controlled and operated railways. African traders were reduced to subordinate roles, and many of the more successful men of the earlier era thought it better to switch to investment in property or to the production of cash crops for sale to the Europeans.

Africans were equally reduced to subordinate roles in other aspects of the processes of change that were being swept into West Africa.

Hitherto they had had a voice in determining how European ideas and ways were to be introduced to African societies or adapted to African conditions. But the colonial expansion could be morally justified only if Europeans chose to believe that they, and they alone, knew what was best for Africa, not only in their own interest, but in that of the Africans also. During the 1860s, on the eve of the expansion, it became obvious that European attitudes towards Africans were beginning to change. Whereas previously Europeans in West Africa had been generally content to note that African societies and ideas often seemed different from those of Europe, they now began to assert that they were also manifestly inferior. Thus the British explorer and consul, Richard Burton, commented in his account of his mission to Dahomey in 1863 that 'the Negro, in mass, will not improve beyond a certain point, and that not respectable'. Following a visit to the Mossi kingdom of Wagadugu in 1888, the corollary to this was pointed out by the pioneer of French power in the Volta basin and the Ivory Coast, L. G. Binger: 'If the European should ever come here, he should come as master.' While the society of western Europe could best be studied through the history of its development since the pioneering glories of Greece and Rome, a new discipline was required for the study of such lowly societies as were found in Africa, that of anthropology (of which Burton was one of the pioneers in Britain). This eschewed historical studies and chose instead to use what were believed to be the principles of Darwinian science. Because Europeans were able to dominate the rest of mankind from the strength of their scientific and industrial society, they were inherently the fittest to rule. Below them the other races of mankind were arranged in a hierarchical order neatly marked out by skin colour, running from white down through the yellows and the browns to inherently primitive and barbaric blacks at the bottom of the scale.

Even the missionaries began to believe that the potential equality of all men before God did not mean that their black converts could be trusted to be responsible Christians on the European model. As early as 1864, Henry Townsend, the pioneer of missionary work in Abeokuta, had opposed Crowther's appointment as bishop on the ground that Africans themselves recognized that Europeans had been entrusted with a special talent to be used for the good of the Africans. By the time of Crowther's death in 1891, Africans were being steadily elbowed out of the higher offices in both church and state in West Africa. No credit was being given them for their own attempts to adapt their societies to the new conditions; the new rulers preferred to deal directly with 'simple savages'. The educated Africans who in 1871 devised a European-style constitution for the Fante Confederation were treated as traitors even though three years were to elapse before Britain could claim them as subjects of a formally constituted Gold Coast Colony. Similar tentatives which were devised in the 1860s and 1890s for the government of Abeokuta were tolerated only so long as they served the convenience of the British government at Lagos. It is hardly surprising that, even before colonial control was fully established, independent African churches had begun to appear alongside those of the missionaries, and that men like Blyden, Africanus Horton, a Creole doctor who had served the British in the Gold Coast, the Yoruba clergyman James Johnson, and J. M. Sarbah, the first Gold Coast barrister, men who had once hoped to see Africans contributing their talents to the work of bringing the continent into the modern world, were already laying the intellectual foundations for a nationalist reaction to European rule.

Chapter 14

The expansion of European power during the nineteenth century, 2:

South, East and North Africa

The Cape of Good Hope at the southern tip of Africa had been of strategic concern to sea-going European nations for almost as long as West Africa had been of commercial interest. In 1795, therefore, following upon the advance of the French Revolution into the Netherlands, the exigencies of Anglo-French maritime and imperial rivalry led Britain to take over the Cape from the representatives of the Dutch East India Company, which was already bankrupt in all but name. Following the Treaty of Amiens, the Cape was restored in 1803 to the Batavian Republic of the Netherlands, but the resumption of the Anglo-French wars led in 1806 to a second British occupation which lasted for rather more than a century. As a result, Britain became involved with a second, initially unexpected, interest in the African continent to rival her earlier interest in West African trade. This was that of European settlement in southern Africa.

European settlement at the Cape had initially been encouraged by the Dutch East India Company, soon after its arrival there in 1652, as a cheap and efficient means by which to support the base which it needed to control entry to the Indian Ocean and to supply its ships sailing to and from the East Indies. While meat could be obtained by barter with the pastoral communities of the local Khoikhoi, European farmers were needed if other foodstuffs were to be supplied. These men would also usefully supplement the garrison of the Company's fort at Cape Town in time of war. But the settlement quickly outran the limited purposes of its founders. By the early years of the eighteenth century, the European farmers (in Dutch, *Boere*; *Boer* in the singular) had been so successful in the area of Mediterranean climate within about fifty miles of Cape Town that, although costs of production were high, they were capable of producing about three times as much as was required by the Company's ships and garrison. But the Company was the settlers' only market, and its officials were determined to pursue its (and sometimes their own) interests irrespective of those of the settlers. It ceased encouraging white settlement and, in an attempt to alleviate the shortage of labour which was a major factor contributing to the high cost of production, fostered the importation of coloured slaves from other African and Asian lands where it did business.

But this served merely to intensify the problems facing the white settlers. The employment of slaves, and also of labourers taken from Khoikhoi society, decreased the employment opportunities for the settlers, and began to breed the belief that manual and artisan work was a fit occupation only for men of colour. The opportunities for more respectable employment in Cape Town were limited, and it became increasingly difficult for whites to make a decent living as farmers employing coloured labour. Increasing numbers of Boers were therefore driven to seek a livelihood in the interior away from Cape Town, by hunting elephant and other game, bartering European trade goods for Khoikhoi cattle and hides (which could officially only be done by agents of the company), and eventually – and increasingly – setting up as cattle-farmers who competed for land with the Khoikhoi. The Boers' possession of muskets and horses, and of a Calvinist faith that they were an elect of God, charged with the duty to civilize a barbarian wilderness, enabled them to push back the Khoikhoi, or to destroy their tribal societies and to incorporate their remnants as a servile class in their own society. (Such San Bushmen as they came across were treated more drastically, as vermin to be hunted and exterminated.)

Because the interior immediately beyond the zone of regular winter rains around Cape Town was an arid one, the trek-Boers (i.e. migrant farmers) had no alternative but to disperse widely over it. It came to be accepted that something like a minimum of 6000 acres was needed to support a Boer family and its retainers and herds. When the British arrived, the total number of Europeans in South Africa was only about 20 000, only about one-third of whom lived outside Cape Town and its immediate environs. Yet in the north the frontier of white settlement was close to the Orange river, over 300 miles from Cape Town, while in the east, always the favoured line of advance, since in this direction lay lands receiving monsoon rains, it lay on the Great Fish river, over 500 miles away. The Company's officials, anxious to avoid embroilment with African peoples which would involve their administration in trouble and expense quite irrelevant to its strategic maritime interest in Cape Town, continually tried to stop or to limit the expansion of settlement, but they lacked the power to achieve anything much more than to antagonize the trekkers still further.

From about 1775, matters reached a crisis in that the lands along the Great Fish river had become a border battleground between the advancing Boers and the southernmost Bantu. The latter were a far more formidable foe than the Khoikhoi, and, like the Boers, they had a growing population always needing more land for cultivation or cattle-grazing. Conflict over the possession of land or grazing rights, and over stolen or straying cattle, was inevitable, and was exacerbated in that Boers and Bantu held very different concepts of property and land tenure. When it seemed that the Cape Town government could do no more than forbid the Boers to cross the frontier and to embroil it in their quarrels, many of the latter formally declared their independence of it in two republics.

This was in 1795, the year when the British first appeared in South Africa. Their aims were essentially the same limited strategic ones that had led the Dutch Company there in the first place. But the British had to take the situation as they found it, and they possessed the resources to set up a far more effective administration than could the Company, especially in its declining years. The early British administrators at Cape Town were military men and, once it was clear – as it was by 1814 – that they were to stay, they accepted that the security of the British interest in South Africa involved both governing the Boers and defending their frontier with the Bantu. By and large the Boers were prepared to put up with the first of these for the sake of the second.

In the later 1820s, however, British policy began to change. The wars with France, which had made possession of South Africa a military necessity, were fading into the past. Opinion in Britain was becoming increasingly critical of the cost of maintaining extensive overseas commitments, especially if they brought no significant commercial returns. In 1825, it was decided to try and reduce the cost of garrisoning the Cape's eastern frontier by settling along it some

5 000 Britons whose menfolk were veterans of the French wars. It was hoped at the same time that this British settlement might serve to moderate features of European society in South Africa which, thanks to the reports of the British missionaries who had been working there since 1799, were increasingly viewed as archaic and illiberal. The missionary propaganda, ably directed by the local London Missionary Society superintendent, Dr John Philip, was drawing particular attention to the maintenance under British rule of a caste system under which coloured men, including Christian converts, had no rights to land, and were in effect a servile class subject to the arbitrary control of white employers. Such complaints attracted attention in a Britain which had already acted decisively against slave-trading, and which was moving towards the abolition of slavery in its colonies and at home towards a considerable programme of humanitarian and political reforms. Legislation was therefore introduced at the Cape to give non-Europeans the protection of law. It was also declared that the cost of defending the frontier of white settlement should fall on the settlers themselves; only the defence of the base at Cape Town was to be an imperial military responsibility.

These changes were profoundly disturbing to Boer society. Settler opinion was little mollified by the establishment in 1834 of a legislative council which, on the argument that a community which was being asked to bear the cost of its own defence should have some voice in the government, included nominated settler representatives. These representatives were not drawn from the frontier, but from the area around Cape Town, and in any case the British governor remained solely responsible both for initiating and administering legislation. When the compensation provided for the South African slaves freed by the British Parliament in 1833 proved to be both less than was expected and slow to materialize, and when in 1836 an energetic governor's attempt to bring order to the eastern frontier by annexing adjacent Bantu lands was not confirmed by the Colonial Office, many frontier Boers decided that they had had enough. They decided that the only course left to them was to move away to the north beyond the limits of British rule, and there to establish independent communities which could determine matters in their own interest.

By 1836–7, the Great Trek was under way. During the next ten years or so something like 14 000 Boer men and women loaded their possessions onto ox-wagons and, together with their livestock and their coloured retainers, emigrated from the Cape Colony. The strategy of this exodus was largely determined by earlier reconnais-sances which had reported that large areas of the better watered more easterly high veld, and a substantial area of very well watered land in the Natal coastlands south of Zululand, were very little occupied by the Bantu. This of course, was a consequence of the recent *Difaqane*. But the Boers did not concern themselves with the fact that these lands were empty of people only because of the military activities of Shaka, of Dingane, his Zulu successor, Mzilikazi and others. What did concern them was that their emptiness seemed to offer a means of outflanking the barrier of the eastern frontier, an opportunity for their expansion and settlement without costly and dangerous fighting in which they might well be overwhelmed by the greatly superior numbers of the Bantu. In fact the trek-Boers were soon made to realize that they would have to fight to secure the new Canaan they sought. But after some initial disasters, they evolved suitable tactics – the laager, or fortified wagon camp, for defence, and the swift, mounted commando raid for attack – to defeat the Zulu and to force Mzilikazi and his Ndebele to retreat north across the Limpopo.

But this was not the end of their troubles. Once the military threats presented by Dingane and Mzilikazi had been removed, the lands which the Boers had taken began to fill up again with Bantu inhabi-tants. A few of these might be useful to Boer society as labourers, but essentially they were regarded by the Boers as unassimilable alien barbarians whose presence placed a continuing military strain on their own small and impoverished communities. Secondly, the British auth-orities in the Cape Colony did not see that the Trekkers, by moving across the Orange river and out of the Colony, had thereby divested themselves of their responsibilities as British subjects. If their actions in any way seemed to threaten the British position in South Africa they should be brought to account.

The Boers certainly could not be allowed to set up a regime indepen-dent of the British interest controlling Port Natal (the future Durban), where there was a harbour to rival those of the Cape, and where, moreover, a few British merchants, trading with the Zulu, and missionaries had settled. Imperial strategy necessitated that Britain must be paramount here, and accordingly in 1843 a new British colony of Natal was proclaimed. Natal had attracted a much larger number of Trekkers than the drier high veld, and, since the Greak Trek had been intended as an escape from outside interference with Boer society, most of these now moved back across the Drakensberg. Thus

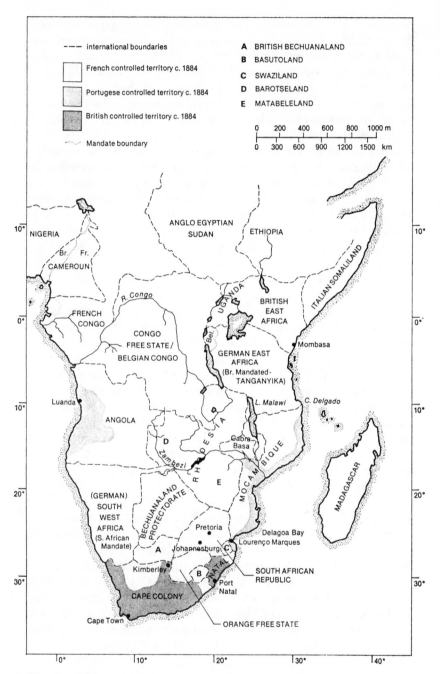

Legend:

- - - international boundaries

French controlled territory c. 1884

Portugese controlled territory c. 1884

British controlled territory c. 1884

······ Mandate boundary

A BRITISH BECHUANALAND
B BASUTOLAND
C SWAZILAND
D BAROTSELAND
E MATABELELAND

| 0 | 200 | 400 | 600 | 800 | 1000 m |
| 0 | 300 | 600 | 900 | 1200 | 1500 | km |

10° NIGERIA

Br. Fr.
CAMEROUN

ANGLO EGYPTIAN
SUDAN

ETHIOPIA

ITALIAN SOMALILAND

R. Congo

FRENCH
CONGO

0°

UGANDA

BRITISH
EAST
AFRICA

Mombasa

CONGO
FREE STATE /
BELGIAN CONGO

Bel.

GERMAN EAST
AFRICA
(Br. Mandated-
TANGANYIKA)

10° Luanda

ANGOLA

L. Malawi

C. Delgado

D

RHODESIA

Cabra
Basa

MADAGASCAR

20° (GERMAN)
SOUTH
WEST
AFRICA
(S. African
Mandate)

Zambezi

E

MOCAMBIQUE

BECHUANALAND PROTECTORATE

Pretoria

Delagoa Bay
Lourenço Marques

A

Johannesburg

C

Kimberley

B

NATAL

SOUTH AFRICAN
REPUBLIC

30° CAPE COLONY

Port
Natal

Cape Town

ORANGE FREE STATE

Map 10 Southern Africa during the era of European expansion

reinforced, the high-veld Boers began to erect two major republics – the South African Republic, in the Transvaal, and the Orange Free State – which seemed to offer some prospect of political stability. After some hesitation, therefore, the British agreed, in 1852 and 1854 respectively, to recognize the independence of these republics. The assumption was that these should do nothing which would serve to upset relations between the British and the Bantu in, or on the borders of, the Cape Colony and Natal.

But the establishment of the Trekker republics as exclusive enclaves in black Africa of white settlers who, as a result of two centuries of economic and social evolution, reinforced by religious conviction and recent practical military and political experience, were determined to deny to non-Europeans any place in their society other than that of a subservient and subordinate labouring class, posed a considerable problem for another predominantly British interest, that of the missionaries. These were by now firmly established in the Cape, and they might make some headway in Natal and in the still independent Bantu territories between it and the Cape Colony. In the Cape, indeed, which in 1852 was granted a representative assembly chosen by an electorate defined by income and property qualifications and not by the colour of a man's skin, it was possible for an educated black élite to evolve which was not dissimilar in character and in its aims from that which was developing in West Africa. But the Transvaal and the Orange Free State were obviously cramping environments for the full realization of missionary endeavours. So, if – as some of them did – the missionaries wanted to carry their message further into the 'dark continent', they were more or less confined to the narrow corridor of Botswana between the western borders of the republics and the Kalahari desert, which equally became a principal route of access to the interior for Cape hunters and traders. But Boer inroads in search of more land were a threat both here and in the lands immediately north of the Transvaal to which the Ndebele had gone. (Ultimately, indeed, missionaries such as John Mackenzie and J. S. Moffatt were to take active roles in the processes by which these territories were placed under British protection during the 1880s.)

Mzilikazi's contact with missionaries dated back to the period before the Great Trek, when his Ndebele were still in the Transvaal. But neither he nor his successor, Lobengula (1870–94), would countenance the conversion of their kingdom. The main value of the missionaries to them was rather as representatives of a British power which might counter the threat from the Boers. So when during the 1840s a young missionary recently out from Britain, David Livingstone, began to chafe at working in southern Africa in a situation too much contaminated by European settlement (and by too many comfortably settled missionaries), and in particular at working in the poor and thinly peopled lands of Botswana squeezed between the Boers and the Kalahari, he decided to strike out even further afield. Eventually, in 1851, he arrived in the fertile and well-peopled Lozi kingdom of the Kololo, which he thought an ideal field for a new missionary venture. But he also appreciated that, both for geographical and political reasons, it would be difficult to maintain regular communication with Loziland from the south. So between 1852 and 1856 he explored the possibility of opening up alternative routes from the west or east coasts. With the support of a small party of Kololo, he marched first from Loziland north-westwards to Luanda on the Angolan coast, and then back again and down the Zambezi valley to Quelimane on the coast of Mozambique.

This first crossing of the continent by a European, and the book in which he narrated it, quickly made Livingstone a national hero in Britain. There was a ready acceptance of his claim that the Zambezi might afford access to fertile, populous and productive central African lands, and that these could and should be civilized by an alliance between Christian missions and British trade, together perhaps with a few selected British farming settlers to offer a practical as well as a moral example of the way to African development. In 1858–64, Livingstone was back in Africa, in command of a scientific expedition sponsored by the British government and equipped with a steamship to prove the navigability of the Zambezi. But the expedition's first major discovery was that, a little way above Tete, the Kabra Bassa rapids (which Livingstone had not seen on his first journey, since he was then travelling on foot and not by water) were an insuperable obstacle. The expedition was therefore diverted up the Shire, the major northern tributary of the lower Zambezi. This led it to the fertile and very densely populated lands south of Lake Malawi and in its basin. With altitude moderating the climate and tempering the fevers met with in the Zambezi valley, these lands, the Shire highlands in particular, seemed better suited for the implementation of Livingstone's idea of development through Christianity, commerce and colonization than anywhere else he had been. It also seemed more urgently needed here than elsewhere because, of course, the inhabitants were experiencing the full weight of the slave trade to the east coast and of Yao and Ngoni pressures.

As will shortly be seen, Livingstone's two major exploring ventures of 1852–6 and 1858–64 quickly unleashed a flood of European interest in the interior of East and central Africa. Initially this was an essentially scientific and humanitarian interest, but it very quickly became an imperial interest as well. Part of the explanation for this was that Europe had already become more involved with affairs on the coast of East Africa than had been the case since the sixteenth century. The origins of this involvement lay once again in the eighteenth-century maritime competition of Britain and France for overseas trade and empire, and specifically in this case in India.

This competition did not at first involve the East African coast very directly. Ships passed closer to it than they had when Europe's main Asian concern had been not with India, but with the East Indies, but the main focuses of strategic interest lay elsewhere, at the Cape of Good Hope, as has been seen, and in the Mascarene Islands. The latter were occupied by the French in 1715, Mauritius – which alone had good harbours – being subsequently taken by Britain in 1810. However, France and Britain gradually became involved in a game in which each sought to counter the influence that it thought the other was seeking to achieve on the east coast. This eventually resulted in what in effect was one of the earliest European treaties seeking to partition Africa, the Anglo-French agreement of 1862. By this agreement Britain accepted the paramountcy of French interests in Madagascar and the Comoro Islands in the Mozambique channel, while France accepted the paramountcy of the British interest at Zanzibar, and thus on the east coast itself.

The genesis of the British interest at Zanzibar can be traced back to another strand in the eighteenth-century competition between France and Britain in India, namely their rivalry for influence in Egypt and the Near East. Prior to the opening of the Suez Canal in 1869, all European trade and naval and military forces going to and from India perforce had to take the long haul round the Cape. But the increasing urgency of the military situation in India meant that both countries came to appreciate the merits of the much shorter route through the Mediterranean and the Near East for the speedy transmission of mail and dispatches. Then as the French began to lose the naval struggle with Britain for command of the high seas, they began to see this route as their main approach to India; hence Napoleon's expedition to Egypt in 1798 and the subsequent British counter-stroke there. Among the other measures taken by Britain to check the French in the Near East was an alliance concluded in 1798 between her East India Company's government at Bombay and the Omani of Muscat. This was intended simply to help keep the French and their allies out of the Persian Gulf. But the Omani also of course had interests on the coast of East Africa, and after 1807, when slave-trading by British subjects became illegal, the alliance acquired a totally new significance.

The responsible British authorities shortly became concerned to stop slaves being imported into their colonies in Mauritius and India. They quickly came to the conclusion that the best way to achieve this was to prevent slaves being sent to them from East Africa. In 1822, therefore, a new Anglo-Omani treaty was negotiated with Seyyid Said (then still resident at Muscat) by a naval captain named Moresby. By its terms, Said agreed to prohibit the traffic in East African slaves east of a line running from Cape Delgado, described as his 'most southern possession in Africa', to a point sixty miles east of Socotra, and thence to Diu Head on the north-west coast of India.

By not only accepting the Moresby Treaty, but also honouring it, Said accepted an immediate loss to the Omani traders, himself included, and to his treasury. But he knew that his navy, however significant in his own corner of the Indian Ocean, was no match for British naval power. Therefore, once he had been convinced that Britain was prepared to use this power against the Indian Ocean slave trade, he thought it better to give up part of this trade to save the rest. Indeed Britain had recognized that to the west of the treaty line, not only that the export of slaves from East Africa might continue, but also that it was exclusively an Omani affair. Even more than this, the Moresby Treaty contained the implication that Britain had recognized, or had even granted, a claim by Said to suzerainty on the whole coast north of Cape Delgado, i.e. to as far south as Portuguese Mozambique. Since in 1822 this was far in advance of the facts, Said was assured not only that Britain would not interfere when he used his navy to turn his claim into reality, but also that his new empire would receive the implicit protection of the world's most powerful naval power.

On the other hand, however, Said and his successors ruling Zanzibar's empire were in no position to resist further pressures from Britain. These naturally increased as British anti-slave-trade opinion became more aware of the extent of the East African slave trade, and of its effects in the interior, as the result of the information gathered by Livingstone and the other explorers and missionaries who entered East and central Africa in his wake. In 1845 and 1873, therefore, the government of Zanzibar accepted new demands from Britain which led first to further restrictions being placed on the export of slaves from East Africa, and then to the outlawing of the trade altogether. The commercial loss was in fact more than made good by the growth of other export trades, such as those in ivory and cloves. But by giving in to foreign pressures, the influence and power of the Zanzibar rulers over their subjects was reduced. They became more and more clients of Britain and of the consuls Britain had been sending to Zanzibar from 1841 onwards. Indeed Britain had gained a point of entry into East African affairs rather similar to those she had gained for West Africa at Lagos and in the consular jurisdiction in the Oil Rivers. But Zanzibar was potentially even more significant than these, for from it there radiated a network of trade and influence extending to as far as Buganda, the upper Congo and Shaba.

It was largely along these trade routes that from 1857 onwards a stream of European explorers, for the most part British and inspired by Livingstone's achievements, began to penetrate the interior of East and central Africa. Within twenty years their work had laid bare the outlines of its geography, the system of great lakes, and the origins and courses of the great rivers, Zambezi, Nile and Congo. Livingstone continued to participate in this work, but his fatal solo expedition of 1866–73 added little to knowledge. Perhaps its major result was to inspire a newspaper proprietor's stunt of sending H. M. Stanley to 'find' him in 1871, for the journalist became an unexpected convert to Livingstone's faith in the urgent importance of injecting Christianity, commerce and colonization into the heart of the dark continent. Stanley returned to Africa as an explorer in his own right. During 1874–7 he made the second major European crossing of the continent, going from Zanzibar to Buganda, and thence to the Congo and down it to the Atlantic. This journey did more than round off the basic work of exploration directed at the interior waterways. It had the two important consequences of leading to the immediate penetration to Buganda of Christian missions, and of helping to consolidate the African interests of Leopold II of the Belgians, who had long been fretting at his introverted little country's lack of interest in overseas empire. After Stanley had appealed without success to Britain to exploit the Congo as a highway along which trade and civilization could be taken to the very heart of the continent, in 1878 he accepted a commission from Leopold to return to the river to establish the posts and to secure the 'treaties' with Africans that were the foundation of the Congo Free State. By 1885, this imposition upon a large area – ultimately some 900 000 square miles – of central Africa of a highly authoritarian European monarchical government, had been accepted by all the great powers.

Leopold sought international support and recognition for this venture essentially on humanitarian grounds. It was, he had said as early as 1876, 'the piercing through the darkness which envelops whole populations . . . a crusade worthy of this century of progress'. He was able to make this claim in large measure because, during the previous twenty years, the main port of entry for the explorers of central Africa had been Zanzibar. Their work would not have been as swiftly successful as it was had they not been able to begin their work by making use of the routes, and often also the technical and logistical support, of the Zanzibar merchants. The explorers therefore had first-hand experience of the east-coast slave trade and its consequences. From Livingstone onwards they had been able to convince Europeans that this was the major bar to the advancement of society in East and central Africa, and that the trade could be halted only by active intervention by Europe.

By the end of the 1870s, indeed, it was becoming evident that something more was needed in the interior than mission stations alone; that the Christian message and moral example were not sufficient by themselves to secure the redemption of African society that the missionaries demanded. Within a few years, the two missions most directly inspired by Livingstone himself had failed. That sent to the Kololo was totally defeated by fever within a few months of its arrival in Loziland in 1860. The Universities' Mission to Central Africa which arrived in the Shire Highlands in 1861 withdrew two years later. It had been decided that the combination of disease and local warfare in the Highlands made its work impossible, and that the only feasible plan for missionary work was a methodical step-by-step approach to the interior from a base at Zanzibar. Even though this was the headquarters of the slaving interest, it seemed at the time the only point at which the resources of the western world could be focussed to support an effective missionary advance into East and central Africa.

When in the later 1870s two Scottish societies did succeed in establishing missions in the Shire Highlands and on the shores of Lake Malawi, part of the explanation lies in the fact that they were supported by a Glasgow trading concern, the African Lakes Company. This gave the missionaries logistical support, and much more besides, for the company was willing to fight the slave trade not only with legitimate trade, but in the last resort with guns also. Some of the missionaries themselves could see no alternative in the troubled conditions surrounding them but to assume some temporal authority over African lands and peoples. *De facto*, then, a British colony was beginning to take shape in southern Malawi. The juridical problems created by this, not least with Portugal and her officials in Mozambique, who argued that the British missionaries and traders were operating in territory long claimed by Portugal, led in 1883 to the appointment of a British consul 'in the territories of the African Kings and Chiefs' of Malawi. Public opinion in Britain required the Foreign Office to give official support to this British interest created in Malawi by the missionaries and the traders, and this might not have been possible had not this interest had such a humanitarian and anti-slave-trade colouring. After this, only short steps were needed for the British in Malawi to launch a military onslaught on the Zanzibari traders operating around the northern end of the lake, and for a formal British protectorate to be declared (1889). In the 1880s also, missionaries were able to gain a permanent footing in Loziland because by this time British traders and political authority were close at hand, while the public demand in Britain for comparable support for the missionaries who had gone to Buganda in 1877 became a major influence in determining the traders' and officials' advance to that kingdom also.

But in none of these cases was the missionary factor the sole determinant leading to positive British imperial action. Bismarck's decision, in 1885, to give official German recognition to the treaty-making activities of agents of the Society for German Colonization in the hinterland of the southern half of the Zanzibar government's sphere of influence on the East African coast, made it impossible for Britain to continue to seek an oversight of affairs in East Africa through her influence with that government. If her interests were not altogether to be excluded from East Africa, it was necessary to partition it with the Germans. This was done by the Anglo-German agreement of 1886, which in effect limited Zanzibar's claim on the mainland to a ten-mile-wide coastal strip, and divided the hinterland to as far as

Lake Victoria into a German sphere in the south and a British sphere in the north. The establishment of a German presence in East Africa, together with the expansive activities of Leopold's agents in the Congo basin, were also important inducements to the consolidation of British interests in central Africa, in Loziland and Malawi, and in the territory between them which is now called Zambia. But the actual form of the British action that was taken in central Africa was largely determined by developments in South Africa consequent upon the discovery of its mineral wealth during 1867–86, while the development of the British interest in Uganda, and in the East African coastlands northwards from the important harbour of Mombasa to Somalia, needs to be seen in relation to the great changes which had taken place in North and North-East Africa since the beginning of the century.

The French and British expeditions to Egypt at the turn of the century initiated a dismembering of the Ottoman empire in Africa, and exposed all northern and north-eastern Africa to strong forces of change springing from the economically and militarily ascendant nations of western Europe that lay close at hand on the northern side of the Mediterranean. In fact each of the four Ottoman provinces in Africa had long been accustomed to acting independently of Istanbul. The rulers of the two richest and best organized, Egypt and Tunisia, seized the opportunity to enlist European skills and capital in attempts to modernize their countries and to achieve viable independence for them. But the odds were against them. They failed to develop sufficient indigenous power to control the alien forces they had encouraged, and which became increasingly rapacious. The end result was that France took over formal control in Tunisia in 1881 and Britain in Egypt in 1882. The other two provinces, the Regency of Algiers and Tripoli, had such weak and ineffective governments that they quickly fell victim to external aggressors. In 1830 France embarked on the conquest that was to give her Algeria, and five years later the Turks themselves sent an army to Tripoli in an attempt to save something from the wreckage of their African empire.

However, not all northern Africa had been part of this empire. In the far west, the Filali sultans of Morocco maintained the nationalist traditions established by the Sa'di dynasty in the sixteenth century. In the event, Morocco retained her independence until 1911, though perhaps this was less because of the Filali regime, which generally lacked the power to control even its own people outside the plains in which lay the larger cities, than because the European powers were so jealous of each other that they long hesitated to take any positive action in a country which, guarding the Strait of Gibraltar from the south, was of universal strategic interest.

In the north-east, of course, the highland kingdom of Ethiopia had survived the rise of Ottoman power as it had earlier survived that of Islam. The decline of the Ottoman empire now enabled it to resume contacts with the rest of Christendom, and notably with Britain and France and, later, with Italy. As the Red Sea became again a major route for international trade, these nations took steps to safeguard their interests in the area. In 1839, Britain took Aden, on the Arabian side of the Bab el Mandeb, to serve as a coaling station, and the French established themselves on the African side at Obok in 1862. Private Italian interests appeared at Assab in Eritrea also in the 1860s, though it was not until twenty years later that the Italian government began to take an active interest in the Horn of Africa. By this time Obok was being developed into French Somaliland, and the British were establishing their Somaliland Protectorate on the coast opposite Aden.

The more ambitious and far-seeing of the Ethiopian barons who were trying to assert themselves in the chaos resulting from the Oromo incursions, which had virtually destroyed the power of the traditional emperor of their country, were able to take advantage of the new situation to develop exports of ivory and other produce and to import firearms. By the middle of the century, the most successful of them, Ras Kasa, had become the undisputed ruler of the northerly provinces of Amhara, Gojam and Tigre. In 1855 he secured his coronation as the Emperor Theodore. But when he failed to receive an answer to a letter which he had sent to his fellow Christian monarch, Queen Victoria of the United Kingdom, he reacted by imprisoning two British envoys and a number of other Europeans. The British government in its turn reacted very much as it was to do against Ashanti five years later. In 1867, a well-organized punitive expedition was sent into Ethiopia. Theodore, who was deserted by many of his vassals, was defeated and committed suicide. But more rational men than Theodore were developing in the same pattern, and the British expedition had convinced them of the necessity of cooperating with the Europeans to secure modern weapons and technology. Theodore's immediate successor as emperor, John IV, wielded even greater power. But he was never strong in the south. Here King Menelik of

Shoa built up a powerful position by conquering Oromo and Somali who had never before formed part of an Ethiopian polity, and by fostering his own commercial contacts with the Europeans. Eventually in 1882 John agreed to come to terms with Menelik, accepting him as his successor to the imperial throne.

When in 1889 Menelik became emperor, he was probably the most powerful indigenous ruler in Africa. By combining military strength with astute diplomacy, he demonstrated that Africans could success-fully compete with Europeans in the business of empire-building in the continent. But in North-East Africa, he was not alone in this respect: a principal preoccupation for both John and Menelik was to stay Egyptian aggression in the area.

In 1798, Napoleon had decisively defeated the archaic forces of the Mamluk oligarchy which for over five centuries had been exploiting the wealth of Egypt. The British forces which three years later brought about the French withdrawal from the country restored the hitherto largely nominal authority of the Ottoman empire. By 1811 the effec-tive ruler of Egypt had become Muhammad 'Ali, an Albanian officer who had made himself master of the substantial Albanian contingent in the army which the Turks had sent to follow up the British victory. But Muhammad 'Ali had no wish to consolidate a foreign authority in Egypt. Like Saladin or the early Mamluks, he sought to create an independent kingdom which would be strong enough to establish its own sphere of interest dominating the adjacent lands of Syria, nearer Arabia and the Nile valley. But he also appreciated that the Napo-leonic invasion had at last demonstrated the inadequacy of traditional Islamic civilization to achieve this purpose in a world which was clearly to be dominated by European science and technology. Egypt, therefore, while remaining Muslim and under local control, must learn from this modern world.

Muhammad 'Ali established an efficient autocracy which extingu-ished the Mamluks as land-owners, restored irrigation and agriculture, established cotton as a major revenue-earning export crop, and began to develop other commercial activities through state monopolies. His major achievement, supported by all his other reforms, was to create a new army trained in modern weapons and tactics by European – largely French – instructors. His fellow Albanians were pushed aside, for Muhammad 'Ali had no desire to see brother officers usurping his authority as he had usurped that of the Ottoman Sultan. Some of the soldiers of the new army were slaves brought in traditional fashion from the Sudan. But increasingly it became something which had hardly been seen in Egypt since the days of the Pharoahs – a national army, with Egyptian conscripts providing the rank and file, and with native Egyptians, educated and trained in state institutions, rising through merit to assume the positions of command.

The purpose of this army, which was supported by adequate naval forces, was to enable Muhammad 'Ali to achieve the strong, independent Egyptian empire that he wanted. From the strictly military point of view, it was universally successful. In the Sudan, the petty sheikhdoms of lower Nubia, ruled by descendants of the Turkish conquerors of the sixteenth century, were quickly overrun, the Funj kingdom of Sennar was occupied, and Kordofan wrested from Darfur. By 1826 an administration was being established, from a capital at the new town of Khartoum at the junction of the Blue and White Niles, to ensure that the resources of the Nilotic Sudan, especially slaves and gold, were available for Egyptian purposes. By 1837, Egyptian troops on tax-collecting forays had advanced up the Atbara and Blue Nile rivers into territory which was not much more than 100 miles away from the old Ethiopian capital of Gondar, and in the 1840s, the Egyptians began to make use of Suakin and Massawa as Red Sea ports for their Sudanese empire.

But it was not until 1865 that the Egyptian authorities finally secured a formal lease to these two ports from the Ottoman government, and this illustrates one of the two political difficulties which prevented Muhammad 'Ali from gaining full benefit from his army's victories. Its early campaigns were technically undertaken in the name of his suzerain, the Ottoman Sultan, who had no military forces of his own of comparable efficiency. But the Egyptian army's successes against the Wahhabis in Arabia or against Greek and Cretan rebels did not win for Muhammad 'Ali the Turkish recognition of Egyptian independence for which he hoped. Instead, the latter campaigns embroiled him with European powers, Britain in particular, which would rather see nominal authority over the Near East remain with a weak Turkish empire than have a real authority wielded by a strong Egyptian government. When finally, in the 1830s, the Egyptian army was turned directly against the Ottoman power, and it seemed that the important province of Syria would pass from its government to Egypt's, the Europeans intervened with force of their own. The result was that in 1840–1 Muhammad 'Ali had to give up his army's Syrian conquests, and content himself with the limited political gain of an acknowledgement from Istanbul that his heirs in the male line would be recognized as its viceroys over Egypt and the Sudan.

Since the government established for Egypt by Muhammad 'Ali was essentially one of personal rule, much of its subsequent history was determined by the capacity and interests of these heirs. His ablest son, Ibrahim, who had commanded the army employed against the Wahhabis and in Greece and Syria, and who acted as co-adjutor with his father in his declining years, predeceased him. The succession therefore passed to two younger sons, 'Abbas (1849–54) and Sa'id (1854–63), and to a grandson, Isma'il (1863–79). 'Abbas was a Muslim reactionary, who endeavoured to reverse his father's modernizing policies. Sa'id, on the other hand, had been educated in France and had European tastes. But he was not interested in the business of government, preferring to enjoy himself in a palace life supported by loans from European financiers. However, Sa'id took one action of the utmost importance. He granted a ninety-nine year concession for the construction of a canal through the isthmus of Suez to Ferdinand de Lesseps, who had once been French consul in Egypt.

This was a notable reversal of a policy maintained by Muhammad 'Ali, who feared that if Europeans were allowed to construct a canal, their interests would grow to control the economic life of Egypt and ultimately also her government. In fact, nothing was done with the concession for some years, mainly because de Lesseps could not raise the considerable capital needed to build the canal. One reason for this was that the Ottoman government would not give the formal approval which was needed before it could be built or operated. This was in part the result of pressure from British governments, which thought that the canal would benefit France and other Mediterranean powers more than it would benefit British shipping, and which preferred therefore that Alexandria be linked to the Red Sea by railways which were being built by British companies.

Eventually, however, the Suez Canal was opened to traffic in 1869, and it rapidly became a commercial success. This was largely a consequence of the more or less simultaneous development of the compound steam engine, which for the first time enabled steamships to undertake long ocean voyages without devoting so much space to coal that they did not have enough to carry a profitable cargo. This meant that, contrary to prediction, the canal was extremely beneficial to Britain, which had the world's largest and most modern merchant marine, and by far the largest share of Europe's trade with Asia.

British ships were soon providing the bulk of the company's business and profits. But the canal was of little benefit to the country through whose territory it ran. The Egyptian government had provided the company with both the land and much of the labour needed for the construction of the canal in return for little more than a substantial block of shares, and these it was soon forced to sell.

Isma'il, during whose reign the canal was opened, with a splendour that included the first production of Verdi's *Aida*, shared his grandfather's vision but lacked his firm grasp of reality. In Egypt itself, he embarked on numerous projects of modernization, building new railways and roads, harbours and irrigation works and also extending education facilities. He also set about the expansion and reform of Egypt's empire in Africa. During the 1860s, three things had become apparent here, in part because of the work of European explorers. It had been established that the White Nile led directly to the fertile and populous lands around the Great Lakes. It became clear that the existing Egyptian administration in the Sudan, closely involved with slave-raiding and encountering serious opposition from the local peoples, needed radical reform and re-orientation if it were to make a truly productive use of the territory it controlled or which it might be expanded to control. Finally, especially with the construction of the Suez Canal, it seemed that Egypt might find alternative and more practicable routes into the interior from the Somali coastlands of the Red Sea and Indian Ocean. Isma'il's policy therefore became one of establishing a modern colonial administration – often making use of European officials – which would stamp out slave trading in the Sudan and extend Egyptian authority further into the interior. So in 1871, the former explorer, Sir Samuel White Baker, occupied Gondokoro on the borders of Uganda; in 1874 Darfur was conquered; and in the following year Egyptian troops landed at Zeila and advanced into the interior to Harar (where they remained until 1885). A similar expedition would have been mounted from Kismayu on the Indian Ocean coast had not Britain intervened to protect the interest of her client at Zanzibar.

But Isma'il followed Sa'id's example by trying to finance all these things by borrowing from Europe. The European financiers and the Egyptian agents who negotiated the loans were none too scrupulous, and it is probable that on average Isma'il's government received no more than £7 ($35) for every £10 ($50) of nominal debt that it incurred. The cost of its borrowing was therefore high. On the other hand, many of the schemes on which the money was spent, however sound in the long term, were not immediately very remunerative. Isma'il was soon forced into the disastrous expedient of borrowing more money, usually on worse terms, to help meet the interest payments he had already incurred. Thus, while his administration brought about a threefold increase in Egypt's foreign trade (though it was greatly helped in this by the cotton famine occasioned by the American Civil War) and a 70 per cent growth of revenue, the really significant facts were the increase in the national debt and in the cost of servicing it. The debt increased no less than thirty-fold, from a modest £3 000 000 ($15 000 000) to £90 000 000 ($450 000 000), involving interest payments amounting to at least £5 000 000 ($25 000 000) a year. These had to come from a government revenue which could hardly be pushed above £8 500 000 ($42 500 000) a year except by a counter-productive increase in the already heavy burden of taxation on the peasantry, the only significant productive section of the community.

It was in these circumstances that in 1875 Isma'il agreed to sell Egypt's shares in the Suez Canal company to a British government whose leader was now as eager to participate in the undertaking as his predecessors had been to oppose it. But this realization of a capital asset could only serve as a temporary palliative; within a year the Egyptian government was unable to keep up interest payments on its foreign debt. Egypt now experienced the calamity feared by Muhammad 'Ali: her government was at the mercy of European financial interests. The French, Austrian and Italian governments, representing a large proportion of the foreign bond-holders, nominated commissioners to manage the debt. Initially the British government held back, holding to its traditional view that it had no responsibility towards those of its citizens who were foolish enough to get into trouble through lending their money to foreigners. However, British bondholders were among those who were bringing actions against the Egyptian government in the special civil courts which Isma'il had instituted to encourage European trade and investment in his country. In 1876 these activities forced him to appoint a Briton and a Frenchman as joint controllers of the Egyptian revenue, and in 1880 these became responsible to a reorganized Debt Commission on which Britain was represented (as also was Germany).

Isma'il's position was now desperate. Egypt could be got out of the difficulties into which his government's extravagance had got her only if her foreign debts were rescheduled to levels which bore some relation to the capacity of her economy to produce money for interest payments and the repayment of capital, and if there were a thorough overhaul of her machinery of government and revenue collection and of the agriculture on which this depended. European intervention was certainly needed to achieve the first, and the second could probably be best achieved – at least within a reasonable length of time – also with European assistance. But Isma'il found that the more he acceded to European pressures, the more he incurred the hostility of the Egyptian army, the rock on which the new Egyptian state had been founded, and the only part of it which was essentially Egyptian in composition and spirit. He therefore vacillated between accommodating the Europeans and joining with the emergent nationalism expressed by the young army officers.

Isma'il's dilemma came to an end in 1879, when the European governments prevailed upon the Ottoman government, still technically sovereign in Egypt, to depose him. His successor, his son Tawfiq (1879–92), proved to be a more amenable tool. Under him there were governments composed of Egyptian ministers, but French and British officials were appointed as the permanent heads of the ministries themselves. The real directors of policy became the British and French controllers of the revenue, Baring (later Lord Cromer) and de Blignières. These secured a re-funding of the debt to a capital value of £80 000 000 ($400 000 000) bearing interest at 4 per cent, and at this level it was just possible to service the debt without totally denuding other services.

But this establishment of foreign control provoked a powerful reaction from the younger army officers led by Colonel 'Arabi Pasha. In 1881 these forced Tawfiq to appoint a new ministry, with 'Arabi as minister of war, and to convoke a quasi-democratic, but hitherto ineffective innovation of Isma'il's, the consultative Council of Notables. Britain and France responded with stiff notes of protest, but when the issue came to the test, France was involved in a domestic crisis, and only Britain was in a position to back up its protest with force. In 1882, Alexandria was bombarded from the sea, and a British army landed and defeated 'Arabi at the battle of Tel-el-Kebir.

Britain was now in sole and complete control of Egypt. Although she made no claim to sovereignty (Egypt was not even formally declared a British protectorate until the outbreak of war with Turkey in 1914), and although her declared policy was to withdraw as soon as a sound administration had been established, for half a century or more Egypt was in effect a colony. It was ruled by British proconsuls, Cromer and his successors (who until 1914 bore only the modest title of British Agent and Consul-General), backed up by a British army of occupation. Britain did provide Egypt with a sound administration, but the British officers sent to run it built up an interest in perpetuating their control and were reluctant to train Egyptians or to concede authority to them. Furthermore, two world wars made Britain extremely unwilling to allow any chance of the Suez Canal falling into foreign hands, and her involvement in Egypt had also involved her in a difficult situation in the Sudan.

The financial difficulties of the Egyptian administration that were evident by 1876, followed by the disappearance from the scene of Isma'il three years later, made it impossible to continue his plans for the Sudan. Slaving and other forms of crude exploitation revived. In 1881 a Sudanese cleric, Muhammad Ahmad, proclaimed himself the Mahdi and launched what quickly became a national uprising which the Egyptian forces were powerless to contain. The Mahdiyya was able to appeal at once to Muslim religious leaders and to slave traders who thought that the Egyptian colonial administration was interfering too much with traditional society, and to smaller men who associated it with slaving, taxation and other kinds of oppression. By the time Britain had taken over the Egyptian government, its authority in the Sudan had been limited to Khartoum and the Red Sea ports. Cromer's opinion was that Egypt could not afford to reconquer its lost empire. General Gordon was therefore sent to Khartoum with instructions to hand the Sudan back to its traditional rulers. But these instructions were not very explicit, and Gordon, who had been a major official in Isma'il's Sudanese service, tried to come to terms with the Mahdi. In the event, he became besieged at Khartoum by the Mahdists, and in 1885, when an expedition to evacuate him was only two days away, the town was overrun and he himself was killed.

For thirteen years, the Sudan became an independent state under the administration of the Mahdi and his successor, the *Khalifa* 'Abdallahi (1887–98). But Britain could not let this situation continue indefinitely. Gordon had ironically become a national hero who should be avenged. More prosaically, the British interest in Egypt, in restoring its administration and commanding the Suez Canal, was thought to involve Britain in taking action to keep foreign powers away from the upper reaches of the Nile river whose waters were so essential to the life of Egypt.

At first the main threat seemed to be to the source of the White Nile, and to come from German approaches to Buganda round the southern end of Lake Victoria. The Imperial British East Africa Company, a strange amalgam of commercial, philanthropic and imperial interests, was therefore formed in 1887 to match the activities of the German company which was operating in the southern half of the Zanzibar hinterland. It secured a lease of the northern half of the Sultan of Zanzibar's coastal strip, was granted a charter by the British government in 1888, and in 1890 established a British presence in Buganda. By this time, both Britain and Germany were rationalizing their positions in East Africa. In 1890, they concluded a new treaty by which, in return for concessions elsewhere, Germany acknowledged Britain's interests in Uganda and at Zanzibar. Each followed this up by recognizing that its East African company was not adequate to maintain its imperial responsibilities in East Africa. The German government took over direct control for German East Africa in 1890; the British government superseded the IBEA Company in 1893, and in the following years constituted formal protectorates for Uganda and for the territory between it and the sea, which ultimately became known as Kenya.

Secondly, Britain became anxious about Italian imperial pretensions in North-East Africa. In 1883 the Italian government took over from the private Italian interests established at Assab, and shortly began to conquer Eritrea; six years later it began to establish a protectorate over the Indian Ocean coastlands of Somalia. The obvious target for these advances was Ethiopia, in which lay the source of the Blue Nile. While the Emperor John IV was endeavouring to maintain the integrity of Ethiopia both against the Italians in Eritrea and against Mahdist pressures from the west, the Italians cultivated Menelik and supplied him with arms (which helped him to occupy Harar). In 1889, when Menelik had become emperor after John had been killed in battle with the Mahdists, they concluded with him the Treaty of Wichale (Ucciali). But while Menelik saw this treaty as one confirming a useful friendship, the Italians interpreted it as marking his acceptance of their protectorate. Thus when Italian forces advanced to implement this, they met with spirited resistance. This culminated in their rout at Adowa in 1896, which meant that Italian imperial ambitions in Ethiopia were held back for forty years.

Apart from Menelik and the Mahdists themselves, Britain's third possible rival for possession of the upper Nile, and in the event the

most serious one, was France. In the Egyptian crisis of 1882, imperially minded Frenchmen felt that they had been cheated by the British
initiative. They therefore entered upon a period of hostility towards
British policies in Egypt and the Nile valley and elsewhere in Africa
which ceased only with the conclusion of the Anglo-French Entente
in 1904. With the Italians still occupying Eritrea, Ethiopia's traditional
window to the outside world, Djibouti, close by Obok in what in
1884 had become French Somaliland, was becoming the main port of
entry for Ethiopia. From it, a French company was already building
a railway towards Menelik's new capital at Addis Ababa. But in the
event Menelik was no more willing to become a French tool than he
had been to be an Italian one, and the French threat that developed
was to the White rather than the Blue Nile, and was mounted from
the west, not from the east.

French expansion in West Africa has already been discussed. But
this had been preceded by the French conquest of Algiers in 1830,
and by the 1880s this had led to the establishment of a very substantial
empire in North Africa. The reasons for the French military action
at Algiers in 1830 were complex, and are not very significant compared
with its results. France could claim that it was acting to stamp out
corsairing, which had tended to revive during the European wars of
1793–1815, and which had led a number of other major sea-powers
to mount occasional punitive actions against North African ports
between 1803 and 1824. But by 1830, corsairing was hardly a sufficient
menace to justify the occupation of Algiers. Secondly, a dispute
between France and Algiers had been simmering since 1798, when
Algerian merchants had provided corn for Napoleon's expedition to
Egypt but had never received payment for it. In 1827 the Dey and
the French consul at Algiers publicly lost their tempers over this issue,
and desultory hostilities followed between the French navy and the
forces of the Dey. Finally, the government of Charles X was looking
for some success abroad which might restore its failing popularity at
home.

This hope proved vain, for Charles X fell a few days after Algiers
had been taken, and the problem of what to do with the conquest
was left to the more liberal and bourgeois administration of Louis
Philippe. This had no thirst for military ventures, and at first it did
little except to occupy the major coastal towns under Algiers – Oran,
Bougie and Bone – to prevent reprisals against French shipping. On
the other hand, it was thought that it would be weak-minded and

dishonourable to return a French conquest to a discredited African regime. Thus in 1834 it was decided to follow a policy of 'restricted occupation'. The whole of the territory over which the Dey had claimed sovereignty was declared to be French, but a French administration would be established only for those coastal districts which had been more or less directly under his control.

But this policy did not work because the traditional leaders of the interior would not acknowledge French sovereignty. Instead they came together under 'Abd al-Qadir, who combined religious authority with considerable executive ability. He declared a *jihad* against the invader, and began to inflict defeats upon the French forces. The French were ultimately forced to recognize that nothing but an outright conquest of the interior would ensure their security in the coastlands. In 1840 this conquest was begun under General Bugeaud. Mobile French columns systematically destroyed Algerian centres of resistance and laid waste the intervening countryside from which these were supported. At first 'Abd al-Qadir was able to survive, in part because of his ability when hard pressed to find refuge in neighbouring Moroccan territory. But finally, in 1847, he was captured and sent into exile. In the same year, Bugeaud was recalled to France; the Ministry of War would not continue his policy of systematically colonizing the conquered agricultural lands, whose native inhabitants had fled into the mountains and steppes, with French peasants supported by government funds. However, continuing resistance from the Algerians to the loss of their best lands meant that Bugeaud's policy of military aggression was continued, with occasional pauses, until 1879, by which time the French frontier had been pushed into the northern limits of the Sahara.

But what thus became the French colony of Algeria was simply the central, and hitherto least organized, part of the Maghrib, the essential ethnic and religious unity of which was demonstrated by the support given to 'Abd al-Qadir and other refugees from the French advance in both Morocco and Tunisia. The security of the Algerian conquest therefore necessitated increasing French interest in both the other territories. In Morocco, however, France's hand was long stayed by the presence of other European interests. Spain still held enclaves at Ceuta and Melilla, and Britain was unlikely to look with favour at any growth of French power directly opposite Gibraltar. Morocco therefore remained free from overt European imperialism until after the Anglo-French Entente and Germany's interventions in its affairs in 1905 and 1911.

But in Tunisia, despite the growing settlement of individual Maltese and Italian immigrants, there was at first no rival European interest to match that of France. The latter had shown that she regarded it as a potential French preserve as early as 1832, when she had mounted a naval demonstration to prevent the Ottoman government securing direct control of Tunis (as it was to do of Tripoli a few years later). Thereafter France offered the Husainid Beys a shield behind which, mindful of events in Egypt, Algiers and Tripoli, they could attempt to modernize their government with the aid of European finance, advisers and technicians. In 1857, Muhammad Bey was the first Muslim ruler in history to grant a constitution (*destour*) under which his country was to be governed. But the same fate overtook the Beys and their ministers as engulfed Isma'il in Egypt. Their modernization programme required more funds than were available from local taxation. They borrowed extensively abroad, some of the money got into the wrong hands, and many of their enterprises produced no immediate revenue. By 1869 the Tunisian government was bankrupt. Internal French difficulties and the newly united Italy's interest in Tunisia for a time held back French intervention. But at the Congress of Berlin in 1878, it was agreed that Tunisia was a French sphere of interest. Three years later, an incident on the Algerian frontier provided the occasion for French troops to occupy the country and establish a protectorate.

France was now mistress of the north-western marches of the Sahara and also established in West Africa to the south of the desert. Since in addition she had begun to prospect for empire in equatorial Africa on the foundations of her earlier colony in the Gabon and the treaties recently made by de Brazza, the Lake Chad basin, which Frenchmen might now approach at once from the north, west and south, began to appear as a central focus for imperial ambitions. During the 1890s this idea began to catch hold on the imagination of the French public. There were grandiose dreams of a single empire linking the Niger to the Congo and the Nile, even of one stretching from the Mediterranean and the South Atlantic to the Indian Ocean. Even if this last proved impossible to reach, it might well be possible to forestall the old enemy, Britain, on the White Nile. In 1897, therefore, a pioneer expedition under Captain Marchand set out from the nearest French base, on the Congo. But two years earlier, though Cromer was not entirely happy about it, the British government had decided that Egypt's finances had been sufficiently restored to permit of mounting a cautious Anglo-Egyptian reconquest of the Sudan. Growing evidence of French intentions, coupled with an appeal from the Italians for an intervention which might prevent Menelik from joining with the Mahdists to drive them into the sea, led to an acceleration of this plan. In September 1898, the massed forces of the *Khalifa* were routed by an Anglo-Egyptian army outside Omdurman, across the Nile from Khartoum, and the reconquest was virtually complete. Thus within a few weeks of Marchand's arrival on the Upper White Nile at Fashoda (the modern Kodok), he found himself face to face with a vastly superior force led by General Kitchener, the conqueror of the Sudan.

In the confrontation at Fashoda, the European competition for power and territory in the northern half of Africa reached its climactic crisis. It had become plain that, since the arrival of Joseph Chamberlain at her Colonial Office in 1895, Britain was at last willing to pursue her interests in Africa to the utmost limits. In the last analysis, France was not prepared to go to war to maintain her claim to the upper Nile, so Marchand was eventually instructed to withdraw. Equally prepared to use force in West Africa, Britain had emerged as the major European aggressor on the African continent. Within a year, she was involved in an all-out struggle to ensure her primacy in southern Africa as well.

Up to the 1870s, the British authorities had been little concerned with the interior of southern Africa. As has been seen, they were prepared to let the Boers escape into it provided that their activities there did not create problems which might adversely affect their strategic interest in the coastline. At first the main danger seemed to be that the land-hunger of the less than 70 000 impoverished Boers who were living in the interior by the 1860s might provoke conflicts with the Bantu masses which they could not contain, and which therefore could embarrass the British administrations in the colonies of the Cape and Natal, which were beginning to achieve a precarious economic viability. In Natal during the 1860s, the lowlands were seen to be suitable for the production of plantation crops, sugar especially. The principal problem was one of securing sufficient labour, for few Bantu were prepared to leave the tribal lands in and around the colony to work on plantations. Natal's tiny European community of 16 000 therefore embarked on the expedient of importing indentured labourers from India, and in so doing added a new complication to the racial problems of South Africa. The 180 000 Europeans in the Cape Colony were in a stronger position, for by the 1860s sheep-farming was beginning to supply funds for modest modern developments like harbour works and the first small railways. The Cape could thus aspire both to self-government and to an economic leadership which might bring all four European communities together with a consequent reduction of Britain's responsibility for South African affairs.

At this point, the hitherto slow pace of change in South Africa was greatly accelerated by the discovery of mineral wealth in the interior. The presence of diamonds was recognized in 1867, and diggers were soon rushing into an area around the confluence of the Vaal and Orange rivers which was found to be exceptionally rich in diamond-bearing soils. This area was known as Griqualand West because it was inhabited mainly by a western branch of the Griqua, a people of mixed but essentially Khoikhoi descent, who had acquired horses, guns, some Christianity, and the Afrikaans language of the Boers from earlier interactions at the Cape. But it lay very close to the frontiers of European settlement of each of the Orange Free State, the Transvaal and the Cape Colony, and each administration strove to control what quickly became a major source at once of wealth and of lawlessness. In 1871, the prize fell to the strongest, the British government at the Cape, which also had an interest in Griqualand West as the starting point for the Cape missionaries' and traders' road to the interior.

The discovery of the diamond fields and their acquisition by Britain for the Cape Colony meant that the latter achieved the means for an economic take-off. By 1880 its diamond exports were worth over £3 000 000 ($15 000 000) a year, and over ten years the trade passing through its ports had more than tripled to some £15 000 000 ($75 000 000) a year. Capital began to flow in from Europe and America. It thus became possible to build major railway lines from all the Cape ports. By 1885 these had reached Griqualand West, 600 miles into the interior, and were pressing at the frontiers of the hitherto isolated republics. At the diamond-mining centre of Kimberley, the industrial revolution in Africa took its first steps. The extraction of the stones from deep 'pipes' of blue ground led swiftly to the supersession of the individual diggers by large, highly capitalized companies, which offered employment to an élite of skilled white workers and to a growing mass of unskilled black labourers. The geographical barriers which had hitherto largely separated the black and white populations of South Africa were broken down by the attraction of the great new wealth to be found in mines and industry, but a potent new barrier, a class barrier defined and fixed by the colour of a man's skin, was put in its place.

In 1872, the Cape was prosperous enough to be granted self-government. Henceforward its affairs were directed not by the British governor, but by its own ministers, responsible to an elected parliament. However, the governor remained responsible for the oversight of British interests in the interior (for which he bore the additional title of High Commissioner). But here the British were disappointed. The federal union of the four European administrations for which they pushed, and which would relieve them of any responsibility for the internal affairs of South Africa, was not achieved. The Cape politicians were not anxious that the other European communities should share in their new-found wealth, nor to be involved in the affairs of substantial areas of territory inhabited mainly by Bantu. These would be expensive to administer, while their possession could well upset the delicate racial balance of their own community with its colour-blind franchise. The Boer republics felt that they had been cheated by the British annexation of Griqualand West. They were determined to maintain their independence and, together with the Boers remaining in the Cape Colony, began to cultivate a sense of Afrikaner nationhood to withstand the growth of wealth and power by the English-speaking settlers who dominated trade and industry, and who were now being reinforced by growing immigration.

But in the Transvaal the treasury was empty, and difficulty was being experienced in defending its lands from attack by neighbouring Bantu peoples. In 1877, therefore, British agents thought that they might tip the balance towards federation by annexing the Transvaal. The plan miscarried completely. Britain was now responsible for defending the Transvaal against the Zulu kingdom, but in 1879, at Isandhlwana, the Zulus cut to pieces a sizeable British force. This defeat was subsequently avenged, but the Transvaalers had seen that the professional British army was not invincible. When they saw no signs of the internal self-government under the Crown which had been promised them at annexation, they rose, and in 1881 inflicted their own major defeat on a British force at Majuba. Britain thereupon again recognized the essential autonomy of their republic subject to a residual British right to oversee its relations with adjacent African peoples and other European governments.

The effect of these events was still further to entrench Afrikaner nationalism, and under Paul Kruger (President from 1883 to 1902), who had participated in the Great Trek as a youth, the Transvaal emerged as its major political champion. If South Africa were to be united, it should not be in a federation dominated by the Cape and its connections with Britain and world trade and industry, but in a republic dedicated to Afrikaner ideals. Attempts to cut the Cape's access to the interior through Botswana were foiled by British imperial annexation. But steps were taken to achieve independence of the Cape and British connections by the grant of a concession for the construction of a railway between the Transvaal's capital, Pretoria, and the Portuguese port of Lourenço Marques (Maputo) on Delagoa Bay. Then in 1886, the republic suddenly found itself with abundant means to achieve all its ambitions. It became apparent that in the Witwatersrand, just south of Pretoria, there lay far and away the world's largest known deposits of gold ore.

Though very extensive, the gold ores of the Transvaal lay at great depths, and even the richest of them rarely yielded more than about £1.50 ($7.50) worth of gold per ton of ore. From the beginning then, profitable mining was only possible with a high degree of technical and economic skills, employing expensive machinery and large quantities of capital. But South Africa had already learnt how to mobilize these on its diamond fields, and very rapidly the Kimberley experience was being repeated on the Witwatersrand, but even more intensively and on a very much greater scale. Diamond production could not be increased beyond a certain level without depressing the price of gem stones (which led inevitably to the monopoly of Kimberley production, then amounting to nine-tenths of the world's supply, achieved by Cecil Rhodes's De Beers Consolidated Mines in 1888). But the demand for gold was inexhaustible. Production increased until within twenty years the powerful companies operating on the Witwatersrand were responsible for one third of the world's output; within forty years they were producing one half.

By 1897, the nominal value of the capital invested in the gold mines, about £60 000 000 ($300 000 000), was about fifteen times that invested in diamond mining in South Africa; the value of the annual output, nearly £11 000 000 ($55 000 000), was more than twice that of the diamond mines; and the number of black labourers employed was about ten times greater. The Transvaal also had readily accessible sources of coal, and the basis for industrialization was now firmly established. Diamond mining had not been able to prevent the world depression from affecting South Africa's foreign trade; in 1885, the year preceding the discovery of the Witwatersrand goldfields, this had been worth just under £13 000 000 ($65 000 000). Twelve years later, in 1897, it had leapt to over £44 000 000 ($220 000 000) and is thought to have accounted for some two-thirds of the foreign trade of all Africa south of the Sahara. South Africa therefore became a major market for European overseas investment. For the first time also it was able to offer worthwhile opportunities to some of the great stream of emigrants flowing out of Europe. The flow to South Africa remained small compared with that to the Americas, or even to Australasia, and in 1911 four out of five of the Europeans living in South Africa had been born there. Nevertheless in the previous twenty-five years, about 400 000 immigrants had arrived, three-quarters of them from Britain.

South African politics were now dominated by two facts. First, the Transvaal was no longer an impoverished backwoods, but the main generator of wealth in South Africa. Kruger's government naturally sought to use some of this wealth to defeat the traditional hegemony of the Cape and the British interest, and to establish an Afrikaner dominion in its place. It was able to complete its Delagoa Bay railway in 1894, and so to fight against the southern power coming up the railways from the Cape and Natal ports, which also reached the Transvaal in the early 1890s. Secondly, however, the alien forces of foreign capital and settlement, predominantly though not exclusively British, which had made the new wealth possible, were now entrenched within the Afrikaner citadel. Pretoria was now threatened by the bustling new mining and financial centre of Johannesburg, only thirty-six miles away. An urban, commercial and industrial ethos was cutting a deep salient into a traditional, rural society. The immigrants who were flocking to exploit the Witwatersrand and the wealth deriving from it were not potential new Boers and Afrikaners; they were 'Uitlanders'. If Boer society and the Afrikaner state were not to be overthrown from within, steps had to be taken to deny them access to the political rights hitherto expected by all Europeans in South Africa.

The challenge posed by Kruger's Transvaal to the forces of change represented by the Cape, Britain and international financial interests was first taken up by Cecil Rhodes. Rhodes had emigrated from Britain as a young man, had made a fortune out of diamond mining and his creation of the De Beers monopoly, and had then become a substantial participant in the Witwatersrand gold-fields. But his base and his heart remained in the Cape, where he had entered parliament in 1880 and ten years later became Prime Minister. Rhodes was much more outward-looking than most Cape politicians of the time. The gist of his politics was that, under the umbrella of British imperial defence, Boer and Briton should come together, first at the Cape, and then throughout South Africa, to create a powerful united base from which white settlement could advance to develop the highland territories of the interior (as only it could do). A Transvaal dedicated to traditional Afrikaner nationalism was a major obstacle standing in the way of the implementation of this policy. This was the more so if it was able to develop an independent foreign policy allying itself with non-British powers, such as Portugal, which laid claim to the central African territories lying between its Mozambique and Angolan colonies, or, even more dangerously, with Germany, which from 1885 onwards was forcefully developing colonies in East and in South-West Africa astride Rhodes's projected line of advance.

During 1883–5, Rhodes had a considerable share in stimulating Britain to take action to check Transvaal encroachment across the Cape's road to the interior through Botswana, action which the Cape government itself was then unwilling to mount. Then, when neither the Cape nor the British government was keen to take on the responsibility, he himself initiated action to make British the lands astride the Zambezi which are now known as Zimbabwe and Zambia. During 1888–90, his agents were busy securing treaties or concessions from the principal African kings of this region, such as Lobengula of the Ndebele and Lewanika of the Lozi. On the basis of these treaties or concessions, and with the resources of his diamond monopoly behind him, in 1889 Rhodes floated the British South Africa Company, with a charter from the British government authorizing it to establish a British administration over the Zambezi territories.

Large though the company's resources were compared with those of other chartered companies of the time, they were not sufficient to enable it immediately to establish an administration over the whole area in which Rhodes's agents had been active. North of the Zambezi, it at first operated by proxy, first by subsidizing the African Lakes Company, and then, from 1891 to 1895, through the embryo administration which the British government was establishing in Malawi, to the expenses of which it contributed. But in 1890 the BSA Company sent out a column of armed police and pioneer settlers to begin to erect the colony of Southern Rhodesia to the south of the Zambezi. This area was of particular importance to Rhodes. It was, of course, the home of the ancient Zimbabwe-Monomotapa kingdoms, and reports from European travellers in it since the 1860s had suggested that it was still rich in gold and other minerals. Moreover it was known that both the Transvaal and the Portuguese were actively concerned to secure it. Therefore, by erecting the white settler colony of Southern Rhodesia in the territory now known as Zimbabwe, Rhodes was both outflanking the Transvaal by denying it access to the north – which he could hope might force it to cooperate more with his plans for a unified South Africa – and expecting to acquire, for the Cape and the British connection, mineral wealth to match that commanded by the republic.

In fact, Rhodes's action only made Kruger and the Transvaalers more determined to fight to preserve their republic and its interests and ambitions. Increasing restrictions were put on the Uitlanders, some of whom began to think in terms of armed rebellion to secure a more amenable government for the Transvaal. Rhodes became increasingly impatient, and at the end of 1895 he authorized his administrator in Southern Rhodesia, Dr Jameson, to enter the Transvaal with the BSA Company police 'to restore order'. But there was no Uitlander rising, and Jameson and his men were ignominiously rounded up.

This fiasco totally destroyed Rhodes's policy. The Transvaalers, descendants of the most diehard element in the Great Trek, and still resentful of the British annexation of their republic in 1877, were now totally convinced that the British interest in South Africa was out to destroy them. More moderate Afrikaners in the Orange Free State and Cape Colony, including many who had hitherto been Rhodes's tacit allies, saw little alternative but to rally behind the Transvaal. The German emperor sent Kruger a telegram congratulating the Transvaal on its victory over the raiders, and though Rhodes's fear of active cooperation between Germany and the Transvaal did not materialize, henceforward all Europe regarded British actions in South Africa as those of an imperial juggernaut seeking to override a small European nation's legitimate claims to independence. On the other side of this ideological conflict, Rhodes, politically discredited and unable to continue as Cape premier, saw the initiative pass to what he called 'the imperial factor'. In his eyes, the British Colonial Office was almost as much an enemy of the true interests of South Africa as the Transvaal had become. The only Europeans who could really understand Africa's problems, and secure a proper development of the continent's material and human resources, were those who actually lived there and had staked their future in it.

The new Colonial Secretary, Joseph Chamberlain, was well aware that South Africa now meant much more to Britain and her imperial interest than a strategic base at the tip of a troublesome sub-continent. It was a rich and essential part of the world economy which Britain could not afford to lose; British power must be mobilized in defence of British capital and settlers. The more than able lieutenant, Sir Alfred Milner, whom Chamberlain sent to South Africa as High Commissioner in 1897, held these views as – or more – strongly. He pressed the Uitlander issue until the Transvaalers saw no alternative but to go to war before Britain could build up an overwhelming military superiority in South Africa. Fighting started in October 1899; three years later, after initial reverses, and through the employment of an army totalling nearly 450 000 men (rather more than the total white population of the two republics, which between them could muster a fighting force of about 85 000), the two Afrikaner republics had been conquered and reduced to the status of British colonies.

Part 4

Africa in the modern world

Chapter 15

The colonial period, 1:

Policies in general and colonies of exploitation in particular

The confrontation at Fashoda in 1898 and the British conquest of the Afrikaner republics in the following three years were the climactic acts in the European partition of Africa. Thereafter there were only loose ends to be dealt with. German intervention in the affairs of Morocco in 1905 and 1911 led to crises which ended in the partition of the country between French and Spanish protectorates, and the creation of a smaller international zone around the key port of Tangier. (Germany herself was bought off by the transfer to her Cameroun colony of a large slice of territory from the French Congo.) In the same year, Italy embarked on the conquests in Tripolitania and Cyrenaica which were to result in her colony of Libya, and eventually, in 1935–6, she was able to accomplish the conquest of Ethiopia which had been denied her in 1896. This left Liberia as the only part of the continent which had never been subjected to the rule of a European colonial power. However, its government was long indebted to European financial interests, and so subject to continual foreign interference. The reason why Liberia did not suffer the fate of Egypt or Tunisia was that neither the British nor the French governments could intervene to add the indifferently governed territory to their adjacent colonies without offending the other and also the United States, which increasingly – if hardly willingly – was forced into the role of becoming a protecting state.

With these relatively minor exceptions, Europe and the world had accepted by 1902 that the whole of Africa was the property of one or other of the European colonial powers, Britain, France, Germany,

Italy, Portugal, Spain and Leopold II of the Belgians (who ruled the Congo Free State in his own right; it did not become the Belgian Congo until 1908). But a large part of this partition had been carried out in Europe itself, at meetings in Berlin, Paris, London and other capitals, at which European statesmen had agreed to boundaries between the competing spheres of interest of their nations that were drawn on small-scale and often not very accurate maps. When these agreements were concluded in Europe, often very little had actually been done on the ground itself in Africa. Sometimes a small military force was in tenuous possession of some strategic point in the area in question – Karonga at the north end of Lake Malawi, the Buganda capital just north of Lake Victoria, Say on the Niger, or Fashoda on the upper Nile. More often, perhaps, a single emissary of a European government or company had raced his rivals to secure the mark of an African ruler to an agreement which could be used in Europe to argue that the territories he claimed to govern had been placed under the protection of that government or company. But it was open to question whether the African ruler understood the agreement in this sense; whether, if he did, he understood its full implications; whether his people accepted his right to act in this way; or whether all the people within the territory he seemed to claim actually acknowledged his jurisdiction.

So when the partition had been completed in Europe, it was necessary to determine where the boundaries between the colonies actually lay on the ground in Africa, and to establish effective occupation of the lands contained within them. The first of these might not be done for anything up to ten or even twenty or more years after the first partition agreements had been signed in Europe. The establishment of effective administrations which were in control of all the territory and people within the boundaries of the colonies was an even more protracted business, which was rarely complete before 1914. Indeed it was by no means an easy task. The areas involved were enormous. France, Britain and Portugal all claimed empires in Africa which were about twenty times the area of their own countries; in absolute terms, the French claims extended over about 3 750 000 square miles, those of Britain over about 2 000 000 square miles. Initially there were no developed communications in these territories. While exploration had often been greatly facilitated by the use of waterways, these proved a disappointment when it came to establishing efficient, reliable and regular means of transport. The courses of even the greatest rivers – the Nile, the Congo, the Niger, the Zambezi – were too often interrupted by cataracts, and most rivers suffered too from seasonal shortages of water which impeded their regular use except by canoes or other small craft. Even before the end of the nineteenth century, it was evident that if the new colonies were to be effectively administered, let alone actively exploited, railways, roads and telegraph lines would have to be built. But for this to be possible, the lands through which they were to run had to be surveyed and mapped – sometimes, even, actually explored. And none of these things could be undertaken until an endless variety of African communities, many of them as yet hardly known to or aware of the outside world, had been made amenable, by agreement with their leaders or by military conquest, to European overlordship. Finally, all these things were expensive in terms of men and money and skills if they were to be done effectively.

The first part of the colonial period, to about 1914 or sometimes even into the 1920s, was thus one in which the main effort was devoted to securing a proper hold of the colonies, to conquering and organizing them. It was equally a time when all the colonial administrations faced the basic dilemma that, until they were firmly in control, and the infrastructures necessary to this effective operation had been established, there was little chance of raising revenue from Africa, and equally little chance that the greater part of it would interest more than a few individual European adventurers, speculators, and evangelists. The generality of Europeans wanted little to do with Africa. They did not want to make careers there; if they had money to spare they could see few enterprises in the continent in which it might seem reasonably safe or profitable to invest; above all, perhaps, they were not keen to pay taxes to pay for the acquisition or adminis-tration of remote and unknown African lands. Sometimes, even colonial offices were not keen to take on responsibility for the new colonies. Thus in British Africa, the first administrations for the Oil Rivers in Nigeria, for Nyasaland (i.e. the modern Malawi), for East Africa and for British Somaliland were set up under the Foreign Office. In the early days of colonization then, the colonial adminis-trations often had no alternative but to make the best use of such stray European agents as lay to hand. It was not unknown to find missionaries pressed into service as administrators, while the relations that developed between the European authorities and speculative capi-talist ventures is a theme to which specific attention is given later in this chapter. But one particular class of, as it were, institutionalized adventurers proved in the early days to be of prime importance.

Between 1871 and 1914 there were few major wars in Europe, so that able and ambitious army officers, if they wanted to exercise command in the field, and so to distinguish themselves and to advance their careers, were naturally attracted to service overseas. Many of the generals of the 1914–18 war – Kitchener, French, Haig, Plumer, Gallieni and Joffre are obvious examples – in fact learnt their trade in Africa. Many others chose to find outlets for their ability and ambition in staying on to govern where they had conquered, thus reinforcing the perhaps inevitably authoritarian flavour of the early colonial administrations. This was enhanced when, after 1918 (as after 1815), many senior officers looked for civil employment; indeed some military experience seems to have been thought a useful qualification for a colonial governorship until at least the 1930s.

The outstanding prototype, at least on the British side, of an army officer turned colonial administrator was Frederick Lugard. In 1888, when he was thirty, after successful early service in India and Burma, the effects of ill-health and an unhappy love affair took him almost incidentally to East Africa, where he was able to distinguish himself in the African Lakes Company's war against the slavers in Malawi. Following this, in 1889–92, he occupied Buganda on behalf of the IBEA Company, and then in 1894 he took service with George Goldie (himself a former army officer), who needed a military force to enable his Royal Niger Company to establish itself in what was to become Northern Nigeria. When, in 1897, military operations there became a Colonial Office responsibility, Lugard was again given command, and in 1900 he became the first High Commissioner (i.e. Governor) of the new colony. After an interlude (1907–12) as Governor of Hong Kong, he was recalled to Africa to amalgamate the Northern and Southern Nigerian administrations, thus creating Britain's most prestigious tropical African colony, and ensuring that his doctrine of 'Indirect Rule' became the accepted ideal of British colonial administration.

Indirect rule, as will be seen, meant that the Europeans sought to control the traditional African rulers, and left to these the more difficult task of keeping order over the mass of the people. It is important to realize that the main burden of imposing European rule on Africans was also borne by Africans. The initiative in the colonial conquests, of course, lay with the European officers; indeed, they not uncommonly acted in advance of formal instructions from their political superiors. (Both Lugard and his French contemporaries in West Africa afford examples of this. Local military commanders were in fact naturally inclined to take a different attitude towards strains arising on their frontiers with as yet unconquered African peoples from that taken by the political authorities at home. While the latter were often hesitant to add to their country's colonial responsibilities and expense, the former equally commonly supposed that the commonsense solution for these strains was to extend their control to the lands on the other side of the frontiers.) But the European commanders' conquests would have been much less easily acceptable had their soldiers also been European. In fact, the rank and file in the colonial armies were Africans. These were much cheaper than Europeans. The latter not only required more in the way of pay, allowances and pensions; to maintain them in the tropics necessitated much more elaborate and extensive commissariat, medical, transport and other ancillary services (and also considerable numbers of African servants and porters). The costs of all this would have been a not inconsiderable burden for European tax-payers. Furthermore, the employment of African soldiers had also the considerable political advantage that no awkward questions would be asked in Europe when they became casualties from disease or in battle.

Because the costs were small, and because the risks of European casualties were not great in relation to the personal and national rewards that might be won, the colonial wars of conquest could continue for many years after the imperial fever of partition was over, without causing adverse comment at home. Under Lugard, campaigning in northern Nigeria continued until 1906 and in eastern Nigeria until 1918. German campaigning in nearby Cameroun was hardly complete before the Germans were themselves ousted by British and French forces (again, largely of African soldiers) in 1914–16. The French colony of Niger immediately north of Nigeria was not finally conquered until the 1920s, and serious fighting continued into the same decade in British Somaliland and the Anglo-Egyptian Sudan. Since these territories were already regarded as European, these wars were thought of less as wars than as police actions, as 'pacifications'. But Europeans could not always deceive themselves in this way. Sometimes, after they thought they had gained control, they found that their demands on the African people for tax or labour or land could provoke a bitter armed reaction which could only be defeated with reinforcements brought from Europe. This was the case, for instance, with the Ndebele and Shona risings of 1896–7 in Southern Rhodesia, and with the Maji-Maji rebellion in German East Africa in 1905–6.

Once Europeans had forcefully imposed their rule on the continent, they continued to rely on Africans to help them govern. The indirect rule to which the British became so attached is but a special, and somewhat extreme example of this. With European men and money so scarce, all the colonial administrations had to enlist the help of African auxiliaries as clerks, messengers, policemen, porters and artisans. The British administrations that were projected into the interior protectorates of Nigeria, the Gold Coast and Sierra Leone could hardly have functioned without the trained and semi-trained manpower available from the coastal colonies. The French in West Africa found ready employment for pensioners from their regiments of Senegalese *tirailleurs*, while in German East Africa, a whole new category of subordinate officials, *akidas*, was recruited from the coastal Swahili.

The colonial conquests were therefore accomplished and, still more, the early colonial administrations were set up, on the cheap. There was very little sense among the early colonial governments that they had any urgent need actively to develop their new colonies. The aim was rather to provide the minimum of force, administration, communications and technical services needed to assert European control. It was supposed that, under this umbrella, the private individual and corporate initiatives which had built western European society would in course of time come to transfer some of their energies to Africa, and so to make the colonies into profitable undertakings. This was not, perhaps, an unreasonable attitude to take towards West Africa, on whose coasts Europeans had been trading for centuries, and where in some areas there had been a notable African response in the production of commodities for the world market. But for most of the rest of sub-Saharan Africa, lack of knowledge and previous experience of the human and physical conditions meant that the risks were too high to encourage European settlers or companies freely to commit themselves except in territories which were known to possess substantial mineral wealth. Even here, private enterprise was selective, for only concentrated deposits of minerals of high value in relation to their bulk could readily repay the costs involved, including building and manning the railways needed to get machinery and stores in from the coast and to get the minerals out. Prior to the second world war, this effectively limited mining operations to the exploitation of gold, diamonds and copper, and essentially in South Africa, the Rhodesias, the Katanga province of the Belgian Congo, and the southern Gold Coast, the first three of which happened also to be climatically suitable for European settlement.

In general, then, if European settlers or companies were to be brought into Africa to bring the continent into the world economy, governments had actively to attract them. In so doing they all too often entered into commitments which could limit their subsequent freedom of action, or even negate their proclaimed aim of making the material and human resources of Africa available for the benefit of mankind. The more intractable problems were to arise from the implantation in Africa of European settlers. But for climatic and medical reasons, settlement was impracticable in the tropical bulk of the continent, and so was restricted to the temperate lands in the extreme north and south and to the highland spine running northwards from South Africa towards Ethiopia. Moreover the problems resulting from settlement were not as quickly evident as some of those which arose when European governments allied themselves with commercial companies. Problems arising in colonies of settlement are therefore dealt with in the following chapter, where they can be viewed in the light of developments in the tropical lowlands of the remainder of the continent.

The leasing or granting of large areas of the colonies to private companies seemed at first to be an obvious means of attracting capital to Africa. Sometimes these companies were formed by the minority pressure groups which, for a variety of reasons, had been arguing in favour of tropical colonies before the imperialist fever had caught on. Indeed such groups could be chartered by the European governments to act as their agents in the acquisition and administration of the colonies for which they had been pressing. But sometimes the companies to which the European governments committed African lands were simply speculative concerns. Their directors and share-holders were gambling on profits to be found from exploiting mines, or forestlands (e.g. for wild rubber or ivory), or from establishing plantations for the production of tropical produce, and were therefore prepared to seek concessions of land or mineral rights or both within the colonies that government initiatives had established.

In fact the line between what may be called 'chartered companies' and 'concession companies' is not an easy one to draw. It is obvious that a commercial concern would not seek or accept a charter giving it the responsibilities as well as the rights of government unless its directors thought that this would help it to undertake commercial activities which would profit its shareholders. On the other hand, in a recently acquired and thinly governed colony, a concession company often needed to take considerable powers of administration if it were to have any chance of successful commercial operation. But from the point of view of the European governments, there was a distinction. A chartered company was thought of as a governing agency whose powers could be altered or abrogated if for some reason its agency proved to be ineffective, unsatisfactory or inconvenient. A concession company, on the other hand, was always supposed to be operating within a framework of law and administration which was provided by the European governments' own colonial authorities.

In the 1880s, both the British and the German governments found it expedient to grant or to recognize powers of government for companies operating in Africa, notably the Royal Niger Company, the Imperial British East Africa Company, the British South Africa Company, and the German South-West and East Africa Companies. But only one of these survived as a governing agency into the twentieth century. The basic weakness was really that no private concern could command sufficient capital to establish proper control over extensive, undeveloped lands inhabited by Africans unused to European rule or actively hostile to it. The companies therefore soon either gave up their burdens, or resorted to expedients which caused trouble for the British or German governments, which as a result were led to take over direct responsibility for the territories involved. The IBEA Company and the two German companies were certainly not strong enough to administer effectively or to quell African resistance to their administrations, and none of them lasted more than a few years. The Royal Niger Company was operating in conditions which allowed it to be a successful trading company. But its commercial interests prevented it from maintaining an impartial administration which could fulfil Britain's obligations to third parties, whether white or black, and eventually too it became involved in competition for territory with French government officials and troops. These factors combined to lead the British government to divest it of its administrative responsibilities at the end of 1899.

The British South Africa Company continued as the governing agency for the two Rhodesian colonies into the 1920s. But it would be fair to say that it survived the troubles in which it involved itself in the 1890s – the Jameson Raid and the Shona and Ndebele risings – by the barest of margins, and that these led to some degree of imperial supervision of its subsequent administration. The BSA Company, created by Cecil Rhodes and thus associated with South African diamond and gold-mining wealth, was by far the best capitalized company of the five, but even so its resources were considerably stretched by the task it had set itself. It was never able to provide more than the barest minimum of administration for its northern colony, and – as has already been mentioned – its shareholders never received any dividends on their substantial investment until after the company withdrew from its administrative responsibilities, in 1923 in Southern and in 1924 in Northern Rhodesia. Its continuance as a governing agency for so long was in fact due to wholly exceptional circumstances, the actual or promised mineral wealth of the Rhodesias, and above all to its close association with South Africa and its policy of encouraging white settlers and sharing political power with them. More will therefore be said about it in the following chapter.

Portugal also employed chartered companies, notably in Mozambique, where in the 1890s administration of the northern quarter of the colony was entrusted to the Niassa Company, and of the provinces of Manica and Sofala, leading up the Zambezi valley, to the Mozambique Company. These companies continued as governing agencies until 1929 and 1942 respectively. But the circumstances here were somewhat different. While British and German governments temporarily found it expedient to entrust some of their nations' African interests to companies, the Portuguese state, virtually bankrupt at the time, was sadly lacking in resources to establish any effective control over the African territories it had long claimed, and feared that it might lose them to stronger powers. Portugal's chartered companies were thus to a considerable extent a device to attract foreign capital to save an important part of her empire, and in this respect at least they served their purpose.

Concession companies were used throughout tropical Africa, though concessions of land, as opposed to concessions of mineral rights, were not very significant in West Africa, except in the south of German Cameroun and, ironically, in the independent Republic of Liberia.

The reason for this was essentially that many West Africans were already well used to meeting European commercial needs, and that in the nineteenth century they successfully developed the production for export of oilseeds (groundnuts, and palm oil and kernels), cocoa, and, to a lesser extent, coffee, bananas and other crops. By and large it proved cheaper for European merchants to buy these commodities from African farmers than to grow them on plantations which they themselves owned and managed. A further factor in the situation was that, by virtue of their long contact and of their increasing involvement in formal European education, West Africans had developed consider-able political expertise in dealing with Europeans. One of the first manifestations of this in a modern form was the creation of political associations to defend African rights from European encroachment, and in particular African rights to land. An association of this kind on the Gold Coast, the Aborigines Rights Protection Society, began a successful agitation against the granting of concessions of land to foreigners as early as the 1890s. By 1914 it had become an established principle of British policy in West Africa that Europeans were not to receive such concessions. There was no such principle in French West Africa, where some Europeans did operate plantations, notably in the Ivory Coast and in Guinea. But they never monopolized production, and in the long run perhaps their main effect was to stimulate the development of African production. Similarly, though the Germans thought plantations necessary in Cameroun, they found they were not required in their other West African colony, Togo, which had shared in the same indigenous development of production for export as the adjacent Gold Coast.

Liberia was a special case. Its thinly populated territory had attracted little European trade in the pre-colonial period, and its government was not entitled to even the limited support from metro-politan sources that was available to a colonial administration. As the strength of the competitive European imperialisms began to press on Liberia, its government became desperate to secure resources to consolidate its hold on the territory it claimed to rule. It embarked on borrowings from European and American bankers without however achieving much in the way of increasing trade or revenue. By 1912, indeed, the principal result was the imposition of a foreign receivership on its customs. The granting in 1925 of a million-acre rubber plan-tation concession to the American Firestone Company (which also provided a new loan to pay off the old debt) was therefore essentially an expedient by which the Liberian government sought to gain the trade and revenue it needed to ensure its political future.

However, the factors inhibiting land concessions in West Africa did not apply to the exploitation of mineral wealth. It seemed obvious that the development of modern mining industry required amounts of capital and of technological skill which could be readily supplied only by Europe or North America. But until the 1930s, although a little mining for tin and coal was developed in Nigeria, only the gold of the Gold Coast was really attractive to western enterprise. European companies began to seek gold concessions here as early as 1877, and by the early 1900s and the advent of railways, the Gold Coast had a mining industry which rivalled that of the Transvaal in sophistication if not in scale. During the 1930s, however, it was appreciated that both the Gold Coast and Sierra Leone possessed large quantities of diamond-bearing alluvial gravels. Concessions were granted to European companies to exploit these, but diamonds could equally be won by individual African diggers, with the result that by the 1950s, especially in Sierra Leone, considerable tensions had developed. By this time too, European industry had become interested in West African deposits of iron ore, bauxite and some other base minerals, especially if they were of high grade and reasonably accessible from the coast, and substantial concessions were granted to exploit these, especially in Liberia, Sierra Leone and French Guinea.

In the British and German colonies in East and central Africa, and also in the eastern highlands of the Belgian Congo, settlers were generally preferred to concession companies for the exploitation of land. In Southern Rhodesia, the BSA Company initially experimented with both, but by about 1900 it had come to the conclusion that settler farmers were more productive. Companies all too often regarded land as a speculative investment; they did not cultivate it themselves, but hoped that a demand for it by settlers would cause its value to rise so that they could profitably dispose of it to them. In Uganda, once it had been linked by railway to the coast, development followed more the West African pattern; African producers began with considerable success to grow crops, cotton in particular, for the world market. But the political circumstances here were unusual, in that Britain had established herself in southern Uganda as much by treaties with the major Bantu kingdoms as she had by conquest, and one strange result of these treaties, especially that with the largest, most accessible and

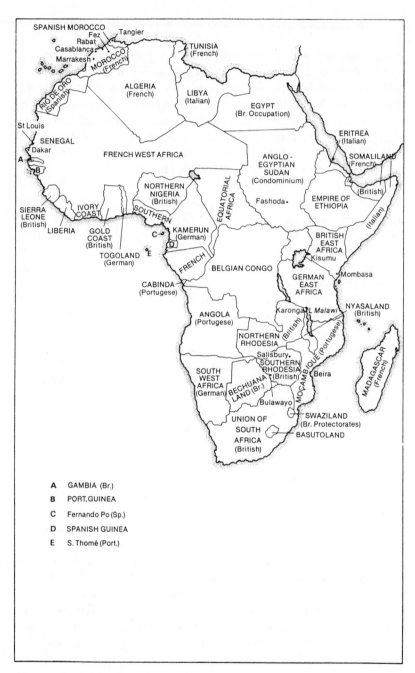

SPANISH MOROCCO
Tangier
Fez
Rabat
Casablanca
Marrakesh •
MOROCCO (French)

TUNISIA
(French)

RIO DE ORO
(Spanish)

ALGERIA
(French)

LIBYA
(Italian)

EGYPT
(Br. Occupation)

St Louis

SENEGAL
Dakar

A

B

FRENCH WEST AFRICA

ERITREA
(Italian)

SOMALILAND
(French)

ANGLO-
EGYPTIAN
SUDAN
(Condominium)

Fashoda •

EMPIRE OF
ETHIOPIA

(British)

SIERRA
LEONE
(British)

IVORY
COAST

LIBERIA

SOUTHERN

GOLD
COAST
(British)

NORTHERN
NIGERIA
(British)

TOGOLAND
(German)

KAMERUN
(German)

C
D
E

FRENCH

EQUATORIAL
AFRICA

BELGIAN CONGO

CABINDA
(Portugese)

BRITISH
EAST
AFRICA
Kisumu

(Italian)

GERMAN
EAST
AFRICA

Mombasa

ANGOLA
(Portugese)

Karonga L Malawi

NORTHERN
RHODESIA

(British)

NYASALAND
(British)

MOÇAMBIQUE (Portugese)

Salisbury •
SOUTHERN
RHODESIA
(British)

Beira

MADAGASCAR
(French)

SOUTH
WEST
AFRICA
(German)

BECHUANA
LAND (Br.)

Bulawayo

SWAZILAND
(Br. Protectorates)

UNION OF
SOUTH
AFRICA
(British)

BASUTOLAND

A   GAMBIA (Br.)

B   PORT. GUINEA

C   Fernando Po (Sp.)

D   SPANISH GUINEA

E   S. Thomé (Port.)

Map 11   Africa in 1914

most responsive kingdom, Buganda, was to establish and to recognize the rights of a class of considerable African landholders.

It was in the lands in and around the Congo basin that a land concession policy was most favoured, and where too the problems attendant on it most quickly became apparent. The position here was that competition between the agents of Leopold II of the Belgians and of the French government had led to these two authorities very rapidly acquiring claims to vast areas of territory which were exceptionally difficult and expensive to control and administer. Their climate was universally unhealthy, much of them was covered by almost impenetrable forest, and their generally scanty populations had hitherto had little contact with the outside world, and were thus generating little trade from which a government revenue might be raised.

The size of the problem facing Leopold was greater than that facing the French. When his parochial little country had shown no significant interest in his plans for empire, he had gone ahead on his own and, though he was a very wealthy individual in his own right, his resources were necessarily limited when compared to those available to a European state. The acquisition and conquest of what became accepted as the Congo Free State, a private kingdom over nearly a million square miles of African territory, left Leopold with nothing to spare to develop it. What were in effect mortgages obtained from an uninterested and unwilling Belgian parliament proved to be quite inadequate to his needs, so in the early 1890s he embarked on two desperate expedients. Complete rights of exploitation of land and minerals over about a quarter of the Congo Free State, mainly in the south-east, which was at once the least accessible part of the kingdom and that with the best mineral prospects, were granted to companies on ninety-nine-year leases. Secondly, and much worse, he converted his administration over much of the remainder of the country itself into the equivalent of a concessions company. It was decreed that all uncultivated land was state property, and that the state had a monopoly of the exploitation of its most immediately valuable assets, wild rubber and ivory. Each African community was compelled to deliver its assessed quota of this produce without payment to the agents of the state.

Where government itself was devoted to exploitation of this nature, abuses and atrocities were inevitable and great. This was the more so as there seemed to be no effective public opinion to check what was going on. Leopold was not responsible to anyone for what his agents did in the Congo; and parliament and opinion in Belgium generally regarded the whole imperial venture as a dirty business which they would rather know nothing about. In the event opinion did eventually catch up with Leopold, but at first it was world opinion rather than Belgian opinion. Leopold's agents were not the only Europeans in the Congo. Indeed they had been preceded by both traders and missionaries from other parts of Europe and from North America. The traders objected that Leopold's activities negatived the freedom of access to the Congo basin guaranteed at the Berlin Conference in 1885; news of atrocities committed in his name began to be spread through the missionaries. Humanitarians, especially in Britain, which had both trading and missionary interests in the Congo, organized a campaign against Leopold's regime, and finally a report from the British consul on the lower Congo, Roger Casement, forced Leopold to realize that an inquiry was necessary. Ultimately, in 1908, he saw no alternative but to transfer his colony to the control of a reluctant Belgian government and parliament.

In 1898, before the disastrous effects of Congo Free State policy were readily apparent, the French government, which already felt its resources sufficiently strained by its commitments in North and West Africa, gave way to the importunities of French financial interests which thought that fortunes might be made from the exploitation of wild rubber in the forests of French Equatorial Africa. Thirty-eight companies were granted leases covering a third of the territory. In theory the French government kept more control over the activities of leaseholders than did the Congo Free State, and its leases were for only thirty years compared with the latter's ninety-nine. But the local French administration was much too thin on the ground to keep a very effective watch on what the companies actually did. To some extent too it was compromised by its acceptance of 15 per cent of their profits in lieu of taxes. There followed much the same sort of scandal as was occurring in the Congo Free State, with the effects of the demands being made on the African people being exacerbated by the continuing impressment by the government of large numbers of porters to support the military operations it was then conducting in Chad. In fact the companies were not adequate to their task, even on their own unenlightened terms. The country was rapidly denuded of its most immediately realizable wealth, and little or nothing in the way of roads or other facilities was provided in return. But still the companies found it difficult to make profits. Probably at least as much

money was lost in French Equatorial Africa in these early years as
was won from it. Thus when the French government began to respond
to mounting criticism of its policy, no great problem was found in
terminating or re-negotiating the concessions. By 1912, the worst was
over, though there was a further scandal during 1921–34, when
perhaps as many as 20 000 conscripted labourers died during the
construction of the railway from Pointe Noire to Brazzaville.

The Congo Free State and French Equatorial Africa may have been
extreme cases, but even so it can hardly be claimed that the results of
the first quarter century of active European colonization in Africa
were impressive. To a considerable extent, the imperialists were
victims of their own propaganda. The continent was not a tropical
treasure box waiting to be opened by the key of colonial rule. Outside
West Africa, few African societies were geared to the production of
profitable commodities for the world market, and therefore able to
provide worthwhile markets for European goods or reasonable
revenues with which the colonial rulers could finance their administrations and see to the sound development of their colonies. Where
there were considerable resources awaiting development, money had
first to be spent on finding and assessing them, and then even greater
investment was commonly required in railways, roads, ports, schools,
hospitals and other facilities before they could be exploited on a
sensible basis. Government, which in the nineteenth and early twentieth centuries generally had a narrow concept of its responsibilities,
could do little in these directions when, because of the low level of
the African economies, it was difficult to raise more than the revenue
necessary to set up and maintain the minimum administration needed
to maintain order. Private enterprise was unwilling to make the large
preliminary investments in infrastructures needed to give its commercial undertakings a chance of success. It preferred to wait for government to open up the colonies; in the meantime, investors would put
their money in enterprises in the developed economies in western
Europe and North America.

The scale and the scope of the early colonial administrations was
very small in relation to the tasks facing them. (Even at the end of
the 1930s, there were only 842 European officials controlling the four
million Africans in the Gold Coast colony. In fact most of these were
in technical jobs; the number holding administrative, police or military
appointments was only 191.) Yet even so these administrations rarely

paid for themselves. Of the four German colonial administrations, only that of Togo ever became independent of aid from the imperial treasury. Of British colonies, Kenya was in receipt of imperial grants-in-aid up to 1911, Uganda up to 1914, and Nigeria up to 1918, and these grants were not to aid development, but simply to bridge the gap between revenue and essential administrative costs. This indeed was the general situation except in those coastal colonies in West Africa which already had some trade which could be taxed even before the colonial period began. Nigeria needed help mainly because the administration of its large and remote northern protectorate was initially separate from that of its commercially flourishing coastal territories. This, of course, was the *raison d'être* for the amalgamation of the two administrations for which Lugard argued, and which he was allowed to effect in 1912–14. The French had earlier taken steps to deal with a similar but even greater problem in their vast West African empire when in 1898 they set up a federal authority at Dakar to oversee the individual colonial administrations. In this way it was hoped that the richer coastal colonies could help subsidize the cost of governing and developing the poorer inland territories. Outside West Africa, it would seem that the only viable colonies by 1914 were Southern Rhodesia and Uganda, the former thanks to the efforts and sacrifices made by the BSA Company and the settlers, and the latter because the railway built from the coast with British tax-payers' money to facilitate control of this strategically important territory had had the incidental result of enabling Bagandan farmers to develop an agricultural revolution on the model of those in the West African coastal colonies.

In general, either little constructive work was done in the early colonial period, or what was done tended to destroy almost as much, or more, as was built. It has already been seen that the attempt to limit formal colonial commitments and to cut costs by employing chartered or concession companies tended to be counter-productive. All too often the result was that the imperial or colonial authorities had to face increased disorder and expense later on, at a time when metropolitan opinion was less favourable to colonial adventures and expenditure than it had been during the imperialist fever of the 1890s. But the company regimes really did not do much more than highlight the dilemma facing almost all the early colonial agents. Without an adequate, assured flow of men and money, it was difficult for them to act constructively with care for the future. There was a natural tendency for them to strip immediately available assets and to place nearly impossible demands upon African societies.

The general view was that the Africans themselves had done remarkably little to develop their vast continent. Therefore, if European capital and skills to do better were initially in short supply, the new colonial authorities felt under an obligation to force the Africans to do more, especially on the large areas of uncultivated land. But they failed to appreciate the restraints imposed by indifferent soils, seasonal and often capricious rainfall, and lack of population. The almost invariable practice of shifting cultivation, in which far more land was always left under forest or bush fallow than was actively farmed, was not necessarily primitive and wasteful, but could be an intelligent response to the environment. The fact that much of the population was not engaged in production except during the short seasons of planting and harvest could also conceal acute shortages of population in relation to the apparent abundance of land. Thus the sequestration of land for plantations or settlers; the impressment of labour to serve European purposes as soldiers, servants, carriers or labourers; or demands for tax that necessitated extra production – all these things could be extremely disruptive of African society, the more so as they followed immediately upon the shock of conquest and its inevitable destruction of lives, crops and other property.

In fact historians have sometimes argued that one of the most immediate consequences of European conquest and colonization in Africa was a major diminution of the continent's scarcest and so most valuable asset, its population. This is most commonly asserted in respect of those territories, such as the Congo Free State and French Equatorial Africa, where the early colonial excesses were most publicized. In the case of the latter, for example, attention is drawn to the fact that *c.* 1900 its population was estimated to be about fifteen millions, that estimates made in 1913–14 varied between about five and ten millions, and that the official figure for 1921 was only some 2 800 000. However, such sequences can be paralleled from colonial territories which were not subjected to concessionary regimes. As has already been said, in the early 1880s, when the French were embarking on their conquest of the western Sudan, responsible and by no means inexperienced administrators talked of gaining for France a new population of eighty-eight millions, while the official figure for all French West Africa for 1913 was less than an eighth of this! There seems little doubt, in fact, that the early colonial propagandists and officials consistently exaggerated the sizes of the populations they sought to add to their empires. Reliable estimates could not begin to be made until they were firmly in control, and then perhaps, since the inhabitants feared that official estimating or primitive head or hut-counting was intended as an aid to the collection of tax, the numbers actually counted tended to be on the low side of reality.

But whatever the actual figures may have been, there can really be little doubt that – during a period when the Europeans were also commonly engaged in warfare, either to make their initial conquests or to put down revolts, or (especially in East Africa) during their own tribal affray of 1914–18, and so deliberately killing Africans and destroying their crops and other property, as well as taking large numbers of carriers away to support their troops – the Europeans' demands for land, labour and tax must have been severely damaging to African society, its population and its capacity for production. It was a supreme irony that these same Europeans justified their actions by the claim that they were bringing civilization to the continent and extirpating the evils of slavery and of slave-raiding and trading which they thought had hitherto held back its progress.

Even before the first world war, the necessity was becoming evident of rethinking the aims and methods of colonial rule. This was perhaps most evident to the Belgian authorities who took over from Leopold's regime in the Congo in 1908. Their answer to the Congo Free State scandals was to keep power firmly in Belgium. Until the very eve of independence in 1960, there was never any question of political rights for the residents of the Congo, whether African or European. Very little freedom of initiative was allowed to the colonial administration, even to its Governor-General, and the purpose of the administration was to maintain a monolithic order under which the wounds of the past would be healed and Belgium would profit from its new acquisition. Gradually some of the old company concessions were renegotiated and reduced, and new, much smaller concessions were granted under strict administrative controls to plantation companies. From about 1919 onwards, plantation production, particularly of palm oil, coffee and rubber, and the indigenous production of coffee, together with the discovery of diamonds (1907) and, above all, the development of the Katanga (Shaba) copper mines, ensured a favourable trade balance for the colony.

While most of the profits of exploitation enriched European and

American investors generally and Belgium in particular, buoyant
revenues made it possible for the colonial government to embark on
schemes of social betterment in fields like health, housing and
education which in their own way were as impressive as anything
seen in Africa during the colonial period. But they were entirely
paternalistic; there was no apparent purpose beyond that of making
the Congolese healthier and fitter assistants to the Belgians in the
exploitation of their country. Thus, for example, in the early 1950s,
while a higher proportion of the population (about one in twelve) was
attending primary school than almost anywhere else in tropical Africa,
the provision of secondary education for Africans was almost non-
existent (there was approximately one secondary school for every 870
primary schools). It was the more easy to maintain this paternalism
because opinion in Belgium still refused to concern itself with the
colony. The Congo continued to be thought of as something which
was not the concern of decent people, and which was best left to the
care of the Ministry of Colonies, the Catholic missions, and a few
major corporations in Brussels. It was thus possible to maintain the
Congo free from unwanted currents of change, rather as though it
were a model factory or zoo. Thus when in the late 1950s the infection
of independence began to seep across its borders, the country was
totally unprepared for it.

The Herero war in South-West Africa and the Maji-Maji rebellion
in East Africa had rather the same effect on German colonial policy
as did the Congo Free State scandals in Belgium. The major difference
was that in Germany the Reichstag, with its contingent of Social
Democrats, felt some responsibility for the colonies and could make
its voice known. From 1907 onwards, there was considerable
rethinking about the policy and the administration needed in the
German colonies. German colonial secretaries were virtually unique
at this time in touring the colonies – foreign as well as German ones
– to see what was going on and what needed to be done. As a result,
the old, automatic Prussian style of authoritarian administration began
to be relaxed. Money was made available not only for such aids to
development as railway building on a considerable scale, but also
for sound research into problems of development in the tropics; for
example, how best to combat animal and human diseases, or how to
improve crops and their yields. By 1914 it would be not unreasonable
to say that German colonial administration was earning the respect
and admiration, if not the love, of the African peoples subjected to

it. But there was no time to see how the new German colonial policies might work out, because, as a result of the 1914–18 war, the German colonies were repartitioned between France, Belgium, Britain and the new self-governing British dominion of South Africa.

Unlike the Belgians and the Germans, the French and the British possessed considerable colonial experience prior to the great expansion of empire in Africa that began in the late nineteenth century. Following the 1789 and 1848 revolutions, the French theory of empire included the belief that colonial subjects were potential citizens who should be assimilated to French culture, and who would be entitled to the same rights as Frenchmen in France, for example, representation in the parliament in Paris. This principle had been established in the island colonies of the West Indies and Réunion, and during the 1870s it was extended to the four *communes* of Senegal, the towns of St Louis, Goree, Rufisque and Dakar which, with their long-established populations of French traders and officials and their mulatto and African auxiliaries, were the base for France's first tropical African colony.

Since the loss of the thirteen North American colonies and the Durham Report on the governance of Canada, the British had accepted that territories under their Colonial Office should have local legislative councils to help their governors frame suitable local laws, and that these councils should include some representatives of the local communities. Initially these representatives might be a minority compared with the government officials who also sat on the legislative council, and they might be nominated by the governor rather than elected by their fellows. Nevertheless the theory was that the legislative councils were the embryos of elective assemblies to which the colonial governments would ultimately become responsible, so that the colonies would become self-governing. In Africa, as has been seen, this had actually happened in the Cape Colony in 1872 and in Natal in 1893, and the other early British colonies, the trading establishments of Sierra Leone, the Gold Coast, Lagos and the Gambia, had all started on the process. By the 1880s, all had legislative councils containing some nominated African members, and these were politically active men who looked forward to the day when they and their kind would control the administration.

But neither the French nor the British thought that their previous experience of colonial government, which in tropical Africa was limited to small coastal trading enclaves with strong European connections, was particularly relevant to the problems involved in controlling large tracts of territory inhabited by Africans who had hitherto been little if at all affected by European influences.

France's new large empire in West Africa started essentially as a military enterprise. To enable France to rule, the major African states, the empires of the Tukolor and Samori or older kingdoms such as Dahomey, were conquered, and their traditional or Muslim systems of government dismantled. Some of the conquerors stayed on as the first civil administrators; other early administrators were influenced by their example, and emphasized the authoritarian and centralizing rather than the republican trends in the French political heritage. France therefore quickly devised for her West African colonies a centralized and authoritarian system of government, with a well-defined chain of command leading down from the Colonial Ministry in Paris, through the Governor-General at Dakar, to the governors of the individual colonies, and their provincial commissioners and *commandants de cercle*, the officers in charge of each district. Africans came into this scheme only as auxiliaries, or at the level of the villages, whose chiefs became the executive subordinates of the French district officer, deriving their authority from him and continuing in office only so long as they retained his confidence.

This authoritarianism was justified by the belief that the *assimilation* of the African masses to French culture and civilization, though still the ultimate justification for colonization, was hardly feasible within the practicable future. So long as Africans remained attached to their traditional or Muslim customs, ways and civil laws, they could hardly become French citizens. The best that could be hoped for was that they could be *associated* with France as her subjects, men and women possessing the obligations of citizenship but not its rights. The acquisition of citizenship became a formal process, involving education in French schools, performing military service and a minimum of civilian French employment, and agreeing to be monogamous and to forswear traditional or Islamic law and custom. In fact before the 1940s, very few Africans had much incentive to qualify for citizenship, since outside the few large towns the impact of France on everyday African life was small and the opportunities were few. Thus by 1939, out of about fifteen million Africans in French West Africa, only about 80 000 were citizens, and only about 2 500 of these had acquired this status other than by the accident of birth in one of the four Senegalese *communes* (which alone had the right to elect a representative to the

French parliament). A similar system and philosophy of government was extended to the federation of the four equatorial African colonies as they were brought under control following the period of conquest and concessions. But here not surprisingly the chances of African participation in the body politic were even smaller.

The situation in British Africa was far less uniform. This was partly because the tradition of local administration in Britain herself was far less subject to centralization than that in France. British colonial governors were allowed appreciably more initiative in relation to local circumstances than were their French colleagues. They would invariably seek the advice of their subordinates, who were in closer touch with African realities, and in normal circumstances, too, they were required to govern with the advice and consent of the legislative councils, to which there was no analogue in the French colonies. But it was also a consequence of the fact that the extension of British authority into Africa was often as much the result of infiltration and agreement as it was of military conquest. Thus in Uganda, the first British agents were missionaries (in the 1870s) and then traders (in the 1880s and 1890s); officials directly responsible to the British government did not appear until after 1893. Much the same pattern may be seen in the colonies of Nyasaland and Northern Rhodesia (i.e. modern Malawi and Zambia). In southern Uganda also, as has been seen, British rule was established as much by agreement with the major African kings as it was by conquest, and this was also the case with the Lozi kingdom in Northern Rhodesia.

On the other hand, as British rule was expanded in coastal districts in West Africa, it did at first take direct forms. Control passed from African kings to European district officers responsible to the colonial governors. But even so, there were significant differences from the French pattern: the degree of initiative left to the colonial governors, the existence of legislative councils imposing some degree of restraint on the exercise of administrative power, and also the fact that initially an appreciable proportion of the colonial administrations was locally recruited. Until about 1900, educated Africans often served as district commissioners, judges, medical officers, etc.; in the 1880s, one quarter of the small senior British establishment in the Gold Coast was black.

There was also appreciable military action in British West Africa. Major kingdoms like Ashanti and Benin were conquered and their administrations dismantled as happened in Dahomey, and British rule was established through the protectorates of Sierra Leone and eastern

Nigeria primarily by force. But perhaps the most spectacular British military conquest, that led by Lugard during 1900–6 against the Fulani emirs in northern Nigeria, led significantly away from direct rule.

The forces available to Lugard were very small, some 2000 to 3000 African soldiers under about 200 British officers and NCOs, one third of whom were always unavailable because they were sick or on leave. If the large, well-organized Fulani emirates had properly coordinated their resistance, it is perhaps open to question whether Lugard's conquest would have succeeded. As it was, by 1903, he was already grappling with the problem of how British control could be administered over a territory three times the size of Britain, and containing something like ten million inhabitants, when his finances did not permit the employment of more than a handful of British officials. (Initially his senior civil establishment, always reduced in effect by sickness and leave, numbered about a hundred.) The answer was never in doubt; it was to be indirect rule. Britain was to control the Fulani emirs, and to allow them to continue with the task of ruling the populace at large.

Essentially this decision was born of expediency. But whereas comparable shortages of men and money also not uncommonly forced the French to begin in a similar manner, they always moved away from it as soon as they could and, as has been seen, they always ended up with a structure in which the political responsibilities of African chiefs were limited to microcosmic units, and very clearly as the direct subordinates of French *commandants de cercle*. However, Lugard and the men he carefully chose to work with him in northern Nigeria (sometimes, indeed, the latter even more than the master himself) tended to push in the opposite direction to the French. It would seem in fact as though there was much in Lugard's own personal experience, and in British colonial experience generally, leading towards the concept that indirect rule was not simply an expedient way of controlling colonies, but also that it was the right way. Lugard himself was not unfamiliar with the native states in British India which in fact dealt with the majority of the populace; he had in effect begun what was indirect rule in southern Uganda; and he had come to Nigeria as the employee of Sir George Goldie, who had certainly proposed to control northern Nigeria through its indigenous governments when his Royal Niger Company had conquered them. Maclean in the Gold Coast in the 1830s, Sir Theophilus Shepstone in Natal between 1845 and 1875, and, outside Africa in the nineteenth century, Raffles at

Singapore and Sir Arthur Gordon in Fiji, had all sought to establish empire in cooperation with local rulers.

So in northern Nigeria, while the Fulani emirates were brought under a general framework of British law (autocratically imposed; there was no question of a legislative council system for northern Nigeria before the 1940s), and some major reforms were imposed on them, for example in methods of taxation and in the abolition of slavery as a status enforceable at law, the local British officials were supposed to act not as *commandants* over their districts, but as British residents at the emirs' courts. It was still the governments of the emirs that levied the taxes (though now they had to pass on half of the proceeds for the support of the central administration and the specialized services provided by their British overlords), and that dealt directly with individual Africans in ways conditioned by custom or by Islamic law.

The system of government which Lugard initiated in northern Nigeria in the early 1900s, and which was then further developed there by his subordinates, was to become a model which all British colonial administrations in tropical Africa sought to emulate. In the first place, indirect rule turned out to be not only an economical, but also an effective way of controlling northern Nigeria, largely because so much of it was subject to Muslim administrations which had the merit of being at once reasonably efficient and reasonably comprehensible in European terms. Secondly, northern Nigeria was a large and important colony, and the united Nigeria of which Lugard went on to be governor-general during 1914–19 was even larger and more important, indeed the premier colony in British tropical Africa. Thus not only was everything that was done there unusually significant, but ultimately it came to require a large number of British administrators. Lugard was a man who insisted both on excellence and in getting things done his way. Many of his subordinates were chosen by him personally; all were strongly influenced by his personality. The best of them naturally secured promotion to governorships and other senior posts in other colonies and took the Lugardian gospel with them. Finally, Lugard was a tireless exponent of his own opinions. His subordinates in Nigeria were bombarded with his 'Political Memoranda', and retirement from Nigeria in 1919 meant only that he acquired a wider field for his propaganda. He set out his views on colonial administration in a book, *The Dual Mandate in British Tropical Africa*, which passed through four editions during the 1920s;

became the British member of the colonial Mandates Commission instituted by the League of Nations in 1919; founded the International African Institute; and ended his career as a peer and the foremost British authority on colonial administration.

By the 1920s, indirect rule had become the official British doctrine for the governance of African colonies, remaining so until the end of the 1940s, and it had been given a philosophical justification. It was by working with and through indigenous rulers that the 'dual mandate' could be achieved of allowing the 'industrial classes' of Europe to gain their due reward for using their 'brains, capital and energy' in developing the resources of Africa, and at the same time of helping its 'native races in their progress to a higher plane'. Though there were some things that needed to be done in Africa – for example, providing and operating modern communications, and medical and agricultural and other technical services – which only the colonial administrations could do, their prime role was to act as a sort of arbiter or umpire. They were to provide a framework of order and of basic justice which would at once provide European capital and skills with the protection they needed to develop African resources, and at the same time protect African society from being radically damaged by this development. The best features of traditional African society and government were to be preserved until Africans were strong enough to stand on their own feet in the new order of things.

In relation to the destruction of African society which had taken place in the early colonial period, there was a great deal to be said for this idea of a European trusteeship for African wards, which became the moral justification for indirect rule. But even by the 1920s, the implementation of indirect rule could run into difficulties which should have led the trustees to question whether it was always the best way in which to fulfil their self-imposed trust. In the event, the questions were asked more by the wards than the trustees.

Indirect rule could hardly be applied to colonies like Southern Rhodesia or Kenya. Here there were white settlers who remained convinced that African society was a barbaric anachronism, who continued to put pressure on it to provide land and labour for their own activities, and who were able to influence or even control the local colonial administrations. There were also obvious problems in the implementation of indirect rule over African societies which had evolved little in the way of overt political authority, in which traditional leadership was still essentially social and religious in

character. The preferred solution here, pioneered by Lugard himself
in those parts of northern Nigeria which had not been subjected to
effective Fulani rule or among the Ibo of eastern Nigeria, was for the
British themselves to create what they called 'Native Administrations'.
But here they were innovating, not preserving, and their innovations
could create as many problems as they solved. Thirdly, there were
regions, such as the southern Gold Coast or Yorubaland, or the
Copper Belt of Northern Rhodesia, where traditional political authority had already been greatly weakened by the new economic opportunities brought by world trade. Here increasing numbers of Africans
were themselves seeking individual wealth and education which were
destructive of traditional society. They therefore had no great interest
in preserving traditional African forms of organization and government, but preferred to push for European forms which seemed more
appropriate to their changing conditions, and which might give Africans themselves a better chance to control the outside forces that were
provoking change.

The main objection to indirect rule was indeed that it could all too
easily become a static system of European control which was not in
the long-term or best interests of the African wards. Some of these
already wanted to jump into the twentieth century, and all of them
needed better training for the new world than could easily or quickly
be provided through developing traditional or supposedly traditional
forms of government. It was difficult to see that these could ever
achieve a scale, sophistication and command of resources to match
those of the new colonial administrations, and which would be needed
if Africans were ever to be able to control the forces of change for
themselves. In fact the British obsession with indirect rule had two
implications which contradicted the trusteeship aim of the Dual
Mandate. Government through traditional chiefs was not easily
compatible with the development of legislative councils into elective
popular assemblies which might control the colonial administrations.
The competence of the legislative councils which had existed in West
Africa before 1900 was not extended to the new interior conquests
like Ashanti or northern Nigeria, and there was no African representation, even by government nominees, on the new councils set up for
the East and central African colonies. Secondly, the development of
a uniform, and supposedly efficient and impartial, colonial service to
hold the balance between private European enterprise and African
interests throughout the vast new empire meant that effectively after

about 1900 Africans were no longer recruited to the colonial administrations.

The successes of indirect rule were in fact few. In northern Nigeria, in Uganda, and in Loziland it served to consolidate and indeed to extend the conservative regimes of Fulani emirs and Bantu kings, while in Ashanti it proved useful in restoring the confidence of a people who had been shattered by military defeat and the exiling of their king, and so in making them amenable to British overrule. Elsewhere its principal success was in Tanganyika (i.e. mainland Tanzania), where during 1925–32, a governor who had served his apprenticeship in Nigeria, Sir Donald Cameron, saw in it the means to make a completely fresh start in governing a territory in which the incessant European campaigning of 1914–18 had caused a major disruption of society, and had totally swept away a German adminis-tration which itself had only just been recovering from the effects of the Maji-Maji rebellion.

The 1914–18 war, in which Britain, France, Belgium and South Africa conquered the German colonies, can be regarded as the last fling of the old imperialism in Africa. Again, for the most part the soldiers used were blacks, though appreciable numbers of South African whites fought in South-West Africa and in German East Africa, and Indian troops were also extensively employed in the latter colony. Togo, Cameroun and South-West Africa (i.e. Namibia) were won relatively easily and quickly. But the conquest of German East Africa was a protracted and bloody business in which the direct casualties on the victors' side alone included the deaths of some 4000 African soldiers and about 30 000 carriers. The victors divided the spoils among them-selves. The French secured the larger parts of Togo and Cameroun, while Britain took smaller eastern zones which were administered together with their adjacent Gold Coast and Nigerian colonies. The lion's share of German East Africa passed to Britain as Tanganyika, though the Belgians took over the small though thickly populated African kingdoms then known as Ruanda and Urundi (now Rwanda and Burundi), while the South Africans secured South-West Africa.

But there was an interesting difference between this secondary partition and the original partition of the 1880s and 1890s. The victors were not allowed to become the absolute possessors of the German territories they had conquered. In 1918, they had subscribed to the Fourteen Points set out by President Wilson of the USA as a basis for the peace settlement. These included the establishment of a League of Nations to provide 'mutual guarantees of political independence and territorial integrity to great and small states alike', and also the principle of self-determination for the peoples in the defeated Austro-Hungarian and Turkish empires. This principle was not specifically enunciated for the German colonial empire. But it was eventually agreed that the conquerors of the German colonies in Africa were to be allowed to administer their conquests only under mandates from the League of Nations which provided that they were to serve as trustees for the advancement of their inhabitants.

The sequestration of African land and the conscription of African labour were expressly forbidden, and the new rulers were required to send annual reports on their administration to, and to submit to periodical inspection from, a Mandates Commission set up by the League.

Wilson's Fourteen Points and the League of Nations and its mandates system seemed to offer hope that the colonial empires in Africa were not intended to be permanent, that international opinion had recognized that one purpose of colonial rule was to create new African nations which would be able to stand by themselves in the modern world. They were certainly interpreted in this sense by the educated élites of coastal West Africa. In Senegal, Lamine Gueye founded a Socialist Party, allied to the Socialists in France, which sought to secure French citizenship and full political rights for all Africans. A Gold Coast barrister, Casely Hayford, launched the National Congress of British West Africa to press for the development of the legislative councils into elected parliaments which would control the colonial administrations and secure dominion status.

But these ventures were significant more as portents for the future than for any practical effects on French or British policy. Even in West Africa, the number of Africans who could comprehend the terms of the argument that their new politicians were opening was far too small to be politically significant. (It can best be measured, perhaps, by observing that although the history of the indigenous press in West Africa can be traced back to at least the 1840s, before the 1940s no newspaper had a circulation greater than about 3000.) Thus, although in broad terms the colonial powers now accepted the principle of trusteeship for their colonial subjects, they saw no need for any urgency in achieving its aims. It was supposed that a century or more would be needed for Africans to reach a state of advancement comparable to that of western Europeans, and so to achieve the common citizenship with the French or Portuguese, or the dominion status within the British Commonwealth, which were thought to be the ultimate goals. (In the Belgian case, the goal was so remote that it had hardly as yet even been defined.)

The second phase of colonial rule, essentially the 1920s and 1930s, was therefore a very static one. The orgy of self-destruction in which Europeans had engaged during 1914–18 had done something to weaken their belief in the innate superiority of their civilization, and as a result they had rather less faith in the permanence of their empires than they had had when they were creating them. But it also made them less confident than they had once been in deliberately bringing change to Africa; even more than before, they thought that it should be left to the action of 'natural' economic forces. European self-assurance was still more weakened by the further disaster of the world depression of the 1930s. But this also led them to question the beneficence of so-called natural economic forces. Consequently it was in the 1930s that there can be seen the first small beginnings of an idea that, if Africa were to be properly developed for the benefit both of its own peoples and of the world at large, colonial governments should play an active role in the process.

Some earlier colonial statesmen, notably Joseph Chamberlain in Britain in the 1890s and Albert Sarrault in France in the 1920s, had urged that if their countries wanted to get real benefit from their new colonial estates, steps must be taken to secure their active development. But very little had actually been done, except perhaps in the German colonies in the brief period between 1907 and 1914. The main stumbling block was the concept that colonies and colonial governments should pay for themselves, and not be a drain on metropolitan resources. But, as has been seen, in the early stages it was very difficult for any colonial government to raise more revenue than was needed to provide for the most basic administrative needs. There was rarely any significant revenue to spare to invest in development projects, or which could be pledged to pay the interest on loans raised for such purposes in the international money market.

In this situation, it was virtually impossible for colonial governments to work out, let alone to implement, coherent plans for the improvement of the material and human resources of the territories in their care. Indeed, prior to the mid-1940s, Sir Gordon Guggisberg, governor of the Gold Coast between 1919 and 1927, was virtually unique in formulating a coherent plan for the development of his colony. This involved improving the colony's transport and technical services so as to make its economy more efficient and productive, so that government could gain more revenue to improve the welfare of its subjects and, above all, to develop a comprehensive educational system which would train Africans to replace expensive European manpower in running the colony. But Guggisberg was unusual among colonial governors of the time. A Swiss-Canadian Jew and a professional engineer whose previous colonial service had been technical and not administrative, he was free from many of the contemporary inhibitions as to the limited responsibilities of government. However, he would never have achieved as much as he did had it not been for the early and continuing success of southern Gold Coast farmers in producing cocoa for sale in the world market. In other words, indigenous economic success was already providing a buoyant government revenue with which he could build. And when, in the world trade depression of the 1930s cocoa prices fell to an average of little more than half what they had been in Guggisberg's time, and less imaginative men had succeeded him as governor, his initiatives were not maintained.

Nevertheless it was this depression which first suggested to the colonial powers that their own interest, let alone Africa's, demanded that some special effort was needed to make funds available to promote development in their overseas territories. The crisis of confidence in the economic system, and the consequent decline in world trade, had produced massive unemployment in the manufacturing countries (in Britain, a fifth of the working population was jobless). Yet a substantial part of the world's producers and customers was subject to the control of the colonial powers; their own actions in their own colonies might therefore serve to help revive world trade and so reduce unemployment at home. If efforts were made to improve conditions and to increase wealth in Africa, then Britain and France and Belgium could sell more goods to its peoples, more Britons and Frenchmen and Belgians would have jobs producing these goods, and they and the industries they manned would be able to buy more foodstuffs and raw materials from Africa, so that the Africans would continue to benefit. What was needed to initiate this beneficial spiral of development was greater European investment in the colonies. If this were not to be forthcoming from the depressed money market, and from private investors who were even more reluctant than before to put their money in African ventures, then it was in the national interest that public money, tax-payers' money, should be invested in the colonies.

The sense, born out of the depression, that the responsibilities of trusteeship might involve active government participation in colonial development, was heightened and given even greater urgency by the predicament that the three major colonial powers found themselves in as a result of the second world war of 1939–45. Once again, self-interest was the spur. Britain, France and Belgium became involved in an all-out struggle in which they needed to mobilize all the resources available to them if they were to stand any chance of survival. They were faced with acute shortages of foreign currencies, especially of American dollars, with which to buy first the weapons and materials they needed to prosecute the war, and then, after it was won, the capital goods and other supplies they needed to rebuild their econ-omies after the strains and destruction of wartime. Furthermore, during 1941–5, traditional sources of such vital raw materials as oil and rubber were denied to them by Japanese advances in the Far East. The Belgian government was forced by German conquest to flee its own country; it was left with only the resources of the Congo to exploit if it were to contribute a worthwhile share to winning the war and regaining Belgian independence. The situation for France after its surrender to the Germans in 1940 was not dissimilar, if initially ambiguous. While the government at Vichy collaborated with the Germans, General Charles de Gaulle built up an alternative Free French government outside France. If this were to have any weight in the councils of its allies and in the post-war settlement, it was vital for de Gaulle to secure the allegiance of the French colonies. To begin with, the administrators in French North and West Africa saw no alternative but to declare for Vichy. However, after initial hesitation, the remoter colonies in equatorial Africa joined de Gaulle, and thus gave him a first territorial base from which to contribute to the continuance of the war. Then in 1942, after British and American forces had landed in Morocco and Algeria, and the tide of war in the Mediterranean was finally turned, all French Africa abandoned Vichy.

But the effects of the depression and the second world war on colonial economic policy in Africa can just as well be illustrated from the example of Britain, for whom the war did not bring enemy occupation. In 1929, two years after the beginning of the turndown in world trade which led into the depression, the British parliament passed its first tentative Colonial Development Act. By this, for the first time the imperial government took general powers to lend or even to grant money to its colonies to help finance projects of economic development. But the funds available under this Act were not to exceed £1 000 000 ($4 800 000) a year, and were to suffice for all British colonies throughout the world. Bearing in mind that there were fifteen colonies in Africa alone, and that even in the worst year of the depression (1931), a medium-sized if relatively prosperous colony such as the Gold Coast could still command a government revenue of £2 280 000 ($10 744 000) (compared with a peak in Guggisberg's time in 1927 of £5 200 000 – $24 960 000), it can be seen that the aid made available under this first Act was minimal. But the principle had been established, and in 1940, the darkest year of the war, a second Act was passed which raised the annual limit to £5 000 000 ($20 000 000). Perhaps more significantly, under the new Act it became possible for money to be lent or granted for colonial welfare as well as for economic projects. It thus became possible to finance or help finance educational or health programmes which might not be directly remunerative in economic terms, but which could bring long-term benefits by increasing the well-being and efficiency of colonial peoples. A third Colonial Development and Welfare Act was passed in 1946, raising the limit to £12 000 000 ($48 000 000) a year, and not long afterwards the concept that there should be any formal limit on expenditure of this kind was quietly forgotten.

After the war, indeed, the colonial period entered into a third phase, in which it became the 'new orthodoxy' for metropolitan and colonial administrations together to plan and to finance comprehensive plans for the economic and social development of the African territories. Thus all the British and French colonial governments were required at the end of the war to produce ten-year development plans. As originally envisaged, £210 000 000 ($840 000 000) was to be spent in this way in the British colonies by 1955. The plans for the French territories were even more ambitious (for example, in the eight colonies of the French West African federation, £277 000 000 ($1 108 000 000) was to be expended. This was essentially because these tended to start from a lower economic base than many of the British colonies, so that their need was greater. It may also be remarked that, while most of the money for development in French

Africa was to come from France, post-war demands in the world market for colonial produce engendered such high prices that the more fortunate British colonies could make substantial contributions to their development plans from their own incomes. The extreme case was the Gold Coast where, with the price for cocoa in the early 1950s ten or more times what it had been in the 1930s, all but £3 000 000 ($12 000 000) of the original £75 000 000 ($300 000 000) cost of its development plan could be found locally.

By the mid-1950s, the African colonies were participating in the world economy as never before. Rates of economic growth, in so far as data exist to measure these, were vastly greater than they had been in the earlier colonial periods. If the value of foreign trade and the amounts available for colonial government revenues are used as indices (and more sophisticated measures are not really available), and if the levels of these are compared for the years 1913, 1935 and 1953, it can be seen that for the Belgian Congo trade increased twentyfold and government revenue sevenfold in the second period, compared with increases of only about two and a half in the first period. The comparable figures for French West Africa are tenfold increases during 1935–53 compared with a twofold increase in trade and a sevenfold increase in government revenue in 1913–35. But two further points must be made, and can be illustrated from Table 5 below comparing factors of increase during the two periods, and the actual amounts of foreign trade and government revenue per head of estimated population in 1953 for five substantial British colonies:

Table 5	Gold Coast	Nigeria	Kenya	Uganda	Northern Rhodesia
1913–35 Factors of increase					
(1) in trade	3	1.5	3	2	25
(2) in government revenue	2	1.5	3	7	6
1935–53 Factors of increase					
(1) in trade	7	13	8	8.5	21
(2) in government revenue	20	10	5	10	33
1953 Value per head					
(1) trade	£37/ $104	£7/ $19.6	£12/ $33.6	£12/ $33.6	£70/ $196
(2) government revenue	£15/ $42	£2/ $5.6	£3.5/ $9.8	£3.5/ $9.8	£15/ $42

The first point is that even where, as in Nigeria, there were substantial increases in trade and revenue during 1935–53, the actual amounts of these could still be very small in relation to the size of the population, which in Nigeria was substantial and may well have been growing faster than wealth was increasing. People in an African colony could still be very poor compared with Europeans. Secondly, the rates of increase could be far from uniform. Thus wealth was increasing more rapidly in a territory like the Gold Coast, where a substantial proportion of the population was already producing for the world market at the beginning of the colonial period, or in Northern Rhodesia, where there had been major mineral exploitation, than in a colony like Kenya which had neither of these advantages.

A similar point to the last can be made about social progress, which was also very uneven. Here useful indices are the proportion of the total population that was attending school in the 1950s, and the ratio between the numbers of secondary and primary schools.

Table 6	School attendance c. 1953		Ratio of number of secondary schools to number of primary schools
	1000s	Approximate % of total population	
Belgian Congo	1000	8.3	1:870
French West Africa	250	1.5	1:25
Gold Coast	430	10.0	1:70
Nigeria	1000	2.9	1:70
Kenya	330	5.5	1:55
Uganda	300	6.0	1:22
Northern Rhodesia	150	8.3	1:560

It is hardly surprising, for example, that the Gold Coast, where European-style schooling had begun to develop in coastal districts from about the 1840s, had far more of its population in school than Uganda, where British rule did not begin until the 1890s. It may also be supposed that European-style educational advance in Nigeria as a whole was held back by the problems raised by poverty and Islam in its large northern protectorate. But beyond this, these figures suggest the importance of political factors in setting social objectives. This point has already been made for the Belgian Congo. It would also seem that while the French were unable or unwilling to educate many of their African subjects, once these had secured a foot on the educational ladder, they had a better chance than most to advance towards the norms of European civilization. It looks also as though the philosophy of indirect rule may have restricted the development of further education in the British colonies generally, and that perhaps the development of Northern Rhodesia through the employment of European capital and settlers in mining enterprise may have produced a further constraint on the higher training of Africans comparable to that operating in the Congo.

This leads to a further and final point about the early stages of the third phase of colonial rule. Although increasing attention was now being given to enhancing the economic, and to some degree also the social development of the African colonies, relatively little attempt was being made to match this with comparable programmes of political training and advancement for the peoples of the colonies. This was to lead to increasing political strains in the 1950s throughout colonial Africa, and not least in the colonies in which European settlers were established. Their particular problems must therefore be examined in the following chapter before turning to the final period of colonial rule in which governments in Europe decided that, having taken steps to tie Africans to the strings of their world economy, the only solution to the political strains was to give way to their colonies' claims for independence.

Chapter 16

The colonial period, 2:
Colonies of settlement

At the climax of the colonial period in the mid-1950s, there were rather more than five million settlers of European descent living in Africa. Unlike most of the officials, technicians, businessmen and missionaries associated with the colonial process, these were Europeans who regarded an African country as their home. These settlers were very few in relation to the total population of the continent, then estimated at about 240 000 000, and they were never more than a small minority in any particular territory. The largest concentrations were in the two temperate zones at either end of the continent, in South Africa, where some three million Europeans constituted about a fifth of the population, and in Algeria, where about a million settlers represented about a tenth of the total.

In the nineteenth and twentieth centuries, the apparent success of white settlement in these two areas had encouraged other Europeans to settle in neighbouring territories with comparable climates and where conditions generally were thought to be not dissimilar. In the belt of highlands running north from South Africa, Southern Rhodesia had about 225 000 Europeans (about 7 per cent of its total population), and there were rather more than 70 000 in Northern Rhodesia (about 3 per cent). There were also sizeable numbers of settlers in the eastern and south-eastern Belgian Congo (about 75 000 in all) and in Kenya (about 60 000), and smaller numbers elsewhere in British East Africa, but in none of these territories did they constitute as much as 1 per cent of the total population. In addition, southern Mozambique had a settler community much of which served to support the European economies in the Transvaal and Southern Rhodesia, which depended on its ports, and some Europeans had been living in Angola since the

sixteenth century. Since about the 1940s, Portugal had been encouraging more of its citizens to emigrate to these two 'overseas provinces'
to secure their economic development and to relieve distress at home.
By 1960, about 200 000 Portuguese were settled in Angola and about
80 000 in Mozambique, where they formed about 4.5 per cent and a
little over 1 per cent of the populations respectively. In North Africa,
the two French protectorates either side of Algeria, Morocco and
Tunisia, had each attracted nearly a third of a million European residents, about 4 per cent and 8 per cent respectively of their total
populations. The Italians had encouraged European settlement in
Libya after their conquest which had begun in 1911. But their rule
there had been ended in 1942, and the number of Europeans remaining
by the 1950s was about 50 000, though this may have been as much
as 5 per cent of the small total population.

Europeans were not the only immigrant settlers in Africa. South of
the Sahara, there were something like a million resident Asians, mainly
from the Indian sub-continent, but also including some Arabs. There
were nearly half a million Asians living in South Africa, and in Kenya
they outnumbered the European settlers by more than three to one.
In North Africa, there was also a considerable population which was
distinguished from the Muslim majority by its adherence to the Jewish
faith. But this was by no means a new development. By the twentieth
century, the North African Jews had as much right to be considered
natives of the lands in which they lived as did the Muslims (some of
whom, of course, were descended from Arabian or Syrian or Turkish
immigrants), or, in Egypt, the Christian Copts. In fact, they were
not always so treated. As a result of French policy, the 150 000 Jews
who were living in Algeria in the 1950s had become largely assimilated
to the European community. And, though Jews had for centuries
played a part in the economic and urban life of Egypt (together with
a motley crowd of Greeks, Turks, Levantines and Europeans), after
the 1956 war with Israel, they were almost entirely expelled.

Although the European settlers in Africa were always a minority
of the population, usually indeed a small minority, and although too
they were not the only immigrant race, they were of major significance
during the colonial period simply because this was a time when European interests sought to dominate the whole continent. Thus their
influence on the local colonial governments was almost invariably out
of all proportion to their numbers. In some cases indeed they secured
control of these governments: this was done *de jure* in South Africa

early in the colonial period, and it was later achieved *de facto* in Algeria and in Southern Rhodesia. Since, too, they were resident in Africa, and so could claim to be more expert in its affairs than their fellows in Europe, and yet maintained familial, financial and other links with the communities in Europe from which they had sprung, it was often possible for them to exert considerable pressures in their own interests on the makers of colonial policy in the European capitals. The European settlers were also significant in that they had for the most part gone to Africa, and had committed themselves, their families, and their fortunes to it, during the high tide of imperialism. When they had arrived, they had had a real superiority over most Africans in military strength, in wealth, in education, technology and organization, and they naturally wanted to maintain the privileged positions they had built up with this superiority. Both for their own security and so that they could continue to exploit African land and labour, settlers continued to deny Africans significant access to the sources of their own power. They therefore continued to maintain a firm faith in the superiority of Europeans, and in their right to rule in Africa, when those in power in Europe itself began to question these beliefs, or at least to doubt whether they had any continuing political relevance.

The early history of white settlement in its southern bastion has already been sketched. In North Africa, of course, European settlement was nothing new. There had been migrations of settlers across the Mediterranean for more than 2000 years before the modern colonial period, the direction of the movement, whether from southern Europe to northern Africa or the reverse, depending on the balance of political and economic power between the two shores. In the nineteenth century, there was no question where this balance lay, and as, from 1830 onwards, the French began to conquer Algeria, there was built up there a colony with a pattern of settlement which was very similar in principle to that which was developing in South Africa.

Following the suppression of a major revolt of the Algerians against French rule which had begun in 1871, Algeria ceased to be primarily a military responsibility. Except for the frontier lands facing the Sahara, which were unsuitable for European settlement and contained only a thin population of pastoralists whose mobility necessitated the continuance of an essentially military control, the country was divided into three large *départements*. In 1881 it was decided to govern these as though they were *départements* of France herself. This decision was strongly influenced by the opposition to military rule shown by the third of a million European settlers. But it ignored certain realities of the situation; for example that the interests of Algerian settler-farmers, producing wine and grain in competition with farmers in France herself, were not necessarily the same as those of Frenchmen at large, and, above all, that the majority of the people in Algeria were not French. Frenchmen were never great emigrants anyway, and few farmers saw much point in moving to Algeria to grow the same crops as they could grow in France on better soils and in more secure conditions. Almost half the Europeans living in Algeria by 1881 had come from impoverished areas of Spain, Italy or Malta, and there were also about 50 000 Jewish residents. Yet all these combined were outnumbered seven to one by close on three million native Algerians. Whereas the Jews had become naturalized French citizens *en bloc* in 1870, and it was easy, especially after 1889, for the Spaniards and Italians to secure naturalization (so that by 1911, only 189 000 out of 715 000 settlers were not French citizens), this was virtually impossible for the Algerians. As Muslims, they could hardly be expected to undertake the renunciation of Koranic law that was involved.

However, the problem of the unassimilated Algerians at first seemed to be less of an issue than that of the Jews, who, though citizens, were also as yet unassimilated, and it was a wave of anti-Semitic agitation among the Europeans that led in 1898 to a major constitutional change. It was accepted that it was unrealistic for Algerian affairs to be dealt with by a variety of separate ministries in Paris as though they were no different from the affairs of France herself. The greater part of government activities in Algeria was placed under the governor-general, and the country was given its own annual budget. This budget, together with the issue of loans and the granting of concessions, required the approval (subject to the final agreement of Paris) of an elected assembly. This was composed of twenty-four French citizens elected by their fellows residing in the 261 *communes de plein exercice* (i.e. the districts which possessed elected local governments on the French model), and twenty-one representatives of the native Algerians who were living in those areas in which there were few citizens, and so little or nothing in the way of elective local government. Some of the latter were indirectly elected, the remainder were nominated. In addition, the governor-general was advised in his conduct of the administration by a *conseil supérieur*, nearly half of whose members were officials or nominees, but the remainder of whom were elected; some of the nominees and a minority of the elected members were Algerians.

In recognition of the Algerian contribution to the French war effort in 1914–18, there was some amelioration of the position of the native Algerians in 1918. It became somewhat easier for them to gain citizenship, and it became possible for some Algerians to become electors in the *communes de plein exercice* even if they were not full citizens. But these measures did not change the basic situation that the majority of the population had little or no voice in the way the country was run.

The successive stages of the French conquest had driven Algerians away from the coastal plains and the adjacent valleys onto the highlands and steppes. The lands so vacated had been granted to individual settlers or to companies which exploited estates of farmland, orchard or forest. The total area thus alienated to Europeans, some 10 500 square miles, was a small proportion of the total area of the colony, which included a large slice of the Sahara, or even of the habitable *départements* (80 000 square miles). But it represented about a third of the territory which had sufficient rainfall to permit of cultivation, and included a very high proportion of the most fertile and accessible lands. By 1913, some 2000 miles of railway had been built through these European areas to allow their produce to be evacuated for export, or for consumption in the large towns which had developed on the coast, and also to facilitate the exploitation by European concerns of the substantial deposits of iron ore and phosphates which had been revealed from the 1870s onwards. With much of the best land in their own country denied to them, and deprived of as good an access to markets, capital and education as was possessed by the Europeans, the agriculture of the native Algerians remained primitive and became increasingly less capable of providing an adequate livelihood for a rapidly growing population. (By the 1950s, the rate of increase was as high as 2.7 per cent per annum.) Many Algerians therefore sought employment on the farms and estates and towns which the Europeans had established. The districts dominated by European agriculture began to fill up with Algerians. They could in fact provide the majority of the population in them, for the cultivation of small farms by individual Europeans and their families did not prove a very rewarding business. By 1954, indeed, the number of Europeans directly supported by agriculture had shrunk to 93 000, less than a tenth of the European total, and nearly nine-tenths of the European land was being exploited in some 6000 large estates. Nearly half of the Europeans were already living in the towns by 1900; by the 1950s the proportion was nearly 70 per cent. Though their populations were swelled by Algerians seeking employment, the towns, especially the larger ones, remained very much European implantations: in 1954, half of Algiers's 590 000 inhabitants were Europeans, and nearly 60 per cent of Oran's 320 000. Thus, while some of the native Algerians, who formed nearly nine-tenths of the total population, continued to survive in poverty on the plateaux and steppes, and, through the courtesy of the French officials who were responsible for the administration of these areas, these secured a minority voice in the government of the country, increasing numbers were obliged to live in areas where most of them had no political rights because they were not citizens. They were a rural and, to some degree also, an urban proletariat which the politically dominant settlers could exploit for their own economic purposes.

The pattern of development pursued under the French in Tunisia and Morocco was not dissimilar in outline. But there was an important difference between the position of the French in Algeria and in the other two countries of the Maghrib, which meant that it did not go to such extremes. Algeria had become French, and its people French subjects, by the fact of French conquest. But Tunisia and Morocco were French protectorates, in which legal sovereignty remained with the local rulers, the Bey and the Sultan respectively. France's assumption of the right to govern these two countries on behalf of their sovereigns followed on the latter's failure to maintain in their lands, so close to Europe, administrations which European governments were prepared to regard as adequate to ensure their nations' interests in them. The government of the Bey of Tunis had become bankrupt in 1869, and an international control had been imposed on its finances. The problem in Morocco was essentially that the government of the Sultan actually controlled less than half the territory claimed by him. At the Algeçiras Conference of 1906, the two European powers with territory bordering on Morocco, France and Spain, had been given authority to police the country. The French protectorates declared over Tunisia in 1881 and over the larger part of Morocco in 1912 (as also the Spanish protectorate over most of the rest of the latter country) thus followed upon earlier and more general European interventions in these two countries' affairs. France would not have been able to secure the dominance of her control without the assent, whether explicit or tacit, of the other European powers.

These international circumstances made it necessary for France to act in Tunisia and Morocco in the names of their indigenous rulers. The heads of her administration were not styled governor or governor-general, but were technically only her Residents-General at the courts of the Bey and Sultan respectively. Although it was Residents-General and their officials who directed policy, and the result was the opening-up of both countries to European capital and settlement, in each case the land was not French territory, and its legal citizens were the native or naturalized subjects of the Bey or Sultan. The possession by a settler of French citizenship was not therefore the automatic passport to political rights and influence that it was in Algeria.

In Tunisia, the economic fruits of French control were impressive. The country had deposits of iron ore to match those of Algeria and of phosphates that were even richer. As in Algeria, French administration provided the security required for capital to come in to mine these and to build the necessary railways and ports. But Tunisia also possessed the largest agricultural potential of any of the three Maghribian territories. Centuries of relatively stable government meant that individual rather than communal land tenure was established at least in the more fertile northern half of the country. The Bey and his ruling class had built up large public or private estates, manned by adequate labour forces. Even before the French protectorate, they had been ready to grant concessions of land to foreigners. One of the first steps taken by the French was to undertake a proper survey, so that land boundaries and security of tenure could be established. European capital and technology and a degree of settlement then quickly produced an agricultural revolution based on the cultivation of cereals, vines and, above all, olives.

But this was not specifically a French, nor exclusively a European, process. The bulk of the settlers attracted to Tunisia, and the majority of the Europeans actually working land, came from Italy, particularly from its impoverished south. By 1911, out of a total European population of 148 000, there were 88 000 Italians and 11 000 Maltese compared with only 46 000 French citizens in Tunisia. The French authorities endeavoured to redress this situation, but there was little new settlement from France (or from Italy, whose government now wanted to colonize Libya), so that by 1931 the European population had increased only to 186 000, compared with 2 160 000 Muslims and

65 000 Jews. French citizens now accounted for just under half the European population, but the increase was due mainly to an active campaign to encourage Italians, Maltese and Jews to naturalize. The peak of European farming settlement had already been reached, but of the 27 000 Europeans living on the land in 1911, the majority were Italians and only a third were French. However, settlers of all nationalities occupied only about a quarter as much land as was exploited by European estate companies, usually French-owned, and about half the productive agricultural land was still being exploited by Tunisians. There was still scope both for local land-owners and for the local, largely Jewish, mercantile class in Tunis to share in the new prosperity.

The French authorities had gained a free hand to direct affairs in Tunisia by raising a loan to buy out the Bey's foreign creditors, and it was their officials who directed the central administration, introducing modern systems of health and education, and providing a system of French law and courts to regulate the affairs of the non-native population. But local government, and the direct taxation of and the administration of justice for the indigenous majority were left essentially to the *caids* and lesser officials of Beylical government. Thus the government of Tunisia under the French was markedly autocratic and bureaucratic in structure, and this was little modified by the institution of purely consultative assemblies, first for the representation of European economic interests and then for nominated Tunisian notables. It was legally difficult for the Europeans to challenge this state of affairs; and indeed they had little cause to do so so long as it was associated with the prosperity of their community, as was certainly the case before the onset of the 1930s depression. Such opposition as there was came from Tunisians who were reaping the advantages of modern education. Remembering that, before the advent of the French, the Bey had offered Tunisia constitutional government, such men began to organize in defence of their people's rights, with the result that by the later 1930s the Neo-Destour Party ('New Constitution') Party, led by Habib Bourguiba, was in open conflict with the French authorities.

In law, the French position in Morocco was the same as that in Tunisia, but the practical circumstances were very different. In Tunisia, once the French controlled the Bey's government, they could control the country. In Morocco, however, the *makhzin* – that is continuing, organized government as distinct from the occasional levying of tribute by force – had rarely penetrated beyond the coastal plains in which lay the major towns. The large upland and mountain zones of the Atlas and the Rif had become recognized as a *bilad as-siba*, a 'land of dissidence', to be left to the Berber tribesmen and their chiefs. At the beginning of the twentieth century, the *makhzin* was in fact at a low ebb. The desire of a brash young sultan, Mulay 'Abd al-Aziz (1894–1909), to Europeanize his country had antagonized many influential subjects, encouraged disorder and increasing European intervention, and finally led to civil war. The first task of the first French Resident-General, General Lyautey (1912–25), was thus to restore order by force. By 1918, French control had been established over the whole of the lands along the frontier with Algeria (which had been a constant source of trouble for the latter's government, and so the main precipitant for the police action which the French had begun in 1907), and elsewhere to rather beyond the previous effective limits of the *makhzin*. But the Atlas was not totally under French control until 1934, and the French were also called upon to help subdue the spirited resistance to the establishment of Spanish control in the Rif that was organized by 'Abd al-Krim during 1921–6.

On the civil front, Lyautey saw his task as one of restoring the prestige of the sultan, and of erecting a modern Moroccan administration, staffed by Frenchmen, alongside the traditional *makhzin*. As the conquest proceeded, so this dual system was extended into the countryside, though with two major differences from the Tunisian model, differences which derived from the need of conquest. One was that there was closer French supervision of the traditional administrative and judicial system. The other was that the most economical way to secure French control over the Berber tribes of the interior was often to come to a political understanding with their major chieftains. Thus if the old *bilad as-siba* was now under control, the nature of this control tended to mark it off from the old *makhzin* lands. This difference was further accentuated by the economic changes initiated by the French. The coastal plains were opened up to economic agriculture and phosphate mining by railways and roads, and the old centres of Fez and Marrakesh, strategically placed on the borders between the two zones, declined in influence compared with coastal towns like Rabat, the French capital, and, above all, Casablanca, which was developed as the major port and commercial and industrial centre. Compared with Tunisia, economic exploitation had to start almost from scratch. Although it was not in accord with the original French agreement with the Sultan in 1912, Lyautey saw little alternative but to encourage settlers (who came from Algeria as well as France) to develop new crops, techniques and industry. By the 1930s, some 160 000 Europeans were living in Morocco. But this was only about 3 per cent of the total population of 5 345 000, and their impingement on Moroccan lands was also not very great. Only about a sixteenth of the cultivable area was in alien occupation, and the vast majority of the Europeans were settled in and around Casablanca and Rabat, where the economic development they had pioneered enabled them to enjoy a very high standard of living. Here too there was a new wage-earning Moroccan proletariat, and the beginnings of a new outward-looking political leadership for this was also emerging from the French educational system to challenge French control and its alliance with the inward-looking Berber society of the interior.

The pattern of European settlement that had emerged in South Africa by the end of the nineteenth century was essentially the same as that in Algeria. Superior force had enabled the settlers to occupy much of the better agricultural land, through which railways were built to enable their produce to reach the world markets. The much more numerous indigenous inhabitants had been penned back into less favourable or less accessible lands where, finding increasing difficulty in supporting a growing population, they served as a reservoir of cheap labour for the European economy. Secondly, the settlers had a monopoly of political power, of capital and of skilled and managerial employment, and were prepared to deny or to limit the non-Europeans' access to these things, both by direct political action and indirectly, e.g. by controlling their access to education.

But the situation in South Africa was much more extreme. When in 1910 the four British colonies of the Cape, Natal, the Transvaal and the Orange Free State joined together to form the Union of South Africa, the total population was just under six million. But some four-fifths of the total land surface was already effectively the exclusive preserve of rather less than one fifth of the population, the 1 276 000 Europeans. This situation was not really ameliorated by the existence as enclaves within the Union or on its borders of three British protectorates in which African land rights were guaranteed, since two of these, Basutoland and Swaziland, were already very densely populated, and most of the third, Bechuanaland, was virtually uninhabitable. Furthermore, in the Union, the European minority had achieved complete power to determine the conditions on which members of the non-European majority might enter, and live and work in the European lands.

The South African settlers possessed this power essentially for three reasons. First, in and around the Witwatersrand, they, and they alone in all Africa, had access to sufficient proven mineral wealth to promote an industrial revolution and an economic take-off. Secondly, in 1910 they, and they alone in Africa, had succeeded in totally emancipating themselves from any control of their affairs from Europe. Thirdly, they were the only settler group in Africa capable of generating a sense of national identity which was quite independent of their original European connections, and which proclaimed that they were totally committed to an African future for themselves and their children.

However secure their position may also have looked in 1910, in the last analysis, the Algerian settlers possessed none of these advantages. Though mineral wealth was not unimportant to them, it bore no comparison in absolute terms with that in South Africa, and, like their agriculture, it could never form the basis for economic strength to compete with the power of their motherland close at hand on the northern shore of the Mediterranean. Their settlement was in fact a simple consequence of the relative balance of economic and political power on the two sides of the Mediterranean; a tidal phenomenon, and so a reversible one. Though the Algerian settlers could and did influence French policy towards their country, they were always part of the French body politic. The ruling majority in this political system always lay in France. If the interests of the French in Algeria conflicted with those of the French in France – as those of their wine- and corn-producing farmers were always apt to do – they could be sacrificed. Finally, if France should decide that the benefits of possessing an extension of itself in Algeria were outweighed by the cost of main-taining it (as eventually the military cost did become too high for the tax-payers and voters in France), then Algeria could be abandoned. And when this happened, since the settlers were really no more than a tidal flow of French society to the further side of the Mediterranean, they could ebb back to the other side (where in fact they had been preceded by a growing tide of Algerians seeking employment in the real centre of wealth as well as of power).

Nevertheless, only eight years before the formation of the Union of South Africa, the power and resources of the British empire had finally won a long and costly war to halt the separatist and nationalist urges of the majority of the white population, the Afrikaners. For the first time for nearly seventy years, British imperial authority appeared to be in complete control of the situation. Milner, the imperial High Commissioner in South Africa, was planning in terms of a generation of British rule over the two conquered Afrikaner republics. Bearing in mind that one of these, the Transvaal, was the major source of wealth for the whole sub-continent, this would also mean that the two self-governing British colonies (one of which, the Cape, had more Afrikaner than English-speaking settlers) would also be subject to the overriding influence of the British imperial interest. During this period, Milner hoped that fresh settlement from Britain would serve to swamp or dissolve Afrikaner nationalist sentiment.

Milner was not specifically aiming at building up a new South African society in which non-Europeans would achieve access to their due share of wealth and political power (although, perhaps, he could suppose that this might be more likely to emerge in a South Africa dominated by a British ethos than by an Afrikaner one). What did concern him was rather to create a political system in South Africa which would ensure that the wealth would continue to be exploited in the British imperial interest.

In the event, however, Milner was the prisoner of a situation beyond his control. In the first place, emigration from the British Isles, which had been running at 150 000 to 200 000 a year from the 1840s to 1900, had dwindled to less than 60 000 a year by the early 1900s. It was composed, moreover, principally of poor people who had nothing to offer but their labour, and these were not attracted to South Africa, where they could not compete with low-paid black workers. Secondly, and perhaps more importantly, when Chamberlain left the Colonial Office in 1903, and still more when the Liberal Party won the 1906 British general election, there was a return to an older British imperial tradition than that of actively exploiting colonial estates. This was the concept that trouble, expense and injustice were bound to arise if any considerable body of European settlers in a British overseas colony was not given a share in the government of that colony and, when their community was large enough and sufficiently self-supporting, if they were not given the right to govern it for themselves. Since this concept was derived primarily from experience in North America and Australasia, which had relatively insignificant indigenous populations, even liberals had failed so far to realize that its application to African territories, with much stronger and more densely settled indigenous communities, might lead to an irreconcilable conflict of racial interests.

Even before his own departure from the scene in 1905, Milner had experienced difficulty in getting the politicians of the self-governing Cape Colony to fall in with his imperial aims, and his policy was totally scrapped by the Liberal government which came to power in Britain in the following year. Most Liberals had agreed with opinion on the European continent that in the South African war of 1899–1902 Britain had unjustly used her imperial might to crush two small European nations which had every right to rule themselves, and many had bitterly opposed the methods which had been employed to secure the final victory. The two conquered territories were therefore quickly granted self-governing constitutions which put them on a par with the Cape and Natal. Both immediately elected Afrikaner governments under leaders determined to gain by constitutional means what had been denied to their predecessors by military defeat, namely freedom for themselves and their people to deal with South African affairs in their own way without foreign interference.

When Milner's successor, Lord Selborne, promoted the idea that the four British colonial governments in South Africa should join together to try and work out common policies for their common inter-colonial problems of railway and customs policies and of African land and labour, he and his advisers were hoping for the emergence of some federal authority which would ensure the overall order needed for the well-being of Britain's considerable economic interests in the sub-continent and so relieve her of any residual responsibility for such problems. Britain therefore deliberately stood aside from the series of inter-colonial conferences which began to meet in South Africa in 1908. These were regarded as entirely the affair of the elected representatives of the four colonies. But only those from the Cape Colony represented any voters that were not European, and the emphasis throughout was on bridging the divisions within the white community. The interests of the non-European majority were hardly touched upon at all. The majority of the delegates were opposed to any extension of the colour-blind, property franchise for parliamentary elections still retained in the Cape, the original mother colony. The best that could be agreed was that each colony would enter the new Union with its existing franchise. The only action in African interests came in fact from outside the conference meetings, when Britain, as the protecting power, was somewhat reluctantly brought to recognize

the strength of the opposition in Basutoland, Bechuanaland and Swaziland to incorporation within white South Africa. In the act passed by
the British parliament to transfer power to the new Union, it was
stipulated that these three territories should for the time being remain
British protectorates, and that their inhabitants' consent would be
needed before they could be added to the Union.

   In the constitutional conferences which led to the formation of the
Union in 1910, and in all its subsequent politics, the initiative lay with
the Afrikaners. Despite immigration (and the growth of the economy
after 1945 was such as to attract a steady trickle of immigrants with
capital or professional skills who felt that South Africa offered a better
chance than did post-war Britain of maintaining the standards of life
which they felt to be their due), a high birth rate has enabled the
Afrikaners to continue to outnumber the English-speaking settlers in
the ratio of about three to two. Though before the 1950s, Afrikaners
could not by and large match the English-speakers in wealth or technical and commercial skills, as a fellow white man, an Afrikaner was
as entitled to a political voice as any English-speaker. Indeed, he
was thought to be better entitled. The poorer rural districts, where
historically most Afrikaners were to be found, were deliberately over-
represented in parliament to offset the power of the urban and industrial centres which were originally dominated by English-speakers.
Above all, the Afrikaners formed a united nation in a sense which the
English-speakers, still thinking of Britain as 'home', and often
obsessed with competition for individual gain, could never achieve in
South Africa by themselves. The Afrikaner leaders had a much clearer
sense of political purpose and direction, indeed were much more
political animals than their English-speaking counterparts. They
sensed too that in any crisis of relations with the African majority,
self-interest would incline the English-speakers, artisan trade unionists
as well as employers, not to rock the white man's boat. It is hardly
surprising, in fact, that all the prime ministers – and, indeed, the great
majority of all government ministers – in South Africa since the
formation of the Union have been Afrikaners. Some of them, notably
Botha, the first prime minister (1910–19), and Smuts (1919–24 and
1939–48), were more concerned than others to carry the English-
speakers with them (and so were apt to lose the confidence of the
majority of the electors, and to give way to more overtly nationalist
leaders, as Smuts did to Hertzog in 1924 and to Malan in 1948). But
essentially they have all belonged to the same nationalist stream, and

in so far as there was an organized opposition to them, it was an opposition not of a liberal party, but of those who wanted to achieve much the same ends more slowly and less blatantly (and all its leaders were also Afrikaners).

Apartheid, the concept that society within the borders of South Africa was made up of a number of distinct nations which should live in their own homelands separate from each other, and that non-Europeans might enter the white homeland only as transient wage-earners with no political status, was not enunciated as a formal political doctrine until 1947, preparatory to Malan's electoral victory of 1948 which finally consolidated the power of the Nationalists. But white South African political action had been moving steadily in this direction ever since the formation of the Union, and irrespective of whether the party in power formally claimed the title of Nationalist. Landmarks on the way were the Native Land Acts of 1913 and 1936, which legally confined the occupation of land by the African two-thirds of the population to 13 per cent of the total area of the country; the whittling away and the eventual abolition of any parliamentary representation for non-Europeans, which was accomplished by a number of measures between 1936 and 1958; and an ever-increasing number of laws from 1911 onwards reserving skilled employment for whites and controlling the manner in which non-Europeans were allowed to enter, live and work in the white areas. From the later 1950s, when the legal framework of *apartheid* had been firmly erected, although the restrictive aspects of the policy continued not only to be maintained but actually intensified, rather more attention was given to what might be termed the positive side of *apartheid* (or 'separate development', as it now became convenient to call it). Steps were taken to make the African areas more genuinely 'homelands', with their own local self-government and with their own facilities, as, for example, university colleges, to replace those to which their inhabitants had once had access in the white areas, and which were now denied to them. But the initiative in such developments remained with the whites, who were reluctant to see final control over these 'Bantustans' pass from the hands of their own parliament and ministers.

Indeed, the policy of developing Bantustans tended rather to show up inherent contradictions in the philosophy of *apartheid*. In the first place, if (to use the figures for 1961, when it was agreed that *apartheid* was not compatible with continued membership of the British

Commonwealth, and the Union became the Republic of South Africa) the expansion of white settlement had divided the 472 000 square miles of South African territory into a large homeland of nearly 411 000 square miles for some 3 000 000 Europeans, and had limited nearly 10 000 000 Africans to a number of separate homelands totalling only some 61 000 square miles, where were the homelands for the other ethnic groups living in the country? The economic interests of the whites, particularly of the nineteenth-century Natal sugar-planters, had resulted in the emergence, particularly in Natal, of a separate Asian group of the population, which by the 1960s numbered some 440 000. An even larger distinct community, the Coloureds, 1 360 000 strong by the 1960s, had emerged from centuries of earlier interaction, essentially in the old Cape Colony, between the Europeans, their slaves and the African populations. In the Cape Province the Coloureds constituted a significant fifth of the total population.

Secondly, the Bantustans which were being set up could hardly be developed to provide adequate homelands for all the Africans. The original 'native areas' in the Union were scattered over some 260 parcels of land, some of which were very small. If they were to be consolidated into effective Bantustan units, some white farmers would have to be removed from good lands which they and their ancestors had long regarded as their own and which they would not want to abandon. Even if this politically difficult operation were successfully accomplished, the Bantustans would still be far too small and poor to support the whole African population. If all the 10 000 000 Africans were to be based on them, they would have a population density of over 160 persons to the square mile. From an agricultural point of view, this would be impossible. The African areas were already over-cultivated and over-grazed, and the consequences in the form of soil erosion and seasonal food shortages were already sufficiently evident. The situation would not be much ameliorated even if the British protectorates could be taken over to add to the land area of the Bantustans. Basutoland and Swaziland were largely mountainous areas which already had densely settled populations of their own, while the habitable area of Bechuanaland was simply a thin strip of country bordering the Kalahari desert. As things were, the inhabitants of the protectorates maintained their strong opposition to the South African system, and in 1966 and 1968 were given their political independence – Basutoland renaming itself Lesotho and Bechuanaland becoming Botswana.

The protagonists of *apartheid* argued that the solution for such problems could lie in directing capital to develop industry in the Bantustans or on their borders, and to ameliorate their agricultural resources. But it was obviously far more profitable for the owners of capital in South Africa, who were the Europeans, to employ it in the developed areas of the country, which were their own European areas, which possessed the mineral resources and adequate infrastructures of transport, housing and other facilities. Above all, the plain fact remained that even if such a transfer of capital did take place, and even if it helped to redress the imbalance of development between the African and the European areas, the white economy was dependent on an adequate supply of black labour. It was not in the European interest that all or even a substantial part of the African workforce should be gainfully supported by the Bantustans. The Europeans were far too few by themselves to man their industries and farms, and to maintain or to develop their levels of output and profitability. Indeed, the more successful their economy, the more dependent it was on African employment and, indeed, on Africans using the wages received in such employment to buy and consume its products.

Something like two-thirds of the African population was already directly or indirectly supported by wages earned in the European sector when the *apartheid* and Bantustan policies became the formal doctrines of the ruling white élite. Despite these policies, the numbers of Africans resident in the European areas, especially in the towns, continued to increase. This, of course, was the consequence of the industrial revolution which had begun with the diamond and gold discoveries of the 1870s and 1880s and with the increasing amounts of capital that had therefore been attracted to South Africa from western Europe and North America. The original mineral discoveries in the Transvaal and Griqualand West were later supplemented by the proving, from the 1940s onwards, of further large gold deposits in the Orange Free State; by the mining of other rare minerals such as uranium and chrome; and by the presence of substantial resources of coal and iron ore which made possible the development of steel manufacture and of heavy industry generally. From the time of the second world war onwards, these basic industries were supplemented by a great flowering of secondary manufacturing industry, so that ultimately the South African economy became virtually self-sufficient. By the end of the 1950s, after a 600 per cent growth in manufacturing industry in only two decades, the economy was generating enough new capital (about £475 000 000 ($1 330 000 000) a year) to enable it to continue its further growth if necessary without any further invest-ment from abroad.

This enormously successful industrial revolution brought equally great social changes. The historical division of the Europeans between Afrikaners and English-speaking settlers ceased to be of major relevance. The Afrikaners ceased to be a poor and embittered, back-ward and inward-looking country folk fighting for survival against the forces of an aggressive, alien, outward-looking capitalism. They themselves became active and prosperous participants in a predomi-nantly urban, industrial and commercial white society. Instead of resisting assimilation, they could now self-confidently set out them-selves to assimilate the English-speaking settlers into a single community, one in which economic materialism was firmly harnessed to the purposes of their uncompromising nationalist leadership. Yet the fact remained that a community of three million Europeans was too small by itself to maintain the prosperity, and the growth of this prosperity, that its members had come to expect. Despite absolute social segregation of the races, despite their use of a considerable part of their wealth and material strength to maintain and to protect their absolute monopoly of political power, the Europeans had ever more need of the non-Europeans, the African masses in particular, who were being ever more integrated into their economy as workers and as consumers. Economic forces were, in fact, demanding that non-Europeans be admitted to ever more skilled jobs, and increasing their purchasing power so that they were *en masse*, if not as individuals, becoming the most significant consumers. Racial, social and political divisions and barriers could not conceal the fact that there was a single economy in South Africa, and that the whole success story of the Europeans as its leaders was in the last resort dependent on the complaisance of the non-European majority.

In retrospect, it seems clear that European settlement was able to take firm root in South Africa as a result of an unusual combination of historical circumstances. There was first the fact that at a very early stage in Europe's relations with Africa, the strategic interest of her major maritime nations seemed to require some formal establishment of European power at the southernmost tip of Africa, which happened also to be in one of the two zones which were climatically hospitable to European settlement. Secondly, because this establishment could

not supply an adequate livelihood for all the settlers brought to maintain it, some of them began at an early stage to disperse over the
interior; and the momentum of this dispersal was maintained because
of the continuing clash of interests between these trekkers and whatever authority was established over the strategic base at Cape Town.
Thirdly, when this European dispersion began, strong African
societies were not established in the immediate hinterland of Cape
Town. The early European colonists found little difficulty in
conquering the weak societies of the Khoisan, and in thus establishing
concepts of European superiority and of a European dominating élite
which were strong enough to prevail when later they came into conflict
with the stronger and better-organized Bantu societies. Fourthly,
there was the discovery that a part of the land which the Europeans
were able to conquer from the Bantu – and a part which at the time
happened by historical accident to be very thinly held by the latter –
was exceptionally rich in mineral wealth. This attracted an exceptional
inflow of European capital, which gave the settler society, firmly
wedded to the concept of its own superiority, more than adequate
means to consolidate both itself and its hold over the non-Europeans.
Finally, it so happened that at the crucial time the external European
power responsible for South Africa was Britain, which was uniquely
conscious of the necessity of eventual self-government for settler
colonies.

During the colonial period, however, it was not generally appreciated that the success of white settlement in South Africa, and its
success in developing the resources of that country, was essentially a
consequence of this unique series of historical accidents. The failure,
or virtual failure, of earlier policies of settlement pursued elsewhere
in sub-Saharan Africa, for example in Portuguese territories, was
ignored or was thought to be irrelevant in the light of the subsequent
great increase in Europe's power and technology. The success of white
settlement in South Africa therefore seemed to suggest that it was a
suitable tool for the development of other sub-Saharan colonies
provided that their climates were not too hostile. However, in the
Belgian Congo, and in Portuguese Angola and Mozambique, it was
only one of a number of expedients, and one moreover which was
rigidly controlled in the metropolitan interest. It was the British
colonies which became the main field for essays of settlement on
South African lines. The principal experiments, the test cases in fact,
were Southern Rhodesia and Kenya. To understand what happened

in these two colonies, their histories need to be looked at in some detail.

The colony of Southern Rhodesia, between the Limpopo and Zambezi rivers, was deliberately planned by Cecil Rhodes as an extension of the Southern African system northwards of the Limpopo. As has been seen, its land was believed to be well endowed with mineral wealth, and it was also important to South Africa as its gateway to the interior beyond the Transvaal. Rhodes was therefore anxious that it should be kept out of the hands of the Afrikaner nationalists, and that it should be occupied and developed as a colony linked to the Cape and British interests. Thus in 1890 a paramilitary police force raised by his British South African Company had been sent with a select body of pioneer settlers to inaugurate his new colony.

Its early years were by no means a success story. Rhodes was acting, and had secured a British government charter for his company, on the assumption that the concessions of mineral and land rights which agents of his had earlier secured from Lobengula, king of the Ndebele, would allow the settlement to be established without the active opposition of this powerful military nation. For this reason, the first settlers were sent to the north-eastern half of the territories claimed by Lobengula, occupied by Shona tribes whom Lobengula regarded as subjects whom he could raid for cattle and slaves, but who were not an integral part of the Ndebele nation. The first settlers were therefore in the remotest part of the country from the point of view of their communications with Bechuanaland and the Cape Colony. They were joined to their bases there only by a long, unmade wagon track which made a detour round the Ndebele lands. They therefore experienced considerable difficulty in working such gold deposits as they could find. They also quickly realized that these deposits were by and large too small and scattered to produce the wealth to match that of the Witwatersrand that they had been led to expect.

In 1893, the BSA Company's administrator in the colony, L. S. Jameson, engineered war with Lobengula as an expedient to try and solve both these problems. The Ndebele were taken by surprise. They offered little resistance to the mobile columns of company troops and settlers with their quick-firing weapons, and Lobengula died while in flight northwards towards the Zambezi. The settlers then quickly spread over his country in search of its expected wealth, while Jameson and the bulk of the BSA Police were shortly withdrawn to Bechuanaland to prepare for Rhodes's projected invasion of the Transvaal.

However, only railways could really solve the transport problems of the settlers and enable mining machinery and other supplies to be brought in expeditiously and reasonably cheaply. But, as will be seen, the BSA Company did not succeed in providing Southern Rhodesia with an effective railway system linking its remote inland colony to the outside world until 1897–1902. In this situation, the early settlers in Matabeleland found little more promise in its gold than they had found in Mashonaland,* and they and the company began to use the Shona policemen recruited to make good the shortage of European police to impress Ndebele land and cattle as alternative sources of wealth.

These activities led in 1896 to a national rising of the Ndebele, few of whose warriors had actively participated in the 1893 war. As a result of the Jameson Raid fiasco, the company had no troops of its own to suppress this rebellion; British imperial troops were therefore called in. But they and the settlers shortly found themselves fighting an even more bitter rising from the Shona. By 1898, when order had been restored, little had been done to make Southern Rhodesia a viable colony, Rhodes had been personally discredited by the Jameson Raid, and the company was heavily in debt.

However, the transport difficulties of the colony were now at last being solved. The BSA Company had early been forced to realize that the most efficient way of gaining access to Mashonaland was not from the south, but by building a railway from the port of Beira in Portuguese Mozambique, which was only some 370 miles away from Salisbury, the seat of the colonial administration, compared with 880 miles from the railhead of the Cape railways in the 1890s, Vryburg (which itself was some 770 miles from the sea at Cape Town). But a railway from the south, to be continued across the Zambezi into the further interior, was naturally central to Rhodes's geopolitical strategy, and initially little money was made available for building the line from Beira. The result was that it was not operating through to the colonial capital of Salisbury (Harare) until 1899, two years after the railway from Vryburg had reached Bulawayo, the principal settlement in Matabeleland. But this line was then temporarily cut by the Afrikaner siege of Mafeking during the South African war. More generally, the war meant a considerable diversion of resources from the development

---

* Matabeleland and Mashonaland are the English names for the two provinces into which the colony was divided, i.e. the south-western half where the Ndebele lived and the north-eastern half inhabited by the Shona.

of Southern Rhodesia. Thus the railway to link Bulawayo and Salisbury, completing a viable transport system for the colony, was not finished until 1902.

Rhodes (who died in 1902) had always intended that, as soon as the settler community was strong enough to bear the burden, responsibility for the administration of the new colony should be transferred to it from the company. This would then be free to profit from the mineral and land rights it held as Lobengula's concessionaire and, after 1893 – as it believed – his successor by right of conquest. By 1898, there were only some 11 000 settlers in Southern Rhodesia. But the company's financial and political difficulties were such that, if it were to escape being superseded by a British Colonial Office administration, and if adequate numbers of settlers were ever to be attracted to the colony, it was thought expedient to begin to share the business of government with them. In that year, therefore, a deal was done with the Colonial Office. The latter sent to Southern Rhodesia an imperial Resident Commissioner to oversee the activities of the Company's administration and the settlers with a view to preventing any further action towards the half million African inhabitants of the kind that had led to the troubles of 1893–7. On the other hand, however, a legislative council, with a minority of settler representatives, was instituted.

But still the colony showed little signs of growth. The provision of railways and mining machinery permitted the operation of a handful of sizeable gold mines. But the profits from these went to the company's commercial associates and to their non-resident shareholders, not to the settlers. Few new settlers came to Southern Rhodesia. The political representatives of the settlers who were there began to complain that the company cared only for its own narrow commercial interests, and that its administration did not do enough to promote settlement or the general economic welfare of the colony. It was argued, for example, that it exploited the settlers by keeping railway rates too high, treated the land of the colony as a commercial asset and not as a public resource, and would not allow the settlers freedom to exploit small pockets of gold ore. The truth was that the company was stretched to find enough money to pay for its administrative costs, let alone to make any profits. But it did eventually dawn on its directors that geology had not provided Southern Rhodesia with a second Witwatersrand, and that if the colony were to have any economic future and the company to receive any reward for its exertions, they must adapt their policy to the actual situation. Their only course in fact was to try and win the settlers to their side in the development of a colony which would rely for its wealth at least as much on agriculture as on minerals.

As early as 1907, when there were still only 14 000 settlers, these were given a majority of representation on the legislative council. Further concessions were made to the settlers in 1914, when the company's charter was due for renewal, and when it badly needed their support. But the settlers had now initiated legal action to test the company's claim that it possessed the land as a commercial asset. Eventually, in 1918, the decision was given that in law the land belonged neither to the company, nor to its government to administer on behalf of the colony's voters, nor to the native inhabitants, but to the British Crown – for whom the company's government had in effect been acting as an agent when it defeated Lobengula. Bereft of what it now saw as its major commercial asset, the company decided that it had no choice but to seek to recover its administrative costs from the Colonial Office and to surrender its charter. Both the Colonial Office and the company thought that the best course for Southern Rhodesia was to become the fifth province of the Union of South Africa. But the predominantly British settlers did not want to become the weakest unit in a larger state whose politics were dominated by Afrikaners. Their own leaders therefore urged that Southern Rhodesia should be allowed to become a self-governing colony, and when in 1922 the issue was put to the voters in a referendum, a sizeable majority supported them.

In 1923, therefore, the British government agreed to the administration of Southern Rhodesia, with nearly a million African inhabitants, being handed over to a settler prime minister and cabinet who were responsible to a legislative assembly elected from a settler population of only 33 000. Few people at the time thought there was anything odd about this. Once union with South Africa had been ruled out, the only feasible alternative would have been a Colonial Office administration. But the Colonial Office, which in any case had to take over from the BSA Company responsibility for the even bigger and poorer colony of Northern Rhodesia, clearly did not want to take on responsibility also for Southern Rhodesia and its independently minded settlers. It preferred to act in the established tradition of granting self-government to an established body of settlers who demanded it as their right as British subjects. If it were objected that in this case these British subjects were far too few to be entrusted with managing the affairs of nearly a million Africans (and, after all, a community of this number of Britons in Britain itself would have had minimal powers of local government and would not have even been allowed to control its own civilian police), a number of things could be said. First, as recently as 1893, the colony of Natal had become self-governing with a non-European population about the same size as Southern Rhodesia's was in 1923, and a white population which was not significantly larger. Secondly, Southern Rhodesia had inherited the colour-blind electoral franchise of the old Cape Colony. Therefore white electors did not have a legal monopoly of political power and, as the non-Europeans gained in wealth and education, their share would become greater. Finally the Colonial Office had reserved power to veto, or to require the modification of, any legislation passed by the Southern Rhodesian assembly which was thought to discriminate unjustly between the races.

In point of fact, the Natal precedent was not a very encouraging one, since in 1906 that colony had faced a serious revolt from its Zulu inhabitants (and one which, like the 1896–7 revolts in Rhodesia, was only put down with the aid of imperial forces), and the two constitutional safeguards were more apparent than real. The Southern Rhodesian whites knew as well as those in the Cape that qualifications for the franchise could be periodically raised so as to keep most non-Europeans out and most Europeans in. In 1939, there were about seventy Africans on a total electoral roll of some 28 000; by 1952, the figures were 380 out of over 45 000. Secondly, if on any particular issue the Britons in Rhodesia were quite determined that what they regarded as their legitimate interests should be protected by discriminatory legislation, in the last resort, the only way the United Kingdom government had of stopping them was to suspend the Rhodesian constitution and to substitute direct rule by the Colonial Office. So far as is known, no British government contemplated taking such a drastic and unpopular step before 1965, and it then proved quite impossible to implement. In practice, therefore, the small settler community in Rhodesia was allowed to build up an apparatus of discrimination against Africans in matters of land (their rights of occupancy were confined to only two-fifths of the colony, usually in areas remote from transport facilities and unattractive to Europeans because of their poor soils or low altitude), employment, residence and mobility which in principle, if not always in degree, resembled the South African practice.

Some explanation for the reluctance of the Colonial Office to interfere in Southern Rhodesian affairs when this programme of control was being initiated in the 1920s and 1930s, may perhaps be found in the fact that throughout this period the survival of the settler community hung on a very fine balance. It took on what was, in relation to its resources, a very substantial debt to contribute to the Colonial Office's repayment to the BSA Company of its administrative costs in establishing the colony, and then, in 1933, to buy out the company's still surviving right to mineral royalties. Furthermore, it was hard hit by the world trade recession of the 1930s. It therefore attracted very little in the way of new European settlement. Net immigration during 1921–41 was less than 18 000, and the white population in the latter year was only 69 000, compared with an estimated African population of 1 400 000.

But by the 1940s, the Europeans had discovered a profitable economic staple in the cultivation of tobacco for export, and in war-time and immediately post-war conditions, their economy began to boom. By the mid-1950s, new immigration had swelled the European population to 160 000. Supported by an African population then officially estimated at some 2 000 000, this made it possible to develop secondary manufacturing industry. In these conditions, the settlers began to chafe at the remaining legal limitations on their self-government. They still had no desire to submerge their individuality within the Union of South Africa, where the Nationalists were now clearly in the ascendant. They therefore concluded that their best chance of gaining complete independence was to engineer an amalgamation of the two Rhodesian colonies and Nyasaland into a new British Central African Union which the British authorities would regard as being strong and wealthy enough to receive the dominion status granted to South Africa in 1910 and, indeed, to stand as a bulwark of British interests to check Afrikaner nationalism.

But in 1923, the very year in which the Southern Rhodesian settlers had been granted responsible government, events in Kenya had forced the British government to reconsider its attitude towards settler colonies. This colony had begun life as the British East African Protectorate, the area between the Indian Ocean and Uganda which needed to be administered to enable Britain to control Uganda, the source of the White Nile, and therefore a foundation of Britain's position in

Egypt. It quickly became apparent that Uganda could not be controlled effectively and economically without a modern means of transporting men and supplies across the 600 miles of territory which intervened between it and the Indian Ocean. So, between 1896 and 1901, some £8 000 000 ($40 000 000) of British tax-payers' money, and labourers brought from British India, were used to build what was called the Uganda Railway from the Indian Ocean port of Mombasa to the nearest point on Lake Victoria, Kisumu, from which steamers could run to Uganda.

The Uganda Railway thus ran to, not through, Uganda, and it was the responsibility of the administration of the BEA Protectorate (which became Kenya Colony in 1920) rather than that of Uganda. The question which immediately arose was how to make the railway pay and to provide some return on what was, at that time, a uniquely large British colonial investment. In the long run, of course, a large part of the answer lay in the growth of Uganda's cotton exports. But the possibility of these was hardly evident before about 1912, and the BEA Protectorate government was more particularly concerned with generating traffic for the railway from its own territory. It was obvious that little would ever come from the 300-mile-wide belt of land that lay between the coast and Nairobi, the headquarters alike of the railway and of the Protectorate administration, situated where the railway began to climb off the coastal plain onto the Kenya Highlands. This was arid country, very unlikely to receive as much as 500 mm (20 in.) of rainfall in a year – which indeed was the case with two-thirds of the whole colony. But the Highlands, with adequate rainfall, good volcanic soils and a healthy climate, seemed ripe for major agricultural development except that they appeared remarkably empty of people. The Foreign Office, which was responsible for British administration in East Africa until 1905, and Sir Charles Eliot, whom in 1901 it had sent as High Commissioner to govern the Protectorate, therefore agreed that these apparently empty Highlands could best be exploited by encouraging their settlement by European farmers.

This was the origin of the land problem which plagued Kenya until its independence and which was the prime cause of the Mau Mau insurrection of the 1950s. The scarcity of African population in the Highlands was in fact a historical accident comparable to that which had led the Afrikaner trekkers in South Africa to think that they could with impunity find new homelands in Natal and on the high veld. It was the result of relatively recent epidemics and famine, and of the interaction between the pastoral Masai and their sedentary Bantu neighbours to the north. Masai raiding had created large grassland reserves which were periodically used for the grazing of their growing herds but which had little permanent human population. But further north, towards Mount Kenya, sheltered from the Masai by belts of forest, there were sizeable farming populations, first and foremost the Kikuyu, whose numbers and whose need for land would rapidly increase once the epidemics were ended and Masai expansion had been checked.

As has been seen, the number of Europeans possessing the capital, skills and patience needed to develop virgin tropical soils by employing and training local labour, and who wished to invest these things and their own future in Africa, was not large. By the 1920s, despite considerable official inducements, less than 10 000 Europeans had come to live in Kenya (and only about a third of these were directly involved in farming). But they had demanded, and had received, their right as British subjects to be represented in the local legislative council, and they had exerted considerable pressure on the local administration and on the Colonial Office in favour of their interests. In particular they had secured that a large slice of the Highlands (eventually defined as nearly 17 000 square miles, about a quarter of all habitable land in Kenya) should be reserved for European occupation, mainly by farmers holding 999-year leases on very favourable terms. The Masai herds were thus confined to less fertile territory to the south of the Highlands, and the farming operations of sizeable populations like the Kikuyu or, near Lake Victoria, the Luo, were legally restricted to defined areas. The Europeans hoped that this would force them out to provide cheap labour for the areas of white settlement – the more so as they were able to secure the imposition of restraints on the African production of commercial crops like coffee. In fact the Europeans' domination of the Highlands, the most productive area of a territory which was generally afflicted with inadequate rainfall for cultivation, eventually so exacerbated a general land hunger that their claim to land became an embarrassment, for their economy could not generate anything like sufficient employment. The Africans most affected were the Kikuyu. By the 1930s, the density of population in their reserve was already some 280 persons to the square mile (compared with 140 for the Luo, which was high enough). However the Kikuyu gained some immediate relief in that the barrier that the Europeans had placed between them and the recent pressure of the

Masai was a permeable one. The settlers were far too few and lacking in resources to gainfully occupy all the White Highlands to which they laid claim, so that some Kikuyu were able to expand onto them as squatters.

However, the Europeans were not the only alien settlers in Kenya; indeed they were outnumbered by Indian settlers by more than two to one. Indians had for some centuries participated in the trade of the East African coastlands. Following the construction of the Uganda Railway, and the importation of Indian labour for its construction, they had rapidly spread into the interior. Some of them were merchants, storekeepers, entrepreneurs and tradesmen on their own account; others, possessing much more sophisticated skills than were at the time readily available to Africans, found useful employment as clerks and artisans in the service of the Europeans. These Indians soon began to object to a situation in which only European settlers were represented in the legislative council and allowed to take up land freely. They could do this effectively because, since India was British, they too were British subjects. Indeed, through the government of India and the India Office in London, they could bring political pressures to bear on the government in Britain to counter the white settlers' connections there.

In 1923, the Colonial Office was induced to look into the Indian complaints. The Colonial Secretary in the Conservative government of the day, the Duke of Devonshire, published a *Memorandum* which promised that the Indians should have some representation in the legislative council and, although they would not in practice be allowed to take up land in the White Highlands, that they would not be subject to segregation in the towns. But, having set out the British government's decisions in the immediate dispute between the Indians and the Europeans in Kenya, the Devonshire *Memorandum* went on, almost as an aside, to make an important declaration of general principle: 'Primarily Kenya is an African territory, and His Majesty's Government think it necessary definitely to record their considered opinion that the interests of the African natives must be paramount, and that if, and when, those interests and the interests of the immigrant races should conflict, the former should prevail.' What had been done in Kenya so far was not going to be rapidly undone. Too much had been pledged to the Europeans in the past to permit of this, or even to give full justice to the Indians' claims. 'But in the administration of Kenya, His Majesty's Government regard themselves as exercising a trust on behalf of the African population, and they are unable to delegate or share this trust, the object of which may be defined as the protection and advancement of the native races.'

This declaration of policy was made, of course, in respect of Kenya alone, and even here its significance was somewhat obscured by its immediate origin in the conflict between the Indian and the European settlers. But if it could be made for Kenya, then logically it could be made also for any other colony in which European settlers were influencing policy but had not yet gained control of the government, as they had in Southern Rhodesia. Seven years later, this was unequivocally spelt out in a further government paper, the *Memorandum on Native Policy in East Africa*, issued in 1930 by Lord Passfield (Sidney Webb), Colonial Secretary in the Labour administration that was then in office. This asserted that Britain's prime responsibility was one of trusteeship for 'native peoples not yet able to stand on their own feet', and it made it clear that self-government of the kind granted to Southern Rhodesia in 1923 would not be granted to other colonies containing settlers until their African inhabitants could participate in it equally with the settlers.

The year 1923 therefore marks a watershed in British policy towards settler colonies in Africa. It was at once the year in which Southern Rhodesia achieved self-government under the old doctrine that any substantial body of Britons in a colony had an automatic claim to it, and the year in which it first became apparent that British governments had appreciated that, in African conditions, the implementation of this doctrine might not be in the interest of the majority of the colony's inhabitants. This recognition by British governments that they had a responsibility towards the non-Europeans who formed the vast majority of their subjects in Africa, and that this responsibility would be traduced if it were shared with or transferred to European settlers, marks an important acceptance of the trusteeship ideals expressed, for example, by Lugard and in the League of Nations Mandate system. However it should also be said that this new doctrine of empire was initially rather a negative one. For many years, very little was done, in Kenya or elsewhere in British East or central Africa, by any active programme of educational, social or economic development, to prepare the African majority for participation in eventual self-government. The real spur in this direction did not really come until the 1950s, and then largely as a consequence of the rapid advance to self-government of colonies in West Africa (which, of course, had no European settlers).

The settler reaction to the new doctrine of an inalienable British trusteeship for the African peoples of the empire was the same throughout East and central Africa. If individual settler colonies could no longer expect rapid advancement to self-government on the Southern Rhodesian model, then larger unions of colonies should be created. It was thought that these would have greater economic potentialities than their component units, so that more capital would be attracted to them and there would be more scope for Europeans in managerial roles. Thus, whatever the position in each member colony, in the larger unions of colonies the British government would have to accept the fact of European leadership.

In East Africa, the settlers' pressure for a union of Kenya, Uganda and Tanganyika, though often very vocal, achieved no more than the eventual establishment, in 1949, of an East African High Commission with its headquarters at Nairobi. This had a central legislative assembly dominated by European members. But its competence was limited to economic matters, in particular to the control of railways and harbours, customs, the post office, research, and other common services for the three territories. There were considerable barriers to its ever developing into a real political union. One of these was the international status of Tanganyika which, on the demise of the League of Nations, had become a Trust Territory of the United Nations, in which British administration continued to be committed to the advancement of its native inhabitants. Another was the steadfast opposition of Uganda, its four major Bantu kingdoms in particular, to any involvement with a socio-political system of the type operating in Kenya.

But there were also the brute facts that the settlers in East Africa were too few and that, even in Kenya, where they were most numerous, their economic position was not strong enough. By the end of the 1950s, the three territories combined still contained less than 100 000 Europeans, two-thirds of whom were in Kenya. In British East Africa as a whole, the Europeans were outnumbered by Africans by about 250:1, and even in Kenya alone the ratio was about 130:1. (They were also outnumbered by Asians by about 3:1 both in East Africa as a whole and in Kenya.) Each of the three territories was exporting between £40 000 000 and £50 000 000 ($112 000 000–$140 000 000) of agricultural produce a year. This was almost entirely African grown except in Kenya, so the European farmers' contribution to the East African total was at best a third. Conversely, while the exports of the three colonies together just about balanced their imports, at about £130 000 000 ($364 000 000) a year, Uganda and Tanganyika individually both had favourable balances of trade, while Kenya's balance was an adverse one of about £27 000 000 ($75 600 000) a year. This was rather more than twice as much as Kenya contributed to the other two territories in services and goods as the seat of the High Commission and as the only territory with anything much in the way of manufacturing industry. In other words, it seems clear that European settlement, as well as leading to a very unequal division of power and wealth between the races in Kenya, was an uneconomic method of developing agricultural resources compared with the response to world market stimuli of African farmers in Uganda and Tanganyika.

In central Africa, however, the situation was rather different, and for a time the settlers were much more successful in getting what they wanted. Southern Rhodesia was already self-governing, so the settlers there had much more power of initiative than their colleagues in Kenya. Secondly, the economies of the three central African territories were more interdependent than those of the three East African colonies, where, although Uganda was reliant on Kenya for her communications with the outside world, Tanganyika was not, and where all three were really competing with each other as producers for the world market of much the same range of agricultural products, such as coffee, cotton, sisal and tea. As in South Africa, the European development of mines, agriculture and industry in Southern Rhodesia had generated a much greater demand for African labour than could be met by her own population, which, though rapidly increasing, was still probably under 3 000 000 in the early 1950s. About a quarter of her African employment was thus taken up by immigrants from the two northern territories. These came principally from Nyasaland, which had an African population about the same size as Southern Rhodesia's but in only a quarter of the area, giving an average population density of eighty to the square mile compared with Southern Rhodesia's twenty per square mile (and about ten per square mile for Northern Rhodesia's population of about the same size but spread over a much larger territory). Conversely, the appreciable industrial development apparent in Southern Rhodesia by the 1950s was dependent on the two northern territories if it were to have a worthwhile local market for its manufactures. Furthermore the railway system of the two Rhodesias was totally integrated, and Nyasaland was also dependent on the same major outlet to the outside world, the port of Beira in Portuguese Mozambique.

But perhaps the most significant difference between the central African colonies and those in East Africa was that the great mineral wealth on which Rhodes had based his plans had at last been developed, though not in Southern Rhodesia or in gold as had been expected, but in the immensely rich deposits of copper ore in Shaba on the border between Northern Rhodesia and the Belgian Congo. These had begun to be exploited by the beginning of the 1930s. By the mid-1950s, copper-mining was responsible for something like nine-tenths of both the exports and the government revenues of Northern Rhodesia. In each of these respects it had become the richest territory in central Africa, both absolutely and even more so in per capita terms. In 1954, against imports of some £125 000 000 ($350 000 000), the three territories combined were exporting commodities worth some £150 000 000 ($440 000 000), of which Northern Rhodesia's contribution was some 62 per cent, Southern Rhodesia's 33 per cent, and Nyasaland's rather less than 5 per cent. On the other hand, Northern Rhodesia's copper mines were dependent for power on Southern Rhodesia, which alone mined coal, and whose cooperation was essential if the Zambezi river, which formed the boundary between the two colonies, was to be exploited for its considerable hydro-electric potential.

The development of the Northern Rhodesian Copper Belt had also changed the political situation in central Africa. The mines provided a great magnet for European urban settlement. The white population of Northern Rhodesia, which had numbered less than 10 000 in 1930, had swollen to nearly 70 000 by the early 1950s. (This compared with some 160 000 in Southern Rhodesia, and a mere 5 000 in Nyasaland, where care had been taken for the agricultural interests of its dense African population.) The growth alike of white population and wealth in Northern Rhodesia was of considerable interest to the settlers in Southern Rhodesia. These had earlier rejected proposals for the amalgamation of the two colonies both in 1917, when it was suggested by the BSA Company as an administrative economy, and in 1930, when it was the Northern Rhodesian settlers' immediate response to the Passfield *Memorandum*. They could then see no advantage in diluting their society by adding to it a vast, poor territory with as many black men as their own and only a handful of whites.

But by the later 1930s the situation had changed sufficiently for the Southern Rhodesian Legislative Assembly to concur with the European unofficial members of the legislative council in the northern colony in pressing for the amalgamation of the two colonies under a constitution conferring complete self-government. Eventually the British government agreed to set up a commission, chaired by Lord Bledisloe, to examine the feasibility of union not only between the two Rhodesias, but with Nyasaland as well. However, in 1939 this reported that, although on economic grounds the case for amalgamation was a good one, and it should therefore be pursued as an ultimate goal, it was not politically practicable in the immediate future because of 'the striking unanimity, in the northern Territories, of the native opposition to amalgamation, based mainly on dislike of some of the native policy of Southern Rhodesia'.

There the matter rested for the war years. But during these and immediately afterwards, the two Rhodesias gained greatly in both economic strength and in European population. Their white politicians, astutely led by Sir Godfrey Huggins (later Lord Malvern) in the south and Roy Welensky (later Sir Roy) in the north, were able in the post-war years to convince both Labour and Conservative leaders in Britain that the economic case for a union of the three central African territories was an overwhelming one. It would, they argued, attract much greater investment in central Africa which would produce development of great value to Britain in her post-war economic difficulties, would raise the standard of living of the African peoples for whom Britain was responsible, and would create a useful British counter-balance to and bulwark against the influence of a South Africa in which, in 1948, the Afrikaner nationalists had won a decisive victory. It was true that African opposition to their scheme was now much more explicit, especially in the two northern territories (which alone had effective political means for its expression), than it was in Bledisloe's day. But they side-stepped this with the idea that union should take the form, not of an amalgamation of the three colonies and their governments, but of a federation. In a federal system, the oversight of African affairs in the two northern territories could remain with local governors responsible to the Colonial Office.

But when in 1953 the Federation of Rhodesia and Nyasaland came into being, it was apparent that this device had not in any way diminished African fears of domination by the settler interest. These were accentuated when the minority of African representatives in the Federal legislature proved unable to stop the European majority from dismantling safeguards against legislation which discriminated against Africans. Indeed the institution of the Federation, together with the contemporary successes of the independence campaigns in British West Africa, provoked the rise in all three territories of popular African nationalist movements determined to wreck it. However, the Federal constitution contained a clause providing that, between 1960 and 1963, its working would be reviewed. This had been inserted because the settler leaders thought that by then they would have proved their case, and that the British government could then be persuaded to remove the last checks on their freedom. In fact this clause proved to be their undoing. In 1960, i.e. at the earliest possible moment, Harold Macmillan's Conservative government set up a commission under Lord Monckton to prepare the ground for this review. This very quickly reported that the strength of African opposition to the Federation was so great that each colony should be given the right to secede from it. When this was accepted by Britain, the two northern territories quickly left the Federation, and their African political leaders soon gained independence for their peoples on the West African pattern.

In 1960, therefore, the bid to extend settler control over tropical Africa north of the Zambezi was finally ended. It had proved to be a weak growth, because there were few Europeans willing to commit the fortunes of themselves and their children to the hard task of developing estates in the tropics, and because it could really flourish only during the high tide of Europe's confidence in its imperial mission. European settlement was now effectively limited to the two temperate zones at either end of the continent where it had taken root before the imperial tide had set in: in South Africa, its Southern Rhodesian extension, and in the adjacent colonies of Portugal, which unfashionably had not abandoned its belief in its original civilizing mission; and in North Africa where, despite its proximity to Europe, the doctrine of European superiority was also about to be abandoned.

Chapter 17

Independence resumed

The political empires that were so proudly and confidently proclaimed over Africa in the later nineteenth and early twentieth centuries as inevitable and permanent extensions of European civilization lasted hardly three generations. By the 1960s, the colonial system was in full retreat. By the end of the 1970s, it had to all intents and purposes disappeared, its outstanding memorial being the embattled garrison of whites settled in South Africa, who had early achieved independence to manage their own affairs free from control from Europe, and who had a dependency of their own in South West Africa – which the rest of the world called Namibia.

The timing of independence for a particular colonial territory or group of territories was often determined by local circumstances and by the manipulation of these by astute African leaders who had equipped themselves with an appropriate anti-colonial ideology. As a result, the story of decolonization in Africa has often been told primarily in terms of the growth of the continent's nationalist movements, *négritude*, pan-Africanism and pan-Islam in particular. But a fuller perspective seems to demand that account should also be taken of changes on the colonial front. Without these it is perhaps open to question whether the African nationalisms would have succeeded, or, at least, have achieved success as quickly as they did.

The changes that developed in the twentieth century in the colonial powers' attitudes to Africa were often inter-linked, and thus mutually reinforcing, in an often bewildering variety of combinations determined by specific historical circumstances in Europe and in Africa. But for purposes of analysis, it seems sensible to stress three main developments. First, as has already been suggested, the two world wars of 1914–18 and 1939–45 and the intervening economic depression served first to undermine western Europe's confidence in its *mission civilisatrice*, and then to lead to a substantial decline in its actual capacity to maintain control of empire. This led, secondly, to an increased readiness to accept that, since one of the avowed purposes of a colonial system, and certainly its moral justification, was a civilizing one, it carried with it its own solvent. Whether or not Europeans liked its results, and however much they may have tried to control these results in their own interest, they could not escape the fact that colonial control was educative. The establishment of any colony involved the setting up of some formal system of schooling for its peoples, if only to make them more efficient servants and instruments for the extraction of its wealth. But beyond this, almost everything the colonial rulers did in Africa – setting up new systems of political control, propagating Christianity, developing new means of transport, introducing new forms of agricultural or mineral exploitation, harnessing sources of power, instituting new industries and technologies, expanding the money and market economy, and, above all perhaps, demanding wage labour for all these and many other activities – was in a broad sense profoundly educative. Inevitably, therefore, Africans learnt to want to do these things for themselves, and in some measure too learnt how to do them, either by adapting their traditional organizations or by taking up European forms of organization.

Thus on the one hand African nationalisms were encouraged, and on the other Europeans could hardly continue indefinitely to deny their claims. In fact, and this is the third major element of change, by the 1950s Europeans were coming to realize that it was not in their interest to deny African claims to political independence. The second major purpose of empire, the harnessing of colonial markets and resources for the benefit of an industrial economy instituted and managed by western Europeans and their allies, had also been achieved. Since this economic harnessing was thought to be inevitable and irreversible, it would not be undone by the removal of *political* controls from Europe. Furthermore it was soon to be seen that any attempts to maintain these controls by force, in the face of local political pressures and in a general climate increasingly hostile to continuing colonial dominion, might actually diminish the economic benefits flowing from what had already been achieved. Thus the necessity to retain empire was as much weakened as had been the will to maintain it.

✻

Decolonization began north of the Sahara, in North-East Africa in particular, in circumstances which had little relevance for the rest of the continent. In the first place, with the single exception of the Ethiopian highlands (which in any case had their own sufficiently idiosyncratic history), this part of the continent had been for centuries firmly part of the Muslim world. It therefore shared in the movement of Islamic reform which began to gather momentum during the course of the nineteenth century, producing not only political opportunists, like Muhammad 'Ali, who felt a need to catch up with western Europe, but also philosophical and political thinkers, who sought to develop Islam itself to demonstrate that Europeans need have no monopoly of modernizing initiatives. The preaching of such men was greatly facilitated by the destruction during the first world war of the Ottoman empire, which in many ways had served as a bulwark behind which traditional Islam had been sheltered from change.

The Ottoman empire was already a dead letter in Africa. Its demise had no practical political effect there other than Britain's 1922 declaration that Egypt was a sovereign kingdom with which she proposed to negotiate an agreement to secure her own interests in respect of such matters as the Suez canal. But there were dramatic changes in the Islamic homelands in nearby Asia which could not but have their effect on the Muslim peoples of North Africa. Turkey passed under the reformist administration of Kemal Atatürk. Elsewhere Arabs secured independence, as under Ibn Sa'ud in most of Arabia, or the promise of independent nationhood under British or French mandates which were intended to be of short duration. Iraq in fact became an independent kingdom in 1932, and the mandates for the other territories did not survive the second world war. By this time also, Jewish settlement in Palestine had provided a potent new spur for a militant Arab nationalism.

Islamic reformism generally, and actual or promised political change in adjacent Arab countries in the Near East in particular, engendered a sense of increasing frustration among the younger generation in North Africa. On the one hand, colonial rule provided them with new – if often restricted – access to modern political and technological thinking. On the other, it gave them no real chance to employ their new ideas other than as subordinate participants in the mechanisms of colonial control. The result was the emergence of nationalist movements which sought to overthrow this control. If all else failed, this should be done by force, in which case the Arab nationalists in Africa would expect practical help as well as inspiration from the Arabs of nearer Asia. But until the second world war, both France and Italy were strong enough in North Africa to feel no need to give any ground, and in their colonies nationalism had no alternative other than to go underground or to retreat into intellectualism.

In Egypt in 1922, however, Britain had unilaterally declared her intention to live up to the promise she had made when she had first occupied the country forty years before. She had expressed her willingness to cooperate with a native Egyptian regime which would accept her particular requirements for the security of her communications with India. There therefore followed many years of more or less open political debate, involving three major protagonists. The first of these was the nationalist party, the Wafd, which was apt to win any free election. But any Wafd government tended to come into collision with one or both of the other protagonists. These were the descendants of Muhammad 'Ali who occupied the throne, first King Fu'ad (to 1936) and then King Faruq, and the British. Both of these had interests that they felt to be threatened by the nationalists, and neither was keen to surrender their traditional powers. Wafd governments therefore tended to be dismissed and replaced by administrations of 'moderates', i.e. representatives of the property-owning class. But these could not depend on the king for support any more than they could hope for support from the people, and they would in their turn give way to a period of palace rule. This would force the moderates to join hands with the Wafd in demanding free elections, and the cycle would then be repeated. Ultimately, however, the Wafd and the British appreciated that neither could readily destroy the basis of the other's power, and that they had better reach an understanding. The result was the Anglo-Egyptian treaty of alliance of 1936. Britain's military occupation of Egypt was to be ended, though for a period of twenty years she was given the right to maintain a limited military strength in a narrow zone astride the Suez Canal.

But within three years, the second world war had begun. North and North-East Africa quickly became major theatres of operations, and their history accordingly diverged even further from that of the rest of the continent. The most immediate consequence of the war was that Britain felt the need to defend Egypt and its canal at all costs against the Italo-German Axis and any allies it might find in the Near East. Instead of the British forces being withdrawn to the canal zone, they were reinforced to meet the immediate threat posed by substantial

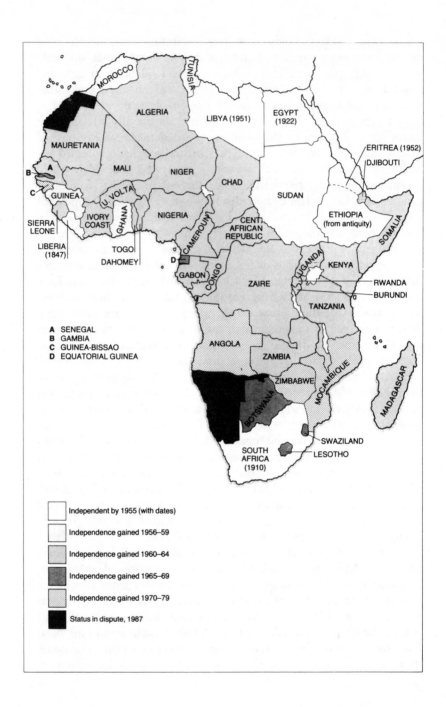

MOROCCO
TUNISIA
ALGERIA
LIBYA (1951)
EGYPT (1922)
MAURETANIA
ERITREA (1952)
DJIBOUTI
MALI
NIGER
CHAD
SUDAN
B A
C GUINEA
U. VOLTA
ETHIOPIA (from antiquity)
SIERRA LEONE
IVORY COAST
GHANA
NIGERIA
CAMEROUN
CENT. AFRICAN REPUBLIC
SOMALIA
LIBERIA (1847)
TOGO
DAHOMEY
D
UGANDA
KENYA
GABON
CONGO
ZAIRE
RWANDA
BURUNDI
TANZANIA

A SENEGAL
B GAMBIA
C GUINEA-BISSAO
D EQUATORIAL GUINEA

ANGOLA
ZAMBIA
MOCAMBIQUE
ZIMBABWE
BOTSWANA
MADAGASCAR
SWAZILAND
SOUTH AFRICA (1910)
LESOTHO

Independent by 1955 (with dates)

Independence gained 1956–59

Independence gained 1960–64

Independence gained 1965–69

Independence gained 1970–79

Status in dispute, 1987

Italian armies flanking the Nile valley and the Red Sea in Libya and Ethiopia. British, Indian and African soldiers experienced surprisingly little difficulty in defeating the Italians in Ethiopia and Somalia. But early British successes in Libya led to the Italians being reinforced by an élite German force, with the result that in 1942 an Axis army invaded Egypt, reaching within sixty miles of Alexandria, and little more than twice this from the Suez Canal itself. Some Egyptians thought that their liberation from the British was at hand. But Britain's understanding with the Wafd held firm, and the threat of force was used to impose a Wafd government on King Faruq.

Later in 1942, Britain and her allies, who now included the United States, were able to mount a major offensive in North Africa. The Italo-German army was decisively defeated at El Alamein, and then chased westwards along the Libyan coastline towards Tunisia. Since France was then under German occupation, an Anglo-American army was landed in Morocco and Algeria with the purpose of advancing westwards into Tunisia to administer the final *coup de grâce*. These landings were initially opposed on the orders of officers faithful to the French government at Vichy. Since Britain and the United States had recently declared, in the Atlantic Charter of 1941, that they sought no 'territorial or other' aggrandizement, and that they respected 'the right of *all* peoples to choose the form of government under which they will live', this French reaction tended to confirm the Maghribian nationalists in their opinion that France was determined to maintain her empire in North Africa at all costs. There was even a brief period early in 1943 when the Germans hoped that the Tunisian nationalist party, the Neo-Destour (i.e. the New Constitution party), would provide civil support for their military occupation. But the allied armies advancing from east and west joined hands, and in May secured the surrender near Tunis of the remaining German and Italian troops. All North Africa from Somalia to Morocco was now firmly under British or French control.

The first result of the second world war in North Africa was thus the destruction of Italy's empire there. It vanished much more completely than Germany's African empire had done as a result of the first world war. From an African point of view, it might even be argued that the German empire lingered on after 1914–18, albeit under new managements, in the shape of the mandates given to Germany's victors to administer her former colonies. Admittedly a mandatory power did not inherit all the rights that Germany had claimed. But it was not insignificant that the League of Nations' supervision over them was entrusted to what was called a *Permanent* Mandates Commission, or that in the mid-1930s, when Britain and France were following a policy of appeasement towards Germany, there was even talk of returning the territories (or some of them) to German administration.

By 1945, however, African empires were no longer sacrosanct. It was not only that the principles of the Anglo-American alliance as set out in the Atlantic Charter were of much more general application than President Wilson's Fourteen Points. It could not be forgotten that the Ethiopia which the Italians had conquered in 1935–6 had been accepted along with other free countries of the world as a member of the League of Nations, and that it had in fact been the first victim of the fascist aggression which Britain, France, the Soviet Union and the United States had belatedly joined together to halt. The campaign of 1940–1 against the Italians in Ethiopia was therefore a war of liberation ending with the restoration of the Emperor who in 1936 had vainly pleaded his nation's cause before the League Assembly. Nor was there any question of placing the older former Italian colonies under long-living mandates administered by the victors. It was accepted from the beginning that their peoples had the same right as others to be ruled by governments of their own people.

The administrations set up by the British after they had occupied Eritrea and Libya were caretaker military governments which were to last no longer than it took to find, train and equip what seemed to be the most appropriate African authority. In Libya, the obvious candidate was the head of the Sanusiyya, a Cyrenaican *tariqa*, founded in 1843, which had consistently resisted first the Ottoman and then the Italian occupation, and which had provided a small contingent of volunteers to fight alongside the British in 1940–3. In 1950, Idris al-Sanusi was elected king of a federal union of Cyrenaica and Tripolitania, and in the following year Libya became an independent kingdom. As for Eritrea, it was difficult to resist Ethiopia's claim that this was one of the first parts of her empire to be lost to her, and that it should therefore be returned. In 1952, therefore, it became a federated province of Ethiopia. As for the Somalis, they had been unruly tribal subjects whether of Italy or Britain. Initially there was reluctance to accept the argument of young Somali nationalists, stimulated by the Italian defeat and the temporary unification of most of their people under British administration, that the time was ripe for the creation of a united Somalia which might quickly become independent. Instead, Italy was given a ten-year commission by the United Nations to prepare her former colony for independence, while Britain embarked on a similar programme in her protectorate. In 1960 these ends were achieved, and the two territories joined in an independent Somali Republic.

Meanwhile the end of the war meant that it should be possible to normalize Anglo-Egyptian relations and to prepare for a new agreement to replace the treaty due to expire in 1956. But Egyptian politics were in a highly unstable condition. The monarchy was determined to redress the humiliation it had suffered in 1942, while the Wafd had compromised itself in the eyes of younger nationalists by its wartime cooperation with the British. Each sought to maintain its influence by none too scrupulous means. Domestic affairs were neglected in favour of forming the Arab League and defending the Arabs in Palestine against the pretensions of the Jewish immigrants to establish a new Israel. Negotiations with Britain broke down more than once, mainly because the Egyptians insisted that the Sudan was Egyptian territory while the British argued that the future status of the country was a matter for its own people to decide. In 1948–9, the incompetence and corruption of palace and orthodox politicians alike was exposed by the crushing defeat inflicted on the Egyptian army in the first Arab-Israeli war. Control seemed to be slipping into the hands of urban mobs inflamed either by Muslim or socialist radicals. But the circumstances of the Israeli débâcle had so disgusted a group of younger army officers, whose leading spirit was Colonel Gamal Abdul Nasser, that, rather in the spirit of 'Arabi Pasha seventy years before, they decided that Egypt needed a completely new start. In 1952 they executed a *coup d'état* which secured Faruq's abdication and exile; in the following year a republic was declared, Nasser shortly becoming its president. The most significant immediate action of Nasser and his colleagues, one which secured them wholehearted popular support, was an agrarian reform which destroyed the landlords who had hitherto dominated the political as well as the economic life of the country. As for external relations, they realistically appreciated that it was more important to rid Egypt of the last vestiges of foreign military occupation than to insist on maintaining her own traditional imperialist ambitions in the Sudan. Agreements were quickly reached with Britain which ended the 1936 treaty, secured the withdrawal of the last British troops from the canal zone by 1955, and in 1953 instituted a three-year transitional period of self-government for the Sudan, at the end of which its people were to decide their own future. In 1956, in fact, the Sudan rejected the maintenance of the link with Egypt and opted for complete independence.

Within a few years after the end of the second world war, therefore, the whole of North-East Africa, from Libya to Somalia, had secured independence from foreign rule. This did not mean, of course, that its problems were at an end. Egypt was to suffer further disastrous wars with Israel and in 1956, under the cover of the first of these, even to see British and French troops reoccupying the canal zone for a brief space, ostensibly in reaction to her nationalization of the Suez Canal Company, and all the other countries were soon to experience violent changes in their forms of government. But the destruction of the Italian empire, and the early British acceptance of independence for Egypt, the Sudan and Somaliland, meant that the prospect of achieving indigenous governments free from European control was earlier and more clearly evident to the peoples of North-East Africa than it was to those of the Maghrib. Here the immediate consequences of the ending of the second world war campaigns in North Africa were quite otherwise. The serious damage done to French authority by the Anglo-American landings and the brief Italo-German occupation of Tunisia, had raised hopes which were quickly dashed. Control from Paris was re-established at the very moment when the North Africans could see that other Arab territories, especially those in the Near East, were achieving complete freedom from colonial tutelage. Algerian, Tunisian and Moroccan nationalists' pleas that the constituent assembly for the new Fourth Republic in France might grant them at least local self-government were brusquely ignored. The most that was achieved for Algeria, in 1947, was a new constitutional statute which extended French citizenship to all Muslims, but which preserved the interests of France and her settlers by giving the 7 500 000 Algerians only as many representatives in the French parliament and in the local territorial assembly as were given to the settlers, who numbered about 1 000 000. In Tunisia and Morocco, the French could retreat behind the fiction that these countries were administered by the governments of their own Bey and Sultan respectively. The result in Tunisia was the speedy resort of the Neo-Destour nationalists to violent dissidence. In Morocco, on the other hand, the greater part of the country was controlled by the French through their alliances with local Berber chieftains who were traditionally hostile to the

Sultan's overlordship. Thus the Sultan himself became the focus for nationalist inspirations. The French tried in 1953 to counter this by inciting the chiefs to rise against the Sultan, whom they then exiled. But this action made him even more of a national hero than before, and armed opposition to French rule shortly began in the working-class districts of the larger cities.

By 1954 the nationalists were in open revolt throughout the Maghrib. The French quickly appreciated that the most serious danger lay in Algeria. This, of course, was where they had most to lose, where there was a really substantial French investment, and where the livelihood, and even the lives, of about a million Europeans seemed to depend on the maintenance of French control. Conversely, it was in Algeria that local society had suffered most severely from the French presence. The modernization of the economy by French settlement as well as French capital meant that foreigners held most of the best lands and most of the more remunerative positions. The native Algerians were being converted into a depressed and frustrated proletariat. Many thought that the best use they could make of their new status as French citizens was to seek employment in France; soon there were as many Algerians in low-status jobs in France as there were Frenchmen occupying the higher status positions in Algeria. But the situation in Algeria itself was such that when, in 1954, one of its nationalist groups decided that there was no way forward but to raise the standard of armed revolt against the French, it quickly became evident not only that the rising could count on the support of Arab nationalists throughout the Muslim world, but also that there was hardly a single Algerian who would oppose it. Within eighteen months a National Liberation Front (FLN) had been formed, and this was waging war throughout the countryside with such success that the French were hard put to it to hold their own.

The crisis in Algeria caused the French to re-assess the situation in Tunisia and Morocco with a view to seeing whether their interests in these two protectorates might not be best preserved by acceding to the nationalists' demands for self-government. In 1954 the principle of this was agreed for Tunisia, and within a year a Neo-Destour government was in office. In Morocco, there were even more dramatic changes. By 1955 there was open revolt in the cities and armed risings had begun in the countryside, where even Berber chiefs now declared for the exiled Sultan. At the end of that year, he was brought back, and early in 1956 France agreed that Morocco should once again be an independent monarchy. This action had immediate repercussions for Tunisia and for the smaller Spanish protectorate in Morocco. The French action against the Sultan in 1953 had been a unilateral one; the Spanish government had continued to regard him as the legitimate sovereign of its zone. When therefore France reversed her policy and recognized the Sultan's independence, Spain had little choice but to follow and to end her protectorate. Independence for Morocco led naturally to a demand for full independence for Tunisia also. But here the monarchy had never served to focus nationalist aspirations; in 1957, therefore, a republic was proclaimed, and Habib Bourguiba, leader of the Neo-Destour throughout all its vicissitudes since its foundation in 1934, became its president.

Meanwhile in Algeria the French were engaged in a full-scale war reminiscent of their original conquest. It was not too difficult for them to police the large cities, where so much of the population was French, but their efforts to control the countryside eventually led to the deployment of an army of 500 000 men and to the use of ever more drastic methods of repression. By 1958, however, the commanders of this army and the settlers were confident that Algeria could be held for France. But Frenchmen in France itself had become increasingly critical of the cost of the war in men and money, and also of the methods being used to wage it, so that the army officers and settlers in Algeria began to doubt whether the governments of the Fourth Republic had the will to maintain the war. They therefore began a revolt of their own. This brought de Gaulle back to power in France, where he shortly instituted a Fifth Republic shorn of the parliamentary doubts and weaknesses which had afflicted its predecessor. De Gaulle was thought of as the strong man who had alone stood up for the honour and integrity of France following her defeat by Germany. So in fact he was, but he was also a pragmatic realist who in 1940 had quickly appreciated the need to win the French colonies to his side. Within little more than a year, de Gaulle had concluded that France's economy and society could hardly survive the strain of maintaining her traditional presence in Algeria. Her own best interests required that the Algerians should be allowed to determine their own future. The immediate consequence was a further settler rising early in 1960. But this received little support from the army, whose rank and file were essentially conscripts, and de Gaulle was not deterred when subsequently some settlers began to resort to terrorism. In 1961, negotiations were opened between the French authorities and the provisional government which the Algerian nationalists had instituted in 1958. Eventually in 1962 it was agreed that the future of Algeria should be settled by a referendum. The result of this was a foregone conclusion, and nine out of every ten settlers left Algeria. The cost of the war to the Algerians had been high. Something like a third of a million of them had lost their lives, and many more of them had been forced to leave their homes, many of which had been destroyed in the fighting. But at least they now had the chance to rebuild their country in their own way.

Africa south of the Sahara was not directly involved in the campaigning of the second world war. Nevertheless the effects of this war, as has already been suggested, were to accentuate the pressures for both economic and educational development, and this was shortly to lead to a demand for political change as well.

This was most clearly and swiftly apparent in West Africa. As has been seen, techniques of economic and political organization had often reached high levels there by the time of the first arrival of European traders on its coasts, and nearly five centuries of continuing European trade had induced further substantial economic change and the beginnings of western education long before formal European colonies were proclaimed. Thus the Europeans who eventually assumed control in West Africa had less need than elsewhere south of the Sahara to enforce 'modernization' upon their subjects. Indeed it was only gradually that the Africans of the coastlands appreciated that they were now supposed to be the servants of the Europeans rather than their partners in change and development. As they did so, it did not take them long to appreciate also that they already had within their grasp a counter to overweening European political domination. This was the organization of a nationalist reaction, which could at once find inspiration in the achievements of West Africans in history, and yet organize itself along the European lines of clubs, professional associations, chambers of commerce and, ultimately, trade unions and political parties. In this way they could join issue with the Europeans on their own ground with the object of being able to take over for themselves the new structures of control and modernization these were erecting.

West Africans were not alone in this. A not dissimilar situation began to develop on the coat-tails of European settlement once it had become firmly established in South Africa. The manner in which the conferences which led to the Union of South Africa in 1910 had

completely ignored the affairs of the non-European majority quickly
led to the emergence of a South African Native National Congress
(later the African National Congress), in which educated African
teachers, ministers of religion, lawyers, journalists and the like joined
together to present their case. But in South Africa this movement of
African political awakening soon found itself in a cleft stick. The
leaders of the ANC, from the Reverend John Dube and Solomon
Plaatje in the early years, to Chief Albert Luthuli and Professor Z. K.
Matthews at the time of its final proscription in 1960, were essentially
reasonable men. They supposed that reasoned, public debate would
serve to hold back or to mollify the stream of measures adopted by
the ruling white minority to circumscribe or diminish the freedom of
non-Europeans. They were unwilling to believe that the white leaders
had no need to heed their arguments unless these were supported by
overt measures of dissent which might seriously inconvenience the
maintenance of the European economy and society – for example the
withdrawal of their labour or the disruption of the pass system which
controlled the movements of non-Europeans. The ANC therefore
tended to lose the initiative to more radical groups which appealed
more directly to the black proletariat, for example the Industrial and
Commercial Workers' Union led by Clements Kadalie in the 1920s,
or the Pan-African Congress initiated by Robert Sobukwe in 1959.
But the activities of such organizations only served to consolidate the
ranks of white hostility to granting non-Europeans any meaningful
rights or shares in their society, and to promote ever more stringent
repression of any dissident political or trade union activity. When
finally in 1960 the PAC inspired massive African opposition to the
pass laws, the result was the Sharpeville massacre; the banning of all
African political activity, the ANC as well as the PAC; and an
apparent ending to all communication between the races in South
Africa except only on the Bantustan terms dictated by the whites.

In East and Central Africa, a combination of early missionary
education and the later pressures of European settlement could also
stimulate African political organization on European or quasi-Euro-
pean lines. An early example was the series of political associations
which arose among the Kikuyu during the Kenyan political crisis of
the early 1920s. There was also considerable political activity in
southern Uganda, which rivalled West African territories in the early
achievement of a relatively high level of post-primary education as
well as in the emergence of a prosperous class of indigenous farmers.

But for many years the aim of political activity here was not the takeover of control from Britain of the colony as a whole, but the modernization of the traditional kingdoms, Buganda in particular, and the defence and development of their agreements with Britain against the threat of an East African Union dominated by Kenya settlers. In Southern Rhodesia, developments followed the South African pattern, albeit about a generation behind and somewhat less hopelessly. The first significant modern protest against European domination was the successful strike organized by African railway workers in 1945. The post-Federation constitution for the colony permitted limited political representation for Africans. Although in the 1960s the more radical African nationalist political parties which had emerged were banned, the European politicians were still prepared to talk with representative African leaders even if they were reluctant to modify their policies to meet their demands.

But, by and large, before the 1950s the numbers of East and central Africans gaining access to any significant level of education were usually too few to sustain continuing political activity of any degree of sophistication. A crude index of this is provided by figures for university graduates. As late as 1960, when most of the colonies were independent or shortly to become so, the numbers of African graduates in vast territories like the Belgian Congo, French Equatorial Africa, or Tanganyika were of the order of fifty or less (compared, for example, with something like 5000 for each of the Gold Coast and Nigeria and nearly 1000 for Senegal).

In these circumstances a more typical reaction to European colonial control and pressures was the formation of separatist 'Ethiopian' churches. What happened here was essentially that Africans took from the missions the basic outlines of Christian belief and enough education to be able to propagate these further. But they rejected the connection between Christianity and the culture and colonial systems that had brought it to Africa, and insisted on developing the religion in ways more adapted to African social needs. Churches of this type were not a new phenomenon, nor, for that matter, were they by any means uncommon in West or in South Africa. The Donatist church and the Coptic churches of Egypt and Ethiopia were of this type, and the first recorded instance south of the Sahara was the Antonine sect in the old Kongo kingdom, whose prophetess, Beatrice, was burned at the stake in 1706. In modern times, their greatest syncretic development may perhaps be found in the numerous Aladura churches of

West Africa. But here, and in South Africa after about 1920, the separatist churches tended to be apolitical, serving as organizational substitutes for dissolving traditional social ties or as other-worldly refuges from current discontents.

In East and central Africa, however, in default of effective properly political organizations, separatist church movements could serve to mobilize active discontent with the colonial situation. In 1915, for example, an abortive revolt against the British in Malawi was led by John Chilembwe, an American-educated African who had built up his own missionary institution. But Chilembwe had few followers, and was perhaps more a politician acting in an apolitical environment than the leader of a properly African church. On the other hand, the Kimbanguist churches in the Belgian Congo and the Kitawale movement – an African development from the American Watch Tower (*kitawale* means 'tower') – in Zambia could take on the guise of massive popular revolts against established authority. (It seems, however, to have been the shape, not the pigmentation, of the authority that was crucial. Thus while after the Belgian Congo had become independent, the major Kimbanguist groups became respectable and, indeed, secured membership of the World Council of Churches, the post-colonial regime in Zambia faced open opposition from 1964 onwards from the Lumpa church founded by Alice Lenshina.)

One further factor needs to be taken into account in explaining why, south of the Sahara, African nationalist movements first took root, and were first successful in gaining their ends, in West Africa rather than elsewhere. This is that West Africa was particularly open to the influence of international ideologies which were critical of the colonial system, or could be developed to criticize it. The depressed state of the black masses in southern Africa perhaps made them equally, or even more receptive of such ideologies. They were an obvious target for international Marxism, for example, and there was for long a tiny but dedicated minority of South African whites keen to help spread its gospel. But in South African conditions, effective political movements based on these ideologies got short shrift from the authorities.

The same was often the case in colonial times in West Africa, where known or suspected communists and their literature and organizations were commonly banned. But coastal West African society had become so open that it was quite impossible to prevent the exposure of its educated class to left-wing and radical ideologies in a general sense.

From at least the 1850s onwards, a swelling stream of West Africans had been going to Edinburgh, London, Paris and other centres for higher education; by the 1920s, the English-speaking ones had begun to go to the United States as well. In such places they could meet with representatives of oppressed coloured peoples from other parts of the world (and also with their dedicated white protagonists). West Africans had an obvious affinity with Blacks from the West Indies and the United States, who were initially more conscious than they were of a need first to defend coloured peoples from the pressures of white dominance, and then to challenge it. English-speaking West Africans were strongly influenced by such major American Black leaders as Marcus Garvey and W. E. B. DuBois. In particular they became involved in the series of Pan-African Congresses dominated by DuBois (though not initiated by him) which met from 1900 onwards in London, Paris, Brussels, Lisbon, New York and Manchester. By the time of the last of these (Manchester, 1945), what had begun essentially as a movement of New World Blacks had become in effect the training school for the future leaders of the independence movements in anglo-phone Africa, and West Africa in particular. And while the English-speaking West Africans were adopting the credo of Pan-Africanism, those from French West Africa were joining with French-speaking West Indians, such as Aimé Césaire, to evolve the parallel doctrine of *négritude*.

Though the approach via Anglo-Saxon culture and the English language was somewhat more pragmatic, and less philosophical or poetic than that through French culture and language, essentially pan-Africanism and *négritude* carried the same message. The black man need not be an inferior replica of the white; he had his own distinctive culture and history behind him. If he and his kind could unite, and absorb what they needed from white culture and not let it absorb them, the African nation would be reborn and could equal or excel anything the whites could do.

By the 1940s men bearing this gospel were returning to West Africa in some numbers, and the situation they found in the coastlands at the end of the second world war was ideal for its propagation. This was especially so in the economically and educationally most advanced colonies, which meant above all the British territories, and especially the southern parts of the Gold Coast and Nigeria (though the nature of the situation, if not perhaps its dimensions, was not dissimilar in Senegal and was becoming so in the Ivory Coast). In these places there were appreciable numbers of Africans who had in some substantial degree emancipated themselves from the constraints of traditional society: professional men; clerks and shopkeepers with at least primary education; growing numbers of wage-earners; and larger numbers of farmers receiving cash incomes from growing crops for the world market, incomes which were relatively high because of the war and post-war shortages of primary produce. To these were now added an important new element, the men who had gained education and significant experience from military service in the war. Many indeed had gained quite new perspectives from fighting alongside white British or French troops against rival white or yellow imperialists in North-East and North Africa, the Far East and in Europe itself. There were something like 200 000 of these men in all, more or less evenly divided between the British and the French colonies. Since the direct or indirect result of their endeavours had been to free lands like Ethiopia, Burma, India and even France from foreign rule, West Africans in general and these men in particular were naturally inclined to ask why this benefit should be withheld from them.

All these people, the ex-soldiers especially, looked for a better life now that the war was over. The ideals of the Atlantic Charter and the United Nations had been well publicized. They believed along with their colonial masters that the war had been a victory over forces of tyranny and oppression. But their own lands were not free. The British had still been putting into place the final coping-stones of indirect rule in the Gold Coast as late as 1943 and 1944. What was first thought on all sides to be the radical advance of establishing African majorities in the legislative councils in the Gold Coast and Nigeria in 1946 and in Sierra Leone in 1948, quickly became regarded as a sterile gesture. Few of the African members were directly elected – and these only by tiny electorates in the major towns; most of them were nominees of the chiefs or the colonial governments, and for all practical purposes the latter could pursue their own policies without hindrance.

There was a comparable disappointment on the French side. Under de Gaulle's wartime leadership, an important conference of colonial officials had been held at Brazzaville in 1944. This had recommended major changes in the structure of the French colonial empire. All France's colonial subjects should become French citizens and, as such, entitled to be represented in the constituent assembly to draw up a new constitution for France and her colonies. The empire should be transformed into a *Union* in which the colonies should share some of the responsibility for their local governance through elected assemblies. Much of this programme was in fact incorporated in the draft constitution of April 1946. But this draft was rejected at a referendum in which French metropolitan voters preponderated, and the eventual constitution of the Fourth Republic, that of October 1946, was less favourable to the colonies. Their people became citizens, but less than equal citizens. They were not all enfranchised, and elections were held in separate colleges which gave undue influence to those – Frenchmen resident in the colonies as well as the small number of Africans – who had been citizens under the Third Republic. The amount of local autonomy given to the colonies and their new territorial assemblies was also less than had been hoped for.

The general sense of frustration was heightened by the circumstances in which Britain and France were embarking on their major programmes of colonial development. These naturally increased Africans' expectations of the new world they were looking for. But, because of world shortages of capital goods, benefits from these programmes were initially far less in evidence than the flood of European technicians, advisers and teachers brought in to implement them. Thus European control and domination seemed to be being consolidated at a time when Africans, the ex-servicemen in particular, were experiencing considerable difficulty in finding suitable opportunities, especially the kinds of employment to which they felt their skills and experience entitled them. Consumer goods were also scarce and expensive, so that the increased incomes of the farmers and wage-earners did not produce the expected benefits. Essentially, of course, this was also a result of the strains imposed on the world economy by the war and by the post-war reconstruction. But because the import-export trade of West Africa was virtually entirely conducted by a handful of major European companies, the average West African could not escape concluding that his economic difficulties were caused by these companies' desire to exploit the situation to make larger profits for their shareholders.

The frustration first boiled over in the Gold Coast, the colony which so far had gained most through the European connection, and which therefore had the highest expectations. In February 1948, there were riots in the larger towns in the south and in Ashanti, in which the principal target became the stores of the major European trading companies. These were a minor disturbance compared with those the

British had faced or were to face elsewhere (for example in India); the official casualty list was 29 dead and 237 injured. But they gave a signal shock to British colonial policy-makers. The Gold Coast had always been regarded as the model colony, the one in which Africans had secured the greatest advancement and prosperity, and one in which there had been signally little violence since the Ashanti revolt of 1900. A commission of inquiry was quickly sent out. This reported forthrightly that the basic problem was that the 1946 constitution for the Gold Coast 'was outmoded at birth', that it was totally inadequate for the needs of what it perceived as a developing new nation. It recommended that the Africans themselves should help frame a new constitution which would be the first step on a rapid advance to self-government, with power being gradually transferred from the irremovable colonial service executive to African ministers responsible to a national assembly.

This proposal was quickly taken up by the British government. This must have judged that Britain could not afford to withstand West African claims to self-government at a time when she was fighting communist revolt in Malaya, and that her economic position in West Africa was strong enough to gain rather than to be undermined by cooperation with a moderate western-trained African nationalist leadership. This was represented by the United Gold Coast Convention, a political association founded in 1947 by J. B. Danquah, a prominent lawyer, and other comfortably circumstanced professional and business men, very much to develop the tradition of Casely Hayford and the National Congress of British West Africa in the 1920s. Danquah and all but one of his leading colleagues were invited to join in shaping the new constitution, and, with relatively little amendment from the Colonial Office, this was duly brought into operation in 1951. But the exception was significant. This was Kwame Nkrumah, an appreciably younger man who in his student days in America and Britain had felt the full force of the new pan-Africanism (he had been a major participant at the Manchester Congress of 1945). He could not see his colleagues as effective leaders of the nation-wide party that he thought was needed to exploit the situation. He thought, indeed, that they were selling themselves to the British. So he broke away from them, found in the current discontents in the southern Gold Coast the mass support he looked for, and channelled this into his Convention People's Party with a programme of 'self-government *now*' and of 'positive action' (e.g. strikes and boycotts) to get it. This immediately brought conflict with the British authorities. But gaol sentences for Nkrumah and his principal lieutenants only served to increase their popularity, and in 1951 the CPP won almost all the seats open to direct election in the new Legislative Assembly. The Colonial Office and the new governor it had sent to the Gold Coast, Sir Charles Arden-Clarke, made the same calculation as had been done in 1948, and Nkrumah and his colleagues were invited to take most of the ministerial seats in the executive council. The two men then cooperated together with unusual political understanding and skill. The result was that, despite some conservative and traditional opposition, especially in the regions, the Gold Coast had by 1957 been converted into an independent member of the British Commonwealth and the United Nations. The European name Gold Coast was cast aside, the new state reviving for itself the name of Ghana, the first West African state known to history.

Once the principle of a rapid advance to self-government had been accepted for the Gold Coast, it could not be denied to Britain's other West African colonies. But each of these presented problems which meant that their progress was somewhat slower. The problem in Nigeria was that it was far from easy to frame a democratic constitution which would be at once workable and acceptable to all regions of such a vast and populous territory. Northern Nigeria was the home of indirect rule, where in fact British influence had served to bolster the power of a traditional and conservative Muslim aristocracy, one looking backwards to an ideal Islam rather than forwards to the new kinds of society which Muslims in northern Africa and the Near East were trying to build. The result was that half or more than half of the population of Nigeria had been more or less deliberately sheltered from the dynamic changes which were affecting the south. Here there were two rival nationalist groupings. The National Council of Nigeria and the Cameroons, led by Nnamdi Azikiwe, an American-educated pioneer of the nationalist style adopted by Nkrumah (who had been in some measure his pupil) in the Gold Coast, had stimulated the Yoruba of western Nigeria to create an originally cultural but ultimately political association of their own, the Action Group, led by Obafemi Awolowo. The result was that the strength of the NCNC tended to become identified with the aspirations of the Ibo of eastern Nigeria, and that the two parties began to compete with each other for support elsewhere in the country.

The immediate response to this situation was to turn Nigeria into a federation, in which the North, East and West could each have a regional administration moving at its own pace and in its own way towards local autonomy. This goal was achieved by the West and East in 1957, and by the North two years later. But the problem of how to secure at the centre a stable and effective government, to which Britain might transfer power, was not effectively solved. Neither nationalist party could achieve control of the Federal government because, on a population basis, the North held half the seats in the Federal Assembly. Eventually the semblance of a democratic majority in the Assembly was put together when the Northern People's Congress – which, despite its name, was a conservative party of the northern emirs and their henchmen – formed a coalition with the more radical nationalist group, the NCNC. The NCNC hoped by this means to get rapid independence for Nigeria, and an increase of its power throughout the country. But for the NPC this was a tactical move designed to restrain the south and to prevent its dynamic emigrants from upsetting their northern society and political system while something was being done to train their own people to take over its administration from the British. The result was corruption, inefficiency, and intolerable strains, especially for the Yoruba of the West and other peoples who were excluded from the machinery of power. Yet it was to this coalition of expediency that Britain in 1960 granted Nigerian independence.

Sierra Leone faced a similar problem to Nigeria in the considerable gap in education and economic advancement between the Creoles of the Colony and the much more numerous inhabitants of the hinterland Protectorate. But for the purposes of British policy this gap seemed to be bridged over by the emergence of a Sierra Leone People's Party led by Milton Margai, a physician from the Protectorate, and independence was therefore granted in 1961. The Gambia was even smaller and poorer than Sierra Leone; indeed it was not easy to see how such a tiny country of only a third of a million people could make a viable independent state. But its people were not willing to lose their identity in a merger with the Senegal, whose territory surrounded them on three sides. They organized themselves politically, and in 1965 secured independence for their country.

The rapid decolonization of British West Africa from 1948 onwards was not without its effect on France's policy towards her adjacent colonies in West and Equatorial Africa. This was most clearly seen in the special case of Togoland. After 1945, the League of Nations mandates were converted into trusteeships under the new United Nations Organization (with the exception of that for South-West Africa, for which South Africa preferred the fiction that the mandate was still in being). British Togoland had always been administered integrally with the Gold Coast, and in 1956, when it was obvious that the latter was about to achieve independence, a majority of its people voted to share in it. This gave the French little option but to grant autonomy to their trusteeship territory (which in 1960 became an independent republic).

But by this time the French were already being rescued from the situation caused by the withdrawal of the promises held out at the Brazzaville Conference, first by their African leaders' astute exploitation of the developing political weakness of the Fourth Republic, and then by the return of de Gaulle to power as a result of the Algerian crisis. If, in 1946, the Africans had got less than they had expected, things were not the same as they were before. They now had a legal basis for political activity in the colonies to offset their control from France. Moreover, even though it took about ten times as many French citizens in Africa as it did French citizens in France to elect a representative in the legislature in Paris which ultimately controlled their destinies, at least every colony was now represented in that legislature.

The first African response to this new situation was to create a *Rassemblement Démocratique Africain* embracing almost all their political representatives, and for this to cooperate with the French Communist Party, the only effective opposition in the French legislature in the later 1940s. But this aroused the implacable hostility of the French administrators in Africa, and during 1948–50 these secured the virtual suppression of the RDA throughout the colonies. Under the leadership of Félix Houphouët-Boigny, a man of some substance from the Ivory Coast, the RDA then changed its tactics. It began to offer the votes of its small but coherent body of representatives in the French legislature to any government which would in return make concessions to the colonies. By the 1950s, the fabric of French politics was such that almost any of the numerous coalition governments of the day needed such support if it were to continue to hold office. Indeed Houphouët and other Africans began to be rewarded with ministerial appointments. In 1956, therefore, Houphouët and the RDA secured the passing of a *loi-cadre* ('outline law'), which permitted the establishment in each colony of a local elected assembly with real powers to control policy and finance.

Not all African leaders were altogether happy with some of the implications of this. The RDA was never strong in Senegal, whose voters, mindful of their long tradition of close association with France, favoured a more independent line, and where Léopold Senghor, the principal apostle of *négritude*, had emerged as a more than able successor to Lamine Gueye. Senghor argued that the *loi-cadre* was breaking up the Federations of West and Equatorial Africa into individual territories that were too small and poor to withstand pressures from France. This policy was particularly disadvantageous to Senegal, which had hitherto gained from being the base for all federal services in West Africa, and it was really beneficial only for those colonies, like Houphouët's own Ivory Coast or, in Equatorial Africa, Gabon, which were experiencing an economic revolution comparable to that in the Gold Coast a generation earlier. Most of the other territories were far too dependent on aid from France to achieve any meaningful autonomy. Within the RDA, these arguments were echoed by Sékou Touré, an appreciably younger man than Houphouët-Boigny, who had never served in French parliaments, but who had built up great strength in French Guinea through his organization of its trade union movement.

Then, in 1958, the Fourth Republic fell and de Gaulle returned to power. De Gaulle decided that the idea that the black colonies were unequivocally French possessions could be as obstructive to French interests as was the maintenance of an untrammelled French presence in Algeria. The constitution of his Fifth Republic therefore advanced the concept of a French *Communauté*. In this Community, the colonies could become 'overseas territories', legally equal with, and as autonomous in internal matters as France herself, and partners with her in a common central government to deal with foreign affairs, defence and overall economic policy. When this constitution was placed before the electorate in a referendum in September 1958, each colony was given the choice of joining the Community or of opting for complete independence outside it.

All the colonies voted for the Community except Guinea. Here Sekou Touré's influence secured a massive 'No' vote, whereupon the French immediately withdrew all their personnel, equipment and aid. But Guinea survived this summary manifestation of what could happen to a colony which did not toe de Gaulle's line. She was immediately offered aid from, and political union with, Ghana, where Nkrumah, on the point of securing a position of absolute power at home, was now devoting his major energies to the goal of bringing about a union of free African states under his messianic leadership. Soon Guinea was also receiving perhaps more realistic aid from Communist countries in Europe and Asia.

Guinea's survival was undoubtedly a factor in determining the leaders of all the other French overseas territories to escape from the mystical bonds with which de Gaulle had sought to snare them. Senegal and the French Sudan took the lead in 1959, joining in what they called the Mali Federation, and then asking for, and receiving, complete independence while remaining within the Community. In fact this federation broke up in the following year, the Sudan keeping the name Mali for itself. Though the two partners' economies were essentially interdependent, they could not agree on priorities for future development. Senegal needed as much aid as she could get just to maintain the top-heavy superstructure she had inherited from the old French West African federation, while Mali's leaders felt the need for a radical developmental approach to improve their impoverished inland territory. Following this experiment, however, all the territorial governments realized that de Gaulle's Community was an unnecessary piece of Gallic embroidery. Each negotiated its own agreement with France under which it was granted complete legal independence. But all except Guinea and Mali, which had taken unacceptable ideological stances, and the Ivory Coast and Gabon, which did not need it, continued to receive from France considerable budgetary, as well as developmental, assistance.

The fever of decolonization was now at its height. It had already reached as far into the continent as the borders of the Belgian Congo, and, the Portuguese possessions excepted, all the remaining colonies went down like ninepins before it until it came up against the *cordon sanitaire* which Rhodesia provided for the whites of South Africa.

In the Congo, the Belgians continued on their way, heedless of what was happening in the rest of the continent, until 1958–9. As late as 1956, a suggestion that they might embark on a thirty-year plan to prepare their colony for independence had been regarded as wildly idealistic. But in 1958, things began to change. A former governor-general of the Congo became Colonial Minister in Brussels, and 'decolonization' was officially mentioned for the first time. Elective councils were introduced for the larger towns, and Congolese political parties began to emerge, albeit mainly on a local or ethnic basis. For the first time, significant numbers of Congolese began to travel outside the Congo to Belgium and elsewhere. Three, including Patrice Lumumba, were able to attend a conference of African independence movements that Nkrumah held in Accra at the end of 1958. The Belgians had realized that, with independence looming for the French Congo, whose capital, Brazzaville, was separated from their Congo capital, Leopoldville (the modern Kinshasha), only by the width of the river, the traditional policy of total isolation for their colony was no longer practicable.

The result, in January 1959, was to inspire the urban proletariat of Leopoldville to take to the streets; it saw independence from European domination as the only possible relief for its social as well as political discontents. The disturbance was more substantial than the Gold Coast riots of eleven years before: the official casualty list was 49 killed and 379 injured (including 49 Europeans). The Belgian response was on the one hand to arrest the local political leaders; on the other to promise independence for the Congo. Within a year, the Belgian government and parliament were negotiating the terms for independence with Congolese leaders (some of whom had been released from gaol for the purpose) representing a plethora of political groups, some half dozen of which were of some size. In May 1960, elections were held for a national assembly, and on 1 July an independent Congo Republic was proclaimed.

The Belgians had taken a massive gamble, calculating in effect that the Congo had been so little prepared for independence that their continued presence would be seen to be essential to the territory's survival. This was true enough in the sense that the Congo was almost completely lacking in the trained men needed to run a modern state, and so had a great need for outside help. But it was also unfortunately true in the sense that no political leader or party in this vast territory commanded anything like a national following. Lumumba, who became prime minister, and his Mouvement National Congolais, came nearest to this, but they held only a quarter of the seats in the Assembly, and nearly half of their strength came from only one of the six provinces. They could not secure the trust of men like Joseph Kasavubu, the Bakongo leader and first president of the republic, and Moise Tshombe, whose power was based in Katanga and on an understanding with the European mining companies; both of these wanted a federal constitution. And within a few days the whole structure was brought down by a mutiny of the African soldiers (none of whom had risen beyond the rank of sergeant) of the *Force Publique*, the combined military and police force essential to the maintenance of order, who thought that independence meant freedom from control by their Belgian officers. The result was mayhem and chaos, and the attempted secession of Katanga, occasioning the intervention of the United Nations (including major contingents of soldiers from other African states) before eventually unity was imposed under General (later President) Mobutu Sese Seke with the help of much Western aid. The country was then renamed Zaire, and its Katanga province became Shaba.

The Congo crisis of 1960–5 was hardly a happy augury for the further extension of decolonization into eastern and central Africa. Indeed, it was a principal factor confirming hostility to the recognition of African rights on the part of all the remaining settler groups, in Portuguese as well as English-speaking Africa. Since in 1962 independence for Burundi and Rwanda, the two African kingdoms which had once been part of German East Africa, but which had then become Belgian mandates and trusteeships, followed logically upon independence for the Congo, the remaining priorities for decolonization were essentially British and Portuguese. In Britain, all political parties were now firmly committed to it. They were able to argue that, settlers notwithstanding, the British East and central African colonies, if less well equipped for African rule than Ghana or Nigeria, were better prepared for it than Zaire had been. Opportunities for higher education had existed for some time, and the legislative councils provided a ready-made means for introducing Africans to the business of conducting government at a national level.

Tanganyika was the most straightforward case. The primacy of African interests in the territory had been stressed in the terms of the League of Nations mandate and the UN trusteeship, so that the few European settlers had been unable to secure an entrenched political position in advance of the Africans, whose representatives first entered the Legislative Council in 1945. The damage done to tribal institutions in the early years of European occupation up to 1918, and the wide spread of the Swahili language and culture, also made it easy for the Tanganyika African National Union, founded in 1954 by Julius Nyerere, an Edinburgh University graduate, to establish a sense of national purpose. Nyerere also excelled at winning the confidence alike of the settlers and of the British administration. The result was that Tanganyika made a smooth transition to independence, which was achieved in 1961. However, early in 1964, there was a violent revolution in nearby Zanzibar, where the Arab regime of the Sultan (itself restored to independence the previous year) was replaced by an African people's republic which quickly aligned itself with the communist world. Almost simultaneously a mutiny in the tiny Tanganyikan army was quelled only with British help. However, Nyerere survived this blow, and shortly sought to control the extremism evident in Zanzibar by effecting the union of the island with his own republic, which was then re-named Tanzania.

Uganda, where Africans had also entered the legislative council in 1945, had even less of a settler problem than Tanganyika. On the other hand, it did face serious difficulties arising from differing levels of development and from local nationalisms. As in Nigeria, the north was economically and educationally backward compared with the south, but here it was the latter which was the home of indirect rule. Indeed, British intervention had more than bolstered up the Bantu kingdoms in southern Uganda. It had provided support to their demands for modernization, more especially in Buganda, and had commonly used their people as its agents for the extension of British power. Initially therefore, Ugandans' claims for independence, and their capacity to organize for it, tended to be compromised by the well-organized sub-imperialism of the Baganda under their *Kabaka*. Eventually however, completely fortuitous circumstances in 1961–2 caused the Baganda to join in a coalition with the nationalist party, led by Milton Obote, which represented the aspirations of most other ethnic groups, and in 1962 Britain felt able to grant Uganda its independence.

From the British point of view, the main problems of decolonization in East and central Africa were likely to arise with those territories in which white settlers had already secured some political devolution in their own interest. As far as central Africa was concerned, however, the institution of the Federation of Rhodesia and Nyasaland had had the incidental result of coalescing African opinion in each territory into a strong nationalist demand for 'one man, one vote'. Once Northern Rhodesia and Nyasaland had left the Federation, therefore, Britain quickly came to terms with the Zambian African National Congress, led by Kenneth Kaunda, and the Malawi Congress Party, headed by

Hastings Banda. In 1964 these two territories became the independent states of Zambia and Malawi respectively.

The situation in Kenya was not so simple. By 1950 the desperate shortage of land for the rapidly growing African population in and around the Highlands, together with the apparent blocking of any openings for African political complaint or advancement, both phenomena caused by European settlement, had created an Algerian-type situation. By 1950, increasing numbers of Kikuyu, the people most affected, were committing themselves by a secret ritual oath to a movement known as Mau Mau. Two years later, Mau Mau activists based in the nearby forests were continually raiding the Highlands and indiscriminately killing settlers and those Kikuyu who were lucky enough to have land or reasonable jobs. The intervention of British troops was needed to restore control and to extirpate Mau Mau, something that was not officially completed until 1959. However, Mau Mau did serve the purpose of convincing the British government that something needed to be done to alleviate African land-hunger and to secure effective African participation in the Kenyan government. But there was then a further problem in that, once normal political life had been restored, the strongest African political party, the Kenya African National Union, seemed to be too much a Kikuyu and Luo party for members of other ethnic groups. In British eyes it was also compromised by the supposed complicity of its leader, Jomo Kenyatta, in the Mau Mau movement. In 1961, it was KANU's rivals who, with support from non-Africans, formed the first national government. Independence had to wait upon Kenyatta's release from detention (1961), which produced first a coalition between KANU and the rival nationalists, and then (in 1963) a decisive electoral victory for Kenyatta and KANU.

Britain was now left to grapple with the situation in Rhodesia. Here the failure of Federation determined the settlers to go it alone. In a general election held in 1962, they secured the return of an uncompromisingly right-wing government, which set about crushing the African nationalist parties and at the same time demanded complete independence from Britain. The British Labour premier, Harold Wilson, supposed that he could talk his Rhodesian counterpart, Ian Smith, into agreeing to at least some concessions to the African majority as the price to be paid for this independence. But he had completely misjudged both his man and the mood of the greater part of the settlers. In 1965, Smith and his government made a unilateral declaration of Rhodesian independence. No country in the world recognized this, not even South Africa. But the rebels could count on the tacit sympathy and support of the whites elsewhere in southern Africa, and the economic sanctions imposed on Rhodesia by Britain and the United Nations could hardly be effective so long as it had free access to the seaports of South Africa and Portuguese Mozambique.

Except for the unresolved problem of Rhodesia, Britain was now free of colonial commitments in Africa. Indeed the dictatorial regimes in Spain and Portugal were the only colonial powers still remaining in 1965. Spain's territories were of relatively minor account. In 1968, she took a leaf out of the Belgian book and precipitately granted independence to Equatorial Guinea, i.e. the islands of Fernando Po and Annobon and a 10 000 square mile enclave of adjacent mainland. For a time, Spain held on to the Spanish Sahara, immediately south of Morocco, which – like Morocco – possessed valuable deposits of phosphates, the natural fertilizer which was becoming of crucial importance to the world's agriculture. But she soon thought it politic to accept the claims of Morocco and Mauritania to divide this thinly peopled territory between them. But until 1974, Portugal, though asserting that she had no colonies, but only some provinces of her land which happened to lie overseas, remained a colonial power in the fullest traditional sense. The result by the mid-1960s in all her three colonies of Guinea, Mozambique and Angola, was that she was facing full-scale guerrilla warfare, actively supported from the adjacent independent territories (as also were guerrilla incursions into Rhodesia). By the early 1970s, half Portugal's national budget was going to support her military forces in Africa, creating a far more serious strain on her economy than ever the Algerian war had done for France. Eventually, in 1974, the Portuguese army and people had had enough and rose in revolt. An early action of the new government was to recognize the African nationalists' claims for the independence of their territories. Since this revolution secured the ending of the dictatorship which had governed Portugal itself ever since 1926, it seemed that Africans were now also extending the benefits of freedom to a European people.

Independence for Mozambique made life much more difficult for the settler community in Rhodesia which ten years earlier had declared its unilateral independence. Hitherto armed opposition to the settler regime had been limited to spasmodic and not very effective raids sent across the river Zambezi from Zambia. But from 1975 onwards the

Rhodesians shared a long eastern land frontier with a Marxist regime
born of ten years' successful military action against the Portuguese
army and air force. Blacks in Rhodesia who wished to fight for self-
government in their own country now found it much easier to obtain
appropriate weapons and relevant military training, and soon guerrilla
warfare had engulfed most of Rhodesia outside the towns. This placed
a growing strain on the material and moral resources of the relatively
small settler society, the more so since the world recession of the
1970s was reinforcing the effect of the sanctions imposed on their
country's trade. By 1977 Ian Smith had been led to realize that international recognition of his regime would come only if the principle
of majority rule were to be accepted. However neither of the two
major African nationalist parties which were hostile to the settler
regime would co-operate with him; indeed they had only recently
come together in a Popular Front, in which the leading spirit was
Robert Mugabe, for the better prosecution of the armed struggle. So
Smith had no alternative but to deal with more flexible African politicians. The result was a new constitution which seemed at once to
promise universal suffrage and yet to preserve a privileged role for
white voters. In 1979 under this constitution, a multi-ethnic government took office under a black prime minister, Bishop Abel Muzorewa, and the country was renamed Zimbabwe-Rhodesia. But this
government was neither able to secure international recognition, nor
to end the war with the nationalists – which indeed was becoming
increasingly bloody and bitter.

As it happened, 1979 was also the year in which one of the regular
conferences of Commonwealth statesmen happened to meet nearby
in the Zambian capital of Lusaka. Leaders of all the independent
African states were firm supporters of the Rhodesian Blacks' struggle,
and were also becoming increasingly worried at its failure to achieve
success and at the damage that was being done to the country. Those
of them that were members of the Commonwealth and at its Lusaka
conference therefore persuaded Mugabe and his colleagues to meet
with Smith and Muzorewa at a round table conference in London
which they had prevailed upon Britain to call. British pressure on
both sides at this conference secured an agreement by which the
unilateral declaration of independence was revoked, and Rhodesia
became temporarily again a British responsibility while a ceasefire was
negotiated, the guerillas were disarmed and demobilized, and elections
were held under a new constitution which secured the principle of

'one man, one vote' but which also for the first seven years gave the white electors 20 seats in a 100 strong legislature. At a general election in 1980, Mugabe's wing of the Popular Front won a decisive victory, and he assumed office as the first prime minister of a new Zimbabwe.

The period of formal European political control of African affairs was now at an end.

Chapter 18

Independent Africa

For most African countries, the change from colonial status to independence had every appearance of being remarkably smooth. Substantial open conflict was really involved only in Algeria, Zaire, Zimbabwe
and the three Portuguese territories. Elsewhere what happened was
little more than that previously identified nationalist politicians and
their supporting party followers slipped quickly and easily into the
controlling positions previously held by the European rulers, and
then, with greater or less speed according to the amount and levels of
training that were available in, or which might be developed for, each
country, Africans were brought in to replace the Europeans who had
hitherto generally monopolized the higher appointments in the civil
administrative and technical services and in the police and the armed
forces. But independence was not the panacea for Africa that the
nationalist leaders had proclaimed, and that most of those who had
supported and voted for them had been led to believe; there were
major problems yet to be faced, and some of these might occasion
serious violence.

However relatively few of these problems arose out of relations
between the new African states. They all became members of the
Organization of African Unity, which was set up in 1963 with headquarters at Addis Ababa, and by and large they respected its guiding
principles of non-interference in the internal affairs of member states
and of respect for their territorial integrity. Although the European
powers had often been accused of marking out the boundaries of their
colonies in Africa with scant respect for the areas occupied by its
ethnic units, it is notable that very few of these boundaries became
the cause of trouble between the governments of the new African

states. Where there has been friction or actual conflict – as has been the case, for example, between Ethiopia and Somalia, Libya and Chad, and Burkina Faso (the former Upper Volta colony) and Mali – it has commonly been the case that the colonial boundary had not been unequivocally determined. The new African rulers were even more at one when they came to consider the last vestiges of European colonial rule on the continent. There was no hesitation in providing training and logistical support – or conduits for arms and instructors from the communist world – for the inhabitants of the Portuguese colonies and of Zimbabwe when they were fighting for their independence. They were also united in their desire to see the end of the whites' monopoly of power in South Africa. But it was quite another matter to organize anything which might actually lead to this end.

South Africa was the most formidable power in Africa south of the Sahara, and by the 1960s the whites who controlled it were in a buoyant mood. With an increasingly successful economy, they had been able to consolidate their political and military strength. Their Afrikaner majority was no longer an embittered, depressed and backward rural community. Their self-confidence fully restored by the economic and social policies of the Nationalist governments which had been consistently returned to power since Malan's initial victory in 1948, the Afrikaners were now competing equally with the English-speakers in education, business and the professions, and they had come to dominate the civil and military services. The English-speaking whites had more and more been brought tacitly to accept the Afrikaner goal of maintaining in Africa a united white nation, pledged to maintain its own version of European society and culture independently of any potentially corrupting influences or pressures coming from outside. In 1960, the all-white electorate took the opportunity given them by the government of Dr Verwoerd to choose by plebiscite to return to the Afrikaner tradition of the Great Trek, declaring that they wished to live in a Republic of South Africa. When, at a Commonwealth Conference in the following year, the leaders of other African Commonwealth countries raised the question of whether the new republic should automatically succeed to the Union of South Africa's membership, Verwoerd's government chose not to submit to the judgement of its peers and withdrew their country from the Commonwealth.

Steadfast in their determination to maintain their position on the continent, the South African whites realized that they needed to come to the best terms they could with the emergent black African states to their north. As they saw it, South Africa's industrial strength made it a natural trading partner for the new states, which they felt must for the most part remain producers and exporters of primary agricultural and mineral commodities. Initially instinct led the South African whites to think that the frontier between the two political and economic systems might lie as far north as the Zambezi. But during the 1970s their leaders came to appreciate that neither the Portuguese colonial and settler system in Angola and Mozambique nor settler society in Rhodesia were robust enough to halt the advance of black nationalism. They recognized that the boundary must be the Limpopo; the best they could hope for further north was that their new black neighbours, whatever their political views, would accept that their lands and South Africa were economically interdependent.

However during the years in which the black nationalists in all three of the territories immediately to the north were fighting to gain control of their lands, white South Africa had always displayed its ideological hostility to them – and had commonly given active aid to their enemies – while most of the practical support for their struggle had come directly or indirectly from the communist world. Such things hardly encouraged them to cooperate with a white South African regime which gave citizenship only to whites; they therefore provided shelter and support to the militants of the African National Congress who had taken to violence after their movement had been outlawed by the South African government following the massacre at Sharpeville. There was the further complication of South West Africa. After the first world war, South Africa had received from the League of Nations the mandate for the administration of this former German colony, but when, after the second world war, the League was replaced by the United Nations Organization, South Africa was alone among the states entrusted with League of Nations mandates in not agreeing that its mandate should be converted into a UN trusteeship.

South West Africa was largely desert or near desert, and it was very thinly peopled except in two areas. Most of the indigenous population, mainly Ovambo, was concentrated in the extreme north close by the border with Angola. However, in the southern half of the country, a belt of highlands between the coastal plain and the Kalahari had attracted European settlement, initially mainly by Germans, but then increasingly by Afrikaners. Just after the Second World War, there were nearly 50 000 whites in a total population of some 430 000. One factor in South Africa's refusal to accept a UN trusteeship agreement was undoubredly a wish to protect the interests of the white minority; another was that the territory possessed appreciable mineral wealth, in diamonds in particular. In due course South African governments began to move to integrate South West Africa with their own republic and its system of apartheid, while the UN took steps to proclaim the illegality of the South African administration in South West Africa and to rename the country Namibia. An important consequence of these developments was the emergence of a South West African People's Organization as a full-blooded nationalist movement. Something like two-thirds of the indigenous population were Ovambo, so naturally they took a leading role in SWAPO, and as the Ovambo were concentrated along the border with Angola, they could hardly help being influenced by the success in that territory of armed resistance to European power. By the early 1970s a considerable element in SWAPO had raised the standard of revolt against the South African regime, and this was soon being sustained by arms, logistical support and training provided from Angola. As part of their effort to defeat the SWAPO revolt, the South African army and air force began to make regular incursions into southern Angola and there to give support to the *União Nacional para a Independência Total de Angola*. This was a southern-based Angolan nationalist movement which had lost out to, and had embarked on revolt against, the *Movimento Popular de Libertação de Angola*, which had taken power in the capital, Luanda, and was in receipt of strong support – spearheaded by Cuban military and technical assistance – from communist sources.

The military activities of the South Africans tended to outrage world opinion. They also proved rather more successful in sustaining UNITA than they were in suppressing opposition to their rule in Namibia. By 1978, the South Africans were coming to the conclusion that they should seek a political solution in Namibia through the creation for the territory of a multiracial regime to which they might hand over responsibility for its administration, and which at the same time could be trusted to have care for their own particular interests in it. While the South Africans found it by no means easy to secure adequate support for such a scheme in Namibia, it not unnaturally incurred outright condemnation from the Black African members of the United Nations with their continuing hostility to the situation within South Africa itself. In the Republic, it was impossible to maintain apartheid without rigid control of the whole black population and continual police activity against anyone, white as well as black, who sought to evade or mitigate or even to criticize the system. To be sure, the idea of separate development for the Blacks was now being actively implemented. Beginning with the Transkei in 1976, autonomy was granted to a number of the larger 'tribal homelands'; the parliament, administration and judiciary of the South African Republic ceased to be responsible for their internal affairs. The idea was that if all the Blacks in South Africa became citizens of one of these 'Bantustans' – or of the three former British protectorates – then all their political aspirations would have been met; any Black who entered the white Republic, whether in search of employment or for any other purpose, would come as a foreigner who would have no right to challenge any administrative controls imposed upon him by the authorities.

But such Bantustans could never be a realistic solution to South Africa's major problem, nor could they ever be really independent of the economic, military and – ultimately – the political power of the over-mighty Republic in which they were encased. They were too small, too poor, and too lacking in resources and developmental potential. No more than the former protectorates could they provide even a minimal standard of living for the mass of the black population of South Africa, a population which was growing at about 3 per cent a year, so that by the mid-1980s it would number some 25 000 000 (compared with about 5 000 000 whites, 3 000 000 Coloureds, and about a million Asians). The Blacks continued to be dependent on the one South African economy, and the great majority of them had no alternative but to work, and for the most part to live, within the borders of the Republic. No country in the world agreed to recognize the new states created by the South African government, and the leaders of some of the largest and proudest of the old Black nations, the Zulu most notably, also regarded their independence as a sham, and refused to countenance it for themselves.

So long as the majority of the inhabitants of the Republic continued to live under a system which denied them political rights, and in which their freedom of movement and their access to employment, education and other social benefits were all subject to control, so it was probably inevitable that the Blacks would increasingly resort to violence. From 1976 onwards, indeed, violence became more and more a part of South African life. On the Blacks' side, it had two main forms. There were more or less instinctive uprisings of young people, particularly in the sprawling townships built outside the cities, and directed not so much against whites and their property as against the life and property of Blacks who went along with the system the whites had erected and who had some authority or status within it. By 1985 disturbances of this kind had become widespread, troops as well as police were being used in attempts to suppress them, and the damage being done and the loss of life involved – Blacks killed by Blacks as well as Blacks killed by the government forces – were so considerable that the government declared states of emergency and forbade independent reporting of any unrest. It seems likely that deaths amounted to something like 1000 a year. Secondly, a militant wing of the outlawed ANC embarked on a campaign of bombing. This was not on a very substantial scale, but it served to confirm the ANC as the leading organization of active hostility to white rule, and the demand for the release from prison of its leader, Nelson Mandela, became a rallying call for almost all the discontented. On the government side, soldiers and police were ever more ready to harrass and assault Blacks and to open fire on them.

The Nationalist governments of J. B. Vorster (1966–78) and P. W. Botha (1978 onwards), which had to face the growing spiral of violence and counter-violence, could not countenance the abandonment of the basic principle of apartheid, but, even before violence became endemic, they began increasingly to see that the continued strict application of the system in all its details might be counterproductive. If, despite the world depression that began in the 1970s, the white minority was to continue to prosper from the economy it commanded, the more it needed the co-operation of the other races. The white community alone could neither provide a large enough market nor sufficient skilled workers. It therefore made sense to grant some recognition to the new trade unions which began to emerge among the black workers during the 1970s. It was seen that it did not make sense to treat all black workers as migrant labourers; the more skilled among them should be allowed to become permanent residents in the townships. Such people need no longer be banned from access to public places, such as hotels and places of entertainment, which had hitherto been reserved for whites only. Mixed marriages became legal (even if the partners in one could find it difficult to find a residential area in which they both might legally live).

No government was yet prepared to consider granting political rights for Blacks within its jurisdiction (these were to be available for them only within the Bantustans), but, with the whites becoming an ever smaller proportion of the total population of what they thought of as their own country, Botha thought it sensible to try and make the Coloured and Asian minorities junior partners in the government of the Republic. To this end a referendum was held in 1984 in which the white voters endorsed a new constitution by which a handful of Coloured and Asian ministers were added to the national cabinet. But this cabinet still remained responsible to an all-white legislative assembly elected only by white voters. However, in addition lesser cabinets of Coloured and Asian ministers were instituted, each of which became responsible for the affairs of its own community to one of two other assemblies, elected by Coloured and Asian voters respectively. The whole tripartite scheme came under an executive president, a role Botha took for himself. It was by no means obvious that the new constitution would achieve what Botha intended. Partnership with the Coloured and Asians, together with the relaxation of the apartheid laws, served to alienate more conservative supporters of the Nationalist Party which had won all the elections since 1948. Yet it was uncertain whether many Coloureds or Asians would think that the new constitution gave their people a fair share of power, and it was certain that most Blacks would look on it as an attempt permanently to exclude them from having any voice in the central government of their own land.

The ever more stringent measures taken to maintain South Africa's apartheid regime – which included the mounting of military raids into other countries which sheltered ANC activists, like Mozambique and Zambia – incurred world-wide criticism. Black African states, which were not in a position to take positive action by themselves in respect of South Africa, had begun to urge concerted international action against the regime as soon as each achieved its independence. By the 1970s more and more was being heard, outside the continent as well as within it, of the need for international action of some kind. But it proved impossible to get agreement on anything more than a ban on the sale of arms to the South African government, and in practice this had little practical result, not least because South Africa's scientists and industry were capable of producing all the weapons its government could require (and, given clandestine access to the relevant foreign designs or designers, these included some of the most sophisticated ones, such as helicopters and jet fighters). By the mid-1980s many nations all over the world were calling for embargoes on trade with, and on investment in South Africa, but it was not possible to secure international agreement for such sanctions. Thus, in the United Kingdom (which, together with the USA, the German Federal Republic, and Japan accounted for the bulk of South Africa's foreign trade), a Conservative government took the line that sanctions would do more harm than good, in that they would be most harmful to Blacks who could not support themselves other than through participation in a successful white-led economy.

South Africa therefore remained a major threat hanging over the future of the continent, constituting a problem Africans had to continue to face and for which there seemed very little hope of finding any quick or peaceful solution. In practice most Africans found they had more immediate problems to worry them in their own countries.

The most common of these problems was that, compared with the Republic of South Africa, the majority of the new states in Africa were not well off. During the 1960s and 1970s, the Republic's economy had been growing steadily at an average rate, in real terms, of 2.5 per cent per annum, with the result that by the beginning of the 1980s the country's gross national product (GNP) was around $2500 per head. It is true that this was not very large when compared with the world's richest nations; the comparable figure for the USA, for example, was over $11 000, and even for the United Kingdom it was nearly $8 000. It is also true that in South Africa wealth was very unevenly distributed between the races. In mining or industrial employment, for example, the salaries of whites were on average at least five times higher than the wages paid to Blacks. More generally, almost all whites were in high income employment while almost all those Blacks who were wage-earning were in low-paid unskilled jobs. In South Africa as a whole, of course, substantial numbers of Blacks had little cash income at all, but lived close to the subsistence level, particularly in the homelands and in the Bantustans (which do not figure in the Republic's statistical returns). Nevertheless, if allowance is made for these things, it is probable that in 1980 the share of the Republic's GNP attributable to its black inhabitants might have been not much less than $1000 per head. Even so, in terms of money, black men and women in the Republic would seem to have been better off than the inhabitants of almost any other country in Africa south of the Sahara.

In 1979, twenty-five of the thirty-nine other countries south of the Sahara for which the relevant data were available were among the world's poorest states, and had mean annual incomes per head between

$110 and $370. A further twelve, ranked as 'middle income countries', had mean annual incomes per head between $380 and $720, with a median figure of $530. In some of the poorer countries, between 1960 and 1979 there had been little or no real growth in per capita GNP; in eight of the thirty-nine, the statistics showed 'negative growth', i.e. their people had actually become poorer. These included three countries in the middle income range: Ghana and Senegal, which in colonial times had been among the most developed lands, and Angola, in which the major new resource of petroleum had become available for exploitation. Only fourteen countries had rates of growth which were as good as, or better than South Africa's, and three of these were the former British protectorates in southern Africa which were closely tied to the Republic's economy (even though one of these, Lesotho, was a 'low income country'). South of the Sahara, only the Ivory Coast and Gabon had GNPs per capita as good as or better than the average share of South Africa's GNP that has been estimated for each of its black inhabitants. The Ivory Coast had a GNP of $1040, whilst in Gabon, where a thin population in a land replete with resources of oil and other minerals meant that growth per annum was 6 per cent, GNP per capita had risen to the high figure of $3280.

It could be argued that a substantial part of the explanation why – Gabon excepted – the other countries of sub-Saharan Africa had not developed wealth to compare with that of South Africa was that they had not succeeded in integrating their economies with the world economy as swiftly and as successfully, and also that they had not as yet embarked on significant industrialization. With independence, therefore, the new leaders of these countries almost without exception embarked on development strategies which involved increasing production for export of primary agricultural and mineral products, and taxing, and borrowing against, the resultant income from the world markets to provide funds for the development and diversification of the economy and the improvement of society. In particular they planned to improve education, health, housing and other amenities, so that more people could live in towns and work in new industries. The output of these industries should mean that less of the national income would need to be expended on imported manufactures, so that more funds would be available to pay interest on foreign borrowings and ultimately to reduce them.

Much the same economic strategy was followed in the five countries north of the Sahara. Although Egypt, Tunisia and Algeria had all anticipated the tropical African countries in their entrance into the world economy, in their ability to attract foreign investment, and in the introduction of industry, Morocco had been very isolated prior to 1912, and before the 1960s Libya had been little more than about a million people existing on the fringes of the desert. Up to the 1960s these five countries were all largely dependent for such foreign earnings as they had on the export of primary agricultural produce, and here, unlike tropical African countries, they often had the disadvantage of competing directly with the more developed agricultures of the European lands that were their neithbours across the Mediterranean. Nevertheless, starting from higher levels than the tropical countries had been able to reach, they were generally able to achieve higher real growth rates, sometimes as high as 6 per cent per annum or even greater. In Libya the situation had been transformed by the mid-1970s through the exploitation of the great petroleum resources that had been found to lie beneath its sands; instead of being one of the poorest countries on the continent, GNP per head shot up to more than $5000. Algeria, with its very much larger population, had also gained from the exploitation of oil and natural gas; by the end of the 1970s, its GNP per head was some $1800. Development in Morocco and Tunisia, though helped by profits from tourism, had been less spectacular; by 1980 they were towards the top of the middle income range with GNPs per head of around $850. Egypt, with its very large population (by the mid-1980s it was to reach 50 000 000), and the continual warfare or threat of warfare with Israel (which lasted until the Sadat–Begin agreement in 1979), was *sui generis*. Its GNP was only about $500 per head, and it was very dependent on subsidies from Saudi Arabia and the other oil-rich but thinly peopled Arab countries, which, in the turbulence of the Middle East, felt a need to have behind them the substantial military forces Egypt's large and comparatively well-educated population could provide.

During the 1960s, the development strategy followed in most African states worked well enough. Real growth in the economies south of the Sahara generally could not match the North African rates, but even so it averaged around 3 per cent a year. But there were obvious limits to the extent to which industrialization could be profitably developed in the sub-Saharan countries, for few of them possessed sufficient population to provide a market large enough to support more than a handful of small secondary industries. A desire to create larger markets had been one of the factors that had led the

British and French to group small colonies together in federations, but these did not survive the colonies' independence. In 1980 there were only nine states besides South Africa south of the Sahara which had attained populations in excess of 10 000 000; these were Nigeria, Ethiopia, Zaire, Tanzania, Sudan, Kenya, Uganda, Ghana and Mozambique. At the same time there were as many as seven mainland states – Equatorial Guinea, Djibouti, Swaziland, the Gambia, Gabon, Guinea-Bissau, and Botswana – which each counted less than 1 000 000 inhabitants.

In the 1970s, however, the standard development strategy began to run into trouble, and by the mid-1980s there were not more than about half a dozen countries in the whole continent which were still experiencing any economic growth in real terms. One reason for this was the great increase in oil prices that occurred during the 1970s. The programmes of modernization and industrialization all depended for their success on adequate amounts of reasonably priced energy being available. Few African countries possess good indigenous sources of energy. South of the Sahara, the geography is generally such that considerable investment – in distribution networks as well as in dams and generating machinery – is needed to produce worthwhile quantities of hydroelectric power, and this investment has not readily been forthcoming except where large transnational corporations have been interested in the production of electricity for their own commercial smelting operations. This has happened really only in Ghana, Guinea, Zaire and Zambia; apart from these, little significant hydroelectric power has been developed outside Nigeria, Cameroun, Uganda, Kenya and Mozambique. Few countries in the continent except South Africa possess substantial deposits of coal; there is virtually no other coal-mining outside Zimbabwe, Zambia, Botswana, Mozambique, Nigeria and Morocco. Most African countries have therefore had to depend on petroleum products for anything between 60 and 90 per cent of the energy required to power their factories and transport, and to give their citizens the possibility of good supplies of power, light and water.

From the 1950s onwards, oil (and sometimes natural gas) began to be extracted from beneath the soils of a number of African countries. Libya, Nigeria, Algeria, Egypt, Gabon, Angola, Tunisia and Congo became significant producers of petroleum products; the first three indeed came to be ranked among the world's major exporters of oil, and – as has already been stated – in per capita terms, Libya and

Gabon became the continent's two richest countries. All the other African states of course had no alternative but to import oil. In the 1960s, this caused little problem; oil, in addition to being an easily portable source of energy, was also a cheap one. But in the 1970s, its price began to rise. At the beginning of the decade, a barrel (160 litres) of crude oil sold for about $1.80. By mid-1973 the price had risen to some $3.00, and then, because the Middle Eastern states which produced so much of the world's petroleum were trying to bring pressure on the western countries which supported Israel in the Yom Kippur war (in which Egypt and Syria sought – with success in the Egyptian case – to regain territory they had lost in previous wars), it shot up to $12 or more. A further substantial increase began in 1979 after Iran deposed its Shah and was invaded by Iraq; by 1981 the price was about $34 (and it was to stay around this level for the next four years before falling to more tolerable figures of $18 or less). This twentyfold increase in the price of oil in the short space of a decade seriously damaged all African development programmes except those of the handful of oil-producing countries, and these suffered with the others from a more general effect of the great rise in oil prices. The oil price rise helped to fuel a world-wide inflation, which meant that the capital and manufactured goods the African countries needed to secure from the developed countries in order to help develop their own lands became much more expensive. This in its turn led to a world-wide economic depression, as a result of which the developed countries bought less of the primary commodities produced by the developing nations, so that the prices of these commodities fell and less money was available to the latter for buying from abroad.

The situation was made worse because during the 1970s it was becoming apparent that, although the great majority of Africans throughout the continent were farmers, more and more African countries were failing to grow enough food to feed themselves, and consequently needed to spend some of the earnings from their exports on importing foodstuffs – thus, of course, diminishing their ability to buy from abroad the goods and services required for their development programmes. The underlying reason for the growing inability of African countries to feed themselves was that for some time their populations had been growing at ever increasing rates. By the 1970s, rates of natural increase (i.e. the excess of births over deaths) throughout the continent were around 3 per cent per annum, a high rate which meant that almost everywhere the number of mouths needing to be fed could be expected to double in rather less than a quarter of a century.* This might have placed a less severe strain on African food production had the development programmes paid more attention to improving life for farmers, by providing the countryside with better facilities in the form of education, medical services, water supplies and the like, and more attention also to encouraging the production and improving the distribution of foodstuffs for domestic consumption. But farmers had been encouraged to grow the crops that could best bring in export earnings, and many of the African commodities that were in demand in the world markets were crops like coffee, cocoa, tea, tobacco, sisal and rubber, which could not be used as domestic foodstuffs. As has been seen, the export earnings were to be used to develop the 'modern' sectors of the economy, the extraction of minerals in demand in the world markets and in particular the development of industry and of the towns that housed the labour and services required by industry and mining. Thus not only was little attention generally given to rural development, but the countryside and the farmers were being taxed and exploited to support the growth of mining, industry and the towns.

As these modern sectors grew, so there were less people available to grow foodstuffs and more people needing to be supplied with them. Labour was attracted from the countryside into the towns by the relatively high money wages offered by industry and the mines. As the towns grew, so they came to offer more and better facilities than were available (or could easily be made available) in the rural areas – electricity and piped water, roads and transport, markets and shops, hospitals and schools, and a great variety of other services and of entertainments. Soon people were being sucked from the countryside into the towns as much by the services and attractions available in them as they were by the employment prospects offered by industry or mining (and, of course, as the towns grew, so more people could find employment in them just by serving those who already lived there).

The temperate zones at each end of the continent had been relatively well equipped with sizeable towns and cities before population growth

* The trend is likely to be reversed in the future if the spread of Aids cannot be halted by a vaccine or other controls. The Aids infection was first recognized in the USA in 1981, but it seems that it had been active in central Africa since at least the early 1970s, and possibly earlier. By 1987 it had spread throughout East Africa and south to the Zambezi, and was entering West Africa. If totally unchecked, it could wipe out the present sexually active generation and the children born to it.

had begun markedly to accelerate. In North Africa, they had been a feature of life for two thousand years or more, and by 1945 there were ten towns with more than 100 000 inhabitants in Egypt (Cairo and Alexandria each had more than a million), nine in Morocco, four in Algeria, and one each in Libya and Tunisia. Towns had also appeared relatively swiftly in southern Africa following upon the growth of white settlement and the early development of mining and industry. By 1945 South Africa had eleven towns with more than 100 000 people and Southern Rhodesia had two. But elsewhere in Africa in 1945, towns and cities of any size had been a rarity; Nigeria had had four cities with more than 100 000 inhabitants, but all the other countries between them possessed only seven. However, in the short space of thirty years after 1945 the number of towns in Africa with more than 100 000 inhabitants grew from 49 to 120 or more. There was hardly a single country which did not have at least one (and Nigeria counted no less than 32). For sub-Saharan Africa, it was estimated that during the 1960s and 1970s the number of people living in towns had doubled, that by 1980 more than a fifth of the people were living in towns, and that – if urbanization were to continue to develop at such a rate – by the 1990s half the population might be expected to be town dwellers.

From 1973 onwards, the problem of growing enough food in Africa to feed its growing and increasingly urbanized population was made much worse because there were a series of successions of years in which the amounts of rain received, particularly in the arid and semi-arid zones between 10° and 30° either side of the equator, were markedly less than the average. Crops failed and pastures became exhausted, with the result that grazing animals died or had to be moved onto lands that had hitherto been able to support crops and a higher level of food production. The result was a series of disastrous famines with which African countries and their governments found it difficult to cope without substantial foreign assistance. They lacked the funds to buy the surplus foodstuffs that western European and North American farmers were producing, nor did they possess the vehicles and the organization needed to distribute substantial quantities of food to large numbers of people who had hitherto fed themselves. After the animals, millions of people were to die, especially if they were infirm, or very young or very old. The survivors fled to swell the populations of the towns, or were brought together in refugee camps with minimal shelter and sanitation, there to be supplied by international relief agencies with what was hoped to be enough food and medical care to permit as many as possible to survive both the famines and the epidemics – of infectious diarrhoea, measles and pneumonia – and the tuberculosis that accompanied them.

Failure of the seasonal rains was nothing new in African history. Experience had taught almost all farmers and cattle-herders living in the lands between the rain forests and the deserts how to survive a single season of less than adequate rainfall, but failure of the rains over two or more successive years – which might well occur at least once in every one or two decades – would always bring famines and epidemics. However, in the past it would seem as though these may have been less cataclysmic. Populations had been much smaller and, because infant mortality had been high and the expectation of life had been shorter, there were fewer younger, older and infirm people to be looked after. Communities were thus leaner and more mobile, and, because there were less people to occupy the land, it was not too difficult to find new lands into which they might move, temporarily or even permanently, if disaster struck their homeland. Furthermore before the twentieth century and the great increase both of population and of 'development', the land itself had been better able to withstand drought. The grasslands were not so heavily grazed, and there had been less demand for trees to be cut down to provide firewood, timber and space for fields and houses. Forests and savannah woodlands alike had been much more able to regenerate themselves, and so to help keep moisture in the soil and to check erosion. But in colonial and post-colonial times the growing populations in the dryer lands had come to have increasingly little room for manoeuvre, and some effort had been made to maintain them on their traditional lands by providing, or helping them to secure, dams and boreholes, better breeds of plants and animals, and artificial fertilizers. It could be even argued that the provision of relief foodstuffs might make matters worse in the long run, enabling people to stay on land which could not be depended upon to support them, and helping them to develop tastes for expensive imported foodstuffs.

By the 1980s, the combined effects of worsening terms of trade, inflation, unchecked population growth and urbanization, the decline of food production, and sometimes famine, had brought many African states face to face with another problem. Payments of the interest due on the foreign loans they had acquired to help finance their development programmes – let alone any repayments of the capital that had been borrowed – were becoming a very high proportion of their GNPs, and were eating up more and more of their diminishing foreign earnings. For Zaire, for example, it was estimated that two-thirds of 1982's export earnings would be required to meet the charges due on its foreign debt in that year together with what was still owed for 1981. The Sudan was in a similar situation. These were both countries in which there had been considerable internal unrest, but the position was not very different in a peaceful and apparently very prosperous country like the Ivory Coast. Here in 1984 it was calculated that the total external debt was equivalent to more than 90 per cent of the GNP! In circumstances like these, many African governments could see no alternative but to ask the International Monetary Fund (IMF) to arrange for the rates of interest on their debts to be reduced and for the periods over which they were to be repaid to be extended. In return for such rescheduling, they were required to agree to considerable restrictions on their freedom to determine their future economic policies.

Such restrictions not unnaturally gave rise to charges that the rich and developed nations that lent money abroad, and which managed bodies like the IMF, were engaged in 'neocolonialism', in that, while the former colonies might have secured political independence, they were still in situations of economic dependency. But most African countries really had no choice in the matter. The plain fact was that in the 1980s the inhabitants of most of the new states were not securing the betterment they had thought would follow independence. Sometimes they were just about holding their own, but often they were actually becoming poorer in that GNP per head was declining. It was declining not only in drought-afflicted low-income countries like Mali, Niger and Ethiopia, but also in what had been regarded as comparatively prosperous middle-income countries such as Kenya, Senegal, Zimbabwe, the Ivory Coast and Tunisia. Even in the oil-exporting countries, all was not plain sailing. While by the mid-1980s, GNP per head in Libya had risen to the dizzy height of something like $10 000, other major oil-producers might not be particularly well off in per capita terms, especially perhaps as oil prices fell away from their 1981 peak. GNP per head in Gabon was estimated to have fallen to about $2800, and in Nigeria, with its enormous population – estimated by 1985 to have grown to 100 000 000 – GNP per head would seem to have remained more or less static around $700. As has been already mentioned, Angola was another oil-exporting country in which GNP per head seems to have remained static at a low level of about $450; conversely, in the non oil-producing country of Ghana, GNP per head seems to have begun to grow during the 1980s, whereas previously it had been declining at a time when elsewhere in independent Africa it had been tending to increase. Explanations for such apparent anomalies can only be found from looking at the political history of the new states.

The governments of the new states were all likely to face political problems arising from difficulties in fulfilling popular expectations aroused by independence. They had almost invariably come to power following success in one or more elections at the time of independence or during the run-up to it. The electoral campaigning had brought to a focus popular consciousness of the great changes brought to Africa during the period of colonial rule. Through the growth of education and literacy, through the increased circulation of newspapers and the prospects for independence voiced in them by the nationalist leaders, through the spread of broadcasting and sometimes also the advent of television, it had become apparent to even the inhabitants of the remotest villages that colonial rule had been no more than a provincial and distant extension of twentieth-century industrial civilization. Now that their countries had been freed from colonial dependency, and had acquired a status in the councils of the United Nations which was legally equal to that of other nations, people expected that the benefits of modern civilization would become more available, and would flow to them more quickly and easily, so that they would all enjoy a higher standard of living. It was supposed that this growth in betterment and in wealth would be the easier since there would no longer be any need to reward the corps of foreigners who had recently been engaged in governing, administering and exploiting their countries. Moreover the new indigenous rulers should be able to ensure that the activities of, and the rewards flowing to, foreign traders and investors would not be decided solely by themselves in their own interests, but would be commensurate with the needs and interests of the new African nations.

But the posts that the new rulers had taken over from the Europeans brought them much higher standards of living in the shape of salaries, housing, cars and other perquisites and status symbols than could possibly be immediately attainable by more than a handful of their electors. The new rulers were also commonly faced with a need to reward the party stalwarts and the local men of influence who had helped them win the votes that had brought them to power. Such people were therefore given government or para-government appointments. Sometimes they were not well qualified for such appointments, and sometimes too there were not enough sufficiently well-remunerated jobs available, so new ones were created for them. Furthermore, these new men who had been brought into the ruling elite all had their own supporters and relations to reward. Therefore the new post-independence governments could appear less efficient and more expensive than the colonial ones they had replaced. The ordinary men and women who had voted them into office would think that too many of the benefits of independence were going to a privileged minority, and too few to themselves. There was a further problem in that, if the lot of the ordinary man and woman was to be improved, the programmes of betterment that were needed usually cost substantially more than was immediately available from local resources, so that post-independence governments were apt to look to the developed countries to assist them in their development plans. But before such plans could possibly begin to generate significant new wealth which would be available to be used for the general good, dissatisfaction was likely to be increased: sizeable sums would have been spent on buying equipment from abroad and in employing foreign experts, and probably also in servicing foreign loans, and doubtless too still more jobs would have been found for hangers-on of the ruling elite.

Growing popular dissatisfaction with the performance of the new African governments did not encourage the leaders of these governments to submit to the verdict of fresh elections. They tended instead to maintain that party politics were an expensive luxury developing nations could not really afford. They would assert that the nationalist party which had won independence – and of which the head of government was often life chairman – represented the political mobilization of the whole nation which was necessary if all its people were to advance and prosper. This thesis might be supported with arguments drawn from the pre-colonial past, for it could be said that in traditional African societies the national will had in general been determined less by any periodic counting of popular votes than by the elders' estimation of what the populace wanted and of what might be good for the nation. But there was of course the difference that the elders had come to their places as guardians of the nation by tradition and inheritance, whereas the post-independence rulers had won theirs by some form of popular election. So if, while failing to provide for the aspirations of those who had elected them, they continued in office for longer than expected, dissatisfaction with their rule could only increase. They would come to be in a position not dissimilar to that of the European colonial rulers. But these in the last resort could maintain themselves in power through their control of military force, and here there was a difference. European governors could rest assured that the European officers who commanded the troops would always defend the colonial regime and stand with them against any opposition to it from its African subjects. But after Africans had succeeded to the command of the military they could choose, when it came to the pinch, whether they should continue to support the government or whether they might claim that the African commanders of African armies were a less corrupt and more efficient élite than the politicians and that the interests of their fellow Africans throughout the country would be better served if they were to take power.

In modern times in Africa, the first example of a civilian regime being overthrown by military action was the coup by army officers in Egypt in 1952 which ended by bringing Nasser to power. Thereafter Africa has witnessed many other military coups; from 1963 to 1987 there were something like sixty occasions on which armed force was successfully used to take over power in an African country; if unsuccessful coups were also to be counted, the number would be substantially larger. Military takeovers tend to be dramatic events of the kind which always attracts more attention in the world news media than the more humdrum aspects of government and administration, so that a common impression has arisen that instability and violence are characteristic of post-independence African history. While it may be questioned whether this history has been any more violent than the contemporary history of many other parts of the world, there is no gainsaying that in Africa military intervention has tended to become a fairly normal means of changing a country's government. But both the circumstances of these interventions and their consequences can vary quite widely.

Sometimes the soldiers have done no more than to arrange for fresh elections to be held, following which power would be handed over to the politicians who won them. More commonly perhaps the soldiers have shared power with civilians. A high-ranking officer would preside over the government and chair a supreme military council. However some civilians might be appointed to this council, and even if this were not the case, the public departments under it might well still be led by civilians, and almost invariably most of the day-to-day business of government would be left in the hands of much the same civilian administrators and bureaucrats, magistrates, policemen and so forth as had conducted it before. In all these cases, such violence as occurred was likely to be essentially symbolic; few or any lives need be lost through the military's usurpation of authority. Nevertheless any military takeover brought with it an in-built danger. If one particular group of soldiers could overthrow constituted authority through the exploitation of their possession of military force (and thereafter enjoy the fruits as well as the responsibilities of power), they were setting a dangerous example for other groups of the military. Rival commanders, lesser officers, even NCOs and ordinary soldiers, might chose to follow this example if they thought the first group had not improved the conduct of government or had been corrupted by power, or simply because they thought they would like a share of the fruits of power for themselves. If a first military takeover were to be followed by this kind of secondary coup, and still more if it were to be followed by more than one such secondary coup, then fighting was likely to occur and, following each coup, the day-to-day conduct of government could well become more military, more arbitrary and more violent.

By the end of 1987, if South Africa and the remoter island states are excluded, more than a third of the independent African states – eighteen out of forty-seven – had never experienced a military take-over, and a further fourteen – nearly another third – had experienced only one. The five states north of the Sahara had all shown consider-able stability. The system of government established by Nasser in Egypt survived the strains of the wars with Israel and the subsequent uncertainties of Middle Eastern affairs, and this despite his premature death in 1970 and the assassination in 1981 of his immediate successor, General Anwar Sadat. In 1969 young Libyan army officers led by Colonel Gaddafi followed the Egyptian example and replaced their country's monarchy with an Arab socialist regime, and in 1965 another military officer, Colonel Boumédienne, ousted the first president of an independent Algeria, Ben Bella. Gaddafi was still in power in 1987, and when Boumédienne died in 1978 there was an orderly succession in Algeria. In Morocco, the monarchy has continued in control. The architect of Tunisian independence, Bourguiba, survived until 1987, when the prime minister he had recently appointed decided that a senile octogenarian should no longer continue as president.

There have also been stable regimes south of the Sahara. In 1987, in eleven of the states in which independence had been achieved in the 1960s (Botswana, Cameroun, Gabon, the Gambia, the Ivory Coast, Kenya, Malawi, Senegal, Tanzania, and Zambia), the government was either still being led by the man who had been in command at the time of independence or, if he had died or retired, power had passed in an orderly manner to an accepted successor. The same was true of six of the second generation of new states which had come into being during 1974–80 (namely Angola, the Cape Verde Islands, Djibouti, Mozambique, São Tomé and Principe, and Zimbabwe). But this did not mean that there had been no violence in these states. In 1964, for example, very soon after their independence, Kenya, Tanzania and Gabon had all experienced mutinies in their armed forces which were only put down by military interventions mounted by their former colonial masters, while in Angola and Mozambique there was hardly less fighting after independence than in the years leading up to it.

The military coups in Egypt and in Libya which had brought Nasser and Gaddafi to power took place essentially because relatively young army officers had concluded that a hereditary monarchy, together with its hangers-on, did not provide a suitable vehicle for the modernization of their country and for securing for the ordinary men and women who inhabited it a just share of its wealth. In their eyes, the system was both too self-interested and too inefficient. Coups which took place in Liberia and Ethiopia were similar in intention. Liberia, of course, was technically not a monarchy but a republic. But ever since 1878 power there had been in the hands of a group of the descendants of the original Afro-American settlers who formed the True Whig Party and who had so managed to manipulate the political machinery that authority in the state had become quasi-hereditary. The election held every four years was always won by the True Whigs so that their leader was always president. During the long period 1943–71, the presidency was held by W. V. S. Tubman, a more than astute politician who saw the need to consolidate the True Whig ascendancy by bringing some members of the indigenous peoples into the machinery of government. After Tubman's death, his chosen successor, W. R. Tolbert, failed adequately to suppress, or to adjust to, criticism from young university-educated radicals who were conscious of what was going on elsewhere in Africa. Dissatisfaction spread to the non-commissioned officers of the army, and in 1980 a young sergeant appropriately called Samuel Doe led a military coup that established a People's Redemption Council, which sought to destroy the old social and political pattern. Whether or not this venture would be successful was not quickly apparent.

However there was no question of the radical changes wrought in Ethiopia by the revolution launched there some six years earlier. Until 1974, Ethiopia had been the oldest monarchy in Africa (indeed it was one of the oldest monarchies anywhere in the world). Apart from the five years of the Italian occupation, since 1918 power had been in the hands of Haile Selassie, who had first been regent for the Empress Zauditu, a daughter of Menelik, but who in 1930 himself became Emperor. Haile Selassie was well aware of the need to modernize structures of administration and society which were still essentially feudal, and he did much to this end, especially perhaps in programmes of education and training. But during the 1960s, when he was in his seventies, he began to run into difficulties. In 1962 he decided that Eritrea's federal status could no longer be tolerated, but within ten years the attempt to make it just another province of Ethiopia had aroused open resistance from an Eritrean Liberation Front which had the sympathy and support of nearby Muslim countries. By this time there was also armed conflict in the Ogaden, one of Menelik's conquests, where the indigenous Somali pastoralists had always opposed any Ethiopian attempt to control their grazing lands. Then in 1972–3 the first of a series of major famines hit the country, and particularly its dryer regions in the north. Haile Selassie's regime failed to deal adequately with any of these problems, not least because of reluctance to give responsibility and authority to those of the new generation it had been at pains to educate and train. From the mid-1960s onwards, demonstrations by students and strikes by workers became increasingly common. Eventually dissatisfaction spread to the army, and in 1974 young officers staged a coup which deposed Haile Selassie (who shortly afterwards died in detention) and declared a socialist republic under a Provisional Military Administrative Council called the *Dergue*.

During the next three years there was continual competition for power between various groups in and around the *Dergue*, each espousing its own particular socialist ideology and supported by its own faction of armed men; many lives were lost. It was not until 1977 that an unchallenged leader of the revolution emerged who was free to attend to the many problems facing the country. This was Colonel Mengistu, under whom Ethiopia was in receipt of substantial aid from communist countries, in particular from the USSR (which among other things was interested in finding bases from which its navy could operate in the Red Sea and the Indian Ocean – a facility which for a time had been found in Somalia). This aid helped Ethiopia to defeat a full-scale invasion from Somalia in 1978, but Mengistu was unable to prevent the revolt in Eritrea from spreading into Tigre and other parts of northern Ethiopia. This revolt, together with widespread resistance to a programme of land reform and collectivization the regime was willing if need be to impose by force, meant that it was particularly difficult for it to cope with the repeated droughts, famines and epidemics afflicting parts of Ethiopia. Some of the worst consequences of these were mitigated by emergency food and medical aid supplied by agencies of the western world, but relief aid, no more than most of what the Ethiopian government might do, could not provide the survivors with hope that their lives might be more stable or secure for the future.

Besides being one of the poorest countries in Africa, Ethiopia suffered from the fact that, even when there was stability at the centre, its government was unable to make its power effective throughout the country. The same problem was faced by the rulers of other large states, especially if – as in Ethiopia – regional dissidents were able to secure arms and other aid from outside the country. In Zaire, Katanga's attempted secession had been backed by support given by Belgian mining corporations and other western interests. When the United Nations troops which had suppressed it had been withdrawn, there were for a long time still many parts of Zaire's large territory in which the writ of the Kinshasa government did not run. Something has already been said of the situation in Angola; the very fact that its MPLA government was Marxist and in receipt of support from communist countries was a natural encouragement to the South African government to provide military support for UNITA (and also to other conservative regimes, for example in the USA, to give it support which was less overtly military). But whereas the main focus for UNITA's activity was in the southern districts of Angola, close to the South African bases in Namibia, the parallel Marxist-oriented government in Mozambique was by the 1980s facing such widespread armed activity from guerilla bands that it could not guarantee control of virtually any part of the country outside its capital, Maputo. South

Africa was naturally suspected of providing arms and other support for the insurgents, the more so perhaps since their activities, by inhibiting movement along the railways between Zimbabwe and the Mozambiquan ports, were forcing Zimbabwe to conduct all its external trade through the Republic. Specifically the South Africans were accused of giving support to the movement called the *Resistência Nacional de Mozambique* (though whether Renamo was in control of all the guerillas, or whether some at least of them were really no more than bandits, was not clear).

There were quite a few countries in which the politicians came unstuck essentially because there was such a paucity of resources that it was extremely difficult for any government to provide the people with any rewards from independence. This was the underlying reality in three of the former French West African colonies: Mali, Niger and the Upper Volta. In the first two cases, the politicians who had brought these countries to independence and who had become their first presidents, Modibo Keita and Hamani Diori, were before long – in 1968 and 1974 respectively – overthrown by military leaders who proved more skilful in retaining power. The territory which was known as the Upper Volta has been less stable, and during 1966–87 experienced no less than five military takeovers of one kind or another. There were clearly problems involved in developing an appropriate government for this equally poor, but much smaller and appreciably more thickly populated territory. (In colonial times the French had never been able to decide whether it was best to amalgamate it with the French Sudan to the north or with the Ivory Coast to the south, or to treat it as a separate unit.) The young army officer, Captain Sankara, who took power in 1983 and changed the country's name to Burkina Faso, favoured a down-to-earth style of government which seems to have annoyed many of those who had hitherto enjoyed the fruits of power, and this may well have something to do with his assassination in 1987.

Initially instability seemed to be endemic in another former French West African territory, Dahomey. Dahomey was not well endowed with natural resources other than the good level of education achieved by many of its people, especially in the south. After independence there was bitter rivalry between three politicians, each of whom had a firm regional base. Their inability to achieve any lasting understanding provoked three military coups in the 1960s before, following a fourth coup in 1972, the military leader, General Kerekou, decided to keep power in his own hands. He thought that a new name was needed for the country and a new ideology for its governance, so the People's Republic of Bénin was proclaimed. In the former British colony of Sierra Leone, central government went through a period of instability after the parliamentary leader who had taken it to independence, Milton Margai, had died in 1964. He was succeeded by his brother, Albert Margai, who planned to institute a one-party state but suffered a narrow defeat at a general election in 1967 at the hands of a more radical party led by Siaka Stevens, a former trade unionist. The commander of the army then mounted a coup to keep Stevens out of power, only to be overthrown by officers who wanted to hold onto power for themselves. But in their turn these were overthrown by some of their rank and file, and Stevens was then able to take office as prime minister. Stevens himself faced a military coup in 1971, but managed to maintain his position with the aid of troops from neighbouring Guinea. Following this he became president and in 1978 instituted a single party state.

The nearby anglophone Gambia, as well as being one of the poorest states on the continent, was also one of the smallest both in terms of territory and of people. Except for its short seaboard, it was also surrounded by Senegal, a country with which it had ethnic continuity. There were therefore many who thought that its future must lie in developing closer relations with its larger francophone neighbour. Nevertheless President Jawara succeeded in maintaining the Gambia as an independent working democracy which held regular elections. In 1981, however, a small group of conspirators attempted a takeover with the help of members of the tiny army, and Jawara's government survived only with the aid of troops sent by Senegal. Following this, the two governments began slowly to institute a Confederation of Senegambia.

Ghana had been the first of the colonies of tropical Africa to secure its independence, in 1957, and it was one of the best developed of them. It possessed a good range of natural resources, and its people, with a relatively high standard of education, had demonstrated they were well capable of exploiting these resources and of managing their own affairs. Kwame Nkrumah, who had brought the country to independence and who shortly became president, then looked for wider fields in which to employ his energy and eloquence. He began to give as much or more attention to urging the cause of independence on the pan-African front as he did to affairs at home. Here a great part of the country's substantial reserves were being expended on projects which brought more prestige than revenue, and little was being done to control politicians and other leaders who put their own interests above those of their country. In 1966 army officers decided that matters had gone too far and seized power when Nkrumah was out of the country. Civilians were enlisted to draw up a new demo-cratic and parliamentary constitution under which elections were held in 1969. But the policies of the party which was then returned to power were circumscribed by an empty treasury, exhausted reserves, and falling prices for Ghana's export mainstay, cocoa. It quickly lost support, and in 1972, led by General Acheampong, soldiers took over again, established a National Redemption Council, and set out to show that they could do better. They did not succeed, and in 1978 Acheampong was deposed by General Akuffo, who promised a return to civilian rule. By this time however there were young officers and NCOs who were being more and more upset both by the performance of their seniors and by the state to which the country had been reduced, and in 1979, led by Flight-Lieutenant Rawlings, these seized power and executed Akuffo and other leading officers. Their first idea was to restore parliamentary government, but when this did not live up to their expectations Rawlings and his colleagues came to the conclusion that nothing less than a 'pragmatic revolution' in Ghanaian society was needed. With this end in view, in 1981 power passed to a Provisional National Defence Council with Rawlings as its chairman.

The Central African Republic (the former Oubangui-Chari colony of French Equatorial Africa), after General Bokassa had seized power there in 1965, provides another, and an extreme case of the ambitions of a ruler totally outreaching the available resources. The consequences here were infinitely worse – indeed they were tragic and terrible – for the natural and human resources available in the Central African Republic were much slighter and more brittle than in Ghana, while Bokassa was very much more of a paranoiac and very much less of a sophisticated statesman than Nkrumah. Bokassa thought his country was his personal fief; he claimed absolute power over his subjects and for justice substituted his erratic and often malignant and cruel whim. In 1976, with Napoleonic style and splendour, he made himself emperor; this proved to be literally his crowning folly. In 1979, when his country was totally bankrupt and he was totally discredited, he was ousted with the aid of a military force sent from France. The restored democratic government was left with an appalling legacy and in 1981 it gave way to a military regime.

In some of the new states, ethnic heterogeneity could sometimes bring serious trouble. This was not always a consequence of European colonialists having bundled different ethnic units together under the single colonial administration. In the very densely populated territories of Rwanda and Burundi, Tutsi pastoral aristocracies had imposed overlordships on majority populations of agricultural Hutu before the colonial era. These overlordships had been perpetuated under European rule, and in both cases the advent of independence unleashed considerable communal violence. In Rwanda this was concentrated in a short period when, on the eve of independence, the Hutu rose against the Tutsi. Many thousands of the latter were slaughtered and the survivors took refuge in adjacent Uganda. In 1973 there was a military takeover led by General Habyarimana who, by the 1980s, was offering the Tutsi guarantees of their position in Rwanda and endeavouring to secure the return of the refugees. In Burundi, the Tutsi monarchy continued until 1966, when it was overthrown by a coup which made a Tutsi officer, General Micombero, president of a republic. The result was to upset the traditional balance the monarchy had maintained with the Hutu. In 1972 the latter rose in a rebellion which was put down with considerable brutality; it is thought that, of some 3 000 000 Hutu, some 100 000 were killed and some 150 000 forced to flee the country. Micombero was overthrown in 1976 by Colonel Bagaza, who espoused socialism but did not satisfy his younger officers, and in 1987 they set up a Committee for National Redemption.

Independence also unleashed ethnic tensions in neighbouring Uganda, with its economically and educationally backward 'stateless' Nilotic societies in the north, and in the south the advanced Bantu kingdoms with which the British had had a special relationship, and which continued to have status under the new constitution. As has been seen, at independence in 1962 there had been an *ad hoc* alliance between Milton Obote, the northerner who led the largest single organized political grouping, and the political chiefs of the Baganda, the leading southern community, so that Obote had become prime minister and the *Kabaka* of Buganda president of the new state. But Obote could not feel secure so long as the *Kabaka* had in his own kingdom an independent source for his authority. In 1966 therefore he used troops of Uganda's army, which was predominantly recruited from the north, to suppress the kingdom of Buganda and to force the *Kabaka* into exile. In the following year, the other traditional kingdoms of the south were also abolished. In using the army to upset established authority in this way. Obote had made a rod for his own back. After extinguishing the kingdoms, his exercise of power became more and more arbitrary, until ultimately, in 1971, the officer who had commanded the assault on the palace of the *Kabaka*, General Idi Amin, a northerner like most of his soldiers, overthrew him and took control. Amin's action secured wide acquiescence, but his use of power was even more arbitrary and less constructive than Obote's had been, and he became more and more ruthless in impatiently using force to deal with real or imagined opponents and critics of his regime. In an effort to regain popularity with his African subjects, he expelled the Asians who dominated Uganda's trade and industry. The result was to ruin the economy, bringing destitution to the towns and inculcating disorder throughout the country. In 1978, when even the army was beginning to dissolve into chaos, Amin was driven to try and regain control by a second reckless expedient; he ordered the army to invade Tanzania (which had given sanctuary to Obote and other Ugandan refugees). This too backfired; very soon it was the turn of Uganda to be invaded, and within a few months the Tanzanian troops had occupied most of the country and Amin had been forced to flee.

President Nyerere of Tanzania took the line that Obote was the rightful head of Uganda's government and that he should be restored to power. With Tanzanian occupation troops providing the only point of stability in the country, the Ugandans did not find it easy to agree on what it was best to do. Eventually in 1980 there was an election which Obote was declared to have won, and during the following two years the Tanzanian soldiers were withdrawn. Uganda then dissolved once more into chaos, with a variety of guerilla bands roaming the country, often ostensibly in support of this or that leader or doctrine, but really doing no more than exploiting the population for plunder and supplies. Obote had no control of the situation. What he thought of as Uganda's army became indistinguishable from most of the competing guerilla bands; eventually in 1985 its commander, General Okello, a northerner in the Amin mould, took the presidency for himself. If there was any way out of this mess, it lay with an unusual leader of guerillas, Yoweri Museveni, an educated man from the west of Uganda who had had some experience as a government minister, who possessed remarkable qualities of leadership and who forged his followers into an unusually well-disciplined and purposeful force. By 1986 he had defeated all his rivals and secured control of the capital, Kampala; it remained to be seen whether order and progress could be restored to such a devastated and divided country.

The Sudan, Uganda's neighbour to the north, and the largest country in Africa, also suffers from a major division between north and south, and it has sometimes been suggested that much trouble would have been avoided and many lives saved had the northern half of Uganda been joined in one country with the southern half of the Sudan. The rationale for this is that the southern Sudanese and the northern Ugandans are both predominantly Nilotes, so that bringing them both under one government might obviate much of the civil strife and bloodshed that has occurred in both countries since independence. (It might be remarked that remnants of Amin's and Okello's armies took refuge in the southern Sudan, establishing bases from which they could continue to intervene in their homeland's difficulties; conversely refugees from warfare in the southern Sudan could always find shelter in northern Uganda.) But just as it was southern Uganda which gained in wealth, education and political experience from increasing contact with the outside world during the colonial period, in the Sudan it was the Muslim and Arabic-speaking north. An independent state on the upper Nile might well be politically united, but it would also be remarkably isolated, and very poor and backward.

The parliamentary system with which the Sudan entered upon independence in 1956 quickly ran into difficulties, and in 1958 General Abboud seized power. He was able to restore effective government in the northern Sudan, but he and his army were unable to make any headway in the southern provinces, where a rebellion had begun in 1955 when the British officials who had hitherto administered them had been replaced by Sudanese who were for the most part northerners. In 1964, after strikes and rioting in Khartoum, Abboud handed power over to civilians who sought to secure peace in the south by proclaiming an amnesty. But parliamentary government was no more successful in dealing with the Sudan's major problem, and in 1969 a group of young officers seized power. Their leader was Colonel Nimeri, who in 1971 became president. At first Nimeri tried to solve the problem of the south by military conquest, but when this had failed – after much blood had been shed, and much hostility provoked

abroad, especially among the Christian churches – he turned to negotiation. In 1972, an agreement was secured which promised autonomy
for the south. But there was still much hostility in the southern Sudan
towards the government in Khartoum; unrest never ceased, and it
began to swell again when, in the later 1970s, Nimeri began to plan
that Islamic law should replace the legal system based on English law
which had hitherto operated in the Sudan. By the time the change
was made, in 1983, a Sudanese People's Liberation Movement was
mounting a major armed rebellion, and the power of the Khartoum
government in the south did not extend beyond the major towns.
However, the adoption of the Shari'a also increased hostility to the
regime from more sophisticated and urban circles in the northern
Sudan, so that in 1984 Nimeri saw fit to declare martial law. This
soon led to his supercession by a minister he had newly appointed,
General Swar al-Dahab, who in 1986 restored parliamentary
government.

Chad, Sudan's neighbour to the west, suffers from much the same
divide as the Sudan, with nomadic Muslim pastoralists in the north
and partly Christian agricultural peoples in the south. But it is less
densely peopled and is much poorer. Indeed it has the misfortune to
be the poorest country in Africa, with a GNP per head which in the
1970s was hardly more than $100 and which by the mid-1980s was
as low as $70 – figures which are about a third of those for the Sudan.
In Chad the advantages of wealth and education, such as they are, lie
with the south and when independence came it was southerners who
dominated the political scene. By 1967 the north was in rebellion and
by the 1970s there was open war in which the northerners were being
sustained by arms and troops sent into Chad from Libya. Gaddafi
was keen to extend his country's influence into Black Africa, and had
the excuse that since colonial times there had been argument over
Chad's frontier with Libya. It was also supposed that the territory in
dispute around Aouzou in northern Chad might contain valuable
minerals. By the later 1970s, only intervention by troops sent by
France was keeping the northerners and their allies from overrunning
southern Chad. By the 1980s African and western diplomats alike
were trying to secure a settlement, but in vain: Libya was putting
more forces into the struggle, while Chad was receiving ever more
military aid from abroad, mainly from France, but also from other
African countries and from the USA.

There was warfare also at the western end of the Sahara, in what had been the Spanish Sahara. King Hassan of Morocco claimed that his country had historical rights to the whole territory, and was not interested in seeing half of it going to Mauritania, as Spain had proposed in 1975. On the other hand, its 70 000 or so nomadic inhabitants saw no need why government should be imposed on them from either Morocco or Mauritania. In 1976, therefore, they established the Polisario Front to fight for a Sahrawi Arab Democratic Republic. This received encouragement and material support from Algeria, which had a long and uncertain desert frontier with Morocco, and had no wish to see any advance of its counter-revolutionary influence. Mauritania lacked the economic and military strength to establish its authority in the western Sahara; indeed its attempt to do so led in 1978 to the collapse of its civil government. When, three years later, civil administration was restored, the Mauritanians chose to recognize first the Polisario Front and then, in 1984, the Sahrawi Republic. Morocco, on the other hand, continued to employ much of its quite substantial military strength in expensive but vain attempts to defeat elusive enemy forces which could always look to Algeria for support and – if necessary – for refuge.

Long-lasting wars, like those in the western Sahara, Chad, the southern Sudan, Ethiopia, and in Angola and Mozambique, meant an incessant drain on the lives of some of the poorest peoples in Africa, and also the destruction of much of what they might be able to do to improve life and secure a better future. But they do not seem to have had quite the same impact on world opinion as the three years of the great civil war that was fought out in Nigeria during 1967–70. The explanation for this is undoubtedly connected with the great wealth of resources that were available to Nigeria – not least the substantial oil-fields in the south-east which began to produce at the end of the 1950s – and with its enormous population, which is thought to have reached the 100 000 000 mark by the mid-1980s, and was by far the largest of any country in Africa. Although the sheer size of this population (twice that of the next most populous country, Egypt) meant that Nigeria's GNP per head, at about $700, was not very remarkable, in the aggregate this was by far the greatest nation in Black Africa. Therefore the decline of this nation into civil war within six years of its independence, the employment in this war of something like half a million soldiers, and the enormous casualties that resulted from it,* were tragedy on the grand scale, and they were treated as such by the media throughout the world.

Nigeria came to independence in 1960 as a federation of three regions, in the north, east and west of the country respectively. The north had a population as large or larger than that of the other two regions put together, and so had rather more seats in the federal legislature than they did. Each region was ruled by a different political party, and each of these parties held a substantial majority of the seats in the region's legislature. In the two southern regions, which had seen more economic and educational development than the larger northern region, these were popular parties each of which was domi-nated by a particular ethnic group, Ibo in the east, Yoruba in the west. In the northern assembly, the majority of the seats was held by a party representing the interests of its traditional and conservative Muslim rulers. At the centre, no government could function without the support of this party; in the event, at independence power lay with an alliance between the northern conservatives and the more radical of the two southern parties, that which held power in the east. The alliance's main achievement was to weaken the west's influence in federal affairs through the creation of a new mid-west region. When the alliance collapsed, as it did in 1964, the northerners kept control with the aid of the mid-westerners and by interfering in the politics of the western region so as to weaken the main Yoruba party. As a consequence, serious disorder developed in the west, while many of the federal civil servants and army officers began to be alarmed at what was happening to their country. Early in 1966, young army officers acted by mounting a coup in which the federal prime minister, the northern party leader, and the puppet prime minister of the west were all among those who were killed. While the rank and file of the army came principally from the southern marches of the northern emirates, the officers were mainly from the south and particularly from Iboland, and it was an Ibo senior officer, General Ironsi, who headed Nigeria's first military administration. The disorder in the west was speedily ended, and a plan was produced to replace the four regions with a large number of more evenly balanced political units. It was now the turn of northerners to be dissatisfied at what they feared was a southern, and particularly Ibo, plot to change the balance

---

* It has been estimated that there were perhaps a million deaths all told, and that civilian deaths from starvation and disease may have outnumbered deaths in battle by something like ten to one.

of power. Soldiers mutinied and killed Ironsi and many other Ibo officers. Military discipline was restored by a Christian northerner, General Gowon, but the many southerners – also predominantly Ibo – who contributed significant expertise to the commerce, services and administration of northern Nigeria began to be attacked. Many lost their lives; perhaps as many as a million fled south as refugees, many of them to swell the already densely populated lands of the eastern region.

Fear of the north was now the dominant factor in eastern political thinking; many felt that dividing Nigeria up into smaller units would only help to perpetuate northern dominance. In the middle of 1967, the Ibo military governor of the region, Colonel Ojukwu, acted by declaring that eastern Nigeria had seceded from the federation and had become the independent state of Biafra. Within a month, the civil war had begun. The Biafrans showed much enterprise and ingenuity in fashioning an army to combat the large forces that the federal government gradually mobilized, and great skill in improvizing to avoid the consequences of the blockade it imposed upon them. In the long run, however, it was a shortage of food and munitions which brought them down. Early in 1970, Ojukwu fled and the Biafrans surrendered. Gowon and his government did a great deal to reconcile them to the new Nigeria that they were hoping to build, but they were less successful in dealing with the many problems of reconstruction that faced them. In 1975, Gowon was forced to give way to another northern officer, General Murtala Muhammad, who pleased the people by producing a timetable for the return of Nigeria to civil rule. Despite Murtala's assassination in 1976, a second Nigerian republic came into being in 1979 with an elaborate constitution involving an executive president, no less than nineteen federated states and an extraordinarily elaborate system of elections. Few people gained from this constitution other than the politicians, who now had even more ways than under the first republic by which public funds might be spent to the benefit of themselves and their supporters. This potentially rich country was soon in substantial financial trouble, and there was general relief when in 1983 the army again resumed control. By 1987, the conservative fiscal policies pursued by the new military rulers made it possible for them to promise the gradual restoration of elective government.

History seemed to be repeating itself; in Nigeria it was obviously open to question whether a restored parliamentary system would be any more successful than its predecessors in providing the country's millions with the stable government they needed. It might be argued, indeed, that such a restoration would run counter to the general current of post-colonial African political development. As has already been said, military takeovers and governments have always secured more of the limelight than stable civilian regimes. But in the last resort in Africa it was commonly of little moment whether a head of government had gained his position by military means or by some civil route. What was often more significant – as much or more with civilians as with soldiers – was that heads of state tended to assume a role akin to that of divine monarchs, presenting themselves as the fathers of the nation from whom flowed all goodness. In the last resort the nation's business was all the business of its leader. It followed that ministers and other functionaries ceased to be responsible to any public opinion, parliament, cabinet, or military council even, but had become the creatures of the ruling head of state. They became in effect his courtiers, depending on him personally rather than on any institutional system for the rewards as well as the privileges of office. Obviously, if such a system became corrupt, if the ruler or his subordinates or both came to serve their own interests rather than those of the nation, then ultimately the situation was likely to be remedied only by the use of violence – and examples of this have already been seen. But many African rulers have been remarkably successful in maintaining their personal ascendancy over substantial periods of years.

The success of these men seems to have had little to do either with the political philosophies they proclaimed, or with the amount and extent of the resources available to implement their policies. Nor did their maintenance of power over substantial periods necessarily bring great benefits to their subjects. Two long-serving rulers claimed to be full-blooded socialists, Sékou Touré, who was president of Guinea from its independence in 1958 until his death in 1984, and Julius Nyerere, who led Tanzania to independence in 1961 and who retired from its presidency in 1986. Sékou Touré was a traditional Marxist who more than once was faced with the necessity of using force to maintain the Stalinist dictatorship he had established, and which provoked both revolts from Guinean citizens who were dissatisfied with the standards of living available under the regime, and rebellions within the ruling party. Although Sékou Touré began by hoping that aid from communist countries would help him develop his country, in reality its economy was always dependent on the sale of metallic ores to western industrial nations. Appreciation of this doubtless helped to soften Sékou Touré's Marxist stance in his later years, when there was little real growth in the economy and he began to move towards closer cooperation with western nations. Nyerere, on the other hand, was a proponent of 'African socialism', which in his case meant eschewing any substantial industrialization and urbanization (in a country which had little mineral wealth), and pursuing *ujamaa*, socialist agriculture. This involved setting up villages with communal landholding and agriculture to serve as self-reliant units for the development of the nation. Nyerere was a modest man possessed of a genuine idealism, but when his schemes were imposed on traditional societies through the medium of a party bureaucracy, the results could be far from happy. When it is appreciated that Tanzania's population doubled during his period of office, it is not surprising that per capita GNP was declining in the early 1980s, when it stood at hardly more than $200. From this point of view, Guinea – with its mineral exports – was better off, with a GNP per head around $300, but both countries were threatened by mounting foreign debts, which during the 1970s had grown more than threefold.

Léopold Sédar Senghor, who was president of Senegal from its independence in 1960 until his retirement twenty years later, was not averse to talking about African socialism. But in practice his country's economy was so closely tied up with the western interests that had invested in it when it was the cornerstone of the Federation of French West Africa, that he had little alternative but to continue to run his country in close cooperation with such interests. The main foreign interest in Senegal – political and strategic as well as economic – was naturally French, and Senghor was in many respects as much a proponent of French culture (and of that of western Europe generally) as he was of *négritude*. It was remarkable how successful he was in maintaining a precarious political balance in a country in which, bereft of its role as a federal headquarters, the economy could never be much more than stagnant. In the 1980s GNP per head began sharply to decline from $450 or more per head to something nearer $350.

In 1987 Kenneth Kaunda, in circumstances not unlike those which had faced Senghor, and with a philosophy which in principle was not dissimilar (however much it may have seemed to differ in many particulars), celebrated his twenty-first year as president of Zambia. This was a considerable achievement because Zambia, with the large investment in the copper mines which produced some 90 per cent of its export earnings, was if anything even more dependent on the western world than Senegal, and serious troubles began to beset it in the 1970s which are reflected in the decline of its GNP from $500 or more per head at the end of the decade to less than $300 by the mid-1980s. Earnings from copper exports were severely reduced by the world depression, and lines of communication on which this land-locked country depended for its foreign trade were interrupted or even blocked by the fighting in Zimbabwe, Angola and Mozambique, and this at a time when droughts often necessitated the import of foodstuffs.

Finally, one may note three long-living leaders who thought that the best future for their countries lay in allying them with western capitalism and in adopting much of its philosophy. Two of these were still in office at the end of 1987, namely Félix Houphouët-Boigny, who became president of the Ivory Coast in 1960, and Hastings Kamuzu Banda, who became prime minister of Malawi in 1963 and its president three years later. The third was Jomo Kenyatta, who became president of Kenya in 1964 and died in 1978, when he must have been more than eighty – an age reached by Banda in 1983 and by Houphouët in 1986. All three may fairly be regarded as the fathers of their countries, countries whose resources are primarily agricul-tural, and which they have ruled very much as though they were their personal estates. This may have been most appropriate for Malawi, a small territory whose limited resources have been stretched to the utmost by its densely settled population; it has remained one of the poorest lands in Africa, with GNP per head not much more than $150. In Kenya, European settlement and capital and Asian settlement had laid foundations during the colonial period for industrialization and urbanization, and Kenyatta's aim was to ensure that the benefits of these things were made available for the modernization of African society. But his successor could not command quite the same breadth of support in Kenya's ethnic patchwork as he did, and population growth made the realization of his aims ever more difficult – as with Tanzania, population passed the 20 000 000 mark in the 1980s.

In the Ivory Coast Houphouët-Boigny was hailed by the western world as the author of an 'economic miracle', and by the end of the 1970s his country was statistically by far the most prosperous oil-importing country in Black Africa, with a GNP per head of more than $1000. This had been achieved by openly encouraging western entrepreneurs to invest in the exploitation of the country's resources – most importantly cocoa, coffee and timber – and in the development of industries and services. From the material point of view, the results were as or more impressive as the development that had earlier been seen in the adjacent anglophone country which had become Ghana. But it was open to question how much of the new wealth had gone to improve the lot of the average Ivorean, who was typically a farmer. Much of it had gone to reward foreign investors and to develop and enrich towns and cities (the capital, Abidjan, became one of the most modern and beautiful of cities in Africa, and one with a substantial European – mainly French – population). When the world trade recession depressed export earnings and drought began to affect agricultural production, it began to seem that the cost of what had been achieved was too high. In particular, it became impossible to service the massive external debt which had been built up, and which per capita was probably the highest in Africa (by 1984 it had mounted to some \$6 750 000 000, or some \$700 per head), and it was necessary to go to the IMF for it to be rescheduled.

As the twentieth century moved towards its close, Africa seemed to be a continent of contradictions. On the one hand, its peoples seemed to have rejected much of the philosophy of individualism and elective democracy the colonial powers had hoped would be one of their main legacies. Almost everywhere in Africa, the philosophy and the style of government were tending to return to African patterns; they were more akin to those of the monarchies of western Europe before the industrial and French revolutions than to those known by Europeans in the twentieth century. Doubtless this was not inappropriate for countries which were still for the most part among the poorest in the world. Except in South Africa, which was still dominated by people of European descent, and in a few pockets elsewhere, in North Africa in particular, Africans were not securing much benefit from industrialization. Rather they were still contributing to the success of the major industrial societies in other parts of the world and, partly because of this, but also because of the general tendency – exacerbated by drought and famine – for African populations to outrun the means available to them for agricultural subsistence, it was now euphemistic to think of Africa as a continent of 'developing' countries. The plain fact of the matter was that almost all African peoples were becoming poorer, and that the gap in wealth between them and the rich nations of the northern hemisphere was perceptibly widening.

On the other hand, Africa was more part of the modern world than it had ever been before, even at the height of the colonial period. One or both of the great world religions of Christianity and Islam were firmly entrenched in every one of its countries, and their influence was growing. More and more Africans were using international langu-ages like English, French and Arabic – often even for domestic purposes. Through growing literacy and the spread of electronic communications, Africans were in constant touch with what was going on elsewhere in the world. They were increasingly demanding – and some of them were enjoying – all that people elsewhere wanted or enjoyed: towns and cities; education and entertainment; bread and bottled beer; radios, refrigerators and motor cars; sports clubs and football internationals. Their states had an established place in the United Nations Organization and in all the other international clubs. Like states anywhere else, they were perfectly capable of mismanaging their own internal affairs but – with some exceptions – they knew how to behave towards their neighbours, how not to interfere in their internal affairs and, sometimes even, how to help them when they were in trouble. Above all, and despite their lack of wealth and the many problems facing almost all of them, Africans were united in believing that their continent had a voice which should be heard in the world, and a distinctive contribution to make to its affairs.

Select bibliography

GENERAL

A work such as this, essaying to survey the whole history of a continent in one short volume, must rely heavily on other writers' more detailed histories. The list that follows is a selective one of those books and articles which have been of particular value to the author in helping to establish his understanding of the history of human society in Africa, together with some general works which may be helpful to readers who would like to have deeper surveys of the history of a particular area or theme. In the interests of brevity, preference has been given to works available in English. It is important to appreciate that the serious study of the African past is a relatively new scholarly activity. As a result, it is only perhaps for relatively modern times that one can be reasonably sure of finding adequate treatments of the major themes in book form. For all earlier periods much important work can be found only in articles in journals. The more important of these journals devoted to the history and archaeology of Africa are perhaps the following:

The Journal of African History, 1960– (Cambridge)
The International Journal of African Historical Studies, 1968– (Boston)
History in Africa, 1974– (Los Angeles)
African Archaeological Review, 1983– (Cambridge)
Journal of the Royal African Society, 1901–43, later African Affairs, 1944– (London)
Revue d'histoire des colonies, 1913–58, later Revue française d'histoire d'outre-mer, 1959– (Paris)
Sudan Notes and Records, 1918– (Khartoum)
Kush, 1953– (Khartoum)
Karthago: revue d'archéologie africaine, 1950– (Tunis)
Hespéris, 1921–59 (Rabat)
Bulletin du Comité d'Etudes Historiques et Scientifiques de l'Afrique Occidentale Française, 1918–38 (Dakar)

Bulletin de l'Institut Français d'Afrique Noire (later Institut Fondamental d'Afrique Noire), 1938– (Dakar)
Transactions of the Historical Society of Ghana, 1952– (Legon)
Journal of the Historical Society of Nigeria, 1956– (Ibadan)
Tarikh, 1965– (Ibadan)
West African Journal of Archaeology, 1971– (Ibadan)
Etudes d'Histoire Africaine, 1970– (Kinshasha)
Azania; Journal of the British Institute of History and Archaeology in East Africa, 1966– (Nairobi)
Tanganyika Notes and Records, 1936– (Dar es Salaam)
The Uganda Journal, 1934– (Kampala)
South African Archaeological Bulletin, 1946– (Claremont, C.P.)

There are two major cooperative histories of Africa. *The Cambridge History of Africa*, edited by J. D. FAGE and ROLAND OLIVER is complete in eight volumes published between 1975 and 1986; the bibliographies and bibliographical essays supporting each of its chapters may be regarded as authoritative guides to the literature at the date of publication of each volume. *The General History of Africa*, sponsored by UNESCO and with parallel editions in English and French, was planned in eight volumes, of which all but vols. 5 (1501–1799) and 8 (Africa since 1935) had appeared by the end of 1987; the bibliographies are not reliable. Note also the two-volume cooperative work edited by HUBERT DESCHAMPS, *Histoire Générale de l'Afrique Noire* (Paris, 1970–71). There are a goodly number of one-volume histories, but for the reasons given the following perhaps merit particular notice:

BASIL DAVIDSON, *Africa: History of a Continent* (London, 1966), and *Horizon History of Africa*, by many hands (New York, 1971); both these are magnificently illustrated. It may be noted, however, that Davidson's book is available in a cheaper format as *Africa in History* (London, 1968); Davidson has also written many other stimulating works of synthesis and interpretation, such as his pioneer *Old Africa Rediscovered* (London, 1959). *Histoire de l'Afrique Noire* by JOSEPH KI-ZERBO (Paris, 1972) is noteworthy as the first major general survey by a black African. *Geschichte Afrikas* by DIEDRICH WESTERMANN (Cologne, 1952) is important as a summary record of the traditional histories of African peoples south of the Sahara, undertaken by a pioneer of African anthropology towards the close of his career.

The most reliable short guide to African peoples and their societies is JEAN HIERNAUX, *The People of Africa* (London, 1974). This is to be preferred to GEORGE PETER MURDOCK, *Africa: Its Peoples and Their Culture History* (New York, 1959). This, despite its title, is not a work of history but an attempt by an ethnographer to assemble the multitudinous peoples of Africa into meaningful groups, to which is prefixed seven chapters of often stimulating but sometimes imaginative interpretation. Seekers after detail may need to refer to the many parts of the still uncompleted *Ethnographic Survey of Africa* edited by DARYLL FORDE (International African Institute, London and Paris, 1950 onwards).

The authoritative survey of the archaeological past of the whole continent by J. DESMOND CLARK, *The Prehistory of Africa* (London, 1970), with its excellent bibliography, is now somewhat dated, as much important new work has since been published. There is an attractively presented, if slighter, more recent overview by DAVID W. PHILLIPSON, *African Archaeology* (Cambridge, 1985); this too has a substantial bibliography. Dating of archaeological sites in Africa is heavily dependent on the radiocarbon technique, and lists of radiocarbon dates, together with appropriate discussion, have been published regularly in the *Journal of African History*. It should be appreciated, however, that the conversion of dates B.P. (i.e. *before* the radiocarbon *present*) is not wholly straightforward; see, for example, HAROLD BARKER, 'The accuracy of radiocarbon dates', *J.Afr.Hist.*, vol. 13, no.2 (1972).

Among historical atlases, there is the inexpensive J. D. FAGE, *An Atlas of African History* (2nd ed., London, 1978) and the magnificent work by many hands which was planned and edited by J. F. ADE AJAYI and MICHAEL CROWDER, *Historical Atlas of Africa* (London, 1985).

From a very large number of comprehensive surveys of the history of particular regions and territories, the following might be particularly mentioned:

HANOTAUX, GEORGES (ed.), *Histoire de la nation égyptienne* (7 vols., Paris, 1931–7)

COLLINS, ROBERT and TIGNOR, ROBERT, *Egypt and the Sudan* (Englewood Cliffs, 1967)

JULIEN, CH.-ANDRÉ, *Histoire de l'Afrique du Nord* (2 vols., Paris, 1951–2) – a history of the Maghrib to 1830; the second volume is available in an English translation edited by C. C. Stewart (1970)

ABUN-NASR, J. M., *A History of the Maghrib* (Cambridge, 1971)

TERRASSE, HENRI, *Histoire du Maroc* (2 vols., Casablanca, 1949–50)

AJAYI, J. F. ADE and CROWDER, MICHAEL (eds.), *History of West Africa* (new ed., 2 vols., London, 1985)

HOPKINS, A. G., *An Economic History of West Africa* (2nd ed., London, 1975)

SURET-CANALE, JEAN, *Afrique noire* (2 vols., Paris, 1964)

HARGREAVES, JOHN D., *West Africa; The Former French States* (Englewood Cliffs, 1967)

DESCHAMPS, HUBERT, *Le Sénégal et la Gambie* (Paris, 1964)

GAILEY, H. A., *A History of the Gambia* (London, 1964)

ROUGERIE, G., *La Côte d'Ivoire* (Paris, 1964)

FLINT, JOHN E., *Nigeria and Ghana* (Englewood Cliffs, 1966)

CROWDER, MICHAEL, *The Story of Nigeria* (4th ed., London, 1978)

CORNEVIN, R., *Histoire du Dahomey* (Paris, 1962)

RUDIN, HARRY R., *The Congo* (Englewood Cliffs, 1967)

DORESSE, JEAN, *Histoire de l'Ethiopie* (Paris, 1970)

LONGRIGG, S. H., *A Short History of Eritrea* (London, 1945)

HOLT, P. M. and DALY, M. W., *The History of the Sudan, from the Coming of Islam to the Present Day* (3rd ed., London, 1980)

OLIVER, ROLAND and others (eds.), *A History of East Africa* (3 vols., Oxford, 1963–75)

OGOT, B. A. and KIERNAN, J. A. (eds.), *Zamani: A Survey of East African History* (Nairobi, 1968)

KIMAMBO, I. N. and TEMU, A. J. (eds.), *A History of Tanzania* (London, 1969)

BIRMINGHAM, DAVID, and MARTIN, PHYLLIS M. (eds.), *A History of Central Africa* (2 vols., London, 1983)

ROBERTS, ANDREW, *A History of Zambia* (London, 1977)

RANGER, T. O. (ed.), *Aspects of Central African History* (London, 1968)

STOKES, ERIC and BROWN, RICHARD (eds.), *The Zambesian Past* (London, 1966)

PACHAI, B. (ed.), *The Early History of Malawi* (London, 1972)

WILSON, MONICA and THOMPSON, L. M. (eds.), *The Oxford History of South Africa* (2 vols., Oxford, 1969–71)

DE KIEWIET, C. W., *A History of South Africa, Social and Economic* (Oxford, 1941)

CHILCOTE, RONALD H., *Portuguese Africa* (Englewood Cliffs, 1967)

African Historical Demography (2 vols., African Studies Centre, University of Edinburgh, 1977 and 1981)

VANSINA, JAN, *Oral Tradition as History* (London, 1985)

Notes to bibliographical lists:
1. In order to save space, titles mentioned in the general section of the bibliography above may not be repeated in the later lists for sections to which they may be particularly relevant.
2. Titles which are relevant to more than one of the sections below are usually given only in the first of such sections.

PART ONE
THE INTERNAL DEVELOPMENT OF AFRICAN SOCIETY
(PAGES 1–140)

General Works

BOVILL, E. W., *Caravans of the Old Sahara* (London, 1933)

BOVILL, E. W. with HALLETT, ROBIN, *The Golden Trade of the Moors* (2nd ed., London, 1968)

CLARK, J. DESMOND (ed.), *Cambridge History of Africa*: vol. 1, *From the Earliest Times to* c. *500 B.C.* (Cambridge, 1982)

CLARK, J. DESMOND, 'The prehistoric origins of African culture', *J.Afr.Hist.*, vol. 5, no. 2 (1964)

CONNAH, GRAHAM, *African Civilizations: Precolonial Cities and States in Tropical Africa – an Archaeological Perspective* (Cambridge, 1987)

COOPER, FREDERICK, 'The problem of slavery in African studies', *J.Afr.Hist.*, vol. 20, no. 1 (1979)

DALBY, DAVID (ed.), *Language and History in Africa* (London, 1970)

EHRET, CHRISTOPHER, and POSNANSKY, MERRICK (eds.), *The Archaeological and Linguistic Reconstruction of African History* (Berkeley, 1983)

FAGE, J. D. and OLIVER, R. A. (eds.), *Papers in African Prehistory* (Cambridge, 1970)

FAGE, J. D. (ed.), *Cambridge History of Africa*. vol. 2, c. *500 B.C.–A.D. 1050* (Cambridge, 1978)

GREENBERG, JOSEPH H., *The Languages of Africa* (Bloomington, Ind., 1963)

HARLAN, JACK R., DE WET, JAN, M. J., and STEMLER, ANN B. L. (eds.), *Origins of African Plant Domestication* (The Hague and Paris, 1976)

HERBERT, EUGENIA W., *Red Gold of Africa: Copper in Precolonial History and Culture* (Madison, 1984)

KLEIN, MARTIN A., 'The study of slavery in Africa', *J.Afr.Hist.*, vol. 19, no. 4 (1978)

LOVEJOY, PAUL, *Transformations in Slavery: A History of Slavery in Africa* (Cambridge, 1983)

MIERS, SUZANNE and KOPYTOFF, IGOR (eds.), *Slavery in Africa: Historical and Anthropological Perspectives* (Madison, 1977)

OLIVER, ROLAND (ed.), *Cambridge History of Africa*, vol. 3, c. *1050–c. 1600* (Cambridge, 1977)

OLIVER, ROLAND and FAGAN, BRIAN M., *Africa in the Iron Age*, c. *500 B.C. to A.D. 1400* (Cambridge, 1975)

SELIGMAN, C. G., *Races of Africa* (London, 1930; rev. ed., 1957), see p. 7 above

SHINNIE, P. L. (ed.), *The African Iron Age* (Oxford, 1971)

WILLIAMS, DENIS, *Icon and Image: A Study of Sacred and Secular Forms of African Classical Art* (London, 1974)

Northern and north-eastern Africa

ADAMS, WILLIAM Y., *Nubia: Corridor to Africa* (London, 1977)

ANFRAY, FRANCIS, 'Aspects de l'archéologie éthiopienne', *J.Afr.Hist.*, vol. 9, no. 3 (1968)

ARKELL, A. J., *A History of the Sudan to 1821* (2nd ed., London, 1961)

AZEGAY, M. W., *Southern Ethiopia and the Christian Kingdom, 1508–1708* (London, 1975)

BECKINGHAM, C. F. and HUNTINGFORD, G. W. B., *Some Records of Ethiopia* (London, 1954)

BELL, H. IDRIS, *Egypt, from Alexander the Great to the Arab Conquest* (Oxford, 1948)

BROUGHTON, T. S. R., *The Romanization of Africa Proconsularis* (Baltimore, 1929)

CHARLES-PICARD, G., *La Civilisation de l'Afrique romaine* (Paris, 1929)

CHARLES-PICARD, G. and C., *Daily Life in Carthage at the Time of Hannibal* (London, 1961)

CHILDE, V. GORDON, *New Light on the Most Ancient East* (rev. ed., London, 1952)

COURTOIS, CHARLES, *Les Vandals et l'Afrique* (Paris, 1955)

DIEHL, C., *L'Afrique byzantine* (Paris, 1896)

DORESSE, JEAN, *L'Empire du Prêtre-Jean* (2 vols., Paris, 1957)

EMERY, W. B., *Archaic Egypt* (Harmondsworth, 1961)

FREND, W. H. C., *The Donatist Church* (Oxford, rev. ed., 1985)

FREND, W. H. C., *The Rise of the Monophysite Movement* (Cambridge, 1972)

GARRARD, TIMOTHY, 'Myth and metrology: the early trans-Saharan gold trade', *J.Afr.Hist.*, vol. 23, no. 4 (1982)

GROVES, C. P., *The Planting of Christianity in Africa*, vol. 1 (London, 1948)

HARDEN, DONALD, *The Phoenicians* (rev. ed., London, 1963)

HAYES, WILLIAM C., *Most Ancient Egypt* (Chicago, 1965)

HIRSCHBERG, H. Z., 'The problem of the Judaized Berbers', *J.Afr.Hist.*, vol. 4, no. 3 (1963)

HOLT, P. M., 'Funj origins; a critique and new evidence', *J.Afr.Hist.*, vol. 4, no. 1 (1963)

LAW, R. C. C., 'The Garamantes and trans-Saharan enterprise in classical times', *J.Afr.Hist.*, vol. 7, no. 2 (1967)

LEVINE, DONALD N., *Wax and Gold: Tradition and Innovation in Ethiopian Culture* (Chicago, 1965)

LEWIS, HERBERT S., 'The origins of the Galla and Somali', *J.Afr.Hist.*, vol. 7, no. 1 (1966)

LEWIS, I. M., 'The Somali conquest of the Horn of Africa', *J.Afr.Hist.*, vol. 1, no. 2 (1960)

MACGAFFEY, WYATT, 'Concepts of race in the historiography of North East Africa', *J.Afr.Hist.*, vol. 7, no. 1 (1966)

PANKHURST, RICHARD, *Introduction to the Economic History of Ethiopia* (London, 1961)

PANKHURST, RICHARD, *The Ethiopian Royal Chronicles* (London, 1968)

RAVEN, SUSAN, *Rome in Africa* (London, 1969)

SERGEW HABLE, SELLASSIE, *Ancient and Medieval Ethiopian History* (London, 1972)

SHINNIE, P. L., *Meroe, a Civilization of the Sudan* (London, 1967)

SPAULDING, JAY, 'The Funj, a reconsideration', *J.Afr.Hist.*, vol. 12, no. 1 (1972)

TADESSE TAMRAT, *Church and State in Ethiopia, 1270–1527* (Oxford, 1972)

TRIMINGHAM, J. SPENCER, *Islam in the Sudan* (London, 1949)

TRIMINGHAM, J. SPENCER, *Islam in Ethiopia* (London, 1952)

ULLENDORFF, EDWARD, *The Ethiopians* (London, 1960)

WARMINGTON, B. H., *The North African Provinces from Diocletian to the Vandal Conquest* (Cambridge, 1954)

WARMINGTON, B. H., *Carthage* (London, 1960)

WHEELER, SIR MORTIMER, *Rome beyond the Imperial Frontiers* (Harmondsworth, 1955)

West Africa

ALAGOA, E. J., 'Long distance trade and states in the Niger delta', *J.Afr.Hist.*, vol. 11, no. 3 (1970)

ALAGOA, E. J., 'The development of institutions in the states of the eastern Niger delta', *J.Afr.Hist.*, vol. 12, no. 2 (1971)

BOSTON, J. S., 'Oral tradition and the history of Igala', *J.Afr.Hist.*, vol. 10, no. 1 (1969)

BRADBURY, R. E., 'Chronological problems in the study of Benin history', *J.Hist.Soc.Nig.*, vol. 1, no. 4 (1959)

CENIVAL, P. DE and MONOD, TH. (eds.), *Déscription de la Côte d'Afrique de Ceuta au Sénégal par Valentim Fernandes* (Paris, 1938)

CONNAH, GRAHAM, *The Archaeology of Benin* (Oxford, 1975)

CONNAH, GRAHAM, *Three Thousand Years in Africa: Man and His Environment in the Lake Chad Region of Nigeria* (Cambridge, 1981)

CONRAD, DAVID and FISHER, HUMPHREY, 'The conquest that never was: Ghana and the Almoravids', *Hist.in Afr.*, vols. 9 and 10 (1982/3)

CRONE, G. R. (ed.), *The Voyages of Cadamosto and Other Documents* (London, 1937)

EGHAREVBA, J. U., *A Short History of Benin* (3rd ed., Ibadan, 1960)

FAGE, J. D., 'Ancient Ghana; a review of the evidence', *Tr.Hist.Soc.Ghana*, vol. 3, no. 2 (1957)

FAGE, J. D., *Ghana: A Historical Interpretation* (Madison, 1959)

FAGG, B. E. B., 'The Nok culture in pre-history', *J.Hist.Soc.Nig.*, vol. 1, no. 4 (1959)

FAGG, B. E. B., 'Recent work in West Africa; new light on the Nok culture', *World Archaeology*, vol. 1, no. 1 (1969)

FAGG, WILLIAM, *Nigerian Images* (London, 1963)

FAGG, WILLIAM, *Divine Kingship in Africa* (London, 1970)

FARIAS, P. F. DE M., 'The Almoravids', *Bull. de l'IFAN*, vol. 29B, nos. 3–4 (1967)

FLIGHT, COLIN, 'The chronology of the kings and queenmothers of Bono-Mansu: a revaluation of the evidence', *J.Afr.Hist.*, vol. 11, no. 2 (1970)

FROBENIUS, LEO, *The Voice of Africa* (2 vols., London, 1913)

Ghana Notes and Queries, no. 9. Special number on the history of the Akan (1966)

GIBB, H. A. R. (trans. and ed.), *Ibn Battuta; travels in Asia and Africa* (London, 1929)

GOODY, JACK, 'The Mande and the Akan hinterland' in VANSINA, J., MAUNY, R. and THOMAS, L. V., *The Historian in Tropical Africa* (London, 1964)

HODGKIN, THOMAS, *Nigerian Perspectives* (2nd ed., London, 1975)

IZARD, MICHEL, *Introduction à l'histoire des royaumes Mossi* (2 vols., Paris, 1970)

JOHNSON, SAMUEL, *The History of the Yorubas* (Lagos, 1921)

JONES, D. H., 'Jakpa and the foundation of Gonja', *Tr.Hist.Soc.Ghana*, vol. 6 (1962)

LABOURET, H., *La langue des peuls, ou Foulbé* (Dakar, 1955)

LEVTZION, NEHEMIA, *Muslims and Chiefs in West Africa* (Oxford, 1968)

LEVTZION, NEHEMIA, *Ancient Ghana and Mali* (London, 1973)

MCDOUGALL, E. ANN, 'The view from Awdaghust: war, trade and social change in the southwestern Sahara from the eighth to the fifteenth century', *J.Afr.Hist.*, vol. 26, no. 1 (1985)

MCINTOSH, RODERICK J. and SUSAN KEECH, 'The inland Niger delta before the empire of Mali: evidence from Jenne-Jeno', *J.Afr.Hist.*, vol. 22, no. 1 (1981)

MCINTOSH, SUSAN KEECH, 'A reconsideration of Wangara/Palolus, island of gold', *J.Afr.Hist.*, vol. 22, no. 2 (1981)

MAUNY, RAYMOND (ed.), *Esmeraldo de Situ Orbis par D. Pacheco Pereira* (Bissau, 1956)

MAUNY, RAYMOND, *Tableau géographique de l'Ouest africain au moyen âge* (Dakar, 1961)

MEYEROWITZ, EVA L. R., *Akan Traditions of Origin* (London, 1952)

MEYEROWITZ, EVA L. R., *The Early History of the Akan States of Ghana* (London, 1974)

MONOD, TH., TEIXEIRA DA MOTA, A., and MAUNY, R. (eds), *Description de la Côte Occidentale d'Afrique, Sénégal au Cap de Monte, par Valentim de Fernandes* (Bissau, 1951)

MONTEIL, CHARLES, *Les Empires du Mali* (new ed. Paris, 1968)

MUNSON, PATRICK J., 'Archaeology and the prehistoric origins of the Ghana empire', *J.Afr.Hist.*, vol. 21, no. 4 (1980)

NIANE, DJ. TAMSIR, *Sundiata: An Epic of old Mali* (London, 1965)

NORRIS, H. T., 'New evidence on the life of 'Abdulla b. Yasin and the origins of the Almoravid movement', *J.Afr.Hist.*, vol. 12, no. 2 (1971)

NORTHRUP, DAVID, *Trade without Rulers: Pre-colonial Economic Development in South-eastern Nigeria* (Oxford, 1978)

PALMER, H. R., *Sudanese Memoirs* (repr. London, 1967)

REINDORF, C. C., *The History of the Gold Coast and Asante* (Basle, n.d.)

RODNEY, WALTER, 'A reconsideration of the Mane invasions of Sierra Leone', *J.Afr.Hist.*, vol. 8, no. 2 (1967)

RODNEY, WALTER, *A History of the Upper Guinea Coast, 1545–1800* (Oxford, 1970)

ROUCH, JEAN, *Contribution à l'histoire des Songhay* (Dakar, 1953)

RYDER, ALAN, *Benin and the Europeans, 1485–1897* (London, 1969)

SHAW, C. THURSTAN, 'Radiocarbon dating in Nigeria', *J.Hist.Soc.Nig.*, vol. 4, no. 3 (1968)

SHAW, C. THURSTAN, *Igbo Ukwu* (2 vols., London, 1970)

SHAW, FLORA, *A Tropical Dependency* (London, 1906)

SMITH, M. G., 'The beginnings of Hausa society, A.D. 1000–1500', in VANSINA, J., *et al.*, *The Historian in Tropical Africa* (London, 1964)

SMITH, ROBERT, *Kingdoms of the Yoruba* (3rd ed., London, 1988)

STEPHENS, PHILLIPS (JR), 'The Kisra legend and the distortion of historical tradition', *J.Afr.Hist.*, vol. 16, no. 2 (1975)

Ta'rikh al-Sudan ed. and trans. HOUDAS, O. (Paris, 1901)

Ta'rikh al-Fattash ed. and trans. HOUDAS, O. and DELAFOSSE, M. (Paris, 1913)

TAUXIER, L., *Le Noir de Bondoukou* (Paris, 1921)

TRIMINGHAM, J. SPENCER, *A History of Islam in West Africa* (London, 1962)

UNDERWOOD, LEON, *Bronzes of West Africa* (London, 1949)

URVOY, YVES, *Histoire des populations du Soudan central* (Paris, 1936)

URVOY, YVES, *Histoire de l'empire du Bornou* (Paris, 1949)

WESTERMANN, D. and BRYAN, M. A., *The Languages of West Africa* (London, 1952)

WILKS, IVOR, *The Northern Factor in Ashanti History* (Legon, 1961)

WILLETT, FRANK, *Ife in the History of West African Sculpture* (London, 1967)

Bantu Africa

ALPERS, EDWARD A., 'Dynasties of the Mutapa-Rozwi complex', *J.Afr.Hist.*, vol. 11, no. 2 (1970)

AXELSON, ERIC, *The Portuguese in South-East Africa, 1488–1600* (Cape Town, 1973)

AXELSON, ERIC, *The Portuguese in South-East Africa, 1600–1700* (Johannesburg, 1960)

BAL, WILLY (ed. and trans.), *Description du royaume du Congo par Filippo Pigafetta et Duarte Lopes (1591)* (2nd ed., Louvain and Paris, 1965)

BEACH, D. N., *The Shona and Zimbabwe, 900–1850* (London, 1980)

CHITTICK, H. NEVILLE, *Kilwa: An Islamic Trading City on the East African Coast* (vols. 2, Nairobi, 1974)

CHITTICK, H. NEVILLE, *Manda: Excavations at an Island Port on the Kenya Coast* (Nairobi, 1984)

CLARK, J. DESMOND, *The Prehistory of Southern Africa* (Harmondsworth, 1959)

COHEN, D. W., 'A survey of inter-lacustrine chronology', *J.Afr.Hist.*, vol. 11, no. 2 (1970)

COLE, SONIA, *The Prehistory of East Africa* (2nd ed., Harmondsworth, 1964)

DALBY, DAVID, 'The prehistorical implications of Guthrie's *Comparative Bantu*', *J.Afr.Hist.*, vol. 16, no. 4 (1975) and vol. 17, no. 1 (1976)

EHRET, CHRISTOPHER, 'Cattle-keeping and milking in eastern and southern Africa; the linguistic evidence', *J.Afr.Hist.*, vol. 8, no. 1 (1967)

EHRET, CHRISTOPHER, *Southern Nilotic History* (Evanston, 1971)

FAGAN, BRIAN M., 'The iron age sequence in the Southern Province of Northern Rhodesia', *J.Afr.Hist.*, vol. 4, no. 2 (1963)

FAGAN, BRIAN M., 'The Greefswald sequence: Bambandyanalo and Mapungubwe', *J.Afr.Hist.*, vol. 5, no. 3 (1964)

FAGAN, BRIAN M., *South Africa during the Iron Age* (London, 1965)

FAGAN, BRIAN M. (ed.), *A Short History of Zambia from the Earliest Times until A.D. 1900* (Nairobi, 1966)

FAGAN, BRIAN M., 'Early trade and raw materials in south central Africa', *J.Afr.Hist.*, vol. 10, no. 1 (1969)

FLIGHT, COLIN, 'Malcolm Guthrie and the reconstruction of Bantu prehistory', *Hist. in Afr.*, vol. 7 (1980)

FREEMAN-GRENVILLE, G. S. P., 'East African coin finds and their historical significance', *J.Afr.Hist.*, vol. 1, no. 1 (1960)

FREEMAN-GRENVILLE, G. S. P., *The East African Coast; Select Documents* (Oxford, 1962)

GARLAKE, PETER S., *The Early Islamic Architecture of the East African Coast* (Nairobi and London, 1966)

GARLAKE, PETER S., *Great Zimbabwe* (London, 1973)

GARLAKE, PETER S., 'Pastoralism and Zimbabwe', *J.Afr.Hist.*, vol. 19, no. 4 (1978)

GRAVEL, PIERRE BETTEZ, 'Life on the manor in Gisaka (Rwanda)', *J.Afr.Hist.*, vol. 6, no. 3 (1965)

GREENBERG, JOSEPH H., 'Linguistic evidence regarding Bantu origins', *J.Afr.Hist.*, vol. 13, no. 2 (1972)

GUTHRIE, MALCOLM, 'Some developments in the prehistory of the Bantu languages', *J.Afr.Hist.*, vol. 3, no. 2 (1962)

GUTHRIE, MALCOLM, *Comparative Bantu: An Introduction to the Comparative Linguistics and Prehistory of the Bantu Languages* (4 vols., Farnborough, 1967–9)

GUTHRIE, MALCOLM, 'Contributions from comparative Bantu studies to the prehistory of Africa', in DALBY, DAVID (ed.), *Language and History in Africa* (London, 1970)

HEINE, B., 'Zur genetischen Gliederung der Bantu-Sprachen', *Afrika and Übersee*, vol. 56 (1972–3)

HIERNAUX, JEAN, 'Bantu expansion: the evidence from physical anthropology confronted with linguistic and archaeological evidence', *J.Afr.Hist.*, vol. 9, no. 4 (1968)

HUFFMAN, T. N., 'The rise and fall of Zimbabwe', *J.Afr.Hist.*, vol. 13, no. 3 (1972)

LAWREN, WILLIAM L., 'Masai and Kikuyu: an historical analysis of culture transmission', *J.Afr.Hist.*, vol. 9, no. 4 (1968)

MAGGS, TIMOTHY, 'The Iron Age sequence south of the Vaal and Pongola rivers', *J.Afr.Hist.*, vol. 21, no. 1 (1980)

MAQUET, JACQUES J., *Le Système des relations sociales dans le Ruanda ancient* (Tervuren, 1954)

NENQUIN, JACQUES, *Excavations at Sanga, 1957* (Tervuren, 1963)

NENQUIN, JACQUES, 'Notes on some early pottery cultures in northern Katanga', *J.Afr.Hist.*, vol. 4, no. 1 (1963)

NURSE, DEREK and SPEAR, THOMAS, *The Swahili: Reconstructing the History and Language of an African Society, 800–1500* (Philadelphia, 1985)

OGOT, BETHWELL A., 'Kingship and statelessness among the Nilotes', in VANSINA, J. *et al.*, *The Historian in Tropical Africa* (London, 1964)

OGOT, BETHWELL A., *History of the Southern Luo* (Nairobi, 1967)

OLIVER, ROLAND, 'The Nilotic contribution to Bantu Africa', *J.Afr.Hist.*, vol. 23, no. 4 (1982)

Papers on Comparative Bantu, *African Language Studies*, vol. 14 (1973)

PHILIPSON, D. W. and FAGAN, BRIAN M., 'The date of the Ingombe Ilede burials', *J.Afr.Hist.*, vol. 10, no. 2 (1969)

PHILIPSON, D. W., *The Later Prehistory of Eastern and Southern Africa* (London, 1977)

POSNANSKY, MERRICK, 'Kingship, archaeology and historical myth', *Uganda J.*, vol. 30, no. 1 (1966)

POSNANSKY, MERRICK (ed.), *Prelude to East African History* (Oxford, 1966)

POSNANSKY, MERRICK, 'Bantu Genesis; archaeological reflections', *J.Afr.Hist.*, vol. 9, no. 1 (1968)

ROBERTS, ANDREW, *A History of the Bemba* (London, 1974)

SASSOON, HAMO, 'New views on Engaruka', *J.Afr.Hist.*, vol. 8, no. 2 (1967)

SUMMERS, ROGER, 'The Rhodesian Iron Age', in FAGE, J. D. and OLIVER, R. A., *Papers in African Prehistory* (Cambridge, 1970)

SUMMERS, ROGER, ROBINSON, K. R. and WHITTY, ANTHONY, *Zimbabwe Excavations, 1958* (Salisbury, Rhodesia, 1961)

VANSINA, JAN, 'Long-distance trade routes in central Africa', *J.Afr.Hist.*, vol. 3, no. 3 (1962)
VANSINA, JAN, *Kingdoms of the Savanna* (Madison, 1966)
VANSINA, JAN, 'Western Bantu expansion', *J.Afr.Hist.*, vol. 25, no. 2 (1984)

PART TWO
THE IMPACT OF ISLAM (PAGES 141–212)

ARNOLD, SIR THOMAS and GUILLAUME, ALFRED (eds), *The Legacy of Islam* (London, 1931)
GIBB, H. A. R., *Muhammadanism* (London, 1949)
HAZARD, HARRY, *Atlas of Islamic History* (Princeton, 1954)
HOLT, P. M., LAMBTON, ANN K. S. and LEWIS, BERNARD (eds), *The Cambridge History of Islam* (2 vols., Cambridge, 1970)
LEWIS, BERNARD, *The Arabs in History* (London, 1950)
ROOLVINK, R., *Historical Atlas of the Muslim Peoples* (Amsterdam, 1957)

ABUN-NASR, J. M., *The Tijaniyya* (Oxford, 1965)
ABUN-NASR, J. M., *A History of the Maghrib* (Cambridge, 1971)
BRETT, MICHAEL, 'Ifriqiya as a market for Saharan trade from the tenth to the twelfth century', *J.Afr.Hist.*, vol. 10, no. 3 (1969)
BRETT, MICHAEL, 'Problems in the interpretation of the history of the Maghrib', *J.Afr.Hist.*, vol. 13, no. 3 (1972)
BRUNSCHWIG, R., *La Berbérie orientale sous les Hafsides* (2 vols., Paris, 1940–9)
CRAWFORD, O. G. S., *The Funj Kingdom of Sennar* (Gloucester, 1951)
CURTIN, PHILIP D., '*Jihad* in West Africa: early phases and inter-relations in Mauritania and Senegal', *J.Afr.Hist.*, vol. 12, no. 1 (1971)
DENNETT, DANIEL C., *Conversion and the Poll Tax in Early Islam* (Cambridge, Mass., 1950)
GAUTIER, E. G., *Le Passé de l'Afrique du nord: les siècles obscurs* (Paris, 1937)
GOUILLY, ALPHONSE, *L'Islam dans l'Afrique Occidentale Française* (Paris, 1952)
HAMPATÉ BA, A., and DAGET, JACQUES, *L'Empire peul du Macina, 1818–1853* (Paris, 1962)
HOGBEN, S. R. and KIRK-GREENE, A. H. M., *The Emirates of Northern Nigeria* (London, 1966)
HOLT, P. M., *Egypt and the Fertile Crescent, 1516–1922* (London, 1966)
HOLT, P. M., *The Age of the Crusades, ... from the Eleventh Century to 1517* (London, 1986)
IBN KHALDUN, *Histoire des Berbères* (trans. de Slane, 4 vols., Paris, 1925–46)
IBN KHALDUN, *The Muqaddimah* (trans. F. Rosenthal, 3 vols., London, 1958)

JULIEN, CH.-ANDRÉ, *Histoire de l'Afrique du nord*, vol. 2 (Paris, 1952)

KENNEDY, HUGH, *The Prophet and the Age of the Caliphates, ... from the Sixth to the Eleventh Century* (London, 1986)

LANE-POOLE, STANLEY, *The Barbary Corsairs* (London, 1890)

LAST, MURRAY, *The Sokoto Caliphate* (London, 1967)

LEVTZION, N. and HOPKINS, J. F. P., *Corpus of Early Arabic sources for West African History* (Cambridge, 1981)

LEWIS, I. M. (ed.), *Islam in Tropical Africa* (London, 1966)

MONTEIL, CHARLES, *Les Bambaras de Segou et du Kaarta* (Paris, 1924)

MONTEIL, VINCENT, *L'Islam noir* (Paris, 1964)

MUHSIN MAHDI, *Ibn Khaldun's Philosophy of History* (London, 1957)

PALMER, H. R., *Sudanese Memoirs* (repr. London, 1967)

ROBINSON, DAVID, *The Holy War of Umar Tal: The Western Sudan in the Mid-nineteenth Century* (Oxford, 1985)

RODNEY, WALTER, 'Jihad and social revolution in Futa Djalon in the eighteenth century', *J.Hist.Soc.Nig.*, vol. 4, no. 2 (1968)

SMITH, H. F. C., 'A neglected theme of West African history; the Islamic revolutions of the nineteenth century', *J.Hist.Soc.Nig.*, vol. 2, no. 1 (1961)

SMITH, M. G., *Government in Zazzau, 1800–1950* (London, 1960)

TAUXIER, LOUIS, *Histoire des Bambara* (Paris, 1942)

TERRASSE, HENRI, *Histoire du Maroc* (2 vols., Casablanca, 1949–50)

TRIMINGHAM, J. SPENCER, *Islam in the Sudan* (London, 1949)

TRIMINGHAM, J. SPENCER, *Islam in Ethiopia* (London, 1952)

TRIMINGHAM, J. SPENCER, *Islam in West Africa* (London, 1959)

TRIMINGHAM, J. SPENCER, *A History of Islam in West Africa* (London, 1962)

TRIMINGHAM, J. SPENCER, *Islam in East Africa* (London, 1964)

URVOY, YVES, *Histoire des populations du Soudan central* (Paris, 1936)

WALDMAN, MARILYN R., 'The Fulani *Jihad*: a re-assessment', *J.Afr.Hist.*, vol. 6, no. 3 (1965)

WANSBOROUGH, JOHN, 'The decolonization of North African history', *J.Afr.Hist.*, vol. 9, no. 4 (1968)

WILLIS, JOHN R., '*Jihad fi Sabil Allah*: its doctrinal basis in Islam, and some aspects of its evolution in nineteenth-century West Africa', *J.Afr.Hist.*, vol. 8, no. 3 (1967)

YUSUF FADL HASSAN, *The Arabs and the Sudan from the Seventh to the Early Sixteenth Century* (Edinburgh, 1967)

CHAPTERS 9–12 (PAGES 213–325)
AFRICA IN THE AGE OF EUROPEAN EXPANSION

General: European activities: the export slave trade

ANSTEY, ROGER, *The Atlantic Slave Trade and British Abolition, 1760–1810* (London, 1975)

AXELSON, ERIC, *The Portuguese in South-East Africa, 1600–1700* (Johannesburg, 1960)

AXELSON, ERIC, *The Portuguese in South-East Africa, 1488–1600* (Cape Town, 1973)

BIRMINGHAM, DAVID, *The Portuguese Conquest of Angola* (London, 1965)

BLAKE, J. W., *West Africa: Quest for God and Gold, 1454–1578* (London, 1977)

BLAKE, J. W., *Europeans in West Africa, 1450–1560* (2 vols., London, 1942)

BOURDON, LÉON (ed.), *Gomes Eanes de Zurara: chronique du Guinée* (Dakar, 1960)

BOXER, C. R., *The Dutch Seaborne Empire, 1600–1800* (London, 1965)

BOXER, C. R., *The Portuguese Seaborne Empire, 1415–1825* (London, 1969)

COUPLAND, R., *East Africa and Its Invaders* (Oxford, 1938)

COUPLAND, R., *The Exploitation of East Africa* (London, 1939)

CRONE, G. R. (ed.), *The Voyages of Cadamosto and Other Documents* (London, 1937)

CURTIN, PHILIP D., *The Atlantic Slave Trade: A Census* (Madison, 1969)

CURTIN, PHILIP D. and VANSINA, JAN, 'Sources of the nineteenth-century Atlantic slave trade', *J.Afr.Hist.*, vol. 5, no. 2 (1964)

CURTIN, PHILIP D., ANSTEY, ROGER and INIKORI, J. E., 'Measuring the Atlantic slave-trade: a discussion', *J.Afr.Hist.*, vol. 17, no. 4 (1976)

DAVIDSON, BASIL, *Black Mother* (London, 1961)

DAVIES, K. G., *The Royal African Company* (London, 1957)

DESCHAMPS, HUBERT, *Histoire de la traite des noirs de l'antiquité à nos jours* (Paris, 1971)

FAGE, J. D., 'Slavery and the slave trade in the context of West African history', *J.Afr.Hist.*, vol. 10, no. 3 (1969)

FAGE, J. D., *States and Subjects in sub-Saharan Africa* (Johannesburg, 1974)

FAGE, J. D., 'Slaves and society in western Africa, c. 1445–c. 1700', *J.Afr.Hist.*, vol. 21, no. 3 (1980)

FREEMAN-GRENVILLE, G. S. P., *The East African Coast* (Oxford, 1962)

GEMERY, HENRY A. and HOGENDORN, JAN S. (eds), *The Uncommon Market: Essays in the Economic History of the Atlantic Slave Trade* (New York, 1979)

GRAY, RICHARD, 'Portuguese musketeers on the Zambezi', *J.Afr.Hist.*, vol. 12, no. 4 (1971)

GRAY, RICHARD (ed.), *Cambridge History of Africa*, vol. 4, c. 1600–c. 1970 (Cambridge, 1975)

GREEN-PEDERSEN, SV. E., 'The scope and structure of the Danish Negro slave trade', *Scand.Econ.Hist.Rev.*, vol. 19, no. 2 (1971)

HAIR, P. E. H., 'The enslavement of Koelle's informants', *J.Afr.Hist.*, vol. 6, no. 2 (1965)

INIKORI, J. E., 'Measuring the Atlantic slave trade: an assessment of Curtin and Anstey', *J.Afr.Hist.*, vol. 17, no. 2 (1976)

INIKORI, J. E. (ed.), *Forced Migration: The Impact of the Export Slave Trade on African Societies* (London, 1982)

LAWRENCE, A. W., *Trade Castles and Forts of West Africa* (London, 1963)

LOCHNER, NORBERT, 'Anton Wilhelm Amo: a Ghana scholar in eighteenth century Germany', *Trans.Hist.Soc.Ghana*, vol. 3, no. 3 (1958)

MAGALHÃES GODINHO, V., *L'Économie de l'empire portugais au XVe et XVIe siècles* (Paris, 1969)

MANNING, PATRICK J., 'The enslavement of Africans: a demographic model', *Canadian J.Afr.Studs.*, vol. 15 (1981)

MANNIX, D. P. and COWLEY, MALCOLM, *Black Cargoes; A History of the Atlantic Slave Trade, 1518–1865* (New York, 1962)

MARKS, SHULA, 'Firearms in southern Africa: a survey', *J.Afr.Hist.*, vol. 12, no. 4 (1971)

MARTIN, EVELYN C., *The British West African Settlements, 1750–1821* (London, 1927)

MAUNY, RAYMOND, *Les Navigations médiévales sur les côtes sahariennes* (Lisbon, 1960)

MEILLASSOUX, CLAUDE (ed.), *L'esclavage en Afrique précoloniale* (Paris, 1975)

MIRACLE, MARVIN P., 'The introduction and spread of maize in Africa', *J.Afr.Hist.*, vol. 6, no. 1 (1965)

PARRY, J. H., *The Age of Reconnaissance: Discovery, Exploration and Settlement, 1450–1650* (London, 1963)

POSTMA, JOHANNES, 'The dimensions of the Dutch slave trade', *J.Afr.Hist.*, vol. 13, no. 2 (1972)

PRIESTLEY, MARGARET, *West African Trade and Coast Society: A Family Study* (London, 1969)

RICHARDS, W. A., 'The import of firearms into West Africa in the eighteenth century', *J.Afr.Hist.*, vol. 21, no. 1 (1980)

RODNEY, WALTER, *West Africa and the Atlantic Slave Trade* (Nairobi, 1967)

STRANDES, JUSTUS, *The Portuguese Period in East Africa* (trans. of 1899 German original, Nairobi, 1961)

THORNTON, JOHN K., 'The demographic effect of the slave trade on western Africa, 1500–1850', *African Historical Demography*, II (Edinburgh, 1981)

VOGT, JOHN, *Portuguese Rule on the Gold Coast, 1469–1682* (Athens, Georgia, 1979)

WHITE, GAVIN, 'Firearms in Africa; an introduction', *J.Afr.Hist.*, vol. 12, no. 2 (1971)

West Africa

AKINJOGBIN, I. A., *Dahomey and its Neighbours, 1708–1818* (Cambridge, 1967)

ARHIN, KWAME, 'The structure of greater Ashanti', *J.Afr.Hist.*, vol. 8, no. 1 (1967)

BOSMAN, WILLIAM, *A New and Accurate Description of the Coast of Guinea* (annotated reprint of 1705 pub., London, 1967)

CURTIN, PHILIP D. (ed.), *Africa Remembered: Narratives by West Africans from the Era of the Slave Trade* (Madison, 1967)

CURTIN, PHILIP D., *Economic Change in Pre-colonial Africa: Senegambia in the Era of the Slave Trade* (2 vols., Madison, 1975)

DAAKU, K. Y., 'European traders and the coastal states', *Tr.Hist.Soc.Ghana*, vol. 8 (1965)

DAAKU, K. Y., *Trade and Politics on the Gold Coast, 1600–1720* (Oxford, 1970)

DAPPER, O., *Umstandliche und eigentliche Beschreibung von Afrika* (Amsterdam, 1670)

FAGE, J. D., *A History of West Africa* (Cambridge, 1969)

FORDE, DARYLL and KABERRY, PHYLLIS (eds.), *West African Kingdoms in the Nineteenth Century* (London, 1967)

FYNN, J. K., *Ashanti and Its Neighbours, 1700–1807* (London, 1971)

GOUCHER, CANDICE L., 'Iron is iron 'til it rust: trade and ecology in the decline of West African iron-smelting', *J.Afr.Hist.*, vol. 22, no. 2 (1981)

JOHNSON, MARION, 'The ounce in eighteenth-century West African trade', *J.Afr.Hist.*, vol. 7, no. 2 (1966)

JOHNSON, MARION, 'The cowrie currencies of West Africa', *J.Afr.Hist.*, vol. 11, nos. 1 and 3 (1970)

JONES, G. I., *The Trading States of the Oil Rivers* (London, 1963)

KEA, R. A., 'Firearms and warfare on the Gold and Slave coasts from the sixteenth to the nineteenth centuries', *J.Afr.Hist.*, vol. 12, no. 2 (1971)

KEA, RAY A., *Settlements, Trade and Polities in the Seventeenth Century Gold Coast* (Baltimore, 1982)

KUMAH, J. K., 'The rise and fall of the kingdom of Denkyera', *Ghana Notes and Queries*, no. 9 (1966)

LATHAM, A. J. H., *Old Calabar, 1600–1891* (Cambridge, 1973)

LATHAM, A. J. H., 'Currency, credit and capital on the Cross River in the pre-colonial era', *J.Afr.Hist.*, vol. 12, no. 4 (1971)

LAW, ROBIN, *The Oyo Empire, c. 1600–c. 1836* (Oxford, 1977)

LAW, ROBIN, 'Trade and politics behind the Slave Coast: the lagoon traffic and the rise of Lagos, 1500–1800', *J.Afr.Hist.*, vol. 24, no. 3 (1983)

MANNING, PATRICK J., *Slavery, Colonialism and Economic Growth in Dahomey, 1640–1960* (Cambridge, 1982)

MAREES, PIETER DE, *Description and Historical Account of the Gold Kingdom of Guinea (1602)*, tr. and ed. ALBERT VAN DANTZIG and ADAM JONES (Oxford, 1987)

POLE, L. M., 'Decline or survival? Iron production in West Africa from the seventeenth to the twentieth centuries', *J.Afr.Hist.*, vol. 23, no. 4 (1983)

RODNEY, WALTER, *A History of the Upper Guinea Coast, 1545–1800* (Oxford, 1970)

RODNEY, WALTER, 'Gold and slaves on the Gold Coast', *Tr.Hist.Soc.Ghana*, vol. 10 (1969)

SMITH, ROBERT S., *Warfare and Diplomacy in Pre-colonial West Africa* (London, 1976)

WILKS, IVOR, 'The rise of the Akwamu empire, 1650–1710', *Tr.Hist. Soc.Ghana*, vol. 3, no. 2 (1957)

WILKS, IVOR, 'Wangara, Akan and Portuguese in the fifteenth and sixteenth centuries', *J.Afr.Hist.*, vol. 23, nos. 3 and 4 (1982)

WILKS, IVOR, *Asante in the Nineteenth Century* (Cambridge, 1975)

Bantu Africa

ALPERS, EDWARD A., *Ivory and Slaves in East Central Africa* (London, 1975)

ALPERS, EDWARD A., 'Trade, state and society among the Yao in the nineteenth century', *J.Afr.Hist.*, vol. 10, no. 3 (1969)

ANSTEY, ROGER, *Britain and the Congo in the Nineteenth Century* (Oxford, 1962)

ATMORE, ANTHONY, CHIVENJE, J. M. and MUDENGE, S. I., 'Firearms in south central Africa', *J.Afr.Hist.*, vol. 12, no. 4 (1971)

BEACHEY, R. W., 'The East African ivory trade in the nineteenth century', *J.Afr.Hist.*, vol. 7, no. 2 (1967)

BIRMINGHAM, DAVID, *Trade and Conflict in Angola* (Oxford, 1966)

CHILDS, G. M., 'The peoples of Angola in the seventeenth century according to Cadornega', *J.Afr.Hist.*, vol. 1, no. 2 (1960)

COHEN, D. W., *The Historical Tradition of Busoga* (Oxford, 1972)

CUNNISON, IAN, 'Kazembe and the Portuguese, 1798–1832', *J.Afr.Hist.*, vol. 2, no. 1 (1961)

CUNNISON, IAN (ed. and trans.), *King Kazembe* (Lisbon, 1962)

DIAS, JILL R., 'Famine and disease in the history of Angola, c. 1830–1930', *J.Afr.Hist.*, vol. 22, no. 3 (1981)

FEIERMAN, STEVEN, *The Shambaa Kingdom: A History* (Madison, 1974)

GRAY, SIR JOHN, *History of Zanzibar from the Earliest Times to 1856* (London, 1962)

GRAY, RICHARD and BIRMINGHAM, DAVID (eds), *Pre-colonial African Trade* (London, 1970)

HEUSCH, L. DE, *Le Rwanda et la civilisation interlacustrine* (Brussels, 1966)

HILTON, ANNE, *The Kingdom of Kongo* (Oxford, 1985)

ISAACMAN, ALLEN F., *Mozambique: The Africanization of a European Institution; the Zambezi Prazos, 1750–1902* (Madison, 1972)

KARUGIRE, S. R., *A History of the Kingdom of Nkore* (Oxford, 1971)

KIMAMBO, I. N., *A Political History of the Pare* (Oxford, 1969)

KIWANUKA, M. S. M., *A History of Buganda* (London, 1972)

LYE, WILLIAM F., 'The *Difaqane*: the *Mfecane* in the southern Sotho area', *J.Afr.Hist.*, vol. 8, no. 1 (1967)

LYE, WILLIAM F., 'The Ndebele kingdom south of the Limpopo river', *J.Afr.Hist.*, vol. 10, no. 1 (1969)

MAINGA, MUTUMBA, *Bulozi under the Luyana Kings* (London, 1973)

MARTIN, PHYLLIS M., *The External Trade of the Loango Coast, 1576–1870* (Oxford, 1972)

MILLER, JOSEPH C., 'The Imbangala and the chronology of early central African history', *J.Afr.Hist.*, vol. 13, no. 4 (1972)

MILLER, JOSEPH C., 'Nzinga of Matamba in a new perspective', *J.Afr.Hist.*, vol. 16, no. 2 (1975)

MILLER, JOSEPH C., *Kings and Kinsmen: Early Mbundu States in Angola* (Oxford, 1976)

MILLER, JOSEPH C., 'The significance of drought, disease and famine in the agricultural zones of west-central Africa', *J.Afr.Hist.*, vol. 23, no. 1 (1982)

MORRIS, DONALD R., *The Washing of the Spears: The Rise and Fall of the Zulu Nation* (London, 1966)

MURIUKI, GODFREY, *A History of the Kikuyu* (Nairobi, 1974)

NEWITT, M. D. D., 'The Portuguese on the Zambezi: an historical interpretation', *J.Afr.Hist.*, vol. 10, no. 1 (1970)

NEWITT, M. D. D., *Portuguese Settlement on the Zambezi* (London, 1973)

NEWITT, M. D. D., 'The early history of the Maravi', *J.Afr.Hist.*, vol. 23, no. 2 (1982)

OGOT, BETHWELL A., *History of the Southern Luo* (Nairobi, 1967)

OLIVER, ROLAND, 'The traditional histories of Buganda, Bunyoro and Ankole', *J.Roy.Anth.Inst.*, vol. 85 (1955)

OMER-COOPER, J. D., *The Zulu Aftermath; A Nineteenth-Century Revolution in Bantu Africa* (London, 1966)

PACHAI, BRIDGLAL (ed.), *Malawi: Past and Present* (Blantyre, 1957)

RITTER, E. A., *Shaka Zulu: The Rise of the Zulu Empire* (London, 1955)

ROBERTS, ANDREW (ed.), *Tanzania Before 1900* (Nairobi, 1968)

ROBERTS, ANDREW, *A History of the Bemba* (London, 1973)

SLADE, RUTH, *King Leopold's Congo* (London, 1962)

THOMPSON, LEONARD (ed.), *African Societies in Southern Africa* (London, 1969)

THORNTON, JOHN K., 'Demography and history in the kingdom of Kongo, 1550–1750', *J.Afr.Hist.*, vol. 18, no. 4 (1977)

THORNTON, JOHN K., *The Kingdom of Kongo: Civil War and Transition, 1641–1718* (Madison, 1983)

VANSINA, JAN, *L'Évolution du royaume de Rwanda des origines à 1900* (Brussels, 1962)

VANSINA, JAN, *The Children of Woot: A History of the Kuba Peoples* (Madison, 1978)

WALTON, JAMES, *African Village* (Pretoria, 1956)

WILSON, ANNE, 'Long-distance trade and the Luba Lomami empire', *J.Afr.Hist.*, vol. 13, no. 4 (1972)

CHAPTERS 13 AND 14 (PAGES 326–388)

THE EXPANSION OF EUROPEAN POWER DURING THE NINETEENTH CENTURY

General

AXELSON, ERIC, *Portugal and the Scramble for Africa, 1875–1896* (Johannesburg, 1967)

BOAHEN, A. ADU, *Britain, the Sahara and the Western Sudan, 1788–1891* (Oxford, 1964)

BRUNSCHWIG, HENRI, *L'Expansion allemande d'outre-mer* (Paris, 1957)

BRUNSCHWIG, HENRI, *L'Avènement de l'Afrique noire* (Paris, 1963)

BRUNSCHWIG, HENRI, *French Colonialism: Myths and Realities* (London, 1966)

CLARENCE-SMITH, GERVASE, *The Third Portuguese Empire, 1825–1975* (London, 1985)

COUPLAND, SIR REGINALD, *The British Anti-Slavery Movement* (repr. London, 1964)

CROWE, S. E., *The Berlin West African Conference, 1884–85* (London, 1942)

FEIS, H., *Europe, the World's Banker* (New Haven, 1930)

FLINT, JOHN E. (ed.), *The Cambridge History of Africa*, vol 5, c. *1790–c. 1870* (Cambridge, 1976)

FRANKEL, S. HERBERT, *Capital Investment in Africa* (London, 1938)

FREUND, BILL, *The Making of Contemporary Africa: The Development of African Society Since 1800* (London, 1984)

GIFFORD, PROSSER and LOUIS, WM. ROGER (eds.), *Britain and Germany in Africa: Imperial Rivalry and Colonial Rule* (New Haven, 1967)

GIFFORD, PROSSER and LOUIS, WM. ROGER (eds.), *France and Britain in Africa: Imperial Rivalry and Colonial Rule* (New Haven, 1971)

GROVES, C. P., *The Planting of Christianity in Africa* (4 vols., London, 1948–58)

HALLETT, ROBIN, *Records of the African Association, 1788–1831* (London, 1964)

HALLETT, ROBIN, *The Penetration of Africa*, vol. 1, *To 1815* (London, 1965)

HAMMOND, RICHARD J., *Portugal and Africa, 1815–1910: A Study in Uneconomic Imperialism* (Stanford, 1966)

HOBSON, C. K., *The Export of Capital* (London, 1914)

HOBSON, J. A., *Imperialism* (3rd ed., rev., London, 1938)

HOPKINS, A. G., 'Economic imperialism in West Africa: Lagos, 1880–92', *Econ.Hist.Rev.*, vol. 21 (1968)

LANGER, WILLIAM L., *European Alliances and Alignments, 1870–1890* (2nd ed., New York, 1950)

LANGER, WILLIAM L., *The Diplomacy of Imperialism, 1890–1902* (2nd ed., New York, 1951)

LENIN, V. I., *Imperialism: The Highest Stage of Capitalism* (London, 1916)

LEROY-BEAULIEU, PAUL, *De la Colonisation chez les peuples modernes* (6th ed., 2 vols., Paris, 1908)

LLOYD, CHRISTOPHER, *The Navy and the Slave Trade* (London, 1949)

NEWBURY, C. W., 'Victorians, Republicans, and the partition of West Africa', *J.Afr.Hist.*, vol. 3, no. 3 (1962)

OLIVER, ROLAND, *Sir Harry Johnston and the Scramble for Africa* (London, 1957)

OLIVER, ROLAND and SANDERSON, G. N. (eds.), *The Cambridge History of Africa:* vol. 6, *From 1870 to 1905* (Cambridge, 1985)

PERHAM, MARGERY and SIMMONS, JACK (eds.), *African Discovery: An Anthology of Exploration* (London, 1942)

ROBERTS, S. H., *The History of French Colonial Policy, 1870–1925* (2 vols., London, 1929)

ROBINSON, RONALD and GALLAGHER, JOHN, with DENNY, ALICE, *Africa and the Victorians: The Official Mind of Imperialism* (London, 1961)

STENGERS, JEAN, 'L'impérialisme colonial de la fin du XIXe siècle: mythe ou réalité?', *J.Afr.Hist.*, vol. 3, no. 3 (1962)

STENGERS, JEAN, 'Une facette de la question du Haut-Nil: le mirage soudanais', *J.Afr.Hist.*, vol. 10, no. 4 (1969)

TAYLOR, A. J. P., *Germany's First Bid for Colonies, 1884–5* (London, 1938)

TAYLOR, A. J. P., *The Struggle for Mastery in Europe, 1848–1914* (Oxford, 1954)

WILLIAMS, ERIC, *Capitalism and Slavery* (Chapel Hill, 1944)

WILSON, H. S., *The Imperial Experience in Sub-Saharan Africa since 1870* (London, 1977)

North Africa

AGERON, CH.-ROBERT, *Histoire de l'Algérie contemporaine, 1830–1965* (Paris, 1964)

BAER, GABRIEL, *A History of Landownership in Modern Egypt, 1800–1950* (1962)

BAER, GABRIEL, *Studies in the Social History of Modern Egypt* (Chicago, 1969)

BERNARD, AUGUSTIN, *L'Algérie* (Paris, 1930)

BERNARD, AUGUSTIN, *Le Maroc* (7th ed., Paris, 1931)

DESPOIS, J. et al., *Initiation à la Tunisie* (Paris, 1950)

DODWELL, H. H., *The Founder of Modern Egypt: Mohammed Ali* (Cambridge, 1931)

FITOUSSI, ELIE and BENOUZET, ANSTIDE, *L'État tunisien et le protectorat français, 1880–1931* (Paris, 1931)

GRAY, J. R., *A History of the Southern Sudan, 1839–1889* (London, 1961)

HILL, RICHARD, *Egypt in the Sudan, 1820–1881* (London, 1959)

HOLT, P. M., *The Mahdist State in the Sudan, 1881–1898* (Oxford, 1958)

HOLT, P. M. (ed.), *Political and Social Change in Modern Egypt* (London, 1968)

JULIEN, CH.-ANDRÉ, *Histoire de l'Algérie contemporaine* (Paris, 1964)

MARLOWE, JOHN, *Anglo-Egyptian Relations, 1800–1953* (London, 1954)

MIÉGE, J.-L., *Le Maroc et l'Europe, 1830–1894* (2 vols., Paris, 1961/4)

SANDERSON, G. N., *England, Europe and the Upper Nile, 1882–1899* (Edinburgh, 1965)

TOURNEAU, R. LE et al., *Initiation à l'Algérie* (Paris, 1957)

VATIKIOTIS, P. J., *The History of Egypt from Muhammad Ali to Sadat* (2nd ed., London, 1980)

West Africa

ADELEYE, R. A., *Power and Diplomacy in Northern Nigeria, 1800–1906* (London, 1972)

AJAYI, J. F. ADE, *Christian Missions in Nigeria, 1841–91* (London, 1965)

AJAYI, J. F. ADE and SMITH, R. S., *Yoruba Warfare in the Nineteenth Century* (Cambridge, 1964)

AKINTOYE, S. A., *Revolution and Power Politics in Yorubaland, 1840–1893* (London, 1971)

ATGER, PAUL, *La France en Côte d'Ivoire de 1843 à 1893* (Dakar, 1962)

AWE, BOLANWE, 'Militarism and economic development in nineteenth-century Yoruba country: the Ibadan example', *J.Afr.Hist.*, vol. 14, no. 1 (1973)

AYANDELE, E. A., *The Missionary Impact on Modern Nigeria, 1842–1914* (London, 1966)

BIOBAKU, SABURI O., *The Egba and Their Neighbours, 1842–1872* (Oxford, 1957)

CROWDER, MICHAEL (ed.), *West African Resistance* (London, 1970)

CURTIN, PHILIP D., *The Image of Africa: British Ideas and Action, 1780–1850* (Madison, 1964)

DIKE, K. ONWUKA, *Trade and Politics in the Niger Delta, 1830–1885* (Oxford, 1956)

DIKE, K. ONWUKA, 'John Beecroft, 1790–1854', *J.Hist.Soc.Nig.*, vol. 1, no. 1 (1956)

DIKE, K. ONWUKA, *Eminent Nigerians of the Nineteenth Century* (Cambridge, 1960)

FLINT, JOHN E., *Sir George Goldie and the Making of Nigeria* (London, 1960)

FUGLESTAD, FINN, *A History of Niger, 1850–1960* (Cambridge, 1983)

FYFE, CHRISTOPHER, *A History of Sierra Leone* (London, 1962)

FYFE, CHRISTOPHER, *Africanus Horton, 1835–1883* (New York, 1972)

GAILEY, HARRY A., *A History of the Gambia* (London, 1964)

GBADAMOSI, T. G. O., *The Growth of Islam among the Yoruba, 1841–1908* (London, 1979)

HARDY, GEORGES, *Faidherbe* (Paris, 1947)

HARGREAVES, JOHN D., *Prelude to the Partition of West Africa* (London, 1963)

HARGREAVES, JOHN D., *West Africa Partitioned*, (2 vols., London, 1974, 1985)

JULY, ROBERT W., *The Origins of Modern African Thought* (London, 1968)

KANYA-FORSTNER, A. SYDNEY, *The Conquest of the Western Sudan: A Study in French Military Imperialism* (Cambridge, 1969)

KIMBLE, DAVID, *A Political History of Ghana: The Rise of Gold Coast Nationalism, 1850–1928* (Oxford, 1963)

KLEIN, MARTIN A., *Islam and Imperialism in Senegal* (Edinburgh, 1968)

LYNCH, HOLLIS R., *Edward Wilmot Blyden, Pan-Negro Patriot* (London, 1967)

METCALFE, G. E., *Maclean of the Gold Coast* (London, 1962)

METCALFE, G. E., *Great Britain and Ghana: Documents of Ghana History, 1807–1957* (Legon, 1964)

NEWBURY, C. W., *The Western Slave Coast and Its Rulers* (Oxford, 1961)

NEWBURY, C. W., *British Policy Towards West Africa* (2 vols., Oxford, 1965)

NEWBURY, C. W. and KANYA-FORSTNER, A. S., 'French policy and the origins of the scramble for West Africa', *J.Afr.Hist.*, vol. 10, no. 2 (1969)

NORTHRUP, DAVID, 'The compatibility of the slave and palm oil trades in the Bight of Biafra', *J.Afr.Hist.*, vol. 17, no. 3 (1976)

PALLINDER-LAW, AGNETA, 'Aborted modernisation in West Africa? The case of Abeokuta', *J.Afr.Hist.*, vol. 15, no. 1 (1974)

PERSON, YVES, *Samori: une révolution dyula* (3 vols., Dakar, 1968–75)

PETERSON, JOHN, *Province of Freedom* (London, 1969)

PORTER, ARTHUR, *Creoledom* (London, 1963)

SCHNAPPER, BERNARD, *La Politique et le Commerce français dans le Golfe de Guinée de 1838 à 1871* (Paris, 1961)

WILKS, IVOR, *Asante in the Nineteenth Century* (Cambridge, 1975)

WILSON, HENRY S. (ed.), *The Origins of West African Nationalism* (London, 1969)

South, Central and East Africa

ABIR, MORDECAI, *Ethiopia: The Era of the Princes, 1769–1855* (London, 1968)

ANSTEY, ROGER, *Britain and the Congo in the Nineteenth Century* (Oxford, 1962)

COOKEY, S. S. S., *Britain and the Congo Question, 1885–1913* (London, 1968)

COUPLAND, SIR REGINALD, *East Africa and Its Invaders ... to ... 1856* (Oxford, 1938)

COUPLAND, SIR REGINALD, *The Exploitation of East Africa, 1856–1890* (London, 1939)

DARKWAH, KOFI, *Menelik of Ethiopia* (London, 1971)

DAYE, PIERRE, *Léopold II* (Paris, 1934)

FLINT, JOHN, *Cecil Rhodes* (London, 1976)

GANN, L. H., *The Birth of a Plural Society: Northern Rhodesia, 1894–1914* (Manchester, 1958)

HANNA, A. J., *The Beginnings of Nyasaland and North-Eastern Rhodesia, 1859–95* (Oxford, 1956)

JAARSVELD, F. A. van, *The Awakening of Afrikaner Nationalism* (Cape Town, 1961)

KIEWIET, C. W. de, *A History of South Africa: Social and Economic* (London, 1941)

LEWIS, I. M., *The Modern History of Somaliland* (London, 1965)

MACMILLAN, W. M., *Bantu, Boer and Briton* (2nd ed., Oxford, 1964)

MARAIS, J. S., *Maynier and the First Boer Republics* (Cape Town, 1944)

MARAIS, J. S., *The Cape Coloured People, 1652–1937* (Johannesburg, 1957)

MARAIS, J. S., *The Fall of Kruger's Republic* (Oxford, 1961)

MARCUS, HAROLD G., *The Life and Times of Menelik II of Ethiopia, 1844–1913* (Oxford, 1974)

MARKS, SHULA, 'Khoisan resistance to the Dutch in the seventeenth and eighteenth centuries', *J.Afr.Hist.*, vol. 13, no. 1 (1972)

MASON, PHILIP, *The Birth of a Dilemma: The Conquest and Settlement of Rhodesia* (London, 1958)

NEUMARK, S. D., *Economic Influences on the South African Frontier, 1652–1836* (Stanford, 1957)

NICHOLLS, C. S., *The Swahili Coast, 1798–1856* (London, 1971)

OLIVER, ROLAND, *The Missionary Factor in East Africa* (London, 1952)

PAKENHAM, THOMAS, *The Boer War* (London, 1979)

RANGER, T. O., *Revolt in Southern Rhodesia, 1896–7* (London, 1967)

ROEYKENS, FR. A., *Léopold II et la Conférence de Bruxelles, 1876* (Brussels, 1956)

ROEYKENS, FR. A., *Léopold II et l'Afrique* (Brussels, 1958)

SCHREUDER, D. M., *The Scramble for Southern Africa, 1877–1895* (Cambridge, 1980)

SIMMONS, JACK, *Livingstone and Africa* (London, 1955)

SLADE, RUTH, *King Leopold's Congo* (London, 1962)

THOMSON, R. S., *La Fondation de l'État Indépendant du Congo* (Brussels, 1933)

WALKER, E. A., *The Great Trek* (4th ed., London, 1960)

PART FOUR
AFRICA IN THE MODERN WORLD (PAGES 389–528)

General

BAETA, C. G. (ed.), *Christianity in Tropical Africa* (London, 1968)
BARRETT, D. B., *Schism and Renewal in Africa* (London, 1968)
BATES, ROBERT H., *Markets and States in Tropical Africa: The Political Basis of Agricultural Policies* (London, 1981)
BUELL, RAYMOND LESLIE, *The Native Problem in Africa* (2 vols., New York, 1928)
CARTER, GWENDOLEN (ed.), *African One-Party States* (Ithaca, 1962)
CARTER, GWENDOLEN (ed.), *Five African States* (Ithaca, 1963)
CARTER, GWENDOLEN, *Politics in Africa* (New York, 1966)
CHILCOTE, RONALD H., *Portuguese Africa* (Englewood Cliffs, 1967)
COHEN, ROBIN (ed.), *African Islands and Enclaves* (London, 1983)
COLEMAN, JAMES and ROSBERG, CARL G. (eds.), *Political Parties and National Integration in Africa* (Berkeley, 1964)
CROWDER, MICHAEL (ed.), *The Cambridge History of Africa:* vol. 8, *From c. 1940 to c. 1975* (Cambridge, 1984)
DAVIDSON, BASIL, *Which Way Africa?* (3rd ed., Harmondsworth, 1971)
DAVIDSON, BASIL, *Africa in Modern History* (London, 1978)
DUMONT, RENÉ, *False Start in Africa* (London, 1966)
FANON, FRANZ, *The Wretched of the Earth* (London, 1965)
FRIEDLAND, WILLIAM H. and ROSBERG, CARL G. (eds.), *African Socialism* (New York, 1964)
GANIAGE, JEAN, DESCHAMPS, HUBERT and GUITARD, ODETTE, *L'Afrique au XXe siècle* (Paris, 1966)
GANN, L. H. and DUIGNAN, PETER (eds.), *Colonialism in Africa, 1870–1960* (5 vols., Cambridge, 1969–75)
GIFFORD, PROSSER and LOUIS, WM. ROGER (eds.), *Britain and Germany in Africa: Imperial Rivalry and Colonial Rule* (New Haven, 1967)
GIFFORD, PROSSER and LOUIS, WM. ROGER (eds.), *France and Britain in Africa: Imperial Rivalry and Colonial Rule* (New Haven, 1971)
HAILEY, LORD, *An African Survey* (London, 1938)
HAILEY, LORD, *An African Survey; Revised* (London, 1957)
HANCOCK, W. K., *Survey of British Commonwealth Affairs, 1918–1939*, vol. 2 (London, 1942)
HASTINGS, ADRIAN, *A History of African Christianity, 1950–75* (Cambridge, 1979)
HODGKIN, THOMAS, *Nationalism in Colonial Africa* (London, 1956)
HODGKIN, THOMAS, *African Political Parties* (Harmondsworth, 1961)
HUNTER, GUY, *The New Societies of Tropical Africa* (London, 1962)

KAMARCK, ANDREW M., *The Economics of African Development* (London, 1967)

LEGUM, COLIN, *Pan-Africanism: A Short Political Guide* (London, 1962)

LEGUM, COLIN (ed.), *Africa: A Handbook to the Continent* (London, 1962)

MUNRO, J. FORBES, *Britain in Tropical Africa, 1880–1960: Economic Relations and Impact* (London, 1984)

NEWITT, MALYN, *Portugal in Africa: The Last Hundred Years* (London, 1981)

PELISSIER, RENÉ, *Les Territoires espagnols d'Afrique* (Paris, 1963)

PERHAM, MARGERY, *The Colonial Reckoning* (London, 1963)

ROBERTS, A. D. (ed.), *The Cambridge History of Africa:* vol. 7, *From 1905 to 1940* (Cambridge, 1986)

ROBSON, P. and LURY, D. A. (eds.), *The Economies of Africa* (London, 1969)

SEGAL, RONALD, *Political Africa* (London, 1961)

SMITH, W. CANTWELL, *Islam in Modern History* (Princeton, 1957)

THOMPSON, V. BAKPETU, *Africa and Unity: The Evolution of Pan-Africanism* (London, 1969)

WORLD BANK, *Accelerated Development in Sub-Saharan Africa* (Washington, 1981)

North Africa

ABBAS, MEKKI, *The Sudan Question* (London, 1952)

AHMED, J. N., *The Intellectual Origins of Egyptian Nationalism* (London, 1960)

AMIN, SAMIR, *The Maghreb in the Modern World* (Harmondsworth, 1970)

ASHFORD, DOUGLAS, *Political Change in Morocco* (Princeton, 1961)

AYACHE, ALBERT, *Le Maroc: Bilan d'une Colonisation* (Paris, 1956)

BAKER, R. W., *Egypt's Uncertain Revolution under Nasser and Sadat* (London, 1979)

BARBOUR, NEVILLE (ed.), *A Survey of North West Africa* (2nd ed., London, 1962)

BERQUE, JACQUES, *French North Africa: The Maghreb between Two World Wars* (London, 1967)

BOURDIEU, PIERRE, *The Algerians* (Boston, 1961)

BOURGUIBA, HABIB, *La Tunisie et la France* (Paris, 1954)

CATROUX, GEORGES, *Lyautey, le Marocain* (Paris, 1952)

DUNCAN, J. S. R., *The Sudan's Path to Independence* (Edinburgh, 1957)

FANON, FRANZ, *A Dying Colonialism* (Harmondsworth, 1970)

FARROD, CHARLES-H., *Le FLN et l'Algérie* (Paris, 1962)

GARAS, FÉLIX, *Bourguiba et la naissance d'une nation* (Paris, 1956)

ISSAWI, CHARLES, *Egypt at Mid-Century* (London, 1954)

JULIEN, CH.-ANDRÉ, *L'Afrique du nord en marche* (Paris, 1952)

KHADDURI, M., *Modern Libya: A Study in Political Development* (London, 1963)

KNAPP, W., *Tunisia* (1970)

LACHERAF, MOSTEFA, *L'Algérie: nation et société* (Paris, 1965)

LANDAU, ROM, *Moroccan Drama, 1900–1955* (London, 1956)

LE TOURNEAU, ROGER, *L'Évolution politique de l'Afrique du Nord musulmane, 1920–1961* (Paris, 1962)

LING, DWIGHT, *Tunisia: From Protectorate to Republic* (Bloomington, 1967)

LITTLE, TOM, *Egypt* (London, 1958)

MARLOWE, JOHN, *Arab Nationalism and British Imperialism* (London, 1961)

MICAUD, CH.-A., *Tunisia: The Politics of Modernization* (New York, 1964)

MIÈGE, JEAN-LOUIS, *Le Maroc* (Paris, 1962)

NASSER, GAMAL ABDUL, *The Philosophy of the Revolution* (Washington, 1959)

SANDERSON, L. P. and G. N., *Education, Religion and Politics in the Southern Sudan, 1899–1964* (London, 1981)

THOMPSON, VIRGINIA and ADLOFF, RICHARD, *The Western Sahara* (London, 1980)

TILLION, GERMAINE, *Algeria: The Realities* (London, 1958)

VATIKIOTIS, P. J., *The Modern History of Egypt* (London, 1969)

WRIGHT, JOHN, *Libya: A Modern History* (London, 1982)

East Africa and the Horn

ARNOLD, GUY, *Modern Kenya* (London, 1981)

BENNETT, GEORGE, *Kenya: A Short Political History* (London, 1963)

CHIDZERO, B. T. G., *Tanganyika and International Trusteeship* (London, 1961)

CLAPHAM, CHRISTOPHER, *Haile Selassie's Government* (London, 1969)

CRANFORD PRATT, R., *The Critical Phase in Tanzania, 1945–1968* (Cambridge, 1980)

HALLIDAY, F. and MOLYNEUX, M., *The Ethiopian Revolution* (London, 1982)

HESS, ROBERT L., *Italian Colonialism in Somalia* (Chicago, 1966)

ILIFFE, JOHN, *Tanganyika under German Rule, 1905–1912* (Cambridge, 1969)

ILIFFE, JOHN, *A Modern History of Tanganyika* (Cambridge, 1979)

INGHAM, KENNETH, *The Making of Modern Uganda* (London, 1958)

LEFORT, RENÉ, *Ethiopia: An Heretical Revolution?* (London, 1983)

LEUBUSCHER, CHARLOTTE, *Tanganyika Territory: A Study of Economic Policy under Mandate* (London, 1944)

LEWIS, I. M., *The Modern History of Somaliland* (London, 1965)

LEWIS, I. M. (ed.), *Nationalism in the Horn of Africa* (London, 1983)

LOFCHIE, M. F., *Zanzibar: Background to Revolution* (London, 1965)

LOW, D. A., *Buganda in Modern History* (London, 1971)

LOW, D. A. and PRATT, R. C., *Buganda and British Overrule, 1900–1955* (London, 1960)

MAGUIRE, G. ANDREW, *Towards 'Uhuru' in Tanzania: The Politics of Partnership* (Cambridge, 1969)

MUNGEAM, G. H., *British Rule in Kenya, 1895–1912* (Oxford, 1966)

MURRAY-BROWN, JEREMY, *Kenyatta* (London, 1972)

NYERERE, JULIUS, *Freedom and Unity* (London, 1966)

NYERERE, JULIUS, *Freedom and Socialism* (London, 1968)

PERHAM, MARGERY, *The Government of Ethiopia* (2nd ed., London, 1969)

ROSBERG, C. G. and NOTTINGHAM, JOHN, *The Myth of Mau Mau: Nationalism in Kenya* (London, 1967)

SAUL, JOHN, *State and Revolution in Eastern Africa* (London, 1979)

SWAINSON, NICOLA, *The Development of Corporate Capitalism in Kenya, 1918–1977* (London, 1980)

THOMPSON, VIRGINIA and ADLOFF, RICHARD, *Djibouti and the Horn* (Stanford, 1968)

TREVASKIS, G. K. N., *Eritrea: A Colony in Transition* (London, 1960)

WOOD, SUSAN, *Kenya: The Tensions of Progress* (London, 1960)

WRIGLEY, C. C., *Crops and Wealth in Uganda* (Kampala, 1959)

West and West-Central Africa

ANSTEY, ROGER, *King Leopold's Legacy: The Congo under Belgian Rule, 1908–1960* (London, 1966)

ASIWAJU, A. I., *Western Yorubaland under European Rule, 1889–1945* (London, 1976)

AUSTIN, DENNIS, *Politics in Ghana, 1946–1960* (London, 1964)

AZIKIWE, NNAMIDE, *Zik* (Cambridge, 1960)

BOURRET, F. M., *Ghana: The Road to Independence, 1919–1957* (rev. ed., London, 1960)

CLAPHAM, CHRISTOPHER, *Liberia and Sierra Leone: An Essay in Comparative Politics* (Cambridge, 1976)

COHEN, ROBIN, *Labour and Politics in Nigeria* (London, 1982)

COLEMAN, JAMES S., *Nigeria: A Background to Nationalism* (Berkeley, 1958)

COQUÉRY-VIDROVITCH, C., *Le Congo au temps des grandes compagnies concessionaires* (Paris, 1972)

CROWDER, MICHAEL, *Senegal: A Study in French Assimilation Policy* (rev. ed., London, 1967)

CROWDER, MICHAEL, *West Africa under Colonial Rule* (4th ed., London, 1976)

CROWDER, MICHAEL and IKIME, O. (eds.), *West African Chiefs* (London, 1970)

D'ABY, J. F. AMON, *La Côte d'Ivoire dans la cité africaine* (Paris, 1951)

DELAVIGNETTE, ROBERT, *Freedom and Authority in French West Africa* (London, 1950)

DELAVIGNETTE, ROBERT, *L'Afrique noire française et son destin* (Paris, 1962)

FOLTZ, WILLIAM, *From French West Africa to the Mali Federation* (New Haven, 1965)

FOSTER, PHILIP, *Education and Social Change in Ghana* (Chicago, 1965)

HARGREAVES, JOHN D. (ed.), *France and West Africa: An Anthology* (London, 1969)

HUBERICH, C. H., *The Political and Legislative History of Liberia* (2 vols., New York, 1947)

HYMANS, JACQUES LOUIS, *Léopold Sédar Senghor: An Intellectual Biography* (Edinburgh, 1971)

KILSON, MARTIN, *Political Change in a West African State: A Study of the Modernization Process in Sierra Leone* (Cambridge, Mass., 1966)

KIRK-GREENE, ANTHONY and RIMMER, DOUGLAS, *Nigeria since 1970: A Political and Economic Outline* (London, 1981)

LANGLEY, G. AYODELE, *Pan-Africanism and Nationalism in West Africa, 1900–1945* (Oxford, 1973)

LEMARCHAND, RENÉ, *Political Awakening in the Belgian Congo* (Berkeley, 1964)

LEVINE, VICTOR T., *The Cameroons from Mandate to Independence* (Berkeley, 1964)

LIEBENOW, J. GUS, *Liberia: The Evolution of Privilege* (1969)

LIERDE, JEAN VAN, *La Pensée politique de Patrice Lumumba* (Brussels, 1963)

LLOYD, P. C., *Africa in Social Change* (rev. ed., Harmondsworth, 1972)

LUGARD, F. C. D., *The Dual Mandate in Tropical Africa* (Edinburgh, 1922)

MACKINTOSH, JOHN P., *Nigerian Government and Politics* (London, 1966)

MORGENTHAU, RUTH SCHACHTER, *Political Parties in French-Speaking West Africa* (Oxford, 1964)

MORTIMER, EDWARD, *France and the Africans, 1944–1960* (London, 1969)

NKRUMAH, KWAME, *Ghana: An Autobiography* (Edinburgh, 1957)

OMU, FRED I. A., *Press and Politics in Nigeria, 1880–1937* (London, 1978)

PEEL, J. D. Y., *Aladura: A Religious Movement among the Yoruba* (London, 1968)

PERHAM, MARGERY, *Lugard* (2 vols., London, 1956–60)

PERHAM, MARGERY, *Native Administration in Nigeria* (new ed., London, 1962)

POST, K. W. J., *The New States of West Africa* (Harmondsworth, 1964)

RIMMER, DOUGLAS, *The Economies of West Africa* (London, 1984)

ST JORRE, J. DE, *The Nigerian Civil War* (London, 1972)

SENGHOR, LÉOPOLD SÉDAR, *On African Socialism* (New York, 1964)

SURET-CANALE, JEAN, *French Colonialism in Tropical Africa* (London, 1971)

THOMPSON, VIRGINIA and ADLOFF, RICHARD, *French West Africa* (London, 1958)

THOMPSON, VIRGINIA and ADLOFF, RICHARD, *The Emerging States of French Equatorial Africa* (Stanford, 1960)

TOURÉ, SÉKOU, *L'Éxperience guinéenne et l'unité africaine* (Bamako, 1959)

TUINDER, B. A. TEN, *Ivory Coast: The Challenge of Success* (Baltimore, 1979)

YOUNG, CRAWFORD, *Politics in the Congo: Decolonization and Independence* (Princeton, 1965)

ZOLBERG, ARISTIDE, *Creating Political Order: The Party States of West Africa* (Chicago, 1965)

ZOLBERG, ARISTIDE, *One-Party Government in the Ivory Coast* (Princeton, 1965)

South-Central and Southern Africa

BARBER, JAMES P., *Rhodesia: The Road to Rebellion* (London, 1967)

BLEY, HELMUT, *South-West Africa under German Rule* (London, 1971)

CARTER, GWENDOLEN M., *The Politics of Inequality: South Africa since 1948* (London, 1958)

DAVENPORT, T. R. H., *South Africa: A Modern History* (3rd ed., London, 1987)

FIRST, RUTH, *South-West Africa* (London, 1963)

GANN, L. H., *A History of Northern Rhodesia to 1953* (London, 1964)

GANN, L. H., *A History of Southern Rhodesia to 1934* (London, 1965)

GRAY, RICHARD, *The Two Nations: Aspects of the Development of Race Relations in the Rhodesias and Nyasaland* (London, 1960)

GREEN, R. and KILJUNEN, M. and K., *Namibia: The Last Colony* (London, 1981)

HAZLEWOOD, ARTHUR and HENDERSON, P. D., *Nyasaland: The Economics of Federation* (London, 1960)

HOUGHTON, D. HOBART, *The South African Economy* (Cape Town, 1967)

KRUGER, D. W. (ed.), *South African Parties and Policies, 1910–1960* (Cape Town, 1960)

LE MAY, G. H. L., *British Supremacy in South Africa, 1899–1907* (Oxford, 1965)

LEYS, COLIN, *European Politics in Southern Rhodesia* (Oxford, 1959)

LODGE, TOM, *Black Politics in South Africa since 1945* (London, 1983)

LUTHULI, ALBERT, *Let My People Go* (London, 1962)

MARKS, SHULA and RATHBONE, RICHARD (eds.), *Industrialisation and Social Change in South Africa, 1870–1930* (Harlow, 1982)

MARTIN, D. and JOHNSON, P., *The Struggle for Zimbabwe* (London, 1981)

MORRIS-JONES, W. H. (ed.), *From Rhodesia to Zimbabwe* (London, 1980)

MUNSLOW, BARRY, *Mozambique: The Revolution and Its Origins* (Harlow, 1983)

PATTERSON, SHEILA, *The Last Trek: A Study of the Boer People and the Afrikaner Nation* (London, 1957)

PIENAAR, S. and SAMPSON, ANTHONY, *South Africa: Two Views of Separate Development* (London, 1960)

ROBERTSON, H. M., *South Africa: Economic and Political Aspects* (Durham, 1957)

ROTBERG, ROBERT I., *The Rise of Nationalism in Central Africa: The Making of Malawi and Zambia, 1873–1964* (Harvard, 1965)

ROUX, EDWARD, *Time Longer than Rope: A History of the Black Man's Struggle for Freedom in South Africa* (2nd ed., Madison, 1964)

SHEPPERSON, G. and PRICE, T., *Independent African: John Chilembwe* (Edinburgh, 1958)

THOMPSON, L. M., *The Unification of South Africa, 1902–1910* (Oxford, 1960)

THOMPSON, LEONARD, *The Political Mythology of Apartheid* (London, 1985)

THOMPSON, LEONARD and PRIOR, ANDREW, *South African Politics* (London, 1982)

VAN DER HORST, S. T., *Native Labour in South Africa* (Cape Town, 1942)

VAN JAARSVELD, F. A., *The Afrikaner's Interpretation of South African History* (Cape Town, 1964)

VAN ONSELEN, CHARLES, *Studies in the Social and Economic History of the Witwatersrand, 1886–1914* (2 vols, Harlow, 1982)

VATCHER, W. H., *White Laager: The Rise of Afrikaner Nationalism* (London, 1965)

WALSHE, PETER, *The Rise of Nationalism in South Africa: The African National Council, 1912–1952* (London, 1970)

WHEELER, DOUGLAS L. and PELISSIER, RENÉ, *Angola* (new ed., London, 1978)

WILSON, MONICA and THOMPSON, LEONARD, *The Oxford History of South Africa*, vol. 2 (Oxford, 1971)

Good information on very recent developments may be found in the volumes of *Africa South of the Sahara* and *The Middle East and North Africa* which are published annually in London, and in the *Annual Reports* of the World Bank from Washington.

Index

Note that some entries are grouped under general headings, e.g. 'crops', 'political movements and parties', 'trade', 'treaties', etc.